NATIONAL UNDERWRIT

a division of ALM Media, LLC

MW00783613

THE TOOLS & TECHNIQUES OF TRUST PLANNING
2ND EDITION

Michael Sneeringer, J.D. and Jonathan Gopman, J.D.

The Tools & Techniques of Trust Planning, 2nd Edition provides advisers with the most up-to-date information about the creation, administration, and modification of trusts for legal and estate planning professionals. Not only does this title deliver an expert overview of general trust information, but it explains how to use specific types of trusts to solve unique planning problems. Explorations of different types of trusts include detailed knowledge about:

- The types of trusts that are most commonly used

- How each type of trust came to be used

- The possible tax consequences for grantors and beneficiaries of using a particular type of trust

- The requirements for each type of trust and how they should be drafted

- How planning professionals such as attorneys, accountants, investment advisers, and trust officers should administer the trust to achieve the client's stated planning goals over the life of the trust

In contrast to academic trust publications that focus on the ramifications of various trust terms and deep case law analysis, this resource provides a refreshing alternative in the form of a succinctly written collection of chapters on trending topics in trust planning.

Completely updated to reflect the 2017 Tax Cuts and Jobs Act, this latest edition of *The Tools & Techniques of Trust Planning* features:

- A new chapter on trust planning topics for blended families

- Updated state, federal, and international law updates for asset protection trusts

- New and more detailed real-world examples of trust planning scenarios that are most commonly encountered by planning professionals

- Current compliance and best practice information to help planners and other professionals avoid common mistakes and improve client satisfaction

For professionals finding themselves in need of reliable tools and expert insights into up-to-date trust planning techniques, this resource covers:

- The Role of Trust Protectors

- Marital Deduction and Bypass Trusts

- 2503(b) and 2503(c) Trusts

- Trusts and Divorce

- Trust Amendments

- Special Needs Trusts

- S Corporations and Trusts

- Grantor Retained Interest Trusts

- And more!

As with all the resources in the highly acclaimed Leimberg Library, every area covered in this book is accompanied by the tools, techniques, practice tips, and examples you can use to help your clients successfully navigate the complex course of trust planning and confidently meet their needs.

Related Titles Also Available:

- *The Tools & Techniques of Estate Planning*

- *The Tools & Techniques of Estate Planning for Modern Families*

- *Tax Facts on Investments*

- *Tax Facts on Insurance & Employee Benefits*

- *The Advisor's Guide to Annuities*

- *Social Security & Medicare Facts*

For customer service questions or to place additional orders, please call 1-800-543-0874 or email CustomerService@nuco.com.

2ND EDITION

The Tools & Techniques of
Trust Planning

LEIMBERG LIBRARY

Stephan R. Leimberg

Jonathan E. Gopman | Michael A. Sneeringer

ISBN: 978-1-949506-45-7
Library of Congress Control Number: 2019939872

THE NATIONAL UNDERWRITER COMPANY
Copyright © 2016, 2019

The National Underwriter Company
a division of ALM Media, LLC
4157 Olympic Blvd., Ste. 225
Erlanger, KY 41018

Printed in the United States of America

ABOUT THE EXECUTIVE EDITORS

Stephan R. Leimberg

Stephan R. Leimberg is CEO of Leimberg and LeClair, Inc., an estate and financial planning software company, CEO of LISI, Leimberg Information Services, Inc., an email newsletter service, and President of Leimberg Associates, Inc., a publishing and software company. He is an Adjunct Professor in the Masters of Taxation Program of Villanova University School of Law and former adjunct at Temple University School of Law. He holds a B.A. from Temple University, and a J.D. from Temple University School of Law. Leimberg is the Editor of the American Society of Financial Service Professionals audio publication, *Keeping Current*.

Leimberg is the author or co-author of numerous books on estate, financial, and employee benefit and retirement planning and a nationally known speaker. Leimberg is the creator and principal author of the entire nine book *Tools & Techniques* series including *The Tools & Techniques of Estate Planning, The Tools & Techniques of Financial Planning, The Tools & Techniques of Employee Benefit and Retirement Planning, The Tools & Techniques of Life Insurance Planning, The Tools & Techniques of Charitable Planning, The Tools & Techniques of Investment Planning, The Tools & Techniques of Risk Management, The Tools & Techniques of Practice Management,* and *The Tools & Techniques of Retirement Income Planning.* Leimberg is co-author of *Tax Planning with Life Insurance* with noted attorney Howard Zaritsky, *The Book of Trusts* with attorneys Charles K. Plotnick and Daniel Evans, and *How to Settle an Estate* with Charles K. Plotnick. He was also a contributing author of the American Bar Association's *The Lawyer's Guide to Retirement*.

Leimberg is co-creator of many software packages for the financial services professional including Estate and Financial Planning *NumberCruncher* (estate planning), *DeCoupleCruncher* (estate planning), *Financial Analyzer II* (financial calculations), *Estate Planning Quickview* (Estate Planning Flow Charts), *Life Settlement NumberCruncher* (life settlement buy-hold analysis), *Planning Ahead for a Secure Retirement* (PowerPoint Client Seminar) and *Toward a Zero Estate Tax* (PowerPoint Client Estate Planning Seminar).

A nationally known speaker, Professor Leimberg has addressed the Miami Tax Institute, the NYU Tax Institute, the Federal Tax Bar, the Notre Dame Law School and Duke University Law School's Estate Planning Conference, the National Association of Estate Planners and Councils, the AICPA's National Estate Planning Forum, the ABA Section on Taxation, and The Annual Meeting of the American Society of Financial Service Professionals. Leimberg has also spoken to the Federal Bureau of Investigation, and the National Aeronautics and Space Administration.

Leimberg was awarded the Excellence in Writing Award of the American Bar Association's Probate and Property Section. He has been honored as Estate Planner of the Year by the Montgomery County Estate Planning Council and as Distinguished Estate Planner by the Philadelphia Estate Planning Council. He is also a recipient of the President's Cup of the Philadelphia Life Underwriters, a two time Boris Todorovitch Lecturer, and the First Ben Feldman Lecturer.

Leimberg was named Edward N. Polisher Lecturer of the Dickinson School of Law and 2004 recipient of the National Association of Estate Planners and Councils Distinguished Accredited Estate Planner award.

Leimberg's LISI email newsletter/data base at www.leimbergservices.com is used daily by thousands of estate, financial, employee benefit, charitable, and retirement planning practitioners.

Jonathan E. Gopman

Jonathan E. Gopman is a partner in Akerman LLP's Naples office and Chair of the firm's Trusts & Estates Practice Group. He is a fellow of the American College of Tax Counsel. He currently serves as Vice Chair of the Asset Protection Planning Committee of the Real Property, Trust and Estate Law Section of the ABA (for the 2016-2017 bar year) and is a Fellow of the American Bar Foundation. Jonathan is an adjunct professor at Ave Maria School of Law, currently serves on its Curriculum Advisory Committee, and chaired its first annual Estate Planning Day Conference held in April of 2014 and continues to serve on the advisory committee for such conference. He is a member of the legal advisory board of Commonwealth Trust Company and STEP. He is AV rated. In 2009, 2010, 2011, 2012, 2013, 2014, 2015, 2016, 2017 and 2018 he was selected for inclusion in *The Best Lawyers in America®* and as a *Florida Super Lawyer* for 2010, 2011, 2012, 2013, 2014, 2015, 2016, 2017 and 2018 and included in Florida Trend's Legal Elite for 2010 and 2011. In the Dec. 2005 and 2007 issues of Worth Magazine he was recognized as one of the top 100 estate planning attorneys in the US.

Jonathan has authored and co-authored numerous articles on asset protection and estate planning and chapters in books on asset protection and frequently lectures on these topics throughout the world. He was a co-author of a prior version of the revised BNA Tax Management Portfolio on Estate Tax Payments and Liabilities, and has been interviewed for and quoted in

a number of publications such as the *New York Times*, Bloomberg, *Forbes, Wealth Manager,* and *Elite Traveler.* He is the originator of the idea for the statutory tenancy by the entireties trust (STET) in 12 § 3574(f) of the Delaware Statutes. His articles and presentations have served as an impetus for changes to the trust laws of several states. In 2011 he was appointed to a special committee of the Nevis government and Nevis International Service Providers Association to revise the Nevis International Exempt Trust Ordinance. He also provided advice and consultation on the proposed revised charging order statute for the Nevis Limited Liability Company Ordinance and together with his colleague, Linda Charity, provided advice and consultation on the content of the proposed banking ordinance in Nevis. He has also provided advice to the government of Nevis on other legislative initiatives. He received his J.D. from The Florida State University College of Law (with High Honors) and his LL.M. in Estate Planning from the University of Miami School of Law.

Michael Sneeringer

Michael Sneeringer is a Senior Associate attorney in the Naples, Florida office of Porter Wright Morris Arthur LLP. He practices in the areas of estate planning, probate administration, and asset protection planning. He is the current Chair of the Collier County Bar Association Trusts & Estates Section. Additionally, Michael's recent activities include: receiving the At-Large Member of the Year 2016-2017, as awarded by the Real Property, Probate and Trust

Law (RPPTL) Section of the Florida Bar; graduating Class II of the Florida Fellows Institute of the American College of Trust and Estate Counsel; serving as the Articles Editor for Probate & Property Magazine, a publication of the American Bar Association's Real Property, Trust and Estate Law Section; and serving as an Executive Council Member of the RPPTL Section of the Florida Bar. In Naples, Florida, Michael is a 2019 graduate of the Growing Associates in Naples™ (GAIN™) program through The Greater Naples Chamber of Commerce.

ABOUT THE CONTRIBUTING AUTHORS

Mary Elizabeth Anderson

Beth is a member of the Trusts, Estates & Personal Planning Service Team with Wyatt Tarrant & Combs LLP in Louisville, Kentucky. She concentrates her practice in the areas of estate planning, trust administration, including issues with estate, inheritance, and gift taxes, trust modifications, business planning, and probate. Beth is an active member of the American Bar Association's Section of Real Property Trust & Estate Law as Group Chair of

the Elder Law and Special Needs Planning Group, Reporter for the Annual Philip E. Heckerling Institute on Estate Planning, and ABA Advisor for the Uniform Laws Commission. She is also the Chair of the Kentucky Bar Association's Probate and Trust Law Section and an Executive Committee Member of the Estate Planning Council of Metro Louisville. Beth has presented at numerous national and regional estate planning events, and been published in *Trusts & Estates* magazine and the *ABA Real Property Trust & Estate Law eReport.*

Recognized as a Kentucky Super Lawyers® Rising Star in 2016, Beth earned her J.D. from the University of Tennessee College of Law and her LL.M from the Philip E. Heckerling Graduate Program in Estate Planning, University of Miami School of Law.

L. Paul Hood, Jr.

L. Paul Hood, Jr. received his J.D. from Louisiana State University Law Center in 1986 and L.L.M. in Taxation from Georgetown University Law Center in 1988. Paul is a frequent and widely-quoted speaker, whose articles have appeared in a number of publications, including *Trusts & Estates, BNA Tax Management Memorandum, BNA Estates, Gifts & Trusts Journal, CCH Journal of Practical Estate Planning, Estate Planning, Valuation Strategies, Digest of Federal Tax Articles, Loyola Law Review, Louisiana Bar Journal, Tax Ideas, The Value Examiner,* and *Charitable Gift Planning News.* He has spoken at programs sponsored by a number of law schools, including Duke University, Georgetown University, New York University, Tulane University, Loyola (N.O.) University, and Louisiana State University, as well as many other professional organizations, including the AICPA and NACVA. From 1996-2004, Paul served on the Louisiana Board of Tax Appeals, a three-member board that has jurisdiction over all State of Louisiana tax matters.

A self-described "recovering tax lawyer," Paul is the author or co-author of three other books, and is the proud father of two boys. Paul lives in Toledo OH, where he serves as a consultant, speaker, and writer, and as Vice President of Thompson & Associates, a charitable estate planning organization.

Larry Rivkin

Larry Rivkin is the co-founder of the law practice Rivkin & Rivkin, LLC, which concentrates in estate planning, estate and trust administration, planned charitable giving, and planning for children with special needs. He is licensed to practice law in Illinois and Florida, has attained his CERTIFIED FINANCIAL PLANNER™ certification, and has been selected as an Illinois Leading Lawyer and an Illinois Super Lawyer.

Larry received his undergraduate degree from Stanford University and his law degree from the University of Chicago Law School, where he was the Lord Bissell Public Service Merit Scholar. He has served as the Chairperson of the Professional Advisory Committee to the Chicago Jewish Federation's Legacies and Endowments Committee and has received the Shirley and Hilton Leibow Award for Service to Individuals with Developmental Challenges.

Yoshimi O. Smith

Yoshimi O. Smith is a co-founding partner of the law firm of Beller Smith, P.L., located in Boca Raton, Florida. She concentrates her practice in the areas of estate and tax planning, estate and trust administration, and business succession planning. Ms. Smith is a graduate of Hofstra University Law School and the State University of New York at Stony Brook. Ms. Smith is admitted to practice law in New York and Florida. She serves on the Estate and Trust Tax Planning Committee, the Probate Law and Procedure Committee, Ad Hoc Fiduciary Licensing Committee, Ethics and Professionalism Committee, and the Wills, Trusts and Estates Certification Review Course Committee of the Real Property, Probate and Trust Law Section of the Florida Bar ("RPPTL"). Ms. Smith is the Probate and Trust Law CLE Vice Chair of RPPTL Section and a member of the Executive Council of RPPTL. She is currently chair of the Probate Committee for the South Palm Beach County Bar Association. Ms. Smith is a frequent speaker on tax and estate planning topics and has published articles and lectured for the NYU Tax Institute, Florida State Bar, New York State Bar Association, Northwest Federal Tax Conference, Palm Beach County Estate Planning Council, Florida Legal Education Association, South Palm Beach County Bar Association, Collier County Bar Association, New York City Bar Association, Portland Tax Forum, National Business Institute, Matthew Bender, Leimberg Services, Thomson Reuters, local estate planning councils, various charities, community and professional organizations.

Mary E. Vandenack

Mary E. Vandenack is founding and managing partner of Vandenack Weaver LLC in Omaha, Nebraska. Mary is a highly regarded practitioner in the areas of tax, high net worth estate planning, asset protection planning, benefits, executive compensation, business succession planning, tax dispute resolution, and tax-exempt entities. Mary's practice serves businesses and business owners, executives, real estate developers and investors, health care providers and tax exempt organizations. Mary is a member of the American Bar Association Real Property Trust and Estate Section where she serves as Co-Chair of the Futures Task Force and Joint Group on Law Practice. Mary is also a member of the American Bar Association Sections on Taxation Section and Business. She is also active in the American Bar Association Law Practice Division and serves as Editor-in-Chief of the Law Practice Magazine. Mary is a frequent writer and speaker on tax, benefits, asset protection planning, and estate planning topics as well as on practice topics including improving the delivery of legal services, technology in the practice of law, building sustainable law firms, and providing increased access to the under-served.

ABOUT THE EDITOR

Jason Gilbert, J.D., M.A., is a senior editor with the Practical Insights Division of The National Underwriter Company, a division of ALM Media, LLC. He edits and develops publications related to tax and insurance products, including titles in the *Advisor's Guide* and the *Tools & Techniques* series of investment and planning products. He also develops content for National Underwriter's other financial services publications and online products. He has worked on insurance and tax publications for more than nine years.

Jason has been a practicing attorney for more than a dozen years in the areas of criminal defense, products liability, and regulatory enforcement actions. Prior to joining National Underwriter, his experience in the insurance and tax fields has included work as a Westlaw contributor for Thomson Reuters and a tax advisor and social media contributor for Intuit. He is an honors graduate from Wright State University and holds a J.D. from the University of Cincinnati College of Law as well as a master's degree in Economics from Miami University in Ohio.

EDITORIAL SERVICES

Connie L. Jump, Senior Manager, Editorial Operations

Patti O'Leary, Senior Editorial Assistant

PREFACE

This book begins where Steve Leimberg's *The Book of Trusts, 4th Edition* left off. We selected the best material from that book to be updated and blended with new content from leading experts in the design and administration of trusts for estate planning purposes.

When lawyers and (especially) clients think of trusts, something old, dusty, and formal may come to mind. Trusts are instruments drafted and implemented to be administered for decades and impose intimidating rules about what can and cannot be done with the property under administration. A closer examination, however, reveals that trusts have proven themselves to be nimble tools that allow planners to not only achieve predetermined goals, but plan for future contingencies. That most daunting aspect of estate planning is not the case law or the tax code, it is the fact that we don't know what the future holds. A solution that seems elegant and powerful today can come to be seen as burdensome decades later when the rules and circumstances have changed in ways that could not have predicted at the outset of planning process.

Uncertainty about the future drives continued demand for trusts. A trust is similar to a living entity, and the people selected to administer a trust, trustees and trust protectors, provide more than algorithmic adherence rules. They are (hopefully!) people who care about the reasons that the trust was established, understand the interests of the beneficiaries, and are mindful of the rules that govern trust administration. This combination of empathy and expertise allows them to use their best judgment to anticipate future problems and resolve current conflicts in ways that preserve the interests of the donor and beneficiaries. In brief, trusts help plan for an uncertain future by providing flexibility and ensuring that decisions about the management and distributions of the trust assets can be made through the exercise of the good judgment of the trustee.

There are plenty of books out there that exhaustively document every possible legal authority for every kind of trust. There are also form books that provide state-by-state breakdowns of every conceivable clause that can be included in a trust. This book is different in that it presents the topic of trust creation and administration from a planning standpoint. Here, trusts are instruments that are designed to help planners deal with problems–today, tomorrow, and well into the future. Every planning need begins with a client's situation: what does the client want, and what are the obstacles to achieving those objectives? The chapters that follow outline many different situations–from tax concerns, to health issues, to dealing with unique types of property–and demonstrate how a trust can help clients meet their current and future planning objectives.

We hope that you are informed by this book, and enjoy it as well. One of the great joys of estate planning is helping clients realize their personal goals, whether through their lives or through their legacies. Trusts are powerful tools for accomplishing those goals, and knowing the right way to use them can bring professional success and personal satisfaction to planners who face these issues every day.

TABLE OF CONTENTS

TRUSTS: WHAT ARE THEY, WHY DO WE USE THEM AND BEST PRACTICES

CHAPTER 1

INTRODUCTION

A *trust* is a legal relationship in which the legal ownership of property is separated from the beneficial ownership of the property. The person (or group of persons) who is considered the legal owner of the trust property, and is therefore responsible for the investments and management of the trust property, is known as the *trustee*, and the persons who receive the income or other benefits of the trust property are the *beneficiaries*. The property that is held by the trustee in trust is sometimes known as the *corpus* or *principal* of the trust.

The person who creates the trust, by transferring the money or property to the trustee, is called the *grantor, settlor, or trustor*. The terms and conditions are usually stated in a written document called a *deed of trust* or *agreement of trust*. (In this book, we will usually refer to the document creating the trust as the *trust document*.)

As will be discussed in other chapters of this book, it is possible for the grantor to be the trustee, for the grantor to be a beneficiary, and for a beneficiary to be a trustee. The only thing that is usually not possible is for the sole trustee to be the sole beneficiary (with no future beneficiaries). In that case, the legal and beneficial interests are said to merge, and the trust is no longer valid. This is called the *Doctrine of Merger*.

It is also possible for a trust to exist without a written trust document. A trust can be created accidentally, which is sometimes called a *resulting* or *constructive* trust. It is also possible in some states to create an oral trust (i.e., by a conversation between the grantor and the trustee, with nothing in writing) In this book, we will be describing trusts created intentionally (sometimes called *express trusts*), and we will hope that the grantor has had the sense to put the terms of the trust in writing, and not merely depend on the memory (and honesty and existence) of the trustee.

HOW DOES A TRUST WORK?

Picture in your mind a box. Let's call that box a trust. Into that box you can put cash, stocks, bonds, mutual funds, the deed to your home, or even life insurance. When you put property into the box, you are "funding" the trust. You can put almost any asset into a trust at any time. You can name a trust as the beneficiary of your personal or group life insurance, pension plan, IRA or other work-related benefits, and you can determine how the proceeds should be administered and distributed at your death.

Once property is put into the trust, it is the responsibility of the trustee to administer the property in accordance with the trust document. For this purpose, "administer" means holding the property and collecting the income, distributing or reinvesting the income, selling the property and reinvesting the proceeds, and making other decisions regarding the investments of the trust, subject always to the instructions in the trust document (which can be very flexible or very restrictive). The trustee must also make the distributions to the beneficiaries required by the trust document and, if the distributions are "as needed" for specific purposes, such as support or education, the trustee may need to decide when the distribution is needed.

For example, Grandfather wishes to set aside $10,000 for his granddaughter, age six, to be used for her college education. Grandfather (the grantor) can give $10,000 to Father (the trustee) to hold in trust for Granddaughter (the beneficiary). Under the terms of the trust, the money is invested as Father decides, and the income and principal may be used for Granddaughter's education as Father decides is appropriate. Any money not spent for education will be paid to Granddaughter at age twenty-five.

THE TRUST DOCUMENT

A trust document will usually spell out the following:

- how – and by whom – and under what guidelines – the assets of the trust are to be managed and invested;

- who will receive the money and assets from the trust;

- how and under what terms and conditions that money is to be paid out (for example, whether money is paid directly to the beneficiary for any purpose, or only paid to a school for the educational expenses of the beneficiary); and

- when money is to be paid (for example, at what ages or in what circumstances the beneficiaries will receive their shares).

In directing how and when money will be distributed, a trust document will usually have different directions for the principal placed in the trust and the income from that principal, such as interest, dividends, or rents. (Capital gains, representing the increase in the value of the property in the trust, are usually considered to be part of the principal even though they are taxable income for tax purposes.) For example, a common arrangement is for one beneficiary to get the income from the trust during his or her lifetime, and principal if the trustee decides it is needed for some purpose specified in the trust document, but the remaining principal will be distributed to someone else after the death of the original beneficiaries.

GRANTORS, TRUSTEES AND BENEFICIARIES

In establishing a trust, the grantor decides:

- what goes into the trust;

- who benefits from the trust;

- the terms and conditions of the trust; and

- who administers the trust and its assets.

Someone is needed to safeguard, invest, and then pay out the assets, or the income from the assets, to the beneficiaries. This someone is the trustee whose obligation may last only a few years or it may run for many generations. There can be more than one trustee, and there can be individuals or corporate trustees such as banks. When several parties are named, they are co-trustees and make decisions jointly (and are jointly liable for mistakes). It is also wise to provide for successor trustees.

The people for whom the grantor set up the trust are the beneficiaries, who receive income from the trust assets, and perhaps also principal, at the age or ages and under the terms and conditions the grantor has specified. The person who is entitled to all of the income from a trust is sometimes called an income beneficiary or life tenant. For example, if the trust instrument says that the grantor is to be paid the income for as long as he or she lives, he or she is the life tenant. If a child is to receive what remains in the trust at a mother's or father's death, he or she is the *remainderman*.

Because the trust is for the benefit of the beneficiaries, not the trustee, the trustee has a legal obligation to act for the benefit of the beneficiaries (consistent with the trust document) and not for the trustee's own benefit. This is often called a fiduciary obligation (from the Latin word for "trust") and a trustee is often referred to as a fiduciary.

TYPES OF TRUSTS

Living Trusts

A trust set up during the grantor's lifetime is an *inter vivos* trust (from the Latin meaning "between living persons) or a living trust. A trust created during a grantor's lifetime is considered to be a living trust even if the trust later receives assets after the death of the grantor. In fact, quite often, the grantor's will "pours over" assets into a previously established living trust just like a funnel could channel assets into a box.

For example, while he was alive, Grandfather could establish a living trust and put cash, real estate, mutual funds, or other assets into that "box." He could name his daughter, a bank or trust company, or himself as the initial trustee of the trust, and he could spell out in detail the duties of the trustee during his (Grandfather's) lifetime. The trustee could be authorized to use Grandfather's assets for Grandfather's care and support, or for the care and support of Grandmother and Grandfather's children and grandchildren. The trust could provide for the disposition of Grandfather's assets following his death. Grandfather could revoke the trust at any time while he was alive. When he died, Grandfather's will could provide that some or all of his assets were to pass from his estate through the pour-over "funnel" into the trust.

Testamentary Trusts

If a trust is created by your will and comes into legal existence at your death, it is a testamentary trust. Some or all of the assets owned in your name at your death can pass from your probate estate into the trust as directed by your will. Why use a testamentary trust? Attorneys use a testamentary trust to save you costs in two ways. First, a testamentary trust reduces the number of necessary documents. Because a testamentary trust is part of the will itself, there is only one document. Compare this to a living trust and a will which requires two separate documents. Second, a living trust may need to have assets transferred to it during your lifetime in order for the trust to be effective. That can means spending time (and perhaps money) transferring the legal title to assets into the trust. It can also mean other administrative and accounting expenses during your lifetime if you are not the trustee. A testamentary trust requires no effort during lifetime (other than signing the will), because the trust will not be funded (that is, no assets will be placed into it) until after your death.

One drawback of the testamentary trust is that if the will is revoked, lost, or otherwise not probated for any reason, the testamentary trust may never come into existence.

Revocable and Irrevocable Trusts

Remember the trust box we discussed earlier? Now picture a string on the box. That string enables you to pull the box back and reach in. You can revoke the trust, take back what you have transferred to it, alter it, amend it, or terminate it. This is a revocable trust. Its advantages of control, flexibility, and psychological comfort are obvious.

Cut the string you hold to the trust box and you have an irrevocable trust. No property can be removed from the trust and nothing can be changed. Once the terms and conditions of the trust are written down and the trust is signed, those provisions are fixed.

Why would anyone give up the control, flexibility, and psychological comfort of a revocable trust to create an irrevocable trust? The problem with a revocable trust is that, as long as the grantor retains the revocation "string," the assets in the trust are still considered to be owned by the grantor for income and estate tax purposes (and are still subject to claims of the grantor's creditors). If you can pull on the string and get the property back, the IRS can pull the income that trust assets earn into your taxable income and pull the property in the trust back into your estate. Generally speaking, the same principles apply to creditors' ability to reach money or other assets in the trust. Irrevocable trusts are usually created to save income tax or estate taxes, and sometimes to protect assets from creditors.

USING A TRUST AS A MEANS TO ADMINISTER OR TRANSFER PROPERTY

Most forms of ownership are very basic, and can deal with only a limited range of possible future circumstances. Also, the rules governing most forms of ownership are fixed by formulas or specific dates or ages, while a trustee can have the flexibility to deal with a variety of changing conditions.

For example, if you want to make a gift to your grandchild, you could simply place money into a bank account or purchase a certificate of deposit or a stock or mutual fund, and title it in the name of your child as custodian for your grandchild under the Uniform Gifts to Minors Act (or Uniform Transfers to Minors Act, whichever is in force in your state). But consider that only one beneficiary is permitted for each account, and the funds must be turned over to your grandchild no later than an age specified by the statute in your state (usually either eighteen or twenty-one). Your state may also impose restrictive rules on how the money should be titled and invested, and for what purposes the money can be spent.

On the other hand, you could establish a trust for your grandchild or grandchildren, and set up incredibly flexible provisions for their future care. All of the money could be placed in one trust, and the trustee could be authorized to use funds for each grandchild's college education. For example, the funds could be held in trust until the youngest grandchild is twenty-five, at which time, regardless of prior distributions, the money would then be divided equally among all of the grandchildren. But if a child was disabled or preferred to have the money remain in the trust because of creditor problems, domestic problems, or lack of money-managing experience, the grandchild (or the trustee) would have the option to withhold or disburse income or principal as they deemed appropriate. Because none of us can foresee the future, the flexibility that a trust can provide is often its most valuable feature.

In many instances, a finely-tuned trust instrument may be not only the best solution to a problem: it may be the only vehicle to solve or deal with an unusual situation. Suppose, for example, you want to make provisions for an individual who because of age, health, location, or relationship with you makes providing for him or her extremely difficult. These situations could include providing for a handicapped person, relatives who live outside of the country, a child born out of wedlock, a friend of the same or opposite sex, and even the care and maintenance of pets. Trusts can contain the provisions necessary to provide for such beneficiaries, and also give a considerable degree of comfort to the person setting up the trust. There are countless other examples of the many and varied special uses for trusts, as a review of this and the following chapters will indicate.

In deciding whether or not to use a trust, you should consider the alternative transfer devices available to accomplish your goals. These other methods of administering or transferring property include powers of attorney, wills, custodial accounts under the Uniform Gifts or Transfers to Minors Act, guardianships, corporations, and family limited partnerships.

Power of Attorney

Under a power of attorney, an individual (usually known as the principal) can designate another person or persons as his or her agent or attorney-in-fact to act on behalf of the principal. The power of attorney can be as broad as the principal wishes, and can usually include the powers to buy and sell investments for the principal, file tax returns, make gifts, and even make medical decisions.

A durable power of attorney is a power of attorney that will remain valid even if the principal should become disabled or even legally incompetent. A power of attorney can become effective immediately after being signed by the principal, or it can take the form of a springing power of attorney, under which the attorney-in-fact can act only after furnishing proof of the principal's disability or incapacity.

Compared to a guardianship or other procedure under state law for the management of the assets of an incapacitated person, a power of attorney is an inexpensive way to arrange for the care and management of an individual's affairs if he or she is unable to manage them because of age, illness, or any other reason. For example, suppose Grandfather was worried that he might become sick or disabled and there would be no one available to handle his money and other assets for him. Grandfather could prepare a durable power of attorney under which he could give his daughter the power to act for him. The power of attorney could spell out all of the circumstances under which Grandfather would want Daughter to act for him, it could indicate the assets that Daughter was permitted to handle for Grandfather, and if it was a durable power of attorney, it would allow Daughter to act even if Grandfather became physically or mentally disabled. (However, the power of attorney would still terminate at Grandfather's death.)

These same asset management goals can also be achieved with a revocable living trust, under which the grantor (or principal) can establish a trust for himself or herself and name a trustee with specific provisions on how that trustee is to act on the grantor's behalf. Compared to a durable power of attorney, which terminates at the death of the principal, the trust vehicle is usually much more flexible, and it can make provisions for the distribution of the grantor's assets following his or her death. (See Chapter 8 on revocable trusts.) However, it may be possible to give an attorney-in-fact powers that cannot be given to a trustee, such as the power to file tax returns for the principal, or the power to make medical decisions. For that reason, it is generally advisable to have both a durable power of attorney and a revocable trust.

Will

A will disposes of property at death. A revocable living trust can achieve the same results. (A revocable living trust is sometimes referred to as a "will substitute.") However, living trusts have at least two advantages over wills:

- A revocable living trust can provide for the management of assets during your lifetime, providing protection in the event of disability due to accident, illness, or old age.

- An irrevocable living trust can receive gifts during lifetime and save estate taxes.

Custodial Accounts

Gifts may be made to minors without giving them outright possession of the property and without establishing a trust. Under the UTMA, the Uniform Transfers to Minors Act, as adopted in most states, property must be transferred to a custodian who holds it as "custodian for the minor under the (name of the state) Transfers to Minors Act."

For example, Grandpa Charlie would like to make a gift of $11,000 to his granddaughter, Lisa, who is six years old. Grandpa Charlie could set up a bank account or purchase securities and title the account with Lisa's mother, Amy, as custodian. The account could be titled "Amy Brody, Custodian for Lisa Brody, under the Uniform Transfers to Minors Act."

The Uniform Transfers to Minors Act has been enacted by practically every state, and the Act sets forth the terms and conditions under which property can be held for a minor child. According to the act, a separate custodian must be appointed for each child, and the age of distribution is usually either eighteen or twenty-one. The cost of setting up the account is negligible, and in many instances where the amount of property in the trust is small and the beneficiary is emotionally mature, this might be preferable to setting up a trust.

There are, however, several advantages that a trust would have over the custodial account. A trust for minors could have more than one beneficiary and trustee, the provisions could be much more flexible, the trust could continue past the age specified by the act (usually eighteen or twenty-one), and it could also include provisions for a successor trustee and for the disposition of the assets at the minor's death.

Guardianships

A guardian is usually appointed by the court for a person who is under a disability, either because of age or mental or physical incapacity. The guardian's duties are established by law and not by the person under the disability. A guardian's actions are usually controlled by the courts very closely, and therefore guardianships provide much less flexibility than trusts. A guardian does not take title to property in his or her name and serves only during the incapacity of the beneficiary. A guardianship is not an alternative that one selects. Rather, it is one that is imposed by state law because of the failure to set up a custodial account or trust for the minor, a power of attorney, or a trust for the incapacitated individual.

For example, if Grandfather names his six-year-old granddaughter the beneficiary of a $100,000 life insurance policy and dies soon afterward, the insurance company would refuse to pay the money directly to Granddaughter at Grandfather's death. It would be necessary for Granddaughter's parents to go to court and have the court appoint a guardian to handle Granddaughter's money until she attains her majority (age eighteen in most states). Had Grandfather established a trust for Granddaughter and named the trust the beneficiary of the policy and the granddaughter as beneficiary of the trust, the court proceedings could have been avoided, and Grandfather could have spelled out how and when and under what terms Granddaughter receives the money.

Joint Ownership

Many people consider joint ownership of property to be a good way of managing property during their lifetimes and as a good way of transferring property at death. However, joint ownership frequently results in disasters.

For example, suppose that Father has died and Mother is getting on in years and is concerned about failing health. She puts her assets in joint names with Son with the expectation that Son will then be able to pay her bills and take care of her assets, but will divide her estate with his sisters after she dies. Mother may even believe that putting the assets in joint names with Son will reduce death taxes. After Mother dies, Son discovers that all of the assets are subject to federal estate tax. He also discovers that he is the owner of the assets under state law, which tempts him to keep the assets for himself, regardless of what his mother intended or his sisters expect. After some bitter arguments with his sisters, he relents and agrees to give them their shares of the assets. Unfortunately, it is too late, because his ex-wife has claimed all of the assets to satisfy his support obligations. If Mother had created a revocable trust, naming Son as trustee, the assets would not have been subject to the claims of Son's ex-wife or other creditors, and the sisters would have been assured of getting the shares Mother intended.

There can be problems even when husbands and wives set up joint checking accounts and brokerage accounts so that both can make deposits and withdrawals during lifetime. There is no federal estate tax at the first death, because the survivor will become the sole owner and the amounts passing to the survivor will qualify for the federal estate marital deduction. However, there could be unnecessary tax at the second death if the assets exceed the unified credit applicable exclusion amount ($1,500,000 in 2005, with scheduled increases in future years—see Appendix B for details), because the unified credit in the first estate was not used. A better alternative might be separate revocable trusts or even a joint revocable trust.

Corporations

There may be estate tax planning advantages, as well as business advantages, in deciding to set up a business as a corporation. Because a corporation is a separate taxable entity, as an employee of the corporation you will be entitled to the same fringe benefits as any other employee. Incorporating gives you a relatively simple and inexpensive way to transfer ownership of corporate assets. Gifts can be made by endorsing shares of stock to your donees or intended beneficiaries, and gifts can be made to children, friends, relatives and charities quickly and easily. Through gifts of stock, family members can be given an interest in the business, but you can keep control. You can also shift the growth in the business to children, and by dividing shares among family members, shift a portion of your estate to your children's lower estate tax brackets. You can also maintain privacy because the transfer of stock in a closely held corporation is not public information.

Whenever the management and disposition of a family business is involved, an attorney should always be consulted about the advisability of incorporating the business. However, a corporation is not a substitute for a trust. In order to control a corporation, you must still own stock, and that stock must be managed during your lifetime and following your death. If you own that stock directly, and not in a trust, you may not be able to control the corporation as you would wish during your lifetime and following your death. Trust arrangements must therefore still be considered along with a corporation.

Family Limited Partnership

Another planning device whose goal is the maintenance and distribution of business and non-business assets is the FLP, the family limited partnership. A limited partnership has two classes of partners—the general partner, who manages and controls the partnership, and the limited partner, whose rights and obligations are similar to those of passive nonvoting investors in a partnership. By setting up a family limited partnership, a parent or parents can maintain control of the assets in the partnership, while at the same time gifting limited partnership interests to their children and reducing the size of the parents' estate. Limited partners are considered less vulnerable to the creditors of a limited partnership, and because of the limitations on transferability, limited partnership interests are considered to be of less value than the underlying obligations represented by the interest. That "reduced value" may lead to very advantageous gift or estate tax discounts.

Example 1. Suppose that the limited partnership owned $1,000,000 worth of General Motors, $1,000,000 worth of IBM, and $1,000,000 worth of Intel stock, and a third party had the choice of either buying $1,000,000 worth of stock directly from a stockbroker or buying a limited partner's one-third interest in the FLP. Which would have a higher value? The limited partnership interest should be worth less than a one-third interest in the underlying stock because it would actually be only a non-controlling interest in a partnership that owned General Motors, IBM, and Intel stock. So the owner of the limited partnership interest might be able to obtain a valuation discount that could lower the value of the limited partnership interest for estate and gift tax purposes.

Example 2. Grandfather has over $1,000,000 in closely held stock and would like to set up a gift-giving program to benefit his children and grandchildren. His lawyer tells him that he could set up a family limited partnership under which he could keep control by making himself or Grandmother a general partner and also limited partners. He and Grandmother could then give their limited partnership interest to their children and grandchildren and still keep a measure of control of their assets because they would be general (that is, controlling) partners. There is also a possibility that when they die, their limited partnership interest could be discounted for death tax purposes.

Although the limited partnership form of owning assets and doing business would, in many instances, be more costly than a trust, individuals with larger estates should consider the use of limited partnerships in their overall estate plans. However, a limited partnership is not a substitute for a trust, any more than a corporation could be a substitute for a trust. In order to control a partnership, you must still own a partnership interest, and that interest must be managed during your lifetime and following your death. If you own that partnership directly, and not in a trust, you may not be able to control the partnership as you would wish during your lifetime and following your death. Many sophisticated attorneys will suggest a marriage of one or more trusts and one or more FLPs.

EXAMPLE: A FAMILY TRUST

The following is an illustration of a family trust without considering any tax implications. Jim and Helen have two children, Greg and Lauren, who are twelve and ten years old respectively. They plan to have Jim's sister, Mona, act as guardian for the children if both of them die. However, their assets plus Jim's life insurance will be approximately $500,000 and they feel this would be too much for Mona to handle on her own.

Jim and Helen could set up a trust that would go into effect only at the death of the survivor of both of them. This could be done in their wills or in a separate trust document. The trust would provide that at the death of both Jim and Helen, all of their money, including Jim's life insurance, would be payable to the Very Secure Bank and Trust Company, who would act as trustee for the children and invest the money for them. The trust could provide that, until their younger child is twenty-two years old and finished with his basic college education, all the money would be held for the children in one trust and would be used for them according to their needs, which Mona could determine, and also for their education. When the younger child is twenty-two, the balance then remaining in the trust could be divided into equal shares, and each child would then receive all of the income from his or her share of the trust. Each child would have the right to withdraw one-half of the principal in his or her trust at age twenty-five, and the balance at age thirty, with the trustee able to use the principal for each child's support, maintenance, health, and education, until his or her thirtieth birthday.

If a child should die before receiving the entire balance in his or her trust, such child's share would go to his or her children, and if he or she had no children, the share would be distributed equally to his or her then-surviving brother or sister. The trust could also have a catastrophe clause that would provide that if something should happen to the entire family, one-half of the balance would go to Jim's family and the remaining one-half to Helen's family.

Through this trust, Jim and Helen could provide professional money management for their children, while at the same time having a trusted family member taking care of their children's every-day needs. The trust could also give Mona the right to replace the bank in the future if she and the children moved to a different area or she was dissatisfied with the way the bank was managing the children's funds.

WHY DO WE NEED TRUSTS?

Properly structured, a trust can be one of the most beneficial methods of holding and transferring property. There are almost unlimited uses for trusts in today's complex society. Trusts are excellent solutions to many different kinds of problems. They can be used to:

- Protect against many of the legal and financial problems of disability and old age;

- Protect people from the financial consequences of bad marriages, bad business decisions, or other legal problems;

- Provide for children (or grandchildren) until they are mature enough to handle their own affairs;

- Avoid estate and inheritance taxes;

- Reduce income taxes;

- Provide professional investment and asset management;

- Prevent family assets like farms or businesses from being unnecessarily divided or sold; and

- Make sure that benefits go to the right people, at the right times, for the right purposes, and in the right amounts.

Trusts offer flexibility, reliability, and confidentiality in situations where publicity is not desired. You can attain your goal with just you and the trustee aware of the nature of your gift and the specific terms of the trust. The terms and conditions in most trusts are not accessible by the public during your lifetime, and they are not filed in a probate proceeding at your death. Therefore, it may be possible for you to make whatever arrangements you wish with complete privacy and confidentiality. Here are two examples of situations in which privacy is often desired:

- Trusts set up for a particular beneficiary of whom the grantor's family is not aware, or with whom the grantor does not wish to be publicly associated. (These could include a trust for another woman or man in your life, a trust for an illegitimate child, or a trust to help a friend or relative pay for a criminal lawyer.)

- Trusts set up to prevent ownership of property from becoming a matter of public record. In many communities, sales of homes and other properties are reported in the local newspapers (as well as in public records, some of which are now accessible through the Internet). Purchasing the property in the name of a trust, with a lawyer or other neutral party as trustee if necessary, can help to keep the identity of the new owner as private as possible.

There are many reasons other than estate or income tax savings for making gifts in trust rather than outright. We call these people-oriented goals. If you examine the list below, you'll find that most of the reasons for making gifts in trust fall into one of these three categories:

1. You want to guarantee proper management for the assets.

2. You want to conserve principal for as long as possible.

3. You want income and principal paid out in the time and manner and to the persons of your choice.

See if any of the following situations apply to you or your beneficiaries:

You are afraid that your beneficiary is unable to handle the asset. If you feel that your spouse, friend, children, grandchildren, niece, nephew, parent, or other beneficiary is unwilling or unable to invest, manage, or handle the responsibility of an outright gift, you should consider making a gift in trust. Minors and legal incompetents are obvious members of this class. So are adults who lack the emotional or intellectual maturity or who do not have the physical capacity or technical training to handle large sums of money or assets

that require constant, high-level decision-making capacity such as a family business.

Legally, a minor cannot buy or sell assets or enter into binding contracts. This means that if property is given to a minor, the property cannot be purchased, sold, exchanged, or mortgaged without the appointment of a guardian of the property of that minor by a court and the consequent accounting to the court for every dollar spent on behalf of the minor. Using an irrevocable trust could minimize or avoid that often expensive, troublesome, and inflexible process.

You fear that your beneficiary will no longer feel dependent on you. You may want the income and estate tax advantages (which we'll describe shortly), but you don't want to put all of the ownership rights in your child or other beneficiary's hands. Suppose you want to start a gift program but you are afraid that if you make no-strings-attached-gifts, your child will begin to feel too independent. Unlike an outright gift, a properly drafted irrevocable trust will not allow a beneficiary to "take the money and run" because he or she will not receive it all at one time and can't get it at whim.

The property is not fragmentable. Perhaps the property doesn't lend itself to fragmentation, but you still want to spread the benefits among a number of people. (For example, a large life insurance policy and its eventual proceeds may be best held by a single trustee, rather than jointly by a half a dozen individuals.)

Say you have ten children and grandchildren. You also have ten acres of real estate, which may be more valuable to them if it is not subdivided into ten one-acre plots. If you placed the real estate into an irrevocable trust, all ten of your children and grandchildren could enjoy the property's growth and income without the need to subdivide it. Upon the occurrence of a specified event (for instance, when the youngest of them reaches age thirty or when the property can be sold for an amount in excess of $100,000 per acre), your trustee could sell the property and divide the proceeds or hold the money for the trust's beneficiaries.

You want to limit ownership. Consider an irrevocable trust in place of an outright gift if you want to limit the class of beneficiaries. For instance, suppose you want to be sure that stock in your family business, the family vacation home, or Grandpop's pocket watch don't end up outside the family. With an irrevocable trust you can make sure that doesn't happen. You can set up a trust that will retain family control and provide protection against the fallout from a beneficiary's unsuccessful marriage, for example, and thus prevent his or her spouse from acquiring that asset. Such ownership restriction is not possible if you make an outright gift.

You don't want the property to return to you once you have given it away. If a parent makes a direct gift to a child and the child predeceases the parent, absent a valid will, the property may return to the parent rather than pass directly to another child under state intestacy laws. To then remove the asset from the parent's estate, he or she would have to make another taxable gift. This second gift may be even more expensive than the first because the asset may have appreciated in the hands of the deceased child. Placing the gift in an irrevocable trust and providing for its ultimate disposition, however, can ensure that it doesn't end up back in your estate.

You'd like to familiarize your trustee with managing your trust. Initially, your irrevocable trust may have only a life insurance policy and a relatively small amount of investable assets in it. You may plan to "pour over" other assets from your probate estate (assets you own in your own name when you die), from a revocable trust you've established during your lifetime, or from a group life insurance plan into the trust. In other words, your trust may be relatively small now but at your death contain a sizable sum of money and other assets. You may want to know now how well your trustee will perform and would like to familiarize the trustee with your assets, your family, your plans, and the relationship of each to the other. Even though the trust is irrevocable, you can give the trustee informal suggestions as to property investment and management.

You desire to protect assets from creditors and predators. You may want to ensure your beneficiary's financial security, yet not make him or her the target of a fortune hunter. You can do this—create significant economic security but protect the beneficiary from himself and others—by using a trust that provides only income, with additional amounts of principal disbursed—at the trustee's sole discretion—for the beneficiary's health, education, maintenance, and support. Alternatively, you could give the beneficiary the right to demand certain limited amounts for specific needs but stipulate that amounts above those levels or beyond those categories of need would be paid out only if the trustee deemed it desirable.

Anyone who cares enough to plan for the future must consider the many ways that trusts can benefit the people and institutions that are important to him or her.

How Can a Trust Help Me Personally?

By establishing a trust with yourself as beneficiary, you can make arrangements for your future care and comfort. Your trust can include provisions for future contingencies. For example, you may have just retired, have set aside money for yourself, and are receiving a pension. Though it appears you have financial security, you are concerned about managing your money, about disability, and about old age.

While you are well, you could be your own trustee. By establishing a trust with a bank or trust company or with a responsible individual as a "back-up" trustee, you could make arrangements to protect yourself from these potential future problems. If you became disabled or for whatever other reason could not or did not want to handle the assets in the trust, the back-up trustee would take your place.

Alternatively, right now you could transfer your assets to a trustee, who would provide professional money management for you and relieve you of the everyday responsibility of handling your money. In the event of your future disability, the trustee would have funds available to use for your benefit, while at the same time continuing to manage the money. At your death, the trust would provide for the disposition of your funds to those persons or institutions you intend to benefit.

Using a Trust for a Spouse

There are many specific instances and examples in this book that explain the advantages of placing all or some of your assets in trust for your spouse at your death. If your spouse isn't accustomed to managing or handling large sums of money, is not a citizen of the United States, is not the parent of all of your children, or your total assets exceed the unified credit exclusion amount ($1,500,000 in 2005, with increases scheduled for future years—see Appendix A for details), a trust would almost certainly be the best method of providing for your spouse at your death. You should also consider a trust for your spouse in the event of his or her future disability. For example, if you are in a second marriage, have children from a prior marriage, and want to make provisions for your spouse at your death but still provide for your own children at your spouse's subsequent death, a QTIP trust is an excellent way to provide for both your spouse and your children. A spendthrift trust is an excellent way to protect your spouse from creditors.

Using Trusts for Children

Although there are many ways to make provisions for minor children, such as custodial accounts and guardianships, in many instances a trust will do a superior job for your children. A trust can provide professional money management for your children's funds, and distribute income to them in the manner and at the ages you select. This is preferable to a custodial account under which funds are distributed to them when the children reach the age specified under state law (usually either eighteen or twenty-one), because, at those ages, children often lack the emotional or intellectual maturity, physical capacity, or technical training to handle large sums of money. A trust can provide for your children's education and treat them equitably—but not necessarily equally—when appropriate.

For example, if one of your children has serious health problems, you may not want to leave your money equally to all of your children. If your daughter is a successful lawyer, but your son is partially handicapped, you might want to consider providing differently for them.

A discretionary trust may be the best means of providing for a handicapped child's needs and preserving his or her government entitlements. When a spendthrift provision is included in the trust document, trusts can also protect your children from claims of creditors (or their spouses).

Moreover, trusts for children can "sprinkle" the trust funds among them to meet their needs as they arise. In most families, the parents keep all of their money in one pot and use the funds for the children as expenses are incurred. For example, if you go into a shoe store with your young son and daughter, and your daughter needs corrective shoes that cost $25 more than the shoes you are buying for your son, you do not put an extra $25 in an envelope for your son. With a sprinkle trust, you can give your trustee the right to pay expenses as they are incurred without the requirement that all of the children receive exactly the same amounts.

Using Trusts to Provide for Dependent Parents

In practically every instance where sufficient funds are available, a trust will be the best way to provide for dependent parents in the event of your death.

For example, if you have been helping to support your parents by giving them $5,000 per year and you want the payments to continue after your death, you could set up a trust for your parents and fund the trust with $100,000. These funds could be invested by the trustees, with the income (let's assume the funds earn 5 percent, i.e. $5,000 a year) paid (and taxed) to your lower income tax bracket parents rather than to you at your higher tax bracket. At your parents' death, the balance remaining in the trust would be distributed to your children. This is preferable to giving the money directly to your parents, who may not be in a position to invest it properly, and whose estates could be required to pay additional death taxes on that $100,000, taxes that could have been avoided had a trust been set up. And something could happen to your parents or their estate plans that results in the entire $100,000 going to their creditors or to other family members instead of back to you or your children.

Using Trusts to Benefit Other Family Members

You should certainly consider trusts if you plan to leave money to grandchildren. Not only can trusts provide your grandchildren's educational needs, but they can also make provisions to distribute the remaining trust assets to the grandchildren at certain ages. If you have a deceased child, you can set up a trust for your son-in-law or daughter-in-law during his or her lifetime, with the trust assets reverting to your grandchildren (or other family members) at your in-law's death.

Trusts can also be used to keep assets such as a home or a business in the family for many years or several generations. If you have no immediate family, you might want to establish a trust to provide for a favorite niece or nephew, for example, or to provide a permanent source of income for a brother or sister who is not a good money manager.

Using Trusts to Provide for Nonfamily Members

There may be certain people who, although they are not legally related to you, are very important, and for whom you would like to provide. Examples might be a close friend or live-in companion or members of your church, synagogue, mosque, or fraternal order. Trusts can also offer the flexibility, reliability, and strict confidentiality in situations where publicity is not desired. Examples of such situations include making provisions for a child born out of wedlock, a close friend of the opposite sex who is not your spouse, or a lover.

Using Trusts to Reduce Gift and Estate Taxes

The federal government may impose a considerable amount of taxes if you attempt to dispose of your assets either during your lifetime (the gift tax) or following your death (the estate tax). These taxes—the federal gift tax, the federal estate tax, and the generation-skipping tax—are in addition to any death tax that your state may impose on your estate or its beneficiaries. In no other area can a properly drawn trust save more money for your intended beneficiaries than in the field of gift tax and estate tax planning.

Perhaps the most widely used tax shelter in the entire estate planning area is the credit shelter trust or, as it is often known, the by-pass trust. Through the use of the credit shelter trust, a married couple can each use their unified credit exclusion amounts ($5,490,000 in 2017) from estate tax, a total for a married couple of $10,880,000 (or even more in future years), even while the surviving spouse has the income and benefit from the entire estate during his or her lifetime. It makes no sense for a married couple with children, whose total family assets exceed the unified credit exclusion amount, not to consider the use of a by-pass trust to save federal estate taxes for their children.

Those persons with estates in excess of $5,000,000 should also have an understanding of how trusts can affect the onerous federal generation-skipping tax. The gift tax law allows every individual to give up to $14,000

in 2017 (adjusted for inflation) each year to as many beneficiaries as he or she wishes. Gifts that fall within this annual exclusion avoid both gift tax and estate tax, so for estates larger than the unified credit exclusion amount, each $14,000 gift could save more than $5,000 in federal estate tax. If your estate has the assets and you have the inclination, you may want to take maximum advantage of the $14,000 annual gift tax exclusion. For example, you may wish to use the $14,000 annual gift exclusion to give assets to each of your children. However, you may not want to make an outright gift to a young child, or even an older child inexperienced with handling money. A trust can be the logical vehicle to use to implement your gift. Once the gift qualifies for the annual exclusion, the terms of the trust are limited only by your imagination. You could set up a minor's trust, in which the money will be held in trust for your child and made available at age twenty-one. Or you could set up an irrevocable trust under which your child would receive the income for the rest of his or her lifetime, with allowances made for educational needs, a wedding, or to purchase a business, and the child could be given the right to withdraw certain amounts of principal at stated ages. Gifts with trusts to utilize the $14,000 annual exclusion can also be made to other family members such as nieces or nephews.

Using Trusts to Make Gifts to Charity

Trusts can enable you to make larger gifts to charity, while saving income taxes and estate taxes at the same time. Instead of an outright undirected gift or bequest to your favorite charity, you could spell out in a trust document the exact way that you would like your funds to be used. For example, instead of making an outright gift of $50,000 to The United Way, you might want to have that money used specifically for needy children in your hometown. Likewise, a bequest of funds to your college could be individualized by setting up a trust to establish a scholarship fund for students in your particular area of expertise or in an area you wish to encourage.

Through the use of a CRT, a charitable remainder trust, you could make a gift that both gives and gives back, i.e, you could make a gift to charity but reserve a specific amount of income for yourself during your lifetime. For example, you could make a gift in trust of, say $500,000, but retain the right to receive a fixed or variable annuity from the trust each year for the rest of your life. Upon making that gift, you would receive a charitable deduction on your income tax return for the value of the gift, less the actuarial value of the annuity interest in the trust you retained. There are many other benefits—to you and to the charity—to making gifts in trust which benefit charity, either during your life or at your death, as explained in Chapter 13.

Using Trusts for Specific Types of Assets

There are trusts specifically designed to purchase and own life insurance. Life insurance that you own on your own life when you die is includible in your estate for federal estate tax purposes. So you can, in effect, essentially double the value of your insurance to your beneficiaries by eliminating the life insurance from your taxable estate through an irrevocable life insurance trust.

There are also revocable life insurance trusts, whose primary purpose is to receive the proceeds from your life insurance policies at your death and hold and invest the proceeds for your beneficiaries on the terms and conditions that you spell out in the trust document. A so-called pourover life insurance trust frequently contains the typical credit shelter trust and marital trusts.

Real estate can often be best handled through a trust. A trust can be used in situations where the real estate in question does not lend itself to fragmentation, but the person establishing the trust desires to spread beneficial ownership among a number of people. For example, land is often more valuable if it is not divided; a single ten-acre tract of land may be worth substantially more than ten one-acre tracts. If a trust is used as a receptacle for the gift, ten beneficiaries could share in the growth and income from the land without necessitating an actual division of the property itself.

If you own several pieces of property of equal value, you could make outright gifts of Parcel A to your son and Parcel B to your daughter. However, unintentionally, you may be treating the children unequally since Parcel A could increase in value, while Parcel B could fall, or the properties could increase or decrease in value or provide income at different rates. By placing both properties in trust and giving both children equal interests in the trust-held property, you could equalize benefits between the children.

If your home has strong sentimental value to you and your family, you might want to consider placing it in trust and reserving the right to live in it for the rest of your life. At your death, a trust could give your spouse or dependent child the right to live in the home for his or her lifetime, with provisions for the trustee to pay the cost of maintaining the home. (Of course, the retention of the right for life to live in the home has federal and state death tax implications). Your family might also save considerable gift taxes through the use of a personal residence trust, placing the home in trust and reserving your right to live in the home for a certain period of years.

Using Trusts to Protect Assets from Creditors

As discussed more fully in Chapter 16, in most states you can set up a spendthrift trust to protect your family's assets from creditors. These trusts can also help protect your children's assets in the event of marital difficulties, and they can protect a professional person's assets from a malpractice lawsuit. For even greater protection, some lawyers are now advocating the establishment of an asset protection trust, which permits the grantor of the trust to safeguard his or her assets by placing them in an overseas trust.

BEST PRACTICES FOR TRUSTS

As discussed above, we learned how trusts work, the different types of trusts, the different uses of trusts and why we need trusts. But what are the best methods to set up trusts? At each phase of trust creation, from the intake stage and even after execution, there are best practices that you should abide by.

Initial Client Intake and Interview

At intake, you need to flesh out whether the potential client is serious about creating a trust. Especially when the client desires to form an irrevocable trust, does the client want to part with dominion and control of the assets? Is the client willing to have additional tax returns prepared?

Is the potential client willing to pay your legal fees? This is probably the most important question that you need to figure out an answer to at the outset. Many clients will want a flat "fixed" fee. However, depending on what you think the client's fee sensitivity is, his or her ability to respond to questions and requests for information, and the client's comprehension to your proposed trust, a flat fee may be hard to discern. But internet based drafting software has made the hourly billing rate harder to justify. You should set expectations as soon as possible to avoid the window-shopping client.

At the beginning of the attorney-client relationship (this might be the initial conference or after the client has signed your engagement letter), you need to flesh out the reasons for the client's desire to create a trust. Questions might include:

- Does the client desire to make gifts of assets to family members or friends?

- Does the client desire to dispose of a business?

- Does the client desire to provide for his or her family in the event of death or incapacity?

- Does the client desire asset protection for his or her assets?

- Does the client desire to save on taxes?

Based on the client's articulated reason, you may need specific types of information:

- **Does the client desire to make gifts of assets to family members or friends?** You will need to know what the asset is and how it is taxed. You will want to know who the beneficiaries are and whether they are minors, have special needs or if they have emotional, psychological or substance abuse problems.

- **Does the client desire to dispose of a business?** For business interests, answers to additional questions become necessary. For example, can the client dispose of such interest by trust? Is there a buy-sell agreement already in place? Are there regulatory issues with disposing of the business interest?

- **Does the client desire to provide for his or her family in the event of death or incapacity?** For this type of planning, the client should provide you with accurate information for such family members. It will be important for the client to tell you who the successor trustees are. You will need to draw out from the client the specific terms that will apply to the trust document (does the beneficiary receive money at a certain age, based on an ascertainable standard, for certain life events like weddings or purchasing a first house, anything else). In an incapacity situation, when might the client return as a trustee?

- **Does the client desire asset protection for his or her assets?** If the client desires asset protection, jurisdiction selection will become important. Should the trust be a foreign or domestic trust? Chapters 16 and 17 discuss asset protection trusts and considerations in greater detail.

- **Does the client desire to save on taxes?** If tax savings are the leading factor, you need to identify what particular types of trusts might be available to the client, based on his or her specific needs: is the asset expected to grow in value (a GRAT?); is the client trying to deplete his or her estate for estate tax purposes (an IDGT?); or does the client desire to intentionally trigger GST tax (a BDIT).

You should ask your client to fill out a client questionnaire resembling the exhibit following this chapter. The questionnaire is crucial to protect yourself in case later on the client's family members blame you for transferring or not-transferring assets of the client. Attorneys in this area of practice will often ask their clients to sign off on such questionnaire attesting that they have informed their attorney as to exact nature and character of their assets. Depending on the type of trust created, an affidavit of solvency might also be appropriate. In such affidavit, the client attests that he or she is solvent before transferring his or her assets to an irrevocable asset-protection type trust. This topic is further discussed in Chapter 16.

Engagement Letter

Have your client sign an engagement letter setting out what you propose to do for the client. It does not have to go into detail as specific as the exact terms of the trust. But describing the type of trust (revocable or irrevocable; if irrevocable the specific irrevocable trust) is appropriate. You should address the letter to the client (as opposed to the client's advisor or your referral source) and both you and the client should sign the letter. The body of the letter could include:

- Which court has jurisdiction over any dispute between you and your client (because your client one day could be suing you on another day);

- Billing details, including:

  o Billing frequency and timing (monthly, quarterly, upon completion);

o Besides legal fees, what else are you billing the client for (postage, long distance calls, conference calls, paper);

o Is there a retainer;

o If billing hourly, what is your hourly rate and does it change annually;

o Will other members of your law firm be working on the file, and if yes, what is their hourly rate; and

o If a fixed fee, what factors determine whether you can charge more than the fixed fee:

♦ What if the client takes an exorbitant amount of time to review the document?

♦ What if the client has significant changes outside of the scope of your initial consultation?

♦ What if there are a significant amount of conferences and e-mails driven by the client?

- Depending on what state you practice in, an explanation of how a joint engagement between a husband and wife would occur;

- A disclaimer that you work with corporate fiduciaries and represent them from time-to-time (if this applies);

- An explanation of attorney-client privilege (something as simple as any conversations where the client copies a third party could eliminate the privilege); and

- How can the client terminate the attorney-client engagement; how can you?

Drafting the Trust

After you have been engaged, it is crucial to timely prepare the trust instrument. You need to set expectations with the client as to how long it will take you to provide the client with a draft. If you know you are getting close to the deadline and will not finish, always proactively reach out to the client to tell him or her that it will be a little while longer (and then give an anticipated date). Never wait for the client to reach out to you to ask where his or her draft is.

Try drafting the trust fresh either from your form document or using a drafting software (Lawgic, Wealth Counsel, Wealth Transfer Planning). You should never use the last trust drafted as a template to start a new trust as most trusts have at least one custom clause or provision. It would be embarrassing for your client to have an unknown name in his or her document and notice it on the day of signing.

At a minimum, before drafting the trust make sure you know:

- The trust name;

- Type of trust (revocable or irrevocable, if irrevocable, what type of irrevocable trust; grantor or non-grantor trust);

- The trust grantor (is it the client or someone else);

- The initial trustee;

- The beneficiaries;

- The dispositive terms applicable to the beneficiaries (what terms are applicable to distributing the assets to the beneficiaries);

- What governing law applies (making sure that you follow any state law prohibition against the unauthorized practice of law); and

- Where is the trust going to be signed?

Add a watermark to the trust instrument. You can do this in Microsoft Word by going to "Page Layout" and then "Background", depending on the version of Word that you have.

Once the trust is drafted, either summarize the dispositive terms in an e-mail or letter to your client. Note areas where the client needs to provide further guidance: who will be the successor trustee, when does the trust terminate, who will be the disaster provision beneficiary (charities selected by the trustee or something or someone else). You should describe what the next steps are in this e-mail or letter.

You should follow up with the client at least weekly once the draft has been sent out. You should aim to have the client sign while the desire to create the trust is fresh on his or her mind. Significant delays will only increase the likelihood that the client never signs the trust instrument.

If your client has changes to his or her trust or needs to fill in some blanks in the trust instrument, always prepare a new version of trust instrument or track changes. This way, your client can see what changed from version 1 to version 2.

Executing the Trust

Not every state has the same execution standards. One state may require no witnesses or notary; other states require witnesses and a notary depending on whether the trust is revocable or irrevocable. Best practices would be for your client to sign every type of trust in the presence of two disinterested witness and a third person who is authorized as a notary public pursuant to state law. Ideally your client should execute the document in blue ink. The witnesses and notary should use blue ink too. Using the same pen is helpful, but not necessary.

Having the grantor initial each page could prevent a later trust contest should the argument center around whether the client signed a particular version of the trust document; but otherwise, initialing each page is not necessary. Other optional formalities might include:

- Using bond paper;

- Bounding the trust in one document with a staple and blue back;

- Having the drafting attorney present (or any attorney for that matter);

- Using signing instructions;

- Using a raised seal notary stamp (may be required depending on state law); or

- Signing multiple original instruments.

It is recommended that each time you have a client execute a trust, you use the same signing ceremony. This avoids any uncharacteristic mistakes that occur when a different approach is taken. You should try and use the same staff members for each signing. In case of your absence, you should make sure that one of your staff members is responsible enough to take on your role. Sometimes the attorney will serve as the witness or notary, other times the attorney will only sit in on the ceremony. If you are going

to be a trustee, co-trustee or successor trustee, it is recommended that you neither witness nor notarize the trust.

If you need a trustee or co-trustee's signature, you should send the appropriate page with signing instructions to said person or organization. Make sure you follow-up with the trustee/co-trustee for the signed page. The trust instrument will not be considered completely executed without it. You do not need the signatures of any beneficiaries or successor trustees.

Post-Execution

You should provide your client with a copy of the executed document through e-mail or mail. If you send the trust document by e-mail, try to encrypt the document or protect it with a password. You will need to send a completed copy of the trust instrument to the trustee/co-trustee once you receive his or her original signature page.

You should prepare a post-execution letter for your client and any of the trustees (this should be one letter; you do not need separate letters for the grantor and trustee). The letter should state the reason for creating the trust, the dispositive terms of the trust and what your client's next steps are (does stock need to be assigned, a bank account created, a tax identification number obtained, etc.). You should sign the letter and you may consider whether it should be e-mailed or sent return-receipt requested (to prove delivery).

You may need to provide your client with multiple paper copies of the trust for your client's bank, broker, financial advisor, and accountant. Make sure you obtain your client's written or e-mail permission prior to sending on to a third party. It is advised as a matter of course that you not provide beneficiaries with copies unless there is a specific reason for doing so.

Depending on the type of trust, the post-execution letter should be sent to your client's accountant. He or she should be made aware of the various tax deadlines that may apply (a gift tax return, a specific tax election, an FBAR filing).

Malpractice insurance carriers tend to advise that if you are not performing any additional work for your client that you send him or her a closing letter, noting that the file is closed and the scope of the engagement has been reached. If there is additional continuing work, a closing letter is not necessary.

TRUST PROTECTORS

CHAPTER 2

INTRODUCTION

The trust protector's role is relatively new in modern domestic trusts. Generally, trust protectors provide oversight of certain trust decisions and allow for a degree of flexibility not easily accommodated by the traditional parties to a trust.[1] While the trust protector's role can be very useful, its role is not precisely defined. For attorney-drafters and settlors, ambiguity in defining the role can be a difficult challenge to address because the statutes among the states are diverse, evolving, and at times inconsistent. There is a dearth of domestic case law interpreting state statutes, and identifying whether the trust protector is a fiduciary (or not) can be tricky. The purpose of this chapter is to provide a broad overview of the role and to identify some of the challenges and opportunities inherent with using trust protectors.

WHAT IS A TRUST PROTECTOR?

There are three traditional roles in trusts: the settlor (sometimes referred to as the grantor, donor or trust creator), the trustee, and the beneficiary. All three roles are required in order to create and operate a trust.[2] In structuring a trust, it is important for the attorney to clearly delineate the relative rights and powers of the parties. For instance, one should address the following:

- Will the settlor, while living, retain the right to remove and replace a trustee?

- Will the beneficiaries retain some right over trustee selection and replacement?

- How broad will the powers of the trustee be in making (or withholding) distributions?

These are just a few basic operational questions that have to be contemplated. Typically, the traditional trust roles are adequate to address most of those concerns.

More profound questions can arise that aren't easily addressed by the traditional roles. For example, the following may arise:

- Should the trust be terminated?

- Should the legal *situs* of the trust be changed?

- Should the trust be amended or beneficiaries changed?

This is where a trust protector can be helpful. The role of trust protector, in short, is a function that carries out an enumerated administrative or strategic purpose not reserved to the trustee, settlor, or beneficiaries. In other words, the trust protector is a non-trustee (and in many cases, a non-beneficiary) who has certain powers over the trust. There is no mandate that the trust protector actually "protect" the trust. The name itself could be anything and has no inherent meaning.[3]

To help interpret the intricacies of the trust protector's role, commentators look to the variety of statutory and case law that exists in the U.S. regarding "trust advisors".[4] Also, there is international common law jurisprudence that can be used for reference purposes.[5]

BRIEF HISTORY OF THE TRUST PROTECTOR ROLE IN THE UNITED STATES

Third party oversight has been part of the U.S. trust law for many years. Prior to the trust protector's emergence, the trust advisor was (and continues to be) used to bifurcate some of a trustee's duties. Prime examples of this bifurcation is giving the trust advisor the power to direct investments or distributions, the power to veto the same, or the power to vote stock.

In the 1980s, the use of foreign asset protection trusts increased in popularity. The strategy involved transferring assets to a non-U.S. professional trustee who would be given vast powers over distribution and other aspects of trust management. Typically, the jurisdictions in which the trusts were based created substantial legal hurdles for creditors seeking to enforce U.S. judgments. To avoid jurisdiction in U.S. courts, the settlor would relinquish direct control over the trust. Understandably, settlors parting with a substantial portion of their wealth were concerned about vesting control in unknown parties thousands of miles away (generally in small islands like the Turks, Caicos and Bermuda). In order to curtail some of their anxiety, settlors employed domestic trusts with trust protectors to retain some level of control without triggering jurisdictional issues in U.S. courts or adverse U.S. tax consequences. It was not uncommon to name a trusted family friend, attorney or other close associate to the role of trust protector with important powers, including power to change the jurisdiction of the trust or the identity of the trustee.[6]

Trust Advisors vs. Trust Protectors

Two questions should be asked at this point in an effort to understand the role of the trust protector:

- Why has there been a rise in the use of trust protectors as compared to trust advisors?

- What's the difference between the protector and advisor?

As discussed, there is no inherent definition to either label. What really matters is how the roles are defined in the trust instrument and state law. Some commentators view the roles as nearly identical in definition; that is "a person who has power to control a trustee in the exercise in some or all of his powers".[7] This approach is not set in stone, and recent thought leadership in this area argues that the nomenclature between the two labels should be given meaning in practice. As Kathleen Sherby comments:

"While the term 'trust advisor' is among the monikers that could be used to refer to a third party

decision maker, this term has been historically and most commonly used to denote the person who provides investment advice to the trustee or for the person who directs the trustee in the exercise of the trustee's traditional roles in administering the trust. Caution should be used when selecting this term to refer to the third party decision maker who is given different powers due to the older body of case law dating back over half a century, under which 'trust advisors', as persons who have the power to control the trustee's exercise of some or all of the trustee's powers, generally with respect to investment decisions but at times with respect to distribution decisions, have usually been found to have the same fiduciary duties as a trustee. These trust advisors were usually exercising one or more of the powers inherently a part of the role of trustee.

"On the other hand, the term 'trust protector' has been used much more recently as the person given the power to perform certain delineated non-administrative decisions relating to the trust but not otherwise inherently a part of a Trustee's role. Most often the trust instrument provides that the trust protector is not acting as a fiduciary, because the powers given to the trust protector are not typically traditional trustee powers."[8]

Such a differentiation between the terms can be helpful in practice, when explaining concepts to clients, and when interpreting trust documents.[9] It will take time for this concept to irrigate the legal landscape.

Is the Trust Protector a Fiduciary?

Why Does This Matter?

The role of fiduciary dates back many centuries. It is an evolving concept, based on a relationship where a person is required to act for the benefit of another person on all matters within the scope of their relationship; one who owes to another the duties of good faith, trust, confidence and candor."[10] It is the highest duty implied by law.

If the role of trust protector is fiduciary in nature, then certain duties of care are owed to the trust beneficiaries, and liabilities may attach for breach of such duties. If it is not a fiduciary role, then what is it? A non-fiduciary power is said to be "personal" to the one wielding it. That is, the power can be exercised without reasonableness; *provided* exercising the power does not *contradict* the settlor's intentions or the governing instrument.

For example, suppose the settlor names his friend, Jordan, as a trust protector with the power to appoint or eliminate trust beneficiaries among the settlor's issue. Without additional information, is this power a fiduciary or personal power? Since the settlor specifically names Jordan, perhaps the power is strictly personal and can be exercised based on Jordan's individual inclination. Personal powers can be exercised for whatever reason provided the exercise is not a fraud on the power. That is to say, the power cannot be used in contravention of the settlor's clear instructions even though the power is technically available. For example, a trust protector with the power to change beneficiaries cannot remove the settlor's family and name the trust protector's family as beneficiaries. That would be an obvious fraud on the power to which a settlor would have never agreed.[11]

What if the trust protector (as in the "office" of trust protector) is given the power? This could be in the nature of a fiduciary. Why else would a settlor give such a broad power to a possibly unknown individual unless it was to further the settlor's intentions? On the other hand, the power to change a beneficiary is not typically exercised by a trustee, and therefore, one could argue that it is not a fiduciary power.[12]

Suffice is to say that the classification of the trust protector as a fiduciary or non-fiduciary is critical for establishing the standard of care owed to the to the trust and its beneficiaries and possible exposure to liability.

Three Schools of Thought

There are three primary schools of thought on how to classify the trust protector role. One trend in the U.S. is to create a default assumption that the trust protector is not a fiduciary. Rationales for this approach vary. One argument is that it encourages people (or trust companies) to serve without the fear of litigation exposure. And, some argue that it allows for competition among the states for trust administration business. States with protective laws tend to be more favored by practitioners and those filling the trust roles. This will be discussed in more detail below.

Another school of thought is the opposite. That is, the default should be that trust protectors are fiduciaries. The primary rationale is that a settlor would not want to appoint someone with great power over the trust who is unaccountable to the courts, and possibly to the beneficiaries.

A third approach is for statutes to be silent, or if a default is stated, to be ambiguous in application. This approach contemplates trust protectors as a fiduciary, not a fiduciary or a quasi-fiduciary. One must look to the powers granted in the trust and statute in order to determine the appropriate categorization.[13]

The bottom line is: be careful and know the state law that applies to your circumstances. In most cases, the trust can be drafted to overcome most deficiencies in the statute. If that is not possible, consider another jurisdiction. We explore some of the vagaries of the prevailing trust protector statutes below.

Uniform Trust Code Approach

Many of the states that adopted the Uniform Trust Code ("UTC")[14] now contain some guidance, vague though it is, on the treatment of trust protectors by virtue of Section 808 regarding directed trusts. The UTC approach is to clearly enumerate that a power to direct is fiduciary in nature. The power to direct can include various actions, such as power over investments, modification or termination of a trust.[15] Specifically, Section 808(d) provides:

> "A person, other than a beneficiary, who holds a power to direct is presumptively a fiduciary who, as such, is required to act in good faith with regard to the purposes of the trust and the interests of the beneficiaries. The holder of a power to direct is liable for any loss that results from the breach of a fiduciary duty."

It is only by looking to the comments to the model statute that we find mention of the term trust protector:

> "'Advisers' have long been used for certain trustee functions, such as the power to direct investments or manage a closely-held business. 'Trust Protector,' a term largely associated with offshore trust practice, is more recent and usually connotes the grant of greater powers, sometimes including the power to amend or terminate the trust."[16]

What about the power to veto a decision by the trustee? The UTC approach treats the power holder as a co-fiduciary. Specifically, the comments provide that "a trustee who administers a trust subject to a veto power occupies a position akin to that of a co-trustee and is responsible for taking appropriate action if the third party's refusal to consent would result in a serious breach of trust."

Importantly, the comments further provide that settlors can specify whether a trust protector is to be held to the standards of a fiduciary. Only by carefully examining the laws of the particular state under which a trust is governed can the efficacy of this commentary be ascertained.

State Laws

With the UTC as the "base line" scenario, one can quickly see the disparate treatment of directed trusts in many of the states that have adopted the UTC as well as many of the non-UTC states. Although examining each state's laws is beyond the scope of this chapter, four primary trends regarding directed trusts among the states have emerged.

1. *States That Have Adopted Section 808 of the UTC in Whole or in Part-* Since inception, the UTC has been adopted in approximately thirty states. Among these states several use Section 808 as sole guidance regarding trust protectors, meaning that there is a rebuttable presumption that third party power holders are fiduciaries.[17]

2. *States That Have Adopted a Modified Version of Section 808-* A number of UTC states not only have enacted Section 808, but provide further statutory guidance for trust protectors.[18] Even among some of the states that have additional statutory provisions dealing with trust protectors, questions still remain due to lack of cross referencing or clarity on which provisions govern.

3. *States That Have Not Adopted the UTC but Have Incorporated Some Provisions for Third Party Advisors into Their Trust Laws-* At least two states, Washington and Texas, have not adopted the UTC, but include provisions for third party power holders that are similar in concept to that of UTC Section 808.[19]

4. *States That Have Neither Adopted the UTC nor Contemplated Third Party Power Holders such as Trust Protectors or Trust Advisors-* Several states have yet to enact any statutes governing trust advisors or trust protectors,[20] and many states still do not differentiate between the two roles

Dealing with Ambiguous Guidance

It is important not to shy away from the use of trust protectors when the role is needed, but it is best to proceed carefully through the fog of uncertainty due to the inconsistency among state statutes and the dearth of domestic case law interpretation. This is not to say that there is no case law. For example, in *Robert T. McLean Irrevocable Trust v. Ponder*,[21] the Missouri Court of Appeals held that a trust protector did not have any powers or duties (actual or implied) to monitor the activities of a trustee in determining whether or not to remove a trustee. This was a case of first impression in Missouri, and the holding should not be viewed as creating a general rule. In addition to *McLean*, and as mentioned above, there are a number of cases involving trust advisors.

This leaves us with the challenge of planning and drafting once the determination is made that a trust protector is needed. There are a handful of strategies to keep in mind:

- Clearly document the settlor's intentions with regard to each enumerated power granted to the trust protector.

- Research the state law very carefully to determine whether:

  o a UTC or other approach has been adopted;

  o a trust protector is presumed to be a fiduciary or not a fiduciary;

  o the powers enumerated in the statute are exclusive or only illustrative;

  o the statutorily presumptive treatment as a fiduciary or non-fiduciary can be overcome through appropriate drafting;

  o there is a difference in state law between trust advisor and trust protector;

  o to what extent a standard of care is owed by the trust protector, whether as a fiduciary or non-fiduciary;

  o if a standard of care is present, what is the liability exposure if the trust protector is found to breach it; and o   consider whether an alternative state's laws should be used, based on the circumstances.

WHEN TO CONSIDER USING A TRUST PROTECTOR

In most circumstances, a trust advisor or trust protector is unnecessary. Decisions regarding distributions, investment management, hiring outside professional advisors (for example, investment managers) and balancing the interests between current and remainder beneficiaries or even the relative interests of current beneficiaries all can and should be managed by the trustee. With a trustee, there is settled law on the applicable fiduciary standard and court oversight. Even bifurcating some of the trustee duties among the trustee and a trust advisor arguably does not diminish the fiduciary aspects of serving as a trust advisor.[22]

Thus, the question remains when should a trust protector be contemplated? What follows is a brief listing of some of the more common situations giving rise to the possible need of a trust protector.

When the Settlor Wants to Reduce Future Court Involvement, Add Privacy to Trust Matters, and May be Sensitive to Tax Issues

Consider the situation in which the settlor is creating a dynasty trust and wants to include flexibility in light of an uncertain future yet also wants to avoid the necessity of seeking court resolution when disputes arise. The following sampling of powers can be considered similar to the powers of a court, and consequently it is difficult to argue that the power holder should be treated as a fiduciary:

- Arbitrate disputes between trustees and/or beneficiaries;

- Modify the trust agreement for purposes of correcting mistakes and taking advantage of tax laws;

- Construe terms of the trust and advising the trustee and beneficiary of the same;

- Alter a beneficiary's interest in the trust;

- Terminate a trust;

- Remove and replace trustees;

- Add or remove beneficiaries to a trust;

- Interpret the rights of a beneficiary to accountings and other trust information;

- Grant, modify or revoke a beneficiary's power of appointment;

- Change the distribution standard; and

- Approve trust accountings and trustee compensation.

Considering the nature of each of the above powers, it would be difficult or impossible for a settlor or trustee to retain any of these powers. The settlor could not retain the powers due to tax reasons (i.e., estate tax inclusion). The trustee could not hold most of these powers because they would create conflicts or be impossible to exercise consistent with fiduciary duties.[23] That leaves the courts–a non-fiduciary. As an alternative to "going to court", a trust protector may be the better solution. State law has to be researched and the trust agreement itself should clarify the nature of each power and the standard of care involved.

When the Settlor Wants to Bifurcate the Role of Trustee

There are times that a settlor may want to bifurcate or delineate a trustee's duties. For example, the assets of the trust might be highly concentrated, thus, giving professional or corporate trustees concern that holding such assets exposes them to undue risk. In such a case, the settlor may want to bifurcate the investment duties from the administrative duties. By further example, in cases where a trust holds special assets (e.g., a closely-held business), the professional trustee may not have sufficient expertise to manage such assets; therefore, the settlor might wish to bifurcate the duty to hold those assets by delegating the responsibility to others with such expertise. Other concerns may be that the settlor does not want all of the power to be held by professionals and wants other people (such as family members) to be involved in important decisions. For instance, in discretionary distribution situations, sometimes, the settlor prefers that family members are involved in that process. These are some common examples where bifurcation or delegation of duties is desired.

The powers below are some (but not all) of the traditional trustee-like powers that can be carved off and assigned to another person:

- Advise as to the exercise and timing of discretionary distributions by a corporate trustee

- Direct or veto the allocation of sale proceeds to income

- Direct or veto the sale of specific assets

- Direct or advise the trustee in making investment decisions

- Advise the trustee on investments generally

- Run a business owned by the trust

- Vote shares of trust owned business or securities

Since the powers above are generally trustee-like, fiduciary duties can be attached to them. For purposes of consistent nomenclature, these powers ought to be assigned to a trust advisor.

When the Settlor Could Retain (or Give Beneficiaries) Powers But Chooses Not To

Certain powers could be held by the settlor or beneficiary without adverse tax consequences or management concerns, but for whatever reason, the settlor may choose not to retain or grant such powers. Some of these powers include the power to:

- Determine or negotiate trustee compensation

- Remove and replace the trustee

- Fill trustee vacancies

- Change the governing law or *situs* of administration

- Approve trustee accountings and waive trustee liability

Each of these powers could have far reaching and unknown consequences on the beneficiaries, and as such, the settlor's intention should be defined by the trust agreement as either a fiduciary or non-fiduciary power.

TIPS AND TRAPS

Assuming the settlor and attorney determine that use of a trust protector is warranted, some best practices are emerging. Fortunately, it seems so, but there is still a long way to go before this becomes a settled part of the trust law landscape. A few things to keep in mind include:

- State law is still unclear and inconsistent.

- Be clear in the trust document which powers apply and what standard of care is owed to each power, as well as the level of possible liability.

- Don't use blanket exoneration clauses. Consider liability questions power by power.

- Avoid using state law that forces fiduciary treatment on the trust protector, if possible. If not, see if the fiduciary treatment can be specifically excluded in the instrument.

- It may be advisable to avoid state laws that presume fiduciary treatment on a trust protector.

- Use consistent nomenclature (i.e., trust protector for non-fiduciary powers; trust advisor for bifurcated trustee powers).

- Give the trust protector discretionary powers, not mandatory powers.

- Include precatory language in the trust regarding the settlor's intention and/or utilize a letter of wishes.

- Give the trust protector power to access the trust document, accountings and all relevant trust information.

- Include a path to removing and replacing the trust protector, and set forth guidelines as to the qualifications of a trust protector.[24]

CONCLUSION

The use of trust protectors in modern domestic trust planning has outpaced the body of law governing such provisions. There is a dearth of case law dealing specifically with trust protectors (although there is a body of law dealing with trust advisors), and state statutes are often inconsistent or confusing. These factors make planning with trust protectors complex. In most situations, it is likely that trust protectors are not needed. Still, many circumstances arise in which the use of trust protectors can aid in enhancing the oversight of trust questions and reduce the potential for litigation. Hopefully, the future will bring better drafted uniform laws and case law to shed further light on the use of trust protectors.

CHAPTER ENDNOTES

1. Generally, the parties to a trust are the settlors, the beneficiaries and the trustee.

2. Some states also require that property (also referred to as corpus or res) be transferred to the trust, and others only require that the property will be funded in the future. Different states differ on this requirement.

3. "[A]t various times, commentators and draftsmen have used alternate titles, such as a trust *monitor, guardian,* and *conservator.*" Alexander A. Bove, Jr., *Trust Protectors: A Practice Manual with Forms,* Juris Publishing, Inc., (2014), Chapter 2.3.

4. Though, there seems to be some question about how similar the roles of trust protectors and trust advisors are. For a more detailed discussion of trust protectors versus trust advisors, see, infra, note 7, and the discussion supra in Section IV of this chapter. The analysis of international origin, case law and statutes are beyond the scope of this chapter.

5. For outstanding source material, see Bove, Trust Protectors: A Practice Manual with Forms, Juris Publishing, Inc., (2014); and Kathleen R. Sherby, In Protectors We Trust: The Nature and Effective Use of "Trust Protectors" As Third Party Decision Makers, University of Miami Heckerling Institute on Estate Planning (2015); and Alexander A. Bove., Jr., The Case Against the Trust Protector, ACTEC Law Journal, Vol. 37:77 (Summer 2011).

6. Richard C. Ausness, *The Role of Trust Protectors in American Trust Law,* Real Property, Trust and Estate Law Journal, Vol. 45 No. 2 (Summer 2010).

7. See Bove, Chapter 2.3, quoting Harvard Law Review Association, *Trust Advisors,* 78 Harvard Law Review 1230 (1965).

8. See Sherby, Section 2.2 (emphasis added), ref. Trust Advisors, 78 Harvard Law Review 1230 (1965).

9. This is not a uniform view. See Bove, *Trust Protectors: A Practice Manual with Forms* (2014).

10. Black's Law Dictionary 658 (8th ed. 2004).

11. To avoid some of these issues, the trust protector language can incorporate a provision that limits the trust protector's ability to take advantage of the trust's assets for personal use.

12. See Sherby, Section 7.3(c)(9).

13. Matthew T. McClintock, LISI Estate Planning Newsletter #2439 (July 21, 1916) at www.leimbergservices.com.

14. The UTC was adopted by the National Conference of Commissioners on Uniform State Laws in 2000, and most recently revised in 2010. A full version of the UTC with comments can be found at www.uniformlaws.org.

15. UTC Section 808(c) enumerates the powers of modification or termination, but the section as a whole contemplates broader powers.

16. Comments to UTC Section 808.

17. According to Sherby's "All States Comparison Chart – Trust Protector/Advisor and Directed Trusts" at University of Miami Heckerling Institute on Estate Planning (2015), beginning on page 13-40, fifteen states have adopted Section 808 as sole guidance: Alabama, Arkansas, Florida, Kansas, Kentucky, Maine, Maryland, Massachusetts, Montana, Nebraska, New Mexico, North Dakota, Ohio, Pennsylvania and West Virginia. Also see "Trust Protectors: The Role Continues to Evolve" by the ABA (March 14, 2018), available online at: https://www.americanbar.org/groups/real_property_trust_estate/publications/probate-property-magazine/2017/january_february_2017/2017_aba_rpte_pp_v31_1_article_huber_trust_protectors/.

18. See, for example, Arizona Revised Statutes, Article 8, 14-10818 which provides, in part, that a trust may provide for the appointment of a protector. Importantly, Arizona's statute creates a default treatment of the trust protector as non-fiduciary. By comparison, see New Hampshire Revised Statutes, Article 12 (Trust Protectors and Trust Advisors), Section 564-B:12-1201, et seq., providing a single definition of trust protector and trust advisor. Regarding the treatment as a fiduciary, New Hampshire adopts a general rule that a trust protector is a fiduciary, but provides for non-fiduciary treatment with respect to each power granted to or reserved exclusively by another trustee, trust advisor or trust protector. Finally, see North Carolina Revised Statutes, N.C. Gen. Stat. Section 36C-8A-3 which calls the third party power holder, simply enough, a "power holder". The term trust protector is not used. Importantly, the presumption as a fiduciary exists except with regard to three enumerated powers. Suffice it to say, states vary with respect to this issue, and thus the planner should understand the nuances of the particular state's law (and governing instrument). Note: This is not an exclusive listing of states.

19. See Texas Code, Title 9, Section 114.0031 and Revised Code of Washington Section 11.100.130.

20. These states include: Connecticut, Hawaii, Iowa, Louisiana, Minnesota, New Jersey, New York, Oklahoma, Utah, California, and Colorado. See, Sherby, Section 6.4

21. 2013 WL 5761058 (Mo. App. 2013).

22. See *Lewis v. Hanson,* 128 A. 2d 819 (Del 1957) (trust advisor's power of consent over various investment decisions rose to level of fiduciary); *Harrington v. Bishop Trust Co., Ltd.,* 43 Haw. 277 (1959) (trust advisor was fiduciary with respect to trust owned stock over which trust advisor had power to vote); *Crocker-Citizens National Bank v. Younger,* 481 P. 2d 222 (Cal. 1971) (fiduciary duties apply to advisors who hold the power of a trustee); *Stuart v. Wilmington Trust Company,* 474 A. 2d 121 (Del. 1984) (power of trust advisor to consent to trustee's decision to make a distribution is fiduciary in nature). Remember that not all cases involving trust advisors or protectors reach the same conclusion. See *Hillman v. Second Bank-State Street*

Trust Company, 153 N.E. 2d 651 (Mass. 1958) (trust advisor had no standing to compel trustee to seek advice prior to making discretionary decisions). Note also the *McLean* case, discussed above, which provides limited guidance on a situation in which a trust protector's inaction was not found to be proximate cause of the depletion of trust assets.

23. The National Conference of Commissioners on Uniform State Laws has drafted a Directed Trust Act which purports to bring additional clarity to the division of power among power holders in contemporary trust planning. Specifically, Section 6(b) provides an exclusive list of powers that may be utilized by a trust director (including five powers that fall under the category of "power of protection"). The comments to the section as well as other sections of the Directed Trust Act analyze the committee's views on the fiduciary obligations pertaining to such powers. Although still in draft form, the Directed The Trust Act will help be a step forward in this area. For a current status of the act, see www.uniformlaws.org/Committee.aspx?title=Directed%20 Trust%20Act.

24. For a more complete discussion on best practices, see Sherby, Section 9.

MARITAL AND BY-PASS TRUSTS

CHAPTER 3

INTRODUCTION

This chapter explains the landscape of the current estate and gift laws, including the unified credit, the concept of portability and the marital deduction. As part of that discussion, marital and by-pass trusts are discussed in detail and how they can work to the planner's advantage as well as disadvantage. Planning concepts are discussed in this chapter as well as the Clayton QTIP trust and the qualified domestic trust.

THE FEDERAL ESTATE TAX UNIFIED CREDIT

The federal gift and estate tax unified credit is a credit against the federal gift tax or federal estate tax that would otherwise have to be paid on either gifts made during life or assets in the estate at death.[1]

This is s a unified credit because the same amount applies whether the assets were transferred during life (i.e. subject to the gift tax) or transferred at death (subject to the estate tax). Only that part of the estate in excess of the applicable exclusion amount is subject to federal estate tax. If a person is married, the unified credit can eliminate estate tax on any part of his or her estate that does not pass to the surviving spouse, and does not qualify for the marital or other available deduction, such as the charitable deduction.

Under the Economic Growth and Tax Reconciliation Act of 2001, the federal estate tax was repealed in 2010. The Economic Growth and Tax Reconciliation Act of 2001 "sunset" in 2011, and the estate tax returned that year. Under the American Taxpayer Relief Act of 2012 (ATRA), the federal gift and estate tax basic exclusion amounts were made permanent and set to $5,000,000

subject to inflation adjustments.[2] The Tax Cuts and Jobs Act introduced in 2017[3] and the Bipartisan Budget Act of 2018[4] doubled the exclusion amount defined under section 2010(c)(3) of the Code, but that doubled amount is subject to sunset in 2026.[5] As of 2019, the basic exclusion amount is $11,400,000 per person. For unmarried individuals the applicable exclusion amount is likely the basic exclusions amount; however, another key provision of ATRA which survived the 2017 Act is the introduction of portability which allows married spouses to transfer any unused exemption amount to the surviving spouse. In 2019, couples can shelter up to $20,800,000 in assets from federal gift and estate taxes meaning very few estates are still subject to estate tax and traditional marital tax planning should be closely reviewed.

PORTABILITY

The American Taxpayer Relief Act of 2012 (ATRA) not only increased the basic exclusion amount, but also, added the ability for a deceased spouse to pass the unused exclusion amount to his or her surviving spouse.[6] Prior to ATRA, if a spouse died with assets included in the estate less than the total value of the applicable exclusion amount that excess exclusion amount was wasted. Planning before portability often required equalization of asset values between the spouses or risked spouses dying out of order with the less wealthy spouse dying first and wasting his or her exclusion amount.

Code section 2010(c) provides that a deceased spouse with a surviving spouse can transfer the deceased spousal unused exclusion amount "DSUE amount" or "DSUEA" to the surviving spouse. The DSUE amount is equal to the unused portion of the deceased spouse's basic exclusion amount.[7] For example, if the deceased spouse did not make any taxable gifts, then upon death the DSUE amount would equal the basic exclusion amount computed in the year the spouse died. However, if the spouse did use some of the basic exclusion amount whether by lifetime gift or because assets in the estate exceeded the basic exclusion amount and did not pass to the surviving spouse, then the DSUE amount equals the total basic exclusion amount less the value of the exclusion amount used. To add numbers to the equations, assume the deceased spouse's estate has a value of $8,000,000, and the terms of the estate plan require funding the credit shelter trust before the marital trust. The $8,000,000 in assets would be added to the credit shelter trust thereby using $8,000,000 of the deceased spouse's applicable exclusion. The estate does not owe federal estate taxes because the total estate value did not exceed the applicable exclusion amount ($8,000,000 is less than $11,400,000), and the remaining deceased spouse's unused exclusion amount $3,400,000 ($11,400,000 - $8,000,000) can be ported to the surviving spouse. Now the surviving spouse has a total applicable exclusion of $14,800,000 (his or her $11,400,000 basic exclusion amount plus the $3,400,000 DSUE amount).

There are some requirements in order to transfer the DSUE amount. For starters the deceased spouse's estate must timely file an estate tax return.[8] Depending on how and to whom assets are transferred there may be relaxed valuation reporting the details of which are beyond the scope of this chapter. The take away is that portability has expanded the options for marital planning including use, order of funding, and timing of funding between credit shelter and marital trusts. Moving forward all marital plans will not be the same by-pass martial trust combination where the by-pass trust is funded first up to the exclusion amount and the marital trust catches the excess. During this period of very large exclusion amounts the marital plan must take into consideration the combined asset values and types of assets of both spouses and the likelihood that one or both spouses will be alive beyond the sunset period. Although it is unknown what will happen post-sunset, there is a concern that any unused exemption over the $5 million (i.e. the doubled amount under the 2017 Act) may be lost. The tax planning purposes significantly change depending on whether the combined asset values are less than $5 million, somewhere between $5 and $11 million, or in excess of $11 million.

THE MARITAL DEDUCTION

Section 2056 of the Code provides that there is an unlimited deduction from the federal estate tax for any qualifying distribution to a surviving spouse. In additional, section 2523 provides that same type of deduction to qualifying gifts made to a spouse during the donor's lifetime. For most married couples, no estate tax deduction is more important—nor is any estate planning tool more powerful—than the federal estate and gift tax marital deduction. This deduction makes it possible in most cases for married couples to leave the decedent's entire estate (or just a portion) to the surviving spouse and pay nothing in federal estate taxes.

The federal estate and gift marital deduction is based on the net value (that is, the gross value of assets less any debts, expenses, or taxes payable on or from the assets) of the property left from one spouse to another at death or given to one spouse by the other during lifetime.[9]

For example, deceased spouse could leave his or her entire estate valued at $10,000,000 to the surviving spouse. Because of the federal estate tax marital deduction, no federal estate tax would be due from deceased spouse's estate and no unified credit would be used on the transfer of the assets to the surviving spouse. In fact, because the marital deduction is unlimited, the estate could be $20,000,000 or even $100,000,000, and in most cases there would be no federal estate tax at the first spouse's death.

By deferring the potential estate tax until the death of the surviving spouse, the surviving spouse not only enjoys the use of the property during lifetime, but also allows Congress more time to change the exemption level or repeal the estate tax altogether. The downfall in this delay is that no one can predict the tax environment in the future nor the possibility that instead of an increased exemption the exemption decreases. Part of the plan for the married couple is determining how many assets should be passed by way of the marital deduction versus sheltering the assets with the application exemption at the first spouse's death.

Disadvantages of the Marital Deduction

The federal estate tax marital deduction can be a valuable estate planning tool. It permits a person to leave all, or any portion of an estate to a surviving spouse without using any exclusion amount or paying federal estate taxes. There is, however, a caveat. When the surviving spouse dies, his or her estate will include not only the assets personally owned, but in addition, the value of any assets the first spouse passed to the surviving spouse. The federal estate tax marital deduction merely defers the potential federal estate tax until the death of the surviving spouse. That delay is important because it gives the surviving spouse the opportunity to use the assets during life. The marital deduction acts as an interest-free loan from the IRS in the amount of the deferred tax, and it's an opportunity to eliminate that tax burden by consuming the assets so that the value of the surviving spouse's estate is less than federal exemption amount. When the surviving spouse dies, there is a risk that all of the assets from the first spouse's death plus all appreciation from the date the surviving spouse received those assets, plus all of the surviving spouse's own assets are taxed at cumulatively higher rates. On the other hand, the longer the surviving spouse lives, the more time is available to gift or consume the property.

Example. Some amount of wealth can be transferred through annual exclusion gifts. In 2019, each person can give away up to $15,000 (this amount is subject to inflation adjustments) per year per donee (including children, grandchildren, siblings, and unrelated people or organizations). Assuming surviving spouse has a taxable estate, if the surviving spouse makes annual exclusion gifts to two children and three grandchildren (five donees) that's $75,000 a year that escapes gift and estate tax altogether and $30,000 in saved estate tax assuming a 40 percent tax estate rate. If this gifting strategy is used over the remaining lifetime of the surviving spouse, a potentially substantial amount of wealth can be transferred to the next generation. Life expectancy tables and software programs such as the *NumberCruncher* Software program (www.leimberg.com) can illustrate the life expectancy of a person at given ages and project the wealth transfer through annual exclusion gifts and other simulations.

Example. A person age fifty has a life expectancy of twenty-eight years.[10] If annual exclusion gifts are made to five donees over for the next twenty-eight years, and those gifted assets earn a modest 4 percent in the market, the surviving spouse could transfer $3,100,000 in annual exclusion gifts thereby saving $1,246,000 in estate taxes. The combined gifts and saved taxes could grow into $5,211,775 over the donor's remaining life. If this strategy started before the first

spouse's death, so that gift splitting could be utilized, the wealth transfer could be as much as $11,186,487!

Over-Using the Marital Deduction

With the high federal estate tax exemption and new portability rules most married couples may want to take full advantage of the marital deduction and push the potential tax deferral to the limits. However, there is a risk that the assets appreciate a great deal more than expected and the total value in the surviving spouse's estate exceeds the combined federal estate tax exclusion.

Suppose, for example, deceased spouse had a $10,000,000 estate and surviving spouse also has $10,000,000 in personally owned assets. Deceased spouse could leave everything to the surviving spouse. Because of the marital deduction, there would be no federal estate tax. And because of portability the deceased spouse's exclusion could be transferred to the surviving spouse. If surviving spouse dies shortly after the first spouse, then it's likely that the total estate (individually owned $10,000,000 plus the assets transferred from the deceased spouse's estate $10,000,000) would pass to the next generation estate tax free because of the combined application exclusion amount of $20,800,000. However, if the surviving spouse lives a modest life for the next several years, and does not take advantage of tax free gifting, but does have a reasonable investment manager, the total estate could easily exceed the $20,800,000 exclusion amount. Or more likely, the combined estate is more than $10 million, but the surviving spouse does minimal or no gifting before the high exclusion sunsets and then dies in a year when the exclusion amount is lower. By pushing all of the assets into the surviving spouse's estate, the appreciation on those assets could result in the estate having to pay federal estate taxes, and make the government the unintended beneficiary of a portion of the present value and future growth of the estate. If instead part of the deceased spouse's assets were distributed to a credit shelter trust, then those assets and their appreciation would pass to the next generation without inclusion in the surviving spouse's estate.

Marital Trusts and the Marital Deduction

Section 2056 (Section 2523 for lifetime transfers) has three major requirements in order for a transfer to qualify for the marital deduction. The surviving spouse must be a United States citizen, the property transferred to the surviving spouse must have been included in the deceased spouse's gross estate, and the property interest must not be a nondeductible terminable interest.[11] Generally, the marital deduction is available for outright transfers, life insurance settlements, and three types of qualified trusts – the estate trust, the general power of appointment trust and the qualified terminable interest property trust.[12]

The federal estate tax marital deduction is available for *qualified* transfers to a surviving spouse. Qualified transfers may be outright as well as transfers made in trusts specifically designed to qualify for the marital deduction. Cash, stocks, bonds, the family home, or other assets passing directly to the surviving spouse under the deceased spouse's Will are not subject to the federal estate tax at the deceased spouse's death.[13] In addition, property jointly owned with the surviving spouse with survivorship rights or tenants by the entirety and passing directly to the surviving spouse also qualify for the estate tax marital deduction. Likewise, life insurance, retirement plans and other beneficiary designated assets payable to the surviving spouse pass estate tax free.[14] The easy way to shelter assets from estate tax is to give them outright to the surviving spouse. However, there may be non tax reasons to avoid outright bequests.

Perhaps, the surviving spouse is unwilling or unable to invest, manage, or handle the responsibility of an outright transfer of a large amount of money, sizable investment portfolio, or a family business. This could be because the first spouse to die always handled the finances or maybe the spouses are looking to protect each other from the consequences of old age and susceptibility of being taken advantage of as each of them grow older including becoming physically, mentally, or emotionally disabled in the future. Creditor and predator protection for the surviving spouse can be very important. Maybe the state's probate process is unwieldy and should be avoided, both in the first estate and the surviving spouse's estate, or the family wants to keep all the details of the estate plan private. Maybe the surviving spouse is not the parent of the other spouse's children, and the deceased spouse wants to provide for the surviving spouse for life, but also wants the remaining assets to pass to his or her children from a previous marriage after the surviving spouse's death. Although the simplest method, an outright bequest to the surviving spouse could derail the family plan. The above are but a few of the issues married couples should consider when deciding how they want to support each other upon the first of them to die.

ESTATE TRUST

A properly drafted estate trust qualifies for a marital deduction. The major advantage of an estate trust over the other two qualifying trusts is that unlike both the general power of appointment marital deduction trust and the QTIP marital deduction trust, an estate trust does not have mandatory income distributions to the surviving spouse. In fact, the estate trust is the only type of marital deduction trust that allows the trustee, at the trustee's discretion, to accumulate rather than distribute the income. Because of currently high tax rates on trust income, income accumulation may not seem advantageous. If the assets consist mainly of non-income-producing property such as closely held business interest, undeveloped real estate, or a large family home, this may be the best choice among the three types of marital deduction trusts. In fact, it may be the only choice. Both the general power of appointment trust and QTIP trust rules require that income be payable annually and that the amount of that income be commensurate with the value of the assets in the trust. For instance, the general power of appointment trust will not qualify for a marital deduction if its only asset is stock in a $7,000,000 family business that pays little to no dividends. The marital deduction may be disallowed if the surviving spouse cannot demand that a non-income-producing asset, such as that closely held business interest, be sold and replaced by an asset that generates income at a rate closer to current market rates. Unfortunately, giving the surviving spouse the ability to force a sale may not be what the deceased spouse (or the family) wanted or intended. An estate trust may be an appropriate martial trust if the non-income-producing property comprises all or a sizable portion of a taxable estate, and the surviving spouse has sufficient assets outside of the trust such that the trust assets nor the income from the trust assets will be needed by the surviving spouse.

Terms of an Estate Trust

An estate trust provides the surviving spouse with a life estate and the remainder is distributed to the estate. In other words, an estate trust stipulates that a surviving spouse is to be paid income from the trust for life whether annually or more frequently, but, at the trustee's sole discretion, that income can be accumulated in the trust. The remainder of the trust, both the unpaid income and principal, must be distributed to the surviving spouse's estate and will pass under the terms of the surviving spouse's will. Due to the fact that no interest can pass to anyone other than the surviving spouse, the trust qualifies for the estate tax marital deduction. Income that is needed for the surviving spouse's support, medical care, education, or other needs can be paid to him or her. The objective of an estate trust is to achieve a balance between attaining the estate tax marital deduction and restricting the surviving spouse's ability to access trust property during his or her lifetime. The cost is that the first-to-die spouse gives up the right to control who receives the property when the surviving spouse dies. That determination is made under the surviving spouse's will.

The Disadvantages of an Estate Trust

One disadvantage of an estate trust is that the surviving spouse has no right to trust income. To give the surviving spouse some control over the trust assets, the trust could provide for a limited withdrawal right. For example the surviving spouse could have a noncumulative right exercisable once year to withdraw an amount of trust assets equal to $5,000 or 5 percent of fair market value of trust assets, whichever is greater. The major disadvantage to the estate trust is that to qualify assets for the estate tax marital deduction the property in the trust must be paid to the surviving spouse's estate at his or her death. Because the assets must be paid to the estate they become subject to all the potential and actual problems of the probate process. The assets are subjected to administrative costs, claims of the surviving spouse's creditors, and a subsequent spouse's right of election against the estate. If these disadvantages are of real concern, because the surviving spouse actually needs to benefit from the trust assets during his or lifetime, or the asset should not be paid to the surviving spouse's estate because the probate process should be avoided or because of creditor concerns, then an estate trust is probably not the right marital trust. An estate trust is a good alternative to the general-power-of-appointment trust or QTIP trust when non-income-producing property is involved and the parties want to make sure that asset is not sold during the surviving spouse's lifetime, or when the surviving spouse has substantial income from other sources. The estate trust could also be used in conjunction with a general power of appointment trust or a QTIP trust if the marital deduction amount is large enough to justify two trusts, and there are income tax saving opportunities by doing so.

GENERAL POWER OF APPOINTMENT TRUST

Allowing the surviving spouse to have complete control over the disposition of the deceased spouse's assets is a constant concern and driving force for enhanced qualified marital deduction trusts. The controlling deceased spouse would like to direct where the assets end up after the surviving spouse's death, but to do so usually runs afoul of the nondeductible terminal interest requirement of the marital deduction rules. Section 2056(b)(5) provides an enhanced alternative for the controlling deceased spouse. The marital deduction is available to a trust that provides at the first spouse's death all of the martial trust's income must be paid to the surviving spouse for as long as he or she lives and no other person can have an interest in the trust assets during the surviving spouse's life.

In addition, the 2056(b)(5) trust must provide the surviving spouse the power to consume, use, give, or leave trust property to anyone. This additional power is called a general power of appointment. In essence, the surviving spouse has a blank check for the assets in the trust. He or she can "appoint" the trust assets to anyone, but in order to qualify for the marital deduction the surviving spouse must be able to appoint the assets to the surviving spouse or the surviving spouse's estate. Any trust assets remaining at the surviving spouse's death will pass to the person or persons specified in the surviving spouse's will, or if the power of appointment is not exercised, then the trust will provide for default takers, usually the grantor's (ie. first deceased spouse's) descendants. If the general power of appointment is exercisable during life, it's referred to as an *inter-vivos* power of appointment, and if the power is exercisable at death by designation in a will or other testamentary instrument, then it is a testamentary power of appointment.

This type of marital deduction trust is appropriately called a general power of appointment marital deduction trust, since the surviving spouse can take all the trust assets whenever desired during lifetime or alternatively leave all the assets to anyone named by will.[15] Typically, the general power is a testamentary power otherwise the purpose of the trust as a protection mechanism during the life of the surviving spouse is undone because the spouse could withdraw all the assets at any point. Merely having the general power is enough to qualify for the marital deduction. The power does not have to be exercised by the surviving spouse to qualify the trust for the marital deduction.[16]

However, the risk to the grantor and benefit to the surviving spouse is that power can be exercised, and therefore, the power may be narrowed tailored to only give the surviving spouse the minimum requirements to qualify for the marital deduction. For example, the power is only a testamentary power to appoint to the surviving spouse's estate. When using a testamentary general power, additional flexibility can be built into the marital trust to protect and care for the surviving spouse such as principal encroachments with a distribution standard of health, maintenance and support or the right to withdraw 5 percent of the trust assets each year. The general power of appointment trust may be useful when planning with an incapacitated spouse who cannot update his or her estate plan nor exercise the power of appointment. The general power of appointment trust simpler than the QTIP trust and unlike the estate trust does not require the assets be distributed to the surviving spouse's estate, but merely included in the value for estate tax purposes.

QUALIFIED TERMINABLE INTEREST PROPERTY TRUST

In addition to qualifying the assets transferred to it for the marital deduction, a Qualified Terminable Interest Property Trust, or QTIP trust, accomplishes an objective that other marital deduction trusts cannot; it allows the deceased spouse to retain control over the disposition of the trust assets after the surviving spouse's death. Prior to 1982, qualifying for the marital deduction required leaving property to the surviving spouse either outright, by will, joint ownership, or as the direct beneficiary of your life insurance, pension plan, IRA, or tax-deferred annuity, or within an estate trust or general power of appointment trust in which the surviving spouse had the power to determine who received the assets when he or she dies.

Recall, one of the requirements of the marital deduction is that the spouse's interest is not terminable. If the surviving spouse's interest is terminable, that is, if the spouse could lose the right to use, possess, enjoy, or dispose of the property upon the occurrence or nonoccurrence of some event (for example, remarriage or having to survive probate of the deceased spouse's estate) or the mere lapse of time, the marital deduction is usually not allowed.[17]

Before the QTIP trust existed, planners and controlling spouses had to choose between qualifying for the marital deduction by giving the surviving spouse the power to dispose of the property or restricting the surviving spouse's interest and thereby ensuring that the property will pass as the deceased spouse wants but the assets will not qualify for the marital deduction. The potential tax consequences of not qualifying for the marital deduction could cause a serious lack of liquidity and insufficient assets to pay the estate taxes resulting in the executor having to sell the very assets the deceased spouse wanted to control. Fortunately, Congress passed a provision that allows certain terminable interest property that would otherwise not be eligible to qualify for the marital deduction.[18] The QTIP trust is particularly useful in second marriages or even in first marriages where, after the death of the first spouse, the second spouse might remarry or decide to leave the property owner's assets to someone other than who the owner would have chosen. A QTIP trust might be the right choice for anyone worried that assets may end up in the hands of a surviving spouse's future spouse, children of a future marriage, the spouse's favorite charity, or frivolously consumed by the surviving spouse.

Absent proper planning the surviving spouse may unintentionally leave assets to the next spouse. If assets were left outright to the surviving spouse, and the surviving spouse dies without a valid will, state intestacy laws may name the surviving spouse's next spouse as the beneficiary of all or a large portion of his or her estate. Even if the surviving spouse dies with a valid will leaving everything to the deceased spouse's children, the second marriage spouse likely has the right to elect against the estate and take an intestate share of the estate regardless of what the will provides. For example, in most states a second spouse could end up with at least the amount he or she would receive if the surviving spouse died without a valid will.

The ability to control the destination of the trust assets is a major advantage of the QTIP trust over other marital trusts. Another advantage is that the deceased spouse's executor can also determine whether all or a portion of the assets will qualify for the marital deduction. Sophisticated plans may contain more than one QTIP trust. Perhaps one for lifetime transfers and another at death, or maybe different trusts for different types of property or when the remainder beneficiaries are not the same.

Terms of a QTIP Trust

Like the general power of appointment trust, the net income of the QTIP trust must be paid at least annually, or more frequently, to the surviving spouse for as long as the surviving spouse lives.[19] But at the surviving spouse's death, the remaining trust assets will pass to the deceased spouse's children or other persons as directed by the deceased spouse. There is no requirement that the surviving spouse has a right to the trust principal either during life or at death.

Four conditions must be met for QTIP treatment to be allowed. The deceased spouse must make a transfer of property. The transfer can be in trust, through insurance proceeds, or in other ways, such as the death proceeds of a nonqualified deferred-compensation plan. The surviving spouse, or donee in the case of a lifetime transfer, must be given the right to all the income, payable at least annually, for life. No one can be given the right to direct that the property will go to anyone other than the spouse as long as that spouse is alive. However, it is permissible to give someone other than the surviving spouse the power to appoint QTIP property if that power can be exercised only after the surviving spouse dies.

The deceased spouse's executor must make an irrevocable election on that deceased spouse's federal estate tax return (i.e. check the box).[20] The election stipulates that, to the extent the QTIP property has not been consumed or given away during the lifetime of the surviving spouse, its date-of-death value (at the surviving spouse's death) will be included in surviving spouse's gross estate. The QTIP trust property is included in the surviving spouse's gross estate and potentially subject to tax in the surviving spouse's estate, even though the surviving spouse is not allowed to take that property or decide who receives it when he or she dies. Of course, it is typically well worth that cost because the surviving spouse may live and enjoy trust income for many years, and the deceased spouse accomplishes his or her dispositive objectives while at the same time delaying potential federal estate taxes.

Disadvantages of a QTIP Trust

At first glance, the QTIP appears to satisfy all needs for all people. Unfortunately, this is not the case. The QTIP trust may not work if all or the bulk of the deceased spouse's estate assets consist of unproductive real estate or interest in a closely held business that does not produce consistent income. If the trust assets are not generating income, the IRS might claim the surviving spouse is not receiving the statutorily required "all income at least annually." The surviving spouse must

be given an interest that is realistically expected to produce income commensurate with its value. Most closely held business interests do not meet this challenge. For example, a closely held business interest providing either no dividends or dividends significantly below the lowest reasonable rate of return on an investment of equivalent fair market value cannot be said to produce an income "commensurate with its value." Without proper planning the marital deduction could be lost because the assets are not qualified.

State law could provide the surviving spouse with the power to require that trust assets be sold and that trust property be made productive in a reasonable period of time. But rather than rely on state law, the terms of the trust should give the surviving spouse the power to demand that "unproductive" (non-income-producing) property be made productive. If the surviving spouse can demand that the trustee sell the stock or other unproductive assets and use the proceeds to purchase income-producing property, the marital deduction can be saved, even if the power is never actually exercised.

Unfortunately, even if the surviving spouse is given the power to demand that the trustee sell the stock, there are practical problems. Assume that the planning objective was to pass the business to the next generation. If the surviving spouse can force a sale, what assurance does the next generation have that they can purchase the family business? The disruption of the family plan by either a minority or majority interest sale to a third party can be frustrating.

If the surviving spouse cannot force the trustee sell the unproductive assets, the surviving spouse can disrupt the plan by electing against the deceased spouse's will. While the spousal election laws of many states merely provide the spouse with a life estate in certain assets, other states grant the spouse an out portion of the estate and potentially trust assets.

If the surviving spouse does not force a sale of trust assets, where will she or he obtain income sufficient to maintain the current standard of living? With proper planning, illiquid non-productive assets can be protected. For instance an irrevocable trust holding a life insurance policy on the deceased spouse could provide the necessary liquidity to provide income to the surviving spouse for life. With income from another source, the surviving spouse may decide to leave the nonproductive property in the QTIP trust. If the surviving spouse directs the trustee of the QTIP trust to sell the nonproductive assets, then the irrevocable trust could purchase the assets. Alternatively, there could be a buy-sell agreement between the irrevocable trust and the estate so that the irrevocable trust could purchase the unproductive assets from the estate so that cash, rather than stock, goes into the QTIP trust.

BY-PASS TRUST

Avoiding federal estate taxes in the first spouse's estate is really simple, qualify everything for the federal estate tax marital deduction by passing it to the surviving spouse. The mark of good estate planning in most family situations is to eliminate, or at least significantly reduce, the federal estate tax at the survivor's death. In other words, to the extent possible, the assets should by-pass estate taxes at both spouse's deaths. Additional tax savings can be realized with the by-pass trust (also called the credit shelter, or family or "B" trust—because it's established in the B clause of the master trust). Rather than leaving the surviving spouse everything, whether outright or in a marital deduction qualifying trust, and have it included in the surviving spouse's estate and potentially subject to estate taxes, an amount up to the value of the federal estate tax exclusion amount (which is $11,400,000 in 2019) can be allocated to the by-pass trust.

Much like its name depicts, this amount by-passes the federal estate taxes when the surviving spouse dies. None of the assets allocated to the marital trust are subject to tax at the first spouse's death because of the marital deduction, and none of the assets allocated to the by-pass trust are taxed because of exclusion amount. As a result, the first spouse's estate, no matter how large it is will not incur federal estate taxes. This is exactly the same tax result as if all of the assets had be distributed to the surviving spouse either outright or in a marital trust. The difference in the two plans is realized at the surviving spouse's death. The by-pass trust is, by definition, designed to avoid the federal estate tax when the surviving spouse dies. Unlike the marital trust, none of the assets in the by-pass trust are included in the surviving spouse's estate. Therefore, the original value and all of the appreciation in the by-pass trust passes to the next generation without being subject to estate taxes in both the spouse's estates.

The current high exclusion amounts shifts the estate tax to income tax analysis away from avoiding estate tax (even at the 40 percent rate) to avoid income tax – specifically capital gains tax on the sale of assets held in the trust. While there are potential estate tax savings in funding the by-pass trust at the first spouse's death, most surviving spouses' estates will be under the available exclusion amount, and all but the very few will be under the combined exclusion amount. Although the tax aspects of a plan may shift the focus away from using a by-pass trust, there are still valid non-tax reasons to use a by-pass trust or other non-martial deduction qualifying trust at the first spouse's death.

Terms of a By-Pass Trust

Unlike the martial trust, there are no requirements for the by-pass trust to provide certain distribution rights or powers to the surviving spouse. The only requirement to consider is not inadvertently adding a right that would trigger unwanted inclusion of this trust in the surviving spouse's estate! The by-pass trust may have the surviving spouse as the sole beneficiary or provide for the surviving spouse and deceased spouse's descendants. By adding the grantor's descendants as permissible beneficiaries, wealth can be transfer down to the next generation during the surviving spouse's life by merely making distributions of the trust assets. If naming more than one beneficiary, it's prudent to give the trustee some guidance as to which beneficiary or generation of beneficiaries should be considered as the primary beneficiary of the trust. Because the children and perhaps grandchildren are beneficiaries of the trust, distributions from the trust are not gifts, and the surviving spouse may still utilize his or her annual exclusion gifting to increase the yearly wealth transfers.

The terms of the by-pass trust can be flexible and should match the goals of the family's estate plan. For example, the trust could provide for distributions of income to the surviving spouse or provide that all distributions of income and principal are discretionary. In addition and in order to preserve these assets for the next generation, the trust may provide that no distributions may be made to the surviving spouse until the marital trust assets are exhausted.

Family dynamics should be considered when adding trust beneficiaries. For example, whether the spouse and children should be beneficiaries of the trust when the spouse may not be the children's parent. There may be resentment or hostile feelings between the different beneficiaries especially if the trustee is allowed to make unequal distributions to the beneficiaries. In addition, a needy child may try to take advantage of a surviving spouse or either by undue influence or other means in order to gain an advantage over his or her siblings.

When the surviving spouse dies, the remaining trust assets pass, not according to the surviving spouse's estate, but under the terms of the trust as set out by the first deceased spouse. Providing the surviving spouse with a testamentary special power of appointment limited to the grantor's descendants can be a flexible tool not only to give the surviving spouse a negotiating point with potential hostile remainder beneficiaries, but also to protect the remainder beneficiaries if trust terms would not adequately protect them at the surviving spouse's death. For example, maybe one of the children is receiving government benefits and the trust terms would disqualify him or her from those benefits.

The larger the estate, the more dramatic the potential tax savings. But even in more modest estates, this combination of trusts can protect against unanticipated asset growth or frugal surviving spouses.. For example, assume the primary spouse has an estate with a value of $11,500,000 (net of expenses and debts) and the other spouse has assets of valued at $800,000. If the primary spouse leaves his or her entire estate to surviving spouse, the unlimited marital deduction will eliminate the tax at the first death. Surviving spouse lives on the after-tax income from the trust, income from his or her individually owned $800,000, and social security. But when surviving spouse dies, the individually owned $800,000 is added to the $11,500,000 received from the first spouse. Therefore, the total taxable estate is $12,300,000 or $900,000 more than the $11,400,000 surviving spouse's basic exclusion amount. The federal estate tax on that $900,000 is $360,000, in 2019. Because the deceased spouse did not use any of the $11,400,000 exclusion, this amount was wasted unless a portability election was made, and given the value of the assets and expectation that the surviving spouse would spend down the assets, a portability election may not have been made.

Now let's change the example. Assume, instead of leaving all of deceased spouse's assets to the surviving spouse, deceased spouse's will directed the assets into a master trust – which, by formula, created two trusts, a marital trust and a by-pass trust. Assume the first $11,400,000 of deceased spouse's $11,500,000 funded the by-pass trust and the balance (the remaining $100,000) funded the marital trust (which likely distributes the assets to spouse outright). The $11,400,000 going into the by-pass trust is included in the taxable estate, but it is excluded from actual tax by the basic exclusion amount, and the deceased spouse's estate owes no tax on this amount. In addition, the remaining $100,000 passing to the marital trust is not subject to tax because of the marital deduction. Now, the assets in the by-pass trust can appreciate in value without being subject to estate taxes or inclusion in the surviving spouse's estate, and the surviving spouse's estate only includes the $800,000 of individually owned assets and the $100,000 in the marital trust. In the next twenty years if this combined $100,000 appreciates in excess of surviving spouse's basic exclusion amount, then the family should be happy with their investment strategy! However, if the assets in the by-pass trust as likely to be sold shortly following the surviving spouse's death, then fully funding the by-pass trust and not taking advantage of a portability styled plan is not the most tax advantageous plan.

Disadvantages of a By-Pass Trust

The price of the estate tax savings potential of the credit shelter by-pass trust are income tax costs in term of carryover basis. At the first spouse's death, the assets receive a basis adjustment, and if the assets are included in the surviving spouse's estate another basis adjustment occurs. Assets in the by-pass trust are not included in the surviving spouse's estate. At the second spouse's death these asset transfer to the remainder beneficiaries, whether outright or in further trust, without receiving an additional basis adjustment.

For decades, estate planners had one goal, avoid the federal estate tax. This was the goal because the income tax consequences were relatively small compared to the estate tax consequences (40 percent or more tax on all assets over $600,000). In today's high estate tax exclusion environment, the focus has shifted to income tax savings because the vast majority of estates are never going to be subject to the estate tax. Basis planning must be taken into consideration when deciding whether to use a by-pass trust.

Under the current high exclusion amount and tax environment, the deceased spouse's plan should direct that all the assets are first paid to a trust that qualifies for the marital deduction. The trust could be a QTIP trust in which only a partial election is made, or the spouse may disclaim a portion of the assets to a different non-qualifying trust (i.e. the by-pass trust). By funding the marital trust first, the surviving spouse, with the help of trusted advisors, can determine whether to include all the assets in the surviving spouse estate for income tax planning or use some of the exclusion amount now (or later through lifetime gifts) to shift assets out of the surviving spouse's estate forgoing the income tax basis adjustment but also reducing the estate tax liability.

In addition, prior to portability, most marital deduction formulas utilized the smallest marital deduction necessary to avoid federal estate taxes. This in turn results in using all of the deceased spouse's exclusion amount and funding the by-pass trust before allocating assets to the marital trust. Given the currently large exclusion amount, many estates today may result in an unfunded marital trusts because the deceased spouse's estate is under the exclusion amount. If the terms of the by-pass trust favor non-surviving spouse beneficiaries over the surviving spouse then the deceased spouse's intention of provided for the surviving spouse for life has been compromised. The surviving spouse may dislike the plan, not to mention the plan drafter, and be forced to elect against the deceased spouse estate merely to receive assets that were intended for his or her benefit. While marital and by-pass trusts can be very useful tax saving plans, it's important to review the mechanics of the plan to ensure that the asset flow matches the spouse's intentions.

CLAYTON QTIP TRUST

The QTIP election provides a great deal of flexibility in estate tax planning because the executor can decide how much of the trust will actually qualify for the marital deduction by making a "partial" QTIP election on the federal estate tax return. Most funding plans direct that the assets will be allocated to one trust, either the marital or the by-pass, then any excess will go to the other trust. The standard formula requires setting the funding scheme before either spouse has died. Having the flexibility to wait until after the first spouse's death to allocate assets between the marital and by-pass trusts would be a nice tool. Following the decisions in the *Clayton* cases, the deceased spouse's executor can utilize this wait and see allocation method.[21] The result is increased flexibility, because the will (or revocable trust) can set up both a QTIP and by-pass trust, and the executor can decide how much of the estate goes into each trust. The deceased spouse's will and the master trust agreement that contains the marital and by-pass trusts need to provide the deceased spouse's executor with the authority to make a partial QTIP election and then provide where the assets not subject to the QTIP election pass. The surviving spouse is the income beneficiary of the QTIP trust and might or might not be the beneficiary of the by-pass trust. The will (or trust) needs to provide that the QTIP trust is funded with whatever fraction of the estate for which the executor makes the QTIP election, and the rest of the estate is distributed into the by-pass trust. An independent executor must make the QTIP election. The surviving spouse cannot be the executor of the estate and make a Clayton QTIP election.

QUALIFIED DOMESTIC TRUSTS

The estate tax marital deduction is not allowed if the surviving spouse is not a United States citizen.[22] If the surviving spouse is a citizen of another country, the deceased spouse's estate will not receive a marital deduction for assets that pass to the surviving spouse and depending on the size of the estate may have to pay the federal estate taxes. Denying a marital deduction in the first estate when the surviving spouse is not a U.S. citizen is revenue motivated. Congress is concerned that the alien-spouse, after having received assets from the deceased spouse's estate, would return home to his or her country along with the inherited money (including the deferred taxes) and beyond the reach of the IRS.

There are exceptions to the general rule that deny the marital deduction when the surviving spouse is not a U.S. citizen. If the surviving spouse becomes a U.S. citizen before the deceased spouse's estate tax return is filed and has been a U.S. resident at all times after the death of the deceased spouse and before becoming a U.S. citizen then the marital deduction is allowed provided that the interest that passes to the surviving spouse would otherwise qualify for the marital deduction. If citizenship is not obtainable or the residency requirements will be not be met, the property passing to the surviving spouse can be placed in a qualified domestic trust (QDOT) and obtain a limited marital deduction.

A QDOT is a trust that benefits the surviving resident alien noncitizen spouse that meets specific requirements. The trust must be created and maintained under U.S. federal or state law. The trust must require that at least one trustee is either an individual who is a U.S. citizen or a domestic corporation. The trust must provide that no principal distributions can be made from the QDOT unless the U.S. trustee "has the right to withhold the QDOT tax from that distribution" without the approval of any other trustee. Similar to qualifying assets in a QTIP, the deceased spouse's executor must make an irrevocable election for QDOT treatment. The QDOT must otherwise qualify as a transfer eligible for the marital deduction under the normal rules applicable to marital transfers.[23]

QDOTs can be into two types. Those that contain assets of more than $2,000,000 at the deceased citizen spouse's death, and those that contain assets of $2,000,000 or less at the deceased citizen spouse's death.[24] QDOTs with asset in excess of $2,000,000 must require that at least one U.S. trustee is a bank, or the U.S. trustee must provide a bond or other security equal to 65 percent of the fair market value of the trust's assets. QDOTs with $2,000,000 or less must meet similar bank-requirement tests or must require that no more than 35 percent of the trust's assets consist of real property located outside of the United States.[25]

Estate tax will be payable at the death of the first spouse to die if a transfer to a resident alien surviving spouse is made in a way that does not qualify under QDOT rules. The transfer will be subject to federal estate tax in the estate of the citizen spouse who predeceases the resident- alien-spouse. QDOTs are substantially different than other marital deduction trusts. The surviving spouse cannot receive principal distributions from the QDOT without paying estate tax. Moreover, the tax is not based on the size of the surviving spouse's estate, but on the size of the deceased spouse's estate. Think of it as an acceleration of the deferred tax in the deceased spouse's estate. The estate tax payable at the surviving spouse's death is computed by adding the assets in the QDOT to the assets owned at the deceased spouse's death. Every time any principal is paid out of the QDOT a new tax must be calculated. Unless there is a financial hardship, the surviving spouse should only receive trust income from the QDOT.

Remember even when qualifying for QDOT treatment a marital deduction does not forgive estate tax but merely delays the realization of that tax. The marital deduction defers the estate tax on the assumption that the deductible property will eventually be included in the surviving spouse's estate. Transfers to surviving spouses who are U.S. citizens can provide the spouse with the opportunity to freely take trust assets, and consume or give the assets away before death without triggering any tax. This cannot be done with a QDOT without generating an immediate estate tax.

Any distribution other than income to the surviving spouse or distribution to the surviving spouse on account of hardship made prior to the surviving spouse's death will result in an immediate tax. A hardship distribution is made in response to an immediate and substantial financial need relating to the noncitizen spouse's health, education, maintenance, or support. At the time of the surviving spouse's death, the entire value of the property in the QDOT will be subject to federal estate tax. There is no way to get asset appreciation

out of the trust without triggering tax. If the trust fails to meet any QDOT requirement, the estate tax will be imposed as if the surviving spouse had died on the date the trust failed the requirement. If the QDOT pays the tax imposed on any of the triggering events above, that payment is considered a taxable distribution that triggers additional tax. In other words, the QDOT's payment of the estate tax on a distribution is itself a distribution (equal to the amount of the tax) subject to a further estate tax. A QDOT is disqualified if the trust uses any device or arrangement the principal purpose of which is to avoid liability for the deferred estate tax.[26]

One solution is to avoid exposure to the QDOT tax by making provisions for the resident-alien- spouse through lifetime transfers. Gift tax rules permit intra-spousal transfers in amounts up to $155,000 per year in 2019. This opportunity is significant for planning purposes, since lifetime gifts to a resident alien spouse do not otherwise qualify for the unlimited marital deduction. To obtain this "super annual exclusion," the gift to the resident alien spouse must qualify under the normal rules for an annual exclusion gift and has to meet the requirements for a marital deduction as if the donee is a citizen. Through effective use of this gift exclusion, the citizen-spouse can transfer substantial assets to the resident alien spouse over time. The surviving spouse can use these assets for his or her support after the citizen spouse dies and thereby reduce the need to fund a QDOT. Moreover, the assets received through the lifetime gifts can avoid all transfer tax to the extent that the resident alien spouse consumes them, and they will qualify for the surviving spouse's unified credit if the resident alien spouse holds them until his or her death. In addition, the resident-alien-spouse is free to take the gifted property outside the United States and avoid U.S. transfer tax entirely if he or she is not a resident at the time of his or her death.

QDOTs and noncitizen planning can be very complex when there is the potential for a taxable estate. The tax imposed on the occurrence of a taxable event proves the QDOT to be a cleverly devised trap for the unwary planner. Different rules and regulations apply depending on different country relationships and treaties. Planning in this area definitely requires additional expertise and

CONCLUSION

The current estate tax exemption of $10,000,000 (as indexed for inflation), the unlimited marital deduction and portability combine together to make estate tax a thing of the past for all but the wealthiest of clients. For those wealthy clients, the use of QTIPS and bypass trusts along with a gifting strategy can literally save millions in dollars.

CHAPTER ENDNOTES

1. I.R.C. Sec. 2010(a); Treas. Reg. 20.2010-1(a).

2. I.R.C. Sec. 2010(c)(2), Treas, Reg. 20.2010-1(d)(2)

3. Pub. L. 115-97 (2017).

4. Pub. L. 115-123 (2018).

5. I.R.C. Sec. 2010(c)(3)(C).

6. I.R.C. Sec. 2010(a)(5)(A).

7. I.R.C. Sec. 2010(c)(4)(B)(ii).

8. I.R.C. Sec. 2010(c)(5)(A); Treas. Reg. 20.2010-2(a).

9. I.R.C. Sec. 2056(a).

10. Social Security Life Expectancy Table, https://www.ssa.gov/oact/STATS/table4c6.html (last accessed on 10/25/16).

11. I.R.C. Sec. 2056(d)(1)(A); 2056(b)(1).

12. I.R.C. Sec. 2056 (b) 5, 6, 7(B).

13. I.R.C. Sec. 2056(a).

14. I.R.C. Sec. 2056(b)(6).

15. I.R.C. Sec. 2056(b)(5).

16. *Id.*

17. I.R.C. Sec. 2056(b)(1)(A); I.R.C. Sec. 2056(b)(1)(B)

18. I.R.C. Sec.2056(b)(1)

19. Treas. Reg. 20.2056(b)-(7).

20. Treas. Reg. 20.2056(b)-7(d)(1).

21. *Clayton v. Comm'r.* 97 T.C. 327 (1991), rev'd, 976 F.2d 1486 (5th Cir. 1992), and abrogated by *Estate of Clack v. Comm'r*, 106 T.C. 131 (1996).

22. I.R.C. Sec. 2056(b)(5)

23. I.R.C. Sec. 2056(b)(5)-(8); Treas. Reg. 20.2056 (c)-2(b)(1)(i)-(iii).

24. Treas. Reg. 20.2056A-2(d)(1)(ii)(A).

25. Treas. Reg. 20.2056A-2(d)(1)(i)(A); Treas. Reg. 20.2056A-2(d)(1)(iii)(C)

26. Treas. Reg. 20.2056A-2(d)(1)(v).

COMMUNITY PROPERTY TRUSTS

CHAPTER 4

INTRODUCTION

The history of community property ("CP") law, a form of joint and concurrent ownership recognized in a handful of states within the United States, originated from civil law practiced in Spain and France. The French and Spanish versions of community property were introduced to the United States as a result of the Louisiana Purchase (contrasted with the original colonies that adopted the common law ("CL") systems from England). Over time, CL and CP laws became the mainstay of legal systems in the United States.

The states (in alphabetical order, that originally adopted and continue to have) a CP regime are: Arizona, California, Idaho, Louisiana, Nevada, New Mexico, Texas and Washington. Most recently, in 1986, Wisconsin adopted a pattern of law that followed the Uniform Marital Property Act ("UMPA") which treats Wisconsin marital property as the equivalent of community property.

MODERN EVOLUTION OF COMMUNITY PROPERTY TRUSTS

In 1998, Alaska passed the Alaska Community Property Act, enacting an 'elective' community property system. The Alaska statute allows residents to elect to classify property as CP (i.e., by agreement). The statute also allows both residents and non-residents, alike, to fund Alaska CP trusts ("AKCPTs") with the intent that property in such trusts are treated as CP (for Federal income tax purposes). In 2010, Tennessee followed suit and enacted an 'elective' statute[1] that allows residents and non-residents to create Tennessee community property trusts ("TNCPT's"). As of July 1, 2016, South

Dakota joined the fray and has a new statute, more akin to Tennessee's version, rather than Alaska's version, that allows residents and non-residents to create South Dakota community property trusts ("SDCPT's").[2]

This chapter discusses the concept of the Community Property Trust ("CPT") and the benefits and burdens of such trusts. We will contrast the varying statutes (i.e., Alaska, Tennessee and South Dakota) and discuss the related Federal income tax issues.

WHAT IS A COMMUNITY PROPERTY TRUST ("CPT")?

For purposes of this chapter, a CPT is a trust created under the laws of the, Tennessee and South Dakota, that allows residents and non-residents to characterize states of Alaska property transferred into those trusts as CP under the laws of those states.

One of the purposes of creating a CPT is to take advantage of the provisions under Code section 1014(b)(6)[3] which allows the income tax basis of community property (whether titled in the name of a decedent, the decedent's surviving spouse, or jointly) to receive a "full" basis adjustment at death.

The Full Basis Adjustment for Community Property

It is said, for income tax purposes, 100 percent of a decedent's CP receives a basis adjustment at death (i.e., the "full" basis adjustment).[4] We use examples to explain this by first looking at the results under a CL jurisdiction and examine the same situations under a CP law regime.

37

HOW IT WORKS

The following examples illustrate the benefit of the full basis adjustment at death.

Common Law Property States

Assume following facts: For the next few examples assume the following:

- Spouse 1 (S1) is married to Spouse 2 (S2).

- Do not have a nuptial agreement.

- They have not inherited anything from anyone.

- All of their wealth was created by their own work, to which they contributed equally.

- S1 predeceases S2.

- At the time of S1's death, the fair market value ("FMV") of the assets was $4 million and the adjusted basis ("A/B") is $1 million.

- S1 leaves everything (that S1 owns) to S2 at the time of S1's death.

These general facts above will apply to the following examples, unless otherwise stated.

Example 1. Assume the general facts and during their married life, until the death of S1, all of the assets were held in an account in S1's individual name. S1's Last Will and Testament leaves all of S1's assets to S2 at his death. Assume S1 and S2 lived in a CL state all of their lives.

In Example 1, because S1 and S2 live in a CL state, S1 is deemed to be the owner of the assets in S1's name. Because S1 owns all of the assets at death (which passes to S2), the basis of such assets in S2's hands will be the FMV of those assets at the time of S1's death (i.e., $4 million). The analysis of how we come to this conclusion is as follows: Code section 1014(a)(1) provides,

" ... the basis of property in the hands of a person acquiring the property from a decedent or to whom the property passed from a decedent shall ... be ...

the fair market value of the property at the date of the decedent's death."[5] [emphasis added]

Code sections 1014(b)(1) through (10), inclusive define the terms, "property in the hands of a person acquiring property from a decedent" and "to whom the property passed from a decedent". In Example 1, Code section 1014(b)(1) would apply and treat the property that S2 received from S1 as having a date of death fair market value in S2's hands (i.e., $4,000,000).[6]

Example 2. Assume the same facts as Example 1, except all of the assets were held by S2 at the time of S1's death.

In Example 2, because S2 had all of the assets at S1's death, and S1 had no assets, nothing passed from S1 to S2, thus, there is no basis adjustment under Code section 1014. Thus, the A/B of S2's assets before and after S1's death will be the same (i.e., $1 million).

Example 3. Assume the same facts as Example 1, except one-half of the assets were owned by S1 at the time of S1's death and the other one-half was owned by S2. Assume that the FMV and A/B of the assets owned by each of S1 and S2 were $2 million and $500,000, respectively.

In Example 3, because S1 had title to one-half of the assets and S2 had title to the other one-half, only S1's one-half would be treated as passing from S1 to S2 as a result of S1's death, so only one-half of those appreciated assets would receive an upward basis adjustment. Thus, as to the one-half of the assets that passed from S1 to S2, under Code sections 1014(a) and (b)(1), S2 would have a basis of $2 million. As to the other one-half, S2 would keep the $500,000 basis. Therefore, S2's basis at S1's date of death would be $2.5 million.

The following table shows the difference in the basis for Examples 1, 2 and 3:

	A/B at the time of S1's Death in S2's hands	FMV at the time of S1's death
Example 1	$4 million	$4 million
Example 2	$1 million	$4 million
Example 3	$2.5 million	$4 million

As we can see, in CL states, only assets that are titled in the decedent's name and pass to another person (i.e., the surviving spouse in our examples) receive a basis adjustment. In Example 1, it was all of the assets; in Example 2, it was none of the assets; and in Example 3, it was one-half of the assets.

Community Property State

In the following examples, we examine the basis adjustment of CP at death.

_____

Example 4. Assume the same facts as Example 1, except that S1 and S2 lived all of their lives in a CP state. Assume that all of their property is CP.

_____

In Example 4, because the property is CP, it is deemed that one-half is owned by S1 and one-half is owned by S2, regardless of where the actual title to such property lies. Thus, at S1's death S1 is deemed to own one-half and that one-half passes to S2 at S1's death, and S2 is deemed to have owned the other one-half of the assets. Based on that ownership, Code section 1014(b)(1) adjusts the basis of S1's one-half of the CP as passing from S1 to S2 to the FMV at S1's date of death. Additionally, Code section 1014(b)(6)[7] adjusts the basis of S2's one-half to the date of death FMV. Thus, the basis of 100 percent of the property in S2's hands will be $4 million (i.e., $2 million adjustment under IRC §§1014(a) and (b)(1) and $2 million adjustment under IRC §§1014(a) and (b)(6)).

_____

Example 5. Assume the same facts as Example 2 (i.e., where title of the property was in S2's hands), except that S1 and S2 lived all of their lives in a CP state.

_____

The result in Example 5 is identical to that of Example 4. The reason for this lies in the fact that since the property was CP, S1 is deemed to own one-half of such property, even though S2 is the title owner of the of the property.[8] Thus, the basis of the property in S2's hands (after S1's demise) would also be $4 million.

_____

Example 6. Assume the same facts as Example 3 (i.e., where title is one-half in

S1's and one-half in S2's hands), except that S1 and S2 lived all of their lives in a CP state.

_____

The result in Example 6 would be the same in Examples 4 and 5, for the same reason (i.e., S1 and S2 are deemed to each own one-half of the property). Thus, the basis in S2's hands would be $4 million.

It is for this reason that it is often said that both halves receive a basis adjustment, or there is a "full" basis step adjustment for CP. Some also refer to this as the "double step-up" in basis. (See Frequently Asked Questions below for further information).

Common Law States that Have Enacted CP Statutes (Hybrid States)

As discussed above, in the last thirty years, four states have enacted some form of a community property statute, in part, based on the Uniform Marital Property Act.[9] They include Wisconsin, Alaska, Tennessee and South Dakota.

In CP states, spouses may own property as "community property". They may also elect out of that form of CP ownership and opt for traditional CL types of ownership (e.g., tenants in common, joint tenants with rights of survivorship or (in some states) tenancy by the entireties).[10] Generally, CP states treat spouses as one unit. And, thus, CP is said to be co-owned by a single unit, and, also co-managed by the unit.[11]

CP can generally be terminated by agreement, dissolution of marriage, and death, but CP states vary on how they treat the termination of property rights. For instance in the case of dissolution of marriage, the states divide on whether the property should be divided on equal or some other form of equitable distribution.

States also divide on other issues. For instance, there is disparate treatment in states with regard to how to treat property of a married couple who are migrating from other CP states and from non-CP states.[12] States are also divided on whether income earned during the marriage is CP or separate property.

States are divided on whether the CP regime should be "optional" or mandatory. This, as we will see, is the basis for the important question of whether the full basis adjustment would work in a state like Alaska, Tennessee, and South Dakota, where the system is optional (i.e., a so-called "opt-in" system). In the traditional CP states (i.e., Arizona California, Idaho, Louisiana, Nevada, New Mexico, Texas and Washington) the systems are mandatory. However in the mandatory states, spouses may convert CP to separate property. Conversion is called "transmutation." An important question comes to mind: Is transmutation elective? If so, this power may impact one's ability to obtain the "double" basis adjustment. As of the time of this writing, the law is not yet fully developed.

Wisconsin

As of January 1, 1986, Wisconsin became the ninth state to have a form of CP by adopting (with modification) UMPA. Wisconsin's version of CP is contained in the Wisconsin Marital Property Act ("WMPA").[13]

The Wisconsin statute governs the property of married persons during their marriage and at death. In cases of divorce, Wisconsin tends to go back to its CL roots and uses an equitable distribution type of distribution scheme. The statue allows residents to "opt out" of the regime by a marital property agreement.[14]

From an income tax standpoint, even though the term used by WMPA is "marital property," the IRS held that "marital property" in Wisconsin will be treated as "community property" for purposes of the full basis adjustment under IRC section 1014(b)(6).[15]

Alaska

As of May 23, 1998, Alaska's "elective" Community Property Act ("AKCPA") became effective.[16] The AKCPA allows married couples, both of whom are Alaskan residents, to elect (by agreement) to classify any part or all of their property as CP for state law purposes.[17] The AKCPA also allows both residents and non-residents to hold property in CPTs,[18] and, if the trusts are properly structured and administered, the property held in such CPT's will be treated as CP for state law purposes.[19]

When the AKCPA was enacted in 1998, Alaska became the first state in over fifty years to have an opt-in community property statute.[20] AKCPA is modeled after the UMPA, thus, it looks a little like the Wisconsin statute, the major difference is that Wisconsin is an "opt out" state (akin to other traditional CP states), whereas, Alaska is an "opt in" state.[21] In other words, residents of Alaska can decide if they would like to take

advantage of the CP statute (or not), because the CP law is not mandatory. Additionally, non-Alaska residents and Alaska residents, alike, could also opt-in to take advantage of the CPT provisions.[22]

Marital Property versus Community Property. It should be noted that even though Alaska based a lot of its law on the Wisconsin version of UMPA, Alaska has changed the nomenclature of the UMPA from "marital property" to "community property".[23] Additionally the terms "individual property" and "separate property" are used, instead of only using the traditional "separate property".[24]

Type of Property at Death of the First Spouse to Die. Upon the death of the first spouse to die (i.e., the decedent spouse), the Alaska's default provision is that CP is owned one-half by the decedent spouse and one-half by the surviving spouse.[25]

Residency Requirement. The married couple does not be need resident in Alaska to create an AKCPT.[26] However, as discussed below, there is a requirement for the trustee to have some nexus with the state. Either or both of the spouses may be a trustee. If the spouse is a trustee, but is not a resident of Alaska, then there is a requirement that a "qualified person" must be a trustee. A qualified person is generally an individual residing in Alaska,[27] a trust company organized under Alaska law with its principal place of business in Alaska,[28] a bank organized under Alaska law that possesses and exercises trust powers and has its place of business in Alaska,[29] and a national banking association (organized under 12 USC 21 – 216d, if such national banking association possesses and exercises trust powers and has its place of business in Alaska.)[30]

Trust Execution. The trust must be signed by both spouses.[31]

Pick and Choose. Spouses may pick and choose the assets that they wish to have treated as CP in the AKCPT.[32] To the extent that there is CP and non-CP, the trustee is required to keep a record of the different types of property.[33]

Present Undivided Interest. The spouse's interest in property designated as CP held in an AKCPT is a present undivided one-half interest in such CP.[34]

Management of CP in the CPT. Either spouse acting alone may manage the CP held in the AKCPT, if so desired.[35]

Gifts- Either spouse may make small gifts from the CPT (currently $1,000).[36] Larger gifts require joint action of the spouses or consent of the non-gift making spouse.[37]

Bona Fide Purchasers. The AKCPT statute protects bona fide purchasers of the trust's CP.[38]

Unconscionability. Alaska wanted to protect the property rights of spouses, since entering into a CPT is akin to entering into a premarital / post-marital agreement. Accordingly, CPTs can be set aside on a number of different bases, including unconscionability,[39] if the CPT was not voluntarily entered into,[40] and other similar reasons.

Special Language in the CPT. The CPT must have the following special language on the front page of the trust.

"THE CONSEQUENCES OF THIS TRUST MAY BE VERY EXTENSIVE, INCLUDING, BUT NOT LIMITED TO, YOUR RIGHTS WITH RESPECT TO CREDITORS AND OTHER THIRD PARTIES, AND YOUR RIGHTS WITH YOUR SPOUSE BOTH DURING THE COURSE OF YOUR MARRIAGE AND AT THE TIME OF A DIVORCE. ACCORDINGLY, THIS AGREEMENT SHOULD ONLY BE SIGNED AFTER CAREFUL CONSIDERATION. IF YOU HAVE ANY QUESTIONS ABOUT THIS AGREEMENT, YOU SHOULD SEEK COMPETENT ADVICE."[41]

Summary of the AKCPT Requirements. The AKCPT must be a written instrument that may be created by any married couple, resident and non-resident alike. The trust must be signed by both spouses. Additionally, the CPT must have at least one qualified trustee and must have the special language, as provided for above. The couple must enter into the trust voluntarily. There are many permissive provisions; thus, the trust could be as flexible as any other estate planning revocable trust.

Tennessee

The Tennessee Community Property Trust of 2010 ("TNCPT") Act became effective on July 1, 2010.[42] The TNCPT Act allows married residents or non-residents of Tennessee to treat property transferred to the TNCPT as community property.[43] Thus, one or both spouses (residents or non-residents of Tennessee) may transmute individually or jointly-owned property to community property by transferring it to a TNCPT.[44]

Marital Property Versus Community Property. Tennessee uses the term "community property" instead of "marital property."[45] The terms individual and separate property are also used throughout the TNCPT Act.

Type of Property at Death of the First Spouse to Die. Upon the death of the first spouse to die (i.e., the decedent spouse), one-half of the property owned by the TNCPT is the decedent spouse's share and the other one-half is the surviving spouse's share.[46]

Residency Requirement. The married couple does not be need to be a resident of Tennessee to create a TNCPT.[47] However, as discussed below, there is a requirement for the trustee to have some nexus with the state.

Trustee. Either or both of the spouses may be a trustee. If the spouse-trustee is not a resident of Tennessee, then there is a requirement that only a "qualified trustee" may be a trustee. A qualified trustee is generally an individual residing in Tennessee,[48] or a business that is authorized to act as a fiduciary in the state of Tennessee under Tennessee statutes section 45-2-1001.[49]

Trust Execution. The trust must be signed by both spouses.[50]

No Pick and Choose. Spouses may designate the property that will be funded into a TNCPT during the couple's marriage.[51] However, once the property is in the TNCPT, it will be CP.[52] This is different than Alaska, where spouses can pick and choose whether property in an AKCPT is CP or not.[53] If property is distributed from the CPT, such property is no longer considered CP.[54] Note, in Alaska, if the CP is distributed from an AKCPT to a spouse, the distributed property remains CP.[55] Thus, in Tennessee, to stay CP, the property must be held in a TNCPT.

Present Undivided Interest. It is not crystal clear if the spouse's interest in property designated as CP held in a TNCPT is a present undivided one-half interest in such CP as to each spouse, because unlike the Alaska statute[56] that so provides, the Tennessee statute is silent on this issue. However, the statute provides that either spouse may amend a TNCPT regarding the disposition of that spouse's one-half interest in the trust.[57] In the event that a creditor wants to reach property, it appears that the creditor of a spouse may reach such one-half of the CP in the TNCPT,[58] and in the event of dissolution of marriage, the CP held in the trust is to be distributed one-half to each of the spouses. Thus, an inference could be made that each of the spouses has an undivided one-half present interest in the TNCPT's property.[59]

Management of CP in the CPT. The Tennessee statute provides that the trust's terms determine who manages the property.[60]

Gifts. Tennessee's statute is silent with regard to making gifts. This is different than the Alaska statute which has specific requirements regarding gifts.[61]

Bona Fide Purchasers. The TNCPT statute is silent with regard to protecting bona fide purchasers of the trust's CP.

Unconscionability. Unlike Alaska's version of the CP statutes, Tennessee is silent about the enforceability of the TNCPT.

Special Language in the CPT. The TNCPT must have the following special language on the front page of the trust.

"THE CONSEQUENCES OF THIS TRUST MAY BE VERY EXTENSIVE, INCLUDING, BUT NOT LIMITED TO, YOUR RIGHTS WITH YOUR SPOUSE BOTH DURING THE COURSE OF YOUR MARRIAGE AND AT THE TIME OF A DIVORCE. ACCORDINGLY, THIS AGREEMENT SHOULD ONLY BE SIGNED AFTER CAREFUL CONSIDERATION. IF YOU HAVE ANY QUESTIONS ABOUT THIS AGREEMENT, YOU SHOULD SEEK COMPETENT ADVICE."[62]

Summary of the TNCPT Requirements. The TNCPT must be a written instrument that may be created by any married couple, resident and non-resident alike. The trust must be signed by both spouses. Additionally, the CPT must have at least one qualified trustee and must have the special language, as provided for above. Unlike the Alaska version of the statute, the Tennessee version is silent on many issues. However, like the Alaska version, there are many permissive provisions; thus, the trust could be as flexible as any other estate planning revocable trust.

South Dakota

As of July 1, 2016, South Dakota is the newest state to enact their version of the CPT trust law, namely the South Dakota Community Property Special Spousal Trust ("SDCPSST") Act.[63] In South Dakota, legally

married couples may classify all or any of their property as "special spousal property" by transferring property to a special spousal trust (the "SDCPT"),[64] which would specifically provide that the trust property is CP.[65]

Marital Property Versus Community Property. South Dakota refers to the property as "special spousal property" and "community property"; the statute does not use the term "marital property".[66]

Type of Property at Death of the First Spouse to Die. Upon the death of the first spouse to die, South Dakota appears to leave it up to the spouses on how the property is to be distributed.[67]

Residency Requirement. The married couple does not be need to be a resident of South Dakota to create a SDCPT.[68] However, as discussed below, there is a requirement for the trustee to have some nexus with the state.

Trustee. Either or both of the spouses may be a trustee. If the spouse-trustee is not a resident of South Dakota, then there is a requirement that a "qualified person" must be a trustee. A qualified person is generally an individual residing in South Dakota.[69] A trust company that has its principal place of business in South Dakota, and a bank or savings association that has trust powers in South Dakota are also qualified persons.[70]

Trust Execution. The trust must be signed by both spouses.[71]

Pick and Choose. Like Alaska and Tennessee, spouses can pick and choose which property they would like to transfer into the SDCPT. Like Tennessee, and unlike Alaska, all of the property transferred into the trust will become CP if defined as special spousal property.[72] The trustee must maintain records of the same.[73]

Present Undivided Interest. South Dakota is unclear of the exact interest of the spouse's property once it is in the trust. However, in the provision regarding amendment and revocation of the trust, it provides that a surviving spouse may amend the trust with regard to such surviving spouse's share. Specifically, the statute reads as follows:

"For purposes of this section, the term, surviving spouse's property, means the property that consists of the surviving spouse's property that is not South Dakota special spousal property and the surviving spouse's share of the special spousal property determined as of the date of the first spouse's death."[74]

The statute is eerily silent on how one determines the surviving spouse's share as determined on the first spouse's death. Perhaps one can infer that since the spouses can determine the rights to the property, etc., one would determine under the trust the amount that the decedent's estate is entitled to and the amount that he surviving spouse is entitled to.[75]

Management of CP in the CPT. Either spouse acting alone may manage the CP held in the CPT, if so desired.[76]

Gifts. Like Tennessee, and unlike Alaska, the statute is silent about a spouse's ability to make gifts of CP in the SDCPT.

Bona Fide Purchasers. Like Alaska, somewhat, the SDCPT statute has some protections for bona fide purchasers of the trust's CP.

Unconscionability. Similar to the Alaskan provision, South Dakota wishes to protect spouses against trusts that are unconscionable when made, if not made voluntarily with knowledge, and entered into unreasonably and unfairly by one of the spouses.[77]

Special Language in the CPT. The SDCPT must have the following special language on the front page of the trust.

"THE CONSEQUENCES OF THIS TRUST MAY BE VERY EXTENSIVE, INCLUDING YOUR RIGHTS WITH RESPECT TO CREDITORS AND OTHER THIRD PARTIES, AND YOUR RIGHTS WITH YOUR SPOUSE BOTH DURING THE COURSE OF YOUR MARRIAGE, AT THE TIME OF A DIVORCE, AND AT THE DEATH OF YOU OR YOUR SPOUSE. ACCORDINGLY, THIS TRUST AGREEMENT SHOULD ONLY BE SIGNED AFTER CAREFUL CONSIDERATION. IF YOU HAVE ANY QUESTIONS ABOUT THIS TRUST AGREEMENT, YOU SHOULD SEEK INDEPENDENT LEGAL ADVICE."[78]

Reference to IRC §1014(b)(6). Interestingly, unlike the Alaska and the Tennessee versions of the law, South Dakota has a special provision that says that property transferred to the trust that is treated as CP in another jurisdiction, will continue to be treated as CP under South Dakota law when and if such property is distributed provided such property would be treated

as CP in the other jurisdiction. Specifically, the statute reads as follows:

For purposes of the application of §1014(b)(6) of the Internal Revenue Code of 1986, 26 U.S.C. §1014(b)(6), as of January 1, 2016, a South Dakota special spousal trust is considered a trust established under the community property laws of South Dakota. For purposes of this chapter, the term special spousal property, means community property for those purposes. Community property as classified by a jurisdiction other than South Dakota transferred to a South Dakota special spousal trust retains its character as community property while in the trust. If the trust is revoked and property is transferred on revocation of the trust, the community property as classified by a jurisdiction other than South Dakota retains its character as community property to the extent otherwise provided by South Dakota law.[79]

Summary of the TNCPT Requirements. The SDCPT must be a written instrument that may be created by any married couple, resident and non-resident alike. The trust must be signed by both spouses. Additionally, the CPT must have at least one qualified trustee and must have the special language, as provided for above. The couple must enter into the trust voluntarily. There are many permissive provision, thus, the trust could be as flexible as any other estate planning revocable trust.

North Carolina – Not Yet Enacted

As of the writing of this chapter, North Carolina was attempting to introduce a CPT regime into legislation. In 2015, they were unsuccessful; however, it appears they are trying to implement a regime similar to the Alaska version.

Florida – Thinking About It

As of the writing of this chapter, the author is the co-chair of a subcommittee of the Florida Bar's Real Property Probate and Trust Law section's Estate Tax Committee. The subcommittee was created to investigate whether it would be worthwhile for Florida to enact a statue similar to one of those above (including Wisconsin, Alaska, Tennessee or South Dakota). One of the purposes is to provide Florida residents with the ability to achieve a full basis adjustment at the time of the first spouse's death for assets held in a CPT. The subcommittee is in its infancy stages and is investigating this thoroughly.

Who are the Parties to a Community Property Trust?

The Trust. As discussed above with regard to the specific states that have enacted CPT statutes, in general, the Community Property Trust must be a written instrument, where one or both spouses transfer property to the CPT, and the CPT must expressly state that some or all of the property contained therein shall be treated as community property under the CPT statutes. Further, the CPT must also contain certain language in capital letters at the beginning of the instrument. Additionally, the CPT could be either revocable or irrevocable by either or both spouses.

Typically, the trust will be a joint revocable trust, which is revocable by both spouses, and the CPT would typically have property that will be considered community property under the state's statute.

The Grantor(s). As detailed above, the grantors will generally be a legally married couple.[80]

The Beneficiaries. The beneficiaries can be the same beneficiaries that are typical under one's estate plan. Thus, we would anticipate that the beneficiaries would likely be the surviving spouse, family members and charity.

The Trustee. Each of the states have a provision that at least one trustee will be a trustee who is a resident of the state. The general reason for this provision is to provide a nexus between the trust and the particular state (e.g., Alaska, Tennessee and/or South Dakota).

Open Issues

When the "next best thing to sliced bread" comes along in the tax world, Treasury and the Internal Revenue Service ("IRS" or "Service") generally get nervous and tend to have a skeptical reaction that something's not right. To proceed in this area where the law is arguably not fully developed, one has to parse the law carefully and examine the pros and cons of the suggested strategy. On examination, what may "not sound right" could turn out to be a sound strategy.

The CPT statutes in Alaska, Tennessee and South Dakota are really wonderful tools, if they work. In today's estate planning environment, where the emphasis has shifted a bit away from transfer taxes,[81] and more to income taxes, these state laws put into play the ability of every married couple to get a full step up in basis for assets held in the CPT and determined to be community property for income tax purposes. So, the big question is whether this strategy (i.e., using a CPT in Alaska, Tennessee or South Dakota) works? Is this the next best thing to sliced bread?

If it works, then anyone with some form of wealth, regardless of whether they meet the state or federal threshold to pay estate tax, may want to consider this as a planning tool to minimize income taxes (both at a state and at the Federal levels).

We then leave it to the reader to analyze the strategy and make a determination of the CPT's efficacy.

CONCLUSION

The "full basis adjustment" as a result of IRC §§1014(b)(1) and (b)(6) is a tremendous benefit for couples who live in CP states, or those who are able to treat property as CP at the time of the decedent spouse's death. As history shows us, the statutes that are currently viewed as providing a tremendous advantage to owners of CP, originally was viewed as a way to remedy an injustice to those same owners. We are fortunate that we've had IRC §1014(b)(6) for roughly seventy years (i.e., since 1948). In light of the greater focus on income taxes, tax basis adjustments become a more significant issue today than it has been in the past. Although not entirely clear, it appears that the CPT statues (like the Alaska version), may offer non-CP residents an opportunity to take advantage of the full basis adjustment. The planner should look at that strategy as a possible method to allow clients the benefit of the full basis adjustment that is generally afforded to CP residents.

FREQUENTLY ASKED QUESTIONS

Question – Why do residents of community property receive such a benefit over common law residents?

Answer – The first clause of IRC §1014(b)(6) states, "... [i]n the case of decedents dying after December 31, 1947 ..." Thus, this law came into effect in the late 1940's. From a social standpoint, at that time, typically the husband[82] had the title to all of the property. Additionally, statistically, the husband predeceased the wife. Thus, absent Code section 1014(b)(6), if 100 percent of the property was CP and titled in the husband's name, then only one-half of the property was deemed to be the husband's property. Thus, only the husband's deemed one-half would receive a basis adjustment under what is now Code section 1014(b)(1), leaving the wife's deemed one-half ownership, without any basis adjustment.

By comparison, if the couple lived in a CL state at that time, and if the property was titled in husband's name (which it generally was) and such property all passed to the surviving wife (which it generally did), the basis in the hands of the wife would be for 100 percent of the property (under the predecessor to Code section 1014(b)(1)). Thus, back in the late 1940's the precursor to the current Code section 1014(b)(6) was put into the Internal Revenue Code of 1939 to give the surviving CP spouse the same result as the surviving CL spouse. Today, many view Code section 1014(b)(6) as an unfair benefit to the surviving community property spouse, but that was not the case when originally enacted in the 1940s!

Question – Who may benefit from a CPT?

Answer – A CPT may be beneficial for those married couples who are in a stable relationship, with children exclusively of that marriage (or think of step or adopted children as being issue of the marriage) and who have the same goals for the distribution of assets upon the first and second deaths.

The CPT has its greatest benefit for those couples who have low basis assets and where the risk of death is unknown (i.e., they both have roughly the same possibility of dying). One of the possible benefits[83] of the CPT is that upon the death of the first spouse to die (the "decedent spouse") the basis of the CPT's appreciated assets is stepped up to the FMV. Thus, the surviving spouse ("surviving spouse") receives 100 percent of the assets with a new FMV basis upon the decedent spouse's death.

Question – Why use a CPT?

Answer – The CPT has both non-tax and tax benefits. It is easy to use, in that you won't have to have two separate trusts for the spouses during lifetime (i.e., it is a joint trust). From an income tax perspective, there is the perceived step up in basis for appreciated assets at the decedent spouse's death. From

an estate planning perspective, the spouses can accomplish all of the estate and generation-skipping transfer ("GST") tax planning in the same manner as if they had separate trusts. From an administrative standpoint, during life, there's probably a little less administration expense, by comparison to separate trust

Question – Are CPTs too good to be true?

Answer – It "may" be too good to be true. We emphasize the word "may", because it might just work. What's important is that if the assets in the trust are considered CP, the provisions under IRC §1014(b)(6) provide that 100 percent of the basis of such property is adjusted. The $64,000 (or $64 million, or $64 billion) question is whether assets are CP (or not).

CHAPTER ENDNOTES

1. The Tennessee Community Property Trust Act of 2010. As noted, some argue that an elective system (i.e., an opt-in system) may be different for income tax purposes upon the death of the first spouse to die.

2. As of the writing of this material, the IRS has not published any rulings taking the position that the property in the AKCPT, TNCPT or SDCPT would be treated as CP for Federal income tax purposes.

3. Unless otherwise stated, the Internal Revenue Code of 1986, as amended, is referred to as "I.R.C." or the "Code".

4. I.R.C. §1014(b)(6). This statement is a bit of an overstatement, because there are two basic requirements that must be met. First, the property must be categorized as CP in a state, territory, possession of the United States or a foreign country. And, second, at least one-half (½) of the CP must be included in the decedent spouse's gross estate for Federal estate tax purposes.

5. Under I.R.C. §1014(a), there are four alternative values that can be used. The most common value is the date of death fair market value ("FMV") and that is the value assumed for purposes of this chapter.

6. Specifically, I.R.C. §1014(b)(1) provides:

   "(b) Property acquired from the decedent - For purposes of subsection (a), the following property shall be considered to have been acquired from or to have passed from the decedent:

   (1) Property acquired by bequest, devise, or inheritance, or by the decedent's estate from the decedent ..."

7. Specifically, I.R.C. §1014(b)(6) provides:

   (b) Property acquired from the decedent - For purposes of subsection (a), the following property shall be considered to have been acquired from or to have passed from the decedent: ...

   (6) In the case of decedents dying after December 31, 1947, property which represents the surviving spouse's one-half share of community property held by the decedent and the surviving spouse under the community property laws of any State, or possession of the United States or any foreign country, if at least one-half of the whole of the

community interest in such property was includible in determining the value of the decedent's gross estate under chapter 11 of subtitle B (section 2001 and following, relating to estate tax) or section 811 of the Internal Revenue Code of 1939; ..."

8. This is akin to Example 4, except in Example 4 the title was in S1's hands. But, because it is community property, title ownership is basically irrelevant. The property is deemed owned one-half by S1 and one-half by S2.

9. To see some of the source material for Alaska's CP law (and arguably Tennessee's and South Dakota's as well) see the Uniform Marital Property Act at http://www.uniformlaws.org/shared/docs/marital%20property/umpa_final_83.pdf. For a good article about the history and intent of UMPA, see, Cantwell, *The Uniform Marital Property Act: Origin and Intent*, Marquette L. Rev., Vol. 68, Iss. 3, Spr. 1985.

10. It is beyond the scope of this chapter to discuss the details of CP and the varying forms of traditional CL ownership. The author only wants to set the stage for analyzing the CP trusts.

11. CP currently does not carry with it the concept of survivorship.

12. Interestingly, CL states are divided on how to treat property of those who have migrated from CP states to CL states, too.

13. Wis. Stat. §766.001(2).

14. Wis. Stat. §766.17.

15. Rev. Rul. 87-13, 1987-1 CB 20.

16. AK Statutes, Title 34, Chapter 77.

17. AK Stat. §34.77.060(a) (2016).

18. AK Stat. §§34.77.030(a) and 34.77.060(b) (2016).

19. AK Stat. §§34.77.030(e) (2016).

20. In 1939 and in 1942, Oklahoma and Oregon, respectively, had enacted elective CP statutes. The primary purpose of those statutes was to take advantage of "income tax splitting" between spouses so that they could take advantage of "running up the brackets" to minimize income tax. Recall that in the early 1940's we did not enjoy joint tax returns between spouses, thus, the goal of the Oklahoma and Oregon statutes was to have spouses elect to treat their property as CP, thus, one-half of each of the spouse's incomes would each be recognized separately, and each spouse could "run up" his and her brackets, thereby reducing the overall income tax to the family unit. Unfortunately, the U.S. Supreme Court decided in *Commissioner v. Harmon*, 323 U.S. 44 (1944), that the "opt-in" statutes (or Oklahoma and Oregon) would not accomplish the income tax benefits that were intended. Soon thereafter Oklahoma and Oregon abandoned the CP regime, and have maintained that stance as of the writing of this chapter.

21. AK Stat. §§34.77.060(a) and (b) (2016).

22. AK Stat. §34.77.060(b) (2016).

23. AK Stat. §34.77.900(3) (2016).

24. AK Stat. §34.77.110(c) (2016).

25. AK Stat. §34.77.155(a) (2016). It should be noted, that spouses may elect to have their property divided on a non-pro rata basis at the time of the death of the first spouse to die. AK Stat. §34.77.155(c).

26. AK Stat. §34.77.060(b) (2016).

27. AK Stat. §§34.77.100(a)(1)(A) – (D) (2016).

28. AK Stat. 34.77.100(a)(2) (2016).

29. AK Stat. 34.77.100(a)(3) (2016).

30. AK Stat. 34.77.100(a)(3) (2016).

31. AK Stat. 34.77.100(a) (2016).

32. AK Stat. §§34.77.100(a); 34.77.100(d); 34.77.110; and 34.77.130 (2016).

33. AK Stat. §34.77.100(h) (2016).

34. AK Stat. §34.77.030(c) (2016).

35. AK Stat. §34.77.040 (2016).

36. AK Stat. §34.77.050(a) (2016).

37. AK Stat. §§34.77.050(b) and (c) (2016).

38. AK Stat. §34.77.080 (2016).

39. AK Stat. §34.77.100(f)(1) (2016).

40. AK Stat. §34.77.100(f)(2) (2016).

41. AK Stat. §34.77.100(b)(2016).

42. TN Code, Title 35, Chapter 17 (being TN ST. §35-17-101 et seq.).

43. TN ST §35-17-105(a) (2016).

44. TN ST §35-17-105(a) (2016).

45. TN ST §35-17-102(1) (2016).

46. TN ST §35-17-107 (2016). Note, following the decedent spouse's death, the surviving spouse may amend the TNCPT as it pertains to the surviving spouse's share. TN ST §35-17-104(b)(1) (2016).

47. TN ST §35-17-105(a) (2016).

48. TN ST §35-17-102(6)(A) (2016).

49. TN ST §35-17-102(6)(B) (2016).

50. TN ST §35-17-103(3) (2016).

51. TN ST §35-17-105(a) (2016).

52. TN ST §35-17-105(c) (2016).

53. *See*, Note 36 and accompanying text, *supra*.

54. TN ST §35-17-105(e) (2016).

55. See, AK Stat. §34.77.030(i) (2016). This is probably because Alaska permits property to be considered CP even if held outside of a trust (at least for Alaskan residents), where in Tennessee, property can only be held as CP inside of a TNCPT.

56. *See*, Note 38 and accompanying text, *supra*.

57. TN ST §35-17-104(b)(1) (2016).

58. TN ST §35-17-106(a) (2016).

59. TN ST §35-17-108(2016).

60. TN ST §35-17-105(d) (2016).

61. *See*, Note 40 and accompanying text, *supra*.

62. TN ST §35-17-103(4) (2016).

63. SD Title 55, Chapter 17 (being SDCL §55-17-1 et seq.).

64. For purposes of consistency with the naming of the Alaska and Tennessee versions of the CPTs (i.e., AKCPT and TNCPT), the author has opted to call the trust a "SDCPT" instead of a "SDSSCPT".

65. SDCL §§55-17-3 (2016).

66. SDCL §55-17-1 (2016).

67. SDCL §55-17-9(3)(2016). Note, following the decedent spouse's death, the surviving spouse may amend the SDCPT as it pertains to the surviving spouse's share. SDCL §55-17-4(2016).

68. SDCL §55-17-1 (2016).

69. SDCL §§55-17-1; 55-3-41 and 55-3-39 (2016).

70. There is an additional requirement for banks and savings associations that their deposits must be insured by the Federal Deposit Insurance Corporation. See, SDCL §55-3-41.

71. SDCL §55-17-1 (2016).

72. SDCL §55-17-3 (2016).

73. SDCL §55-17-8 (2016).

74. SDCL §55-17-4 (2016).

75. SDCL §55-17-9(3) (2016).

76. SDCL §55-17-9(2) (2016).

77. SDCL §55-17-14 (2016).

78. SDCL §55-17-2 (2016).

79. SDCL §55-17-5(2016).

80. By definition, there can be no community property without a legally married couple.

81. Generally, we refer to "transfer taxes" as the estate, gift and generation-skipping transfer (or "GST") taxes.

82. Note, same sex marriage was not allowed in the United States at that time, so for the married couple, the term "husband" and "wife" was the norm, whereas, today, we tend to use the term "spouse" or "spouse 1"and "spouse 2".

83. Below, we discuss the income tax issues with the basis adjustment at death and why we say that there is a "possibility" that the basis of the assets in the CPT can be adjusted at death to the date of death value.

2503(b) AND 2503(c) TRUSTS

CHAPTER 5

OVERVIEW

Leaving money or assets to minors presents difficult planning considerations that should be carefully considered. Assets should never be given outright or in installments to young beneficiaries when they do not have the intellectual and emotional maturity to manage the assets appropriately without supervision. Yet parents or grandparents often want to provide for their children or grandchildren's care and education but have the control and flexibility over the transfer to the beneficiary that only trusts can provide. Trusts can also offer a significant tax advantage thereby allowing the grantor to be generous without giving up control.

Several types of trusts used for minor or young individuals can be effective wealth transfer tools. The Section 2503(c) minor's trust and Section 2503(b) mandatory income trust are among the simplest and most common forms of trust used. The most common feature is that gifts to such trusts qualify for the federal gift tax annual exclusion. As a result, both these trusts can achieve protection for children and grandchildren and valuable tax benefits.

Generally, gifts in trust do not qualify for the federal gift tax annual exclusion. Code section 2503(b) requires the donee of a gift to have the present right to use, possess or enjoy the property. Section 2503(b) trusts (commonly referred to as the "mandatory income trust") is a 2503 trust that qualifies for the gift tax annual exclusion by requiring all the income from the trust to be distributed annually. A Section 2503(c) minor's trust is another type of 2503 trust. Congress recognized many years ago the problems that can occur when making gifts to minors. Consequently, it created the Section 2503(c) minor's trust as a statutory exception to the rule that a gift of a future interest

does not qualify for the annual exclusion provided the trust meets the strict qualification requirements set forth therein.

2503(c) MINOR'S TRUST

The first variation of a 2503 trust is the Section 2503(c) trust. A 2503(c) trust is an irrevocable trust that satisfies the specific requirements set forth under section 2503(c) of the Internal Revenue Code. One of the main advantages of a 2503(c) trust is that it allows transfers that satisfy the requirements of 2503(c) to qualify for the annual gift tax exclusions. Despite the relative specificity contained in the statute, a Section 2503(c) trust permits a surprising degree of flexibility in the design of the trust document. Consequently, it is often a more useful vehicle for making gifts to minor children than is apparent on the face of the statute.

REQUIREMENTS

Section 2503(c) of the Code creates three basic requirements in order for transfers to qualify for the annual exclusion:

1. The property and income from the trust may be expended by or for the benefit of the beneficiary, before he reaches age twenty-one;

2. The property, to the extent not so expended, must pass to the beneficiary on attaining age twenty-one; and

3. In the event the beneficiary dies before attaining age twenty-one, any remaining trust property and undistributed income must be paid to the

beneficiary's estate or as the beneficiary may appoint under a general power of appointment.[1]

Benefit Requirements

The first requirement of Section 2503(c) is that the trust must give the trustee the discretion to expend trust income and principal for the benefit of the beneficiary before the beneficiary attains the age of twenty-one years.[2] Actual expenditures are not required; it is sufficient for the trustee to merely be granted that discretion.[3] However, failure to state that the trustee has discretion to make expenditures of principal and income will result in the loss of the annual exclusion.[4]

To satisfy this requirement, Treasury Regulations section 25.2503-4(b)(1) provides that the trust cannot place "substantial restrictions" upon the exercise of the trustee's discretion to make distributions to or for the benefit of the beneficiary while the beneficiary is a minor.[5] Neither the Code nor regulations define "substantial restriction". However, there have been several cases and rulings that help delineate the scope of the restrictions that can be imposed on the trustee's discretion. Footnote As a result, trust provisions regarding distributions must be carefully examined since some standards have been deemed "substantial restrictions" while others are not.

The Service takes the position that any restrictions that exceed those imposed upon a guardian under applicable state law could result in the loss of the annual exclusion.[6] State laws may vary in the standard imposed upon a guardian. Thus a provision requiring a trustee to take into account the financial resources of the beneficiary or his or her parents' will result in the loss of the annual exclusion.[7] In Revenue Ruling 69-345, the trustee's discretionary power was subject to the limitation requiring the trustee to take into consideration other resources available to the beneficiary and other payments made to the beneficiary for the beneficiary's benefit. The Service ruled the requirement that the trustee take into consideration the beneficiary's needs was held to be a substantial restriction on the exercise of the trustee's discretion given the surrounding circumstances of the family's economic position.

A provision limiting distributions to only events of accident, illness, infirmity, disability or other emergency affecting the trust beneficiary, will be considered a substantial restriction on the trustee's discretion to make distributions and will cause a gift to the trust to fail to qualify as a present interest under Section 2503(c).[8] Similarly, if the trustee may only make distributions upon the demand of another person on the beneficiary's behalf, the trustee's discretion to make distributions is subject to a substantial restriction.[9]

Not all distribution standards will be deemed substantial restrictions for purposes of 2503(c) and considered a gift. A general standard that is reflective of need will qualify as a present interest for the annual exclusion.[10] In *Williams v. United States*,[11] the Court of Claims held that a clause authorizing distribution only when, in the opinion of the trustee, the beneficiary was in need of additional funds, did not constitute a substantial restriction on the trustee's discretion, and, as a result, the trust qualified under Section 2503(c).

In Revenue Ruling 67-270, the Service ruled that a trust agreement is deemed to meet the requirements of Section 2503(c) for purposes of expending trust income and principal for the benefit of the beneficiary when in addition to providing for a beneficiary's health or education, a trust provides for distributions which have no objective limitations such as welfare, happiness and convenience and when read as a whole approximates the scope of the term "benefit" as used in Section 2503(c) of the Code. Therefore, a standard of distribution for the beneficiary's support, care, education, comfort and welfare, and to accumulate any income not so needed, will qualify under Section 2503(c).[12] Similarly, a trust instrument that authorized the trustee to make distributions in such amounts and at such times as the trustee in his or her sole discretion deemed necessary for the proper care, maintenance, support, and education of the beneficiary qualifies as a gift of a present interest.[13]

Finally, the fact that the trustee may not make such distributions in a manner that will serve to discharge the grantor's legal obligation to support the trust beneficiary will not be considered a substantial restriction, as such a statement merely duplicates the rights of the minor under state law.[14]

The case law shows that the Service has allowed a few minor deviation from the general requirement that the trustee have discretion to distribute income and principal of the trust for the welfare and benefit of the minor. However, any substantial restrictions on the trustee's discretion will fail, and relatively minor restrictions are likely to invite a challenge by the Service.

In order to increase the likelihood that the distribution standard of the trust satisfies the benefits requirement and qualifies for the annual exclusion, the trustee should be given a broad discretionary authority, without standards, to make distributions for the benefit of the beneficiary in the trustee's sole discretion. Such a standard will certainly satisfy the benefits requirement. This is often a wise course of action even without the statutory requirements. Giving the trustee the broadest possible discretion, will allow the trustee to deal with any unexpected situations that may arise. If this standard is considered too broad for the client, then a more subjective standard for the beneficiary's support, care, education, comfort and welfare can be used, but an added condition that the distribution will always be greater than those imposed on guardians under local law is suggested.

"Passing" Requirement

The second requirement of Section 2503(c) is that the trust must provide for all accumulated income and principal remaining in the trust to be distributed to the beneficiary when he or she reaches age twenty-one.[15] To satisfy this requirement, the trustee must either distribute the trust to the beneficiary, or in the beneficiary's discretion, no later than when the beneficiary is age twenty-one. This is a major hurdle for most donors since they often prefer to postpone the enjoyment of trust corpus beyond age twenty-one to allow for the beneficiary to have greater judgment and maturity.

Initially, the Service interpreted this requirement as prohibiting the continuation of the trust past the beneficiary's twenty-first birthday.[16] Thereafter, the Service lost several cases[17] which failed to follow the ruling. Subsequently, the Service reevaluated its earlier position and revoked the earlier revenue ruling and issued Revenue Ruling 74-43.[18]

Currently, there is more flexibility in structuring a 2503(c) trust than might otherwise be expected from the face of the statute. Revenue Ruling 74-43 established two instances where the passing requirement is satisfied:

(1) where the beneficiary, on reaching twenty-one, has a continuing right to terminate the trust by giving written notice to the trustee; and

(2) the beneficiary, on reaching twenty-one, has a right during a limited period to compel immediate distribution of the trust corpus by written notice to the trustee. In either case, the failure to elect would result in the trust's continuation for an additional period specified in the instrument thereby delaying distributions to the beneficiary to a later age.[19]

Although this type of trust gives the beneficiary the right to actually receive a distribution of corpus, in many cases this right will not be exercised, and the trust will continue by its own terms for the period originally designated in the instrument. If an extension of the trust occurs, the income tax treatment of the trust will change. This is discussed further below.

The withdrawal right given to the beneficiary is akin to a Crummey demand right. Adequate notice is given to the beneficiary and the withdrawal right may terminate after a reasonable period of time. Similar to Crummey withdrawal powers, the beneficiary should be given a reasonable time frame during which the beneficiary can exercise the right to withdraw the trust property. There is no clear definition of what constitutes a reasonable time frame. However, the Service has approved time periods of thirty and sixty days.[20]

It is not necessary for both the income and principal of a trust to qualify for the annual exclusion under Section 2503(c). A gift in trust can qualify for the annual exclusion as to a portion of the beneficiary's income interest even if it does not qualify as to the beneficiary's interest in trust corpus.[21] This trust is commonly referred to as a 2503(c) income trust.

In *Herr v. Commissioner*,[22] the donor created the trust for the benefit of minors wherein the income satisfied the requirements of a 2503(c) trust, but the corpus did not. The court held that the gifts of income to the beneficiary qualified for the annual exclusion, whereas the gifts of corpus did not. The case was affirmed on appeal and has been followed elsewhere since. In Revenue Ruling 68-670, a grantor established a trust where the beneficiary did not have an interest in the trust corpus but satisfied the requirements of Section 2503(c) with respect to trust income. The Service ruled that the right to receive trust income until the beneficiary reached the age of majority, or until the beneficiary's earlier death, met the requirements of Section 2503(c) and was not treated as a future interest, even though the beneficiary had no interest in the trust corpus. This ruling demonstrates the Service's consent to the concept that the principal and income interests of a single trust can be segregated for purposes of determining Section 2503(c) qualification.

The ability to segregate income and corpus offers several planning opportunities for those donors that prefer to postpone the enjoyment of trust corpus beyond age twenty-one. The trust can be structured to qualify the income interest for the Section 2503(c) requirements, with the distribution of corpus postponed until a later date. The actuarial value of the income interest would then qualify for the gift tax annual exclusion and the excess value of the assets over the actuarial value of the income interest is deemed a future interest for which a gift tax return must be filed and a gift tax paid (or unified credit expended). The income interest will need to be sufficiently large to fully use the annual exclusion. As a result the postponement of the trust corpus will be attractive. 2503(c) requires in the event of the beneficiary's death before attaining age twenty-one that both all undistributed net income and principal be distributed to the beneficiary's estate,[23] or the beneficiary be given a general power of appointment as defined in section 2514(c) of the Code. Again, there is more flexibility in designing the terms of the trust than might otherwise appear on the surface of the statute. The goal of this section is to ensure estate tax inclusion for property that receives the benefit of the gift tax annual exclusion. Therefore, the Service has interpreted the requirement for disposition at death to be read in the alternative, requiring that one of the two be present in the trust document. Generally the requirements under this section have been strictly construed.

Distributions to Beneficiary's Estate Requirement

In order to satisfy the requirement that the assets pass to the beneficiary's estate, it is important not to go beyond simply naming the beneficiary's estate if the beneficiary dies before the age of twenty-one.

Several cases have held that a direction passing the assets to the beneficiary's "heirs at law", "next of kin" or "living descendants" is not equivalent to making it payable to the minor's estate for purposes of Section 2503(c)(2)(B).[24] Passing the assets to the minor's heirs or descendants rather than the minor's estate circumvent legislative intent to tax the trust assets in the minor's estate should the minor die before age twenty-one. It

also removes the minor's ability to direct the disposition of the assets by will.

Passing the assets to the beneficiary's estate on a contingent basis will also fail to satisfy the requirement of passing the assets to the beneficiary's estate. In *Messing v. Commissioner,*[25] the gifts to the trust were considered gifts of a future interest because the trust provided that the assets were to pass to the beneficiary's issue, or if there were none, to the beneficiary's estate.

Although the Code allows the assets to pass to the beneficiary's estate if the beneficiary dies before age twenty-one, it may not be wise to do so. Naming a minor's estate will subject the assets to probate of the minor. If the beneficiary lacks capacity to execute a will because the beneficiary is a minor, then the assets will pass by intestacy likely back to the minor's parents who were the donor's to the trust in the first place thereby defeating the tax planning involved. The general power of appointment may then be the better alternative.

General Power of Appointment

In order to satisfy the contingent requirement of a 2053(c) trust, the donor can grant the beneficiary a general power of appointment if the beneficiary dies before age twenty-one. The general power of appointment granted can be exercisable either by will or during lifetime. The power may be granted even if under state law the beneficiary is under a disability because he or she is a minor and lacks the capacity to exercise the power.[26] To satisfy this requirement, the trust instrument should not define the beneficiary's capacity in a manner that is greater than set forth under state law. In *Gall v. U.S.,*[27] the trust limited the beneficiary's ability to exercise the power of appointment before the age of nineteen which was the age of testamentary capacity under state law. This limitation was said to be more restrictive than the limitation imposed by state law since state law also granted testamentary capacity to a married beneficiary who is at least eighteen years of age. As a result, the trust failed to qualify under Section 2503(c). Consequently, for estate tax purposes, if a testamentary general power of appointment is granted to a minor, the value of the trust will be included in the minor's estate for federal estate tax purposes.[28]

If the beneficiary fails to validly exercise the general power of appointment, the trust agreement may provide for a default appointment of the trust assets.[29] This is similar to the alternative disposition that is used in the absence of the exercise of such power found in most trust documents. This allows the grantor of the trust the ability to control the disposition of the property in the unlikely event that the beneficiary dies before age twenty-one. It also allows the assets to pass in continuing trust to other beneficiaries, which is ordinarily recommended when such other beneficiaries are minors.

The trust can also provide the beneficiary with a special power of appointment rather than a general power of appointment, but if the power is not validly exercised, the trust property would be payable to the beneficiary's estate.[30] Collectively, the cases show that the trust instrument should not include a disposition of trust assets, other than to the beneficiary's estate that cannot be defeated by the donee's exercise of power of appointment.

As explained, the use of the general power of appointment allows for greater drafting flexibility and control than having the assets pass to the beneficiary's estate. However, great care should be taken in drafting the provision to adhere to the case law and IRS rulings because of the strict construction used in many cases. Drafting mistakes may not be corrected because retroactive reformation of a trust is not available to modify a trust to satisfy the annual gift tax exclusion requirements.[31]

TAX CONSEQUENCES

Estate Tax Beneficiary

As discussed above, the third requirement of a 2503(c) trust provides that when a beneficiary dies before reaching age twenty-one, the assets in the trust must be distributed either to the beneficiary's estate or be subject to a general power of appointment. Therefore in the event of the beneficiary's death before age twenty-one, the trust will be subject to estate tax in the beneficiary's estate.

If the beneficiary dies after the age of twenty-one and the beneficiary automatically receives the assets in the trust, the beneficiary becomes the owner of the trust assets and as such will be subject to estate taxation. Similarly, if the beneficiary was granted a power of withdrawal which the beneficiary exercised and subsequently died before the trust was distributed, the

assets of the trust will be included in the beneficiary's estate.

Donor or Donor's Spouse

Generally, a 2503(c) trust will not cause estate tax inclusion in the grantor's estate or the spouse of the grantor. However, if either the grantor or the grantor's spouse serve as trustee of the trust, estate tax inclusion may be triggered. The first requirement that the trustee must have discretion to expend trust income and principal for the benefit of the beneficiary before attaining the age of twenty-one years causes the property to be included in the donor's estate under the provisions of Sections 2036(a) and 2038 if the donor is serving as trustee and held the power upon death before termination of the trust.[32]

Estate inclusion can also occur for the donor's spouse if the spouse serves as trustee. If the spouse trustee can use the trust assets to discharge a support obligation, the trust assets will be included in the estate of the spouse.[33] Once the minor is emancipated, the support obligation expires. However, the expiration may be considered a lapse of a general power of appointment causing the spouse to have made a gift to the trust.

Income Tax

During the initial term of the trust, income will be taxed to the trust unless the income is distributed. The result will be the same even if the donor is serving as the trustee of the trust. In instances where the distribution discharges a parent's support obligation, the parent will be taxed on the income.

After the beneficiary's twenty-first birthday, the income from the trust will be taxed to the beneficiary as a grantor trust. If the beneficiary receives the trust assets either by the terms of the document or exercises a withdrawal right, the beneficiary becomes the owner of the trust assets and will be subject to any income. If the beneficiary fails to withdraw the trust funds and the trust continues, the failure of the beneficiary to exercise the withdrawal is deemed a withdrawal and re-contribution of the funds by the beneficiary for income tax purposes. This results in the beneficiary being considered the grantor of the trust for income tax purposes under Section 677(a). The trust then ceases to be a separate taxpayer for income tax purposes and the beneficiary is taxed on all trust income, whether or not distributed.[34]

GST Tax

The generation-skipping transfer (GST) tax is a tax that is imposed on transfers of property made from one generation to another generation which is two or more generations below the transferor's generation (e.g., a transfer of property from a grandparent to a grandchild).[35] Many individuals are familiar with the gift tax annual gift tax exclusion under Section 2503(b) of the Code. However, many are surprised to learn that there is a separate annual exclusion rule under the GST tax provisions of the Code for gifts made in trust.[36]

While gifts made to a Section 2503(c) trust qualifies for the gift tax annual exclusion, there are additional rules that must be satisfied for a gift to qualify for the GST tax exclusion. Under Section 2642(c) of the Code, a gift to a trust will not qualify as an annual exclusion gift for GST tax purposes unless: (1) during the life of the beneficiary, no portion of the trust may be distributed to (or for the benefit of) any person other than such beneficiary; and (2) if the trust does not terminate before the beneficiary dies, the assets of such trust will be included in the beneficiary's gross estate. A gift to a Section 2503(c) trust should qualify for the annual exclusion for GST tax purposes because the trust must be included in the beneficiary's estate under Code section 2503(c) if the beneficiary dies prior to attaining the age of twenty-one, which is one of the requirements under Section 2642(c).[37]

Planning and Drafting

When to Create a 2503(c) Trust

The 2503(c) trust can be created early on in the beneficiary's life to take advantage of the annual exclusion and the growth of trust assets, but it cannot be created before birth of the beneficiary. A minor's trust cannot be established for an unborn child and qualify for the annual exclusion because the property must pass to the beneficiary upon attaining age twenty-one and if he or she dies before such age it must pass to the beneficiary's estate or the beneficiary must be granted a general power of appointment. Since neither of these conditions can be fulfilled if the fetus dies before birth, the gift does not qualify for 2503(c) treatment.[38]

If state law permits, the creation of a 2503(c) trust before the termination of a Uniform Transfer to Minors Act (UTMA) or Uniform Gifts to Minors Act (UGMA) account can be a helpful planning tool. Often, there is

a desire to prevent a child from accessing funds held in a UTMA or UGMA account upon termination. The child may not be emotionally or intellectually equipped to receive the funds at that time. States like Florida and Illinois permit the custodian of the UTMA or UGMA account to transfer the funds to a 2503(c) trust rather than directly to the child, thereby prolonging the time the child has to access the funds.[39]

Trustee Selection

As discussed above, neither the donor of a Section 2503(c) trust nor the donor's spouse should serve as trustee of the trust. If the donor serves, the assets of the trust may be includable in the donor's gross estate under the provisions in Sections 2036(a)(2) and 2038(a). As to a donor's spouse who has a legal support obligation and serves as trustee, the trustee's discretionary power would constitute a general power of appointment with adverse estate tax consequences.[40] A relative or friend can be a good choice. A corporate fiduciary or trusted advisor are often willing to serve and bring valuable experience to the position of trustee.

Multiple Beneficiaries

In cases where a 2503(c) trust is to be established for multiple beneficiaries, the grantor has two options; create multiple identical trusts for each beneficiary or create one trust for all beneficiaries. The former is certainly easier to draft and simple to understand. For ease of administration, the latter may be more appealing. The mechanics of the drafting would require that a separate share be created for each beneficiary and the gifts to the trust be split equally among the separate shares. However, it is critical that each trust contain all of the requirements set forth therein in order to qualify for the annual exclusion.

2503(b) TRUSTS (MANDATORY INCOME TRUSTS)

The second variation of a 2503 trust is the 2503(b) trust. A 2503(b) trust is an irrevocable trust in which the beneficiary is entitled to receive all of the principal from the trust, either for the beneficiary's life or a fixed term. Upon termination of the income interest, the trust can be distributed as the grantor directs. The trust allows for the gift to qualify for the annual gift exclusion without requiring that the beneficiary have access to the trust at age twenty-one.

Requirements

Mandatory Income Distributions

None of the stringent 2503(c) trust requirements discussed in the prior section are imposed on a 2503(b) trust. The only requirement of a 2503(b) trust is that all trust income must be distributed to the trust beneficiary at least annually. Therefore, except insofar as a 2503(b) trust requires mandatory income distributions, this creates for great drafting flexibility since the trust may last for a term of years (period certain), or for the life of the trust beneficiary.

In order to qualify as a mandatory income trust, the income interest must be an absolute right to which the beneficiary is entitled to under all circumstances. A trust where the trustee has discretion to make income distributions will not qualify. The trustee cannot be empowered to accumulate income, even during the beneficiary's minority, and the actuarial tables cannot be used to value the income interest.[41] Nor can the grantor retain the right to extend the term of the income interest as doing so will not qualify the additional income interest for the gift tax annual exclusion.[42] Furthermore, the retained power by the grantor to extend the trust may arguably be considered a power to alter the beneficial enjoyment of the trust resulting in the inclusion of the trust in the grantor's estate under section 2038.

Commencement of Income Interest

The mandatory income requirement requires that the income interest begin immediately, without delay in its commencement. A delay of even a few months converts the income interest into a future interest which will not qualify for the gift tax annual exclusion.[43]

Readily Ascertainable Income Interest

The gift tax annual exclusion of the income interest can be lost if the value of the income interest is not readily ascertainable. The income interest is ascertainable if the beneficiary receives all of the income of the trust and principal distributions can be made for the beneficiary's benefit.[44] The trustee may also be given the power to distribute principal to the beneficiary, but the trustee cannot divert principal or income to another beneficiary.[45] Similarly, the beneficiary can have a lifetime power of appointment without prejudicing the gift tax annual exclusion.[46]

Investment of Trust Assets

In order to pay income currently to the beneficiary, the trust must invest in income-producing assets. If they are not, the income interest cannot be valued. The trust cannot authorize the trustee to invest in nonproductive assets (even if the trustee never exercises the power), otherwise it will render the income interest illusory and disqualify the income interest for the gift tax annual exclusion.[47] The annual exclusion can also be lost if the trust instrument allocates gains or losses on the sale or other disposition of principal to income.[48] Again, the income interest cannot be valued because of the uncertainty of sales of assets and the income that they will produce.

Power to Allocate Receipts and Disbursement

The trustee of a Section 2503(b) income trust should not be given broad powers to allocate receipts and disbursements between income and principal, otherwise, it may jeopardize loss of the gift tax annual exclusion. A trustee that is given a power to allocate receipts and disbursements in a manner different from that local law, may make it difficult or impossible to ascertain the value of the income interest.[49]

Spendthrift Provisions

A spendthrift clause is a restriction in a trust document that precludes the beneficiaries from transferring or encumbering their interests in the trust prior to the date of distribution from the trust. Caution should be taken in including a spendthrift clause in a Section 2503(b) income trust with respect to the income interest of the beneficiary. The gift tax annual exclusion is not jeopardized by a spendthrift clause that prohibits a beneficiary's assignment of the income rights in advance of actual distributions from the trust.[50] However, a spendthrift clause under which the trustee may withhold income from an incompetent or wasteful beneficiary probably does render the value of the income interest unascertainable and disqualifies the gifts for the annual exclusion.[51]

Principal Distributions

A 2503(b) trust can provide for principal distributions but only to the beneficiary that is receiving the income distributions. The income or principal of the trust cannot be made to another beneficiary that is not the income beneficiary. As a result a discretionary trust for multiple beneficiaries will not suffice.

TAX CONSEQUENCES

Gift Tax

Whenever a donor transfers assets to a 2503(b) trust, the entire value of the assets transferred to the trust will be deemed a gift. However, only a portion of it will qualify for the gift tax annual exclusion. A gift has two parts: the income portion and the remainder portion. Only the actuarial value of the income portion will qualify for the gift tax annual exclusion.[52] The actuarial value of the income portion is determined on the basis of the IRS tables using the 7520 rate. The remainder of the trust will be deemed a gift of a future interest which does not qualify for the annual exclusion and is fully subject to gift taxation. Thus, a gift to a Section 2503(b) trust even for an infant still creates at least a small future interest transfer, requiring a gift tax return to be filed and the use of the donor's unified credit or payment of a gift tax.

Income Tax

A 2503(b) trust can be structured either as a grantor trust or a nongrantor trust, without jeopardizing gift tax annual exclusion eligibility. How a 2503(b) trust is taxed for income tax purposes will depend on how it's structured.

In order to trigger grantor trust status, the grantor can retain or give to a nonadverse party a nonfiduciary right to reacquire trust assets by substituting assets of equivalent value without causing the trust to be included in the grantor's gross estate for federal estate tax purposes.[53] However, grantor trust status should not be triggered by giving the trustee the right to distribute income or principal to other beneficiaries, or give someone the right to add trust beneficiaries during the term of the current beneficiary's income interest. Either of these powers will violate the mandatory income requirement of a 2503(b) trust.

If the trust is not considered a grantor trust, a nongrantor 2503(b) trust, like any other irrevocable trust, must have its own tax identification number and file annual income tax returns. Since all of the income of a nongrantor 2503(b) trust must be distributed to the beneficiary, it renders the beneficiary, rather than the trust, taxable on that income. However, a nongrantor 2503(b) is a separate taxpayer for capital gains and losses, and any other items of income, deduction, or credit is properly allocated to trust principal. The grantor of a Section 2503(b) trust will also be taxed on any trust income actually used to pay for the support of a beneficiary whom the grantor is legally obligated to support.[54]

Planning and Drafting

When to Create a 2503(b) Trust

Similar to a 2503(c) trust, a 2503(b) trust can be created early on in the beneficiary's life to take advantage of the annual exclusion, but the beneficiary must be alive for the trust to be created. A 2503(b) trust for an unborn beneficiary cannot qualify for the annual exclusion because the unborn beneficiary does not have an unrestricted right to the property transferred to the trust and is not a gift of a present interest.[55]

Trustee Selection

The requirement that a Section 2503(b) income trust pay all of its income to the beneficiary, makes trustee selection somewhat simpler than it is for many other trusts. It is possible for the grantor to serve as trustee of a 2503(b) trust. In order for the grantor to do so and not trigger grantor trust status and inclusion in the grantor's estate, the grantor as trustee cannot have the authority to distribute principal or the authority must be restricted to a definite and ascertainable standard such as health, education, maintenance and support.[56]

If someone other than the grantor is appointed to serve as trustee, that person can be given broad discretionary powers to distribute principal without regard to an ascertainable standard. The person can even be a related or subordinate party to the grantor and not trigger grantor trust status or inclusion in the grantor's estate since the trust has only one income beneficiary and principal distributions are charged to the principal share of that income beneficiary.[57]

Comparing 2503(c) and 2503(b) Trusts

Both a 2503(b) and a 2503(c) trust have their advantages and disadvantages. Both should be explored to find the best fit for the particular needs and goals of the grantor. The key difference between the two trusts is the distribution requirements. One of the attractive features of a 2503(c) trust is that the trustee has very broad discretion regarding the distribution of income and principal until the beneficiary reaches age twenty-one. But, a donor concerned about providing the beneficiary with access to trust funds at age twenty-one would prefer a 2503(b) trust since there is no mandatory access at age twenty-one. A 2503(b) trust is also appropriate when the donor wants the trust assets to pass to a different beneficiary after the income beneficiary's income interest terminates. The annual mandatory income distributions will also limit the growth of the trust principal.

The eligibility of the gift tax annual exclusion is also a factor that should be considered. With a 2503(c) trust the donor will get the benefit of the annual exclusion on the full value of the assets transferred to the trust, whereas with a 2503(b) trust only the actuarial value of the income interest will be eligible for the gift tax annual exclusion. Regardless of which of the two trusts are selected, the trusts generally are limited in their use. When donors are considering annual gifts to minor beneficiaries, however, these trusts should be considered as an alternative.

CHAPTER ENDNOTES

1. I.R.C. §2503(c); Reg. §25.2503-4(a).

2. Treas. Reg. §25.2503-4(a)(1).

3. *Mueller v. Comm'r.*, 23 AFTR2d 69-1864, 69-1 USTC ¶ 12,582 (WD Mo. 1969); *Pettus v. Comm'r.*, 54 TC 112 (1970).

4. *Thebaut v. Comm'r.*, 361 F2d 428 (5th Cir. 1966).

5. Treas. Reg. §25.2503-4(b)(1).

6. Rev. Rul. 69-345, 1969-1 CB 226; see also *U.S. v. Baker*, 236 F.2d 317 (4th Cir. 1956); *Heidreich v. Comm'r*, 55 TC 746 (1971); Ill. *Nat'l Bank of Springfield v. U.S.*, 756 F. Supp. 1117 (C.D. Ill. 1991); *Williams v. United States*, 378 F2d 693 (Ct. Cl. 1967); *Ross v. United States*, 348 F2d 577 (5th Cir. 1965); see, also, Rev. Rul. 59-78, 1959-1 C.B. 690 (citing Baker, 236 F.2d 317).

7. Rev. Rul. 69-345, 1969-1 CB 226.

8. *Faber v. U.S.*, 439 F.2d 1189 (6th Cir. 1971); *Illinois Nat'l Bank of Springfield v. United States*, 756 F. Supp. 1117 (C.D. Ill. 1991); *Pettus*, 54 T.C. 112 (1970).

9. *Wood v. Comm'r.*, 16 TC 962 (1951).

10. *Heidrich*, 55 T.C. 746 (1971).

11. *Williams v. US*, 378 F2d 693 (Ct. Cl. 1967).

12. Rev. Rul. 67-270, 1967-2 C.B. 349.

13. *Craig v. Comm'r.*, T.C. Memo 1971-254.

14. Ill. Nat'l Bank, 756 F. Supp. at 1120; *Upjohn v. U.S.*, 72-2 USTC 12,888 (W.D. Mich. 1972).235 Rev. Rul. 69-345, 1969-1 C.B. 226.

15. I.R.C. §2503(c)(2)(A).

16. Rev. Rul. 60-218, 1960-1 C.B. 378, revoked by Rev. Rul. 74-43, 1974-1 CB 285.

17. *Heidrich v. Comm'r.*, 55 T.C. 746 (1971); *Perkins v. Comm'r.*, 27 TC 601 (1956); *Griffith v. Comm'r.*, 63-1 USTC ¶ 12,124 (SD Tex. 1962).

18. Rev. Rul. 74-43, 1974-2 CB 285.

19. *Id*; Treas. Reg. §25.2503-4(b)(2); Priv. Ltr. Ruls. 8936032, 8817037, 8729018.

20. PLRs 8521089, 7824035, 7805037.

21. *Comm'r. v. Herr*, 303 F.2d 780 (3d Cir. 1962), aff'g 35 T.C. 732 (1961); *Pettus*, 54 T.C. 112 (1970); *Quatman v. Comm'r.*, 54 T.C. 339 (1970); see, also, Rev. Rul. 68-670, 1968-2 C.B. 413.

22. *Herr v. Comm'r.*, 35 TC 732 (1961), aff'd, 303 F2d 780 (3d Cir. 1962).

23. Rev. Rul. 73-287, 1973-2 CB 321.

24. *Ross v. Comm'r.*, 652 F.2d 1365 (9th Cir. 1981), aff'g 71 T.C. 897 (1979); *Clinard v. Comm'r.*, 40 TC 878 (1963); *Messing v. Comm'r.*, 48 TC 502 (1967) ("surviving issue"); *Heath v. Comm'r.*, 34 TC 587 (1960).

25. 48 TC 502 (1967).

26. I.R.C. §2503(c)(2); Treas. Reg. §25.2503-4(b); Rev. Rul. 75-351, 1975-2 CB 368.

27. *Gall v. U.S.*, 521 F.2d 878 (5th Cir. 1975), cert. denied, 425 U.S. 972 (1976).

28. 44 Reg. §25.2503-4(b).

29. Treas. Reg. §25.2503-4(b)(3).

30. Priv. Ltr. Rul. 8320007 (Feb. 1, 1983). See *Ross v. Comm'r*, 71 TC 897 (1979), aff'd, 652 F2d 1365 (9th Cir. 1981) (distinguishing "heirs at law" from "estate").

31. *Van den Wymelenberg v. US*, 397 F.2d 443 (7th Cir. 1968), cert denied, 393 US 953 (1968); *Davis Samuel v Comm'r.*, 55 TC 416(1970).

32. I.R.C. §§2036(a) and 2038.

33. Regs. §20.2041-1(c)(1).

34. Priv. Ltr. Rul. 8142061.

35. I.R.C. §§2601, 2611, 2612, 2613, 2621, 2622 and 2623. There are certain exceptions to the imposition of the tax, such as the predeceased ancestor exception. See, e.g., I.R.C. §2651(e).

36. See §2642(c).

37. See, e.g., Priv. Ltr. Rul. 9321055 (February 26, 1993); Priv. Ltr. Rul. 9218040 (January 30, 1992).

38. Rev. Rul. 67-384, 1967-2 CB 348.

39. Fla. Stat. §710.116 and 760 ILCS 20/15.

40. I.R.C. §2041(a)(2); Treas. Reg. §20.2041-1(c).

41. *Skouras v. Comm'r.*, 14 TC 523 (1950), aff'd, 188 F2d 831 (2d Cir. 1951); *Perkins v. Comm'r.*, 1 TC 982 (1943), nonacq. 1943 CB 38; *Edwards v. Comm'r.*, 46 BTA 815 (1942), aff'd, 135 F2d 574 (7th Cir. 1943); see also Regs. §25.7520-3(b)(2)(ii).

42. Rev. Rul. 76-179, 1976-1 CB 290.

43. See Rev. Rul. 75-415, 1975-2 CB 374; *Hessenbruch v. Comm'r.*, 178 F2d 785 (3d Cir. 1950); Rev. Rul. 67-384, 1967-2 CB 348; *Faulkner v. Comm'r.*, 41 BTA 875, 876 (1940).

44. See Reg. §25.2503-3(c), Ex. 4.

45. Regs. §25.2503-3(c) Ex. 3; Regs. §25.7520-3(b)(2)(ii).

46. *Newlin v. Comm'r.*, 31 TC 451 (1958) , acq. 1960-1 CB 5.

47. See also Regs. §20.7520-3(b)(2)(v); *Stark v. United States*, 477 F2d 131 (8th Cir.), cert. denied, 414 US 975 (1973); *O'Reilly v. Comm'r.*, 973 F2d 1403 (8th Cir. 1992), rev'd, TC Memo. 1994-61.

48. Rev. Rul. 77-358, 1977-2 CB 342.

49. See Rev. Rul. 77-358, 1977-2 CB 352. See also explanation of this ruling in GCM 37141 (May 3, 1997).

50. Rev. Rul. 54-344, 1954-2 CB 319.

51. Priv. Ltr. Ruls. 8347090 and 8248008; Rev. Rul. 85-35, 1985-1 CB 328.

52. Rev. Rul. 68-670, 1968-2 CB 413.

53. Rev. Rul. 2008-22, 2008-1 CB 796.

54. I.R.C. §677(a); see also *Braun v. Comm'r.*, TC Memo. 1984-285.

55. Rev. Rul. 67-384, 1967-2 CB 348.

56. I.R.C. §674; *Leopold v. United States*, 510 F2d 617 (9th Cir. 1975); *Jennings v. Smith*, 161 F2d 74 (2d Cir. 1947); *Hurd v. Comm'r.*, 160 F2d 610 (1st Cir. 1947); *Estate of Bell v. Comm'r.*, 66 TC 729 (1976); *Estate of Pardee v. Comm'r.*, 49 TC 140 (1967); *Estate of Nettleton v. Comm'r.*, 4 TC 987 (1945), acq. 1946-1 CB 3.

57. I.R.C. §674(b)(5)(B).

IRREVOCABLE LIFE INSURANCE TRUSTS

CHAPTER 6

USE OF IRREVOCABLE LIFE INSURANCE TRUSTS

Estate planners usually encounter some form of insurance when examining a client's schedule of assets. The primary utility of life insurance in the tax planning context is the opportunity it provides to transfer future benefits at a reduced present cost. An irrevocable life insurance trust (ILIT) is a useful estate planning device used to manage life insurance policies and dispose of policy proceeds. ILITs are very popular because of their enormous transfer tax savings.

When the insured is the owner of a life insurance policy, the proceeds of the policy will be subject to estate tax when the insured dies. Rather than the insured being the owner of a life insurance policy, an ILIT serves as the owner and beneficiary of the policy. An ILIT is an irrevocable, non-amendable trust established for the purpose of being the owner and beneficiary of one or more life insurance policies. When properly drafted, the ILIT allows the proceeds of the life insurance policy held in the trust to avoid estate taxation. Although transfer tax savings is the primary reason for creating life insurance trusts, there are also non-tax advantages of holding a life insurance policy in trust. The trust provides liquidity for taxes, financial support for the insured's beneficiaries, spendthrift protection and can even provide meaningful advantages when planning for elective share rights of a surviving spouse.[1]

GENERAL STRUCTURE

An ILIT is usually established by formation of the trust, followed by the contributor (usually the insured) assigning an existing insurance policy to the trust or the trustee of the trust buying a policy directly from an insurance company.

The insured retains no benefits in the trust.[2] If the trust only contains a life insurance policy or policies, during the insured's lifetime, premiums are typically paid by the insured making annual gifts to the trustee of the trust in an amount sufficient for the trustee to pay the premiums of the life insurance policy. At the insured's death, the insurance company pays the policy proceeds to the trust, and the trust assets are then administered and distributed in accordance with the terms of the trust instrument. If the insured's estate is in need of liquidity, the trustee may lend money to the insured's estate or use the proceeds to purchase assets from the insured's estate, provided the trustee has such authority under the trust instrument.

ESTABLISHING THE TRUST

Establishing an effective life insurance trust always begins with a properly drafted trust instrument. Immediately thereafter, the life insurance policy should be transferred to the trust and consideration should be given to the ongoing trust administration issues such as income tax reporting and payment of premiums. Although these tasks may appear basic and rudimentary, they are critical to the success of the trust and for the estate, gift, and generation-skipping transfer tax benefits to be realized.

Purchase or Assignment of Life Insurance Policy

The main purpose of creating an insurance trust is for the trust to hold life insurance. The trust can acquire ownership of the life insurance policy by either purchasing a policy or by the grantor transferring an existing policy to the trust by gift. Once the trust becomes the owner of a life insurance policy, it should immediately name itself as the beneficiary of the insurance policy. If the trust is the applicant, owner and beneficiary of the life insurance policy from the outset, none of the death benefits will be included in the grantor's gross taxable estate because the grantor has no "incidents of ownership" over the policy.[3] In cases where an existing policy is transferred to the trust by the grantor, the grantor must survive for three years after the insurance is transferred to achieve estate tax exclusion.[4]

Funded v. Unfunded Trust

An ILIT may be funded or unfunded. A funded trust contains assets other than life insurance policies. The assets are often investment accounts held to produce sufficient income to pay the insurance premiums. Funding the trust has the additional benefit of allowing future appreciation of the assets to be sheltered from estate taxation. An unfunded trust contains only life insurance policies. The trustee of an unfunded ILIT is dependent on cash gifts from the grantor to pay the premium payments that become due. The cash contributions are often made annually, and are sheltered (or partially sheltered) from gift taxation by giving trust beneficiaries a power to withdraw contributions made to the ILIT.

These powers to withdraw, commonly known as "Crummey powers" (discussed at greater length below), cause the contributions to be "present interest gifts" allowing them to qualify for the gift tax annual exclusion. A typical ILIT is in funded and produces no income. Accordingly, there is no need to determine how the trust will be treated for income tax purposes. In cases where the ILIT is funded, the income tax consequences and the applicability of the grantor trust rules must be considered.

Types of Life Insurance

The type of life insurance that will be held by an ILIT should be carefully considered. The best practice is to examine the situation of each client to obtain the most appropriate insurance product to meet the client's objectives. However, when the main purpose for establishing the ILIT is to provide estate liquidity, term life insurance is usually a poor choice for an ILIT policy because the insured may outlive the policy term. A renewable term insurance may not even be adequate, because the premiums usually increase with each renewal and many companies will not issue new term policies

for individuals at more advanced ages. Therefore, for an ILIT, permanent coverage is suggested instead to term coverage. Many life insurance trusts are funded with permanent life insurance because it provides certainty that it will pay out regardless of when the insured dies.

Payment of Premiums

It is critical that the premium payments on life insurance be paid promptly when due. Failure to make timely premium payments could result in the policy lapsing. If the trust is funded and has the assets available to pay the premiums, then it should do so in a timely manner. If the trust is not funded and is dependent on the grantor transferring proceeds to the trust for the trust to pay the premiums, it is important for the trustee and the grantor to coordinate in advance for the timely payment of the premium.

The policy premium can be paid either directly by the grantor or by the trustee of the trust after receipt of monies transferred into the trust by the grantor. Either way, it will be considered a gift to the trust[5] and the payment of the policy premiums will not be considered an incident of ownership in the policy which would compromise the tax benefits of the trust.[6] Nevertheless, it is recommended that the policy premiums be paid by the trustee after receipt of funds, rather than by direct payment to the insurer. The insured's direct payment of the premiums makes the entire arrangement somewhat contrived and the formalities of the Crummey powers which are discussed below become somewhat more complicated. As a result, the grantor typically will pay the premiums on the life insurance held by the trust by making a gift to the trust. The trustee will then use the gifted funds to pay the policy premium.

Establishing a Bank Account

The trustee of an ILIT may wish to open a bank account with a local bank after the trust is established. If the premiums are to be paid directly by the insured and the trust does not anticipate making any current disbursements, the trustee need not open a bank account until additional funds are added to the trust either by the grantor or when the proceeds of the life insurance policy become payable to the trust. More often, and the better practice for the payment of the premiums, is for the insured to make contributions to the trust and the trustee pay the premiums directly. In this case, the trustee should open a bank account for the trust.

GIFT TAX CONSIDERATIONS

Generally, any assets contributed to an irrevocable life insurance trust will be considered a taxable gift to the beneficiaries of that trust. Provided the grantor does not retain the right to designate new beneficiaries, or to change absolutely the interest of the beneficiaries, or any other power which would render the gift incomplete, transfers to the trust will be construed to be completed gifts. Fortunately, due to the use of the gift tax annual exclusion, the valuation of any life insurance policy transferred to the trust and the use of the unified credit, in most cases, no gift tax will actually be paid. Nevertheless, a primary consideration in creating an ILIT is to avoid incurring a gift tax. Securing the gift tax annual exclusion for contributions made by the grantor to the trust becomes of critical concern after execution of an ILIT.

When a Gift is Made

The contribution of a life insurance policy on the life of the grantor, or on the life of anyone else, will be considered a taxable gift to the beneficiaries of the trust. Whether the gift qualifies as a transfer of a present interest eligible for the annual exclusion will be determined by the terms of the trust.[7] Similarly, when the grantor makes the transfer to the trust to pay the policy premiums, the grantor is making a gift to the beneficiaries of the trust. The result does not change if the gifts are made directly or indirectly to the trust.[8] To avoid incurring a gift tax, it is important to secure the gift tax annual exclusion for the payment of the policy premiums by the grantor. The trust terms will once again determine whether such premium payments are gifts of a present interest qualifying for the gift tax annual exclusion.

Unless the gifts are covered by the annual exclusion, the transfers will be considered taxable gifts. As a result, some of the grantor's applicable credit amount will be used or gift tax may be owed. To ensure that gifts to the trust qualify for the gift tax annual exclusion, the most common drafting technique is to give one or more beneficiaries a right known as a "Crummey" power enabling the beneficiary to withdraw amounts contributed to the trust.

Valuation of Gift

The advantage of gifts of life insurance is that the value of the property transferred is modest compared to the value upon the death of the insured. This built-in appreciation makes it an ideal property for gifts. The general rule is that the value of a life insurance policy on the date of the gift is the replacement value.[9] However, the manner by which the replacement cost is determined varies depending on the nature of the policy:

- If the policy was newly issued and is transferred to the trust immediately after receipt, the value of the gift is determined based on the net premiums already paid.[10]

- If the life insurance policy is paid up and no further premiums are necessary to keep it in force for the life of the grantor, the value of the gift is the replacement cost which is the price the insurer would charge for the same policy on the life of a person of the same age of the insured on the date it is transferred to the trust.[11]

This value is usually obtained from the life insurance company. When the policy premiums are still due and ongoing, the policy's cash value is used to determine the gift amount. The gift tax value is the sum of the policy's interpolated terminal reserve[12] plus any unearned premiums,[13] less any loans outstanding against the policy.[14] Finally, term policies are valued by using the portion of the last premium which covers the period beyond the date of the gift.

The regulations also provide that all relevant facts and elements of value must be considered in every case when determining a policy's value. Therefore, the general rule that the value of a life insurance policy on the date of the gift is based on the replacement value is subject to increase or decrease based on the health of the insured at the time of the gift. In special circumstances, the IRS has argued an increase in value due to the insured being uninsurable or rated near death.[15]

In order to minimize the gift tax cost when contributing a life insurance policy to an ILIT, several techniques may be considered. One technique is to borrow a portion of the cash value out of the policy before it is transferred to the trust. The creation of a loan against the policy will lower the gift tax value of the policy. The loan amount should not be more than the grantor's net cost, which is the total of the premiums paid less any tax-free dividends, the grantor has received. Another technique is to divide a large policy into smaller policies and contribute them to the trust over a period of time using the annual exclusion to minimize or eliminate the taxable gift amount.

When transferring cash or any other type of property to the ILIT, the gift amount is the value of the asset transferred to the trust.[16] The most efficient way to minimize the gift tax cost of contributions to an ILIT is to maximize the use of the gift tax annual exclusion. This is usually accomplished with the use of the Crummey power.

Annual Gift Tax Exclusion

Pursuant to Code section 2503(b), a gift tax annual exclusion may apply to present interest gifts made to each donee during a calendar year. In addition, if one spouse makes a gift to an individual donee and the non-donor spouse consents, the donor-spouse may exclude up to two annual exclusions to each donee. This is called "gift splitting".[17] A present interest is an "unrestricted right of the immediate use, possession or enjoyment of property or income from property".[18] Gifts of future interests do not qualify for the annual exclusion.

When a gift is made to a trust, the beneficiaries of the trust, not the trust, are the donees. Generally, a gift made in trust is not a present interest gift and is at least in part, a future interest.[19] Consequently, gifts to an irrevocable life insurance trust for the payment of premiums will not, in and of themselves, qualify for the annual exclusion. In order to create a present interest gift for annual gifts to an ILIT, a Crummey power is ordinarily used. There will be a gift tax annual exclusion for each beneficiary that is given a Crummey power.

Crummey Powers

Crummey powers, named after a court case in which the taxpayer's surname was Crummey, gives trust beneficiaries the power, exercisable annually for a limited period of time, to withdraw the annual cash transfers to the trust.[20] This immediate, but temporary, right to withdraw the gifts made to the trust makes transfers to an ILIT a present interests which qualify for the federal gift tax annual exclusion. This is true even though the withdrawal power lapses. Generally, Crummey powers lapse if they are not exercised when the specified period expires, and the trustee is then free to use the recently transferred funds for premium payments. In practice, Crummey powers are rarely exercised. To many, the Crummey notices discussed below seem like burdensome technicalities. However, given the tax benefits that they offer, it is critical to stress the importance of these "technicalities" to the client.

For the Crummey power to give rise to a present interest, the trust beneficiary must be legally and technically capable of immediately possessing or enjoying the gifted property and must have had a reasonable opportunity to

do so. To constitute a reasonable opportunity to exercise the withdrawal right, the beneficiary must be:

1. aware that the right exists;[21] and

2. be given a reasonable amount of time within which to exercise the right of withdrawal.[22]

Knowledge of Withdrawal Right

In order to qualify for the gift tax annual exclusion, the beneficiary must be aware of the right of withdrawal and be given actual notice of the right as well as an opportunity to exercise the right.[23] In the event the holder of the withdrawal power is an unemancipated minor, the parent of such minor must be given actual notice.[24] If a trustee is the parent of the minor, the trustee does not have to give himself or herself written notice of the withdrawal right.[25] In all events, the power to withdraw must be actual and not illusory. So long as the beneficiary receives actual notice of the withdrawal right, i.e. a Crummey notice, this requirement is satisfied.[26]

Most trust instruments provide that the trustee must notify the Crummey power holder of the right of withdrawal. However, it should be noted that the Service has held that a notice given at the time of execution of the trust is sufficient and notice to the beneficiaries upon each subsequent gift to the trust is not necessary.[27] The method of providing notice varies greatly among trustees. Some trustees provide notice and request that beneficiaries acknowledge receipt; others do not request receipt; others require receipt and waiver; and some send a one-time written notice. Whichever method used, the trustee should establish sufficient evidence of compliance with Service requirements in the event of an audit.

Time of Withdrawal

In order to qualify for the gift tax annual exclusion, the beneficiary granted a Crummey right of withdrawal must have a reasonable amount of time within which to exercise the right of withdrawal after receiving the notice. The trust should then provide a time period within which such power can be exercised. However, the time period should be as short as possible. By limiting the withdrawal to as short a period of time as may be permitted, the beneficiaries will have less of an opportunity to elect to make a withdrawal. Furthermore, this minimizes the time within which the beneficiary could die holding such power which could cause the amount subject to the power to be included in the beneficiary's estate.

The Service has approved a period of time as short as thirty days within which the right to withdraw may be exercised before the right lapses.[28] Therefore, it is recommended that the withdrawal period specified in the trust instrument be at least thirty days before lapses.

Naming Beneficiaries with Withdrawal Rights

Ideally, the trust instrument should ensure that during the life of the grantor, there are a sufficient number of persons holding a Crummey withdrawal right to enable the total amount of the annual premiums to qualify for the annual exclusion. This is usually accomplished by giving current and contingent beneficiaries a withdrawal power.[29] However, if the power holder has minimal or no interest in the trust other than the withdrawal power, the Service has repeatedly attacked these arrangements as shams and refused to deem it a present interest qualifying for the annual exclusion.[30]

Satisfying the Withdrawal

Although beneficiaries that are granted a Crummey withdrawal right to have the right to make such withdrawal, it is not often exercised. Nevertheless, in order to benefit from the gift tax annual exclusion, the trust beneficiary must be assured of receiving some amount of trust corpus, should the beneficiary make such demand.[31] If a gift is less than the aggregate withdrawal powers given to the beneficiaries, the trust agreement should specify that each beneficiary may withdraw only a pro rata share of the gift.[32] If the only asset in the trust is the life insurance policy that has no cash value, the donor should make the gift to the trustee for the trustee to hold the money for a reasonable time after notice to the beneficiaries, and only thereafter have the trustee pay the life insurance policy premiums. This will insure that the funds are available should the beneficiary exercise his or her right of withdrawal.

5 x 5 Powers

For gift tax purposes, a Crummey withdrawal power is considered a general power of appointment.[33] Normally, the holder of the power does not use it and allows it to lapse unexercised each year. The lapse of a Crummey power is deemed a release of the power of appointment that in turn is considered a gift to other trust beneficiaries,[34] to the extent it exceeds the greater of $5,000 or 5 percent of the trust principal.[35] If lapses exceed the $5,000/5 percent safe harbor, the Crummey power holders will be taxed as having made a gift and will have to draw upon their

gift tax exemption amount to shelter the resulting taxable gifts from gift tax. Each beneficiary who allows his or her Crummey withdrawal power to lapse has only one $5,000/5 percent safe harbor exception available each year.[36] Therefore, if the beneficiary is the beneficiary of the several trusts, only one exception is permitted.

Annual Exclusions for Significant Premiums

To avoid a gift by the beneficiary, the Crummey power given to each beneficiary is often limited to the greater of $5,000 or 5 percent of the trust principal if the gift is less than the gift tax annual exclusion amount.[37] But when the gift exceeds the gift tax annual exclusion for each beneficiary, the dilemma is whether to limit the shelter to the full annual exclusion or limit the shelter to the $5,000/5 percent safe harbor to protect the beneficiary. There are several methods for drafting Crummey provisions which avoid the gift tax consequences of exceeding $5,000/5 percent safe harbor and take advantage of the gift tax annual exclusion:

- *Immediate Vesting in Primary* Beneficiary – The trust can provide for distributions of trust property to the estate of the primary beneficiary who is the holder of the Crummey power in the event the beneficiary dies prior to the trust termination. This avoids a current gift from a primary beneficiary to the remainder beneficiary as a result of the lapse. If the beneficiary survives until the termination of the trust, the assets in the trust would become his property. In that event, however, the entire trust property would be includable in the beneficiary's estate, which could be undesirable.

- *Power of Appointment* – As another option, the beneficiary can be given a general or limited power of appointment over the trust property. This makes the gift incomplete and therefore there is no taxable transfer on the lapse of the withdrawal power.[38] If the beneficiary dies before termination of the trust, the value of the trust will be included in the beneficiary's gross estate.[39] The same result is possible with a limited power of appointment. If the beneficiary dies before the termination of the trust possessing only a limited power, only the portion of the trust determined by multiplying the value of the trust at the beneficiary's death by a fraction that reflects the percentage of the trust property that previously lapsed should be included in the beneficiary's estate.

- *Hanging Power* – The final option, and the most commonly used to avoid the gift tax consequences of exceeding $5,000/5 percent safe harbor and yet take advantage of the gift tax annual exclusion, is the "hanging power." With the hanging power, each year, the amount of the withdrawal power up to the $5,000/5 percent safe harbor lapses, and the excess carries over to the next year. The excess amount is then "suspended" or "hangs" until such time as the grantor discontinues making additions to the trust. In subsequent years, the carryover power will lapse to the extent gifts in those years are less than the $5,000/5 percent safe harbor amount.

If using this hanging power technique, the powerholder should not expressly decline to exercise a Crummey Power because then the power may not "hang." Furthermore, the amount of the lapse cannot be tied to the gift tax ramifications of the powerholder. In that case, the gradual lapse will be disregarded as a condition subsequent for gift tax purposes.[40] As a result, the amount of the lapse must be determined prospectively. Hanging powers are most useful when either the policy premiums are of short duration, or the trust continues for a substantial time after the death of the insured, thereby enabling the power to lapse in years when no additional gifts are made to the ILIT. The hanging power may have adverse estate tax consequences for the beneficiary which are discussed in greater detail below.

Gift Splitting

For gift tax purposes, Code section 2513 permits a married individual to make a gift to a third party and, with the consent of his or her spouse, treat it as having been made one-half by the actual donor and one-half by the spouse.[41] Gift splitting permits a spouse who has adequate assets to make gifts which are sheltered from gift tax by both his or her own annual exclusion and unified credit as well as those of his or her spouse. To qualify, both spouses must be US citizens or resident aliens and they must be legally married.[42] The gift splitting election will apply to all gifts made during the year to a particular tax return relates.[43] If spouses do not want to split all gifts, the gifts should be made in different calendar years.

When a gift is made to a trust, the transfer generally qualifies for gift splitting if the nondonor spouse is not a beneficiary of the trust. However, if the nondonor spouse is a discretionary beneficiary, it is not always clear whether gift splitting is available. The transfer will qualify for split-gift treatment only if the interest transferred to third parties is ascertainable and severable from the interest transferred to the spouse.[44] The portion of the transfer allocated to the third-party beneficiaries will then qualify for split-gift treatment, while the portion allocated to the non-donor spouse will not. If the respective portions of the transfer allocable to the non-donor spouse and to the third-party beneficiaries cannot be ascertained, none of the transfer qualifies for gift splitting.

There are only a few cases and rulings involving the availability of gift splitting when the spouse is a permissible beneficiary of the trust.[45] While the authority is sparse, it is possible to draw several conclusions from the cases and rulings. If the donor can establish that the likelihood of distributions to the spouse is negligible, the spouse's interest can be disregarded so that gift splitting will be available. If the trust provides for an ascertainable standard for distribution, it may be possible to quantify the value of the spouse's interest, so that gift splitting will be available for the remaining portion of the gift. The problem with this test for taxpayers and their return preparers is that the proof required to satisfy the eligibility for gift splitting is a factual inquiry. As such, it will rarely be certain whether gift splitting is available when the trust allows for encroachment upon principal to or for the benefit of the spouse. Consequently, the best approach may be to report each donor's gifts separately, rather than electing gift splitting in a year that includes a gift to such a trust.

ESTATE TAX CONSIDERATIONS

The ability to remove life insurance proceeds from an estate is one of the primary reasons for utilizing an ILIT. In order to successfully remove the insurance proceeds from the grantor's estate, there must be a completed gift of the property to the ILIT[46] and the terms of the trust must be structured to avoid inclusion under sections 2035 to 2042 of the Internal Revenue Code. Each one of these sections is discussed below.

Section 2035 and the Three-Year Rule

Under Section 2035, if the insured transfers a life insurance policy to a third party such as an ILIT within three years of the insured's death, then the policy proceeds will be included in the insured's estate for estate tax purposes.[47] The simplest and safest way to avoid this result is to have the ILIT apply for and own the policy from the outset. If the trustee of an ILIT purchases the insurance policy directly from the insurer, Section 2035 is inapplicable because there was no "transfer" from the decedent. But, even momentary ownership of the policy by the insured within three years of his or her death will require inclusion of the full policy proceeds in the insured's estate. Therefore, the trustee should apply for the insurance policy, with the ILIT as the owner and beneficiary of the policy.

If an existing policy is gifted to an ILIT, then the grantor must survive three years for the insurance proceeds to avoid estate inclusion under Section 2035.[48] The relevant time of transfer is when the gift is complete for gift tax purposes. This typically occurs when dominion and control over the transferred property is relinquished.[49] The amount of the policy that is included in the insured's estate under Section 2035 will depend on the payor of the policy premiums. If the insured paid the premiums during the period of time before death, then the full value of the proceeds are includible in the insured's estate. However, if the trustee paid the premiums during that time, the proportionate amount of proceeds paid by the trustee will be excluded from the insured's estate.[50] Thus, if at all possible, the trustee should pay the premiums with funds received from someone other than the insured.

The three year rule of Code section 2035 only applies to gratuitous transfers. It does not apply to a bona fide sale of a life insurance policy for full and adequate consideration.[51] Therefore, a bona fide sale of an existing insurance policy to an ILIT should escape inclusion under 2035. However, under Code section 101(a)(2), the sale of a policy triggers the transfer-for-value rule. Under that rule, a "non-exempt" transferee will have to report a portion of the death proceeds as taxable income when the insured dies. The portion includible as taxable income is the face amount of the policy less any consideration paid (purchase price and subsequent premiums). The IRS has indicated that a sale of a life insurance policy to a "grantor" trust, of which the insured is treated as the owner for federal income tax purposes, will either not be treated as a "transfer for valuable consideration," or, if so treated, will be deemed to be a transfer of the policy to the insured -- one of the exempt transferees under the transfer-for-value rule.[52] Thus, if the ILIT is a grantor trust, the insured's sale of the policy to the ILIT for full and valuable consideration avoids both the three year rule and the transfer-for-value rule.

Sections 2036 to 2038 and 2041

The insurance proceeds may also be included in the decedent's estate if the trust is not properly structured

to avoid Code sections 2036 to 2038 and 2041. An ILIT should be drafted in a manner so that the grantor will not have any retained interests under sections 2036(a)(2) and 2038:

- Code section 2036 will cause inclusion in the gross estate if the grantor retains a beneficial interest in the insurance policy.

- Section 2038 will cause inclusion if the grantor transferred insurance to the ILIT and retained the power to alter, amend or revoke the beneficial enjoyment of the insurance policy or the ILIT. Therefore, the trust should be irrevocable, and the grantor should have no power to alter, amend, revoke or terminate the trust. The grantor should also relinquish any present or future interest in the trust. The trustee should not have the ability to use trust assets in a manner that would subject the assets to inclusion in the grantor's estate, including allowing the grantor to borrow any part or all of the trust assets, allowing any person to dispose of any part of the principal or income of the trust for less than adequate consideration, and allowing the trustee to revest title to any part of the trust in the grantor.

- Lastly, if the grantor holds a power of appointment over the policy or the ILIT, Code section 2041 will cause inclusion. For this reason, the grantor should not hold a power of appointment.

Section 2042 and Incidents of Ownership

In order to avoid inclusion in the grantor's estate, the grantor must not have any "incidents of ownership" in the trust or the underlying insurance policy.[53] The term incidents of ownership is defined very broadly and includes:

1. the power to change the beneficiary of the policy;

2. the power to surrender or cancel the policy;

3. the power to assign the policy or revoke an assignment; and

4. the power to pledge the policy as security for a loan or to obtain a loan against the surrender value of the policy.

All of these incidents of ownership should be vested in the trustee and not the grantor. A "reversionary interest" in the policy or its proceeds, which is the possibility that the policy or its proceeds may return to the decedent or decedent's estate, is also an incident of ownership.

Payment of Estate Taxes

Often, life insurance is obtained for the specific purposes of providing estate liquidity. However, insurance proceeds that are received by the executor are includible for tax purposes if the proceeds are received by or for the benefit of the decedent's estate.[54] Inclusion also occurs when the proceeds are received by someone other than the decedent but that person is bound to use the proceeds to discharge the decedent's estate obligations. If the terms of the ILIT bind the trustee to pay the decedent's taxes, debts or other charges which are enforceable against the estate, the proceeds subject to the obligation will be includible in the insured's gross estate.[55] To avoid this adverse tax

consequence, the ILIT should permit, but not obligate, the trustee to lend money to or purchase assets from the estate, thereby providing the estate with the needed liquidity without triggering estate inclusion.

Direct Incidents of Policy Ownership

If at death the decedent possessed incidents of ownership in the policy, exercisable either alone or in conjunction with another person, the insurance proceeds are includible in decedent's gross taxable estate. The terms of the policy generally dictate whether the decedent possessed an incident of ownership in the policy. The term "incidents of ownership" generally signifies that the insured or his estate has the right to the economic benefits of the policy. However, it is not limited to ownership of the policy as a matter of law but includes direct rights over the policy. Examples of some of these rights that are and are not considered incidents of ownership are shown in Figure 6.1.

Figure 6.1

INCIDENTS OF OWNERSHIP	
Considered Incidents of Ownership	**Not Considered Incidents of Ownership**
• The power to change the beneficial ownership in the policy or its proceeds, or the time or manner of enjoyment thereof • The power to obtain from the insurer a loan against the surrender value of the policy • The retained right to repurchase the policy from an assignee • The power over the choice of settlement options.[1] • The right to modify or designate a beneficiary or contingent beneficiary[2] • The power to prevent or veto a person from changing a beneficiary by withholding consent (a "negative" or "veto" power)[3] • The power to modify the time and manner of payment of policy proceeds • The right to elect optional modes of settlement of proceeds of employer provided life insurance on a decedent's life.[4]	• A veto power that gave the insured the power over the designation of the beneficiary[5] • The power to cancel insurance provided through an employer by terminating employment[6] • The power to convert group-term insurance into ordinary insurance by terminating employment.[7]

1. Treas. Reg. §20.2042-1(c)(4); TAM 9128008.
2. *Chase Nat'l. Bank of New York, Ex'r. v. U.S.*, 278 US 327 (1929); *Nance v. U.S.*, 430 F.2d 662 (9th Cir. 1970); *Broderick v. Keefe*, 112 F.2d 293 (1st Cir. 1940); *Est. of Richard A. Henry v. Comm'r.*, TCM 1987-119).
3. *Eleanor M. Schwager*, 64 TC 781 (1975); Rev. Rul. 75-70.
4. Rev. Rul. 81-128.
5. *Estate of Rockwell v. Comm'r.*, 779 F.2d 931 (3d Cir. 1985).
6. *Landorf v. U.S.*; Rev. Rul. 72-307.
7. Rev. Rul. 84-130.

Ownership in Corporation or Partnership

Incidents of ownership can also be present through the decedent's ownership interest in a corporation or partnership. If the decedent owns the more than fifty percent (50 percent) of the voting stock of a corporation, the incidents of ownership that the corporation possesses over an insurance policy on the insured shareholder's life will be attributed to the insured.[56] However, the rule will not apply to the extent the proceeds are payable to the corporation or payable to a third party in satisfaction of a corporate debt.

On the other hand, life insurance owned by a general partnership and insuring a partner's life is generally not includible in the partner's gross taxable estate.[57] Similarly, in the case of limited partnerships, no inclusion results from a policy insuring a majority limited partner where the policy is owned by a limited partnership and the insured cannot exercise incidents of ownership.[58]

Reversionary Interest

Incidents of ownership over a life insurance policy can be triggered if the grantor retained a reversionary interest in the policy. A reversionary interest is the possibility that the policy or its proceeds may return to the decedent or his estate and a possibility that the policy or its proceeds may become subject to a power of disposition by the decedent.[59] The reversionary interest can arise by the express terms of the policy or by operation of law. The reversionary interest will cause estate inclusion, if the value of the reversionary interest immediately before the decedent's death exceeded 5 percent of the value of the policy.[60] If the value does not exceed 5 percent of the value of the policy immediately before death, the reversionary interest is disregarded. Furthermore, the possibility that the decedent might receive a policy or proceeds either by an inheritance or as the surviving spouse under a statutory right of election does not automatically result in inclusion.

Substitution of Assets

A grantor trust is a trust that is considered a disregarded entity for income tax purposes. Grantor trusts are popular and useful estate planning devices. ILITs are often grantor trusts. One of the common ways to structure an ILIT as a grantor trust is to give the grantor the power to substitute trust assets with assets of equivalent value. For many years, practitioners were wary of allowing a substitution of assets where life insurance was involved for fear that the proceeds of life insurance would be included in the grantor's estate under Section 2042. Revenue Ruling 2011-28 clarified the issue and declared that the use of a power of substitution, by itself, would not constitute an incident of ownership under Section 2042, and thus the life insurance policy or its proceeds would not be includible in the grantor's gross estate.

To fall within the parameters of Revenue Ruling 2011-28, the grantor's retention of the power to acquire an insurance policy held in trust by substituting other assets of equivalent value must be exercisable by the grantor in a nonfiduciary capacity, the trustee must have the fiduciary obligation (under local law or the trust instrument) to ensure the grantor's compliance with the terms of this power by ensuring that the properties acquired and substituted are of equivalent value, and the substitution power cannot be exercised in a manner that can shift benefits among the trust beneficiaries.

Creditors' Rights Doctrine

Pursuant the creditor's right doctrine, if a creditor has the ability to reach the assets of a trust, the gift made to the trust is not considered a completed gift.[61] If the gift is incomplete, then the property will be includible in the grantor's gross taxable estate.[62] Therefore, if the life insurance policy held by an ILIT is subject to creditor's claim, then the policy is includible in the grantor's estate. Whether a creditor can recover from an ILIT is determined by state law.

Estate Taxation of Crummey Powers

The beneficiary of an ILIT who possesses a Crummey withdrawal power on the date of death, or has allowed the Crummey withdrawal power to lapse before the date of death, can experience adverse estate tax consequences.

- *Unlapsed Powers*- Beneficiaries holding Crummey powers hold general powers of appointment. As a result, if a beneficiary dies while holding a Crummey power that has not lapsed, the property subject to the withdrawal right will be included in the beneficiary's gross taxable estate.[63] This is often the issue with hanging powers. If the beneficiary dies prior to the termination of the trust, the aggregate amount of the hanging power in existence at the date of the beneficiary's death will be included in the beneficiary's estate for federal estate tax purposes.

- *Lapsed Powers*- Generally, property which is subject to a general power of appointment that is released or allowed to lapse by the powerholder will be included in the power holder's estate under Sections 2035 to 2038 if the property had been owned by the powerholder before transfer to the trust.[64] As a result, the annual lapse of a Crummey withdrawal power will subject the property covered by the power to inclusion in the beneficiary's estate. However, pursuant to Section 2041(b)(2), to the extent the lapse of the withdrawal power exceeds the $5,000/5 percent safe harbor, only the excess would be includible in the beneficiary's estate.

INCOME TAX CONSIDERATIONS

Grantor Trusts or Separate Taxpayer

The income generated from an ILIT will typically be taxed to the trust as a separate entity or to the beneficiaries that receive distributions. Alternatively, the grantor will be taxed on the income generated by the ILIT if the grantor is treated as the owner under the grantor trust rules of Code sections 671 to 679. Typically, an ILIT will only hold the insurance policy and funds for a limited time to pay policy premiums. This results in minimal or no taxable income. Therefore, in the usual case, it is of no consequence to determine whether the trust is a separate income tax entity or whether the income is attributable to the grantor. However, when the ILIT is funded, and upon death of the insured, the status of the trust as a separate entity or as a grantor trust must be considered.

Making an ILIT a Grantor Trust

Generally, it is desirable for an ILIT to be deemed a grantor trust for income tax purposes. The grantor trust status shelters the trust beneficiaries from averse income tax consequences caused when the trust is deemed a separate taxpayer. It also enables the sale of the insurance policy without triggering an income tax on the death benefits. If a decision is made to make the ILIT a grantor trust, there are numerous powers that accomplish this result. However, some powers destroy the main purposes of preventing the

inclusion of the insurance proceeds in the grantor's gross estate for estate tax purposes and should be avoided. There are other powers which, if properly structured, can trigger grantor trust status and yet avoid estate tax inclusion.

Desirable Powers

There are four grantor trust powers which can be included in the terms of an ILIT that will trigger grantor trust status for income tax purposes without risking estate tax inclusion. The first power is the ability to pay premiums for policies that are owned by the ILIT on the grantor's life.[65] Generally, because trust income may be applied to pay premiums on life insurance on the grantor's life, any taxable income will be taxed to the grantor under the grantor trust rules, thereby making the trust a grantor trust.[66] Although the statute clearly provides that grantor trust status will be triggered if income "may" be used to pay premiums, there are some cases that predate the rule which provide that it is not available if the trust had to use income to pay the premiums.[67] Therefore, to assure grantor trust treatment, it is wise to include other provisions that assure grantor trust status without compromising transfer tax treatment.

Second, if the grantor's spouse is a mandatory or possible income beneficiary of a funded ILIT, then the trust will be considered a grantor trust.[68] The concern with this approach is that the grantor trust could be terminated prematurely if the grantor's spouse predeceases or divorces the grantor. Therefore, a different grantor trust trigger is preferred.

Third, a trust will be deemed a grantor trust if a nonadverse party has the power to add beneficiaries to the trust other than after-born or after-adopted children.[69] It is advisable that this power be given to an independent trustee to permit the addition of a charity. This will trigger grantor trust status while preventing inclusion in the grantor's estate.

Finally, the power to substitute trust assets with assets of equivalent value will trigger grantor trust status.[70]

Undesirable Powers

There are certain powers that should be avoided as a way to triggering grantor trust status because they will cause estate tax inclusion. The grantor's retention of a reversionary interest in the income or principal of the trust that exceeds five percent (5 percent) should not be used.[71] The grantor's retention of the power to control the beneficial enjoyment of income or principal without the consent of an adverse party[72] or to retain administrative powers, such as the power to borrow without adequate interest or security, should be avoided.[73] The grantor should not retain the power to revoke the ILIT.[74] Although all these powers will trigger grantor trust status, they will also trigger estate tax inclusion.

Crummey Powers

The existence of Crummey Powers can have potential income tax consequences for the holder of the withdrawal right. However, the beneficiaries will not have any income tax consequences if the grantor is treated as the owner of the trust under the grantor trust rules. Section 678(a) provides that trust income is taxed to the Crummey power-holder since the power-holder has the power to vest the trust corpus in himself. However, Section 678(b) provides that Section 678(a) does not apply if income would otherwise be taxed to the grantor. But Code §678(b) applies only to a "power over income." In fact, a Crummey power is a power over trust principal. Despite this distinction, the IRS has ruled that trust income is taxed to the grantor rather than to the Crummey power-holder.[75]

If the grantor is not treated as the owner of an ILIT, then the beneficiary is treated as the owner under the grantor trust rules of that portion of the trust over which the beneficiary has the power to vest the principal in himself or herself.[76] This is the case even if the beneficiary is a minor and lacks capacity to withdraw the power. It is the existence of the power, not the capacity to exercise such power that determines whether the person other than the grantor is treated as the owner of any portion of the trust.[77]

Transfer-for-Value Rule

At times, it is desirable for an ILIT to purchase an insurance policy from an old trust, a corporation or an employer. Life insurance proceeds payable by reason of the insured's death are generally not included in the recipient's gross income.[78] However, all or a portion of the proceeds may become taxable income under the transfer-for-value rule.[79] The rule applies whenever a policy is transferred for valuable consideration. Under the transfer-for-value rule, if an insurance contract is transferred for value, the proceeds are taxable income to the beneficiary at the insured's death to the extent the proceeds exceed basis.[80]

Section 101(a)(2)(B) provides exceptions to the transfer-for-value rule to avoid the income taxation upon the sale of a life insurance policy. If the transfer of a policy is to the insured, a partner of the insured, a partnership in which the insured is a partner, or to a corporation in which the insured is a shareholder or officer, the proceeds of the insurance will not be taxable income. In Revenue Ruling 2007-13, the IRS stated that the transfer between the insured and a grantor trust (if the insured is the grantor) falls within the exemption and will not trigger income tax.

GENERATION-SKIPPING TRANSFER (GST) TAX CONSIDERATIONS

The federal generation-skipping transfer (GST) tax is a separate tax in addition to federal gift and estate taxes. Congress intended that the federal gift and estate tax laws would apply to transfers of wealth from members of an older generation to members of the next younger generation such as parents to children. Taxpayers determined to avoid gift and estate taxes by structuring wealth transfers so they would "skip" the next generation or benefit multiple younger generations through a single transaction by leaving assets directly to grandchildren and great grandchildren. Congress implemented the generation skipping transfer (GST) tax as a backstop to the estate and gift tax to cover situations in which property was transferred through several generations. The GST tax imposes a tax on transfers that "skip" a generation.

GST for ILITs creates some uncommon situations which require the draftsperson to carefully examine the GST ramifications of all ILITs. Life insurance is an ideal asset for multi- generational planning because of its inherent appreciation, all of which can be exempt from GST taxation. When an ILIT provides benefits to multiple generations or to "skip" individuals, the GST tax consequences should be considered. But a possible GST tax trap awaits if the insured and the insured's descendants do not die in the usual order.[81] An unexpected death order may require allocation of some (or all) of the transferor's GST tax exemption to avoid taxation. For some, the GST allocation is not desired because all trust assets pass to nonskip persons like the grantor's spouse and children. In this case, the

GST aspects of the trust must be examined to opt out of the automatic GST allocation rules.

Generally, GST tax is imposed on transfers made during lifetime or resulting upon death to a beneficiary who is two or more generations younger than the transferor. Such a beneficiary is generally referred to as a "skip person."[82] For example, if a grandparent makes a transfer to an ILIT for the benefit of a grandchild, excluding the child as a beneficiary, the grandparent will have made a transfer that is a direct skip. GST tax is also imposed on "indirect skips" known as "taxable terminations" and "taxable distributions."[83] An example of a taxable termination is when the trust principal is distributed to a grandchild after the death of the parent of the grandchild who was a beneficiary of the trust. An example of a taxable distribution is where a trust permits income or principal to be distributed to a grandchild of the transferor and the trustee makes such distribution.

Transfers to an ILIT may be shielded from GST tax in two ways: (1) the GST tax annual exclusion;[84] and (2) the GST exemption. Many estate planning professionals believe that any gift that qualifies for the annual exclusion is also exempt from GST tax. That was true when the GST tax first was enacted, but Congress has since narrowed the exclusion. For transfers after March 31, 1988, a gift to an ILIT that qualifies for the gift tax annual exclusion does not necessarily qualify for the annual exclusion for GST tax purposes. For GST tax purposes, an annual exclusion gift is nontaxable only if made outright or to a trust with one beneficiary whose interest is vested, or when the trust assets are includible in beneficiary's gross estate.[85] In most typical ILITs with multiple beneficiaries, the transfers will not qualify for the annual exclusion and the grantor must allocate GST exemption to the trust to make it GST exempt.

Predeceased Ancestor Rule and ILITs

Often, a typical ILIT is structured for the benefit of the grantor's spouse and children. If everyone dies in the usual order with the grantor first, followed by the spouse and then children, GST is not an issue. However, a possible GST tax trap awaits if the grantor and his descendants do not die in the usual order.

The predeceased ancestor rule provides that a transfer to a grandchild, or more remote decedent is not a generation-skipping transfer if the transferor's descendant who was also the descendant of the donee

is deceased.[86] The predeceased ancestor rule, however, applies only if the ancestor is deceased at the time of the transfer.[87] In the case of an ILIT, the transfer occurs when gifts are made to the trust to pay premiums and as the Crummey powers lapse. Because this occurs before the distribution to the skip person, payment to such a skip person would be a generation-skipping transfer.[88] The unexpected generation-skipping transfer may require allocation of the transferor's GST tax exemption.

Allocation of GST Exemption and Automatic GST Allocation

Each taxpayer has a GST tax exemption amount which may be allocated during life or at death. The allocation of the GST exemption is used to minimize the eventual GST tax on transfer to or distributions from the trust. The transferor's unused GST tax exemption is allocated by: (1) the taxpayer making an affirmative allocation on a gift tax return filed for the year in which the taxpayer makes a transfer; or (2) by "automatic allocation" if the transfer was a considered an "indirect skip" to a "GST trust".[89] Due to the issues caused by the automatic allocation rules discussed below, it is recommended that an affirmative election in or out of GST be made on a timely filed tax return.

In 2001, Congress provided for the automatic allocation of GST exemption to transfers to trusts that do not result in an immediate GST tax but which may incur GST tax later.[90] This automatic allocation to "indirect skip" transfers eliminated the problem of missed GST exemption allocations to ILITs designed to be generation-skipping trusts. The grantor's GST exemption was automatically applied to the trust under the indirect skip rules even if the grantor failed to file a gift tax return. The definition of a "GST Trust" to which the indirect skip rules apply is very broad and covers most trusts unless the trust falls into a narrow group of exceptions which are as follows:

1. If 25 percent of the trust corpus must be distributed to or may be withdrawn by one or more non-skip persons before the date that the individual attains age forty-six, on or before one or more dates specified in the trust instrument that will occur before the date that such individual attains age forty-six, or upon the occurrence of an event that, in accordance with regulations prescribed by the Secretary, may reasonably be expected to occur before the date that such individual attains age forty-six;

2. If the trust instrument provides that more than 25 percent of the trust corpus must be distributed to or may be withdrawn by one or more individuals who are non-skip persons and who are living on the date of the death of another person identified in the instrument who is more than ten years older than such individuals;

3. Those trusts any portion of which would be included in the gross estate of a non-skip person (other than the transferor) if such person died immediately after the transfer;

4. If the trust grants non-skip persons withdrawal rights equal to twice the annual exclusion amount, and the transferor transfers an amount greater than the annual exclusion in the first year;

5. If the trust is a charitable lead annuity trust or charitable remainder trust; or

6. If the trust is a charitable lead unitrust with a non-skip person holding the remainder interest.[91]

The broad reach of the automatic allocation rules can cause virtually any trust created for the benefit of family member to be considered a GST trust. In the common situation where the beneficiaries of the trust are the grantor's grandchildren and younger generations, the ILIT itself is considered a skip person.[92] In other situations where the beneficiaries of the trust are the grantor's children and grandchildren, it would be considered a GST trust subject to the automatic allocation rules. In both of these instances, the allocation of GST exemption is preferred to exempt the trust from GST taxation.

However, in some situations, the settlor would not want GST exemption automatically allocated to the trust. At times, an ILIT is structured for the benefit of the surviving spouse, upon whose death the trust assets are to be paid to the grantor's children, either outright or in further trust. In this case, the ILIT would not likely be subject to GST tax. Under the GST automatic allocation rules, the GST exemption would be allocated to the trust even though the trust assets may never pass to grandchildren. If the settlor is not filing a gift tax return for gifts to the ILIT, or is not making the proper election on the gift tax return to elect out of the indirect skip rules, his or her GST exemption may be depleted unintentionally. To avoid this result, the taxpayer should elect out of the automatic GST exemption allocation.[93]

The allocation should occur on the gift tax return for the year the transfer was made. The transfer will then be determined according the value on the date of transfer.[94]

GST and Crummey Withdrawal Powers

The Crummey notices contained in many insurance trusts can cause several adverse GST tax consequences that need special consideration. In certain instances, the Crummey notices can prevent the automatic allocation of GST tax to apply. In other instances, it may result in a double GST exemption allocation or a delay in allocation.

Crummey Withdrawal Powers and the Automatic Allocation

In certain circumstances, a hanging Crummey power can prevent the automatic allocation of GST tax. The automatic allocation only applies to transfers made to a "GST trust." Under one of these exceptions, a trust is not a GST trust if any portion of it would be included in the gross estate of a non-skip person (other than the grantor) if such person died immediately after the transfer. This exception would appear to apply to Crummey trusts in which a spouse, child or other non-skip person holds a hanging power because the amount subject to the hanging power would be includible in such beneficiary's estate.

To prevent all Crummey trusts from falling outside the definition of a GST trust, the statute provides an exception to the exception. The value of transferred property is not deemed to be includible in the gross estate of a non-skip person to the extent of the annual exclusion amount. Thus, if the hanging power applies to an amount with respect to all non-skip beneficiaries of a Crummey trust that falls within the annual exclusion amount, the trust will be considered a GST trust, resulting in automatic allocation of GST tax exemption. However, in the subsequent year, if an additional annual exclusion gift is made, it may not qualify as a GST trust in that year. Therefore, it is advisable that an affirmative election or GST allocation be made with regard to transfers to the trust.

Double GST Allocation

An individual's GST exemption can only be allocated to property over which the individual is the transferor.[95] Therefore, is it important to determine the identity of the transferor. The transferor for GST tax purposes is the decedent for transfers subject to the estate tax and the donor for transfers subject to the gift tax. For purposes of GST tax, a transfer is subject to estate tax if the property is includible in the decedent's gross estate.[96] A transfer is subject to gift tax if gift tax is imposed (without regard to exemptions, exclusions, deductions and credits).

If the lapse is in excess of the $5,000/5 percent safe harbor, the grantor is the transferor for the amount up to the $5,000/5 percent safe harbor. The powerholder may be the transferor over the excess depending on the federal gift tax consequences of the lapse. If the powerholder has been given a special or general power of appointment, causing the gift to be incomplete, the grantor will remain the transferor, which would require an allocation of GST exemption to the entire gift.

If the lapse results in a completed gift because the powerholder is not given a power of appointment or a hanging power, this results in the grantor being the transferor up to the $5,000/5 percent safe harbor and the powerholder being the transferor over the excess.[97] The powerholder will then have to allocate the powerholder's GST exemption to the amount over the excess of the $5,000/5 percent safe harbor. The amount of allocation for the grantor would be the entire gift to the trust (including the amount allocated by the powerholder), if the allocation of exemption is automatic or if the exemption is claimed on a timely filed gift tax return. Therefore, the lapse of a Crummey notice in excess of the $5,000/5 percent safe harbor can cause the double GST exemption allocation by the grantor of the trust and the powerholder of the Crummey power.

ETIP Rules and Crummey Withdrawal

A GST exemption cannot be allocated to property until the close of the estate tax inclusion period (ETIP). The ETIP is the period where transferred property would be included in the transferor or the spouse of the transferor's gross estate (other than by reason of Section 2035) if the transferor's were to die.[98] A withdrawal power held by the spouse could constitute in an ETIP which would prevent GST allocation by the transferor until the lapse of the power. But a limited exemption is created if the power of withdrawal is limited to the $5,000/5 percent safe harbor. Other Crummey withdrawal powers, such as a hanging power, would constitute an ETIP. Therefore, if the grantor wishes to allocate GST to an ILIT in which his spouse is a beneficiary, the spouse's Crummey withdrawal power should be limited to the $5,000/5 percent safe harbor amount.

RECIPROCAL TRUST DOCTRINE

The reciprocal trust doctrine is a judicial doctrine which was created to determine who is to be treated as the grantor for tax purposes when there are two related or reciprocal trusts. The first case to recognize the doctrine was *Lehman v. Comm'r.*,[99] although the seminal case that establishes when trusts are "reciprocal" is *United States v. Estate of Grace.*[100] In *Estate of Grace*, the Supreme Court of the United States held that the reciprocal trust doctrine applies when trusts are "interrelated, and that the arrangement, to the extent of mutual value leaves the settlors in approximately the same economic position as they would have been in had they created trusts naming themselves as life beneficiaries."[101]

The doctrine "uncrosses" trusts in situations where related parties create two trusts where each grantor is the beneficiary of the other trust. The doctrine treats each person as if they were the grantor over the trust in which they are the beneficiary. It is not uncommon for married people to each create an insurance trust naming the other spouse as a beneficiary. Doing so may trigger the reciprocal trust doctrine, causing both trusts to be included in the estate of the respective grantor. To avoid this bad result, the trusts should different enough to avoid the issue. This can be accomplished by altering the beneficiaries of the trusts or the manner and amount in which the beneficiaries receive their interest.

PROVIDING ESTATE LIQUIDITY

An ILIT is often used as a mechanism to provide estate liquidity to pay estate taxes when the assets of the estate are hard to sell or are illiquid and where the client does not wish to sell the assets. Business owners and clients with real estate holdings usually encounter this problem. A properly drafted ILIT can ensure that insurance proceeds are tax-free and provide for liquidity without forcing an estate to sell estate assets to meet obligations.

Although an insurance policy may be obtained for the specific purposes of providing estate liquidity, the ILIT should not instruct the trustee to pay the estate of the insured any amounts needed for estate debts, expenses and taxes. As discussed above, doing so will cause the proceeds to be included in the insured's gross estate under Section 2042. Instead, proceeds can be made available to the executor for liquidity by permit the trustee to lend money or purchase assets from the estate without risking inclusion. To avoid inclusion, the authority of the trustee must be discretionary and not mandatory. The loan or purchase of the estate assets should also be on the same terms as an arms-length transaction. The purchase should be at fair market value to avoid the possibility of it being considered a taxable distribution. Similarly, the loan should contain a reasonable rate of interest, provide a repayment schedule, and be secured by estate assets as collateral.

TRUSTEE SELECTION

The choice of trustee over an ILIT should be made with great caution. A practitioner and client should discuss in detail the factors that should dictate the proper choice of trustee. Some relevant factors include the trust's purpose, duration, the trustee's duties and fees, and tax consequences.

Insured as Trustee

To avoid any implication that the insured retained any incidents of ownership over a life insurance policy, the insured should not be the trustee of an ILIT.[102] The regulations state that a decedent is considered to retain an incident of ownership in the policy if:

1. the insured trustee could have exercised trust powers over the policy for his benefit;

2. the insured has transferred the policy or any of the consideration for purchasing and maintaining the policy to the trust; or

3. the giving of the trust powers to the insured as trustee was part of a prearranged plan involving the insured.[103]

Although it is possible for the insured to serve as trustee of the trust, it is not recommended. Making the grantor/insured a trustee of an ILIT is an invitation for problems with the IRS and should be avoided.

Beneficiary as Trustee

Generally, a beneficiary should not be named as sole trustee, but may be named as co-trustee as long as the beneficiary's discretionary powers are limited to avoid adverse tax consequences. The beneficiary should not be permitted to have discretion to pay out principal or income to himself or to any person that he or she has a legal obligation to support to avoid the power being considered a general power of appointment.[104] If the grantor insists on appointing a beneficiary as trustee, then the power to distribute principal and income should be limited to an ascertainable standard (i.e., maintenance and support).[105]

Insured with Right to Change Trustee

When creating irrevocable trusts like an ILIT, clients often want to retain an unrestricted right to remove and replace a trustee. There used to be a concern that the power to remove and replace a trustee always causes the powers of the trustee to be attributed to an insured/trustee.[106] Revenue Ruling 95-58 clarified that the powers of a trustee will not be attributed to a grantor for purposes of Section 2036 or Section 2038 so long as the remover had to appoint a successor who was not a related or subordinate party within the meaning of Section 672(c). Thereafter, the IRS extended Revenue Ruling 95-58 to Section 2041.[107] In PLR 200314009, the IRS extended the rational of Revenue Ruling 95-58 to Section 2042 and ruled that a grantor's power to appoint trustees of an insurance trust would not cause inclusion of policy proceeds under Section 2042(2). However, neither a private letter ruling nor a technical advice memorandum may be cited as precedent under Section 6110(k)(3). Therefore, the safest course of action is not to give the insured trustee removal or replacement power. If really desired, the power can be given to another family member, preferably one who is not a beneficiary unless the trustee powers are limited by an ascertainable standard.

PRUDENT INVESTOR RULE

The Uniform Prudent Investor Act (UPIA) is a model statute that sets the standards governing a trustee's acts. It applies to ILITs and governs the conduct and practices of an ILIT trustee. The UPIA replaces the prudent person rule with the prudent investor rule.[108] The prudent investor rule requires a trustee to invest and manage trust assets as a prudent investor would.[109] It considers the purposes, terms, distribution requirements and other circumstances of the trust. The evaluation of a trustee's investments follows the modern portfolio theory.[110]

The modern portfolio theory does not look at an individual investment in isolation but rather looks at the portfolio as a whole. The overall investment strategy must have risk and return objectives tailored to the trust. The trustee is allowed to invest in any kind of property or type of investment.[111] However, the trustee must diversify the investments of the trust unless the trustee determines that the trust does not require diversification.[112]

From the inception of a trustee's term, the trustee is required to review the trust assets and implement an investment strategy that follows the prudent investor rule.[113] The trustee has a continued duty to monitor the investments.[114] Other duties imposed on the trustee include the duties of loyalty and impartiality.[115] The trustee must invest and manage the trust assets for the sole benefit of the beneficiaries. If the trust has more than one beneficiary, the trustee must act impartially in investing and managing the trust assets. This requires the trustee to take into account the different interests of the beneficiaries and the inherent conflict between an income beneficiary and a remainder beneficiary.

Most insurance trusts will only hold a single life insurance policy during the life of the insured. The donor may not want the trustee to be held to the standards of the prudent investor rule. The grantor should consider overriding the prudent investor rule and preempting it by specific language in the trust.[116]

The grantor can reduce or eliminate a trustee's duties that would otherwise be applicable under the prudent investor rule of the governing state. For example, the grantor may eliminate the trustee's duty to monitor the policy's performance and the duty to diversify. Eliminating the duty to diversify will allow the trustee to retain the original insurance policies in trust. The grantor can even reduce or eliminate the trustee's duty to search the marketplace for better performing policies that have become available.

Some states have enacted statutes that reduce or eliminate the trustee's duties relating to life insurance held in trust. Other states have enacted statutes which have gone so far as to relieve a trustee from liability stemming from the management of life insurance as an investment.[117] For example, Delaware's statute relieves the trustee of an ILIT from liability which arises from the trustee's failure to make certain investigations regarding the viability of the insurance policy as a sound investment.[118] Florida's statute removes the trustee's duty to manage the policy as an investment.[119] It also removes the trustee's liability to beneficiaries for any loss sustained with respect to the insurance policy.

COMMUNITY PROPERTY CONSIDERATIONS

When the grantors reside in a community property state, an additional twist occurs that requires special attention to be paid to the drafting and funding of the ILIT. Community property is any property earned or accrued during marriage, with the exception of gifts and inheritances. This community property concept presents a problem if the grantors are married and intend the ILIT to insure the life of one spouse for the benefit of the other.

When the spouse of the insured is intended to be a beneficiary of the trust, then the beneficiary spouse must not be a grantor of the trust to avoid inclusion under Code section 2042. If community property dollars are used to fund the ILIT, then both spouses are considered grantors. In this event, one half of the proceeds belongs to the decedent's spouse and is included in the surviving spouse's taxable estate upon the surviving spouse's death.[120] To avoid this result, only separate property of the insured should be used to fund the trust, so that the uninsured spouse will not be considered a grantor. If the married couple does not have separate property, then an agreement between the spouses to partition the community property into equal shares of separate property should be considered. Only funds from separate property should be used to make gifts to the ILIT.

TAX CUTS AND JOBS ACT OF 2017

The Tax Cuts and Jobs Act of 2017 (TCJA) made sweeping changes in many areas of the federal tax law. In the context of estate and gift taxes, TCJA increased the basic exclusion amount under Code section 2001(c)(3(C) from $5,000,000 to $10,000,000, (adjusted further for inflation, or $11,400,000 in 2019). The doubling of the exclusion amount eliminated the need for many individuals to purchase or maintain existing life insurance policies to pay a federal estate tax. Nevertheless, the cancelation of existing policies should be done with great caution. The increased exclusion amounts are temporary and are scheduled to sunset in 2026, or even sooner if there is a change in legislation. If the policyholder survives the sunset, the insurance may once again be needed. If the policy is cancelled, the policyholder can develop medical problems during that time thereby losing their insurability. Instead, in some instances, the ILIT can be repurposed to meet different needs like premature death and liquidity.

CHAPTER ENDNOTES

1. Under the Uniform Probate Code and in some states, life insurance held by the decedent at the time of death is subject to the surviving spouse's right of election. Unif. Prob. Code §2-205(1)(iv); Minn. Stat. §524.2- 205(1)(iii). In contrast, life insurance held by a life insurance trust is generally not included in the augmented estate, even under the Uniform Probate Code.

2. Treas. Reg. §20.2042-1(c)(2).

3. I.R.C. §2042.

4. I.R.C. §2035(a).

5. Rev. Rul. 72-307.

6. I.R.C. §2042.

7. Reg. §25.2503-3(a).

8. Rev. Rul. 72-307.

9. Treas. Reg. §25.2512-6(a).

10. *Id*.

11. Treas. Reg. §25.2512-6(a), Ex. 3.

12. This is the amount the insurer set aside to meet the obligations under the policy as of the date of the transfer.

13. This is the premiums that were paid and that will carry the insurance beyond the date it was transferred to the trust.

14. Treas. Reg. §25.2512-6(a), Ex. 4.

15. *Estate of Pritchard v. Comm'r.*, 4 T.C. 204 (1944).

16. Treas. Reg. §25.2511.1(h)(8).

17. I.R.C. §2513.

18. Reg. §25.2503-3(b).

19. Reg. §§§25.2503-3(b)-(c), Examples (1) and (2).

20. *Crummey v. Comm'r.*, 397 F.2d 82 (9th Cir. 1968).

21. Rev. Rul. 81 – 7, 1981-1 CB 474; Priv. Ltr. Ruls. 7946007 and 8806063.

22. Priv. Ltr. Ruls. 8004172, 8006048, 8126047, 8545076, 8616027, 8701007, 8712014, 8813019, 8922062 and 923-2013.

23. Priv. Ltr. Ruls. 7946007, 7947066, 8014078, 8024084 and 9232013.

24. Priv. Ltr. Ruls. 8138102, 8138170, 8138171, 8308033, 8806063 and 9232013.

25. Priv. Ltr. Rul. 9030005.

26. Rev. Rul. 81 – 7, 1981-1 CB 474; Priv. Ltr. Ruls. 7946007 and 8806063.

27. Priv. Ltr. Rul. 8121069.

28. Priv. Ltr. Ruls. 8004172, 8126047, 8308033, 8545076, 8616027, 8701007, 8712014, 8813019, 8922062 and 9232013.

29. *Cristofani v. Comm'r.*, 97 T.C. No. 5 (1991).

30. Priv. Ltr. Ruls. 8727003 and 9045002.

31. Rev. Rul. 80-261, 1980-2 C.B. 279.

32. Rev. Rul. 80-261.

33. I.R.C. §2514(c).

34. I.R.C. §§2014(b) and 2514(e), PLR 9804047.

35. I.R.C. §2014(e).

36. Rev. Rul. 85 – 88, 1985–2 C.B. 201.

37. Priv., Ltr. Ruls. 7939061, 8003033, 8003152, and 7947066.

38. Treas. Reg. §25.2511-2(b) and (c); PLR 8229097, and PLR 8517052.

39. I.R.C. §2041.

40. *Comm'r. v. Proctor*, 142 F.2d. 824 (4th Cir. 1944); TAM 8901004.

41. I.R.C. §2613(a).

42. I.R.C. §2513(a)(1).

43. I.R.C. §2513(a)(2).

44. Treas. Reg. §25.2513-1(b)(4).

45. Rev. Rul. 56-439, *Robertson v. Comm'r.*, 26 T.C. 246 (1956); *O'Connor v. O'Malley*, 57-1 USTC ¶11,690 (D. Neb. 1957); *Kass v. Comm'r.*, T.C. Memo 1957-227; *Falk v. Comm'r.*, T.C. Memo 1965-22; *Wang v. Comm'r.*, T.C. Memo 1972-143.

46. Treas. Reg. §§§25.2511-2(b) and (c).

47. I.R.C. §2035.

48. I.R.C. §2035(a).

49. See Treas. Reg. §25.2511-2.

50. *Estate of Silverman v. Comm'r.*, 61 TC 337 (1973).

51. I.R.C. §2035(d).

52. Rev. Rul. 2007-13.

53. Treas. Reg. §20.2042-1(c)(2).

54. Treas. Reg. §20.2042-1(b)(1).

55. *Id*.

56. Treas. Reg. §20.2042-1(c)(6).

57. Priv. Ltr. Ruls. 9623024 and 9725009.

58. *Estate of Knipp v. Comm'r.*, 25 T.C. 153 (1955), aff'd. on another issue, 244 F.2d 436 (4th Cir.1957), cert. denied, 355 U.S. 827 (1957); *Watson v. Comm'r.*, 36 T.C.M. (CCH) 1084 (1977), *Estate of Fuchs v. Comm'r.*, 47 T.C. 199 (1966), acq., 1967–1 C.B. 2; *Estate of Infante v. Comm'r.*, 29 T.C.M.(CCH) 903 (1970); *Estate of Tompkins v. Comm'r.*, 13 T.C. 1054 (1949).

59. Treas. Reg. §20.2042-1(c)(3).

60. Treas. Reg. §20.2042-1(c)(3).

61. Rev. Rul. 77-378; I.R.C. §2036(a)(1); Treas. Reg. §25.2511-2(b).

62. Rev. Rul. 77-378.

63. I.R.C. §2041(a)(2).

64. I.R.C. §§§2041(a)(2) and 2041(b)(2).

65. I.R.C. §677(a)(3).

66. I.R.C. §677(a)(3); *Rand v. Comm'r.*, 40 B.T.A. 233, 238–39, aff'd., 116 F.2d 929 (8th Cir. 1941).

67. Priv. Ltr. Rul. 200228019.

68. I.R.C. §677(a)(1-2).

69. I.R.C. §674(c).

70. I.R.C. §675(4). See also Rev. Rul. 2011-28.

71. I.R.C. §§673, 2037.

72. I.R.C. §§674 and 2036(a)(2).

73. I.R.C. §§675 and 2036.

74. I.R.C. §§§676 and 2038.

75. Priv. Ltr. Rul. 9141027.

76. I.R.C. §678(a)(1); Treas. Reg. §1.671-3(a)(3).

77. Rev. Rul. 81-6.

78. I.R.C. §101(a)(1).

79. I.R.C. §101(a)(2).

80. I.R.C. §101(a)(2).

81. I.R.C. §2632(d)(1).

82. I.R.C. §2613(a).

83. I.R.C. §2611.

84. I.R.C. §2642(c).

85. *Id.*

86. I.R.C. §2651(e).

87. I.R.C. §2651(e)(1).

88. I.R.C. §2612(b).

89. I.R.C. §2632(c)(3)(B).

90. I.R.C. §2632(c).

91. Treas. Reg. §26.2632-1(b)(2).

92. Treas. Reg. §26.2612-1(d)(2)(1).

93. I.R.C. §2632(c)(5).

94. I.R.C. §§2632(c) and 2642-2(a)(1). If there is no allocation until after the death of the grantor, the inclusion ratio is determined according to the post-death value of the property.

95. I.R.C. §2631.

96. Treas. Reg. §26.2652-1(a)(2).

97. I.R.C. §2654(b)(1); Treas. Reg. §26.2654-1(a)(2)(i).

98. Treas. Reg. §26.2632-1(c)(2).

99. 109 F.2d 99 (2d Cir.), cert. denied, 310 U.S. 637 (1940).

100. *U.S. v. Estate of Grace*, 395 U.S. 316 (1969).

101. *Id.* at 324.

102. Treas. Reg. §20.2042-1(c)(4).

103. Rev. Rul. 84-179.

104. I.R.C. §2041.

105. Priv. Ltr. Ruls. 9030005 and 8916030.

106. Rev. Rul. 79-353, 1979-2 C.B. 325, revoked by, Rev. Rul. 95-58, 1995-2 C.B. 191.

107. Priv. Ltr. Rul. 9607008.

108. The UPIA has been enacted in forty-three states, the District of Columbia and the U.S. Virgin Islands.

109. UPIA §2(a).

110. UPIA §2(b).

111. UPIA §2(e).

112. UPIA §3.

113. UPIA §4.

114. Comment to UPIA §2.

115. UPIA §§5 and 6.

116. UPIA §1(b).

117. See, e.g., Del. Code §3302(d); Fla. Stat. §736.0902; North Dakota §59-17-01; Pennsylvania §7208; South Carolina §62-7-802; and West Virginia §44-6C-1.

118. Del. Code §3302(d).

119. Fla. Stat. §736.0902.

120. Treas. Reg. §20.2042-1(b)(2).

TRUSTS AND DIVORCE

CHAPTER 7

INTRODUCTION

Trusts are estate planning tools which are commonly used even with the simplest of estate plans. Trusts can be created to serve a variety of different purposes, and can be drafted in a variety of different ways. These days, trusts are routinely used as tools for gifting, asset management, tax shelter and protection from creditors. In cases of married couples, a spouse might be the beneficiary or a grantor of a trust. Depending on the facts and circumstances, the trust may be entirely separate from the divorce proceedings or it may be an integral part of property division between the spouses. The confluence of multiple marriages, multiple divorces, and the common use of trusts requires attention to be paid at all stages of the couple's relationship to the impact divorce may have on a trust.

USE OF TRUSTS BEFORE MARRIAGE

Before marriage, a couple is often encouraged to consider a premarital contract to effectively protect their respective property rights and financial interests. The simplest way to delineate who gets what in a divorce is through a detailed prenuptial agreement. The three basic reasons for entering into a premarital contract are to address issues in contemplation of death, to address issues upon dissolution of marriage, and to govern the relationship during marriage. Not all nuptial agreements provide for all three situations, but wise practitioners will discuss all three scenarios with the client.

Historically, couples have created prenuptial agreements prior to entering into a marriage to protect assets brought into the marriage. A prenuptial agreement is an agreement made before marriage which defines the rights and obligations of the parties if the marriage ends because of a divorce or the death of a spouse. Most states require full financial disclosure prior to execution of a prenuptial agreement in order for the agreement to be valid. In an ideal situation, a divorcing couple already would have provided for division of their property and assets through a prenuptial agreement, but in most divorce cases this is not clear-cut. Prenuptial agreements also have a high risk of being overturned for many reasons, including insufficient financial disclosure or disclosure of assets, lack of independent counsel, duress or coercion. For some couples, even suggesting a prenuptial agreement can ruin wedding plans.

Planning Note: Under Code Sections 71 and 215, alimony was includible in income to the recipient and deductible by the payor. The Tax Cuts and Jobs Act of 2017 permanently repealed those sections but provided a "grandfathering exemption" allowing alimony to remain deductible for divorce decrees or separation agreements entered into before December 31, 2018. It does not appear that prenuptial agreements entered into before December 31, 2018 fall under the definition of "divorce decree or separation agreement" for the purposes of the grandfathering exemption. Therefore, even if a premarital agreement explicitly states that the prior law is to apply, if the divorce occurs after December 31, 2018, the law in effect at the time of the divorce should govern. Accordingly, advisors should review existing premarital agreements to determine how they may be impacted by this new law.

In the absence of a premarital agreement (or even if a prenuptial agreement is in place but it relies on the definition of separate property), there is a great need for proper asset protection planning prior to entering into a marriage to protect the assets brought into the marriage. There are ways to keep separate property from becoming marital property without a prenuptial agreement, but it may take some extra effort. The client can take steps unilaterally prior to the marriage to minimize the complications of divorce by maintaining the separate character of the client's separate property. Trusts are one of the most viable options to accomplish this goal.

Revocable Trusts

Pursuant to the laws of most states, with respect to married couples, there are two types of property classification: marital property and separate property. During a divorce proceeding, one of the primary tasks of the court is to categorize all of the property as either separate property or marital property. Categorizing this property is very important, as it will affect the distribution of property at divorce. When property is deemed a spouse's separate property, it belongs to one spouse. Separate property is generally not divisible in divorce, so the other spouse will have no right to it and the spouse who owns the separate property will get to keep the entire property interest at divorce.

Under some state's family law statutes, when spouses fail to keep their separate property truly separate, it can become marital property, meaning it is property owned jointly by the couple. Separate property loses its separate property status if it is commingled with marital property. For instance, the re-titling of property brought into the marriage by one spouse into the names of both spouses as co-owners can convert that property from separate to marital property.

At a minimum, the client should be advised to "keep separate, separate" by maintaining existing assets in the client's name and opening bank and brokerage accounts in the client's individual name (perhaps with a designation "separate account"), and by depositing only separate property into such separate property accounts. Contemporaneous records showing the source of any and all separate deposits should be retained in the event proof of separate character of the account is needed later.

The better option is to place separate premarital property in a revocable trust. The benefit of a separate property revocable trust is that it helps the client to avoid comingling the premarital assets with post-marital assets. The creation and funding of a revocable trust prior to marriage may be an effective way to maintain the separate character of the grantor's assets. Using a revocable trust could make the entire issue of separate property, and its appreciation, a moot point upon divorce. Upon showing that the revocable trust only contained premarital assets, those assets should pass to the contributing spouse alone. Where the revocable trust and/or prenuptial agreement is insufficient protection for the client, as an added measure, the trust can be a Domestic Asset Protection Trust, which is discussed below.

Domestic Asset Protection Trusts

Given the issues surrounding prenuptial agreements, there has been a migration towards alternative vehicles to protect assets brought into a marriage. One such alternative is a Domestic Asset Protection Trust (DAPT).

Traditionally, a grantor cannot set up a trust for his own benefit and have it be protected from creditor's claims (a "self-settled trust").[1] Until relatively recently, a self-settled trust in the United States with a grantor as a discretionary beneficiary would be ineffective to remove the trust assets from the reach of creditors. Most states provide creditors with access to trust assets to the extent distributions can be made to the grantor.

The prohibition on self-settled trusts has been lessened over the last two decades. Today, seventeen states allow for the formation of DAPTs and thirteen non-DAPT states recognize varying self-settled techniques.[2]

A DAPT is an irrevocable trust designed to shield assets from the grantor's creditors, including future ex-spouses. DAPTs are usually structured as wholly discretionary trusts, providing the independent trustee with absolute discretion to make distributions to beneficiaries including the grantor. The principal purpose for using a DAPT is asset protection to insulate the grantor's assets from the reach of future creditors. Secondarily, DAPTs can be used for transfer tax planning.

In the context of divorce, DAPTs can be utilized in lieu of, or in conjunction with, a prenuptial agreement. The attractive feature of the DAPT is that the creation prior to marriage does not require the consent of the future spouse and there is no obligation to disclose the DAPT or its assets to a future spouse. As a result, DAPTs are being used more frequently as an alternative to a prenuptial agreement because it removes the tension that may be created by establishing a prenuptial agreement.

Most states provide that premarital assets which are not comingled with marital assets are generally exempt from equitable distribution. A DAPT will typically result in protection from equitable distribution since the assets in the trust are, by the very nature of the trust, separated from marital assets (assuming that marital assets are not also contributed to the trust). A DAPT places the trust assets beyond the reach of the spouse, effectively making the property held in the trust "separate property." Consequently, the transfer of premarital assets into a DAPT prevents the assets from becoming subject to equitable distribution, or available for alimony or child support.

Despite the benefits of a DAPT, its use in the marriage context is limited and there is still uncertainty surrounding the efficacy of this technique. Therefore, they should be used cautiously and the client should be informed of the risks and limitations which are discussed below.

Statutory Requirements

DAPTs are a creature of state law and are governed by state statute. A review of the state's applicable statute must be conducted to ensure all formalities are followed. In general, a DAPT must comply with the following requirements:

1. it must be irrevocable;

2. it must appoint an independent trustee who is a resident of the governing jurisdiction;

3. it must have a spendthrift provision; and

4. it must incorporate the law of the DAPT jurisdiction to govern the trust's validity, construction, and administration.

Timing

Unlike premarital agreements which must be entered into prior to the marriage, DAPTs can be created at any time. However, when DAPTs are used in the marital context, for the client to shield assets from being considered part of the marital estate subject to equitable distribution, alimony and child support, the trust must typically be created well in advance the marriage.

DAPTs have limited use in protecting assets from an ex-spouse if the DAPT was created during the marriage. If the trust was created after the parties entered into the marriage, the DAPT may be subject to attack as a possible fraudulent conveyance, particularly if the DAPT is created in close proximity to or in contemplation of filing for divorce. Moreover, the DAPT may fall within an exception wherein no protection is afforded to the assets. For example, nine states provide that a spouse is an exception creditor (i.e., no asset protection will be provided) with respect to alimony if the spouse was married to the grantor before or on the date of transfer of assets to the trust.[3] Thus, in these states, there will be no asset protection from the spouse if the spouse was married to the grantor before or on the date of transfer of assets to the trust. In several other states, child support is an exception creditor.

Similarly, a spouse may also be an exception creditor with respect to property division upon divorce if the spouse was married to the grantor before or on the date of transfer of assets to the trust.[4] Alaska, for example, provides that an ex-spouse will be an exception creditor if assets were transferred to the trust during the marriage or within thirty days of the marriage, unless the grantor gives written notice to the other party to the marriage of the transfer.[5]

For a discussion of the ability of a spouse to reach trust assets after a divorce for payments due for alimony or child support, see "Trust during Divorce" below. For a discussion of whether a trust constitutes a property interest subject to division in divorce, see "Inclusion of Trusts in the Marital Estate" below.

Resident vs. Nonresident Use

The likelihood that the DAPT will insulate trust assets from creditors, including spouses, depends primarily on whether it is created by a resident or nonresident of the DAPT state. The greatest likelihood for asset protection comes from the use of a DAPT by a resident of the DAPT state. A DAPT that is properly created may be used successfully by a resident of a DAPT state.

When the grantor of the DAPT is not a resident of the DAPT state, an interesting issue remains as to whether the nonresident of a DAPT state may form a

DAPT under one of the DAPT state's laws and obtain desired asset protection. This issue involves a conflict of laws analysis and requires looking at a variety of factors, including the grantor's intent, determination of a meaningful nexus or connection between the grantor and the DAPT state, and public policy of the non-DAPT state. In fact, whether the nonresident's home state has a strong public policy against DAPTs has been a significant factor to determine which state's laws apply. A recent case, *In re Huber*, stands for the proposition that a DAPT is invalid under a conflict of laws analysis where the non-DAPT state has a strong public policy against asset protection for self-settled trusts.[6] Additionally, for residents of states which have enacted the Uniform Voidable Transactions Act, Section 10 of the Act, along with new Comments to the Act, provide that the applicable law is that of the debt's principal residence, indicating that a transfer to a DAPT by a resident of a non-DAPT, Uniform Voidable Transactions Act state is voidable.[7] In a divorce proceeding, the non- DAPT state may apply its own laws and invalidate the DAPT, thus exposing its assets to the reach of an ex-spouse. The grantor's state of domicile or the location of trust assets could be determinative. If the non-DAPT state has a strong public policy against self-settled trusts, this could result in the invalidation of the DAPT.[8] Recent case law has considered this conflict of laws issue for residents of non-DAPT states. For example, the Supreme Court of Alaska recently held that an Alaska statute cannot grant Alaska exclusive jurisdiction over fraudulent transfer actions against an Alaska trust.[9] In light of these considerations, a practitioner should proceed with caution when establishing a DAPT for a non-resident.

If the client is a non-resident of a DAPT jurisdiction and still wants to avail itself of the protection afforded by a DAPT jurisdiction, he or she will have to achieve a sufficient nexus with the DAPT jurisdiction. The nexus is usually established by complying with the requirements needed upon formation of the trust under state law. Almost all of the DAPT statutes have requirements to establish *situs* within the jurisdiction. As an illustration, the requirements include:

1. depositing some or all of the trust's assets within the state;

2. having an in-state trustee (resident, bank or trust company); and

3. having all or part of the trust administered in state.

The in-state trustee should maintain records, prepare or arrange for the preparation of tax returns, and materially participate in the administration of the trust. Establishing the *situs* in and nexus with the DAPT jurisdiction will allow the non-resident grantor to establish the trust, but it will not ensure or guarantee that the grantor's domiciliary state will honor the DAPT asset protection.

USE OF TRUSTS DURING MARRIAGE

Trusts created during a marriage must be drafted with flexibility to account for changes in circumstances for a grantor. Given the high rate of divorce, trusts can be drafted to account and plan for divorce. Caution must be taken, however, so as not to incorporate provisions that are contrary to public policy or to shift assets out of the marital estate in an inequitable fashion.

Drafting Provisions in Anticipation of Divorce

Provisions may be included in a trust document in the event the grantor gets divorced. The grantor may also have concerns about trust beneficiaries' future divorce and the beneficiary's spouse gaining access to the trust funds upon divorce. Thus, trust documents for clients must be tailored with great flexibility and foresight to address the client's needs and future contingencies.

Termination of Interest upon Divorce

It is common that, during a couple's marriage, a grantor-spouse will create an irrevocable trust and name his or her spouse as a beneficiary. Life insurance trusts, personal residence trusts, and spousal lifetime access trusts are a few examples. These trusts and many others are irrevocable and cannot be modified after creation.[10] Therefore, it is prudent to include clauses in the trust document that provide flexibility to account for change in circumstances such as a divorce.

In situations where the grantor and the spouse divorce, it is often suggested to have the trust provide that, upon divorce, the spouse's interest in the trust terminates. Such provision would eliminate all of the spouse's interest in the trust and would, in effect, treat the spouse as having predeceased the grantor and may impact the income tax treatment of the trust as discussed below. Although effective in some circumstances, in others, such a provision may not be the best approach. The automatic removal of a spouse may frustrate the grantor's intent. The grantor may want to provide for the spouse in the same fashion had the divorce not occurred, such as, for example, where the couple have minor children together. Also, the couple may divorce and then remarry in the future. If the provision is desirable, the clause should be structured to become effective upon the court issuance of an order granting the divorce. It is inadvisable to automatically disinherit the spouse upon the filing of a divorce action because a divorce petition can always be withdrawn.

An alternative to the divorce termination provision is the floating spouse provision. The floating spouse provision defines the spouse not by name but in a more generic manner to hedge the risk of divorce or death of a prior spouse. The spouse is defined as the person the grantor is married to from time to time. This means that if the grantor and grantor's spouse get divorced, and the grantor gets remarried, the new spouse is a discretionary beneficiary in place of the former spouse.

The trust documents could also provide a mechanism for the spouse to be removed from any fiduciary position (e.g. trustee or trust protector) upon divorce. In this case, it may be desirable for the provision to be triggered once the divorce action is initiated. An independent trustee can be given the authority to remove a divorced spouse.

Grantor Trust Status

Generally, a trust is a separate taxpayer responsible for payment of its own income taxes. When a trust is treated as a "grantor trust," the grantor will be taxed on the income generated by a trust. This is accomplished if the grantor is treated as the owner under the grantor trust rules of Internal Revenue Code sections 671 to 679. The trust becomes subject to these rules if the grantor, the grantor's spouse or a nonadverse party retains certain powers with respect to the trust. Selection of the power used to trigger grantor trust status is important as the grantor may later decide he wants to terminate grantor trust status. The grantor trust rules are often invoked to allow the grantor to pay the income taxes on the trust's income, thus leaving the assets to appreciate income tax-free and maximize the growth in the trust.

Under section 672(e), a grantor is deemed to hold any power or interest held by someone who was a spouse of the grantor at the time the trust was created. When the spouse of the client is a trust beneficiary or trustee, the trust will be deemed a grantor trust whereby the grantor will be responsible for payment of income taxes attributable to the trust. A divorce will not terminate grantor trust status. Therefore, it is bad enough that the divorced spouse is a trust beneficiary, the grantor may also be stuck paying the income taxes on the trust's income, post-divorce. To avoid this problem, removing the spouse's rights as a beneficiary, trustee and powerholder as discussed above, will cause the trust to be treated as a nongrantor trust (assuming no other powers are triggering grantor trust status).

Termination of former spouse's interest is not always possible. For example, with a lifetime QTIP trust, if the former spouse's right to income is subject to termination upon the occurrence of a specified event, such as divorce, it will not satisfy the qualifying income interest for life requirement.[11] This means that following divorce, the *inter vivos* QTIP trust income must continue to be distributed to the spouse.

Under prior law, Section 682(a) stated that notwithstanding the general taxation of the grantor-spouse under the grantor trust rules, upon divorce, trust income that is distributed to a former spouse will be included in the former spouse's gross income. When the spouse's rights could not be terminated, Section 682 was intended to override the grantor trust rules and cause trust income that is distributed to a spouse to be included the spouse's gross income. The Tax Cuts and Jobs Act (TCJA) of 2017 permanently repealed section 682, as well as sections 71 and 215 (former Code Section 71 dictated that gross income includes amounts received "as alimony or separate maintenance payments" and Section 215 allowed the alimony payor to take an income tax deduction for alimony paid). For divorce decrees entered into after December 31, 2018, alimony is no longer includible in gross income by the recipient spouse, nor is it deductible by the payee spouse. Accordingly, because Section 682 is repealed, trust income is taxed to the grantor under the grantor trust rules of Section 672(e). The IRS recently clarified that Section 682 will continue to apply with regard to trust income payable to a former spouse who was divorced or legally separated under a divorce or separation agreement executed on or before December 31, 2018, unless such instrument is later modified and the TCJA changes apply to the modification.[12]

Provisions that Promote Divorce

Trusts or trust provisions may be held invalid if found to be contrary to public policy. If there is a condition which encourages or promotes a divorce in a trust document, the provision is invalid.[13] A provision that conditions the distribution from a trust on the beneficiary's securing a divorce from their current spouse will be deemed invalid.[14] Similarly, a trust provision which provides a financial reward for a beneficiary obtaining a divorce from their spouse may be invalid as a violation of public policy.[15]

The Restatement (Third) of Trusts expanded the breadth of public policy considerations in trusts by holding that an intended trust or trust provision is invalid if it is contrary to public policy.[16] It invalidates a condition that "tends to encourage disruption of a family relationship or to discourage formation or resumption of such a relationship."[17]

As discussed above, it is proper for the trust instrument to provide that a beneficiary's interest and fiduciary position terminates upon divorce. Such a provision attempts to discourage divorce. On the other hand, when a trust document conditions the distribution from a trust to a beneficiary on the beneficiary's securing a divorce, such a provision promotes divorce and is against public policy.

Equalizing of Estates

In order to maximize the potential use of the applicable exclusion amount in estate planning for a married couple, in many instances, each spouse will adopt a will or revocable trust which provides for the creation of the trust at death of the first spouse to hold assets equivalent to the applicable exclusion amount in trust for the benefit of the surviving spouse for life (known as a credit shelter trust). Although portability has eliminated the need to create a credit shelter trust in order to use the applicable exclusion amount of each spouse, for many, a credit shelter trust is still the preferred method of transferring assets with married couples. Often, a credit shelter plan or structure is defeated if, at the death of the first spouse, there are no assets in that spouse's estate to pass through the terms of the will or trust. Consequently, in conjunction with the structure, estate planners frequently recommend the division of assets between spouses to equalize their estates. This rearrangement of assets may create several potential issues in the event of a later divorce

regarding the characterization of assets as "marital" or "separate".

If assets were originally titled in one spouse's name and treated as separate property, the transfer of these assets to the other spouse may be treated as a gift and consequently become separate property of the other spouse. In this scenario, the gifted assets are no longer treated as separate property of the transferring spouse, but rather may be characterized as separate property of the recipient spouse.[18] Consequently, this issue should be considered before any transfers are made.

Establishing Trusts for Third Parties

All non-community property states have adopted some form of an equitable distribution regime should a couple file for divorce. Equitable distribution typically gives a court the discretion to divide the spouse's property in a fair but not necessarily equal manner. The more common form of equitable distribution among states divides the spouse's property into marital and separate property and then fairly divides the marital property among spouses. During the course of the marriage, a client-spouse often creates trusts as part of his or her estate plan which benefits the grantor's heirs. If a client-spouse does so and gifts assets to such trusts, the marital estate would be reduced by the value of the assets transferred to the trust and the assets would be excluded from equitable distribution. The assets in the trust are shifted out of the reach of the spouse and into the hands of the trustee of the trust for the benefit of the beneficiaries.

However, there is a great risk in establishing a trust and making gifts to such trust when the divorce is imminent and done with the intent to reduce the marital estate. The dissipation of martial assets is the wasting of assets that would otherwise be distributed during the divorce. When there is the unjustified wasting of marital assets through gifts or fraudulent conveyance to a third party or a trust for a third party thereby depleting the marital assets, it will be considered dissipation of assets. The spouse may assert a claim of dissipation, declaring that the assets were transferred prior to a divorce proceeding in an effort to reduce what would otherwise have been available in an equitable distribution.

A court may take intentional dissipation of marital assets into account when determining equitable distribution. Florida, for example, begins with the premise that distribution should be equal unless there is a justification for an unequal distribution based on all relevant factors.[19] One such factor is the intentional dissipation, waste, depletion, or destruction of marital assets after the filing of the petition or within two years prior to the filing of the petition.[20] Numerous courts throughout the country have found assets to have been dissipated.

- *In re Marriage of Rai*–the court provided that a party can be found guilty of dissipation even though the act occurred prior to separation or prior to the commencement of the dissolution proceedings.[21]

- *In re Marriage of Paulsen*–the trial court properly considered whether pre-separation actions constituted dissipation.[22]

- *In Monte v. Monte*–the court held that the intentional dissipation of assets by one party is no more than a fraud on the marital rights to the detriment of the other spouse. The court thus held that such dissipation is chargeable to the dissipating spouse.[23]

Thus, if contemplating the establishment of a trust for heirs of third parties without the consent of the spouse, the aforementioned risks must be considered. If a trust is established, it is recommended that the trust contain spendthrift provisions to protect the beneficiary's creditors and spouse from attaching those assets as described below.

Asset Protection Trusts

During the marriage the client-spouse may also be the recipient of monies from third parties such as his or her parents or grandparents. To protect those assets from the reach of the spouse, any and all of *inter vivos* and testamentary gifts to the client-spouse by others should be placed by the donor in an asset protection trust for the client-spouse's benefit. The spendthrift provisions will help not only insulate the interest from the claims of the client-spouse's creditors, but also any claims of the spouse, the spouse's successors or creditors. A spendthrift clause typically states that a beneficiary may not assign or convey his or her beneficial interest. This type of trust language is called "spendthrift" because it prevents a careless beneficiary from squandering their inheritance. If the grantor prohibits the beneficiary from assigning their beneficial interest then the beneficiary's creditors cannot force

the assignment to pay the beneficiary's debts. A recent Massachusetts case, *Pfannenstiel v. Pfannenstiel* held that a husband's interest in a trust created by his father for the benefit of him and ten other beneficiaries could not be attributable to the husband as part of the equitable division of marital assets because he had no control over the trust and could only receive distributions at the trustees' discretion.[24] This case serves as meaningful guidance for the states with similar equitable division statutes.

The inclusion of a statement in the trust agreement that it is the grantor's intent that any and all interests of the client, as well as any and all distributions of the trust, are the client's separate property may not be conclusive, but may prove to be persuasive in future litigation.

A completely discretionary trust where distributions are within the sole and absolute distribution of an independent trustee is preferable. Additionally, where there are multiple trust beneficiaries, having a single trust for all beneficiaries instead of separate trust for each is also preferable. Having the client-spouse serve as trustee of the trust is not recommended, although some states acknowledge that doing so will not disqualify the trust as being a spendthrift trust.[25] However, some states have creditors that are exempted from the spendthrift provision. As many as thirty states provide some type of "exception creditor" where a beneficiary's children and/or former spouse may have the right to reach trust assets that are otherwise protected from creditors. For a detailed discussion, see "Trusts during Divorce" below. Therefore, carefully planning, drafting and administering the trust could prove to be persuasive in maintaining the client's interests in the trust, as well as distributions from the trust, as separate property.

TRUSTS DURING DIVORCE

There are many financial decisions to be made in a divorce, and one very important one is what to do about your estate plan. During the divorce proceeding, existing revocable trusts should be revisited and irrevocable trusts should be examined to determine how it will be impacted by the divorce.

Creation of Testamentary Trusts during Divorce

During a divorce, it is important to take into account that a spouse may die prior to a divorce becoming final.

The surviving spouse may then be entitled to receive an elective share. The elective share is a percentage of a deceased spouse's estate that a surviving spouse is entitled to receive upon the death of a spouse. Under the Uniform Probate Code, the share varies based on the length of the marriage with the maximum amount a surviving spouse can take being 50 percent when the marriage lasts fifteen years or longer.[26] States vary in the amount and manner that the surviving spouse is entitled to receive and how the amount can be satisfied.

In some jurisdictions, state statutes allow the elective share to be satisfied with an elective share trust. An elective share trust is a trust for the benefit of the spouse that counts towards the satisfaction of the elective share amount due to the surviving spouse. Therefore, instead of the surviving spouse receiving an outright amount, the amount can be left in trust. This may be preferable since the donor spouse can control the disposition of the assets upon the surviving spouse's death. In a blended family, where the grantor has children from a prior marriage, this type of trust is especially useful. Florida and North Carolina, for example, permit the creation of elective share trusts.[27] In Florida, the terms of the trust will establish the percentage amount of the trust that will be used to satisfy the elective share. Other states such as Oregon, will count Qualified Terminable Interest Property (QTIP) and credit shelter trusts that name the surviving spouse as beneficiary, towards satisfaction of the elective share.[28] Therefore, if recognized by the client's jurisdiction, establishing a trust to satisfy an elective share in the event of death during a pending divorce is a good alternative to an outright disposition.

Inclusion of Trusts in the Marital Estate

Under common law, a spouse is awarded property based on title to the property. Any property titled in the name of one spouse is given to that spouse. Over the last several decades, this rule has changed with non-community property states adopting equitable distribution statutes. Under an equitable distribution regime, the division of property in a divorce is based in equity and is fact driven. This can lead to unpredictable decisions that stretch the rules in order to produce a just result. There has also been a movement towards expanding the types of property and interests that are considered in a property division.

Generally, property acquired during a marriage by gift, bequest, devise, or inheritance is not considered marital property subject to equitable distribution. In the context of trusts, the key question becomes whether trusts created by the divorcing spouse or created by a third party for the benefit of a divorcing spouse is considered part of the marital estate. The inquiry becomes whether the trust interest constitutes "property". The answer to this question varies widely from jurisdiction to jurisdiction. The answer depends on factors such as the grantor of the trust, governing law provision of the trust, jurisdiction of the divorce proceeding and the interest held by the divorcing spouse. Generally, if the interest is too tenuous, contingent, remote or speculative in value, it will not constitute property.[29]

Revocable Trusts

Revocable trusts have become commonplace in many jurisdictions and are used as will substitutes to dispose of assets upon death while avoiding probate. Where the divorcing spouse is the grantor of a revocable trust and retains the power to revoke the trust, the trust property is treated as owned by the grantor and handled accordingly. When the divorcing spouse is a beneficiary of a revocable trust created by a third party (e.g., parent of the spouse), the beneficiary's interest is not a property interest during the life of the grantor. The interest is a mere expectancy, not an interest in property that is considered in the division of marital property.[30]

Irrevocable Trusts

When a beneficiary's interest is in an irrevocable third-party trust, whether the interest is part of the marital estate subject to equitable distribution is less clear. Interests in trusts may be considered marital property depending on the jurisdiction of the trust, the divorce proceeding and the trust's terms.

The recent trend is shifting towards considering a beneficial interest in a third-party trust as marital property. Several states, including Colorado and Massachusetts, now take into consideration an interest in a trust in a divorce. Even if a beneficial interest in a third-party trust is not considered marital property, it may still be taken into account by a court in fashioning an equitable distribution of marital property. However, other states, such as California, Arizona, Nevada and New Mexico do not follow this trend and preclude an interest in a third-party settled trust as marital property.

These states deem the interest in third-party settled trust separate property.

However, more and more states are considering a beneficiary's interest in a third-party trust as a marital asset subject to equitable distribution. Generally, the inquiry then focuses on whether the beneficiary has a property right in the trust or merely an expectancy right. In establishing the trust interest as part of the marital estate those states often examine the beneficiary's present possessory interest, presently exercisable withdrawal right of their interest, and the distributions terms and standard, if any, in the trust document.

Income Interest

When the beneficiary has in income interest in a third-party trust, whether an income interest is considered a marital asset depends on the discretion given to the trustee under the trust instrument and state law. Generally, a mandatory right to income in a trust will increase the likelihood that the interest being considered a marital asset. A mandatory income right resembles a property right more than an expectancy because it is a guaranteed right to income. When a beneficiary's right is discretionary, the asset resembles an expectancy right and normally precludes the interest from becoming a part of the marital estate. However, states laws differ with how they treat the interest so the appropriate state laws must be examined.

Mandatory Income Interest

Generally, a mandatory income interest of a beneficiary is considered property for equitable distribution purposes since the beneficiary has a legally enforceable right in the stated amount or percentage of whatever income is produced.[31] Although there may be uncertainty in the amount of income which the trust may actually produce, it does not prevent the income interest from constituting property. The uncertainty in the amount is only a factor in valuation, but does not affect the classification of the interest as property.[32]

Certain states do not follow this general rule and have held the contrary. For example, in Colorado, when the beneficiary has no interest in the corpus and no right to control how the corpus is invested, the income is a merely gratuity interest deriving from the benefit of the grantor.[33] Delaware simply does not consider a mandatory income interest to be divisible property.[34]

Discretionary Income Interest

Generally, when the beneficiary's right to receive income is dependent entirely on the trustee's discretion, the income interest is not considered property.[35] In a recent case, the Massachusetts Supreme Judicial Court held that a spouse's income interest[36] in a third-party ascertainable standard trust was not subject to division as part of the equitable distribution.[37] The court held that the spouse's interest was no more than an expectancy because it was so speculative. However, the court noted that on remand, the judge may consider the expectancy as part of the "opportunity of each spouse for future acquisition of capital assets and income" in the judge's determination of a revised equitable division of marital property. Some states, such as New Hampshire, North Dakota and Oregon, take a contrary position and consider income interests for divorce purposes.[38]

Remainder Interest

States differ in their analysis of the factors to consider in establishing the remainder interest in a third-party trust as part of the marital estate. Some states are guided by the distinction between vested and unvested interests. Other states look to determine whether the interest is possessory or the interest can be reduced to possession. Lastly, some states focus on the distinction between discretionary and non-discretionary trusts.

When a divorcing spouse holds a remainder interest in a third-party trust, some jurisdictions require it to be a vested interest before it is considered property for purposes of marital division. Some states consider vested remainders in discretionary trusts to be marital property.[39] On the other hand, an unvested remainder does not constitute a property interest because it is deemed too speculative to be considered a property right.

States such as Connecticut and Wyoming hold that an unvested remainder interest in a discretionary trust does not constitute marital property.[40] Some states such as North Dakota, Oregon and Vermont do not draw any distinction between vested and unvested and merely consider all remainder interests to be property.

However, not all jurisdictions will analyze the property ownership distinction the same way. Delaware, Indiana, Pennsylvania and Wyoming will not consider an interest in a trust for purposes of equitable distribution until the interest becomes possessory (e.g., the possession of a general power of appointment or right of withdrawal that is presently exercisable). The courts will examine whether the spouse has a present enforceable right to the assets of the trust. The interest must be a present possessory right to be considered property subject to marital division. Alternatively, the interest is considered property when the beneficiary can make the trust asset possessory.

Finally, other states will analyze the beneficiary's interest based on the discretion given to the trustee of the trust. For example, in *Pfannenstiehl v. Pfannenstiehl*, the Massachusetts Supreme Judicial Court, the highest appellate court in the state, examined the trust provisions and the discretionary standards to reach their conclusion that the trust interest was not considered property.[41] The court's determination was based on the conclusion that the right to receive distributions was dependent entirely on the trustee's discretion thereby making the interest too speculative to be considered property.

Governing Law and Forum Shopping

Trust instruments typically contain a governing law provision. Such provision will state which law will govern the administration and validity of the trust's terms. However, the governing law provision will not control for purposes of equitable distribution in a divorce proceeding. Instead, the jurisdiction where the divorce is located will control and dictate what is considered "property" for purposes of the property division. Forum shopping can have a great influence on the outcome of a divorce. Whether a trust interest is marital property can mean the difference of millions of dollars. The state where the beneficiary lives at the time of the divorce may govern in the determination of property rights.

Trusts and Alimony

The examination of the trust terms is also important for purposes of determining the impact on the computation of spousal alimony. A beneficiary's interest in a trust will generally be taken into consideration as a resource when a court determines the amount of support that is payable.[42] The income and principal of a discretionary or support trust may be a factor in determining whether the trust beneficiary has the ability to pay alimony. This result may differ among jurisdictions and state statutes. For example, a New Jersey case, *Tannen v. Tannen* held that a beneficial interest in a purely discretionary trust was not an asset that could be considered for the purposes of determining an alimony award.[43]

Transfers in Trusts upon Divorce

When a couple divorces, a court or the parties often require trusts to be created by one spouse for the benefit of the other in connection with the marital settlement agreement and the divorce action. The trusts are structured to take effect either during the life of the spouse or upon death. A common example is the creation of a life insurance trust to hold a life insurance policy that is required to be paid to the divorcing spouse or the couple's children. An alimony trust is also a common trust created upon divorce to fund the support payments required to be made to a divorcing spouse. Some of the trusts that may be created upon divorce pursuant to court order or a marital settlement agreement are discussed below.

Specific Trusts Used in Connection with a Divorce

Alimony Trusts

Historically, a type of trust that was commonly created pursuant to a divorce decree was an alimony trust (also known as a "Section 682 Trust" because this Code Section dictated the income tax consequences).[44] An alimony trust was often used when the transferor spouse was concerned about a spouse not being able to financially handle a lump sum settlement. It provided the recipient spouse with comfort in knowing that the support obligation would be satisfied. Additionally, alimony trusts helped to remove the tension of divorced spouses having to interact with one another over a support obligation as the recipient spouse would look to the trustee for payment.

The TCJA repealed Section 682, thus preventing the use of alimony trusts in divorces after December 31, 2018. Today, a spouse who creates a trust to administer and maintain alimony payments will be taxed under the grantor trust rules, specifically Section 672(e). The IRS clarified that Section 682 will continue to apply with regard to trust income payable to a former spouse who was divorced or legally separated under a divorce or separation agreement executed on or before December 31, 2018, unless such instrument is later modified and the TCJA changes apply to the modification.[45]

Annuity Trusts

As part of a marital settlement agreement, a spouse may accept a trust in lieu of a lump sum outright distribution. When the spouse wants to be assured a fixed return and not rely on trust income, an annuity trust may be an ideal solution. This type of trust will pay the spouse a fixed amount each year.

The benefit of the annuity trust is that the trust will not be subject to the "zero-valuation rule" of Code section 2702. The zero-valuation rule applies when a transfer of an interest in trust is made to or for the benefit of a member of the transferor's family and the transferor or any applicable family member (e.g., the transferor's spouse) retains an interest in the trust. The rule then values the retained interest at zero which means that the entire value of the transferred property is treated as a gift.

The trust will not be subject to the "zero-valuation rule" if it satisfies the qualified interest regulations which provide that:

1.   the annuity amount be paid at least annually at a fixed amount that does not exceed 120 percent of the amount payable in the preceding year;

2.   during the trust term, the trust is prohibited from making distributions to anyone other than the beneficiary;

3.   the term is for the life of the beneficiary, for a specified term of years, or for the shorter of the two; and

4.   prepayment of the interest is prohibited by the trust. (The trust may permit income in excess of the annuity amount to be paid to the beneficiary.)[46]

Qualified Personal Residence Trusts

A substantial asset of the marital unit is typically a personal residence. Generally, upon divorce, one of the spouses wants to continue to use the marital residence or vacation home subsequent to a divorce. The divorce may present an opportunity to create a Qualified Personal Residence Trust,[47] which serves as a useful tool to accomplish the desired goal of occupancy while providing significant gift and estate tax savings to the transferor. The terms of the trusts must meet the strict requirements set forth under Code section 2702 and the

corresponding regulations. If structured correctly, the trust can provide the spouse the ability to reside in the residence free of rent for a term of years. At the end of the term, the trust can be distributed to the couple's children.

Irrevocable Life Insurance Trusts

Life insurance is an asset that is commonly used in connection with marital settlement agreements. It is often used to complement alimony payments or serves as a means to support the couple's children in the event of a spouse's premature death. However, when the life insurance policy is owned by the insured spouse, upon the insured spouse's death, the death benefits will be includable in his or her estate for estate tax purposes.[48] An Irrevocable Life Insurance Trust (ILIT) would avoid this result if the trust is the owner and beneficiary of the life insurance policy. The trust terms can benefit the spouse and/or the couple's children in whatever manner is directed in the trust instrument. If properly structured, the trust can provide financial support and tax savings.

TAX CONSEQUENCES

When a couple divorces, a marital settlement agreement and/or divorce decree often requires assets and monies to be transferred between spouses and possibly to the couple's children. Even if spouses do not have the intent to benefit one another through gifts, the transfers to trusts pursuant to a divorce decree or marital settlement agreement must comply with all tax transfer laws to avoid adverse tax consequences. The gift and estate tax laws do not depend upon the existence of a subjective donative intent. All transfers will be subject to transfer taxation unless it is subject to a deduction or exclusion. Consequently, the income, estate and gift tax ramifications of any transfers made to and from a trust upon the couple's divorce will need to be examined.

Income Tax Consequences

Generally, when a transfer is made to a trust pursuant to a marital settlement agreement and/or divorce decree there is no gain or loss on the transfer of property to a trust if the transfer is incident to the divorce for the benefit of a former spouse.[49] The same is true if the transfer satisfies a spouse's support obligations. The tax basis of the transferred property will typically be the adjusted basis of the transferor immediately before the transfer unless negative basis property is transferred.[50]

Once the transfer is made to the trust, the terms of the trust will then dictate how the trust is taxed for federal income tax purposes. The income tax consequences of the trust itself will be governed by the normal rules of the income taxation of trusts under the Internal Revenue Code. The trust will generally be taxed as either a simple or complex trust pursuant to Subchapter J of the Internal Revenue Code or as a Grantor Trust under Sections 671-679 of the Internal Revenue Code. If the trust is a simple or complex trust, the trust or its beneficiaries will be taxed on the trust income. If the trust is a grantor trust, the transferor spouse will be taxed on the trust income to the extent the transferor is deemed to own the trust. If the transferor is treated as only owning a portion of the trust, the trust will be taxed on the portion not owned by the transferor.

As discussed above, the income tax consequences of alimony trusts created before December 31, 2018 are governed by Section 682 and the transferee spouse will be taxed on the income of the trust that the transferee is entitled to receive.[51] If the trust is structured as a grantor trust, the transferor will be taxed on the excess income that is not distributed to the transferee spouse.[52] If a portion of the payments from the trust are required to be made for the support of the transferor's children, then the transferor is taxed on the income attributable to the payments.[53] For arrangements entered into after December 31, 2018, Section 682 is repealed and the trust will be taxed under the grantor trust rules of 672(e).

Planning Note: Practitioners should review the tax status of alimony payments under an existing divorce decree. If there has been a modification, the date of the modification and whether the TCJA changes expressly apply to the modification should be determined.

Gift Tax Consequences

When a couple enters into a marital settlement agreement, to avoid gift taxation, all transfers required to be made must qualify for the marital deduction, otherwise the transfers will need to be considered as made for adequate consideration in money or money's worth. Normally, the consideration is satisfied by:

- the relinquishment of support rights;

- the relinquishment of rights to equitable division of property; or

- being made pursuant to a divorce decree.[54]

When a transfer is made to a trust, the transferor can rely on the gift tax marital deduction if the transfer of property is made to a qualified terminable interest property (QTIP) trust.[55] A QTIP trust requires all income to be paid to the transferee spouse and prohibits payments from being made to anyone other than the spouse during the spouse's lifetime. An election on a gift tax return is required by the transferor spouse.[56]

If the transfer does not qualify for the marital deduction, to avoid any adverse gift tax consequences, the transfer to a trust can be structured to qualify for a gift tax exception. Certain property settlements qualify for an exception to gift taxation if the transfer is made in connection with a written marital settlement agreement. To qualify for the exception:

1. there must be a final divorce within one year before or two years after, execution of the marital settlement agreement; and

2. the transfers must be either in settlement of marital or property rights or to provide a reasonable allowance for the support of children of the marriage during minority.[57]

Transfers in trust for a spouse will qualify for the exception even when periodic payments are required to be made after the divorce.[58] Section 2516 transfers will also be exempt from the "zero valuation rule" of Section 2702.[59]

Estate Tax Consequences

The estate tax consequences of trusts created in the context of a divorce will depend on the includibility of the transferred property in the transferor and transferee's gross estates. The transferor can potentially be subject to estate tax consequences under Sections 2035 through 2038 and 2042 of the Internal Revenue Code.

The risk of inclusion is dependent on the rights retained by the transferor and the chance of transferred property being returned to the transferor's estate upon the death or remarriage of the transferee spouse. Whether there is inclusion under Sections 2035 through 2038 also depends on whether there was a bona fide sale for an adequate and full consideration in money or money's worth. If so, all or a portion may be shielded from estate tax.

The transferee spouse might have the transferred property included in his or her gross estate if either the transfer to the trust qualifies for the marital deduction or the transferee spouse is considered the transferor of the trust. For example, inclusion may result in the transferee's gross estate if the transferee is given a general power of appointment, the trust is a QTIP trust or the remainder of the trust is payable to the transferee's estate.[60]

TRUSTS AFTER DIVORCE

During a couple's divorce, property, assets and debts are often divided, and custody and support of any children will be determined. Because of these major changes in a person's life, it is recommended that the client update their estate planning documents and other beneficiary designations including life insurance and retirement accounts once the divorce is finalized. Often, estate planning documents include revocable trusts (also referred to as living trusts). The revocable trust should be revised to change the beneficiaries and the fiduciary appointments and remove the spouse, if desired.

Invalidation of Trust Terms upon Divorce

Although it is strongly recommended that upon divorce a client revisit his or her estate plan, often times this advice is not followed or the client fails to do so in a timely manner. In some states, there is no immediate need to revise a client's revocable trust upon entry of the final judgment of dissolution of marriage. Some state statutes provide recourse by automatically voiding any provision in the trust that effects the client's spouse.[61] For example, in Florida, unless the trust instrument or judgment for dissolution of marriage or divorce expressly provides otherwise, any provision in a revocable trust that was executed prior to the annulment of the marriage or entry of a judgment for dissolution of marriage or divorce that affects the client's spouse

will become void upon annulment of the marriage or entry of a judgment for dissolution of divorce.[62] The statute treats the spouse as having died on the date of divorce. The statute also has the same effect on fiduciary positions such as trustee. The Uniform Probate Code (UPC) has a similar provision in section 2-804.

Even where this fallback exists, if circumstances change, such as remarriage, then revisions to the revocable trust become necessary if the client wishes to provide for his or her new spouse in their estate planning documents. In Florida, if the spouses divorce and then remarry, the dispositions to the former ex-spouse are still void, and are not "revived" by the couple's remarriage.[63] The revocable trust will need to be revised in order to again effectively dispose of assets to the spouse. Section 2-804 of the UPC on the other hand, will revive all dispositions and designations to a former spouse made via a revocable trust.

State law can only go so far with regard to a decedent's probable intentions regarding former spouses. There is the whole world of irrevocable estate planning devices that involve spouses as vested beneficiaries. Irrevocable funded trusts present the most common situation. State laws are not going to extend into eliminating or modifying vested, irrevocable benefits. Thus, it is paramount for the client to address or take into account spousal rights in irrevocable trusts as part of the divorce process or within the terms of the documents, as discuss above.

Attaching Trust Funds

When assets in an irrevocable trust are involved in a divorce proceeding, two issues are frequently encountered. The first issue is whether the beneficiary's interest in a trust, constitutes a property interest subject to division in divorce. The second separate issue is whether the former spouse of a beneficiary of a spendthrift trust or a discretionary trust (or both) created by a third party (such as the beneficiary's parent) can reach the beneficiary's interest in the trust to satisfy an award of alimony or child support. The second issue is discussed herein.

The Uniform Trust Code (UTC) has been adopted in thirty-one states. Under the UTC and the laws of the states that have adopted the UTC or a similar variation, regardless of whether a trust has a spendthrift provision or the trust is a discretionary trust, a beneficiary's child and/or former spouse may have rights to reach the trust assets that are otherwise protected from creditors. Sections 503 and 504 of the UTC deals with the exception creditors of a spendthrift trust and discretionary trusts. Discretionary and spendthrift trusts under Article 5 of the UTC are not protected from claims of a former spouse who holds a judgment in the form of support (a "support judgment").

Spendthrift Trusts—General Rule and UTC

Generally, a spendthrift trust is a trust that restrains voluntary and involuntary alienation of all or any of the beneficiary's interest in the trust.[64] Trusts in which the interest of the beneficiary cannot be assigned by the beneficiary or reached by the beneficiary's creditors are known as spendthrift trusts. Spendthrift trusts are free from creditor's claims because the grantor has explicitly provided, through the incorporation of a spendthrift provision in the governing instrument, that the trust funds shall be exempt from the claims of the beneficiary's creditors. The spendthrift trust carries out a stated intent of the grantor.

Sections 501 to 503 of the UTC address spendthrift trusts. Pursuant to UTC Section 501, if a beneficiary's interest in a trust is not subject to a spendthrift provision, a court may authorize a creditor or the assignees of the beneficiary to reach the beneficiary's interest in the trust by attachment of present or future distributions for the benefit of the beneficiary. However, when a trust includes a valid spendthrift provision, a beneficiary may not transfer his or her interest in the trust and a creditor or assignee of the beneficiary may not reach any interest or distribution from the trust until the beneficiary receives the interest.[65] A Comment to UTC Section 502 states that unless one of the exceptions applies (as discussed below) a creditor of the beneficiary is prohibited from attaching a protected interest and may only attempt to collect directly from the beneficiary after payment is made from the trust.

Spendthrift Trusts—Exception for Certain Creditors

UTC Section 503 and various state statutes provides various exception creditors who can reach interests in spendthrift trusts. Among them are a beneficiary's child, spouse, or former spouse. UTC Section 503(b) provides that "[a] spendthrift provision is unenforceable against: (1) a beneficiary's child, spouse, or former spouse who

has a judgment or court order against the beneficiary for support or maintenance..." Section 503(a) defines a "child" as including "any person for whom an order or judgment for child support has been entered in this or another State." Section 503(c) states that "a claimant against which a spendthrift provision cannot be enforced may obtain from a court an order attaching present or future distribution to or for the benefit of the beneficiary..."

The Comments to Section 503 state that "[t]he exception for judgments or orders to support a beneficiary's child or current or former spouse is in accord with Restatement (Third) of Trusts... and numerous state statutes. It is also consistent with federal bankruptcy law, which exempts such support orders from discharge." Consequently, this is very strong authorization for attaching present or future distributions from the trust.

Discretionary Trusts—General Rule and UTC

Discretionary trusts are trusts in which distributions to the beneficiary are left within the discretion of the trustee. The discretion can be general without regard to any ascertainable standard or limited to a reason for the distribution (e.g. health, education, maintenance and support). For maximum asset protection, however, it may be advisable to avoid distributions based on an ascertainable standard and have distributions be purely at the discretion of the trustee.[66]

The effect of a discretionary trust is to limit the extent of the beneficiary's interest in the trust so that the beneficiary's interest will only come into existence when and to the extent that the trustee decides to make a distribution. A creditor cannot compel the trustee to pay anything to the creditor because the beneficiary could not compel payment to themselves or application for their own benefit.[67] Even when a trust is subject to an ascertainable standard, if the beneficiary cannot compel payment or compel application in any way except for the restricted purpose set out in the terms of the trust, creditors cannot reach the trust.[68] Courts generally will not substitute their judgment for the judgment of a trustee as long as the trustee exercises the trustee's judgment in good faith and within reasonable bounds. Under the UTC, Section 504(b) provides that other than as provided in Section 504(c), whether or not a trust has a spendthrift provision, a creditor of the beneficiary may not compel a distribution that is subject to the trustee's discretion even if the discretion is expressed in the form of a standard or the trustee has abused the discretion.

Discretionary Trusts–Exception for Certain Creditors

Similar to spendthrift trusts discussed above, the UTC provides exceptions to the general rule. In the marital context, UTC Section 504(c) contains an exception dealing with a beneficiary's child, spouse, or former spouse. It provides:

"To the extent a trustee has not complied with a standard of distribution or has abused a discretion:

(1) a distribution may be ordered by the court to satisfy a judgment or court order against the beneficiary for support or maintenance of the beneficiary's child, spouse, or former spouse; and

(2) the court shall direct the trustee to pay to the child, spouse, or former spouse such amount as is equitable under the circumstances but not more than the amount the trustee would have been required to distribute to or for the benefit of the beneficiary had the trustee complied with the standard or not abused the discretion."

As a result, the UTC and those states that have adopted a version above or similar version, exempt the beneficiary's child, spouse, or former spouse from the trust protection.

Exemptions for Certain Creditors under State Law

Of the states that adopted the UTC, some states have adopted provisions of UTC Sections 503 and 504 in their entirety, other states have modified 503 and 504 in part by limiting or expanding the scope of exception creditors and other states have reserved or omitted adoption of either 503 or 504, relying instead on either common law or other reasoning. Therefore, state laws differs significantly, even among the states adopting the UTC, with respect to the power of the former spouse or child to enforce rights against spendthrift and or discretionary trusts created by a third-party.

In some states, such as Florida, it is unclear whether a former spouse with a support judgment could garnish assets held in a discretionary trust. In the Florida case of *Berlinger v. Casselberry*, the court ruled that a spouse has the right to garnish assets held in a discretionary trust. Other states provide greater protection for discretionary trusts. For example, Nevada specifically disallows claims of spouses, former spouses, children, or dependents.[69] Section 166.080 of the Nevada statutes provides that no spouse, former spouse, child or dependent shall be a beneficiary unless named or clearly referred to as a beneficiary in the writing. In South Dakota, a trustee of a spendthrift trust may directly pay any expense on behalf of such beneficiary and may exhaust the income and principal of the trust for the benefit of such beneficiary regardless of whether a beneficiary has an outstanding creditor.[70] If the trust contains a spendthrift provision, no creditor may force a distribution nor reach a present or future support distribution with respect to a mandatory or support interest.[71] In the case of discretionary trusts, a creditor cannot reach assets in the trust. The term "reach" is defined as including by garnishment or attachment.[72] Further, a discretionary interest is explicitly defined as a "mere expectancy," and creditors cannot force a distribution with regard to a discretionary interest.[73] In light of the fact that as many as thirty-one states provide some type of exception creditor access to spendthrift trusts or discretionary trusts, those beneficiaries known to have exposure, may want to consider changing the *situs* of the trust to a more protective jurisdiction.

Powers of Appointment

Trusts are often drafted wherein a beneficiary is given a power to modify the interests of the beneficiary in the trust. The common law rule is that appointive assets covered by an unexercised general power of appointment, created by a person other than the donee, cannot be reached by the donee's creditors. Until the donee exercises the power, the donee has not accepted control over the appointive assets that gives the donee the equivalent ownership of them. The nongrantor holder of a general power of appointment cannot be compelled to exercise it.[74] However, once the power is exercised, the property subject to the power is accessible by the powerholder's creditors.

Some states, the Restatement (Third) of Trusts and the UTC take a different position and hold that creditors of the holder of a non-self-settled general power of appointment can reach the property even if the power is unexercised. The Restatement (Third) of Trusts provides that an unexercised general power of appointment is an ownership equivalent power.[75] The UTC states that creditors of a holder of a general *inter vivos* power of appointment who is not the settler will have access to property subject to the power even during periods when power is unexercised.[76]

The results differ, however, when the power is a special power of appointment. Property subject to a special power of appointment generally cannot be reached by the holder's creditors whether or not the power is exercised, except to the extent required by the rules of law relating to fraudulent conveyances. One court held that a limited power of appointment is distinguished from a general power of appointment, finding that the holder of a general power of appointment is generally considered the owner of the underlying property whereas the holder of a limited power of appointment does not have any interest in the underlying property.[77]

Self-Settled Trusts

As discussed above, a self-settled trust is a trust created by a party who may also be a beneficiary of the trust. If the trust is irrevocable, the universal common law is that the assets in the trust are subject to the donor's creditors.[78] The creditors can reach the maximum amount which the trustee could pay under the terms of the trust to the beneficiary.[79]

Several states including Alaska, Delaware, Hawaii, Missouri, Nevada, New Hampshire, Ohio, Rhode Island, South Dakota, Tennessee, Utah, Virginia and Wyoming have enacted self-settled trust legislation designed to protect self-settled trusts from creditors. With a DAPT, the donor is usually a discretionary beneficiary and, by statute, creditors of the donor are not permitted to reach the assets of the trust, provided certain criteria are met.

In certain cases, specific creditors, such as a spouse, may be excluded from the list of creditors who cannot attach trust assets. In other cases like Alaska, Nevada, Virginia and Wyoming, a spouse or former spouse is not an exception creditor regardless of when the parties were married.[80] For example, Alaska's statute allows the creation of a self-settled spendthrift trust which denies spousal claims even if the marriage existed at the time of the trust's creation. Delaware enacted a similar but not identical statute.[81] This may allow a client to create a pre-marriage self-funded spendthrift trust which is protected from the new spouse without having to use a pre-nuptial agreement as discussed above in Section II herein.[82]

CHAPTER ENDNOTES

1. See, e.g., Restatement (Second) of Trusts §156 (1959).

2. American College of Trust and Estate Counsel (ACTEC), "ACTEC Comparison of the Domestic Asset Protection Trust Statutes," (Updated through August 2017); available on line at: https://www.actec.org/assets/1/6/Shaftel-Comparison-of-the-Domestic-Asset-Protection-Trust-Statutes.pdf.

3. Delaware, Mississippi, New Hampshire, Ohio, Rhode Island, South Dakota, and Tennessee.

4. Alaska, Delaware, Mississippi, New Hampshire, Ohio, Rhode Island, South Dakota, Hawaii, Missouri, and Tennessee.

5. AS §34.40.110(l).

6. *Waldron v. Huber (In re Huber)*, 493 BR 798.

7. Note, however, the new provisions to the Uniform Voidable Transactions Act have received considerable criticism and commentary. See, e.g., George D. Karibjanian, Richard Nenno, and Dan Rubin, "Uniform Voidable Transactions Act: Are Transfers to Self-Settled Spendthrift Trusts by Settlors in Non-APT States Voidable Transfers Per Se?", *Bloomberg BNA* (July 13, 2017).

8. See Restatement (2d) of Conflicts of Laws, §270.

9. *Toni 1 Trust v. Wacker*, 2018 WL 1125033 (Alaska, Mar. 2, 2018); see also, Steve Oshins discussion on "*Toni 1 Trust v. Wacker*: DAPT Fraudulent Transfer Statutes Note Exclusive, But Yet Again No Discussion about whether Non-Resident Can Use a DAPT," LISI Asset Protection Planning Newsletter #360 (March 6, 2018).

10. There are, in fact, a number of ways to modify irrevocable trusts, which are discussed in a separate chapter. Some examples include judicial modification, non-judicial modification, and decanting.

11. Treas. Reg. §§25.2523(f)-1(c), 25.2523(e)-1(f).

12. Notice 2018-37, IRB 2018-18.

13. Restatement (Second) Trusts §62 Comment E (1959).

14. An exception allows for a beneficiary's interest to be accelerated in order to provide funds needed for living and other expenses incurred as a result of a divorce. Restatement (Second) Of Prop.: Donative Transfers §6.1 Comment E (1983); Restatement (Second) Of Trusts §62 Comment E (1959).

15. Restatement (Second) Trusts §62 Comment D (1957). Restatement (Third) of Trusts §29 "General Notes on Clause (c)" (2003).

16. Restatement (Third) of Trusts §29 (2003).

17. *Id.* at Comment J.

18. *In re Marriage of Weiler*, 258 Ill.App.3d 454, 629 N.E.2d 1216 (5th Dist. 1994); In re Marriage of Lee, 246 Ill.App.3d 628, 615 N.E.2d 1314 (4th Dist. 1993) mandate recalled 623 N.E.2d 1361, appeal denied 153 Ill.2d 560, 624 N.E.2d 808.

19. Fla. Stat. §61.075(1).

20. Fla. Stat. §61.075(1)(i).

21. 189 Ill.App.3d 559, 565, 136 Ill. Dec. 922, 545 N.E.2d 446 (1989).

22. 677 P.2d 1389, 1390 (Colo. App. 1984).

23. 212 N.J. Super. 557 (App. Div. 1986).

24. *Pfannenstiehl v. Pfannenstiehl*, 475 Mass. 105 (2016).

25. See Fla. Stat. 736.0504(3).

26. UPC §§2-202, 2-203.

27. Fla. Stat. §§732.2025(2), 732.2095(2)(b); N.C.G.S. §§30-3.2(3c)(g), 30-3..3A(e).

28. §13(2)(b) of HB 3077.

29. Restatement 2d Trusts §162; Restatement 3rd Trusts §56 Comment A.

30. See, e.g., *In re Marriage of Githens*, 204 P3d 835 (Or. App. 2009) and *In re Estate of Knickerbocker*, 912 P2d 969 (Utah 1996).

31. Oregon, New Hampshire and North Dakota.

32. Restate (Third) of Trusts §56, Comment A; UTC §501.

33. *In Re Marriage of Guinn* 93 P.3d 568 (Col. Ct. Ap. 2004).

34. See *Sayer v. Sayer*, 492 A.2d 238 (Del. 1985).

35. *D.L. v. G.L.*, 61 Mass. App. Ct. 488, 811 N.E. 2d 1013 (2004).

36. The spouse's interest was a discretionary interest where the trustee had the sole discretion to distribute income and principal, in equal or unequal shares to an open class of the donor's then living issue to provide for the comfortable support, health, maintenance, welfare and education of each or all members of such class.

37. *Pfannenstiehl v. Pfannenstiehl*, 88 Mass. App. Ct. 121, 37 N.E.3d 15 (2015), *rev'd* 475 Mass. 105 (2016).).

38. See *Fox v. Fox*, 592 N.W.2d 541 (N.D. 1999).

39. See *Lauricella*, 409 Mass. 211, 565 N.E.2d 436 (1991); *Henderson v. Collins*, 267 S.E.2d 202 (Georgia 1980); *Burrell v. Burrell*, 537 P.2d 1 (Alaska 1975); *Moyars v. Moyars*, 717 N.E.2d 976 (Ind. Ct. App. 1999); *In re Marriage of Bentson*, 656 P.2d 395 (Or. Ct. App. 1999).

40. See *Rubin v. Rubin*, 527 A.2d 1184 (Conn. 1987) and *Storm v. Storm*, 470 P.2d 367 (Wyo. 1970).

41. *Pfannenstiehl v. Pfannenstiehl*, 88 Mass. App. Ct. 121, 37 N.E.3d 15 (2015), *rev'd* 475 Mass. 105 (2016).

42. *Athorne v. Athorne*, 100 NH 413, 128 A.2d 910 (1959); *Rosenberg v. Rosenberg*, 64 Md. App. 487, 497 A.2d 485 (1985), cert. denied, 305 Md. 107, 501 A.2d 845 (1985).

43. *Tannen v. Tannen*, 3 A.3d 1229 (NJ Super. AD 2010). Md. Est. & Trusts §14-402(a)(2).

44. I.R.C. §682.

45. Notice 2018-37, IRB 2018-18.

46. I.R.C. §2702(b); Treas. Reg. 25.2702-3.

47. I.R.C. §2702(a)(3)(ii); Treas. Reg. 25.2702-5(c).

48. I.R.C. §2042.

49. I.R.C. §1041(a); PLR 201901003

50. I.R.C. §§1041(b)(2), (e).

51. I.R.C. §682.

52. I.R.C. §671(a).

53. Treas. Reg. §1.682(a)-1(b).

54. Typical spousal support and child support obligations are not considered gifts since they are given pursuant to a divorce decree and consideration is given by satisfying the foregoing obligations and the spouse releasing all interests in the other spouse's property. Rev. Rul. 77-314; Rev. Rul. 68-379; *Estate of Glen v.Comm'r.*, 45 TC 23 (1966); and *Estate of Waters v. Comm'r.*, 48 F.3d 838 (4th Cir. 1995); *Harris v. Comm'r.*, 340 US 106 (1950). See Rev. Rul. 60-160.

55. I.R.C. §§2523, 2056(b)(7).

56. I.R.C. §6075(b).

57. I.R.C. §2516.

58. Rev. Rul. 57-506; PLRs 200616008, 200832021.

59. Treas. Reg. §25.2702-1(c)(7).

60. I.R.C. §§2041, 2044.

61. See e.g. 706 ILCS 35/1.

62. Fla. Stat. §736.1105.

63. See *In re Estate of Guess*, 213 So. 2d 638 (Fla. 3d DCA 1968); *In re Estate of Bauer*, 161 So. 2d 678 (Fla. 1st DCA 1964).

64. Restatement (Third) of Trusts (2003), §58, General Comment.

65. UTC §502(c).

66. *Pfannenstiehl v. Pfannenstiehl*, 88 Mass. App. Ct. 121, 37 N.E.3d 15 (2015), *rev'd* 2016 Mass. LEXIS 591 (Mass. Aug. 4, 2016).

67. Restatement (Second) of Trusts §155 Comment B (ALI 1959).

68. *Id.*

69. Nevada Revised Statutes §166.090.

70. South Dakota Codified Laws §55-1-35.

71. South Dakota Codified Laws §55-1-42.

72. South Dakota Codified Laws §55-1-24(6).

73. South Dakota Codified Laws §55-1-43(1)-(2).

74. *State Street Trust Co. v. Kissel*, 302 Mass. 328, 333, 19 N.E. 2d 25 (1939).

75. Restatement (Third) of Trusts §56, Comment B.

76. UTC §505(b)(1).

77. *Cooley v. Cooley*, 628 A.2d 608 (1993).

78. *Ware v. Gulda*, 331 Mass. 68, 117 N.E.2d 137 (1954); *State Street Bank & Trust Co., v. Reiser*, 7 Mass. App. Ct. 633, 389 N.E.2d 768 (1979); Restatement (Second) of Trusts §156 (1957); Restatement (Third) of Trusts §58. (2003); Uniform Trust Code §505(a)(1); Restatement (Third) of Trusts §25.

79. Restatement (Third) of Trusts §58, Comment E. See also Uniform Trust Code §505(a)(2).

80. R.I. Gen. Laws §§18-0.2.1et. seq.; Nev. Rev. Stat. §166.040.

81. Del. C. Ann. Title 12 §§3570-3576.

82. Alaska Stat. §34.40.110(h).

REVOCABLE LIVING TRUSTS

Technically, a revocable trust is a trust to which the grantor transfers all or part of the grantor's assets during lifetime, while retaining the right to the trust's income, the right to withdraw (or add to the trust) assets, and the right to revoke or modify the trust and recover all of the assets. The right to revoke the trust can be retained by the grantor or it can be shared or given to another person.

The most important point is that, as its name implies, a revocable trust is one that can be revoked or modified in any way at the whim of the grantor (sometimes called the "settlor" or "trustor"). Trust assets can be recovered or the terms of the trust can be changed at the discretion of the grantor. The right to alter or amend the terms of the trusts can be spelled out in the trust document specifically. The death of the settlor or legal incompetence will automatically make a revocable trust irrevocable. At either of those two events, no one can alter, amend, revoke, or terminate your trust unless the trust instrument otherwise provides.

To be revocable, a trust must state just that. It is extremely important to state in the trust document "I reserve the right to revoke this trust" (or words to that effect). Otherwise, the grantor will not have the right to alter, amend, revoke, or terminate the trust in most states, and the trust will be irrevocable once it is set up and funded (i.e., once assets have been placed into it). This is very important: In most states, a trust is irrevocable unless it clearly states that it is revocable.

If the grantor and the grantor's spouse both contribute property to the trust, the trust should specifically state whether the right to amend or revoke can be exercised by either the grantor or the grantor's spouse, or if they both must sign any amendment or revocation. It should also state whether the power to revoke extends only to what has been contributed or if it applies to both contributors' portions, and whether the power to revoke continues after one has died.

ADVANTAGES OF SETTING UP A REVOCABLE LIVING TRUST

There are a number of advantages to creating a revocable living trust, including the management of assets, control of the assets and their distribution, favorable transfer mechanisms, the ability to "forum shop" for the right jurisdiction, insulation of the assets, and advantages to unmarried or divorced settlors. Another advantage is that third parties may be more inclined to accept the authority of a trustee over that of an agent under a durable power of attorney. In many ways, it is helpful to view a revocable living trust as a "souped up" durable power of attorney.

Management and Investment of Assets

A grantor can be relieved of the burden of managing or investing stocks, bonds, real estate or other assets. This could be particularly true if someone inherits a large sum of money or assets requiring considerable time or management. A corporate or other professional trustee may be a good solution.

If someone is not married, cares for himself or herself, and is concerned about management of financial affairs when they are old or ill, a revocable living trust can serve as a particularly useful financial management safety net. Without a trust, the family might have to suffer the expenses, delays, and restrictions of going to court and obtaining a court-appointed conservator to hold assets and manage the family financial affairs. A revocable trust can help avoid the expensive, complex, aggravating, and in some cases embarrassing court process if the family has to request that a court declare a family member incompetent. Nor will the investments be restricted to the usually very conservative types of allowable investments that are forced upon a conservator by state law. By coordinating a well-drawn durable power of attorney with a revocable trust and a step-up trustee (who will "step up" and take over if necessary), the grantor can be assured financial matters will be handled carefully if disabled. If the disability ends, the grantor can resume trusteeship over the assets in the trust. The combination of durable power of attorney and revocable living trust offers much more flexibility than a power of attorney alone, and it eliminates the difficulty that agents or attorneys-in-fact sometimes encounter when dealing with banks and stock brokerage firms.

The grantor may be worried (or certain) that the beneficiaries don't have the experience, inclination, and time, or the legal, mental, or emotional capacity, to handle responsibilities of the trust. Gifts to minors and mental, physical and emotional incompetents can fall into this category. Under law (and as a practical matter), a minor cannot make decisions or take actions regarding stocks, bonds, real estate, or other property unless and until the minor is emancipated. Appropriate actions can be taken if that same property is placed in trust for the minor. This allows the sale, exchange, or mortgage of property given to a minor child or other relative without the expensive, inflexible, and troublesome process involved when a guardian must be appointed. Through a revocable trust, a successor trustee can be given the discretionary power on behalf of a beneficiary who is ill or for any other reason is not capable of handling the assets and income needing to be managed.

Distribution and Control of Assets

The single most important reason many people choose a revocable living trust over other alternatives is that it accomplishes all their other objectives, while enabling them to retain almost total control of the assets they place into the trust. The combination of lifetime control and continuing flexibility to meet unknown future contingencies but still accomplish other non-tax savings goals is an appropriate solution for many people.

Living trusts enable the grantor to control the manner and timing of asset distribution. A revocable living trust can postpone full ownership until the donees are in a better position to handle the income and the property itself. For instance, if the beneficiaries are legally adults but they lack the emotional or intellectual training, experience, demeanor, physical capacity, or willingness to handle large sums of money or assets that require constant, high-level decision-making ability, a revocable living trust may be a viable solution.

A living trust makes it so the grantor does not have to make the all-or-nothing-at-all decision of an outright gift. It can be specified that the income and capital that beneficiaries are to receive is to be spread out over a period of time, or, better yet, kept in trust, since assets are worth more in trust to the beneficiaries than they are free of trust, where they are exposed to the beneficiary's creditors and predators. A trust can be used to create rewards for behavior the grantor wants to promote. An example might be providing extra payments of income or capital on the achievement of certain goals. Such trusts are called incentive trusts.

Some people are reluctant to make outright gifts to children or others because they want to maintain a degree of control over those individuals. They fear that once their children or other beneficiaries receive a significant amount of income or capital, they will be less dependent (financially or psychologically) on them. With a revocable living trust, the grantor can maintain some control over a beneficiary.

Yet another control-related reason for setting up revocable living trusts is that, in some states, they minimize the possibility that details about assets owned and their disposition will become public knowledge. Unlike a will, which becomes a matter of public record once it is filed in the appropriate local court, in many states a revocable trust is not required to be filed anywhere that would open its provisions to public scrutiny. In most states, an inventory of the assets that will pass under a will must be filed in court, and so the assets, too, become subject to inspection. Only a few states make the same information available if the assets are held in trust. Privacy can become important if interfamily conflicts are anticipated. In that case, the relative privacy available through a revocable living trust may be an important factor. No one need know how much another beneficiary receives or upon what terms. This may be a major advantage if a child is being disinherited or getting a different level of income or capital.

Effective and Efficient Transfer

A revocable living trust can serve as a unifying receptacle for a multitude of assets. Because a trust can be named as recipient of almost any type of asset and because the grantor (or others) can transfer cash, stocks, bonds, or other property such as a vacation home into a revocable living trust at any time, the grantor can use the trust to unify not only the mix of assets owned now but also assets obtained in the future. That unification will be monitored and administered by one person (or party) or by co-trustees working together who can see the whole investment picture.

Another aspect of unification is that, if rendered mentally incompetent by a stroke or other disability, additional assets received can be added to your trust by others. (This should be specified in the power of attorney that the holder of that power is authorized to add property to the trust.)

Forum Shopping

Within reasonable limits, the grantor can designate which state's law will govern the administration of the trust and the interpretation of its terms. This means that the trust does not necessarily have to be governed by the laws of the grantor's own state. The grantor can pick a state where the laws are more favorable to accomplishing the trust objectives, and stipulate in trust the desire that the interpretation of trust terms be governed by "State X."

The choice of forum can be a significant advantage if one of the objectives is to allow the trust to continue longer than might otherwise be permitted under the grantor's own law, reduce a surviving spouse's rights to a statutory share of the estate, or lessen the threat of a will contest, because laws in these areas vary greatly from state to state, and another state may have laws that are much more favorable. Forum shopping should be considered if another state has a more favorable law dealing with creditors' rights or charitable bequests, and the grantor's intentions may be thwarted under the laws of the home state.

Insulating Assets

Generally speaking, by "wrapping" the trust around assets, it makes it harder for someone to disturb plans to distribute property the way the grantor sees fit. A well-drawn trust is better able to withstand an attack than a will drawn shortly before death—which is a very good reason to establish a trust now, rather than take a chance and create one in a will (that is, a "testamentary" trust).

Insulating assets is particularly important if provisions in a will that may be controversial or apt to stir up a family dispute.) If there is any suggestion that the will might be challenged, the grantor should consider a revocable living trust. In a few states, a revocable living trust can even help defeat a challenge by a surviving spouse who "elects against" the will (i.e., exercises a statutory right to take a share of the estate determined under state law regardless of the terms of the will).

A trustee can usually use trust assets to defend against an attack on the validity of the trust. Although the intended beneficiaries may still be bearing the costs of their own defense, it may help to discourage a claimant to realize that, even if the attack on the trust is successful, the claimant will have had to pay the legal fees of both sides to the dispute.

Unmarried and Divorced Clients

Revocable trusts can be a very good choice for an unmarried individual or someone married more than one time. Both situations are strong indicators that a revocable living trust might be appropriate and should definitely be considered. An unmarried individual who is living with another person will often wish to provide for his or her partner. Typically, that partner will have no state law survivorship rights. Worse yet, the property-owning individual may have relatives who will inherit that property if there is no will. This is a perfect recipe for a will contest, and it could easily lead to a bitter fight—almost certainly to a probate delay. The living trust can help avoid the entire problem because it will not be offered for probate; none of the disappointed relatives need know of the terms, or even the existence, of the trust and the assets it conveys.

A revocable trust may also be indicated for divorced clients in states that require an "affidavit of heirship" (essentially a family tree) and a copy of any divorce decree when an unmarried person dies. What if the marriage was terminated but there is no easily accessible evidence to prove it? (Perhaps the divorce occurred forty years ago.) A revocable trust may avoid the delay, aggravation, and cost of searching for the evidence of a prior valid divorce.

Individuals who have married more than once would often like to make provisions for children of a former marriage, but they want to keep the terms and amounts private. A revocable trust is an excellent vehicle for accomplishing this objective.

DISADVANTAGES OF A REVOCABLE LIVING TRUST

Revocable trusts also come with some disadvantages, including claims by creditors and potential tax issues.

Claims of Creditors

This might still be possible in some states, but is increasingly unlikely. The currently prevailing view (and the position of the Uniform Trust Code) is that the assets of a revocable trust are subject to the claims of creditors of the settlor whenever the probate estate of the settlor is insufficient to pay those debts. So the grantor can't protect oneself or beneficiaries by placing assets into a revocable living trust, and avoidance of probate does not guarantee any creditor protection.

In some cases assets, may be at a greater risk by transferring them to a revocable trust than if left by will. For instance, in many jurisdictions creditors of the probate estate have only four to six months to make their claims. Yet the creditors of a revocable trust may have no such short deadline, although it may be possible to establish a procedure and time limits for bringing claims in the trust instrument itself. In many states, a creditor can file a claim for payment years after death, assuming the claim is filed within the statute of limitations—as long as six or seven years for a mortgage, credit card, or other contract claim in some states. Furthermore, some states (such as Florida) will not honor a homestead exemption (which allows a homeowner to designate a house and land as his or her homestead and then exempt that homestead from execution for the homeowner's general debts) from creditors if the deed is registered in the name of a revocable trust.

The IRS as Creditor

If the trustee distributes assets in the revocable trust before the IRS (the most senior creditor of all) is satisfied that the federal estate tax has been paid, the trustee can be held personally liable for any unpaid tax. Because the assets in the revocable trust are part of the taxable estate,[1] any distribution to beneficiaries is at the trustee's personal peril until the executor receives a "closing letter" from the IRS for the federal estate tax. Tax liens for income taxes incurred during lifetime can also be attached to revocable living trust assets. And a trustee in bankruptcy (a court-appointed party representing your creditors) can revoke a trust in order to obtain the cash and to sell trust property to satisfy personal creditors.

SETTING UP A REVOCABLE TRUST

The trust instrument (sometimes called a trust indenture) should spell out all the terms and conditions for distributions of income and principal. It should identify the beneficiaries (which can include the grantor and the grantor's spouse), either by name or by class (for example, "my grandchildren"). The trust must also specify when distributions should be made during lifetime and following death, any conditions or restrictions on distributions (only after a certain age, or only for certain purposes), and the amounts or portion to be distributed to each beneficiary. Trustees are usually given investment and administrative powers by law, but it is a good idea to eliminate uncertainty by listing the powers of the trustees in the trust document. It may also be desirable to expand or restrict the normal powers of the trustee in order to carry out your particular planning objectives.

The grantor must fund the trust initially and maintain the funding of the trust during its existence. This means legally changing the ownership of assets from the grantor's name alone (or the grantor's name and the grantor's spouse's name jointly) to the name of the trustee (even if you are the sole trustee). It is very important that assets held in the trust's name be segregated from personal assets by retitling them. A trustee must keep separate records and hold cash in a bank account in the trust's name.

The trustee will then hold the legal title to the assets in the trust. It is the trustee's job to invest and safeguard trust assets, file tax returns (if needed) and pay the trust's income tax liabilities, pay out income and principal in accordance with the terms of the trust, and generally carry out the terms and conditions of the trust.

As new assets are acquired, you must also change ownership to the trust, or better yet, acquire ownership originally in the name of the trustee. Before 1997, the IRS had taken the position that gifts from a trust fall within a special class of gifts that are still included in the gross estate for federal estate tax purposes if death occurs within three years after the gift. So in the past, it was usually recommended that gifts intended to qualify for the annual gift tax exclusion not be made from a revocable living trust. Fortunately, the Internal Revenue

Code was amended by the Taxpayer Relief Act of 1997 to eliminate this problem.

OPERATION OF THE REVOCABLE TRUST

Operating a revocable trust involves several important considerations during the settlor's lifetime and after the settlor's death. There are additional considerations to bear in mind depending on what type of assets are put into the trust.

During the Settlor's Lifetime

The living trust serves as a kind of special savings account, separating the trust assets from the settlor's individual assets even though the trust assets are always available for withdrawal. Let's assume that the settlor retitled whatever assets that the settlor wanted in the trust's name and have held back a modest checking account for day-to-day living expenses. The trust assets continue to produce the same income or capital growth that they produced before being transferred into the trust. The income earned by the trust is deposited into the trust's checking, savings, or money market accounts, or reinvested in the securities held in the trust's brokerage account. The settlor generally can withdraw all or any part of the income and principal from the trust at any time, or the trustee can pay bills for the settlor. The settlor can also revoke the trust and withdraw all the assets whenever the settlor wants and at any time (or at least until the settlor dies, becomes incompetent, or voluntarily amends the trust to make it irrevocable).

Upon Death

The trust becomes irrevocable upon death just like a will is irrevocable upon death. After any debts, taxes, or other expenses have been paid, trust assets will be distributed to the persons named, and under the terms and conditions specified in the trust document, just like a will directs the distribution of an estate. The settlor can specify that part or all of the assets of the trust should continue to be held in the trust and that the trust continue for many years (even in perpetuity).

The revocable trust may be given a "split personality" at death—that is, the trustee can be directed to split a single trust into two or more smaller trusts to

accomplish various planning objectives. For instance, a revocable trust could be divided into one or more of the following types of trusts:

- **A qualified terminable interest property (QTIP) trust** is to provide income for life to the settlor's surviving spouse. A QTIP trust qualifies for the federal estate tax marital deduction, so there is no federal estate tax (and usually no state death tax) on the transfer to the trust. At the death of the settlor's spouse, all of the assets in the trust will be part of the spouse's taxable estate,[2] but the assets will pass to the beneficiaries named, so that the settlor can be sure the settlor's assets will pass to the settlor's children even if your spouse should remarry or have children from a prior marriage.

- **A qualified domestic trust (QDT),** which is a special form of trust for a surviving spouse who is not a U.S. citizen. It is NOT the same as a marital deduction trust.[3]

- **A "family" or "by-pass" trust,** which can provide income and other benefits to the settlor's spouse and children, but will not be subject to federal estate tax at the death of the settlor's spouse. This kind of trust is usually funded with an amount that is free of federal estate tax due to the federal estate tax applicable exclusion amount, so the assets in the trust will escape federal estate tax at both the settlor's death and the death of the settlor's spouse. For this reason, the family trust is often called a credit equivalent by-pass trust or credit shelter trust. No matter how much the assets in this trust increase in value after the settlor's death, the entire amount can by-pass any tax at the spouse's death, which can save hundreds of thousands of dollars in taxes and sometimes more.

- **Charitable Split-Interest Trusts,** such as a charitable remainder trust or charitable lead trust, if the settlor want to benefit both the settlor's family and charity.

Types of Property

Any property that can be owned in the settlor's own name can be placed into a revocable living trust. The settlor can put cash, stocks, mutual funds, bonds, real estate, or any other asset that the settlor owns into a trust. The settlor can even put life insurance into a trust, or name the trust as beneficiary of life insurance. (The settlor can also name a trust as a beneficiary of your pension or profit-sharing plans, or an individual retirement account, but the settlor can't transfer the actual assets of the retirement plan or IRA into the trust without realizing taxable income and perhaps incurring penalties for premature withdrawals. Assets can be transferred at the time the trust is set up, and assets can be added any time up until death.

TERMINATING A REVOCABLE TRUST

Revoking a revocable trust will enable the trust creator to resume possession and title to the assets. If the right to revoke the trust is reserved, a written letter from to the trustee (even if that trustee is yourself) is all that should be necessary to end the trust and recover the assets. The letter to the trustee should state the wish to revoke the trust. It should also specify that assets in the trust should be retitled in your name.

Power of Appointment

Some lawyers insert a power of appointment provision that essentially gives the holder of that power the right to demand trust assets be paid to the party specified. If the power of appointment is a "general power," the grantor has the right to demand that the trustee pay the assets directly to the grantor or any other power designated. Holding a general power is like having a blank check that can be written against trust assets. It gives the holder the absolute right to recover all the assets placed into the trust at any time before death. Powers of appointment are the "magic carpet" of estate planning because assets can be yanked out from under one beneficiary and magically placed for the benefit of another.

It may also be possible to revoke a trust by will. The settlor can state in in a revocable living trust that the settlor has the right to revoke the trust by will as well as during the settlor's lifetime, in which case the trust assets would be distributed to the executor of settlor's estate. However, if the trust becomes irrevocable prior to death because the settlor either released the revocation power or became incompetent prior to death, there is a metaphysical problem with trying to revoke an irrevocable trust. Therefore, it's best that if the settlor wishes to retain a power to revoke at death by will, the settlor retain a testamentary power of appointment over the trust.

Another way a trust can be terminated is through the trustee's discretionary power to make principal distributions to the settlor. If the trustee invades the principal for the settlor and pays out all the trust's assets, it will terminate. (A trust must have assets or a res to exist.)

Incapacity

If legally incapacitated because of mental illness (such as Alzheimer's disease), the grantor will not be able to revoke the revocable trust. The power to revoke may still exist, but will not be able to exercise the power if legally incompetent, just like not being able to sell property or sign contracts. However, if a durable power of attorney to a spouse, child, other relative, or friend, that person may be able to act to revoke the trust or at least make withdrawals from the trust for the grantor's benefit, or to make gifts that will reduce the death taxes otherwise payable by the beneficiaries.

In most states, the person to whom the settlor has given a durable power of attorney will not be able to revoke the trust or withdraw from the trust unless very stringent requirements have been met. At a minimum, the durable power itself must specifically allow the agent and attorney-in-fact to revoke or withdraw from the trust, and the trust itself must clearly allow for that action.

TERMS OF THE TRUST

The terms of the trust can be designed to deal with a variety of different circumstances, including a grantor acting as trustee, designation of beneficiaries, and claims of heirs.

Trustee of Own Trust

The grantor or spouse (or both together) can serve as the trustee of the grantor's own trust, either alone or with any other person. Instead of oneself, the trustee can be a child or other relative, a friend, a legal or financial advisor, a corporate fiduciary such as a bank trust department, or any combination of them.

There are obviously advantages in serving as the trustee of one's own trust, including complete control over all investments. The grantor, acting as trustee, can write him or herself a check from the trust at any time.

Because a revocable trust is generally ignored for income and estate tax purposes,[4] there are no tax disadvantages in serving as the trustee of one's own revocable living trust. However, there may be tax complications if the settlor's spouse or other family members serve as trustees after death.

There are some potential non-tax disadvantages in naming oneself as the sole trustee. If one of the purposes of the trust is to provide for continued management of investments and other assets in the event of disability, then serving as the sole trustee may result in complications or delays. Mental or physical abilities may deteriorate gradually, through age or illness, and the grantor may inadvertently neglect the management of the trust assets, or even mismanage or waste assets, because of diminishing abilities. Even if a successor trustee recognizes the grantor's disability and steps in to take control of the trust, the disability might prevent *the* grantor from resigning, in which case the successor trustee might have trouble getting the banks or brokers who are holding trust assets to accept the authority of the successor trustee. So a court proceeding may be needed to officially remove oneself as trustee and qualify a successor.

Even if the grantor serves successfully as sole trustee until death, the successor trustee may have difficulties in gaining control of all trust assets. In the past, most banks and brokers were satisfied with a copy of the trust document and a death certificate. However, more and more financial institutions are becoming concerned by the possibilities unknown trust revocations or amendments, invalid trusts, or even fraud by those claiming to be the successor trustee. As a result, more and more financial institutions are requiring court approval of the successor trustee before turning over trust assets.

A trusted family member, such as a spouse or a child, should serve as a co-trustee during the trustee's lifetime, even if the grantor/trustee continues to perform all of the services of trustee. Having a co-trustee named on bank or brokerage accounts should eliminate or simplify the transfer of assets or control of the trust assets upon death or disability. A bank or a financial institution can also be considered for co-trustee.

Trust Document when Serving as Own Trustee

With only a few rare exceptions, the terms of any trust created should be in writing. This is because others are affected by the trust:

- The trustee who is responsible for managing, safeguarding, investing, and paying out trust principal and income and who holds legal title to trust assets. While the settlor might be the sole trustee while living, someone else will have to serve as trustee upon the settlor's death or disability, and that other trustee will need to know what the settlor wanted done with the trust assets.

- The trust's beneficiaries are the equitable title holders to the assets of a revocable living trust, for whom the trustee serves and who are entitled to the benefits of trust assets and income. How are they to know whether they have gotten what they are supposed to get if the trust is not in writing? There are often disputes among trust beneficiaries when a written trust is vague or ambiguous. Imagine the possibilities for litigation when there is nothing in writing at all?

- The IRS and state tax authorities need to determine tax liabilities based on the terms of the trust. In the absence of written evidence of the terms of the trust, the trust may be ignored for tax purposes, and the tax liabilities might be considerably greater than what the settlor intended or expected.

- Banks, brokers, mutual funds, creditors, and others who buy, sell, lend, or who have other dealings with the trust and its assets need to be sure that they are dealing with the right trustee and that the trustee has the proper power to sell or invest the assets.

All of these parties need an accurate recording of the terms of the trust and written documentation of the trustee's authority to act on behalf of the trust and its beneficiaries.

The trust document—sometimes called a deed of trust, trust indenture, or trust instrument—serves as evidence of the agreement between the grantor and trustee and lets the beneficiaries, federal and state taxing authorities, and others who deal with the trustee know:

- Who is to serve as trustee

- Who are the beneficiaries to be paid income or principal from the trust, and when and how much they are to be paid;

- What powers the trustee will have to sell, buy, or manage trust assets, and whether those powers are expanded or limited from what is otherwise allowed or provided by law. Each state gives trustees certain powers (and responsibilities). The settlor can expand the powers (and therefore the flexibility) of the trustee, or the settlor can choose to restrict the trustee's ability to purchase or hold certain assets or take certain actions. For instance, if the settlor is fiscally conservative and don't want the trustee to take certain risks or purchase certain types of assets, the settlor can specify that in the trust instrument, although extreme caution is advised here because if the trust will exist for a long time, there may be no way to ascertain what types of assets will be safe investments out into the future.

- How much compensation will be paid to the trustee.

Whether there are any special limits on the liabilities or responsibilities of the trustee. The settlor can exonerate the trustees (other than the settlor) from certain liabilities or impose responsibilities beyond what the applicable state's law normally provides. For certain types of trust investments or trustee decisions, it may be necessary to limit the liability of the trustees in order to entice a trustee to accept the duties and responsibilities of trustee. For example, if the settlor wanted a family business to continue to operate as long as a least one of the settlor's children is active in the business, the settlor could direct the trustees to continue the business and exonerate the trustees for any liability for business losses or for the failure to diversify the trust assets.

Beneficiaries

There is almost unlimited flexibility in naming beneficiaries. The settlor can name the settlor as the primary beneficiary during the settlor's lifetime. The settlor can also specify that the settlor will receive all of the income from the trust annually, along with whatever principal the settlor want or need, at whatever dates or in whatever installments, and under whatever terms, the settlor specifies in the trust instrument.

Any individual can be a beneficiary—even a minor or an adult who is legally incompetent—because the beneficiary does not need to manage any property, only receive the benefits from the trust. (Of course, if the beneficiary is a minor or legally incompetent, it may be necessary to have a guardian appointed to receive the income or principal if the trustee does not have the power to hold the income or principal for the beneficiary and apply it for his or her benefit. In order to avoid the need for guardians, most trusts have provisions for minor or disabled beneficiaries.)

The settlor doesn't have to identify any beneficiaries by name. The settlor can specify, for example, that "income is to be paid annually or more frequently to my children." In fact, beneficiaries don't even have to be alive when the settlor creates the trust. The law requires only that beneficiaries be an identifiable and definite class or group, such as spouse, children, grandchildren, nieces, or nephews. The settlor could, therefore, include children or grandchildren not yet born as beneficiaries—even if the settlor has no children at the time the settlor sets up and funds the trust.

Beneficiaries do not have to be related to the settlor. For example, the settlor can name a friend or employee as the beneficiary of your trust. Charities and other organizations can also be named as beneficiaries, including corporations, other trusts, partnerships, federal, state, and local governments, and even foreign governments. However, complications can arise if the beneficiary is an unincorporated association or other organizations unable to hold legal title to property.

The settlor ordinarily cannot name a dog, cat, or other pet as a beneficiary of the trust, because a pet cannot own property or sue in court, and so cannot receive money from the trust or sue in court to enforce the trust, although pet trusts have come into being in some jurisdictions. (The settlor can name an individual as a beneficiary with the request that the money from the trust used to take care of the pet. However, this is not legally binding and is sometimes called an "honorary" trust.)

Claims of Heirs

In most states a revocable trust will not provide a significant bar to the claims of heirs with no more protection than a will. Generally speaking, a will can be contested on any the following grounds:

- Lack of testamentary capacity (i.e., competence).

- Fraud.

- Mistake.

- Undue influence.

- Failure to comply with formal requirements (witnesses and other formalities of execution).

Generally speaking, a revocable trust or other lifetime transfer can be contested on any of the following grounds:

- Lack of donative capacity (i.e., competence).

- Fraud.

- Mistake.

- Undue influence.

- Failure to comply with formal requirements (lack of valid corpus, trustee, or other element of a valid trust).

In other words, there is really no substantive difference in the laws regarding the validity of wills and the laws regarding the validity of revocable trusts (aside from mechanical differences in the formalities of wills and the formalities of trusts). A successful will contest usually requires that the decedent, at the time of signing the will, didn't understand the extent of his or her property, didn't know who the natural objects of his or her bounty were, didn't understand the consequences of signing the will, or didn't comply with state law requirements to make a valid will. The degree of mental capacity needed to transfer assets to a trust will vary from state to state, and there might be a significant distinction in the degree of capacity needed between making a valid will and making a valid revocable trust in some states.

If legal capacity is an issue, the difference may be quite important, and it should be researched by an expert in estate planning and administration. However, the difference between a will and trust is usually procedural. The trustee of a revocable trust is usually not required to give notice to heirs at law or other potential claimants, so it is possible that the trust could be distributed after death before any disgruntled heir is able to locate the trustee and begin any legal challenge to the trust. Also, the fact that a trust exists during the lifetime of the grantor, and the grantor lives with the trust for several years before his or her death, may help convince the court that the grantor knew what he or she was doing.

Surviving Spouses

A revocable trust provides little protection against the claims of surviving spouses. In most states, the surviving spouse can "elect against a will" and other transfers by a decedent. This right, called an "elective right," typically allows a surviving spouse to take a specified share of real and personal property (often one third) regardless of what the settlor's will provides—even in the absence of fraud, undue influence, or failure to meet statutory requirements for a valid will. In other words, a surviving spouse can claim a portion of the settlor's estate—including assets held in a revocable living trust—even if the will and revocable trust are completely valid, but this presupposes that the assets in the trust form part of the "augmented share" on which the elective share is based. Of course, even in those relatively few states that do allow one spouse to block the other spouse's elective rights by transferring assets to a revocable living trust, if it can be shown that the transfer was specifically to do just that—to perpetrate a "fraud" on the other spouse—the courts may find this to be an unfair practice and invalidate the transfer.

Divorce

The revocable living trust does not provide any protection to the grantor in the case of divorce. In fact, they can create problems that would not arise under a will.

Probate laws in many states will automatically revoke any gift to a spouse by will if divorced before death. So if in the will, the settlor leaves a spouse the settlor's entire estate, and the settlor then then gets divorced, but the settlor forgets to change the will, in those states, the ex-spouse will receive nothing and the settlor's property will be distributed as if the ex- spouse had predeceased the settlor. Likewise, if the settlor named a spouse as executor or executrix of the will and the settlor dies after getting divorced but before the settlor changed the will, that provision is automatically negated in many states.[5]

This protection is usually not afforded to those with revocable trusts. In most states, there is no automatic change in the settlor's trust merely because the settlor becomes divorced, although this is changing. The settlor may therefore be stuck with an ex-spouse who is both a trustee and/or beneficiary of a revocable trust with assets that the settlor have placed into the trust. Of course, the settlor could always revoke the trust and recover the assets—assuming the settlor does so before death or mental incapacity.

Some lawyers will include provisions in a trust that specifically state that the settlor's spouse must still be married to the settlor at the settlor's death in order to be a beneficiary (and most married couples will accept those kinds of standardized provisions without offense or anxiety about the state of their marriage). Another way to solve this problem is to use a "floating spouse" definition in the trust instrument that provides that the settlor's spouse is the person to whom the settlor is married at the time. However, no matter what estate planning tools or techniques the settlor used, we suggest that the estate planner review all of them immediately upon a divorce (or better yet, adjust them appropriately as the settlor proceeds in the divorcing process).

COORDINATING REVOCABLE TRUST WITH THE REST OF THE ESTATE PLAN

The revocable living trust should not, by itself, be viewed as the perfect (or sole) solution to estate planning problems. It is only one of many tools, and it must be coordinated with other tools and techniques by knowledgeable planners as part of an overall estate plan.

Wills

An adult citizen or resident alien living anywhere in the United States, should have an up-to-date valid will with or without a living trust. Why? As already mentioned, no matter how masterfully drafted the revocable living trust might be, it is operative only for property that has been placed into it. If, for any reason, the settlor hasn't retitled an asset and made the trustee the owner, that asset will pass under the terms of the will (that is, through probate), rather than

according to the provisions of the trust. None of the advantages of a revocable living trust are possible for these assets.

No matter how meticulous the individual is in retitling property to a revocable trust, it is often the case that all assets will not be actually held in the name of the trust at death. There can be some asset (a car, household items, a tax refund or jewelry, for example) that was overlooked. That asset will pass through intestacy if there is no valid will at death.

If the estate is large enough to require an estate tax return ($11,400,000 in 2019), the IRS will prefer to deal with a formally appointed executor—someone qualified by state law to act on behalf of the estate. If an executor has not been appointed, the trustee will be considered the "executor" by default, and able to make various tax elections available to the estate.[6] (If there is no executor or administrator officially appointed by the court, then any person in actual or constructive possession of any of the estate property, including the trustees of a revocable living trust, may be considered an executor.) This is not always a great result. Generally, it is better to specify an executor in the will and name at least two backups in case one of them cannot serve (or will not serve, or ceases to serve) for whatever reason, before completing the administration of the estate.

There is one more extremely important reason for a will. Some key non-tax objectives can be achieved only through a will. For example, a will can name a guardian of the person for each of the children. This is not possible in a trust.

Durable Power of Attorney

Every adult should execute this relatively simple and inexpensive legal document and make sure it is constantly updated. A power of attorney is a document that gives a spouse, child, other relative, or trusted friend (the agent and attorney-in-fact) the legal right to act on the principal's behalf as the principal could have acted (or in more limited ways, if the settlor decides to grant limited powers). A "durable" power ensures that the rights given to the person or persons named as the attorney-in-fact (or agent) are not nullified due to physical, mental, or emotional disability. The durable power of attorney should specifically authorize the agent and attorney-in-fact to add to a revocable trust, as well as withdraw from the trust to the extent needed for support (or to make gifts for tax planning purposes). The revocable trust should also specify that the attorney-in-fact can withdraw from the trust for those purposes.

spouses. Last, a revocable trust should never be used in isolation as an estate planning tool. At a minimum, a will is required along with the trust as well as a durable power of attorney.

CONCLUSION

A Revocable trust is a financial planning tool. Like any tool, there are good uses of the tool and uses that result in less than desirable results. The revocable trust is a great instrument for someone who may want to give up management of assets but still control how they are used. On the other hand, a revocable trust is not a good tool for using against creditors, unhappy heirs and

CHAPTER ENDNOTES

1. IRC Sec. 2038.
2. IRC Sec. 2044.
3. IRC Sec. 2056A.
4. IRC Secs. 676 and 2038.
5. *See, e.g.,* UPC Sec. 2-804.
6. IRC Sec. 2002.

Figure 8.1

SAMPLE FORM TO TRANSFER TITLE

DATE: January 1, 2005
FROM: Charles Parker
TO:
RE: Transferring Title to Revocable Living Trust

To Whom it May Concern:

I have established a Revocable Living Trust solely for my benefit, and would like to transfer title of my account with you to the name of my Revocable Living Trust.

My account should be titled as follows:
"Charles Parker, Trustee
U/D/T dated January 1, 1998,
F/B/O Charles Parker"

Please change your records to reflect this change.
Asset to be transferred: _____ Refer to account no.:_____
There is no consideration for this change to title. If you have any further questions, please contact me at 215-555-4343.

Sincerely,

Charles Parker

INTER VIVOS QTIP TRUSTS

CHAPTER 9

Marital deduction trusts also can be formed during lifetime. This chapter is about one form of a marital deduction trust formed during the grantor's lifetime.

INTRODUCTION

A qualified terminable interest property (QTIP) trust is a form of marital deduction trust permitted by Code sections 2056(b)(7) and 2523(f) of the Code.[1] Under sections 2056(b)(7)(B) and 2523(f)(2) of the Code, QTIP is any property that is transferred by a donor or decedent spouse (a "Donor") in which a donee or surviving spouse (a "Spouse") has a "qualifying income interest for life" and that is subject to a QTIP election. A Spouse has a qualifying income interest for life if the Spouse is entitled to all of the income from the property in such trust, payable at least annually, and no person has the power to appoint any property in the trust to any person other than to the Spouse. In drafting a QTIP trust, estate planners often fail to consider methods of optimizing certain aspects of the trust such as asset protection planning and allocating income to the ultimate beneficiaries.

ADVANTAGES OF INTER VIVOS QTIP TRUSTS

Inter vivos QTIP trusts have a number of advantages associated with them, including:

- The grantor spouse is responsible for the income tax on trust income during the marriage, which is a transfer that is not subject to the gift tax.

- Utilizing the less wealthy spouse's transfer tax applicable exclusion amounts.

- Leveraging donor spouse's GST Tax exemption via a reverse QTIP election.

- Donor Spouse can be given secondary life estate in donee spouse's inter vivos QTIP trust.

- The grantor spouse controls the ultimate disposition of the trust property.

DISADVANTAGES OF INTER VIVOS QTIP TRUSTS

The inter vivos QTIP trust is not perfect and comes with a number of disadvantages, including:

- The grantor spouse is responsible for the income tax on items of ordinary income during the marriage without any access to the trust for reimbursement.

- The lifetime QTIP could provide that any authority to make discretionary principal distributions terminates upon divorce, as well as eliminating or curtailing other rights given to the donee spouse (such as being a trustee). However, the income interest must continue uninterrupted for life post-divorce in order to qualify as a QTIP trust, unlike a Spousal Lifetime Access Trust (SLAT), which can use a "floating spouse" provision which says that for all purposes of the trust the term "spouse" refers to the person to whom the grantor is presently married.

POTENTIAL USES OF INTER VIVOS QTIP TRUSTS[2]

Inter vivos QTIP trusts can be quite handy in estate planning. Some of the potential uses include:

- Funding lifetime or testamentary use of the applicable exclusion amount or even the DSUE amount of the donee spouse.

- Funding use of the GST Tax exemption of the donee spouse.

- Funding lifetime use of the applicable exclusion amount of the donor spouse.

- Funding a grantor by-pass trust.

- Minority interest planning.

- Donee of excess value, if any, of a defined value gift or sale.

- Sales to intentionally defective grantor trusts.

- Income tax basis adjustment planning.

- Creditor protection planning.

- Elective share minimization planning.

DISTRIBUTION OF INCOME

Most QTIP trusts provide for the distribution of income on a quarterly or more frequent basis; however, mandating distributions in this manner is not required to qualify for the marital deduction. The terms of a QTIP trust or applicable local law need only direct the trustee to distribute income annually. More frequent distributions can be permitted under the terms of the trust, however, it is recommended that the discretion to make such distributions be given to a disinterested or independent trustee. For example, an income distribution provision in a QTIP trust could provide:

> The Trustees shall pay the net income from the QTIP Trust, at least annually or at such more frequent intervals as the Independent Trustee in its sole, absolute and uncontrolled discretion deems appropriate, to the Settlor's Spouse during his/her life.

A provision in the QTIP trust should also be included to fix the date for the mandatory distribution of income, *e.g.*, December 31 of each year, with all other potential distribution dates during the year being discretionary distribution dates. A marital deduction savings clause is also recommended for inclusion in the document.[3]

Under Treasury Regulations sections 20.2056(b)-5(f)(4) and 25.2523(e)-1(f)(3), income from a QTIP trust can be applied by the trustee "for the benefit of the spouse" rather than making a direct distribution of such income to a Spouse. To enhance the provisions of a QTIP trust, the trustee can be given the flexibility to apply the income for the benefit of the Spouse.

Stub Income

Many QTIP trusts provide for the payment of "stub income" to the Spouse's estate. Stub income is the income earned during the period immediately following the last distribution of income and ending at the Spouse's death. Under Treasury Regulations sections 20.2056(b)-7(d)(4) and 25.2523(f)-1(c)(1)(ii), distribution of such income is not required for the trust assets to qualify for QTIP treatment. This trust should contain a provision directing its stub income to be distributed to the successor beneficiaries or successor trusts. A specific provision in the trust is recommended because the laws of many states direct stub income to be distributed to the Spouse's estate. For example, Subsection (2) of Florida Statutes section 738.303 provides in relevant part:

> When a mandatory income interest ends, the trustee shall pay to a mandatory income beneficiary who survives that date, *or the estate of a deceased mandatory income beneficiary whose death causes the interest to end*, the beneficiary's share of the undistributed income that is not disposed of under the terms of the trust. (Emphasis added.)[4]

By way of example, a provision in a QTIP trust directing stub income to be paid to the successor estate or beneficiary could provide:

> Upon the death of the Settlor's husband, the Trustee shall deal with the balance of the principal of the QTIP Trust, together with any net income then on hand, as provided in Article ____.

The stub income rule in Treasury Regulations sections 20.2056(b)-7(d)(4) and 25.2523(f)-1(c)(1)(ii) can also be used to enhance the creditor protection aspects of the

Spouse's mandatory income interest in the QTIP trust. In this regard, Section 155(1) of the Restatement (Second) of Trusts provides in relevant part:

> [I]f by the terms of a trust it is provided that the trustee shall pay to or apply for a beneficiary only so much of the income and principal or either as the trustee in his uncontrolled discretion shall see fit to pay or apply, a transferee or creditor of the beneficiary cannot compel the trustee to pay any part of the income or principal.[5]

Comment (c) to section 155, however, provides that the foregoing rule applies only when the trustee may, in its absolute discretion, refuse to make any distribution to or for the benefit of a beneficiary. As previously mentioned, the income interest in a QTIP trust is a mandatory interest, meaning the income from the trust must be distributed to the Spouse annually as long as the Spouse is living. According to the comment, the rule set forth in section 155 "is not applicable where the trustee has discretion merely as to the time of payment, and where the beneficiary is ultimately entitled to the whole or to a part of the trust property."[6] The beneficiary's interest may be reached by a creditor if the provisions of the trust agreement require the trustee to distribute to or apply for a beneficiary any portion or all of the income or principal of the trust. Thus, the question is whether a mandatory income interest in a QTIP trust can be designed to avoid the exception to the rule in section 155 that is set forth in comment (c).

The mandatory income interest in a QTIP trust should be able to be structured so that the Spouse is not entitled to receive anything from the trust, whether income or principal, unless living on the mandatory income distribution date. To accomplish this result the stub income must be directed to be distributed to a successor beneficiary or trust rather than the Spouse's estate. As previously explained, a QTIP trust may provide for distribution of its income on an annual basis and require the Spouse to be living on such date to receive the income. If the Spouse dies prior to the distribution date, the stub income can be required to be distributed to a beneficiary other than the Spouse's estate. In such a case, it is unlikely that a creditor should have the ability to reach the Spouse's income interest until its distribution from the trust. Comment (e) of section 155 supports this conclusion, providing in relevant part:

> If by the terms of a trust it is provided that the trustee shall pay to or apply for a beneficiary so much of the income and principal or either as the

trustee in his uncontrolled discretion shall see fit to pay or apply, and upon the death of the beneficiary shall pay to another person all of the income and principal not so paid or applied, a transferee or creditor of the beneficiary cannot compel the trustee to pay over any part of the trust property.[7]

Of course, inclusion of a spendthrift provision can also further protect a Spouse's income interest in a QTIP trust as well as a provision enabling the trustee to apply the trust income for the benefit of the Spouse.

Many QTIP trusts contain provisions granting a Spouse the right to direct the trustee to make all assets productive of income or direct the trustee not to retain unproductive assets without the Spouse's consent. The genesis of such a provision is found in the language of Treasury Regulations sections 20.2056(b)-7(d)(2), 20.2056(b)-5(f)(1), 25.2523(f)-1(c)(1)(i) and 25.2523(e)-1(f); however, such a provision is not required to qualify for QTIP treatment.[8] It is sufficient for the trust to manifest the Donor's intent that the Spouse be given the requisite income interest in other ways. It is suggested that alternative provisions be used to ensure the Spouse is given the requisite income interest in the trust to qualify for QTIP treatment. For example, a provision in a QTIP trust could provide:

> To the extent that the Settlor's personal representative makes a QTIP election for the Marital Trust, the Settlor intends, by the provisions of this Article, to obtain for his/her estate the advantage of the marital deduction or other similar benefit, if any, which may be available under the Federal estate tax law applicable to the Settlor's estate. No provision of this Agreement shall apply to the Marital Trust to the extent that its being made applicable would defeat the intent expressed in the preceding sentence. Furthermore, the amount of net income distributed to the Settlor's Spouse from the Marital Trust shall never be less than the amount required to be treated as "income" under the marital deduction provisions of the Internal Revenue Code and the Treasury Regulations issued thereunder, and the composition of such net income shall include all items within the meaning of the term "income" in the marital deduction provisions of the Internal Revenue Code and the Treasury Regulations issued thereunder. Accordingly, the Settlor's Spouse shall have substantially that degree of beneficial enjoyment of the trust estate of the Marital Trust during his/her lifetime that the principles of the law of trusts accord to a person who is unqualifiedly

designated as the life beneficiary of a trust and the Trustees shall not exercise their discretion or apply any provision of this Agreement in a manner that is not consistent with this intention. The Trustees shall invest the trust estate of the Marital Trust so it will produce for the Settlor's Spouse during his/her life an income or use that is consistent with the value of the trust estate and with its preservation.

A spendthrift provision that prohibits the voluntary or involuntary transfer of an interest in a trust by a Spouse will not cause the trust to fail to qualify for QTIP treatment. Such a provision is condoned by Treasury Regulations sections 20.2056(b)-5(f)(7) and 25.2523(e)-1(f)(7). Nevertheless, a spendthrift provision that provides that a Spouse's income interest will be forfeited or converted to a discretionary interest would cause a trust to fail to qualify for QTIP treatment.[9]

CLAYTON QTIP TRUSTS

Use of a *Clayton* style QTIP trust is condoned by Treasury Regulations sections 20.2056(b)-7(d)(3) and 20.2056(b)-7(h), Example (6). Under the terms of a *Clayton* style QTIP trust, if a personal representative fails to make a QTIP election over all or a portion of the trust property, such property (or portion thereof) will be disposed of in an alternative disposition that typically would not qualify for a marital deduction such as to a wholly discretionary trust for the benefit of a Spouse and other beneficiaries.[10] Such alternative disposition does not affect the marital deduction with respect to the remaining QTIP property. Many states have disclaimer statutes that prohibit a beneficiary from disclaiming an interest in property if the beneficiary is insolvent.[11] Whether a disclaimer can defeat the claim of a creditor of an insolvent disclaimant may depend on applicable law, including federal tax law.[12] A Spouse's mandatory income interest in a QTIP trust is a valuable interest in property that could be the subject of a disclaimer. Although a spendthrift provision may prove helpful in thwarting the claims of potential creditors to reach a mandatory income stream, a Clayton style QTIP trust could provide additional flexibility to a Spouse experiencing creditor issues. Where applicable law might not permit an insolvent Spouse to disclaim a mandatory income interest, it may not be able to prevent a personal representative (particularly an independent party serving in such capacity) from failing to make a QTIP election, thereby diverting all or a portion of the trust assets to another more protected form of disposition.[13]

For estate and gift tax purposes, Treasury Regulations sections 25.2523(f)-1(d)(1) and (2) and 25.2523(f)-1(f) Examples (10) and (11) permit a Donor of an *inter vivos* QTIP trust to retain a secondary life interest in the trust if the Donor survives the Spouse.[14] Inclusion (or potential inclusion) in the Spouse's estate under Code section 2044 is deemed to cleanse the trust of any taxable strings under sections 2036 and 2038 of the Code. This cleansing process is deemed to occur despite existing authority in the tax law that would seem to mandate a different result.[15]

CLAIMS OF CREDITORS

Under the trust law of most states, a Donor's creditors can reach the Donor's interest in the trust to satisfy claims against the Donor.[16] In most jurisdictions in the United States, one should be mindful that, although the QTIP Regulations result in a transfer for estate and gift tax purposes, a creditor's ability to "bust the trust" should remain the same. In other words, the cleansing process for federal transfer tax purposes should not affect the self-settled nature of the trust for state law purposes. The application of the Self-Settled Trust Doctrine may be avoided by establishing (or moving) this type of QTIP trust in a jurisdiction that has reversed the doctrine. A few states have reversed this doctrine by statute.[17] In such states, a settlor, regardless of his or her state of residence, can establish a self-settled trust and remain eligible to receive discretionary distributions of income and/or principal from the trust. If the statutory guidelines of such states are followed and the formalities of the trust relationship are adhered to, it should be possible for a Donor to obtain some degree of creditor protection for a wholly discretionary interest in the secondary trust. Perhaps greater creditor protection can be achieved by structuring the arrangement in one of many foreign jurisdictions that permit asset protection trusts, but this hardly is a foregone conclusion and not without risks.

If asset protection is important to the Donor, care should be taken in structuring this arrangement and selecting the appropriate jurisdiction to establish the trust. For instance, in the facts of Examples (10) and (11) of Treasury Regulations section 25.2523(f)-1(f), the Donor retains a mandatory right to receive income in the secondary trust. Under the laws of some asset protection trust jurisdictions, the creditor protection benefits of an asset protection trust otherwise granted to a settlor may be negated by retention of a mandatory income interest; however, some states seem to permit retention of a mandatory income interest in a trust by a settlor without the loss of the asset protection benefits granted by the act.[18]

To obtain asset protection benefits for a Donor's secondary life interest in an *inter vivos* QTIP trust, a Donor will need to consider establishing the trust in a jurisdiction that has reversed the Self-Settled Trust Doctrine. Additionally, if the Donor retains a mandatory income interest in the trust, the Donor may be even more limited in the jurisdictions where the trust can be established in order to secure creditor protection under local law.

Many states grant exemptions from the claims of creditors for assets held in certain retirement plan accounts.[19] In some states, this exemption applies not only to the plan participant or account owner but also the designated beneficiary of the account following the owner or participant's death. Designating a QTIP trust as the beneficiary of the proceeds of a retirement account may have an adverse effect by rendering a portion of the value of such account subject to the claims of a beneficiary's creditors, thus stripping away some of the benefit granted by the exemption. For instance, under Florida's statute, all of the income paid from a protected retirement plan continues to be exempt from the claims of a beneficiary's creditors after it is distributed from the plan. Nevertheless, if income from such an account is first required to be distributed to a QTIP trust, it will be necessary for the trustee to distribute such income to or for the benefit of the Spouse. If the Spouse receives the distribution outright, creditors may be able to seize the income in the hands of the Spouse because the Florida exemption may not protect such income. To enhance the asset protection aspects of a QTIP trust one must consider the effect of state law exemptions on the assets that may be used to fund the trust.

Under Examples (7) and (8) of Treasury Regulations section 26.2652-1(a)(5), the estate tax liability imposed on the transfer of the value of the assets in a Reverse QTIP trust can be paid from a source other than the Reverse QTIP trust without adversely affecting the trust's inclusion ratio. For example, the tax liability can be paid from a non-exempt QTIP trust, if any, or from the Spouse's own assets. To the extent possible, the Donor's estate plan and the Spouse's estate plan should take advantage of this rule and properly apportion the payment of the estate tax liability on the assets in a Reverse QTIP trust to a source such as the non-exempt QTIP trust or the Spouse's own assets.

In Field Service Advice 199920016, the issue was whether there had been a disposition of a Spouse's income interest in a QTIP trust under §2519 of the Code because of an investment of the trust assets in a family limited partnership (FLP). The Spouse and her daughter were co-trustees of the QTIP trust and the Spouse, her daughter, two of her daughter's children and the QTIP trust formed the FLP. The daughter and her two children received general partnership interests in exchange for capital contributions of cash to the FLP and the daughter also received a limited partnership interest in exchange for a capital contribution of certain assets to the FLP. The Spouse and the QTIP trust received limited partnership interests in exchange for capital contributions of cash and securities. The daughter was appointed as the managing partner of the FLP. As managing partner, she possessed "sole discretion with respect to distribution decisions" from the FLP.[20] The limited partners were prohibited from participating in the operation or management of the business of the partnership. Interests in the FLP were freely transferable to parents and descendants of partners, however, a transfer to any other person or entity would trigger an option in the other partners to purchase the assigned interest for 70 percent of its fair market value. In holding that the contribution of trust assets to the FLP was not a disposition under Code section 2519, the F.S.A. provided:

> [Spouse]'s conversion of the trust assets into FLP interests is not the typical disposal of the income interest envisioned under the provisions of section 2519. By converting the trust assets into FLP interests, she has disposed of the corpus rather than the qualifying income interest. Facially this appears to be a permissible conversion. Thus, in order to invoke 2519, the conversion of the trust assets must work such a limitation on her right to the income as to amount to a disposition of that income. Although the conversion to partnership interests could yield this result, it does not necessarily follow. An investment in a partnership, despite possible restrictions on distribution, could be, under the right circumstances, a very lucrative investment.

The ruling recognized that while the managing partner had the power to withhold distributions from the FLP, under the facts of the case the Spouse had continued to receive the same proportionate share of the income from the assets in the FLP. Additionally, the Spouse did nothing that affected her right to receive the income from the trust. Finally, the ruling recognized that a QTIP trust "can be originally funded with partnership interests or, for that matter, closely held stock" and those types of investments could possibly distribute no income in a given year.[21] According to the ruling, "The right to annual income is not tantamount to a fixed right to yearly income, rather it is a right to any income to the extent it exists, on at least an annual basis."[22]

Providing the trustee of a QTIP trust with the flexibility to invest trust assets in limited liability entities such as corporations, limited partnerships and limited liability companies can enable the trustee to better protect the assets of the trust from potential creditors, provide additional flexibility to structure investment of the trust assets and provide opportunities to reduce the Spouse's estate and gift tax liability. This discretion should not hinder the qualification of the trust for the marital deduction.[23] Thus, to enhance the assets protection aspects of a QTIP trust, the trustee should be given the discretion to invest trust assets in limited liability entities such as corporations, limited partnerships and limited liability companies.

Additional planning opportunities may exist if the QTIP trust is designed to permit the donee spouse to assign his or her income interest in the trust.[24] To qualify for the marital deduction, a QTIP trust must be drafted to meet the requirements set forth in the Code. For example, the Spouse must be given the right to receive all of the income from the trust at least annually and no other person is permitted to have a current interest in the trust during the Spouse's life. Nevertheless, QTIP trusts are too often drafted to provide the Spouse with interests or rights that can be attractive to creditors of the Spouse. These rights are not necessary to qualify the trust for the marital deduction and in many respects are contrary to the fundamental purpose of a trust, that is, to protect the trust assets from creditors, indiscretions and inability of the beneficiary.

INTER VIVOS QUALIFIED TERMINABLE INTEREST PROPERTY TRUSTS

An *inter vivos* QTIP trust ("QTIP Trust") can be created by a settlor for the settlor's spouse by gifting assets to such trust, specifically assets valued up to an amount designed to utilize the creator spouse's remaining applicable exclusion amount. A QTIP election *must* be made with respect to any gift to this QTIP Trust. As a result of the QTIP election, the trust will be includible in the estate of the settlor's spouse for estate tax purposes.[25] The gift by the settlor to the trust will (must - it would seem) qualify for the unlimited marital deduction. The

QTIP Trust may contain provisions that provide for the donor-settlor following the donee-spouse's death. The trust assets should not be subject to the claims of the donor's creditors although the trust is self-settled. The following discussion highlights fourteen states that currently have QTIP Trust legislation,[26] with a particular focus on Florida and less of an emphasis on the states with QTIP Trust legislation and domestic asset protection trust legislation.[27] While Arizona became the first state to enact such stand-alone legislation,[28] Indiana is the latest.[29]

Florida

Although the term "self-settled trust" is not used in the Florida Trust Code, section 736.0505 of the Florida Statutes establishes rules related to revocable and irrevocable trusts created by a settlor where the settlor retains a beneficial interest in the trust. The inclusion of a spendthrift provision is irrelevant.[30]

Under Florida law, the assets of a revocable trust are subject to the claims of the settlor's creditors during the settlor's lifetime, however, only to the extent such assets would not be exempt from creditors' claims if held directly by the settlor.[31] Therefore, a settlor's homestead held by his or her revocable trust should remain exempt under Florida law (but not necessarily Federal bankruptcy law).[32]

With respect to the assets of an irrevocable trust, a creditor or assignee of a settlor may reach the maximum amount that can be distributed to or for the benefit of the settlor.[33] If there is more than one settlor, the amount that may be reached may not exceed the portion of the irrevocable trust attributable to the settlor's contribution. Subsection (1)(b) conforms to the holding in *In re Witlin*,[34] that is, that a beneficiary who is also the settlor may not use the trust to shield his assets from creditors.[35] If the trustee has the discretion to distribute the entire income and principal to the settlor, the effect is as if the settlor had not created the trust for purposes of placing the settlor's assets beyond the reach of his or her creditors.[36]

Drafting irrevocable trusts as "wholly-owned grantor trusts" for federal income tax purposes is a common technique used by estate planners to enhance the benefits of such trusts by effectively permitting tax-free gifts when the grantor pays income taxes attributable to trust assets. Still, it may be desirable to grant the trustee a discretionary power to pay such taxes or reimburse the settlor. Although not found in the Uniform Trust Code, the Florida Trust Code ensures that such discretionary power will not subject an irrevocable trust to the claims of creditors under the general rule established in Florida Statutes section 736.0505(1)(c).[37] This provision provides in relevant part:

> [T]he assets of an *irrevocable* trust may not be subject to the claims of an existing or subsequent creditor or assignee of the settlor, in whole or in part, solely because of the existence of a discretionary power granted to the trustee by the terms of the trust, or any other provision of law, to pay directly to the taxing authorities or to reimburse the settlor for any tax on trust income or principal which is payable by the settlor under the law imposing such tax.[38]

As a result of this provision, the state legislature may have unwittingly added Florida to the list of asset protection states. Normally such a decision is made with substantially more consideration. Issues related to this provision include:

1. There is no time limit on reimbursement. Thus, in theory a trustee can accrue a reimbursement account for several decades and reimburse the settlor for a tax liability incurred many years in the past. While policy arguments can be made to permit reimbursement for a tax liability incurred within the statute of limitations for a tax return, permitting reimbursement for tax liability incurred beyond that point is ridiculous unless the state has made a conscientious decision to become an asset protection trust jurisdiction. Such a decision was not the case in this instance.

2. As a result of the issue identified above, Florida has unwittingly added a new exemption to its laws. Practitioners are certainly obligated to discuss the use of this potentially substantial exemption with their clients.

3. The provision could have been drafted to prevent abuse by mandating the formula for determining the maximum amount that the trustee could distribute to the settlor. Some methods of constructing such a formula might have been to mandate that the trustee can pay up to:

    a. *the highest marginal rate of tax.* Thus, the income generated by the assets in the trust is assumed to be taxed at the highest rate applicable to the settlor.

    b. *its proportional share of the tax liability.* Thus, all income generated by the assets in the trust is assumed to be taxed at the settlor's average tax rate.

    c. *the lowest possible tax rate applicable.* Thus, the settlor's remaining income from sources other than the assets in the trust is assumed to be taxed at the higher rates applicable to the settlor.

4. Although potentially difficult under certain circumstances, the provision could have prevented abuse by directing that any tax payments be made directly to the appropriate taxing authority rather than reimbursing the settlor for such amounts. Of course, one could argue that such a provision would be too restrictive.

5. Is the payment by the settlor of the settlor's tax liability subject to the fraudulent transfer statute? The funds could one day be returned to the settlor pursuant to a discretionary distribution. At first blush, it would seem that such payment should not be a fraudulent transfer, however, inequitable results will be caused to a creditor because of this provision if the fraudulent transfer statute is not applicable. How will the bankruptcy law treat this provision?

6. Can distributions be made from the reimbursement account *for the benefit of* the grantor rather than having to be distributed directly to him? The statute provides no guidance in this respect.

7. The provision applies even though the grantor trust may be designed to receive gifts that are incomplete for federal gift tax purposes. This can lead to serious abuse of the statute.

8. A tax reimbursement provision is not appropriate for use in every type of grantor trust. For instance, such a provision should never be used in a general power of appointment marital trust,[39] a QTIP trust,[40] a Section 2642(c) trust or Section 2503(c) trust. Additionally, if it is necessary for a trust to

qualify as a skip person for GST tax purposes, a tax reimbursement provision should not be included in the trust agreement.[41]

During the period a *Crummey* Power or other power of withdrawal may be exercised, the powerholder is treated in the same manner as the settlor of a revocable trust to the extent of the property subject to the power.[42] Since the purpose of this commentary is to examine the types of self-settled trusts that are now permitted to be used in Florida to shield trust assets from the creditors of a settlor, a discussion of the treatment of *Crummey* Powers and other types of withdrawal rights granted to third parties in a trust is beyond the scope of this article. The authors would respectfully point out that the peculiar characteristics of this provision may fundamentally change the way *Crummey* Powers and other lapsed withdrawal rights are taxed for federal income tax purposes.

The asset protection benefits of marriage are numerous and in the case of trust law in Florida were increased when Section 736.0505(3) became effective. Section 736.0505(3) Florida Statutes provides:

- Subject to the provisions of s. 726.105, for purposes of this section, the assets in:

  a. A trust described in s. 2523(e) of the Internal Revenue Code of 1986, as amended, or a trust for which the election described in s. 2523(f) of the Internal Revenue Code of 1986, as amended, has been made; and

  b. Another trust, to the extent that the assets in the other trust are attributable to a trust described in paragraph (a),

  shall, *after* the death of the settlor's spouse, be deemed to have been contributed by the settlor's spouse and not by the settlor.

This provision creates *an exception* to the self-settled trust doctrine. It protects the assets in a self-settled trust from the claims of a creditor of the settlor. The exception relates to any trust interest for the benefit of the settlor that is established after the death of the settlor's spouse when the settlor created and funded an *inter vivos* general power of appointment or QTIP marital trust for the initial benefit of the settlor's spouse and the trust interest for the settlor follows the death of the settlor's spouse. A settlor can fund an *inter vivos* QTIP trust for the settlor's spouse by gifting assets to such trust. A QTIP election *must* be made with respect to any gift to this QTIP trust. As a result of the QTIP election, the trust will be includible in the estate of the settlor's spouse for estate tax purposes.[43] The gift by the settlor to the trust will (must - it would seem) qualify for the unlimited marital deduction. The QTIP Trust may contain provisions that provide for the settlor following the donee-spouse's death. The trust assets should not be subject to the claims of the settlor's creditors although the trust is self-settled. According to Section 736.0505(3), the settlor would *not be treated* as the settlor of the trust. Other considerations include:

1. **The Reciprocal Trust Doctrine.** Can the reciprocal trust doctrine be applied to uncross trusts created contemporaneously by spouses for the benefit of each other?[44] The reciprocal trust doctrine is a theory that treats two trusts as created in consideration of the other, such that the settlor of trust 1 is deemed in law to be the "settlor" of trust 2, and as having made a transfer under which the settlor retained an interest in the income from the property of trust 2 for life such that trust 2 is includible in the settlor's gross estate.[45]

   If the reciprocal trust doctrine is applicable, what period is sufficient between one spouse establishing and funding a trust and the other spouse doing the same to avoid the application of the doctrine? Would the federal government be concerned about the application of the reciprocal trust doctrine in this instance?

   If Florida courts will apply the reciprocal trust doctrine in a manner similar to the way it is applied under Federal tax law, it would seem possible to structure an arrangement with sufficient care to avoid a problem at the state level. It should be noted, however, that there is no existing guidance on this issue in Florida.

2. **Recommending the QTIP.** It may be malpractice to not recommend that spouses each establish QTIP trusts for the other, although this is far from certain and will depend upon the specific facts of the situation. Any estate planning conference with clients should certainly now include a discussion of the benefits of creating a QTIP Trust in Florida under Florida Statutes section 736.0505(3) by at least one spouse.

3. **Making the QTIP Election.** The protection afforded to the successor trust or trusts is

dependent upon a Federal tax election in the case of a QTIP trust and the trust containing the proper provisions to ensure it qualifies as a marital trust under either of Code sections 2523(e) and 2523(f).[46]

In PLR 201025021, the Service apparently mistakenly granted the taxpayer an extension to make a QTIP election for a gift to a QTIP Trust. Could a private letter ruling issued by the Service affect the substantive law of Florida in regards to a trust created pursuant to Florida Statutes section 736.0505(3)?[47] It should be noted that PLR 201025021 was revoked by PLR 201109012 and then reinstated in PLR 201233011, which granted the taxpayer relief pursuant to Code section 7805(b). If the *inter vivos* QTIP election is not **timely** made, the election is ineffective, and this defect cannot be cured because the requirement of timely filing is **statutory**. This is unlike the testamentary QTIP election, which can be made late on a **first-filed** federal estate tax return, even if it is filed late. Failure to timely file the QTIP election has been held to be **malpractice**.

a.   Nevertheless, it should serve as a lesson to attorneys who plan in this area and to litigators attacking and defending such trusts that rulings issued by the Service and decisions in tax cases in court can affect the outcome of litigation under Florida law. For example:

b.   What is the purpose of the specific reference to Florida Statutes section 726.105? Does this preclude the application of section 726.106?

c.   How will this provision be applied to property added to the QTIP trust during the donee-spouse's lifetime that cannot qualify for the marital deduction?

d.   How will this provision be applied to property held in a trust for which only a partial QTIP election has been made?

4.   **Florida Practice.** Serious public policy concerns may exist regarding the application of this statute and similar to Section 736.0505(1)(c), it is questionable whether the Florida legislature carefully considered some of the ramifications

of the statute it enacted. For example, consider the situation where A creates and funds a trust for the benefit of his spouse B. A retains a secondary life interest following B's death that can either be wholly discretionary or include a mandatory income interest for potential QTIP treatment based on a formula or a *Clayton* type QTIP election.[48] Two months after the gift A and B are involved in a car crash. B dies and three unrelated individuals are severely injured in the accident. A is at fault. A's gifts to the QTIP Trust were not fraudulent under the applicable Florida fraudulent transfer rule. At the time of the accident B has not filed his gift tax return. The gift tax return may not be due for almost a year or more in some cases if the gifts were made in early January. Whether A's creditors from the car accident can collect on a judgment from the assets in the trust will depend on whether A makes a QTIP election. Is this a fair result?

What happens if there is a disposition of the donee-spouse's income interest in the original trust prior to the donee-spouse's death? For gift tax purposes it might be difficult to imagine a donee-spouse renouncing his or her income interest, however, it might happen for other non-tax reasons. If the assets in the original QTIP Trust pass to a successor trust or trusts for the benefit of the settlor-spouse, it appears that the assets in the trust will not be protected from the settlor-spouse's creditors during the donee-spouse's lifetime. This contingency should be addressed when drafting the trust agreement.

In any states with QTIP Trust legislation, practitioners should carefully review their Uniform Disclaimer of Property Interests Act to see how it may benefit a client seeking to implement this type of trust arrangement.

Section 736.0505(3) also presents some unique estate planning opportunities. Practitioners should carefully review *Bonner Est. v. U.S.*,[49] and *Mellinger Est. v. Comm'r*,[50] and similar cases in an effort to uncover these potential planning opportunities.

5.   **Additional Planning Concerns.** This strategy cannot work if the donee-spouse is not a US citizen as the transfer would not qualify for the marital deduction.[51] If the donee-spouse and

settlor-spouse divorce, they may be unaware of the potential continuing obligations of the settlor of a QTIP Trust to pay income taxes on trust capital gains post-divorce, despite the settlor having no right to trust distributions or access to trust assets to pay such capital gains taxes.[52]

If the initial transfer of the assets to the trust by the settlor was a fraudulent conveyance, the protections discussed, above, would be superseded by fraudulent transfer law. The extended bankruptcy fraudulent transfer period of ten years applicable to transfers to self-settled trusts should apply to this trust arrangement.[53] Since little or no case law exists to provide guidance on the application of section 548(e)(1) to this type of trust arrangement, practitioners can only speculate on this issue.[54] Furthermore, while in most instances the use of a QTIP trust as the lead interest trust would be more attractive so that the underlying assets held in the trust are protected from the donee-spouse's creditors, in regards to section 548(e)(1), it may be more prudent to use a general power of appointment trust as the lead interest trust. Although not completely clear, it may be that the use of such a trust would cleanse the successor trust from the application of the ten-year rule under section 548(e)(1).

It is important to note that the mandatory income interest in the trust remains vulnerable to attack by a creditor. While the interest itself may be protected by use of a spendthrift provision, income distributed directly to the beneficiary is certainly at risk for attachment.

If the property transferred to the trust has a *situs* outside of Florida that is located in a jurisdiction that has the Self-Settled Trust Doctrine, the law of that jurisdiction would most likely apply to such property held in the trust. In such a situation the asset protection features of this trust might not be available to the settlor following the donee-spouse's death. As previously stated, in Florida, the protection afforded to the successor trust or trusts is dependent upon a Federal tax election in the case of a QTIP trust and the trust containing the proper provisions to ensure it qualifies as a marital trust under either of Code sections 2523(e) and 2523(f). This does not appear to be the case in other states that have or may soon have similar laws.

Arizona

Arizona Revised Statutes Article 14-10505A.2. provides in relevant part:

- Subject to the requirements of this section, with respect to an irrevocable trust, a creditor or assignee of the settlor may reach the maximum amount that can be distributed to or for the settlor's benefit. If a trust has more than one settlor, the amount the creditor or assignee of a particular settlor may reach may not exceed the settlor's interest in the portion of the trust attributable to that settlor's contribution. This paragraph does not apply to any trust from which any distribution to the settlor can be made pursuant to the exercise of a power of appointment held by a third party or abrogate otherwise applicable laws relating to community property. A creditor of a settlor:

  a. Shall not reach any trust property based on a trustee's, trust protector's or third party's power, whether or not discretionary, to pay or reimburse the settlor for any income tax on trust income or trust principal that is payable by the settlor under the law imposing the tax or to pay the tax directly to any taxing authority.

  b. Is not entitled to any payment or reimbursement that is to be made directly to any taxing authority.[55]

Arizona Revised Statutes Article 14-10505E provides in relevant part:

- For the purposes of this section, amounts and property contributed to the following trusts are not deemed to have been contributed by the settlor, and a person who would otherwise be treated as a settlor or a deemed settlor of the following trusts shall not be treated as a settlor:

  1. An irrevocable *inter vivos* marital trust that is treated as qualified terminable interest property under section 2523(f) of the internal revenue code if the settlor is a beneficiary of the trust after the death of the settlor's spouse.

  2. An irrevocable *inter vivos* marital trust that is treated as a general power of appointment trust under section 2523(e) of the internal revenue code if the settlor is a beneficiary of the trust after the death of the settlor's spouse.

3. An irrevocable *inter vivos* trust for the settlor's spouse that does not qualify for the gift tax marital deduction if the settlor is a beneficiary of the trust after the death of the settlor's spouse.

4. An irrevocable *inter vivos* trust created by the settlor's spouse for the benefit of the settlor, regardless of whether or when the settlor also created an irrevocable *inter vivos* trust with respect to which such spouse is a beneficiary.[56]

Arizona Revised Statutes Article 14-10505F provides in relevant part:

• For the purposes of subsection E, a person is a beneficiary whether so named under the initial trust instrument or through the exercise by that person's spouse or by another person of a limited or general power of appointment.[57]

Unlike Florida, Arizona, as well as several other states,[58] statutorily provide that the initial settlor of any irrevocable *inter vivos* trust created for the settlor's spouse will not be deemed to have been contributed by the settlor if the settlor is the beneficiary of the trust after the death of the settlor's spouse, even if there is no QTIP election. At first glance, the Arizona statute appears to create great asset protection and the possibility of the enhanced estate tax benefits that are afforded to credit shelter trusts as compared to QTIP Trusts (*i.e.*, all appreciation of assets in the credit shelter trust would avoid future estate taxes and regardless of whether the applicable exclusion amount is reduced the assets in a credit shelter trust should not be subject to estate tax inclusion). There are, however, two potential pitfalls to the statute:

1. the trust must have its *situs* in Arizona and be subject to income tax there; and

2. there is no provision similar to Treasury Regulations section 25.2523(f)- 1(f), Example 11 that assures that the initial settlor will not be subject to estate tax under Code sections 2036 or 2038. As a result, the IRS could take the position that despite state law, the initial settlor has an interest under sections 2036 and 2038 of the Code, resulting in estate tax inclusion.[59]

It would also seem possible under Arizona law to design the lead trust without a mandatory income distribution provision so all distributions to the spouse

could be solely within the trustee's discretion. Perhaps the lead trust could also be designed such that gifts to the trust would not constitute completed gifts for Federal gift tax purposes.

North Carolina

On June 27, 2011, a new subsection (c) was added to N.C.G.S. section 36C-5-505 to provide:

• Subject to Article 3A of Chapter 39 of the General Statutes, for purposes of this section, if the settlor is a beneficiary of the following trusts after the death of the settlor's spouse, the property of the trusts shall, after the death of the settlor's spouse, be deemed to have been contributed by the settlor's spouse and not by the settlor:

a. An irrevocable *inter vivos* marital trust that is treated as a general power of appointment trust described in section 2523(e) of the Internal Revenue Code.

b. An irrevocable *inter vivos* marital trust that is treated as qualified terminable interest property under section 2523(f) of the Internal Revenue Code.

c. *An irrevocable inter vivos trust of which the settlor's spouse is the sole beneficiary during the lifetime of the settlor's spouse but which does not qualify for the federal gift tax marital deduction.* [Emphasis added.]

d. Another trust, to the extent that the property of the other trust is attributable to property passing from a trust described in subdivision (1), (2), or (3) of this subsection.

For purposes of this subsection, the settlor is a beneficiary whether so named under the initial trust instrument or through the exercise of a limited or general power of appointment.

Note that the North Carolina self-settled trust statute, similar to the statute in Arizona, does not require the initial trust to qualify for the Federal gift tax marital deduction. It would also seem possible under this statute to design the lead trust without a mandatory income distribution provision so all distributions to the spouse could be solely within the trustee's discretion. Perhaps the lead trust could also be designed such that gifts to the trust would not constitute completed gifts for Federal gift tax purposes.

Like Arizona, a QTIP election is not required.[60] North Carolina might be attractive as a jurisdiction to create QTIP Trusts as it does not have a Rule Against Perpetuities.[61] However, North Carolina is one of five U.S. states to exert its jurisdiction to assess income tax on non-grantor trusts determined by the residence of the beneficiaries of the trusts.[62] It should be noted that the fiduciary income tax was held to be unconstitutional as imposed upon the income earned and accumulated by an out-of-state trust in *The Kimberly Rice Kaestner 1992 Family Trust v. North Carolina Dep't of Rev.*[63]

Michigan

Effective April 1, 2010, Section 700.7506(4) of the Michigan Compiled Laws provides in relevant part:

- An individual who creates a trust shall not be considered a settlor with regard to the individual's retained beneficial interest in the trust that follows the termination of the individual's spouse's prior beneficial interest in the trust if all of the following apply:

  a. The individual creates, or has created, the trust for the benefit of the individual's spouse.

  b. The trust is treated as qualified terminable interest property under section 2523(f) of the internal revenue code, 26 USC 2523.

  c. The individual retains a beneficial interest in the trust income, trust principal, or both, which beneficial interest follows the termination of the individual's spouse's prior beneficial interest in the trust.[64]

Little has been written by Michigan practitioners on Michigan's QTIP trust statute. A discussion on Michigan trust law is outside the scope of this commentary.

Maryland

Effective October 1, 2013, Section 14-116 of the Maryland Estates and Trust Code provides in relevant part:

1. Interests in grantor and qualified terminable interest property trusts.

   a. In general. An individual who creates a trust may not be considered the settlor of that trust with regard to the individual's interest in the trust if:

      (1) That interest is the authority of the trustee under the trust instrument or any other provision of law to pay or reimburse the individual for any tax on trust income or trust principal that is payable by the individual under the law imposing that tax; or

      (2) All of the following apply:

         (i) The individual creates or has created the trust for the benefit of the individual's spouse;

         (ii) The trust is treated as qualified terminable interest property under §2523(f) of the Internal Revenue Code of 1986; and

         (iii) The individual's interest in the trust income, trust principal, or both follows the termination of the spouse's prior interest in the trust.

   b. Rights of creditors. A creditor of an individual described in subsection (a) of this section may not attach, exercise, reach, or otherwise compel distribution of:

      (1) Any principal or income of the trust;

      (2) Any principal or income of any other trust to the extent that the property held in the other trust is attributable to a trust described in subsection (a)(2) of this section;

      (3) The individual's interest in the trust; or

      (4) The individual's interest in any other trust to the extent that the property held in the other trust is attributable to a trust described in subsection (a)(2) of this section.

(c) Construction of section. This section may not be construed to affect any State law with respect to a fraudulent transfer by an individual to a trustee.[65]

Maryland law includes similarities to Florida, including each's susceptibility to fraudulent transfer laws and limitations with regards to a proactive QTIP election.[66]

Kentucky

Effective July 15, 2014, Section 386B.5-020(8)(a) of the Kentucky Uniform Trust Code provides in relevant part:

- (8)(a) For the purposes of this section, amounts and property contributed to the following trusts are not deemed to have been contributed by the settlor of the trust, and a person who would otherwise be treated as a settlor or a deemed settlor of the following trusts shall not be treated as a settlor:

  1. An irrevocable *inter vivos* marital trust that is treated as qualified terminable interest property under Section 2523(f) of the Internal Revenue Code of 1986, as amended, if the settlor is a beneficiary of the trust after the death of the settlor's spouse;

  2. An irrevocable *inter vivos* marital trust that is treated as a general power of appointment trust under Section 2523(e) of the Internal Revenue Code if the settlor is a beneficiary of the trust after the death of the settlor's spouse;

  3. An irrevocable *inter vivos* trust for the spouse of the settlor that does not qualify for the gift tax marital deduction if the settlor is a beneficiary of the trust only after the death of the settlor's spouse.

- (b) For the purposes of this subsection, a person is a beneficiary whether so named under the initial trust instrument or through the exercise by that person's spouse or by another person of a limited or general power of appointment.

- (c) For purposes of this section, the settlor shall be any person who:

  1. Created the trust;

  2. Contributed property to the trust; or

  3. Is deemed to have contributed property to the trust.[67]

Kentucky's statute is almost identical to the Arizona statute except for Arizona's provision authorizing "reciprocal" spousal trusts and the definition of "settlor" in Section 386B.5-020(8)(c), Kentucky Revised Statutes.[68]

South Carolina

Effective January 1, 2014, Section 62-7-505 of the South Carolina Trust Code provides in relevant part:

(a) Whether or not the terms of a trust contain a spendthrift provision, the following rules apply:

  (2) With respect to an irrevocable trust, a creditor or assignee of the settlor may reach the maximum amount that can be distributed to or for the settlor's benefit. If a trust has more than one settlor, the amount the creditor or assignee of a particular settlor may reach may not exceed the settlor's interest in the portion of the trust attributable to that settlor's contribution.

(b) For purposes of this section:

  (2) the assets in a trust that are attributable to a contribution to an *inter vivos* marital deduction trust described in either Section 2523(e) or (f) of the Internal Revenue Code of 1986, after the death of the spouse of the settlor of the *inter vivos* marital deduction trust are deemed to have been contributed by the settlor's spouse and not by the settlor.

It should be noted that even South Carolina practitioners have cautioned whether a non-South Carolina resident should create such a trust.[69]

Oregon

Effective 2013, Section 130.315 of the Oregon Uniform Trust Code provides in relevant part:

(4) The assets of an irrevocable trust that are attributable to a contribution to an *inter vivos* marital deduction trust described in section

2523(e) or (f) of the Internal Revenue Code, as in effect on December 31, 2012, after the death of the spouse of the settlor of the *inter vivos* marital deduction trust shall be deemed to have been contributed by the settlor's spouse and not by the settlor.

(5) The assets of an irrevocable trust for the benefit of a person, including the settlor, are not subject to claims of creditors of the settlor to the extent that the property of the trust is subject to a presently exercisable general power of appointment held by a person other than the settlor.

(6) Subsections (2) and (3) of this section do not apply to a person other than a settlor who is a beneficiary of a revocable or irrevocable trust and who is also a trustee of the trust, if the power to withdraw for the person's own benefit is limited by an ascertainable standard.[70]

Little has been written by Oregon practitioners on Oregon's QTIP trust statute. A discussion on Oregon trust law is outside the scope of this commentary.

Texas

Effective September 1, 2013, Section §112.035 of the Texas Property Code provides in relevant part:

(g) For the purposes of this section, property contributed to the following trusts is not considered to have been contributed by the settlor, and a person who would otherwise be treated as a settlor or a deemed settlor of the following trusts may not be treated as a settlor:

(1) an irrevocable *inter vivos* marital trust if:

(A) the settlor is a beneficiary of the trust after the death of the settlor's spouse; and (B) the trust is treated as:

(i) qualified terminable interest property under Section 2523(f), Internal Revenue Code of 1986; or

(ii) a general power of appointment trust under Section 2523(e), Internal Revenue Code of 1986;

(2) an irrevocable *inter vivos* trust for the settlor's spouse if the settlor is a beneficiary of the trust after the death of the settlor's spouse; or

(3) an irrevocable trust for the benefit of a person:

(A) if the settlor is the person's spouse, regardless of whether or when the person was the settlor of an irrevocable trust for the benefit of that spouse; or

(B) to the extent that the property of the trust was subject to a general power of appointment in another person.

(h) For the purposes of Subsection (g), a person is a beneficiary whether named a beneficiary:

(1) under the initial trust instrument; or

(2) through the exercise of a limited or general power of appointment by:

(A) that person's spouse; or

(B) another person.[71]

Like in Arizona, no QTIP election is required in Texas; Texas practitioners have discussed that there has been no documented reasoning for such statutory language.[72]

Indiana

Indian House Bill No. 1083, introduced January 5, 2016, became effective July 1, 2016. It added rules for the interpretation of QTIP Trusts, providing that, under certain circumstances, an individual who contributes assets to a trust and whose spouse is a beneficiary of the trust at the time of the contribution may not be considered to be or treated as a settlor of the trust.[73] The full text of Indiana Statutes section 30-4-2.1-18 provides:

(a) This section shall be liberally construed to carry out its intent.

(b) This section applies to:

(1) a trust created after June 30, 2016; and

(2) any rights or interests created after June 30, 2016, in a trust existing before July 1, 2016.

(c) The following definitions apply throughout this section:

(1) "Donee spouse" means the individual who is:

(A) the spouse of the donor spouse at the time of the donor spouse's contribution to a trust; and

(B) a beneficiary of the trust to which the donor spouse contributes assets.

(2) "Donor spouse" means an individual who contributes assets to a trust that provides that the individual's spouse is a beneficiary at the time of the contribution.

(3) "General power of appointment" has the meaning set forth in Section 2041(b)(1) of the Internal Revenue Code (26 U.S.C. 2041(b)(1)) or Section 2514(c) of the Internal Revenue Code (26 U.S.C. 2514(c)).

(4) "Internal Revenue Code" means the Internal Revenue Code of 1986 (26 U.S.C. 1 et seq.), as amended.

(d) An individual described in any of the following may not be considered to be or treated as a settlor contributing assets to the trust described in the same subdivision:

(1) A donor spouse with respect to an irrevocable *inter vivos* marital trust that contains the provisions required under Section 2523(f) of the Internal Revenue Code (26 U.S.C. 2523(f)), regardless of whether the donor spouse is a beneficiary of the trust after termination of the donee spouse's interests in the trust.

(2) A donor spouse with respect to an irrevocable *inter vivos* marital trust that contains the provisions required under Section 2523(e) of the Internal Revenue Code (26 U.S.C. 2523(e)), regardless of whether the donor spouse is a beneficiary of the trust after the termination of the donee spouse's interests in the trust.

(3) An individual with respect to an irrevocable trust in which the individual is a beneficiary and the individual's spouse is the settlor, regardless of whether or when the individual is the settlor of a second irrevocable trust in which the individual's spouse is a beneficiary.

(e) For purposes of this section, an individual is a beneficiary of a trust if the individual:

(1) is named as a beneficiary of the trust under the initial trust; or

(2) acquires a beneficial interest in the trust as a result of the exercise of a limited or general power of appointment by a donee spouse, beneficiary, or other person.

(f) An individual who contributes assets to a trust may not be considered to be or treated as a settlor of the trust because, under the trust instrument or any other provision or law:

(1) the trustee may pay or reimburse the individual for a tax on trust income or principal that is taxable to the individual under chapter 1, 2, or 2A of the Internal Revenue Code and comparable income taxes imposed by state and local taxing authorities;

(2) the trustee may apply trust assets to payment of premiums on the life of the individual or the individual's spouse, within the meaning of Section 677(a)(3) of the Internal Revenue Code (26 U.S.C. 677(a)(3)); or

(3) the individual has a power described in Section 675 of the Internal Revenue Code (26 U.S.C. 675).

Unlike Florida, Indiana's statute does not contain the proactive statutory language requiring a QTIP election.[74]

POTENTIAL EFFECTS OF VOIDABLE TRANSFER LAW ON QTIP TRUSTS

As noted in the discussion of Florida law, above, if the initial transfer of assets to the QTIP Trust by the settlor was a fraudulent conveyance, the protections described previously would be superseded by fraudulent transfer law, as well as the extended bankruptcy fraudulent transfer period applicable to transfers to self-settled trusts.[75]

Adopted by the National Conference of Commissioners on Uniform State Laws, the Uniform Voidable Transactions Act (UVTA) is billed as the replacement of the Uniform Fraudulent Transfers Act.[76] As of August, 2016, the UVTA has been adopted in nine states – California, Idaho, New Mexico, North Dakota, Minnesota, Iowa, Kentucky, North Carolina and Georgia – and introduced in Indiana, Massachusetts, Michigan, New Jersey, New York, Rhode Island and South Carolina.[77]

The criticisms of the UVTA have focused on the official comment's application on various estate planning techniques: techniques which are allowed in one state, however, not allowed or recognized in another.[78] For QTIP Trusts in particular, Sections 4 and 10 of the UVTA could potentially affect their use by a debtor in state X who formed a QTIP Trust using the laws of state Y, or moves to state X from state Y.[79] Thus, in a state that has no QTIP Trust legislation like California and New York, and then adopts the UVTA, query whether the state has unintentionally outlawed QTIP Trusts?

CONCLUSION

A QTIP Trust provides practitioners with another trust option, albeit more akin to an asset protection trust. Funding a QTIP Trust during a married couple's lifetime makes use of the applicable exclusion amount of the donee spouse while enabling the grantor to have access should the beneficiary spouse predecease.

CHAPTER ENDNOTES

1. Unless otherwise indicated, all section references are to the Internal Revenue Code of 1986 (hereinafter the "Code").

2. For more on the potential uses of inter vivos QTIP trusts, see, e.g., Richard S. Franklin, "Lifetime QTIPs: Why They Should Be Ubiquitous in Estate Planning?" 65th Annual Tulane Tax Institute (2016).

3. See e.g., Rev. Rul. 75-440, 1975-2 C.B. 372; TAM 199932001; and PLR 8440037.

4. Fla. Stat. §738.303(2).

5. Restatement (Second) of Trusts §155(1).

6. Restatement (Second) of Trusts §155(1), cmt. c

7. Restatement (Second) of Trusts §155(1), cmt. e.

8. See e.g., TAMs 8638004 and 9237009.

9. See e.g., Miller v. U.S., 267 F. Supp. 326 (M.D. Fla. 1967); and TAM 8248008.

10. A Clayton style QTIP trust gets its name from the trust in Estate of Clayton v. Com'r., 976 F.2d 1486 (5th Cir. 1992). A line of related cases with similar holdings also exist. See e.g., Robertson Est. v. Com'r., 15 F.3d 779 (8th Cir. 1994), rev'g 98 T.C. 678 (1992); Spencer Est. v. Com'r., 43 F.3d 226 (6th Cir. 1995), rev'g 64 T.C.M. 937 (1992); and Clack Est. v. Com'r., 106 T.C. 131, acq. in result only, 1996-2 C.B. 1 (AOD 1996-011).

11. See e.g., Fla. Stat. §739.402.

12. See e.g., Drye v. U.S., 528 U.S. 49 (1999); Choate v. Tubbs, W.D. Tenn., No. 01-1288-T, 4/4/03; Laughlin v. Nouveau Body and Tan (In re Laughlin), 602 F.3d 417 (5th Cir. 2010).

13. Of course, this planning may come with a price, that is, the potential loss of the use of the credit for the tax on prior transfers under §2013 of the Code and the loss of the benefit of the marital deduction.

14. See also PLR 200406004.

15. See e.g., Herzog v. Com'r., 116 F.2d 591 (2d Cir. 1941) (but c.f., Vanderbilt Credit Corp. v. Chase Manhattan Bank, N.A., 100 A.D.2d 544, 473 N.Y.S.2d 242 (2d Dept. 1984)); Wells v. Com'r., T.C. Memo 1981-574; Estate of Uhl, 241 F.2d 867 (7th Cir. 1957); Estate of German v. U.S., 85-1 U.S.T.C. ¶13,610 (Ct. Cl. 1985); Outwin v. Com'r., 76 T.C. 153 (1981); Paolozzi v. Com'r., 23 T.C. 182 (1954); Estate of Paxton v. Com'r., 86 T.C. 785 (1986); Rev. Rul. 76-103, 1976-1 C.B. 293; Rev. Rul. 77-378, 1977-2 C.B. 347; PLR 9332006; PLR 8829030; PLR 8037116; PLR 9837007 and PLR 9332006.

16. See Restatement Second Trusts Section 156(2) (providing, "[w]here a person creates for his own benefit, a trust to support or a discretionary trust, his transferee or creditors can reach the maximum amount which the trustee under the terms of the trust could pay to him or apply for his benefit." As mentioned, this black letter rule is commonly referred to as the "Self-Settled Trust Doctrine.").

17. See discussion in Ch. 15.

18. See also Alaska Stat. §34.40.110(b)(3)(A); Del. Code Ann. Tit. 12 §3570(11)b.4.; 2005 SD S.B. 93 §2(2)(d); Utah Code Ann. §25-6-14(7)(f)(iii).

19. See e.g., Fla. Stat. §222.21.

20. Presumably this discretion was subject to the business judgment rule under applicable state law.

21. See e.g., PLR 199915052.

22. F.S.A. 199920016.

23. See Id.

24. See e.g., PLR 201243004; Bramwell & Kanaga, LISI Estate Planning Newsletter #2040 (Dec. 20, 2012) at http://www.leimbergservices.com.

25. I.R.C. §2044.

26. Ariz. Rev. Stat. Ann. §14-10505(E); Del. Code Ann. Tit. 12 §3536(c); Fla. Stat. §736.0505(3); Ind. Stat. §I.C. 30-4-2.1-18; Ky. Rev. Stat. Ann. §386B.5-020(8)(a); Md. Code Ann., Est. & Trusts §14.5-1003; Mich. Comp. Laws §700.7506(4); N.H. Rev. Stat. Ann. §564-B:5-505; N.C. Gen. Stat. §36C-5-505(c); Or. Rev. Stat. §130.315(4); S.C. Code Ann. §62-7-505(b)(2); Tenn. Code Ann. §35-15-505(d); Tex. Prop. Code Ann. §112.035(g); Va. Code Ann. §64.2-747.B.3.; Wyo. Stat. Ann. §4-10-506(f).

27. Delaware, New Hampshire, Tennessee, Virginia and Wyoming have enacted domestic asset protection trust legislation.

28. Ariz. Rev. Stat. Ann. §14-10505(E) became effective January 1, 2009.

29. As of August 2016, see Ind. Stat. §I.C. 30-4-2.1-18, which became effective July 1, 2016.

30. Fla. Stat. §736.0505(1).

31. Fla. Stat. §736.0505(1)(a).

32. *In re Cocke*, 371 B.R. 554 (Bankr. M.D. Fla. 2007).

33. Fla. Stat. §736.0505(1)(b).

34. 640 F.2d 661 (5th Cir. Fla. 1981).

35. *See In re Witlin*, 640 F.2d 661 (5th Cir. Fla. 1981).

36. *See* Unif. T. Code §505, comments.

37. *See* Fla. Stat. §736.0505(1)(c).

38. Fla. Stat. §736.0505(1)(c).

39. *See* I.R.C. §2523(e).

40. *See* I.R.C. §§2056(b)(7) & 2523(f).

41. *See* I.R.C. §2613.

42. Fla. Stat. §736.0505(2)(a).

43. *See* I.R.C. §2044.

44. For an excellent discussion of this issue see Rothschild & Akhavan, "Creditor Protection – The Reciprocal Issue for Reciprocal Trusts (It's Not Just About Estate Taxes)," 38 Est. G. & Tr. Jrnl. 187 (Mar.-Apr. 2013). See also *Security Trust v. Sharp*, 77 A.2d 543 (Del. Ch. 1950); Ariz. Rev. Stat. Ann. §14-10505(E)(4); and Restatement (Third) of Trusts, §58(2), cmt. f, Reporter Note's cmt. f.

45. *Security Trust Co. v. Sharp*, 32 Del. Ch. 3, 6 (1950).

46. *See* I.R.C. §§2523(f)(4) & 6075(b). These sections of the Code provide the rules and time limitations for making the QTIP election for an inter vivos QTIP trust.

47. For an excellent analysis of PLR 201025021 see Steiner, "PLR 201025021: IRS Grants Extension of Time to Make QTIP Election for *Inter Vivos* Transfer," LISI Estate Planning Newsletter #1699 (Sept. 16, 2010) at http://www.leimbergservices.com.

48. The decision to make the Clayton QTIP election may (should) be vested in an independent fiduciary.

49. 84 F.3d 196 (5th Cir. 1996).

50. 112 T.C. 26 (1999), *acq.*, AOD 1999-006 (better known as the Fredericks of Hollywood estate).

51. *See* I.R.C. §2523(f).

52. *See* Nelson & Franklin, "*Inter Vivos* QTIP Trusts Could Have Unanticipated Income Tax Results to Donor Post-Divorce," LISI Estate Planning Newsletter #2244 (Sept. 15, 2014) at http://www.leimbergservices.com.

53. *See* §548(e)(1) of the Bankruptcy Code.

54. Perhaps this uncertainty simply dictates that this type of trust arrangement be established as an offshore trust structure that complies with all of the requirements of Florida law, see discussion on offshore trusts in chapter ___.

55. Ariz. Rev. Stat. Ann. §14-10505A.2.

56. Ariz. Rev. Stat. Ann. §14-10505E.

57. Ariz. Rev. Stat. Ann. §14-10505F.

58. Indiana, Kentucky, North Carolina and Texas.

59. *See* discussion at Nelson, Asset Protection & Estate Planning – Why Not Have Both? In the Forty-Sixth Annual Heckerling Institute on Estate Planning at 17-1 (Matthew Bender 2012).

60. *See* discussion regarding Ariz. Rev. Stat. Ann. §14-10505E, above.

61. N.C.G.S. §41-23.

62. N.C.G.S. §105-160.2; 17 NCAC 6B.3724(b).

63. 2016 WL 3585978 (N.C. App. Ct, 2016).

64. Mich. Comp. Laws §700.7506(4).

65. Md. Code Ann., Est. & Trusts §14.5-1003.

66. Md. Code Ann., Est. & Trusts §14.5-1003(c).

67. Ky. Rev. Stat. Ann. §386B.5-020(8)(a).

68. Compare Ky. Rev. Stat. Ann. §386B.5-020, with AZ Rev. St. §14-10505(E).

69. *See* Collins, *Asset Protection Trusts in South Carolina*, LISI Asset Protection Planning Newsletter #284 (Feb. 25, 2015) at http://www.leimbergservices.com.

70. Or. Rev. Stat. §130.315.

71. Tex. Prop. Code Ann. §112.035(g).

72. *See* Ripp & Jetel, *Asset Protection Trusts . . .in Texas?*, LISI Asset Protection Planning Newsletter #280 (Feb. 5, 2015) at http://www.leimbergservices.com.

73. House Bill No. 1083, available at http://iga.in.gov/static-documents/0/3/0/d/030d6422/HB1083.01.INTR.pdf.

74. *See* discussion regarding Ariz. Rev. Stat. Ann. §14-10505E, above.

75. *See* §548(e)(1) of the Bankruptcy Code.

76. *See* Kenneth C. Kettering, *The Uniform Voidable Transactions Act; or, the 2014 Amendments to the Uniform Fraudulent Transfer Act*, 70 THE BUSINESS LAWYER 778, 779 (Summer 2015).

77. *See* Uniform Law Commission, Enactment Status Map & Legislative Tracking, available at http://www.uniformlaws.org/LegislativeMap.aspx?title=Fraudulent%20Transfer%20Act%20-%20now%20known%20as%20Voidable%20Transactions%20Act.

78. See discussion in Karibjanian, Wehle, Lancaster & Sneeringer, *The Uniform Voidable Transactions Act and its Effect on the Estate Planning Community*, Steve Leimberg's Asset Protection Planning Newsletter #316 (Mar. 14, 2016), *available at* http://www.leimbergservices.com; Karibjanian, Wehle, Lancaster & Sneeringer, *The New Uniform Voidable Transactions Act: Good for the Creditors' Bar, But Bad for the Estate Planning Bar? - Part Two*, Steve Leimberg's Asset Protection Planning Newsletter #317 (Mar. 15, 2016), *available at* http://www.leimbergservices.com; and Karibjanian, Wehle, & Lancaster, *History Has Its Eyes on UVTA - A Response to Asset Protection Newsletter #319*, Steve Leimberg's Asset Protection Planning Newsletter #320 (Apr. 18, 2016), *available at* http://www.leimbergservices.com.

79. A discussion of the UVTA is outside the scope of this chapter. See discussion in Karibjanian, Wehle, Lancaster & Sneeringer, *The New Uniform Voidable Transactions Act: Good for the Creditors' Bar, But Bad for the Estate Planning Bar? - Part Two*, Steve Leimberg's Asset Protection Planning Newsletter #317 (Mar. 15, 2016), *available at* http://www.leimbergservices.com.

SUPPLEMENTAL NEEDS PLANNING

CHAPTER 10

INTRODUCTION

According to a recent study by Center for Disease Control and Prevention scientists, approximately 61 million adults in the United States (or approximately one in four U.S. adults) live with a disability.[1] When the number of children in the United States who have a disability is added, this number becomes much higher. As a result, a sizable percentage of modern families in the United States are impacted by disability. This chapter focuses on the particular estate planning issues faced by such families.

This chapter is not intended to provide an exhaustive discussion about Medicaid and other public benefit qualification issues (particularly for the elderly) or about the administration of supplemental needs trusts. Instead, it is intended to bridge the discussion of traditional estate planning issues (taxes, trust law, etc.) with planning to preserve eligibility for public benefits. In particular, it will focus on practical estate planning guidance for parents, grandparents, and siblings of a child or adult with special needs.

The chapter begins with a basic review of relevant public benefits law, moves to a discussion about supplemental needs trusts and alternatives to supplemental needs trusts (such as ABLE accounts), continues with drafting and planning issues related to supplemental needs trusts and the coordination of those trusts with other estate planning documents, and concludes with special situations and tax issues related to supplemental needs trust planning.

It is important to note that, while this chapter will summarize relevant public benefit rules and discuss supplemental needs trusts and other alternatives for proper planning in light of those rules, some of the planning alternatives and pitfalls will vary from state to state. The amount of written federal guidance on public benefits and supplemental needs trusts is far less than in other areas, such as federal tax law, leaving more room for administrative interpretation. Practitioners have reported variation in interpretation and enforcement from state to state. Moreover, Medicaid is a program jointly funded by the federal government and the states, with states having a degree of flexibility in structuring and administering their own programs. As a result, planners are strongly advised to seek expertise within their state of practice as they address their clients' specific issues.

PUBLIC BENEFIT PROGRAMS

Public benefits for individuals with qualifying disabilities can be divided into two eligibility categories: (i) entitlement benefits and (ii) need-based benefits. Eligibility for entitlement benefits, such as Social Security Disability Insurance (sometimes referred to as "SSDI" or simply as "Disability") and Medicare, is based on a combination of a qualifying disability and a prior work record of the person with a disability or of his or her deceased, disabled, or retired parent, and such benefits do not have asset limitations. Individuals who qualify for SSDI automatically qualify for Medicare two years after their SSDI qualification.

In contrast, eligibility for need-based benefits, such as Supplemental Security Income (SSI) and Medicaid, is based on a combination of having a qualifying disability and meeting income and resource limits.

In the case of both entitlement benefits and need-based benefits, there is a component that provides monthly income (SSDI or SSI) and a component that pays for medical care (Medicare or Medicaid).

These primary public benefit programs are reflected on the following chart:

	Entitlement	Need-based
Income	SSDI	SSI
Medical	Medicare	Medicaid

Impact of the Affordable Care Act

For more than a generation, Medicare and Medicaid partially filled a gap in medical coverage for certain individuals with disabilities under the age of sixty-five who were unable to work at all (or at least unable to work at a job that included health care insurance benefits) and whose preexisting conditions made it difficult, and in some cases impossible, to obtain private coverage.

However, many individuals with disabilities were not able to access Medicare because they did not have a sufficient work history to qualify for SSDI and thereafter Medicare (and could not qualify based on another family member's work history) and were not able to meet the resource limitations of Medicaid without substantially depleting their assets. The Affordable Care Act further closed the gap in coverage for individuals with disabilities by loosening resource limitations for Medicaid coverage, thereby making it available for a larger pool of low-income families, subject to state participation in that expansion.[2] It also prohibited private insurers from denying coverage based on preexisting conditions. As a result, many individuals with disabilities can now access health coverage without needing to transfer most of their assets to a d(4)(A) supplemental needs trust (sometimes referred to as a "Payback Trust")[3] or a d(4)(C) pooled trust[4] (both discussed later in this chapter).

Long-term Residential and Skilled Nursing Care

Medicare Part A generally covers skilled nursing care in a facility such as a rehabilitation hospital or nursing home for a limited time (twenty days without a co-pay, and an additional eighty days with a co-pay). Medicare does not cover such skilled nursing care after an initial one hundred days. Furthermore, private health insurance generally does not pay for any long-term care.

In contrast, for qualifying individuals, Medicaid generally pays for such care without a time limit and, in some states, also pays for day rehabilitation programs and residential services for adults with disabilities. Because of the high cost of long-term institutional care, qualification for Medicaid is extraordinarily valuable for individuals who need to live in a structured residential facility for an extended period of time, even if the individual already qualifies for Medicare.

IMPORTANCE OF SSI AND MEDICAID FOR ESTATE PLANNING PURPOSES

Although SSDI and Medicare are extremely important benefits for individuals with disabilities who qualify for them, they do not have direct estate planning implications. If an individual is receiving SSDI and/or Medicare, a gift or inheritance will not impact those benefits.

In contrast, eligibility for SSI and Medicaid can be lost if a gift or inheritance is structured improperly. As a result, this chapter will focus on preserving eligibility for SSI and Medicaid.

Basic Eligibility Requirements

An individual is eligible for SSI benefits if the person:

- is age sixty-five or older, blind, or disabled;

- is a U.S. citizen residing in the U.S., or a permanent resident, subject to certain exceptions; and

- meets the income and resource limits.[5]

The definition of "disabled" and the specific limitations on resources and income are summarized below. Because Medicaid is a joint federal-state program with states having a degree of flexibility to determine program eligibility, there is not a uniform Medicaid eligibility standard applicable in all states. However, many states adopt the SSI eligibility rules for their Medicaid programs so that, in those states, if an individual qualifies for SSI, they will automatically qualify for Medicaid. Accordingly, this chapter will focus on the SSI eligibility rules.

Definition of "Disability"

For SSI purposes, "disability" is based on an inability to engage in substantial gainful activity because of a medically-determinable physical or mental impairment that is expected to last for a continuous period of at least twelve months or result in death. The specific statutory language follows:[6]

"(3)(A) Except as provided in subparagraph (C), an individual shall be considered to be disabled for purposes of this subchapter if he is unable to engage in any substantial gainful activity by reason of any medically determinable physical or mental impairment which can be expected to result in death or which has lasted or can be expected to last for a continuous period of not less than twelve months.

(B) For purposes of subparagraph (A), an individual shall be determined to be under a disability only if his physical or mental impairment or impairments are of such severity that he is not only unable to do his previous work but cannot, considering his age, education, and work experience, engage in any other kind of substantial gainful work which exists in the national economy, regardless of whether such work exists in the immediate area in which he lives, or whether a specific job vacancy exists for him, or whether he would be hired if he applied for work. For purposes of the preceding sentence (with respect to any individual), "work which exists in the national economy" means work which exists in significant numbers either in the region where such individual lives or in several regions of the country.

(C)(i) An individual under the age of eighteen shall be considered disabled for the purposes of this subchapter if that individual has a medically determinable physical or mental impairment, which results in marked and severe functional limitations, and which can be expected to result in death or which has lasted or can be expected to last for a continuous period of not less than twelve months.

(ii) Notwithstanding clause (i), no individual under the age of eighteen who engages in substantial gainful activity (determined in accordance with regulations prescribed pursuant to subparagraph (E)) may be considered to be disabled.

(D) For purposes of this paragraph, a physical or mental impairment is an impairment that results from anatomical, physiological, or psychological abnormalities which are demonstrable by medically acceptable clinical and laboratory diagnostic techniques."

In determining whether employment constitutes "substantial gainful activity," the Social Security Administration looks at whether monthly remuneration for that employment typically exceeds a certain threshold amount. In 2019, for example, the monthly substantial gainful employment threshold for blind individuals was $2,040 and for non-blind individuals was $1,220. In other words, if a person works at, or could work at, a job paying that threshold amount or more, they will not qualify as "disabled" for SSI purposes.

The Social Security Administration provides detailed information on whether an individual will qualify as disabled and how it makes that determination at https://www.ssa.gov/planners/disability/dqualify4.html.

Resource Limitations

To be eligible for SSI, a person may not own more than $2,000 in "countable resources."[7] Countable resources include cash (not including the current month's income), bank accounts, income-producing real estate (other than one's residence), stocks, bonds, and other securities, life insurance with a cash value in excess of $1,500, and assets held for the person in most types of trusts.

However, certain resources are excluded for purposes of determining SSI eligibility. These "non-countable resources" include, most notably:

- a home serving as principal place of residence;
- personal effects and household goods;
- one motor vehicle;

- life insurance (with limitations);

- burial funds (with limitations) and burial space;

- certain self-support resources (*i.e.*, goods used to generate income, such as supplies for a small business), with limitations; and

- an ABLE account (discussed later in this chapter) of up to $100,000.[8]

As noted above, trust assets generally are considered resources of the beneficiary. In particular, trusts directing or authorizing a trustee to distribute principal as necessary for a beneficiary's support or maintenance are considered fully available to that beneficiary, even if that beneficiary is only one of many beneficiaries. While the trust document may grant the trustee discretion to decide if distributions are required, the beneficiary may go to court to enforce a distribution if that beneficiary has, for example, a support or maintenance need that the trustee is not meeting. Therefore, the trust assets are considered available to each beneficiary for SSI and Medicaid purposes.

There is a special rule for Uniform Transfers to Minors Act (UTMA) and Uniform Gifts to Minors Act (UGMA) accounts. Unless a UTMA or UGMA account is funded with assets belonging to a minor, then, before the minor reaches the age of majority under state law, such accounts are generally not counted as resources of the beneficiary of those accounts.[9]

Finally, for a child under the age of eighteen, the assets of the child's parents are generally considered resources of the child.[10] Therefore, most individuals with living parents do not become eligible for SSI and Medicaid before age eighteen.

Transfers

In general, an individual with a disability who does not meet the SSI resource limitations may not simply transfer assets to others or to a trust in order to divest himself or herself of sufficient assets to meet those limitations. Most transfers for less than fair market value will trigger a period of ineligibility.[11] However, there are exceptions to that general rule. Most notably, transfers to a supplemental needs trust described in 42 U.S.C. 1396(d)(4)(A) trust, a pooled trust described

in 42 U.S.C. 1396(d)(4)(C), or, subject to certain annual contribution limitations, an ABLE account will not trigger a period of ineligibility, as discussed in more detail later in this chapter.

Income Limitations

For purposes of SSI eligibility, a claimant cannot have monthly "countable" income that, in the aggregate, exceeds the Federal Benefit Rate ($771 for a single person in 2019).[12] Income is considered to be any type of receipt - whether in cash or in kind - that the claimant could use to meet their needs for food or shelter (excluding a host of specific items, such as food stamps, income tax refunds, and the proceeds of a loan). Three types of income are considered: earned income, unearned income, and in-kind income, as further described below.

Earned income is earnings from wages or self-employment. Certain exclusions apply in computing countable earned income, including, but not limited to, $65 per month of earned income, one-half of earned income over $65 per month, and up to $10 per month of infrequent or irregular earned income. An individual who earns more than the SSI threshold for the year in question ($1,220 per month in 2019, if the individual is not blind) is considered by Social Security to be engaging in substantial gainful activity and will likely not receive SSI at all. It is possible for a person who has some earnings to be eligible for a reduced SSI payment.

Unearned income is cash (or assets that are readily convertible to cash) that is received other than from work, such as investment income, alimony, child support, gifts, and trust distributions. As with earned income, certain exclusions apply in computing countable unearned income, including, but not limited to, the first $20 per month in unearned income (other than income based on need), scholarship funds used for paying educational expenses, and payments for providing foster care. Unearned income over $20 per month will reduce an individual's SSI dollar for dollar. If an individual receives over a certain amount of unearned income per month ($791 in 2019), that individual will not be eligible for SSI.

In-kind income is any food or shelter item that an SSI recipient receives for free or at a reduced cost from a third-party, including his or her parent or a supplemental needs trust. Receipt of in-kind income will reduce SSI, but generally never by more than one-third of the recipient's monthly benefit.[13]

Finally, for a child under the age of eighteen, the income of the child's parents is generally considered income of the child.[14]

THE ROLE OF SUPPLEMENTAL NEEDS TRUSTS AND SUPPLEMENTAL NEEDS TRUST ALTERNATIVES

Historically, given the public benefit rules discussed above, if parents wished to leave assets in excess of $2,000 for the benefit of their child with special needs, they had only two choices. They could leave assets directly to the child or to a traditional health, support, maintenance and education trust for the child's benefit, in which case the child would be disqualified from SSI and Medicaid until those assets were substantially exhausted. Alternatively, to preserve need-based government benefits for a child with special needs, parents could leave assets to a sibling of the child or to another close family member or friend, with the hope that the recipient would use those assets for the child's benefit. However, the recipient would be under no legal obligation to use the assets for that purpose, and, in some cases, circumstances could frustrate the parents' best intentions. For example, the other family member or friend might have their own financial hardship or creditor issues, or might marry a spouse who is not supportive of using funds to provide for the individual with special needs.

Over the last few decades, it has become possible to set aside funds to enrich the life of an individual with disabilities without disqualifying that individual from SSI or Medicaid. Subject to various rules discussed below, funds for the benefit of an individual with special needs can now be held in (i) a third-party funded supplemental needs trust, (ii) a first-party funded supplemental needs trust, (iii) a pooled trust, or (iv) an account created under The Stephen Beck, Jr. Achieving a Better Life Experience (ABLE) Act.

Third-Party Funded Supplemental Needs Trusts

The most common and flexible type of supplemental needs trust is a third-party funded supplemental needs trust. It may be created and funded by anyone other than the individual with a disability. Often, it is created by that individual's parents, grandparents, or sibling by lifetime or testamentary gift. The trust funds may be used to enhance the beneficiary's quality of life by providing goods and services not covered by government benefits. Upon the beneficiary's death, the remaining trust assets may be distributed to other beneficiaries designated by the trust grantor, without any Medicaid reimbursement requirement.

Legal authority for third-party funded supplemental needs trusts originated with case law in many states, and, subsequently, some states codified that authority by statute. From the Social Security Administration's perspective, a supplemental needs trust is one in which the beneficiary has no legal authority to terminate the trust and receive the trust principal, no right to mandatory distributions, and no ability to direct the use of the trust for his or her support and maintenance. "If an individual does not have the legal authority to revoke or terminate the trust or to direct the use of the trust assets for his or her own support and maintenance, the trust principal is not the individual's resource for SSI purposes."[15]

First-Party Funded Supplemental Needs Trusts

As noted previously, an individual with a qualifying disability for SSI purposes but who does not meet the SSI resource limitations may not simply transfer assets to others or to a trust in order to divest himself or herself of sufficient assets to meet those limitations. However, an exception applies for transfers to a trust described in subsections (A) or (C) of 42 U.S.C. 1396(d)(4).[16]

The Omnibus Budget Reconciliation Act of 1993 specifically authorized supplemental needs trusts for funds in control of an individual with disabilities under the age of sixty-five.[17] These trusts are often known as "payback trusts," "OBRA trusts," or, most commonly "(d)(4)(A) trusts" (which is how they will be referred to for the rest of this chapter) in reference to the federal statutory provision that authorized them. They offer a way to preserve public benefits for an individual with disabilities who has or acquires assets in his or her own name (or otherwise in a form that is deemed available to the individual), such as by gift, inheritance, or lawsuit settlement, and they must be for the individual's "sole benefit."

The initial 1993 OBRA legislation that authorized d(4)(A) trusts required that such trusts be created by a parent, grandparent, or legal guardian of an individual with a disability, or by a court. However, the Special Needs Trust Fairness Act (a part of the 21st Century Cures Act which was passed by Congress and signed into law by President Obama on December 13, 2016) loosened this requirement by also authorizing an individual with a disability to create a d(4)(A) trust for his or her own benefit. In addition, the Social Security Administration updated the applicable section of its Program Operations Manual System to clarify that, if a d(4)(A) trust is established by the agent of an individual with disabilities under a power of attorney, it will be deemed to have been established by that individual.[18]

Whether a d(4)(A) trust is established by the individual trust beneficiary, the individual trust beneficiary's parent, grandparent, or guardian, or a court, that individual's own assets may be transferred to the d(4)(A) trust before the individual reaches the age of sixty-five, without incurring a penalty for purposes of Medicaid or SSI eligibility. As with a third-party funded supplemental needs trust, a d(4)(A) trust may be used to enhance the beneficiary's quality of life by providing goods and services that are not covered by public benefits. However, unlike a third-party funded trust, if assets in a d(4)(A) trust remain at the beneficiary's death, Medicaid must be reimbursed from those trust assets for any benefits it provided to the beneficiary during his or her life.

Pooled d(4)(C) Trusts

An alternative to a privately-created supplemental needs trust is a pooled trust that is created and maintained by a non-profit association.[19] Under a pooled trust arrangement, funds for multiple beneficiaries with disabilities are pooled for investment management purposes under a common trust agreement, but each beneficiary has his or her own separate sub-account within the trust for his or her own sole benefit. Most estate planners are familiar with donor-advised charitable funds in which an umbrella organization manages the fund and administers charitable grants, while individuals establish sub-accounts within the fund into which they can make charitable gifts and from which they can recommend charitable grants. In practice, pooled trusts operate much like donor-advised charitable funds, except that the funds are administered not for the benefit of charities, but for the benefit of individuals with disabilities.

As noted above, the 1993 OBRA Legislation did not authorize an individual with a disability to establish his or her own d(4)(A) trust. Instead, it required that a d(4)(A) trust be established by the individual's parent, grandparent, or guardian, or a court. In contrast, the 1993 OBRA legislation did authorize an individual with a disability (as well as their parent, grandparent, or guardian, or a court) to establish a pooled trust for that individual. As a result, prior to the passage in 2016 of the Special Needs Trust Fairness Act, which for the first time allowed individuals with disabilities to establish their own d(4)(A) trusts, pooled trusts were particularly valuable when an individual with a disability had no living parent or grandparent.

Unlike a d(4)(A) trust, funding for a pooled trust may be done before or after the beneficiary reaches the age of sixty-five years. However, in some states, funding after the age of sixty-five years may result in a period of SSI and Medicaid ineligibility. If a resident of one of those states receives assets, such as by inheritance, after the age of sixty-five years, they might explore Medicaid-planning options, like any other person over the age of sixty-five years with assets, which are outside of the scope of this chapter.

Pooled trust assets are exempt for purposes of SSI and Medicaid eligibility during the beneficiary's life, but, unless the funds are retained in trust by the nonprofit association to benefit other beneficiaries of the pool, they too are subject to Medicaid reimbursement at the beneficiary's death.

The nonprofit associations that manage pooled trusts typically have account minimums, charge fees based on account size, and maintain investment control. Sometimes the associations will permit the person creating the account to name a distribution advisor.

With regard to to privately-created supplemental needs trusts, the disadvantages of a pooled trust are reduced control, potentially-higher fees, and, if funded with third-party money, Medicaid reimbursement or retention in trust for other members of the pool at the beneficiary's death. Pooled trust advantages include the ability to fund the trust after the beneficiary reaches age sixty-five (subject to state law), fewer administrative burdens, and the opportunity to exempt funds for SSI and Medicaid eligibility purposes even when the beneficiary has no suitable private trustee options.

The Academy of Special Needs Planners maintains a directory of pooled trusts by state:[20]

ABLE Accounts

In 2014, Congress passed and President Obama signed the ABLE Act, adding a new section 529A to the Internal Revenue Code and authorizing states or agencies thereof to establish tax-advantaged accounts for individuals with "marked and severe functional limitations" beginning before age twenty-six.

An individual may qualify for an ABLE account in one of two ways. First, an individual may qualify by applying for and receiving Social Security benefits due to blindness or disability that commenced before the individual reached the age of twenty-six years.[21] Alternatively, an individual may qualify if the individual, the individual's parent, or the individual's guardian certifies that the individual is blind and such blindness occurred before the age of twenty-six, or has a medically determinable physical or mental impairment, which (i) commenced before the individual attained the age of twenty-six, (ii) results in marked and severe functional limitations, and (iii) can be expected to result in death or has lasted or can be expected to last for a continuous period of not less than twelve months. The disability certification must be supported by a copy of the individual's diagnosis relating to the individual's relevant impairment or impairments, signed by a physician meeting the criteria[22] of the Social Security Act.[23]

With regard to qualifying for an ABLE account through a disability certification, the applicable Internal Revenue Code section (529A) authorizing ABLE accounts and the proposed Treasury regulations accompanying that section required that the disability certification and related physician's diagnosis be filed with the Treasury Secretary. However, to reduce the administrative burdens associated with ABLE accounts, the IRS subsequently issued a notice (pending final Treasury regulations which have not yet been issued) specifying that the disability certification and physician's diagnosis need not be filed with the Treasury Secretary when the ABLE account is opened, but instead the individual need only certify under penalties of perjury that they meet the qualification standards and

that they will retain a copy of the applicable physician's written report making the diagnosis and provide it to the ABLE program or IRS upon request.[24] The Social Security Administration has adopted this same rule for ABLE account eligibility in its program operations manual.[25]

Although ABLE accounts are funded with after-tax dollars, ABLE account earnings are exempt from income tax if the account is used only for "qualified disability expenses." Qualified disability expenses are expenses related to the beneficiary's blindness or disability, including education, housing, transportation, employment training and support, assistive technology and personal support services, health, prevention and wellness, financial management and administrative services, legal fees, expenses for oversight and monitoring, and funeral and burial expenses.[26] If ABLE account funds are distributed for any purpose other than "qualified disability expenses," except as a result of the beneficiary's death, then, unless the distribution is returned by a prescribed date, the income earned on those funds is taxable and there is an additional 10 percent tax on that income.[27]

A variety of limitations apply to ABLE accounts. Contributions to an ABLE account may be only in cash, and total contributions to an ABLE account in any calendar year from all sources generally may not exceed the gift tax annual exclusion amount from a single donor to a single donee for that year (*e.g.*, $15,000 for 2019), except that, effective as of January 1, 2018 and until January 1, 2026, ABLE account beneficiaries with employment earnings may contribute into their ABLE accounts an additional amount up to the lesser of the federal poverty line for a one-person household (for 2019, $12,490 in the Continental U.S., $14,380 in Hawaii, and $15,600 in Alaska) or their employment earnings that are includible in their gross income for that calendar year (*i.e.*, not deferred into an employer retirement plan),[28] and may claim the retirement savings contributions tax credit (often known as the "saver's credit") for those contributions.[29]

States must provide limited investment discretion to participants,[30] and must establish maximum funding amounts to avoid excess contributions.[31] In addition, for SSI eligibility purposes, only the first $100,000 in an ABLE account is treated as exempt from the SSI resource limit.[32] Although no similar maximum funding rules currently apply for Medicaid eligibility purposes. ABLE accounts, like d(4)(A) trusts, must provide for Medicaid reimbursement out of remaining account assets at the beneficiary's death if the state files a claim for reimbursement.[33] Some states might elect not to seek payback recovery from the ABLE account assets of beneficiaries that were residents of the state at death.

ABLE accounts are modeled after Code section 529 college savings plans. Like those plans, states may establish their own ABLE account programs and open those programs not only to residents of their state but also to residents of other states. On June 1, 2016, Ohio became the first state to launch an ABLE program, and other states followed suit in rapid succession. As with establishing and funding 529 college savings plans, the process for establishing and funding an ABLE account is determined by the applicable state ABLE program. The ABLE National Resource Center currently maintains a directory of the various state ABLE programs.[34]

Effective as of January 1, 2018 and until January 1, 2026, a 529 college savings plan for a beneficiary may be rolled over into an ABLE account for that beneficiary or a "member of the family" of that beneficiary, with the rollover counting toward the ABLE account contribution limits for the year of the rollover.[35] In other words, in any given year, the amount rolled over from a 529 college savings plan to an ABLE account for a particular beneficiary, when combined with other contributions to that ABLE account in that year, may not exceed the annual contribution limit. The ability to roll over amounts from a college savings plan to an ABLE account is particularly helpful because parents, grandparents, and other family members sometimes fund 529 college savings plans before they are aware of a disability that might make college unlikely. In those cases, the rollover allows for the transfer of funds to another tax-advantaged vehicle that better meets the particular needs of the beneficiary.

ABLE accounts offer flexibility in certain situations that supplemental needs trusts and pooled trusts do not. For example, an individual whose disabilities are significant enough to meet the SSI disability threshold but who is reasonably high functioning can control his or her own ABLE account even though he or she could not control his or her own supplemental needs trust or pooled trust. For relatively modest funds, ABLE accounts are often more cost effective to administer than supplemental needs trusts and pooled trusts. This cost effectiveness makes them especially suitable for individuals with disabilities who have less than the gift tax annual exclusion amount of countable assets, or who have multiple years before applying for SSI and/or Medicaid and can substantially deplete their assets by contributing the maximum permitted to an ABLE account each year over multiple years before such application.

In addition, it is not uncommon for families and friends of individuals with disabilities (particularly those who became disabled as a result of an accident) to plan small fundraisers for them. In most cases, contributions to a third-party supplemental needs trust create gift tax issues because those contributions will generally not qualify for the gift tax annual exclusion. In those cases, establishing an ABLE account for the individual with a disability will generally avoid any gift tax problem, as long as the total value of contributions from all parties in a given year does not exceed the gift tax annual exclusion limit for a single donor to a single donee in that year.

For many individuals with disabilities, ABLE accounts will not replace supplemental needs trusts but may instead provide a helpful complement to them.

COMPARING SUPPLEMENTAL NEEDS TRUSTS, POOLED TRUSTS, AND ABLE ACCOUNTS

Figure 10.1 compares the salient features of first-party supplemental needs trusts, pooled trusts, third-party supplemental needs trusts, and ABLE accounts.

Figure 10.1

	d(4)(A) SNT	d(4)(C) Pooled SNT	3d-Party SNT	ABLE Account
Who Can Create	Individual with a disability, his or her parent, grandparent, or guardian, or the court	Individual with a disability, his or her parent, grandparent, or guardian, or the court	Anyone other than individual with a disability	Anyone, including individual with a disability
Who Can Fund	Individual with a disability (subject to the seeding discussion below)	Anyone, but generally will be funded just by individual with a disability	Anyone other than individual with a disability	Anyone
Timing of Funding	Before individual with a disability reaches 65	Anytime, subject to period of ineligibility in some states if funded after age 65	Anytime	Anytime
Annual Contribution Limits	None	None	None	The gift tax annual exclusion amount from all contributors (plus additional amount when funded with employment earnings of individual with a disability)
Total Funding Limits	None	None	None	Each state will have its own total funding limit, but only $100,000 of account is exempt for SSI purposes
Beneficiary	Any individual with a disability	Any individual with a disability	Any individual with a disability and, in some cases, others	Any individual with a disability who was blind or disabled before age 26
Number of Such Trusts/Accounts Permitted	Unlimited	Unlimited	Unlimited	One
Income Taxable?	Yes	Yes	Yes	No, if used for qualified disability expenses
Third-Party Contributions Qualify for Gift Tax Annual Exclusion	N/A generally	N/A generally	No	Yes
Medicaid Reimbursement at Beneficiary's Death	Yes	Yes	No	Yes
Remainder Beneficiary after any Applicable Medicaid Reimbursement	Any individual or organization specified by the trust grantor	Determined by Pooled Trust Master Agreement	Any individual or organization specified by the trust grantor	Beneficiary designated in account agreement

PLANNING WITH SUPPLEMENTAL NEEDS TRUSTS: ARE THEY NEEDED?

When considering a particular situation where there is a family member with special needs, the first question is whether a supplemental needs trust is needed or desired at all. That question, in turn, centers on three issues.

Does the Individual Have a Qualifying Disability? Not every individual with special needs will meet the disability threshold for SSI and Medicaid. Unless the individual has already qualified for SSI, SSDI (which uses the same disability threshold), or Medicaid, the family needs to consider whether that individual has an identifiable disability that is expected to last for more than one year or result in death, and that makes the individual unable (or is likely to make him or her unable as an adult) to engage in substantial gainful activity. If the individual does not, then a supplemental needs trust generally will be unnecessary, but more traditional long-term trust planning with a third-party trustee likely will be desirable. In some cases (such as when the individual is young and it is not yet clear how independent he or she will be as an adult), the determination will not be simple. In those cases, the family members doing the planning will need to make their best guess regarding whether there is a reasonable likelihood that the individual will meet the disability threshold in the future.

Are There Sufficient Assets to Protect? If the family has only very modest means and no significant life insurance, then, even if the individual meets or will likely meet the disability threshold, it might not be worth the cost or administrative burden of supplemental needs trust planning. Instead, in those situations, a pooled trust or ABLE account might be sufficient, if any planning is needed at all.

Would the Family Prefer to Self-Fund the Beneficiary's Needs? Although supplemental needs trusts generally may be used for any purpose other than those that duplicate what the government is providing, they do typically include one material restriction – the requirement that distributions be made not to the beneficiary, but instead directly to providers of goods and services for the benefit of the beneficiary. When the beneficiary is relatively high functioning and desires maximum independence, and his or her eligibility for public benefits is uncertain, a family might choose to bypass a supplemental needs trust in order to preserve greater flexibility in structuring the trust, keeping in mind that until the trust assets are substantially depleted, the beneficiary will be ineligible to receive means-tested public benefits. This choice is most prevalent among families that have millions of dollars to dedicate for the individual with special needs or a philosophical aversion to relying on government benefits if at all possible. It is important to note that some states offer therapeutic programs that are open only to Medicaid recipients and do not allow private payment, so that a decision not to pursue a supplemental needs trust and thereby forego potential Medicaid eligibility will make those programs unavailable.

TIMING AND METHOD OF TRUST CREATION AND FUNDING

When to Create a Supplemental Needs Trust. Generally, once a determination is made that supplemental needs trust planning would be necessary or desirable for an individual with special needs, that individual's family members (or close friends) should create a supplemental needs trust document (or documents), and coordinate such documents with their other estate planning documents. As noted below, except with the limited exception of seeding d(4)(A) supplemental needs trusts in certain states, creating the trust document or documents does not mean actually funding the trust or trusts. Instead, by creating the trust document or documents, the family has created a structure to be activated when needed.

Which Type of Supplemental Needs Trust to Create. A third-party trust should be considered whenever one or more family members or close friends desire to leave an inheritance to an individual with special needs. In contrast, a d(4)(A) trust may not be needed if proper advance planning can be done. Specifically, before applying for SSI or Medicaid, families that are planning for an individual with a disability can be careful to ensure that the individual either never has significant assets in his or her own name, substantially spends down those assets for the individual's benefit, or, subject to the contribution limitations, contributes them to an ABLE account.

However, even when a family has done careful planning to significantly reduce the likelihood that a d(4)(A) trust will be needed, they might consider creating one anyway when they create a third-party supplemental needs trust. The provisions of a d(4)(A) trust are typically very similar to those of a third-party supplemental needs trust, so the incremental drafting time to add a d(4)(A) trust when a third-party trust is already being drafted typically is modest. In addition, it is always possible that the individual with a disability will receive assets in his or her own name or in a traditional health and support trust due to an unanticipated inheritance, a gap in planning of other family members, or a lawsuit settlement. Before the Special Needs Trust Fairness Act allowing the trust beneficiary or his or her agent under a power of attorney to establish a d(4)(A) trust, and before the availability of ABLE accounts, having a parent or grandparent of the beneficiary proactively create a d(4)(A) trust at the same time they create a third-party supplemental needs trust provided insurance that the d(4)(A) trust will be available if it is ever needed. While that remains an option worth considering for families that are doing advance supplemental needs trust planning, it is less compelling in some cases now that there are increased options to address the situation of an individual with a disability subsequently receiving assets.

When to Fund a Supplemental Needs Trust. A third-party supplemental needs trust generally should be funded at the death of a parent, grandparent, or other family member or close friend as part of their estate planning. Lifetime gifts by parents or other third parties are generally not recommended because of the loss of flexibility over the use of those funds (*e.g.*, the parents may not generally take back the funds contributed to a third-party funded supplemental needs trust). Instead, parents and other third parties will often prefer retaining the assets during life but using them to pay for goods and services for their child or other loved one with a disability, subject to any gift tax implications.

In contrast, a d(4)(A) trust should be funded prior to an individual with disabilities applying for SSI or Medicaid, if he or she has over $2,000 of countable assets without either immediate expenses on which to spend those assets or the ability and desire to contribute them to an ABLE account. Alternatively, if an individual with disabilities is already receiving Medicaid or SSI and then receives additional assets other than SSI, SSDI, or employment earnings, the d(4)(A) trust should be funded at that time, subject to any applicable rules, and report the funding to the Social Security Administration and/or applicable Medicaid authority.

It should be noted that, because the assets and income of a parent generally will be counted when determining SSI or Medicaid eligibility for an individual under eighteen, most individuals under eighteen will not qualify for SSI and Medicaid. In the case of an individual under eighteen who has more than $2,000 of countable assets and does not expect to apply for SSI and/or Medicaid until age eighteen due to his or her parents' assets or income, consideration should be given to whether the child's assets may be spent for his or her needs or contributed to an ABLE account subject to the account limitations before he or she reaches eighteen to avoid the need to fund the d(4)(A) trust and deal with trust administration issues.

Seeding d(4)(A) Trusts in Certain States. As noted previously, Section d(4)(A) trusts may be established by the beneficiary's parent or grandparent, as well as by the beneficiary, the beneficiary's guardian, or a court. Many practitioners long assumed that "established by" in the context of a beneficiary's parent or grandparent meant simply taking the action to create the trust but not also funding it, since d(4)(A) trusts are intended to be funded with the beneficiary's own assets. However, the Social Security Administration has taken the position that "established by" means not only executing the relevant trust document, but also actually funding (seeding) the trust with a modest amount, unless the law of the state in which the trust is created allows an "empty" or "dry" trust (effectively, a trust without corpus).[36]

In states that require corpus to have a valid trust, the Social Security Administration is unlikely to accept a schedule of property listing a nominal amount (*e.g.*, $10) at the end of the trust as meeting that requirement, even if such a schedule might be sufficient for other trust law purposes. Therefore, it is recommended that, if a parent or grandparent creates a d(4)(A) trust, they first fund (or, in the Social Security Administration's terms, "seed") it with a nominal amount of their own assets prior to funding it with any of the beneficiary's assets. If a d(4)(A) trust will be funded with the beneficiary's assets shortly after creation, the parent or grandparent can accomplish this seeding by first making a small initial contribution to the trust account before any deposit is made of the beneficiary's assets. If the d(4)(A) trust will not be funded with the beneficiary's assets shortly after creation, it is recommended that the parent or grandparent open a trust bank or brokerage account to hold a small initial contribution from them to be best protected from a future Social Security Administration challenge based on lack of seeding, recognizing that doing so will create some additional administrative burdens.

How to Fund a d(4)(A) Supplemental Needs Trust. If the beneficiary with a disability has the capacity to control his or her own assets, the beneficiary can transfer those assets to the d(4)(A) supplemental needs trust once it has been created. If the beneficiary does not have such capacity, then an agent for the beneficiary under a proper power of attorney or a trustee for the beneficiary under a trust that is not exempt for public benefit purposes can transfer the beneficiary's individual or trust assets to the d(4)(A) supplemental needs trust if the governing document or state law authorizes such a transfer. If the beneficiary is under a guardianship, an order of the court having jurisdiction over the guardianship will be required to fund the supplemental needs trust. Likewise, if the supplemental needs trust is being funded pursuant to a court settlement, authorization from the court having jurisdiction over the settlement will be required.

If the beneficiary has an IRA or qualified retirement plan, he or she likely will have to liquidate that IRA or plan in order to transfer its assets to a supplemental needs trust. Doing so will trigger recognition of trust income, however, if the beneficiary is under 59½, the 10 percent early withdrawal penalty might be avoided if the beneficiary meets the disability exception to that penalty.[37] There have been some instances where the custodian of an inherited IRA has been willing to transfer that inherited IRA into the participant's supplemental needs trust without liquidating it and without treating the transfer as a taxable distribution. In the case of an inherited IRA, that approach has been supported by some private letter rulings.[38] However, as of the date of this writing, it does not appear that such a transfer can be accomplished without taxable distribution treatment with a person's own, non-inherited IRA.[39] In cases where there is a large inherited IRA, it might be worth exploring whether a transfer of that IRA to a supplemental needs trust is feasible.

If an individual funds a d(4)(A) trust, the creation and funding of that trust will need to be reported at the time of creation and funding (or, if later, at the time of application for public benefits) to the Social Security Administration and/or the governmental body that administers the Medicaid program in the individual's state of residence. That reporting will trigger a review of the trust terms and funding by the Social Security Administration or Medicaid body to determine if the d(4)(A) trust qualifies as an exempt asset.

How (and to What Extent) to Fund a Third-Party Supplemental Needs Trust. When parents create a third-party supplemental needs trust for their child with special needs, they need to determine how that trust will be funded and with how much that trust will be funded. In most cases, while the parents are alive, it will be advisable for the parent who is the settlor not to fund the third-party supplemental needs trust but instead to retain the assets, pay directly for the child's needs, and retain flexibility to adjust to changing circumstances, while putting in place a plan to fund the third-party trust at the parents' death. That plan could involve funding via the parents' wills or trusts. IRAs and other retirement plans are generally not ideal options for funding because of their built-in income tax and because it is more difficult with supplemental needs trusts, than with other trusts, to incorporate provisions allowing for distributions over the beneficiary's life expectancy. In some cases, where the parents want to guaranty that the third-party supplemental needs trust will be funded with at least a minimal amount, it will be helpful to use a life insurance policy payable to the trust. In the case of a married couple, a second-to-die policy can be valuable in this context just as it sometimes is when trying to create a liquidity source for estate taxes.

The more difficult question often is how to determine the appropriate amount of assets with which to fund the third-party supplemental needs trust. Parents might approach this question in a similar manner as to how much life insurance to obtain – by estimating, in a conservative manner, how many dollars the child will need from the trust over the remainder of the child's life, in light of available public benefits, and then working backward into a funding amount. The calculation is complicated by the uncertainty of life expectancy, the future of public benefits, and many other factors. Financial advisors who specialize in helping families that have children with special needs can offer valuable assistance with making these determinations.

If parents have multiple children, one of whom has special needs, they should consider whether they wish to treat their children equally for inheritance purposes, direct a larger share of their estate to the supplemental needs trust for the child with special needs, or direct the first portion of the estate to the supplemental needs trust up to a desired funding amount and then allocate the rest for their other children. If the last of these approaches is desired, funding the supplemental needs trust with life insurance, as noted above, can be a useful approach.

PRIMARY TERMS OF SUPPLEMENTAL NEEDS TRUSTS

Restrict Amendment and Revocation. The beneficiary of a d(4)(A) or third-party supplemental needs trust should never be granted the authority to amend or revoke the trust. If the beneficiary has a guardian, that guardian likewise should never be granted amendment or revocation authority because that authority will be imputed to the beneficiary.

It is strongly recommended that the trustee or another third-party be given the authority to amend a d(4)(A) or third-party supplemental needs trust for the limited purposes of (i) changing the governing state law to the law of the state in which the beneficiary resides, (ii) complying with applicable public benefits law, and, if desired, (iii) updating the trustee succession. In the case of a d(4)(A) trust, no trustee or third-party should have any additional amendment authority or any revocation authority.

In the case of a third-party trust, while not mandatory, it may be prudent to likewise avoid granting revocation authority or additional amendment authority to any trustee or third-party. Such a prohibition is more restrictive than it sounds. Until the third-party trust is actually funded, the parents or other creators can effectively accomplish an amendment or revocation by creating a new third-party supplemental needs trust and directing assets to it (instead of to the prior third-party supplemental needs trust) at their deaths, or by eliminating the funding of the existing supplemental needs trust.

Express the Grantor's Intent. In addition, it is important to express the grantor's intent to enrich the quality of the beneficiary's life by preserving the beneficiary's eligibility for public benefits while setting aside funds for the beneficiary's needs that are not covered by public benefits.

Be Mindful of the Sole Benefit Rule for d(4)(A) Trusts. In the case of a d(4)(A) trust, the trust must be for the "sole benefit" of the individual with disabilities. Therefore, while the trust may have remainder beneficiaries after Medicaid reimbursement upon the death of the individual with disabilities, the trust must not have any other beneficiaries during the individual's life. The Social Security Administration has clarified that there may be collateral benefits to a third party without violating this rule. For example, if a d(4)(A) trust pays for a television for the individual

with disabilities, others may watch that television, and, if a companion takes the beneficiary to a museum, the trust may pay for the museum tickets for both the beneficiary and the companion.[40] However, as discussed later in this chapter, the draftsperson must be careful not to include trust provisions that run afoul of the sole benefit rule, such as an early termination provision.

A third-party supplemental needs trust is not bound by the sole benefit rule, so it can have other beneficiaries during the life of the individual with disabilities. However, with third-party trusts, it is sometimes cleanest to include only the individual with disabilities as a beneficiary during his or her life, and doing so could allow the trust to be a "qualified disability trust," as defined in Code section 642(b)(2)(C) (also referred to herein as a "Qualified Disability Trust"), for income tax purposes, as discussed later in this chapter.

Place Distributions in Trustee's Sole Discretion and Limit to Supplementing, but not Replacing, Public Benefits. A supplemental needs trust should not include any mandatory distribution provisions or withdrawal rights. In addition, distributions should not be subject to any standards such as health, support, maintenance, and education, but instead should be left entirely in the trustee's discretion. In some states, a trust where distributions are entirely in the trustee's discretion with no distribution standards might be sufficient to keep the trust from being a countable asset. In other states, distributions need to be further limited to those that supplement, but do not replace, public benefits that the beneficiary is receiving. Specifically, the trust should provide that no distributions may be made for the beneficiary's food, shelter, or medical care unless and until all benefits are exhausted.

Limit Distributions to Providers of Goods and Services. If a trust merely authorizes the trustee, in the trustee's sole discretion, to make distributions to the beneficiary (and not merely for the benefit of the beneficiary), but the beneficiary has no power to compel distributions, that authorization should not technically cause the trust principal to be counted as the beneficiary's resource for Medicaid and SSI eligibility purposes. However, some practitioners report that, in their states, the mere authorization of distributions to the beneficiary causes the public benefit authorities to treat the trust as an available resource. Moreover, actual distributions to the beneficiary will count as unearned income to the beneficiary for SSI purposes. *Therefore,* *it is strongly recommended that the trust document not authorize distributions to the person with disabilities but instead limit them to direct payment to providers of goods and services.*

Ideally, the trust document should include with the trustee's powers the specific authority to pay advocates and care managers for the beneficiary. In addition, in the case of a third-party supplemental needs trust (but not a d(4)(A) supplemental needs trust), the trust can give the trustee authorization to make gifts on the beneficiary's behalf to his or her loved ones, but doing so (or otherwise allowing distributions to individuals other than the beneficiary) will result in the trust not constituting a qualified disability trust for income tax purposes, as discussed later in this chapter.

Since discretionary distributions from a supplemental needs trust effectively can be made for any purpose other than duplicating or replacing those covered by public benefits, the trust document itself need not include a detailed list of permissible third–party distributions. Some practitioners prefer to include a short list of example distributions in their trust documents, and others prefer not to include any list at all. If a list is to be included in the trust document, it should be carefully circumscribed to avoid listing any expenses that might be deemed problematic.

For reference only, the following is a non-exclusive list of distributions to third parties for the beneficiary's benefit that typically fall within the purposes of a supplemental needs trust to the extent such expenses are not covered by public benefits.

- Books and movies (including streaming services)

- Case management and advocacy services

- Classes and lessons (including college tuition)

- Clothing and linens (including cleaning expenses)

- Club memberships

- Dental expenses

- Electronics, including cell phones, tablets, computers, and internet service (as well as training and adaptive technology for any electronics)

- Entertainment, including cable TV service, concerts, theater, and sporting events

- Hearing aids (and batteries) and eyeglasses

- Furniture

- Haircuts, manicures, pedicures, and personal grooming services and supplies

- Health insurance premiums for private insurance

- Hobby supplies and sporting goods

- Home repairs and modifications (*e.g.* wheelchair accessibility)

- Household supplies (non-food), including cleaning supplies and paper products

- Job coach

- Medical treatment, drugs, co-pays, and devices

- Personal care attendant

- Prepaid funeral contracts

- Private hospital or nursing home room

- Therapy (including rehabilitation, speech, physical, occupational, music, and art)

- Transportation expenses (subject to discussion of transportation expenses later in this chapter)

- Vacations

Designate Trustees and Successor Trustees. The trustee is responsible for investing trust assets, engaging with the beneficiary to determine the beneficiary's needs over time, making distributions from the trust for the benefit of the child while avoiding distributions that would jeopardize the beneficiary's eligibility for public benefits, maintaining records of all trust income and expenditures, and doing required tax reporting, all in accordance with the terms of the trust agreement and applicable law. The trustee must be careful to administer the trust in a manner that will not cause a reduction or loss of the child's public benefits. As a result, one of the most important choices in doing supplemental needs trust planning is selecting a succession of trustworthy trustees that have the time and financial savvy necessary to serve effectively. The choice has become more challenging because, in recent years, a number of banks and trust companies have made the business decision not to serve as trustees of supplemental needs trusts due to the complexity of administration and the risk of liability.

In many cases, the beneficiary's parents may be trustees, power of appointment holders, or default remainder beneficiaries. However, in certain limited cases where a minor beneficiary of a funded trust is eligible for public benefits despite a look-through to the parents' assets and income, naming a parent as trustee could be problematic in that the trust income could be deemed to be the income of the parents, thereby placing the beneficiary's eligibility at risk.[41] Also, a parent's role as trustee, power of appointment holder, or default remainder beneficiary could cause estate tax inclusion for him or her, so estate tax exposure should be considered in connection with any powers or interests he or she might have under the document.[42] See the section below for a discussion regarding the income tax consequences.

Provide for Medicaid Reimbursement in d(4)(A) Trust. In the case of a d(4)(A) trust, at the beneficiary's death and before any distributions to remainder beneficiaries, the trust must direct the trustee to reimburse all states that provided Medicaid assistance to the beneficiary for all Medicaid payments made *during the beneficiary's life* (and not merely for those made since the trust was created). However, the trust may provide that taxes and reasonable administration expenses be paid prior to Medicaid reimbursement.

At the time of the beneficiary's death, the trustee will have an obligation to report to the Medicaid authorities that the beneficiary has died and to seek an accounting from those authorities of what has been paid by Medicaid during the beneficiary's life.

Designate Remainder Beneficiaries. Remainder beneficiaries are the persons or charities that will receive any remaining trust assets after the beneficiary with a disability has died, taxes and trust administration expenses have been paid, and, in the case of a d(4)(A) trust, Medicaid has been reimbursed and any other required payments have been made.

DRAFTING RECOMMENDATIONS FOR SUPPLEMENTAL NEEDS TRUSTS

Use a Stand-Alone Supplemental Needs Trust. When confronted with a family situation that includes a beneficiary with a disability, many practitioners have routinely included a paragraph or article in their form will or trust documents limiting distributions to that beneficiary to those for supplemental needs. While such a paragraph or article is better than not addressing the supplemental needs issue at all, it is not ideal in two important respects.

First, standard trusts often include boilerplate provisions (such as a provision to allow a trustee to terminate a small trust in favor of a trust beneficiary) that are helpful for other purposes but can create a reason for a public benefits authority reviewer to treat the trust assets as countable resources. Second, if a parent or grandparent creates a supplemental needs trust for their child or grandchild under a will or revocable trust that does not become effective until the parent or grandparent's death, there is no existing trust to which other family members or friends can direct assets.

In contrast, a stand-alone supplemental needs trust can be carefully crafted to avoid the inclusion of boilerplate provisions that are problematic for public benefit eligibility purposes, and the stand-alone trust creates an immediate repository for assets from other family members for the beneficiary with a disability.

As discussed later in this chapter, the one exception to the use of stand-alone supplemental needs trusts is when the beneficiary is the spouse of the creator of the trust.

Authorize Amendments to Comply with Applicable Public Benefits Law. As noted previously, because the relevant public benefits law (or interpretations of that law) might change, or the beneficiary might move to a different state with different rules from the state in which the supplemental needs trust was created, it is crucial for any supplemental needs trust to authorize the trustee or another party to amend the trust at any time to comply with applicable public benefit law and to change the governing law of a trust, as well as to make any such amendment retroactive to the creation of the trust.

In addition, the trust document should include a savings clause that all provisions of the trust are intended to comply with applicable public benefits law and, to the extent they do not comply, they are deemed void. However, in practice, the Social Security Administration does not always give effect to such clauses.

The Social Security Administration's internal guidance provides that, whenever the Social Security Administration determines that an individual is ineligible for benefits because of excess resources[43] that include a countable trust, the agent must cite:

- The applicable section of the trust containing the problematic language or issue;

- The Program Operations Manual System (POMS) citation that contains the policy requirements on that subject; and

- Language indicating where the POMS can be found online. [44]

This guidance, combined with the trust amendment power discussed above, should provide the family with an opportunity either to challenge the determination regarding the alleged problematic trust provision or amend the trust to remove or change that provision so that it complies with Social Security Administration regulations.

Direct Use of d(4)(A) Trust Assets before Those of Third-Party Trust. If a beneficiary has both a d(4)(A) trust and a third-party trust, it will be helpful to authorize the trustee of the d(4)(A) trust to exhaust assets of the d(4)(A) trust first before distributions are made from the third-party trust and to authorize the trustee of the third-party trust to withhold distributions until the assets of the d(4)(A) trust are exhausted. These authorizations will provide guidance for the trustees, while obtaining the likely desired result since the d(4)(A) trust will be subject to Medicaid reimbursement at the beneficiary's death, while the third-party trust will not.

Avoid Early Termination Provisions in d(4)(A) Trusts. Drafters of supplemental needs trusts have long faced the challenge of how to address changes in law or circumstances or to protect trust assets if they are deemed by the public benefit authorities to be available to the trust beneficiary. In the past, a common approach was to include in the trust a provision that would terminate the trust and distribute the assets to the remainder beneficiaries or others if the assets were deemed available to the beneficiary with a disability.

This provision has been referred to as an "early termination" or "kickout" provision.

In 2013, the Social Security Administration ruled that, except in certain narrow cases, an early termination provision in a first-party d(4)(A) trust violates the sole benefit requirement for d(4)(A) trusts and therefore the assets of a trust that includes such a provision count as an available resource of the trust beneficiary.[45] As a result, such early termination provisions should not be used in a d(4)(A) trust, and instead (as discussed above) a clear amendment provision can be relied upon to allow the trust to comply with the applicable law.

While the Social Security Administration ruling on early termination provisions applies specifically to first-party trusts, one should consider avoiding an early termination provision in a third-party trust as well. Such a provision will often be inconsistent with the grantor's intentions and might prevent the trust from being deemed a "qualified disability trust" for income tax purposes. Also, as noted above, any concern about protecting the trust from public benefit authority challenges can be better addressed through an amendment power.

Finally, in at least one first party d(4)(A) trust situation, the Social Security Administration has treated a standard general trust merger power (i.e., a provision in the trust's financial powers that authorizes the trustee to merge the trust into another trust with substantially similar provisions without explicit reference to first satisfying the trust's Medicaid reimbursement provisions) as an impermissible early termination provision. Therefore, at least in first party d(4)(A) trusts, a general merger provision should be avoided.

Avoid Provisions that Undermine Supplemental Needs Trust Rationale. The underlying rationale of a supplemental needs trust is that the beneficiary has significant disabilities and needs funds to enrich the quality of the beneficiary's life. However, especially in the case of a beneficiary with mental disabilities, including provisions that cast doubt on the extent of the beneficiary's disabilities should be avoided. For example, although the beneficiary could technically be given a limited power of appointment at death, granting the beneficiary such a power might give the impression that the beneficiary is not sufficiently disabled and, therefore, should generally be avoided.

Consider Authorizing Trustee to Fund an ABLE Account for the Beneficiary. Incorporating the discretionary power for the trustee of a supplemental needs trust to fund an ABLE account for the beneficiary can add helpful flexibility. The applicable Social Security Administration rules now explicitly provide that transferring funds from a supplemental needs trust to an ABLE account for the same beneficiary will not constitute income to the trust beneficiary.[46] Because an ABLE account is typically subject to Medicaid payback at the account beneficiary's death, a discretionary power to fund an ABLE account, subject to the funding limitations for such accounts, is more beneficial in d(4)(A) supplemental needs trusts than in third-party trusts.

Use Caution with Transportation Expenses. For many years, it was believed that funds from a supplemental needs trust, including a d(4)(A) trust, generally could be used to pay for travel expenses of a family member or friend of the trust beneficiary to visit that person since such visits would be beneficial to the trust beneficiary. However, to avoid perceived abuses, a few years ago the Social Security Administration enacted a rule to allow payments from a d(4)(A) trust to a third-party for travel expenses, but only for specific enumerated purposes. In April 2018, the Social Security Administration updated its operating manual, and one of the updates was to expand the enumerated purposes for which third-party travel expenses could be made from a d(4)(A) trust. Under the 2018 updated rule, such payments would violate the sole-benefit rule of d(4)(A) trusts except in the following cases:

- Payment of third-party travel expenses to accompany the trust beneficiary and provide services or assistance that is necessary due to the trust beneficiary's medical condition, disability or age.[47]

- Payment of third-party travel expenses to ensure the safety or medical well-being of the trust beneficiary in either of the following two cases: (i) travel for a service provider to oversee the trust beneficiary's living arrangements when the beneficiary resides in an institution, nursing home, other long-term care facility (for example, group homes and assisted living facilities), or other supported living arrangements; and (ii) travel for a trustee, trust advisor named in the trust, or successor to exercise his or her fiduciary duties or to ensure the well-being of the beneficiary when the beneficiary does not reside in an institution.[48]

Therefore, in d(4)(A) trusts, it is recommended either not to explicitly mention third-party travel expenses, or, if there is a compelling desire to reference them, to explicitly limit them as described above and as they may be further limited under the applicable public benefit rules.

Consider Allowing Some In-Kind Support and Maintenance Once Public Benefits Have Been Exhausted. As a general rule, if the beneficiary of a d(4)(A) or third-party supplemental needs trust is receiving public benefits, neither trust should be used for food or shelter, unless and until public benefits have been exhausted. Instead, trust assets may generally be used to provide those goods and services that enrich the quality of the beneficiary's life and which are not provided for by public benefits. Therefore, food and shelter (for example, the beneficiary's groceries, meals, and basic housing expenses such as rent, mortgage payments, real estate taxes, homeowner's insurance, gas, electricity, water, and sewer) should be paid first from the beneficiary's public benefits before being paid from either trust.

However, in certain cases, it may be in the beneficiary's best interests for shelter expenses and, more rarely, for food expenses, to be paid by the d(4)(A) trust or the third-party trust, if the trusts do not outright prohibit such payments. Therefore, the trust document might permit (or at least not prohibit) such payments, bearing in mind that if such expenses are actually paid by the trustee, this assistance will be considered "in-kind support and maintenance" and likely will reduce the beneficiary's SSI.

Consider Power of Appointment Provisions. In order to provide added flexibility regarding distributions at the beneficiary's death, it might be helpful to grant a person (other than the beneficiary) a power of appointment, effective at the beneficiary's death, to family members of the beneficiary, other persons or charities, or a residential facility in which the beneficiary resided during life. However, if the trust is expected to be the beneficiary of an IRA or qualified retirement plan, and if the trust is otherwise intended to be an accumulation trust for IRA distribution purposes, then such a power of appointment might be problematic.

Do Not Be Too Clever in Drafting. Estate planners often pride themselves on their ability to draft with finesse and cleverness to achieve a desired substantive result while taking advantage of a tax opportunity or avoiding a tax problem. In the supplemental needs trust context, those who take chances in their drafting do so at their peril.

Unlike federal taxation, about which there are volumes of regulations and rulings and thus available authority on almost any tax issue that might arise in practice, the regulations and rulings in the public benefits area are more scant and leave greater room for administrative interpretation. In addition, due to budget limitations, those reviewing supplemental needs trusts and determining whether the trust assets count as available resources generally are not lawyers, let alone trust lawyers, so their interpretations sometimes lack a broader understanding of trust documents. As a result, in the supplemental needs trust context, it is best to stick with simple, clear, tried-and-true language, and save the cleverness for other contexts.

DRAFTING RECOMMENDATIONS FOR OTHER ESTATE PLANNING DOCUMENTS

When incorporating a supplemental needs trust for a particular family into one's planning, there are a number of drafting issues to consider:

Discretionary Distribution Provisions in One-Pot Spray Trusts. Often trust documents will include trusts that authorize a trustee to make distributions for one or more of a class of multiple beneficiaries. These trusts are sometimes referred to as one-pot trusts or spray trusts. For example, it is common for the will or revocable living trust of a married individual to leave the portion of his or her assets that is sheltered by the federal and any applicable state estate tax exemptions at his or her death to a separate trust to provide health, support, maintenance, and education distributions for his or her spouse and descendants. Such as trust is typically called a "Family Trust," "Residuary Trust," or "Credit Shelter Trust." Importantly, if one of the testator's or grantor's descendants has a disability, then that descendant's inclusion as a permissible health, support, maintenance, and education beneficiary, even if only one of many such beneficiaries, will make the trust deemed to be an available resource to him or her for SSI and Medicaid eligibility purposes. To avoid this outcome, the trust should prohibit the trustee from making any distributions to that descendant, and should instead authorize the trustee to distribute assets for that

descendant's benefit to that descendant's third-party supplemental needs trust.

"Crummey" Withdrawal Rights. Short-term withdrawal rights (often referred to as "Crummey powers"[49] from the case) are commonly given to trust beneficiaries in an irrevocable life insurance trust or in certain gift trusts in order to qualify a grantor's trust contributions for the gift tax annual exclusion. However, if a beneficiary with a disability has withdrawal rights, then the amounts subject at any time to a power of withdrawal will be considered an available resource to that beneficiary, and, even if that beneficiary allows that withdrawal right to lapse, the portion of the trust contribution over which the beneficiary's withdrawal right lapsed will typically be treated as if the beneficiary contributed that amount to the trust. This will prevent the trust from being treated wholly as a third-party trust, and, in some cases, the public benefit authorities might argue that the entire trust should be considered to be a first-party trust. As a result, when supplemental needs trust planning is done for an individual, that individual should not be given Crummey or other trust withdrawal rights.

Gifting Provisions in Property Powers of Attorney and Revocable Trusts. It is common for the lifetime provisions of a revocable living trust and the enumeration of powers in a durable property power of attorney to authorize the trustee or property agent to make lifetime gifts on the grantor's or principal's behalf. Often, that authorization is limited to gifts that qualify for the gift tax annual exclusion under Code section 2503(b) or the tuition and medical exclusion under Code section 2503(e). However, contributions to a supplemental needs trust for an individual with a disability typically will not qualify for either of these exclusions. Therefore, if the grantor or principal wants to authorize the trustee or agent to fund a supplemental needs trust on his or her behalf, then specific language authorizing transfers to a supplemental needs trust should be included in the applicable gifting provisions of the durable property power of attorney and revocable trust. In addition, when the gifting provisions do not include a general authorization to make gifts that qualify for the gift tax annual exclusion (which would include ABLE account contributions), it might be desirable to include specific authorization to fund an ABLE account for a family member with a disability.

Guardianship Designations. It is routine for estate planners to include guardianship designations in a will when the testator either currently has children who are under eighteen or might have children in the future. However, if the testator has an adult child with a disability who either is currently under a guardianship or conservatorship or could be in the future, it is desirable to include the parents' preferred guardianship designations either in a will or other suitable document under the law of the state in which that child resides so that, in the event of a future guardianship proceeding, the parents' wishes can be considered by the court in making its determination of what is in the best interests of the adult child.

In addition, if the child already is under a guardianship, one should consider whether applicable state law would allow for the appointment of a successor or stand-by guardian with court approval while the current guardian is acting, to provide for a smooth transition in the event the current guardian dies or otherwise ceases to act in the future.

Amendment and/or Trust-to-Trust Transfer Provisions. Since many trusts may remain in existence for a long time, the grantor often will not know at the time the trust is created whether any present or future trust beneficiary will have a significant disability that would otherwise make them eligible for means-tested public benefits but for their beneficial interest in the trust.

Therefore, even in situations where there is no current special needs situation, it can be helpful to include in other trust documents provisions by which the trustee or a third-party trust protector may (i) amend the trust to restrict any interest of a beneficiary with a disability to a supplemental needs interest, or (ii) authorize in the trust's financial powers or facility of payment provisions the transfer of the trust assets to a separate supplemental needs trust for the benefit of a trust beneficiary. This latter power will allow for the decanting of a trust to another more suitable trust without worrying about whether the trust meets the requirements of a state decanting statute and without having to jump through the hoops of any such statute.

Separate Life Care Plan or Letter of Intent. Parents of an individual with disabilities carry with them every day a detailed knowledge of their child's medical, developmental, and social history, how that history impacts their child's daily life, what practices help their child function in the best possible way, and what activities to avoid. While it is difficult for a trustee to stand in the shoes of any person, it is especially difficult when the child has special needs. A life care plan is an organized comprehensive document that details the

medical, developmental, social, and related needs and habits of an individual with disabilities. It is not a legal document, but rather an informational guide to assist those who would have legal authority in the parents' absence. To plan for the future of a child with special needs in the most comprehensive way, a life care plan is a valuable counterpart to a supplemental needs trust and should be considered by every parent who does planning for their child with special needs. There are now consultants with specialized skills to assist in the development of such plans.

COORDINATION WITH OTHER DISPOSITIVE INSTRUMENTS

Supplemental needs trust planning does not end with the creation of a well-drafted supplemental needs trust or trusts. It is critical that the supplemental needs trust(s) be complemented by other dispositive instruments that direct all assets for the individual with a disability not to that individual directly but instead to the third-party supplemental needs trust for that individual.

Wills and Other Trust Documents of Other Family Members and Friends. The wills and trust documents of the beneficiary's family members and friends need to be carefully worded to ensure that any interest for the beneficiary be directed to his or her third-party supplemental needs trust. This includes not only current beneficial interests and remainder interests at death, but also contingent reminder interests. For example, grandparents (or potential grandparents) frequently leave their assets to their children in equal shares but further provide that, if a child predeceases them leaving one or more descendants who survive them, the share that otherwise would have passed to the child shall instead pass to the child's descendants. Where the child has a son or daughter with a disability for whom the child has created a third-party supplemental needs trust, it is important for the grandparents' documents to include a proviso that, if any assets would otherwise be distributable to the grandchild with a disability, they should instead be allocated to that grandchild's third-party supplemental needs trust.

The following is an example letter to family members and friends to alert them of this issue:

Dear Family Members and Friends:

We have created a supplemental needs trust for our daughter, Jane, in order to enrich the quality of her life while preserving her eligibility for means-tested government disability benefits. Accordingly, if you desire to include Jane as a beneficiary of your estate plan or to make any lifetime gifts to Jane, please direct any such inheritance or gift to "The Jane Doe Supplemental Needs Trust, dated _____," to be administered according to the terms of that trust.

Retirement Plan and Life Insurance Beneficiary Designations. As all good estate planners and financial advisors know, not all assets pass by the terms of wills and trusts. Life insurance policies, IRA and other retirement plan accounts, and payable-on-death or transfer-on-death financial accounts pass upon the death of the insured, participant, or owner not pursuant to his or her will or trust but pursuant to his or her applicable beneficiary designation. Therefore, where a third-party supplemental needs trust has been created for an individual with a disability, it is crucial that the beneficiary designations of that individual's loved ones avoid naming as primary or secondary beneficiary that individual or a traditional health and support trust for his or her benefit, but instead name the individual's third-party supplemental needs trust or another trust that will fund the third-party supplemental needs trust.

However, while naming the individual's supplemental needs trust is preferable, for public benefits purposes, to naming the individual outright or naming a health and support trust for the individual, doing so in the case of IRAs and qualified retirement plans might raise complications for income tax purposes. A properly drafted supplemental needs trust will not qualify, for IRA distribution purposes, as a "conduit trust" (*i.e.*, a trust that requires the trustee to distribute to a particular trust beneficiary all retirement plan distributions it receives).[50] Therefore, if an IRA or qualified retirement plan is payable to a supplemental needs trust and stretching distributions over the individual beneficiary's life expectancy are desired (instead of a requirement that the entire IRA or qualified retirement plan be distributed and taxed within five years of the participant's death), care must be taken to structure the trust as a qualifying "accumulation trust." Alternatively, if the mix of assets is sufficiently diversified, it might make more sense to fund the supplemental needs trust solely with assets other than IRAs and qualified retirement plans and to leave any IRAs and qualified retirement plans to other beneficiaries.

SPECIAL SITUATIONS

Fixing Problematic Trusts. One challenging question that frequently arises is how to address an irrevocable trust in which an individual with a disability has a beneficial interest that was not properly structured as a supplemental needs trust, either because the disability was not anticipated at the time the trust was drafted or because the drafting attorney was not experienced with supplemental needs trust planning. In those cases, two steps are typically recommended.

First, the trust should be reviewed to determine if the trustee or any other person has a power that can be exercised to direct any assets for the benefit of the individual into a supplemental needs trust. For example, does the trust include a provision by which a trust protector or a mentor may modify the trust for this purpose? Does the trust include an explicit provision by which the trustee is authorized to transfer property from the existing trust to a new trust? Does the trust grant any beneficiary a power of appointment that could be exercised to direct trust property to a different trust?

Second, if the trust itself does not include any provisions authorizing a desired fix, one should consider whether a state decanting statute is available to solve the problem. Decanting statutes are those that allow a trustee to transfer property of the existing trust to a new trust in certain situations, even if the trust document does not explicitly include that authority. Some states have decanting statutes that specifically authorize transfers to supplemental needs trusts in certain cases.

Planning for a Child Whose Eligibility for Public Benefits is Uncertain. Sometimes, when planning for a child with special needs whose medical and developmental circumstances are evolving, it is not clear whether that child will ultimately be eligible for public benefits. Depending on the child's state of residence, it might be possible to leave that child's inheritance to a fully-discretionary trust for the child's benefit that also grants the trustee discretion to transfer the trust assets to a separate supplemental needs trust for the child, while still preserving the child's eligibility for public benefits. The safer approach would be to leave the child's inheritance to a supplemental needs trust. Then, if the child does not ultimately receive public benefits, the supplemental needs trust can be used for any purpose for the child, bearing in mind that distributions will generally have to be made not to the child, but directly to providers of goods and services for the child.

Supplemental Needs Trust for a Spouse. There are special rules related to the assets and income of a spouse for purposes of Medicaid eligibility. As a result, planning with supplemental needs trusts for a spouse is more limited than for other family members. For example, in some states, a supplemental needs trust for a spouse may be created only under a will and not under an inter vivos trust document.[51] Guidance should be sought from a local practitioner with expertise on these issues before creating a supplemental needs trust for the grantor's spouse.

Transfers to a Supplemental Needs Trust for Transferor's Child to Accelerate the Transferor's Own Eligibility for Public Benefits. As noted above, transfers by an individual that is seeking to qualify for SSI or Medicaid generally will trigger a period of ineligibility for benefits. However, there are exceptions to this rule. In addition to the exceptions for certain transfers to a d(4)(A) trust or d(4)(C) pooled trust for the benefit of the transferor, there are exceptions for transfers to a supplemental needs trust for the sole benefit of the transferor's disabled or blind child[52] and for transfers to a supplemental needs trust for the sole benefit of any other disabled or blind individual under the age of sixty-five.[53] Therefore, if a person who is trying to become eligible for public benefits desires to provide for a child of his or hers that is blind or disabled or another individual under the age of sixty-five that is blind or disabled, that person can accelerate his or her eligibility and provide for that child or other individual by transferring his or her assets to a sole benefit supplemental needs trust for that child or other individual.

Personal Injury/Medical Malpractice Settlements. When an individual with a disability is to receive settlement proceeds or monetary damages from a personal injury lawsuit, the receipt of such an award by that individual personally could render them ineligible for current or future public benefits. As a result, it is advisable to consider allocating such an award to a d(4)(A) trust for the benefit of the individual.[54] However, extra caution should be taken before any such proceeds are actually paid to the individual or transferred to the individual's d(4)(A) trust, particularly if a structured settlement is to be awarded or where a state may have an existing lien for medical services that were already rendered to the individual (or where another party, such as Medicare or a private insurance company, has some basis for recovery out of the award prior to the funding of a d(4)(A) trust).

Child Support for Child over Eighteen with Disabilities. In a state which allows or mandates a parent to pay child support for the benefit of a child with disabilities over the age of eighteen, consideration should be given to irrevocably assigning that child support to a supplemental needs trust for the child's benefit pursuant to a court order, so that the child's SSI will not be reduced or eliminated. If, as is the case in most states, the applicable state law treats the support payments as representing the child's right to income, the funds should be directed to a d(4)(A) trust rather than a third-party trust.[55] Although child support may not be paid directly to an ABLE account, if the d(4)(A) trust authorizes the trustee to fund an ABLE account for the trust beneficiary, it might be possible for a d(4)(A) trust to receive child support payments and then transfer some or all of the amounts received to an ABLE account, subject to the ABLE account contribution limitations.

Alimony payments. Similarly, alimony payments (sometimes referred to as "maintenance" payments), which are legally assignable, will not constitute income if they are irrevocably assigned to a trust, such as by court order.[56] Because the former spouse was legally entitled to receive the alimony payments, the funds must be directed to that individual's d(4)(A) trust.

Divorced Parents. Sadly, the rate of divorce is especially high among parents of children with special needs. While, in such cases, each parent could create their own supplemental needs trust or trusts for their child with special needs, administering multiple trusts with different trustees and remainder beneficiaries can be difficult and could put the trustees into the difficult bind of determining which trust or trusts should be spent first (*e.g.*, the trust created by one parent or the trust created by the other). If possible, it would be desirable for the parents to agree on the supplemental needs trusts, perhaps by compromising on the trustee succession and remainder beneficiaries, while doing the rest of their estate planning separate from one another. (See discussion on special needs trusts in the context of divorce in Chapter 2 on "Planning for Divorce.")

Potential Conflict between Parent or Grandparent and Beneficiary. When engaging in supplemental needs trust planning, the family member doing the planning may have different interests and desires than those of the individual with special needs who is the intended beneficiary. For example, a parent or grandparent might wish to create a d(4)(A) trust for an individual with disabilities who has significant assets in order to preserve that individual's eligibility for means-tested public benefits. However, that individual, if competent, might be reluctant to transfer those assets to the d(4)(A) trust due to his or her loss of control over those assets or might wish to establish his or her own d(4)(A) trust with desired terms (*e.g.*, remainder beneficiaries after the required Medicaid payback and trustee succession) that differ from those desired by the parent or grandparent. In those cases, the attorney or other adviser needs to carefully consider who they are representing. It may be prudent for the individual with disabilities to have his or her own counsel to explain to him or her the potential benefits of the d(4)(A) trust and the possibility of creating his or her own d(4)(A) trust, and to help him or her fund the d(4)(A) trust, if desired.

TAX ISSUES WITH SUPPLEMENTAL NEEDS TRUSTS

Income Taxation of d(4)(A) Trusts. Most first-party d(4)(A) trusts meet the definition of grantor trusts as to the beneficiary under Code section 677. A grantor trust is one in which the trust income passes through to the grantor (generally understood to be the person whose assets were used to fund the trust, and who may be different from the person who actually executed the trust instrument). Section 677 treats as a grantor trust any trust "whose income without the approval or consent of any adverse party is, or, in the discretion of the grantor or a non-adverse party, or both, may be distributed to the grantor or the grantor's spouse; held or accumulated for future distribution to the grantor or the grantor's spouse." Therefore, if the trustee of a d(4)(A) trust is not a remainder beneficiary of the trust and is, therefore, not adverse to the beneficiary, the trust should qualify as a grantor trust.

At the same time, many first-party d(4)(A) trusts also meet the definition of a "qualified disability trust" under Code section 642(b)(2)(C). Under that section, for a given taxable year, a qualified disability trust is a trust established for the sole lifetime benefit of a person under the age of sixty-five years who has been determined by the Social Security Administration to have been disabled for some portion of the taxable year. Where there has been such a determination of disability, a first-party d(4)(A) trust clearly fits within this definition. A qualified disability trust is generally taxed like a complex trust, except that instead of having the $100 personal exemption typically available to trusts, it is allowed the higher personal exemption to which individuals are entitled.

In light of both section 677 and section 642(b)(2)(C) arguably applying to first-party d(4)(A) trusts, tax professionals and commentators differ in their treatment of them. Some argue that grantor trust status always trumps other income tax categories, and, therefore, first-party d(4)(A) trusts should clearly be reported as grantor trusts. Others argue that because section 642(b)(2)(C) was specifically designed for supplemental needs trusts, it should trump the grantor trust rules and apply instead when the trust meets that section's requirements. Note that, because distributions from a properly-drafted supplemental needs trust must always be in the trustee's discretion (instead of being mandatory), such a trust will never be a simple trust for income tax purposes.

As a practical matter, grantor trust status may be beneficial for tax purposes in that the beneficiary's individual marginal income tax rate likely will be less than the trust's marginal income tax rate. On the other hand, qualified disability trust status may be beneficial because the increased personal exemption combined with the ability to deduct expenses might yield tax savings. In addition, as noted earlier, the eligibility rules for SSI and Medicaid include income limits. Although the applicable Social Security Administration rules do not treat earnings of a d(4)(A) trust as income to the beneficiary for SSI eligibility purposes unless the trust directs, or the trustee makes, payment of those earnings to the beneficiary,[57] by treating the trust as a separate taxpayer, no income will pass through to the beneficiary's income tax return. This treatment can avoid having to reference the applicable rules or otherwise explain to the Social Security Administration or the state authority administering the Medicaid program why that income for tax purposes does not count as the beneficiary's income for public benefit eligibility purposes.

Ultimately, the tax preparer will need to decide how to report the trust. If the trust is reported as a grantor trust, a clear paper trail of trust income should be established by obtaining a separate taxpayer identification number for the trust (grantor trusts generally may report under either the grantor/beneficiary's social security number or under a separate taxpayer identification number) and by filing annual grantor trust reporting returns for the trust. In addition, the trust document should provide that, if the trust is treated as a grantor trust for federal income tax purposes:

- the trustee shall pay directly to the taxing authority any income tax liability of the beneficiary resulting from trust income;

- the beneficiary shall not have any right to or interest in any such funds;

- such funds shall not be treated as a resource, or a distribution of income, to the beneficiary; and

- any tax refund shall be paid directly to the trustee to the extent that such refund is attributable to amounts previously paid by the trustee.

Income Taxation of Third-Party Trusts. If a parent, other family member, or friend of the beneficiary with a disability funds a third-party supplemental needs trust for that individual, it will be a grantor trust as to the grantor (the parent, other family member, or friend) if the grantor is the trustee, retains a power of appointment over the trust assets, or is a remainder beneficiary.[58] Depending on the overall tax and financial situation of the parties, grantor trust status as to the trust funder might or might not be desirable, and, therefore, the income tax implications should be considered when deciding whether to give the grantor any such authorities or interests in the trust document.

If the trust is not a grantor trust, its income tax status for a particular year will depend on the current trust beneficiaries. If the trust was established for the sole lifetime benefit of an individual with disabilities under the age of sixty-five years, and that individual has been determined by the Social Security Administration to be disabled for at least a portion of the taxable year, then it will be a qualified disability trust for that taxable year.[59] Otherwise, the trust will be a complex trust for that taxable year. As with first-party supplemental needs trusts, a properly-drafted third-party supplemental needs trust should never be a simple trust because distributions will always be in the trustee's discretion.

Estate Tax Inclusion with d(4)(A) Trusts. Because d(4)(A) trusts and d(4)(C) pooled trusts are typically funded with the separate assets of the trust beneficiary, upon the beneficiary's death they are generally includible in the beneficiary's estate for estate tax purposes under Code section 2036, subject to an estate tax deduction for any Medicaid reimbursement obligation. When these trusts are particularly large, such as when they are funded out of a large personal injury or medical malpractice settlement, consideration should be given to incorporating helpful provisions for transfer-tax planning purposes. For example, it might be desirable to include a provision in the trust directing the trustee,

absent a contrary direction in the beneficiary's will, to contribute to the payment of estate tax that portion of the estate tax attributable to inclusion of the trust assets in the beneficiary's estate. In addition, if the trust assets are substantial, interests of remainder beneficiaries may be left in trust (rather than distributed outright) in order to exclude the assets from those remainder beneficiaries' estates and to possibly exempt them from generation-skipping transfer tax, subject to the lifetime beneficiary's available GST exemption. If the d(4)(A) trust is being created via court approval, it will be necessary to explain to the court the reasons for the tax planning.

Estate Tax Inclusion with Third-Party Trusts. The assets of a third-party supplemental needs trust will generally not be includible in the trust beneficiary's estate at the beneficiary's death because the beneficiary should not have a general power of appointment over those assets.

If the trust grantor is the trustee or retains a power of appointment and also funds the trust by lifetime gift, then the trust assets at the grantor's death will be includible in the grantor's estate for estate tax purposes. If, in the more common case, the grantor establishes the trust but funds it only by testamentary transfer (and not by any lifetime transfer), then the trust itself will have no assets at the grantor's death includible in the grantor's estate, but the assets used to fund the trust at the grantor's death might be includible in the grantor's estate.

Gift Tax Issues Related to Supplemental Needs Trusts. As noted in the section of this chapter regarding drafting recommendations, a beneficiary with a disability should not be given withdrawal rights (including Crummey withdrawal rights) over a third-party supplemental needs trust. As a result, gifts to the trust cannot qualify for the gift tax annual exclusion as to that beneficiary. This rule can be problematic when a family wishes to hold a fundraiser for the trust beneficiary and have donors contribute to that beneficiary's third-party supplemental needs trust because those gifts would technically be reportable by the donors.

In contrast, transfers to an ABLE account will qualify for the gift tax annual exclusion, bearing in mind that, in any calendar year, annual contributions from all sources combined cannot exceed the gift tax annual exclusion amount for one donor to one donee (which is $15,000 for 2019). As a result, as noted earlier, an ABLE account may be particularly helpful where several family members or friends wish to make small gifts for the beneficiary or where there will be a fundraiser for the beneficiary.

If an individual makes a contribution to a third-party supplemental needs trust and is the trustee of that trust, retains a power of appointment, or has a reversionary interest in the trust, then the contribution to the trust will not constitute a completed gift but instead the contributed assets will remain in the contributor's taxable estate.

CONCLUSION

Planning for the many modern families that have a loved one with a disability does not need to be unduly complex. However, it does require much more than simply adding a supplemental needs trust paragraph or article to an otherwise standard will and trust document. Instead, it requires a clear understanding of the different alternatives available to a family when there is a family member with a disability, the rules governing those alternatives, an ability to apply those rules to the family's particular factual situation and goals, and a recognition of when to seek specialized assistance. When done wrong, the costs are high in that an individual with a disability who would otherwise be able to access important public benefits could lose their eligibility. When done right, it can bring tremendous comfort and security to the individual and their family, as well as psychic rewards to the practitioner. We hope this chapter has provided helpful, practical guidance to allow you to do it right.

CHAPTER ENDNOTES

1. Okoro CA, Hollis ND, Cyrus AC, Griffin-Blake S. Prevalence of Disabilities and Health Care Access by Disability Status and Type Among Adults — United States, 2016. MMWR Morb Mortal Wkly Rep 2018;67:882–887.

2. The expanded Medicaid medical coverage provisions in those states that have participated in the Affordable Care Act's Medicaid expansion are generally subject to income, but not asset, limitations. In contrast, the long-term care and other longstanding provisions of Medicaid separate from the Affordable Care Act include both income and asset limitations. For convenience, when Medicaid is referred to throughout the rest of this chapter, that reference is to traditional Medicaid with its asset as well as income limitations.

3. So called, because it is authorized and established pursuant to 42 U.S.C. §1396p(d)(4)(A).

4. So called, because it is authorized and established pursuant to 42 U.S.C. §1396p(d)(4)(C).

5. 42 U.S.C. 1382c(a)(1), 42 U.S.C. 1382(a)(1), and Social Security Program Operations Manual Systems (POMS) SI 00810.001.

6. 42 U.S.C. 1382c(a)(3).

7. 42 U.S.C. 1382(a)(3)(B); 20 C.F.R. 416.1201; and POMS SI 01110.003.

8. 42 U.S.C. 1382b(a); 20 C.F.R. §§416.1203-416.1204, 416.1210-416.1239, 416.1245, and 416.1247; POMS SI 01110.210; POMS SI 01130.740.C.3.

9. POMS SI 01120.205D(3).

10. 20 C.F.R. §416.1202.

11. POMS SI 01150.110.

12. 20 C.F.R. §416.1100-1182.

13. 20 C.F.R. §416.1130-1157.

14. 20 C.F.R. §416.1165.

15. 20 C.F.R. §416.1201; POMS SI 01120.200.

16. 42 U.S.C. 1382(b)(e)(5).

17. 42 U.S.C. 1396p(d)(4)(A).

18. POMS SI 01120.203C2a.

19. 42 U.S.C. 1396p(d)(4)(C); POMS SI 01120.203B2a.

20. Available online at: specialneedsanswers.com/pooled-trust.

21. Internal Revenue Code (I.R.C.) §529A(e)(1)(A).

22. 42 U.S.C. 1395x(r)(1).

23. I.R.C. §529A(e)(1)(B).

24. I.R.C. Notice 2015-81

25. POMS SI 01130.740

26. I.R.C. §529A(e)(5).

27. I.R.C. §529A(c)(3).

28. I.R.C. §529A(b)(2).

29. I.R.C. §25B(d)(1)(D).

30. I.R.C. §529A(b)(4).

31. I.R.C. §529A(b)(6).

32. POMS SI 01130.740.

33. I.R.C. §529A(f).

34. http://www.ablenrc.org/.

35. I.R.C. §529(c)(3)(C)(i)(III) and I.R.C. §529(e)(2).

36. POMS SI 01120.203f.

37. I.R.C. §72(t)(2)(A)(iii).

38. See P.L.R. 200620025 and P.L.R. 201116005.

39. See P.L.R. 200117042.

40. POMS SI 01120.201F.3.a

41. 20 C.F.R. §416.1202.

42. I.R.C. 2036.

43. The rules for which can be found at POMS SI 01110.003 Resources limits for SSI benefits.

44. Social Security Administration Emergency Message EM-16012, dated March 2, 2016, secure.ssa.gov/poms.nsf/Home?readform.

45. POMS SI 01120.199 Early Termination Provisions and Trusts.

46. POMS SI 01120.201I.1.c.

47. POMS SI 01120.201F.3.b.

48. POMS SI 01120.201F.3.c.

49. *Crummey v. Comm'r*, 392 F.2d 82, (9th Cir. 1968). Named for the first person to use a trust structure whereby gifts to a trust qualify for annual exclusion treatment by providing the recipient a window of time (often thirty days) to take immediate control of the gift.

50. For a discussion of certain limited planning situations, where a conduit trust might be paired with a separate third-party supplemental needs trust for a child with special needs, see Grassi Jr., Sebastian V. and Welber, Nancy H., "Estate Planning with Retirement Benefits for a Special Needs Child: Part 2 – Trusts as Beneficiaries of Retirement Plan Assets," American Bar Association, 23 *Probate & Property Magazine* 60 (Sept./Oct. 2009).

51. 42 U.S.C. §1396p(d)(2)(A) provides that an individual shall be considered to have established a trust if the individual's assets were a part of all of the trust corpus and the individual's spouse (among others) established such trust other than by will.

52. POMS SI 01150.121.2.

53. POMS SI 01150.121.2.

54. POMS SI 01120.201C(2)b, citing a trust funded with settlement proceeds from a doctor's insurance company to be considered a trust funded with the individual's assets.

55. POMS SI 01120.200.G.d.1 and POMS SI 01120.201.C.2.b, providing that when court-ordered child support to be paid directly into the trust, the Social Security Administration will consider it to be irrevocably assigned to the trust and will not count it as income.

56. POMS SI 01120.200.G.d.1.

57. POMS SSI 01120.201J.1.a.

58. I.R.C. §674.

59. I.R.C. §642(b)(2)(C).

HOLDING SUBCHAPTER S STOCK IN TRUST (AND ESTATES) SUBCHAPTER J MEETS SUBCHAPTER S

CHAPTER 11

INTRODUCTION

The purpose of this chapter is to give an overview of the Subchapter S corporation ("S Corp")[1] rules for holding S Corp stock in trusts during the grantor's lifetime and after death. We begin with some basic S Corp requirements and then delve into the shareholder rules as it applies to trusts and estates.

An S Corp is subject to the rules under Subchapter S and Subchapter C of the Internal Revenue Code. To the extent that a provision is covered under Subchapter S, it trumps the Subchapter C rule.[2] Thus, when dealing with distributions, redemptions, and attribution rules, quite often the planner must be familiar with both the Subchapter S and Subchapter C rules, since some of the Subchapter S rules will supersede the Subchapter C rules.

CORPORATE LEVEL REQUIREMENTS OF AN S CORPORATION

There are a number of corporate level rules that are particular to an S Corp.[3] For instance, the corporation must be a domestic corporation,[4] it may not be an ineligible corporation,[5] it can only have a limited amount of shareholders,[6] the shareholders must be of a certain type (i.e., individuals, trusts and estates),[7] and it may only have one class of stock.[8]

Classes of Stock

An S Corp can only have "one class of stock".[9] The regulations speak in terms of the stock conferring identical rights to distribution and liquidation proceeds,[10] and instruct as to when stock confers such identical rights to distribution and liquidation proceeds.[11] Specifically, the regulations provide that a difference of voting rights is allowed.[12]

It is important to review not only the stock certificate and articles of incorporation to determine if there is one class of stock, but also the bylaws, shareholder agreements, compensation and/or employment agreements, as well as other governing provisions of relevant agreements, to see if those other documents create substantial rights to cause the corporation to have a second class of stock.[13] Documents alone won't tell the full story. Facts and circumstances also weigh on the determination of whether a corporation has one class of stock. Any distribution (actual, constructive or deemed) that differs in timing or amount will be given appropriate tax effect.[14] To determine if there is more than one class of stock, generally only those shares outstanding are considered.[15]

Number of Shareholders

There can be a maximum of 100-shareholders in an S Corp. Estates and certain trusts can be shareholders as well as individuals.[16]

Generally determining the number of shareholders is easy. However, in closely-held family business settings, because of the various attribution rules that apply to related persons, determining the number of shareholders is a bit tricky.[17] Generally, each individual is counted as one person. But in the family setting, where spouses own stock, they are treated as one person.[18] Additionally, under the family attribution rules, members of a family with a 'common ancestor' are treated as one person. Thus, if stock is held by four siblings and their sixteen children, all of those individuals will be treated as one shareholder for the 100-shareholder rule.[19] Thus even though twenty individuals are owners of the stock, for the 100-shareholder rule, there is only one shareholder. Effectively, because of this very liberal family attribution rule, with a closely held S Corp owned primarily by family members and trusts for family members, the 100-shareholder rule will generally not be in jeopardy.

An estate is generally treated as one person for the 100-shareholder rule.[20] Note for spouses, the estate of a deceased spouse and a surviving spouse are treated as one person.[21] Likewise, the estates of a deceased couple are also treated as a single person if both spouses were U.S. citizens or residents.[22]

There are a few different types of trusts that qualify as S Corp shareholders. The three most common are: the Electing Small Business Trusts ("ESBT"),[23] the Qualified Subchapter S Trusts ("QSST"),[24] and grantor trusts.[25] As with all trusts, there are different persons who have different beneficial interests (e.g., some are current and vested, some are future and vested, some are contingent and unvested, some are vested subject to divestment, some are entitled to income, while others are only entitled to principal, etc.). Understanding this issue and the multitude of interests that a trust beneficiary could have, the Regulations provide a practical approach for ESBTs in that they only count the "potential current beneficiaries" for purposes of the 100-shareholder limitation.[26]

A "potential current beneficiary" is any person who at any time is entitled to a distribution of income or principal (whether mandatory or discretionary).[27]

If a trust beneficiary has a power of appointment, it is disregarded for purposes of this rule. Thus, any donees of such power are not considered potential current beneficiaries, unless the power is exercised in favor of that particular donee (or donees).[28]

The "potential current beneficiaries" are treated as shareholders of the S Corp. If there are no potential current beneficiaries for a particular year, then the trust is treated as the shareholder.[29]

If a trust holds S Corp stock at any point in time, it is important to review the trust instrument to determine the potential current beneficiaries, so that one could determine if the 100-shareholder rule is in jeopardy. If the shareholder limit is exceeded at any moment, the corporation will no longer qualify as an S Corp.

It is important to understand that the "potential current beneficiary" test is used only for the purpose of determining if the 100-shareholder limitation is met (or not). Separate and apart from this are rules regarding whether a trust qualifies as a QSST or ESBT. For rules on beneficiaries (called "eligible beneficiaries"), see the section below.

All of the shareholders must elect S Corp status. Provided that none of the S Corp requirements are violated, the corporation is taxed as a pass-through entity (i.e., with the shareholders being are taxed on a per diem, pro rata basis).[30]

ELIGIBLE SHAREHOLDERS

An S Corp can only have certain types of shareholders. We separate the shareholders as those that are eligible during lifetime and those that are eligible after the death of the shareholder.[31]

Lifetime Eligible Shareholder. Generally, all individuals,[32] other than non-resident aliens,[33] are permitted shareholders. An individual may own stock as a joint tenant, tenant by the entireties and as a tenant in common.[34]

Grantor Trust. There are two types of grantor trusts that are eligible shareholders: (i) grantor trusts where the grantor is treated as an owner under Code sections 671 through and including 677, and (ii) grantor trusts where someone other than the grantor is treated as an owner under Code section 678.[35]

Grantor is treated as Owner. Trusts that are treated as wholly grantor trusts[36] are permitted as shareholders.[37] The statute provides that the "deemed owner" will be treated as the shareholder.[38] If the trust is not a wholly owned grantor trust, it will not be a shareholder. The trust may qualify as an ESBT, however.[39]

Joint Grantor Trusts by Married Couples. Literally, Code section 1361(c)(2)(A)(i) requires that "an" individual own all of the trust. Thus, on its face, it appears that joint grantor trusts would not qualify. However, Treasury Regulation section 1.1361-1(e)(2) and a few private rulings seem to allow married couples to own a grantor trust that may own S Corp stock.[40]

Non-Grantor is treated as Owner. *Crummey* power holders can be considered the owner of a grantor trust as a result of Code section 678, if the trust is otherwise a wholly owned grantor trust as to the *Crummey* power holder. In this case, such person will be the deemed shareholder of the S Corp stock. The IRS has issued many rulings on this topic.[41]

Upon the grantor's death, the trust may be an eligible trust for a period of two years. See After Death Eligible Shareholders discussion below. The estate of the "deemed owner" (generally the estate of the grantor of the grantor trust) will be considered the shareholder for income tax reporting purposes.[42]

Qualified Subchapter S Trust ("QSST"). The QSST can be a S Corp shareholder. In order for a trust to be treated as a QSST it must meet the following statutory requirements:

- during the life of the current income beneficiary, there shall be only one income beneficiary of the trust;[43]

- any corpus distributed during the life of the current income beneficiary may be distributed only to such beneficiary;[44]

- the income interest of the current income beneficiary in the trust shall terminate on the earlier of such beneficiary's death or the termination of the trust,[45]

- upon the termination of the trust during the life of the current income beneficiary, the trust shall distribute all of its assets to such beneficiary,[46] and

- all of the income (within the meaning of Code Section 643(b)) is distributed (or required to be distributed) currently to 1 individual who is a citizen or resident of the United States.[47]

Additionally, the trust's terms must always provide that the first four statutory requirements will always be met for the trust to qualify as a QSST.[48]

Example 1. The terms of the trust are silent with respect to corpus distributions. Further distributions of corpus to a person other than the current income beneficiary are permitted under local law during the life of the current income beneficiary.

Because the terms of the trust do not preclude the possibility that corpus may be distributed to a

person other than the current income beneficiary, the trust cannot qualify as a QSST.[49]

Importantly, the determination of whether the terms of a trust meet all of such requirements depends upon: (a) the terms of the trust instrument, and (b) applicable local law.[50]

Election Requirements. The QSST election cannot take effect until the S Corp has filed its S election (on Form 2553). The QSST may make a concurrent S Corp election by executing the third page of the Form 2553. If, during life, the S stock has been transferred to a non-grantor trust[51] that qualifies as a QSST, the current income beneficiary of the trust must make the election by signing a statement with the following information:

- name, address, and taxpayer identification number of the current income beneficiary, the trust, and the corporation;[52]

- statement that the election is being made under section 1361(d)(2);[53]

- the date on which the election is to become effective;[54]

- the date on which the stock of the corporation was transferred to the trust;[55] and

- all information and representations necessary to show that

  o under the terms of the trust and state law:

    ♦ during the life of the current income beneficiary, there will be only one income beneficiary;[56]

    ♦ any corpus distributed during the life of the current income beneficiary may be distributed only to that beneficiary;[57]

    ♦ the current beneficiary's income interest will terminate on the earlier of the beneficiary's death or upon termination of the trust;[58] and

    ♦ upon the termination of the trust during the life of such income beneficiary, the trust will distribute all its assets to such beneficiary;[59]

o the trust is required to distribute all of its income currently, or that the trustee will distribute all of its income currently if not so required by the terms of the trust;[60] and

o no distribution of income or corpus by the trust will be in satisfaction of the grantor's legal obligation to support or maintain the income beneficiary.[61]

There is no pre-printed form for this election; thus, the drafting attorney should prepare a statement with the above requirements on the statement.[62]

Simple and Complex Trusts Qualifying as QSSTs. A complex trust may qualify as a QSST if the trustee distributes all of the income annually. A simple trust will qualify (regardless of whether the income is actually distributed). A careful reading of the requirements is essential to determine whether the trust will qualify as a QSST.

The QSST election is required to be made within the sixteen-day and two-month period beginning on the date that the S Corp stock is transferred to a trust that would not otherwise be considered an eligible shareholder (e.g., a grantor trust

If an S election terminates because of a late QSST election, the corporation may request inadvertent termination relief under the IRS' revenue procedure or by private letter ruling. The IRS issued Rev. Proc. 2013-30[63] to simplify late elections (not only for QSSTs, but also for ESBTs and other elections, as well as to eliminate significant user fees). If the beneficiary does not meet the simplified method requirements, then the beneficiary must file for a letter ruling.[64] To assist the taxpayer, the IRS added some very helpful flowcharts (at the end of the revenue procedure).[65]

ELECTING SMALL BUSINESS TRUST ("ESBT")

Electing Small Business Trusts ("ESBTs"), introduced in 1997, are eligible to hold S Corp stock.[66] Consistent with Congress' desire to make ESBTs better estate planning vehicles,[67] ESBTs may have multiple income beneficiaries, accumulate income, sprinkle both income and principal among the various beneficiaries, and serve as generation-skipping transfer vehicles. This makes them generally more flexible than QSSTs.

To qualify as an ESBT, the trust must provide that:

- the trust must be a trust (although obvious, it is a statutory requirement);[68]

- only individuals, estates and certain charitable organizations[69] are permissible beneficiaries;[70]

- no interest in the trust may be acquired by purchase;[71] and

- the trustee made an election under Code Section 1361(e)(3).[72]

Further, the ESTB must not:

- be a QSST;[73]

- be a tax-exempt trust;[74]

- be a charitable remainder trust;[75] and

- be a foreign trust.[76]

Interestingly, a grantor trust may elect to be an ESBT.[77]

The Beneficiaries of an ESBT

An ESBT may only have individuals,[78] estates,[79] or certain charitable organizations as beneficiaries.[80] The Regulations provide that the beneficiaries of an ESBT include any person who has a present, remainder, or reversionary interest in the trust.[81]

Generally, either a trust or an individual could be considered a beneficiary of the ESBT. For trusts to be considered an ESBT beneficiary, the trust must qualify as a "distributee trust". A distributee trust is a trust that receives (or may receive) a distribution from an ESBT, whether the rights to receive the distribution are fixed or contingent, or immediate or deferred.[82] If the distributee trust is a charitable organization defined in Code Section 170(c)(2) or (3), then the trust could be considered the beneficiary. If the distributee trust is a trust that is not such a charitable organization, then the regulations require that one looks through the trust to determine the beneficiaries.[83]

Example 2. Assume that a trust is created for surviving spouse ("SS") for life and remainder in trust for children for life. The beneficiaries of the ESBT are SS and the remainder trust.

Since the remainder trust is not a charitable organization defined under Code Section 170(c)(2) and (3), one must look through the remainder trust to determine the beneficiaries. In this case, SS and the decedent's children are the beneficiaries of the ESBT.

———————————

The purpose of determining the "beneficiaries" of the trust is solely to determine whether the "beneficiary" is an eligible shareholder. Thus, it is critical to review the rules to determine who are the "potential current beneficiaries" and the "eligible beneficiaries" of the "potential" ESBT.

The Election Requirements

The election must be made by the trustee (who must sign and file a statement, with the service center where the S Corp files its income tax return (the "election statement")), by executing a statement that meets the requirements set forth below.[84]

The election statement must include the following:

- the name, address, and taxpayer identification number of the trust, the potential current beneficiaries, and the S Corp in which the trust currently owns stock;

- an identification of the election as an ESBT election made under Code Section 1361(e)(3);

- the first date on which the trust owned stock in each S Corp;

- the date on which the election is to become effective (not earlier than fifteen days and two-months before the date on which the election is filed); and

- certain representations signed by the trustee.[85]

The election must be filed within the same time requirements for filing a qualified subchapter S trust (QSST) election.[86] Like QSSTs, the IRS has permitted late elections for ESBTs.[87] Unlike a QSST, an ESBT cannot make a protective ESBT election. Any attempt to make an election would cause the trust to be an ineligible shareholder and effectively terminate the S election for the S Corp. Relief may be available under Code Section 1361(f) if an inadvertent, ineffective election is attempted.[88]

Income Tax. A trust that qualifies as an ESBT may make an ESBT election notwithstanding that the trust is a wholly-owned grantor trust. If a trust makes a valid ESBT election, the trust will be treated as an ESBT for income tax purposes as of the effective date of the ESBT election.[89] An ESBT has only one employer identification number (EIN). If an existing trust makes an ESBT election, the trust continues to use the EIN it currently uses. If an ESBT election is effective on a day other than the first day of the trust's taxable year, the ESBT election does not cause the trust's taxable year to close.[90]

The termination of the ESBT election (including a termination caused by a conversion of the ESBT to a QSST) other than on the last day of the trust's taxable year also does not cause the trust's taxable year to close. If, during the taxable year of an S Corp, a trust is an ESBT for part of the year and an otherwise eligible shareholder for the rest of the year, the taxable income is allocated between the two owners of trusts under Code Section 1377(a), as discussed above.

Voting trusts. The use of voting trusts in estate planning is allowed but is not common[91] Nonetheless, understanding voting trust issues with an S Corp is necessary. There is little statutory guidance as to the requirements to qualify a voting trust for S Corp purposes; however, the Regulations provide a short list of items for the voting trust to qualify as a S Corp shareholder, as follows:

- a written agreement delegating the right to vote the stock to one or more trustees;

- trust distributions be made to the beneficial owners of the stock;

- the stock pass to the beneficial owners at the end of the trust term; and

- the trust terminate at a specific date or event (under state law or under the terms of the agreement).[92]

Further, to qualify as a voting trust, the "beneficial owners must be treated as the owner of their respective portions of the trust under Subpart E and the trust."[93]

AFTER DEATH ELIGIBLE SHAREHOLDERS

In addition to being qualified shareholders during life, QSSTs[94] and ESBTs[95] are the two most common (but not the only) types of shareholders that can also hold S Corp stock after the death of an individual.

During Estate / Trust Administration. In the estate settlement process, there are two other possible trusts that would qualify as shareholders:

- Trusts that were grantor trusts during the life of the grantor (hereinafter, "Continuing Grantor Trusts"); and

- Trusts that receive S Corp stock from a decedent's estate (hereinafter, "Testamentary S Trusts"); however, this type of trust only qualifies for a limited duration of two years after the trust receives the property from the estate.[96]

Additionally, an estate qualifies as a shareholder.[97]

Continuing Grantor Trusts. If S Corp stock was held by a grantor trust before death, the trust (which is no longer a grantor trust because of death) is permitted to hold the S Corp stock for a maximum period of two years after the grantor's death.[98] No special election is necessary to allow the Continuing Grantor Trust to continue to hold the S Corp stock.

Testamentary S Trusts. As set forth above, an estate may transfer or a Qualified Revocable Trust, may make a deemed transfer of) S Corp stock to a "Testamentary S Trust" and such recipient trust would qualify as an eligible S Corp shareholder for a period of up to two years after the date of the transfer (or deemed transfer).[99] The two-year period is shortened upon disposition from the trust to another eligible shareholder (e.g., a QSST or an individual).[100]

Estates. In addition to the four trusts[101] that can be shareholders during the settlement process, decedent's estates can be shareholders, too.[102] Interestingly, unlike the two-year limitation for the Continuing Grantor Trust and the Testamentary S Trusts, the statute does not place a limit on the period of time that an estate can hold S Corp stock. In fact, in an older case decided before the re-write of subchapter S in 1982, the Court held that S Corp stock could be held in the estate for a reasonable time. Beyond that "reasonable time" the

beneficiaries would be considered the owners of the S Corp stock.[103]

In a revenue ruling issued almost thirty years ago under the "old" subchapter S provisions and prior to the re-write of Code section 6166 the IRS held that "the administration of the estate will not be considered unreasonably prolonged for purposes of Code section 641(a)(3),[104] and thus the estate will continue to be an eligible shareholder within the meaning of Code section 1371(a) for the period during which the estate complies with the provisions of Code section 6166."[105] Thus, if an estate qualifies for the benefits of Code section 6166 and the qualifying entity or entities are S Corp stock, then, during the Code section 6166 payment period (assuming that the estate continues to meet all of the requirements under Code section 6166) the estate could hold the S Corp stock.

The following examples illustrate the various entities that can be shareholders during the settlement process:

Example 3. A held S Corp stock in her revocable trust (RT) which is solely for her benefit and can be revoked by A at any time. Upon D's death the trust provides for the creation of a credit shelter trust and marital QTIP trust for her spouse, B, for life and remainder to A's children.

Analysis: During A's lifetime, the S Corp stock is held in a grantor trust, which is an eligible shareholder. Upon A's death, the S Corp stock could continue to be held in A's now irrevocable estate administration trust (i.e., the Continuing Grantor Trust) for a period of two years.

If the S Corp stock is distributed during the two-year period to another trust, the trustee (and perhaps the beneficiaries) of that trust would have to qualify as a beneficiary. It is likely that a QSST or ESBT election would thereafter be made.

At the end of the two-year period, if the S Corp stock is still held in the estate administration trust, the trustee would have to either make an ESBT or QSST election.

Example 4. Let's assume the same facts as in Example 3, except in this case let's assume that instead of titling stock in the RT, A holds the S Corp stock in her individual name. Let's further assume that A's Will is a pour-over will that pours-over to her Revocable Trust (i.e., the then irrevocable estate administration trust at A's death).

During life, A is an eligible shareholder because she is an individual. At death, A's estate becomes a shareholder. The stock can be held in the estate for a reasonable time.[106] When the personal representative distributes the stock to the RT (which is now an irrevocable estate administration trust), the S Corp stock could be held in a transitional / administrative trust (i.e., a Testamentary S Trust) for a period of two years after the personal representative distributed the stock from the estate. Thereafter, again, depending upon the terms of the trust, the trustee could distribute shares to an ESBT or QSST. In this case, there were five different possible shareholders (i.e., the individual, the estate, the Testamentary S Trust, the QSST and ESBT) from the date of death through the administration process.

Example 5. Let's assume the facts of Example 3, and further assume that A held stock both in her individual name and her revocable trust (both of which are eligible shareholders). At death, her estate and the revocable trust become shareholders. In this example, the S Corp stock could possibly be held in her estate, a Testamentary S Trust, a Continuing Grantor Trust, an ESBT and/or a QSST.

Summary

The examples demonstrate that during the relatively short period of administration, various entities can hold the S Corp stock. Importantly, the income tax implications for the different entities are different (as discussed below). Thus, because there is a possibility that the S Corp stock could be held by up to five or six different entities, and all of which are taxed in slightly different manner, one must be cognizant of these implications and the effect it has to all of the parties (i.e., the trust, the estate and their respective beneficiaries).

TAX IMPLICATIONS OF SHAREHOLDERS – WHO IS THE SHAREHOLDER?

An S Corp generally does not pay federal income taxes,[107] rather, items of income, deduction, gain, loss and credits (hereinafter "tax attributes") are "passed through" to the shareholder.[108]

Where trusts are the record holders of the S Corp stock for state law purposes, depending upon the type of trust there are three possible persons who are subject to the S Corp's tax attributes:

- the grantor of the trust (or actually the deemed owner of the trust);

- the trust; and/or

- the trust beneficiary(ies).

In the case of an ESBT, it is possible for all three (i.e., the deemed owner, the trust and the beneficiary) to be subject to tax attributes. What further complicates the issue is the allocation of fiduciary income and principal when the trust is taxed on the pass-through income. Thus, understanding who is subject to the tax attributes is important, if not critical.

Individuals as owners of S Corp Stock. Individuals are the easiest shareholders understand. The rule is simple: tax attributes are allocated to that individual based upon his or her pro rata, per diem ownership.[109]

Grantor Trusts. Tax attributes are allocated to that deemed owner based upon the deemed owner's ownership on a pro rata, per diem ownership.[110]

QSSTs

During the QSST's income beneficiary's lifetime, the tax laws provide that such income beneficiary is treated akin to a grantor of a grantor trust, in that the beneficiary is treated as a deemed owner and the QSST's tax attributes are allocated to the income beneficiary based on pro rata, per diem ownership.[111] Special rules apply when the QSST disposes of the stock during life (discussed next) and when the beneficiary dies.

If Stock is Disposed during Life. If the S Corp stock is disposed during the income beneficiary's lifetime, solely for determining the tax consequences of such disposition (i.e., gain and/or loss on disposition), the income beneficiary is <u>not</u> treated as deemed owner.[112] The theory here is that the if the stock is disposed (e.g., sold) the trust (with respect to that disposed stock) is no longer deemed to be a QSST; therefore, under regular income tax trust rules, the trust is deemed to be owner of the stock and the tax attributes from the sale are attributed to the trust (and not the current beneficiary).

Congress recognizes two exceptions that should apply in the event of a disposition:

- Code Section 469 – passive activity loss carryover issues; and

- Code Section 465 - at-risk limitation issues.[113]

The rationale behind these exceptions was to ensure that if the rules of Code Sections 469 and 465 limited losses or deductions during the time that the S Corp stock was held by the QSST, thus, limiting the losses directly at the income beneficiary level, that upon disposition, the same income beneficiary should be able to take advantage of the recapture provisions of Code Sections 469 and 465 that attempt to release the loss carryovers upon disposition of a passive or at-risk activity, respectively.

Example 6. Assume that J is the beneficiary of a QSST (owning S Corp) created for him by his father, L, and that the QSST sells the S Corp stock to an unrelated 3rd party.

As of the date of the sale, the QSST election terminates as to the stock sold and any gain or loss recognized on the sale will be recognized by the trust (i.e., J, will not recognize the income from the sale).

Thus, the portions of the trust other than the portion consisting of S Corp stock are subject to subparts A through D of subchapter J of chapter 1, except as otherwise required by subpart E of the Internal Revenue Code (i.e., the grantor trust rules).[114]

Example 7. Let's assume the same facts as Example 6, except let's assume that the QSST distributes the S Corp stock to J, the income beneficiary.

Similar to the result in Example 6, in this case, the QSST election terminates as to the distributed stock and the consequences of the distribution are determined by reference to the status of the trust apart from the income beneficiary's terminating ownership status under Code Sections 678 and 1361(d)(1). Thus, the portions of the trust other than the portion consisting of S Corp stock are subject to subparts A through D of subchapter J of chapter 1, except as otherwise required by subpart E of the Internal Revenue Code.[115]

K-1s- Who gets them? The income beneficiary of the QSST should receive the K-1 each year from the time that the trust becomes a QSST. The pro rata, per diem rules for the allocation of the tax attributes apply for the first and last year that the income beneficiary is the deemed owner of the S Corp stock in the QSST.

When Beneficiary of QSST Dies

While S Corp Stock is held by Trust. Upon the income beneficiary's death taxation depends upon whether the trust "continues" or "terminates" under local law. Simply, if the trust terminates, a new election must be made within two years from the income beneficiary's date of death; whereas, if the trust continues no new election is necessary.

If the trust terminates, as of the date of the income beneficiary's death, the estate of the income beneficiary is treated as the shareholder of the S Corp stock held by the QSST (or former QSST as the case may be).[116] The estate ordinarily will cease to be treated as the shareholder for purposes of Code Section 1361(b)(1) upon the earlier of (a) the transfer of that stock by the trust or (b) the expiration of the two-year period beginning on the day of the income beneficiary's death. If the trust continues to hold the stock beyond the two-year period the corporation will no longer be an eligible S Corp.

If the trust continues then no new QSST election needs to be filed, the successor income beneficiary is taxed on the tax attributes of the S Corp on a pro rata, per diem basis.[117]

The determination of whether a trust continues or terminates is dependent upon state law. The regulations provide examples to illustrate the point.[118]

Example 8. Shares of stock in Corporation X, an S Corp, are held by Trust A, a QSST for which a QSST election was made. B is the sole income beneficiary of Trust A. On B's death, under the terms of Trust A and under local law, the trust is deemed to continue for the benefit of J and K, where J and K become the current income beneficiaries of Trust A. J and K each hold a separate and independent share of Trust A within the meaning of section 663(c). J and K are successive income beneficiaries of Trust A, and they are treated as consenting to B's QSST election.

Example 9. Assume the same facts as in Example 8, except that on B's death, under the terms of Trust A and local law, Trust A terminates and the principal is to be divided equally and held in newly created Trust B and Trust C. The sole income beneficiaries of Trust B and Trust C are J and K, respectively. Because Trust A terminated, J and K are not successive income beneficiaries of Trust A. J and K must make separate, new QSST elections for their respective trusts to qualify as QSSTs, if they qualify. The result is the same whether or not the trustee of Trusts B and C is the same as the trustee of trust A.

Planning Pointers: The authors often see the second example in practice. Thus, the consulting attorney should remember to consider making new elections upon the death of an income beneficiary of a QSST.

ESBTs

By comparison to QSSTs, ESBTs may have multiple income beneficiaries and there are no income and/or principal distribution requirements. Simply put, ESBTs may provide the trustee with mandatory or discretionary income and principal distribution powers. It is for this reason that the ESBT is viewed as a good estate planning vehicle. However, the cost of the flexibility is a potential for higher income taxes.

Income Tax Issues

The ESBTs' rules are analogous to complex trust income tax rules. Like complex trusts, generally all of the income is taxed to the trust or the beneficiary (depending upon DNI and distributions).[119] To determine what rules apply, the Regulations provide that the ESBT may be divided into one, two or three possible 'portions' ('portions' is the name given in the Treasury's regulations, thus, the authors follow that convention) to determine taxability.

The regulations provide if a trust holds assets other than S Corp stock, there will be an "S portion" and a "Non-S portion."[120] If only S Corp stock is owned by the trust, then there will only be an "S portion." And, with respect to those portions, either the grantor or the non-grantor trust rules will apply.

Once the S portion and the Non-S portion are determined, as to each portion, the trustee determines if any part of the portions are grantor trusts. If so, then the portions are separated into grantor trust portions and non-grantor trust portions. Effectively, the grantor trust portions of both the S portion and the Non-S portion would be combined and reported to the deemed owner of the grantor trust. The non-grantor trust portions are subject to the normal non-grantor trust rules under subparts A – D of subchapter J of the Code.

S Portion. The S portion is that portion of the trust that consists of S Corp stock. The S portion is then divided into that portion what is (a) not treated as a grantor trust and (b) that portion that is treated as a grantor trust.[121]

The ESBTs tax attributable to the S portion of the S Corp stock is determined under special rules.[122] The tax on the S portion is determined by reference to normal income tax rules with a few modifications. The two most notable of these are: (a) there is no exemption amount, and (b) the income tax rate for the income attributable to the S Corp stock will be taxed at the highest marginal income tax rate.[123]

Most importantly, the S Portion is taxed to the ESBT. This means that the trust pays the income at the highest marginal rates, and any distributions to the beneficiaries pass tax free. An example is provided below that illustrates this point.

Non-S Portion. The Non-S Portion, unlike the S Portion, is generally taxed under the regular rules for taxing trusts with no S Corp stock. Thus, to the extent that a part of that trust is a grantor trust, then the regular grantor trust rules apply. To the extent that part of that trust is not a grantor trust and to the extent that items of S Corp income, deduction, etc., were not caught under the S Portion rules, they will be combined with the Non-S portion and the normal non-grantor trust rules would apply.[124]

Grantor Trust Portion. The tax attributes related to the grantor trust portion of the ESBT are taken into account on the deemed owner's income tax return in accordance with normal grantor trust rules.[125] Recall that the deemed owner could be either the grantor of the trust or someone other than the grantor under Code Section 678.

The regulations have a wonderful example that details how the Grantor Portion, S Portion and Non-S Portion work in tandem. The authors suggest that the reader take the time to work through the example to better understand the rules. The following examples are based on that comprehensive example.[126]

Example 10. Assume that a trust ("T") has a valid ESBT election. B, an individual, has a 10 percent grantor trust portion in T. No other person is treated as the owner of any other portion of the Trust under subpart E. T owns stock in X, an S Corp and in Y, a C corporation. Further assume that during 20X1, T receives a distribution from X of $5,000, all of which is applied against T's adjusted basis in the X stock in accordance with Code Section 1368(c)(1). T receives $1,000 as a qualified dividend from Y. Assume no deductions. Trust makes a distribution of $1,000 to its beneficiary, A.

B is taxed on 10 percent of X's and Y's taxable income (i.e., 10% of $5,000 and 10% of $1,000). T is taxed on 90 percent of the $5,000 (or $4,500) at the highest marginal rate as the S Portion; and 90 percent of the income from Y (i.e., 90% of $1,000 or $900) is reduced by the personal exemption of $100 (i.e., net is $800), and thus passes out to A as a qualified dividend.

Example 11. Same facts as Example 10, except that T sells all of its stock in X to a person unrelated to T and its beneficiaries, and realizes a capital gain of $5,000. This 10 percent of the gain (or $500) passes to the B (i.e., the grantor trust portion) and 90 percent gain (or $4,500) is taken into account by the S portion and is taxed

using the appropriate capital gain rate found in Code Section 1(h) to T.

Example 12. Same facts as Example 10, except Y is not a corporation; rather it is a partnership and has taxable income of $1,000. Further, X, the S Corp, makes a distribution of $2,000 to T, which then distributes the same amount to A.

In this case, B is taxed on 10 percent of X's and Y's taxable income (i.e., 10% of $5,000 and 10% of $1,000). T is taxed on 90 percent of the $5,000 (or $4,500) at the highest marginal rate as the S Portion; and 90 percent of the income from Y (the partnership) (i.e., 90% of $1,000 or $900) is reduced by the personal exemption of $100 (i.e., net is $800), and thus passes out to A as pass-through taxable income. Note: of the amount that passes to A, only $800 is taxable to A and $1,200 is a non-taxable distribution.

Grantor Trusts. For the maximum two-year time period that a Continuing Grantor Trust is permitted to be an eligible shareholder (i.e., after the death of the grantor), even though the trust is a shareholder for state law purposes, for federal income tax purposes, the estate of the deemed owner (i.e., the decedent) and not the Continuing Grantor Trust is required to report the tax attributes.[127]

It is not necessary that the estate pour-over to the Continuing Grantor Trust. However, when this happens, the results of this could be quite peculiar. The following examples demonstrate the anomalies.

Example 13. Assume L has a revocable trust ("RT") that is treated as wholly a grantor trust, and during life, L places 100 percent of S Corp stock (called "S, Inc.") into RT. Further assume L dies on January 31, 20X1, and that L's probate estate pours-over into L's RT. L's RT creates standard A-B trusts for L's spouse, J, for life and remainder outright to L's and J's children. Further, both of the A-B trusts qualify as QSSTs.

When L dies RT will be considered an eligible shareholder under Code Section 1361(c)(2)(A)(ii) for a period of two-years (i.e., RT will be a Continuing Grantor Trust). Upon the expiration of the two-year period, or if the stock is funded in the A-B trusts and a QSST election is made to take effect sooner, RT ceases to be a Continuing Grantor Trust, and the stock will be held by the QSSTs.

During the period of administration, effectively, L's estate would report the taxable attributes of S, Inc., on the estate's Form 1041. Since the A-B trusts will be the only beneficiaries, and since J is the income beneficiary of the trusts, to the extent of DNI distributions, ultimately J, the surviving spouse would report the income on J's income tax return. Since RT is the owner of the stock for state law purposes, any distributions from S, Inc. to RT would pass through to J as income distributions.

———————————

Example 14. Let's assume the same facts as Example 13, except that RT is not a revocable trust; rather it is an intentionally defective grantor trust ("IDGT") that was irrevocable for state law purposes and that L's will does not pour-over into that trust.

In this case, the tax ramifications pass to the surviving spouse, J (to the extent that there are DNI distributions); however, the economic benefit passes to the beneficiaries of the IDGT.

———————————

Planning Opportunity: This may be a planning opportunity for the family, because if they want to sell the assets or the stock in the family S Corp, the family might want to take the following steps: (1) not elect QSST treatment; and (2) partially redeem the S Corp stock before the two-year time period. If it is their desire at some later point in time, consider selling the balance of the S Corp stock. The benefit of this is that the tax attributes are borne by the estate, but the assets flow to the trust. This would be especially beneficial from a generation-skipping transfer ("GST") tax planning perspective (i.e., where the trust is GST exempt).

———————————

Code Section 645

A trustee of a so-called "qualified revocable trust" ("QRT")[128] and the personal representative of an estate are allowed to make an election (i.e., the "section 645 election") to combine the incomes of the two entities (i.e., the QRT and the estate) and to report the income as part of the estate for the section 645 election period.[129] The section 645 election period (discussed in detail below) begins on the decedent's date of death and ends on the earlier of the distribution of all of the assets from the QRT and estate, or the day that is the day before the so-called "applicable date."[130] If an estate tax return was not necessary, the applicable date is the date that is two years from the decedent's death.[131] If an estate tax return was required, the applicable date is the later of the day that is two years after the decedent's death or six months after the date of the final determination of the estate tax liability.[132]

Treat the Trust like an Estate. Effectively, by making a section 645 election, if the Continuing Grantor Trust qualifies as a QRT, the income of the Continuing Grantor Trust is combined with the estate's income and reported on the estate's income tax return.[133] The rules applicable to the Continuing Grantor Trust (e.g., the two-year holding period) would not apply, because such trust would be treated as part of the estate. Stated differently, during the section 645 election period, the S Corp stock can be held by the Continuing Grantor Trust for state law purposes, yet be taxed for federal income tax purposes as if it were held by an estate.

What happens after termination of the section 645 election or transfer of S Corp stock from the QRT?- Under the regulations, after the section 645 election period terminates[134] or if the QRT transfers the S Corp stock, the succeeding trust will be considered a Testamentary S Trust (i.e., with a two-year period beginning from the end of the section 645 election period) without regard to whether the successor trust would qualify as a permitted shareholder.[135]

Private Letter Ruling 200529006 provides some guidance to an estate holding S Corp stock and making a section 645 election.[136] This PLR provides us with a few planning suggestions:

First, Rev. Rul. 76-23[137] is still being cited by the Service, which stands for the proposition that S Corp stock may be held by an estate during the Code section 6166 payment period and holding the stock in an estate for that period (which could be as long as fifteen years) will not be deemed to be a prolonged period of time.

Second, if a section 645 election is made, even though the S Corp stock is held by a trust for state law purposes, it will be deemed to be held by the estate for income tax purposes and the theory behind Revenue Ruling 76-23 will apply. Therefore, if the section 645 election is made the decedent's estate is deemed as if it owned the stock for federal income tax purposes, even though the S Corp stock would have been held by a trust at the time of death (and not the decedent's estate). If the estate qualifies for Code section 6166 treatment, the holding of the S Corp stock is still subject to the section 645 election period (i.e., which begins at the date of death and generally ends twelve months after the estate tax is finally determined).[138] In cases where an estate tax closing letter is sent by the IRS, it would be roughly twelve months from the date of the closing letter, and it is not extended by Code section 6166. Thus, after the twelve month period, the trust is deemed to transfer the property to a testamentary trust, thereby creating another two-year holding period in that trust. As one could see, the secion 645 election could significantly extend the period of time that S Corp stock is held in a trust or estate other than a QSST or ESBT.

TESTAMENTARY S TRUSTS

Like the Continuing Grantor Trust, during its two-year holding period, the Testamentary S Trust becomes the shareholder for state law purposes, and for federal income tax purposes the estate will report the income, gains, losses, etc.[139]

Estates. If an estate is a shareholder the tax attributes from the S Corp flows thru to the estate.[140]

In the year of death, there will be at least two shareholders sharing the tax attributes of the S Corp:

- the decedent; and

- the decedent's estate.

In general, the decedent's final return (sometimes referred to as the "Final 1040") will generally report the decedent's pro rata share of the tax attributes through the date of death, and the estate will report its pro rata share of tax attributes from the date of death to the end of the taxable year of the estate. Combined, the tax attributes reported by the decedent and her estate would total the same amount as if the decedent lived through the end of the year.

During the settlement process, through various elections, some of the tax attributes could be arranged to be reported more by one party (e.g., the decedent on his Final 1040) or by her estate on its first income tax return (the "First Form 1041").

Elections Available for Apportionment of Income

In general, the S Corp's tax attributes for the entire tax year are allocated on a per diem basis to the shareholder based upon the shareholder's pro rata ownership.[141]

Separate Year Election – Code Section 1377(a)(2). Upon a shareholder's death,[142] if an S Corp elects with the consent of all "affected shareholders", the S Corp may terminate the corporation's tax year with respect to that decedent shareholder, thereby creating two tax years (i.e., one before death, and one after death) for that shareholder and his or her estate.[143] The tax attributes before death would be allocated pro rata to the decedent's Final 1040 and the tax attributes for the S Corp's tax year after death would be allocated pro rata on the estate's First Form 1041.[144] An "affected shareholder" is the decedent and the decedent's estate.[145] Thus, the personal representative of the estate would be the person consenting to the request.

The S Corp must attach a statement to the corporation's timely filed income tax return (i.e., the Form 1120S) for the tax year in which the decedent-shareholder died. The election must include the following:

- a declaration by the S Corp that it is electing under Code Section 1377(a)(2) and Treas. Reg. section 1.1377-1(b) to treat the taxable year as if it consisted of two separate taxable years;

- information setting forth when and how the shareholder's entire interest was terminated (e.g., death);

- the signature on behalf of the S Corp of an authorized officer of the corporation under penalties of perjury; and

- a statement by the corporation that the corporation and each affected shareholder consent to the S Corp making the terminating election.[146]

There is no formal IRS form for this election, thus, the tax preparer simply prepares a document that would include the requisite information and have the appropriate persons sign the document.

Estate Income – DNI / FAI. Income allocated to the estate is reportable on the estate's income tax return (i.e., Form 1041). Pass-through ordinary income becomes part of distributable net income ("DNI"), and in general, pass-through capital gain is not included in DNI.[147] The character of the receipt of the assets from the corporation for fiduciary accounting income ("FAI") purposes and the dispositive terms of the will would dictate whether, the pass-through income stays in the estate or passes outright to the beneficiaries of the estate.[148]

PLANNING POINTERS

During Life. In terms of lifetime planning, there are times that various trusts may own stock of an S Corp. When a trust converts from one type of trust to another, or if the deemed owner changes (e.g., where the trust is treated as a grantor trust as to the grantor (under Code Section 675(4)) and the grantor releases the power so that it is treated as a grantor trust as to the beneficiaries (under Code Section 678)), there is authority under Code Section 1377(a)(1) and the Treasury Regulations to make an election under Code Section 1377(b) if it is beneficial to the taxpayers.[149]

Let's use the following example to understand the benefits of the Code Section 1377 election.

Example 15. Let's assume (a) Sophie owned 50% of the stock in SH Corp., an S Corp and that the other 50 percent is owned by a trust (the "Trust") that Sophie created. The trust is a grantor trust by reason of Code section 675(4)[150] where her child, Richard, the beneficiary, but for Sophie's Code section 675(4) power, would be treated as the owner, (b) Sophie and SH Corp. have the same tax year (a calendar year), (c) SH Corp. will recognize $1.2 million for the year, where most of that capital gain will be recognized from the sale of its only asset on January 31, and (d) there will be a total of $120,000 of municipal interest income (i.e., tax-free income) earned evenly over the entire year. Let's assume that on February 1, after the major transaction, Sophie "turned off" her Code section 675(4) power, so that she is no longer the deemed owner under the grantor trust rules. Rather, her only child, Richard, who

is the beneficiary of the trust, is the grantor (under Code section 678).

If we use the default rule, the pro rata per diem income on Sophie's Federal income tax return ("Sophie's Form 1040") would be $650,000 (approximately 100% of 1/12th and 50% of 11/12th) of long term capital gain; $65,000 (approximately 100% of 1/12th and 50% of 11/12th) of municipal income. Her child, Richard, through the Trust, would reflect (approximately $550,000 of capital gain (i.e., 50% of 11/12th of long-term capital gain; $55,000 (approximately 50% of 11/12th) of municipal income.

If SH Corp. makes an election under Code Section 1377(a)(2) and Sophie consents, they could elect to allocate income as earned. Sophie would pick up the entire capital gain (i.e., 100% of $1.2 million) and $65,000 of municipal interest income and Richard will pick up only $55,000 of municipal income.

In this case, approximately $550,000 of capital gain is borne by Sophie. If Sophie's capital gains rate is 20 percent, Sophie would pay $110,000. What this translates to is a tax-free gift of $110,000. To simplify this example, the tax imposed under Code section 1411 is ignored.

Thus, by simply toggling between the grantor status, and taking advantage of the Code Section 1377(a)(2) election, Sophie (in the above example) transferred tax-free value to her child, Richard.

After death. Likewise, if there will be a substantial change of income before and after a change in ownership (e.g., the decedent's date of death), it may make some sense to make the election under Code Section 1377(a)(2). Recall, the election does not affect the other shareholders of the S Corp; the election only affects the person who has changed ownership (e.g., the decedent in the case of death). Thus, one could adjust the amount of income that flows to either the decedent's Final Form 1040 or the estate's First Form 1041.

Example 16. Let's assume the same facts as Example 15, except that on February 2nd, after the grantor trust toggle had been shifted to Richard, Sophie died unexpectedly.

If we use the default rule, the pro rata per diem income on the Sophie's Form 1040 would be $650,000 (approximately 100% of 1/12th and 50% of 11/12th) of long-term capital gain; $65,000 (approximately 100% of 1/12th and 50% of 11/12th) of municipal income. Richard, through the Trust, would reflect (approximately $550,000 of capital gain (i.e., 50 % of 11/12th of long term capital gain; $55,000 (approximately 50% of 11/12th) of municipal income.

If SH Corp. elects and Sophie's personal representative consents, they could elect to allocate income as earned. Sophie's estate would pick up the entire capital gain (i.e., 100% of $1.2 million) and $65,000 of municipal income and Richard will pick up only $55,000 of municipal income.

The benefit (vis-à-vis Example 15) may be slightly increased if Sophie's estate is subject to estate tax, since the extra income tax liability (of $110,000) would be allowed as a deduction against the gross estate, and therefore, decrease the estate tax payable at Sophie's death. If Sophie is subject to a 40 percent estate tax, this would translate to an extra benefit of approximately $44,000.

Thus, as a result of properly using the Code section 1377 election, Sophie and her family could continue to shift value from Sophie's generation to Richard's generation.

CONCLUSION

As Professor James J. Freeland, once said, "Subchapter S and subchapter J were not written by the same folks!" Meaning simply that the income tax rules under the subchapter S corporation rules may not always be in sync with the income tax rules that govern estates and trusts, and in certain circumstances reach anomalous results. The key is to understand the rules and to see how to take advantage of the rules for the taxpayer's particular situation.

CHAPTER ENDNOTES

1. For purposes of this outline, a corporation taxed under Subchapter S of the Code will be called an "S Corp" and a corporation taxed under Subchapter C will be called a "C Corp". All references to the Internal Revenue Code of 1986, as amended, shall be referred to as the "Code" or "I.R.C.".

2. I.R.C. §1371(a).

3. For a detailed analysis of all of the requirements, *see,* Eustice, Kuntz & Bogdanski, *Federal Income Taxation of S Corporations,* 5th Ed., 2015 & Supp. 2016-1, Warren Gorman and Lamont, and Bittker & Eustice, *Federal Income Taxation of Corporations and Shareholders,* 7th Ed. (2000 & Supp. 2015-3), 2015, Warren Gorman and Lamont.

4. I.R.C. §1361(b)(1) and Treas. Reg. §1.1361-1(b)(1). We do not discuss the intricacies of the domestic corporation requirements in this chapter. See, Eustice, *Federal Income Taxation of S Corporations* for more details.

5. I.R.C. §1361(b)(1) and Treas. Reg. §1.1361-1(b)(1). We do not discuss the intricacies of the ineligible corporation prohibition in this chapter. See, Eustice, *Federal Income Taxation of S Corporations* for more details.

6. I.R.C. §1361(b)(1)(A) and Treas. Reg. §1.1361-1(b)(1)(i). We discuss the number of shareholder rules in section 0., *infra.*

7. I.R.C. §1361(b)(1)(B) and (C) and Treas. Reg. §1.1361-1(b)(1)(ii) and (iii). We discuss the shareholder requirements throughout this chapter.

8. I.R.C. §1361(b)(1)(D) and Treas. Reg. §1.1361-1(b)(1)(iv) and -1(l). We discuss the shareholder requirements throughout this chapter.

9. I.R.C. §1361(b)(1)(D) and Treas. Reg. §1.1361-1(b)(1)(iv) and -1(l).

10. Treas. Reg. §1.1361-1(l)(1).

11. Treas. Reg. §1.1361-1(l)(2).

12. Treas. Reg. §1.1361-1(l)(1).

13. Case law, private letter rulings and Treasury Regulations provide guidance on whether the specific corporation has one class of stock. It is beyond the scope of this chapter to discuss the topic; however, the reader is encouraged to review the pertinent corporate documents to ensure that the one class of stock rule is not violated.

14. Treas. Reg. §1.1361-1(l)(2)(i).

15. Treas. Reg. §1.1361-1(l)(1). Accordingly, even if an agreement, under the corporate documents, call for a second class of stock (e.g., preferred stock) if such second class of stock is not outstanding, it will be ignored. Suffice to say, if the agreement allows for a second class, one should look to eliminate that provision so long as the corporation desires to be an S corp.

16. I.R.C. §1361(b)(1)(B) and Treas. Reg. §1.1361-1(e). A custodian or guardian holding S Corp stock is also allowed. And, estates in bankruptcy are considered "estates" for the rule.

17. I.R.C. §1361(b)(1)(B) and (c)(1)(B).

18. I.R.C. §1361(c)(1) and Treas. Reg. §1.1361-1(e)(2). Note: although husbands and wives are treated as one person for the 100-shareholder rule, they are generally treated as separate persons for all of the other rules for S Corps. Further, divorced spouses are treated separately.

19. I.R.C. §1361(c)(1)(B) and Treas. Reg. §1.1361-1(e)(3)(i). There are a complex set of look-through rules in connection with trusts to determine if persons are members of a family. Additionally, there are rules related to how many generations one must review to see if one is a member of the family. If two or more individuals (after applying the rules) are deemed to be members of a family, then those individuals will only be counted as one shareholder. If you believe that you will run up against the 100 shareholder limitation, you should carefully review the member of the family rules to see if you can take advantage of family attribution.

20. I.R.C. §1361(c)(1) and Treas. Reg. §1.1361-1(e)(1). A decedent's estate counts as one shareholder. The term estate includes the estate of an individual in bankruptcy under Title 11 of the United States Code. See Treas. Reg. §1.1361-1(b)(2).

21. I.R.C. §1361(c)(1)(A)(i) and Treas. Reg. §1.1361-1(b)(2).

22. Treas. Reg. §1.1361-1(e)(2).

23. I.R.C. §1361(e).

24. I.R.C. §1361(d)(3).

25. A grantor trust is generally defined as a trust all of which is treated under subpart E of part I of subchapter J of the Code (i.e., Code §§671 – 679 (inclusive)) that is owned by an individual who is a resident and citizen of the U.S. This is the definition under Code §1361(c)(2).

26. Treas. Reg. §1.1361-1(m)(4)(i).

27. I.R.C. §1361(e)(2).

28. I.R.C. §1361(e)(2) and Treas. Reg. §1.1361-1(m)(4)(vi)(A). This rule applies as of August 14, 2008.

29. I.R.C. §1361(c)(2)(B)(v) and Treas. Reg. §1.1361-1(m)(4)(vii).

30. I.R.C. §1366(a)(1) and Treas. Reg. §1.1366-1(a)(1). Additionally, the character of items of income, loss, deduction, credit, etc., at the corporate level passes-through to the shareholder under I.R.C. §1366(b). The shareholders take into account his or her pro rata share on a per diem basis under I.R.C. §1377(a)(1) and Treas. Reg. §1.1377-1(a)(1).

31. For purposes of this chapter, since the focus is on estate planning with S Corp, our coverage of the 100-shareholder limit is cursory. The reader is encouraged to review the rules on his or her own. See generally, I.R.C. §1361 and Treas. Reg. §1.1361-1.

32. I.R.C. §1361(b)(1)(B).

33. I.R.C. §1361(b)(1)(C).

34. Treas. Reg. §1.1361-1(e)(1).

35. Note: prior to 1981, a "non-grantor" could not be considered a "deemed owner".

36. For a good outline on grantor trusts, see, Zaritsky, *Open Issues and Close Calls – Using Grantor Trusts in Modern Estate Planning*, 43rd Heckerling Institute on Estate Planning (Jan. 2009). See, also, Danforth and Zaritsky, 819 T.M., *Grantor Trusts: Income Taxation Under Subpart E.*

37. I.R.C. §1361(c)(2)(A)(i). The statute literally states, "A trust all of which is treated (under subpart E of part I of subchapter J of this chapter) as owned by an individual who is a citizen or resident of the United States." Thus, the individual must be a U.S. citizen or resident. If the trust is not deemed wholly owned by the grantor, then the trust could be partially a grantor trust and partially an ESBT. See discussion of ESBTs below in section 0 of this chapter.

38. I.R.C. §1361(c)(2)(B)(i).

39. *See*, discussion of ESBTs in section 0 of this chapter.

40. Favorable rulings following the Treasury's regulations include: PLRs 201345024, 200652006, 200824011 and 200747001.

41. The IRS has issued a number of private rulings on this particular issue. For a current discussion on this topic, see Section III of Zaritsky's Open Issues and Close Calls titled "Grantor Trusts and *Crummey* Powers." See also, PLRs 200147044 and 9625031, where IRS privately ruled that the trust with a *Crummey* power qualified as a shareholder under I.R.C. §1361(c)(2)(A)(i) because the *Crummey* beneficiary was considered the grantor and the

trust was considered a wholly owned grantor trust (by reason of I.R.C. §678(a), and the *Crummey* beneficiary of the trust was the shareholder for income tax purposes under I.R.C. §1361(c)(2)(B)(i)). See also, PLR 9009010 and 9140047. But see, an old PLR (8336018) which had an interesting twist to the *Crummey* provision, which caused the trust not to be treated as a grantor trust (Note: Today, this could be saved by an ESBT election). In a series of rulings, PLRs 200011054, 200011055,200011056 and 200011058, the IRS ruled that a trust that gives beneficiaries withdrawal rights (i.e., *Crummey* powers) that lapse will treat the trust as a grantor trust under §678 even after the lapse, therefore, the so-called *Crummey* beneficiaries become grantors of the trust. In light of rising income tax rates, the reader may want to review these PLRs to see if it is beneficial to shift the S Corp income to the junior generations (i.e., the *Crummey* beneficiaries). See PLRs 200729005, 200729006 and 200729007 where *Crummey* powers existed, yet the grantor retained the powers under I.R.C. §675(4) to exchange assets. In those rulings, the IRS ruled that if the "facts and cI.R.C.umstances" illustrated that the powers were properly used, that the grantor / creator of the trust (by reason of I.R.C. §675(4) is the owner for the period of time until the power of substitution was relinquished. Thereafter, the IRS ruled that the beneficiaries would be considered the grantors under §678. This is an interesting taxpayer-friendly ruling.

42. I.R.C. §1361(c)(2)(B)(ii). See also, Treas. Reg. §§1.1361-1(h)(1)(ii) and 1.1361-1(h)(3)(i)(B).

43. I.R.C. §1361(d)(3)(A)(i) and Treas. Reg. §1.1361-1(j)(1)(ii)(A).

44. I.R.C. §1361(d)(3)(A)(ii) and Treas. Reg. §1.1361-1(j)(1)(ii)(B).

45. I.R.C. §1361(d)(3)(A)(iii) and Treas. Reg. §1.1361-1(j)(1)(ii)(C).

46. I.R.C. §1361(d)(3)(A)(iv) and Treas. Reg. §1.1361-1(j)(1)(ii)(D).

47. I.R.C. §1361(d)(3)(B) and Treas. Reg. §1.1361-1(j)(1)(i).

48. Treas. Reg. §1.1361-1(j)(1)(iii).

49. Treas. Reg. §1.1361-1(j)(1)(iii).

50. Treas. Reg. §1.1361-1(j)(2)(ii)(A).

51. Under the regulations, grantor trust status trumps QSST status, thus, by definition if the S Corp stock is transferred to a grantor trust, a QSST election cannot be made. Treas. Reg. §1.1361-1(j)(6)(iv).

52. Treas. Reg. §1.1361-1(j)(6)(ii)(A).

53. Treas. Reg. §1.1361-1(j)(6)(ii)(B).

54. Treas. Reg. §1.1361-1(j)(6)(ii)(C).

55. Treas. Reg. §1.1361-1(j)(6)(ii)(D).

56. Treas. Reg. §1.1361-1(j)(6)(ii)(E)(1)(i).

57. Treas. Reg. §1.1361-1(j)(6)(ii)(E)(1)(ii).

58. Treas. Reg. §1.1361-1(j)(6)(ii)(E)(1)(iii).

59. Treas. Reg. §1.1361-1(j)(6)(ii)(E)(1)(iv).

60. Treas. Reg. §1.1361-1(j)(6)(ii)(E)(2).

61. Treas. Reg. §1.1361-1(j)(6)(ii)(E)(3).

62. In looking for a pre-printed form, the authors found that most of the research software available had some suggested forms which had all of the requisite information.

63. Rev. Proc. 2013-30, 2013-36 IRB 173. This revenue procedure generally took effect on September 3, 2013, and supersedes prior revenue procedures, including: Rev. Proc. 2003-43, 2003-23 IRB 998, Rev. Proc. 2004-48, 2004-2 C.B. 172, Rev. Proc. 2004-49 (in part), 2004-2 C.B. 210, Rev. Proc. 2007-62, 2007-2 C.B. 786, Rev. Proc. 97-48, 1997-2 C.B. 521 (in part), and Rev. Proc. 98-55, 1998-2 CB 643.

64. I.R.C. §1362(f) and Treas. Reg., §1.1362-4.

65. See exhibits at the end of Rev. Proc. 2013-30.

66. ESBTs were introduced to the Code as part of P.L. 104-188, Small Business Job Protection Act of 1996 (August 20, 1996).

67. According to the House and Senate Committee reports, the rationale of introducing the ESBT was to facilitate family estate planning with regard to trusts owning S Corp stock. S. Rep. No 104-281, Senate Finance Committee Report on HR 3448, the Small Business Job Protection Act of 1996 (P.L. No 104-188), (June 19, 1996) and H. R., Rep. No. 104-586, House Ways and Means Committee Report on the Small Business Job Protection Bill of 1996 (P.L. 104-188) (May 23, 1996). Both Committee reports stated that the "reason for change" was as follows:

   "The Committee believes that a trust that provides for income to be distributed to (or accumulated for) a class of individuals should be allowed to hold S Corp stock. This would allow an individual to establish a trust to hold S Corp stock and 'spray' income among family members (or others) who are beneficiaries of the trust. The Committee believes allowing such an arrangement will facilitate family financial planning."

68. I.R.C. §1361(e)(1)(A) and Treas. Reg. §1.1361-1(m)(1)(i).

69. I.R.C. §1361(e)(1)(A) provides that organizations described in I.R.C. §170(c)(2), (3), (4) or (5) or an organization described in I.R.C. §170(c)(1) which holds a contingent interest in the trust and which is not a potential current beneficiary, qualify as a beneficiary. I.R.C. §1361(e)(2) defines a "potential current beneficiary".

70. I.R.C. §1361(e)(1)(A)(i) and Treas. Reg. §1.1361-1(m)(1)(i).

71. I.R.C. §1361(e)(1)(A)(ii) and Treas. Reg. §1.1361-1(m)(1)(iii).

72. I.R.C. §1361(e)(1)(A)(iii) and Treas. Reg. §1.1361-1(m)(2).

73. I.R.C. §1361(e)(1)(B)(i) and Treas. Reg. §1.1361-1(m)(1)(iv)(A). However, the regulations allow an ESBT to convert to a QSST and vice-versa. See generally, Treas. Reg. §1.1361-1(j)(12).

74. I.R.C. §1361(e)(1)(B)(ii) and Treas. Reg. §1.1361-1(m)(1)(iv)(B).

75. I.R.C. §1361(e)(1)(B)(iii) and Treas. Reg. §1.1361-1(m)(1)(iv)(C).

76. I.R.C. §1361(c)(2)(flush language).

77. Treas. Reg. §§1.1361-1(m)(4)(ii) and (v). The regulations explain in detail how to allocate income based upon the status of the trust (i.e., ESBT or grantor trust).

78. I.R.C. §1361(e)(1)(A)(i) and Treas. Reg. §1.1361-1(m)(1)(ii)(D). Note, one must be sure that the beneficiary is not a non-resident alien ("NRA"). If the NRA is an eligible beneficiary, so long as the NRA is not a "potential current beneficiary" the trust may qualify as an ESBT; however, when the NRA becomes a "potential current beneficiary" then this may disqualify the ESBT status and potentially the S Corp status, too. See, PLRs 200522005, 200522004, and 200522003.

79. I.R.C. §1361(e)(1)(A)(i) and Treas. Reg. §1.1361-1(m)(1)(i). It is clear that the estate of a decedent can be a beneficiary of an ESBT, but the ESBT regulations do not mention whether the estate of an individual in bankruptcy under Title 11 of the United States Code could be a beneficiary.

80. I.R.C. §1361(e)(1)(A)(i) and Treas. Reg. §1.1361-1(m)(1)(i).

81. Treas. Reg. §1.1361-1(m)(1)(ii)(A).

82. Treas. Reg. §1.1361-1(m)(1)(ii)(B).

83. Treas. Reg. §1.1361-1(m)(1)(ii)(B).

84. Treas. Reg. §1.1361-1(m)(2)(i). Note: The regulations also provide logistical guidance, when there is more than one trustee acting, on how to make an election if there are multiple S Corps, and what happens if the service center where one files the S Corp return changes.

85. Treas. Reg. §§1.1361-1(m)(2)(ii)(A) through (E) inclusive. The representations of the trustee include: (1) the trust meets the definitional requirements of I.R.C. §1361(e)(1); and (2) all potential current beneficiaries of the trust meet the shareholder requirements of I.R.C. §1361(b)(1).

86. Treas. Reg. §1.1361-1(m)(2)(iii).

87. *See*, Notes 63 - 65 and accompanying text.

88. Treas. Reg. §1.1361-1(m)(2)(v).

89. Treas. Reg. §1.1361-1(m)(3)(i).

90. Treas. Reg. §1.1361-1(m)(3)(iii).

91. I.R.C. §1361(c)(2)(A)(iv), as clarified by Treas. Reg. §1.1361-1(h)(1)(v).

92. Treas. Reg. §1.1361-1(h)(1)(v).

93. Treas. Reg. §1.1361-1(h)(1)(v). It is not clear what this means. Does this mean that there are actually separate trusts? Recall, that for grantor trust treatment the trust must be wholly a grantor trust as to the deemed owner. Does this mean that the trust is bifurcated based on ownership? Hopefully, there will be clarification in the future.

94. I.R.C. §1361(d).

95. I.R.C. §§1361(c)(2)(A)(v) and (e).

96. I.R.C. §1361(c)(2)(A)(iii).

97. I.R.C. §1361(b)(i)(B).

98. I.R.C. §1361(c)(2)(A)(ii).

99. I.R.C. §1361(c)(2)(A)(iii) and Treas. Reg. §§1.1361-1(h)(1)(iv)(A) and (B).

100. I.R.C. §1361(c)(2)(A)(iii) and Treas. Reg. §§1.1361-1(h)(1)(iv)(A) and (B) and –1(h)(3)(i)(D).

101. That is, Continuing S Trusts, Testamentary S Trusts, ESBTs and QSSTs.

102. I.R.C. §1361(b)(i)(B).

103. *Old Virginia Brick Company, Inc. v. Comm.*, 367 F2d 276 (4th Cir. 1966). The Appeals court sided with the opinion of the Tax Court, quoting the Tax Court's reasoning that an estate is considered terminated "once the period necessary for the performance of ordinary administrative duties is ended." Thus, the estate should only be held open for a reasonable period and the assets should be held in the estate for such period. In reviewing the legislative history of subchapter S, the authors notes that the eligible shareholders before the re-write of the law in 1982 were similar to the eligible shareholders under the then-new law. See, Legislative History of Subchapter S Revision Act of 1982 (P.L. 97-354) S Rep. No. 640, 97th Cong., 2d Sess. (1982). Thus, it appears that the precedent of *Old Virginia* would likely be followed today. *See also*, Treas. Reg. §1.1361-1(h)(1)(ii).

104. Today, the reference would be to Code §641(a).

105. Rev. Rul. 76-23, 1976-1 C.B. 264.

106. *See* Note 103 and accompanying text.

107. This is true for an S Corp that has been an S Corp from its inception and continued to be an S Corp for all time. If the S Corp was once a C Corp and had accumulated earnings and profits, then it is possible for the S Corp to pay an income tax. It is beyond the scope of this chapter to discuss these issues.

108. I.R.C. §1366(a)(1) and Treas. Reg. §1.1366-1(a)(1). Additionally, the character of items of the tax attributes at the corporate level passes-through to the shareholder under I.R.C. §1366(b). The

shareholder takes into account his or her pro rata share on a per diem basis under I.R.C. §1377(a)(1) and Treas. Reg. §1.1377-1(a)(1).

109. *See*, Note 108.

110. *See*, Note 108.

111. *See*, Note 108. See also, I.R.C. §1361(d)(1)(B).

112. Treas. Reg. §1.1361-1(j)(8). The provisions of this regulation are contrary to the original position that the IRS once held in Rev. Rul. 92-84, 1992-2 C.B. 216. The Service ruled that the income beneficiary of a QSST rather than the trust itself, recognizes gain or loss when the trust sells all or part of its stock in an S Corp, even if under local trust law the gain or loss is allocable to corpus rather than to income. In 1995, the IRS issued TD 8600, 1995-2 C.B. 135, which added Treas. Reg. §1.1361-1(j)(8), and which became effective for taxable years beginning after July 21, 1995.

113. I.R.C. §1361(d)(1)(C).

114. Treas. Reg. §1.1361-1(j)(8).

115. Treas. Reg. §1.1361-1(j)(8).

116. Treas. Reg. §1.1361-1(j)(7)(ii).

117. Treas. Reg. §1.1361-1(j)(9)(i).

118. Treas. Reg. §1.1361-1(j)(9)(ii)(Examples).

119. In fact, the rules regarding income taxation are set forth under Treas. Reg. §1.641(c)-1 (i.e., the regulations under subchapter J and not subchapter S).

120. Treas. Reg. §1.641(c)-1(a).

121. I.R.C. §641(c)(1)(A) and Treas. Reg. §1.641(c)-1(b)(2).

122. *See*, I.R.C. §641(c). The instructions for Form 1041 provide guidance on how the income should be reported for income tax purposes.

123. I.R.C. §641(c)(2)(A) and Treas. Reg. §1.641(c)-1(e)(1) (for the highest rate); and I.R.C. §641(c)(2)(B) and Treas. Reg. §1.641(c)-1(e)(2) (for the denial of the exemption). In addition to the above, the Code and regulations provide that the only items of income, loss, deduction, or credit taken into account are: (1) the items required to be taken into account under I.R.C. §1366 (see, I.R.C. §641(c)(2)(C)(i) and Treas. Reg. §1.641(c)-1(d)(2)); (2) gain or loss from the disposition of S Corp stock (including gain when distributions are in excess of basis), except that capital losses are allowed only to the extent of capital gains (see, I.R.C. §641(c)(2)(C)(ii) and Treas. Reg. §1.641(c)-1(d)(3)(i); (3) to the extent provided in the regulations, state or local income taxes and administrative expenses to the extent allocable to items (1) and (2) (see, I.R.C. §641(d)(2)(C)(iii) and Treas. Reg. §1.641(c)-1(d)(4)(i); and (4) for S Corp taxable years beginning after 2006, any interest expense paid or accrued on indebtedness incurred to acquire stock in an S Corp. I.R.C. §641(d)(2)(C)(iv).

124. Treas. Reg. §1.641(c)-1(g)(1).

125. Treas. Reg. §§1.641(c)-1(b)(1) and 1.641(c)-1(c).

126. Treas. Reg. §1.641(c)-1(l).

127. I.R.C. §1361(c)(2)(b)(ii). Treas. Reg. §1361-1(h)(3)(i)(B) provides,

"[i]f stock is held by a trust defined in paragraph (h)(1)(ii) of this section, the estate of the deemed owner is generally treated as the shareholder as of the day of the deemed owner's death. However, if stock is held by such a trust in a community property state, the decedent's estate is the shareholder only of the portion of the trust included in the decedent's gross estate (and the surviving spouse continues to be the shareholder of the portion of the trust owned by that spouse under the applicable state's community property law). The estate ordinarily will cease to be treated as the shareholder upon the earlier of the transfer of the stock by the trust or the expiration of the 2-year period beginning on the day of the deemed owner's death."

When a spouse dies with S Corp stock that is community property, the portion of S Corp stock deemed to be the decedent spouse's share shall become the decedent's estate's share and such estate shall be the shareholder of such portion for Federal income tax purposes. I.R.C. §1361(c)(2)(B).

128. For purposes of this discussion, we will assume that a standard revocable trust (i.e., where the grantor has the right to revoke, amend, alter and/or modify the trust) typically used in basic estate planning qualifies as a QRT.

129. I.R.C. §645(a).

130. I.R.C. §645(a).

131. I.R.C. §645(b)(2)(A).

132. I.R.C. §645(b)(2)(B).

133. Treas. Reg. §1.645-1(a).

134. Treas. Reg. §1.645-1(h)(i).

135. See, Treas. Reg. §1.1361-1(h)(1)(iv)(B).

136. Private Letter Ruling 200529006 (July 22, 2005). Actually, when obtaining the PLR, the reader will find that the questions presented to the IRS appear to address Code §6166; however, the Service gratuitously discusses Code §645. The author found other rulings where Code §645 was mentioned, but there was no analysis of the particular code section.

137. *See*, Note 105 and accompanying text.

138. Treas. Reg. §1.645-1(f)(2)(ii) provides (in part) that if an estate tax return is required to be filed, the applicable date is the later of two years after death or six months after the final determination of estate tax liability. Generally speaking, the date of the final determination of estate tax liability is six months after the issuance of an estate tax closing letter. Thus, the two six-month periods are combined, which totals 12 months. Note that on its website, the IRS announced that estate tax closing letters will only be issued upon request for all estate tax returns filed on or after June 1, 2015. This policy raises some questions about the continued reliance on the "12 month" rule, and future guidance hopefully will be issued. It is the authors' belief that the 12 month rule continues to apply.

139. I.R.C. §1361(c)(2)(B)(iii) and Treas. Reg. §1361-1(h)(3)(i)(D).

140. I.R.C. §1366.

141. I.R.C. §§1366 and 1377(a)(1).

142. Treas. Reg. §1.1377-1(b)(4) explains that under I.R.C. §1377(a)(2) death of a shareholder qualifies as a termination of a shareholder's interest.

143. I.R.C. §1377(a)(2).

144. Treas. Reg. §1.1377-1(b)(1).

145. Treas. Reg. §1.1377-1(b)(5)(ii).

146. Treas. Reg. §1.1377-1(b)(5)(i)(A) – (D).

147. I.R.C. §643(a)(3) and Treas. Reg., §1.643(a)-3.

148. *See*, section 0, discussing the issue of where a revocable trust is treated as part of an estate (i.e., the §645 election).

149. *See*, Treas. Reg. §1.1377-1(a)(2)(iii). Also see an example of converting from a QSST to an ESBT under Treas. Reg. §1.1377-1(c) Example 3.

150. The power that causes the trust to be a grantor trust is the power of substitution.

GRANTOR RETAINED INTEREST TRUSTS

CHAPTER 12

INTRODUCTION

This chapter discusses some of the estate freezing and trust transfer techniques in use today. The freezing techniques discussed in this chapter are Grantor Retained Interest Trusts, which include the grantor retained income trust (GRIT), the grantor retained annuity trust (GRAT), and the grantor retained unitrust (GRUT).

An estate freeze is a transaction that essentially caps the tax value of an asset and simultaneously transfers that asset and all subsequent appreciation and income to another party, usually someone in a younger generation. The freeze does this in a way that shifts post-transfer appreciation and income to the recipient, free from additional federal (and, in most cases, state) transfer tax.

In response to the success that taxpayers enjoyed in estate freezes, primarily through GRITs and entity recapitalizations, Congress first enacted Code Section 2036(c) back in 1987. However, because that statute was ambiguous and arguably failed to cover some types of estate freezes, Congress replaced it in 1990 with an entirely new chapter of the Internal Revenue Code: Chapter 14, which contains Code Sections 2701-2704.

The heart of Chapter 14 is the breadth of its applicability to transactions between "members of the family," which includes a transferor's spouse, any ancestor or descendant of the transferor, any sibling of the transferor, and any spouse of any of those included people.[1] Therefore, Chapter 14 has stopped many estate freezes between family members, including the old GRIT and most recapitalizations into common and preferred interests. However, because many couples today are not legally married and not otherwise related to each other or members of each other's family for tax purposes, Chapter 14 has no applicability to transactions between those couples. Note, however, that pre-Chapter 14 law applies to those couples (but without the repealed Code Section 2036(c)).

WHAT IS A GRANTOR RETAINED INTEREST TRUST?

A grantor retained interest trust is an irrevocable trust to which a grantor may transfer assets, such as a personal residence, closely held business interests, or other assets that generate income and have substantial appreciation potential, while retaining an interest for a period of years and potentially reducing future estate taxes. Principal, at the end of the specified period of years, will pass to a noncharitable beneficiary, such as the grantor's partner, child or grandchild of the grantor, or a trust for their benefit. Three types of trusts that can be especially useful in which the grantor retains an interest are the GRIT, GRAT and GRUT.

GRIT

In a GRIT, a grantor transfers property to an irrevocable trust and retains the income for a term of years, after which the trust property passes to the principal beneficiaries. A GRIT, which was commonly used for gifts of income producing property[2] to family members before the adoption of Code Section 2702, is now generally limited to transfers of a personal residence or certain tangible property, such as artwork, in situations where the grantor retains the use and enjoyment of the property during the term of the trust and the property passes at the end of the term to members of the grantor's family. The GRIT is a particularly effective tool in the arsenal of an estate planner for shifting income-producing property of persons such as unmarried couples and those who are not legally related (i.e., not members of the same family). In the case of the personal residence GRIT, the trust will usually be a Qualified Personal Residence Trust (QPRT) unless the grantor and the ultimate recipient are not members of the same family, in which case the old-fashioned GRIT can work quite well. The GRIT also usually employed a contingent reversion to the grantor, which further reduced the value of the gifted remainder interest.

GRAT

In a GRAT, the grantor transfers property to an irrevocable trust and retains a right to payment of an annuity that can be expressed as a fixed dollar amount or, much more commonly, a fixed percentage of the initial fair market value of the property that is transferred to the trust for a fixed period of time (e.g., two years). Much more specific information about GRATs is included below.

GRUT

A GRUT allows the grantor to transfer property to an irrevocable trust and retain a right to payment of a fixed percentage of the value of the trust property (determined annually) for a fixed period of time (e.g., three years). Because the GRUT really is a "leaky freeze," i.e., the grantor retains a share of the asset appreciation as measured by the unitrust payout that grows as the asset appreciates in value, it has little practical utility as an estate freeze technique in most estate plans.

WHEN TO USE GRANTOR TRUSTS

In all of these types of trusts, the grantor is essentially making a current gift of a future interest in trust assets to the remainder beneficiary. Because these transfers are of a future interest, the gift tax annual exclusion is inapplicable.

If the grantor survives the selected term—depending on the value of the trust property remaining at the end of the term—significant tax savings may be realized with the GRIT, GRAT, and GRUT. However, under Code Section 2702 (described in more detail in the next section), with respect to most GRITs between members of the same family (as defined in Code Section 2704(c)(2)), a grantor will now be treated as making a gift of the entire property transferred to the trust (rather than a gift of the discounted value of the remainder) if certain family members are designated as the remainder beneficiaries. A GRIT holding a personal residence (such as a QPRT) is a notable exception to this rule. As noted previously, a couple that is not legally married and not members of the same family as defined in Code Section 2704(c)(2) can use a GRIT quite effectively. A GRIT does not have to comply with the strict governing instrument requirements for GRATs and GRUTs in the Code Section 2702 regulations, and, thus, is much more flexible and can be more effective than a GRAT, particularly for appreciating property that generates little income (e.g., closely-held entity interests).

The use of grantor retained interest trusts are usually indicated:

1. When the client is single and has a substantial estate upon which federal estate taxes are certain to be paid.

2. When a married couple has an estate in excess of the couple's combined applicable exclusion amount, ($11,400,000 in 2019).

3. When income producing property is located in more than one state and unification and probate savings are desired, the GRAT, GRUT or GRIT would serve to transfer ownership in a manner that would avoid ancillary administration.

4. When the client desires protection from will contests, public scrutiny, or an election against the will if the grantor survives the trust term.

5. If the remainder interest of the GRIT passes to someone other than those family members listed in Code Section 2702,[3] such as a partner, niece, nephew, or unrelated friend.

6. If the client wishes to use an alternative to (or be used in conjunction with) a recapitalization or other freezing technique that has the added advantages of gift tax leverage and possible estate tax savings.

7. When there is a high probability that the client will outlive the trust term that is needed to obtain a low present value gift to the remainder beneficiary.

8. When the client has assets so substantial that a significant portion can be committed to a remainder beneficiary without compromising his own personal financial security.

9. When the client has a high tolerance for complexity and a strong incentive to achieve gift and estate tax savings (rather than taking the direct but potentially more tax-costly approach of making an immediate gift).

ADVANTAGES OF GRANTOR RETAINED INTEREST TRUSTS IN GENERAL

1. These techniques are generally a "What have we got to lose?" proposition (i.e., the worst case scenario is if the client does nothing).

2. If the property appreciates more rapidly than the Code Section 7520 rate (a complete history and current rates are available at no charge from http://www.leimberg.com) and the grantor survives the trust term, then the trust is successful and transfers excess wealth free from transfer taxes.

3. The grantor, by paying the income tax on the trust's income (because it is a grantor trust for federal income tax purposes) can achieve the so-called "tax burn" and essentially transfer wealth to the trust's beneficiaries free from gift tax. This is because payment of the income tax on trust income by the grantor is not a gift even though it benefits the remainder beneficiaries of the trust, who essentially are relieved from the tax burden.[4]

4. Can pass appreciation while retaining a cash flow stream.

5. Can take advantage of Code Section 7520 interest rate blips relative to current market rates.

6. Permits leverage in calculation of gift tax.

7. Great for working with gifts of partnership/LLC interests to leverage the applicable exclusion amount through the additional use of valuation discounts,

although the proposed regulations under Code Section 2704 may limit this additional leverage.

8. Expressly sanctioned in the Internal Revenue Code. This advantage should not be understated, particularly for clients who are risk averse, as other techniques may present far greater risk of uncertainty as to the law.

9. S corporation stock can be placed in a grantor retained interest trust because it is a grantor trust for income tax purposes since the grantor usually will be entitled to all of the trust income. However, caution is important to ensure that the *entire* trust is a grantor trust for income tax purposes. Clearly, even a GRIT, GRAT or GRUT can be a partially grantor trust for income tax purposes unless the grantor is given additional rights or powers to make it a wholly grantor trust.[5] Thus, it is important to make sure that it is a wholly grantor trust.

10. Client can serve as trustee, at least during the time in which the grantor retains an interest. However, it is not recommended that the grantor continue to serve as trustee of any continuing trust that results at the end of the term of the GRIT, GRAT, or GRUT.[6]

DISADVANTAGES OF GRANTOR RETAINED INTEREST TRUSTS IN GENERAL

1. Expense of set up, including valuation costs, can be significant.

2. Mortality risk (i.e., risk that the settlor will not survive the trust term), leading to some estate tax inclusion risk.

3. Property must generate enough positive cash flow to pay the distribution amount, or the underlying property has to be sold (capital gain to grantor) or given back to the grantor (which defeats the estate planning purpose), and cannot be in the form of promissory notes.[7]

4. Asset must grow at a rate faster than the Code Section 7520 rate, or so-called hurdle rate, in order for more wealth to pass to the remainder beneficiaries.

5. Despite previously asserting includability under Code Section 2039, IRS now says that the proper inclusion section is Code Section 2036.

6. Risk of trust failure to be tax qualified as gift of whole value of asset placed in trust. In other words, if the interest in a GRAT or GRUT (but not a GRIT between persons who are not members of the same family for purposes of Code Section 2704(c)(2)) retained is not a qualified interest (as defined in Code Section 2702(b), explained in the Qualified Interest Section), then the value of the retained interest is zero, which means that the gift is of the entire amount put into the GRAT or GRUT.[8]

7. Inability to "zero out" (as stated by the IRS[9]). However, the Tax Court did not agree, and it invalidated the regulation that had made it impossible to zero out.[10] Nevertheless, President Obama's tax proposals would have eliminated the right to zero out GRAT's and would have imposed a ten-year minimum term on the GRAT to eliminate the practice of so-called "rolling GRATs" where short term (e.g., two-year term) GRAT is established, and then if the grantor survives that term, the property is "re-GRATed" to a new GRAT, and so forth, but these proposals were never enacted, and President Trump's proposals thus far haven't included these proposals.

8. Cannot be used effectively with precision for GST tax purposes.[11]

9. Limited payout design flexibility for a GRAT or GRUT, especially when compared to an installment note, which may be tailored to a particular situation with unequal payments of principal and interest. The only flexibility for a GRAT or GRUT is that a payment in a subsequent year can increase only to the extent the fraction or percentage does not exceed 120 percent of the stated dollar payout or fixed fraction or percentage payable in the preceding year.[12]

10. Gift-splitting with a spouse should not be used in grantor retained interest trusts.[13]

REQUIREMENTS

A few of the most important grantor retained interest trust requirements are summarized here. Code Section 2702 (including Qualified Interests) is discussed at the end of this section. It is important to note that GRITs do not have to comply with all of the following rules and restrictions. There is further discussion in the section entitled GRATs: Beyond the Basics.

An irrevocable trust must be established. A GRIT, GRAT or GRUT must provide that the grantor retains the right to income, annuity, or unitrust payments for a specified number of years (there is no limit to how few or how many years, although a one-year term might not be permissible for a GRAT or GRUT), and a GRAT and GRUT must contain a number of required provisions set forth in the regulations under Code Section 2702 that are described below in a separate section entitled GRATs: Beyond the Basics. As noted later, the longer the specified term of the GRIT, GRAT or GRUT, the greater the value of the retained interest and, therefore, the lower the taxable gift that the grantor is making to the ultimate beneficiaries. Of course, the longer the term of the grantor's interest, the greater the risk that the grantor will not survive the trust term. These calculations can be performed instantly using NumberCruncher software.

Obtain evidence of the value of the assets placed in the GRIT, GRAT, or GRUT. It is strongly recommended that one or more qualified appraisers value the property at the time of transfer to the trustee of the trust. In fact, if the GRAT or GRUT payment requires distribution of trust assets to the grantor, appraisals of the distributed property also must be obtained to ensure that the proper amount is being distributed. Failure to distribute the correct amount per the trust instrument could be a fatal flaw to a GRAT or GRUT.

The grantor should retain a mandatory income, annuity, or unitrust interest in a GRIT, GRAT, or GRUT to keep the valuation exercise at a mere actuarial computation. The trust instrument should expressly provide that the trustee has no discretion to withhold payments from the grantor (or possession of the trust property from the remainder beneficiary). Payments should be made annually or more frequently, again for valuation purposes, although this is a governing instrument requirement for a GRAT and GRUT.[14]

Grantor should be given only an annuity or unitrust interest (or possibly a noncontingent reversion). There is no requirement that the fixed annuity amount be the same for each year. The only requirement for a GRAT or GRUT is that the annuity paid in a given year not exceed 120 percent of the amount that was paid in the prior year.[15] The trustee generally should be specifically prohibited from making distributions in excess of the annuity or unitrust amounts. While a GRAT or GRUT can provide for payment of income in excess of the annuity or unitrust amount to the grantor, the value of the gift of a remainder interest is not reduced by the value of such an excess income provision.

Once grantor's retained interest expires, neither the grantor nor any other donor to the trust should act as trustee. Retention of an interest as a trustee could lead to estate tax exposure. If the grantor's spouse acts as trustee, consider the potential economic and income tax consequences because the trust probably will continue to be a grantor trust for income tax purposes, which may or may not be desirable, depending upon the situation. It is recommended that if the trust is going to remain in place as a grantor trust for income tax purposes as to the grantor after the term of the grantor's interest that some escape provision, perhaps held by a trust protector or third party that could turn grantor trust status off. The trust instrument also could permit the powerholder to renounce the power or right that made the trust a grantor trust for income tax purposes.

Code Section 2702 Requirements

In valuing a transfer in trust to, or for, the benefit of a member of the transferor's family, Code Section 2702(a) provides that all retained interests in trusts involving a transfer to a member of the same family that are not qualified interests are valued at zero. The amount of any gift is then determined by subtracting from the value of the property the value of the retained interest.[16] This is the so-called subtraction method of value. Code Section 2702 specifically does not apply to: (1) incomplete gifts (determined without regard to whether there is consideration); (2) personal residence trusts; (3) charitable remainder annuity trusts and pooled income funds; (4) charitable lead trusts (if the only interest other than the remainder or a qualified annuity or unitrust interest is the charitable lead interest); and (5) certain charitable remainder unitrusts.[17]

Code Section 2702 does not apply to assignment of remainder interests in trusts if the only retained interest is distribution of income in the sole discretion of an independent trustee, as defined in Code Section 674(c), and certain property settlement agreements.

The following definitions apply under Code Section 2702:

1. In determining whether a remainder beneficiary is a member of the transferor's family, such term includes an individual's spouse, any ancestor or lineal descendant of an individual or an individual's spouse, any brother or sister of the individual, and any spouse of any such individual.[18]

2. An interest is retained by the transferor if it is payable to the transferor or transferor's spouse, an ancestor of the transferor or of the transferor's spouse, or the spouse of any such ancestor.[19]

3. A transfer in trust includes a transfer to a new trust or an existing trust or an assignment of an interest in an existing trust, but not a transfer resulting from exercise of a power of appointment that would not constitute a taxable gift (e.g., lapse of a "Crummey" power that does not exceed the "5 or 5" limitation); or a disclaimer.[20]

4. A retained interest is one held by the same individual both before and after the transfer to the trust.[21]

Qualified Interests

Qualified interests are valued under Code Section 7520, which requires that the interest be valued at approximately 120 percent of the applicable federal midterm interest rate under Code Section 1274(d)(1) for the month into which the valuation falls. All other transfers between members of the same family are valued at the full fair market value of the property, since the retained non-qualified interest is valued at zero. In other words, if the retained interest is not a qualified interest, there is no reduction in the gift for the value of the retained interest. As noted previously, these rules are inapplicable between persons who are not members of the same family, meaning that GRITs and other types of split-interest gifts are permissible.

A qualified interest is:

1. a qualified annuity interest;

2. a qualified unitrust interest; or

3. a qualified remainder interest.[22]

Qualified Annuity Interests (in a GRAT)

A qualified annuity interest is an irrevocable right to receive a fixed amount, measured either by a dollar amount or a percentage of the initial value of the GRAT, as finally determined for federal gift tax purposes, at least annually, payable to or for the benefit of the holder of the term interest (i.e., the transferor or an applicable family member). A withdrawal right, whether or not cumulative, does not qualify, and neither does the issuance of a note or other debt instrument from the trustee.[23]

The annuity payment can be a fixed dollar amount or a fixed percentage of the initial value of the trust, as finally determined for gift tax purposes.[24] Income in excess of the fixed amount can be distributable to the transferor, but it is not considered in valuing the retained interest.[25] Subsequent contributions must be prohibited.[26] If the annuity is based on a percentage of the initial value of the trust, there must be a provision in the GRAT or GRUT instrument to adjust for incorrect valuation similar to the rules of Treas. Reg. Sec. 1.664-2(a)(1)(iii).[27] Payment in the situation of a GRAT using a taxable year can be made after the close of the taxable year of the trust if made by the filing date for the trust income tax returns, determined without regard to extensions.[28] An annuity amount payable based on the anniversary date of the creation of the trust must be paid no later than 105 days after the anniversary date.[29] The annuity can be based on a fixed dollar amount or percentage of the value of the trust, and it cannot vary except to the extent that the amount (or percentage) in any year does not exceed 120 percent of the amount (or percentage) from the preceding year.[30]

Qualified Unitrust Interests (in a GRUT)

A qualified unitrust interest is an irrevocable right to an annual payment of a fixed percentage of the net fair market value of the trust assets, to be determined annually.[31] Rules similar to those applicable to annuity trusts also apply here. Combinations of annuity and unitrust payments are not permitted. However, the trust may permit payment of the greater of an annuity or unitrust amount, to be valued at the higher of the two values.[32]

Rules Applicable to GRATs and GRUTs

Any payments to persons other than the grantor are prohibited.[33] The term of the trust must be stated either as a period of years or the term holder's life (or the shorter of the two).[34] Successive term interests for the same individual are permitted, but the

governing instrument must provide that there can be no provision for commutation of any interest.[35] The transferor can retain a reversionary interest in either the GRAT or GRUT, contingent upon death during the trust term, but the reversion is valued at zero for gift tax purposes.[36] This is not so in a GRIT, where reversionary interests reduce the value of the gift of the remainder.

Qualified Remainder Interests

A qualified remainder interest is the right to receive all or a fractional share of the trust property on termination of all or a fractional share of the trust, and includes a reversion.[37] It must be noncontingent (i.e., payable to the beneficiary or the beneficiary's estate in all events).[38] All interests in the trust (other than the noncontingent remainder interests) must be qualified annuity interests or qualified unitrust interests.[39] Payment of income is not permitted in excess of the annuity or unitrust amount to the holder of the qualified annuity or unitrust interest.[40] The right to receive a monetary amount or the original value of the corpus does not qualify.[41]

The retention of a remainder interest is a relatively rare estate planning technique, because any increase in the value of the transferred property is included in the transferor's taxable estate, and unless the remainder (reversion) is valued at less than 5 percent of the value of the transferred property, the grantor will be taxed on the income in any case.

Subsequent Transfers of Retained Interests

A reduction of taxable gifts or adjusted taxable gifts is permitted if the individual subsequently transfers an interest in a trust that was valued under Code Section 2702.[42] The amount of the reduction is the lesser of (a) the increase in taxable gifts resulting from the application of Code Section 2702, or (b) the increase in the transferor's subsequent taxable gifts, or taxable estate, which results from the subsequent transfer.[43] The rule applies to testamentary transfers only if a term interest in the trust is included in the transferor's taxable estate solely by reason of the operation of Code Section 2033, or a remainder interest is included in the transferor's taxable estate, and such interest was valued under Section 2702.[44] Where spouses have split gifts, the adjustment is allocated one-half to each spouse, but one spouse may assign this adjustment to the other.[45]

Example 1 GRAT.[46] Assume that a sixty-five-year-old widow, Agnes Bonnette, is in a 40 percent gift tax bracket. Assume further that the Code Section 7520 rate is 3.2 percent because the transfer was made in February 2019. Agnes places her $10,000,000 securities portfolio into an irrevocable trust. The trust provides that Agnes will have a 6 percent GRAT annuity for a ten-year term. At the end of that time, the property in the trust will continue to be held in trust for her children.

The present value of her right to the GRAT payment for ten years is $ 5,066,280 .506628 × $10,000,000). Because the entire value of the securities portfolio placed in trust is $10,000,000 and the annuity interest that Agnes retained is $600,000, the value of the future interest gift she makes to the remainder beneficiaries (her children) is the difference ($10,000,000 − $5,066,280), $4,933,720. This entire amount ($4,933,720) is a taxable gift, because the gift tax annual exclusion is allowed only for gifts of a present interest. This amount, $4,933,720, can be sheltered by the gift tax applicable exclusion amount ($11,400,000 in 2019). Consequently, Agnes will pay no federal gift tax unless she has already exhausted her gift tax applicable exclusion amount, in which case, at a 40 percent gift tax rate, the gift tax would be $1,973,488.

If the $10,000,000 property appreciates at an after-tax rate of 5 percent and earns 3 percent per year, then the property will be worth $13,016,689 by the end of the ten-year term. If, however, the property appreciates at an annual rate of 3 percent (but still earns 2 percent per year), then the property would be worth $10,031,425 at the end of the ten-year term.

Should Agnes die before the term expires, the trust assets would be included in her estate at their values as of her date of death, and there might not be any federal death tax savings.

However, if Agnes survived the ten-year period (no matter by how short a period of time), none of the trust assets would be included in her estate. Assuming the property appreciated at an after-tax rate of 6 percent, at a 40 percent estate tax rate, an approximation of the savings would be $5,206,676 (40% × $13,016,689). If the estate tax were discounted to reflect that it would be payable ten years later than the gift tax, then the savings, on a time value of money basis, would be less. Furthermore, because the property would not pass through probate, probate costs on the asset would be avoided.

GRATs and GRUTs can provide similar gift, estate and GST tax discounts. A married couple could each establish GRATs and GRUTs (or split-gifts) so as to utilize each spouse's applicable exclusion amounts. However, in light of the portability rules, the creation of a GRAT or GRUT by each spouse may become less important for tax savings.

Example 2 GRIT.[47] In February 2019, Adam Martinez, age fifty-five, sets up a fifteen year GRIT with a $15,000,000 property that is expected to wildly appreciate for his unmarried partner, Yulieski Altuve, retaining the income during the term and a contingent reversionary interest. Adam's gift at the creation of the GRIT is $7,668,600. At a 12 percent after-tax growth rate, the property is expected to be worth $82,103,486 at the end of the GRIT term.

TAX IMPLICATIONS

1. Absent other factors, if the grantor outlives the specified term, none of the trust's assets should be included in the grantor's estate, because the grantor has retained no interest in trust assets at death. Code Section 2036 (retained life estates) applies only if the grantor retained the right to possess or enjoy the property or the income it produces: (a) for life; or (b) for a period not ascertainable without reference to the grantor's death; or (c) for any period which does not, in fact, end before the grantor's death. The grantor generally should not serve or continue to serve as trustee after the end of the term interest in the trust, in order to avoid control over the trust that could subject the trust assets to estate taxation pursuant to Code Section 2036(a)(2).

2. The gift to the remainder beneficiary is a gift of a future interest. Therefore, it cannot qualify for the gift tax annual exclusion.

3. Because a GRIT, GRAT, or GRUT should be a grantor trust for income tax purposes, the grantor will be liable for income tax on ordinary income earned by the trust.[48] Nevertheless, it is important to make certain that the entire trust is a grantor trust for income tax purposes because it is possible for a trust to be a partial grantor trust.

4. If the grantor lives beyond the specified term, there should be no further transfer tax because the gift was complete upon the funding of the trust.

5. The taxable portion of a gift made after 1976 is considered an adjusted taxable gift because the entire present value of the gift to the remainder beneficiary is taxable. However, using a GRIT, GRAT, or GRUT can transfer a rapidly growing asset at an extremely low transfer tax cost. This results in a significant leveraging of the applicable exclusion amount. Perhaps more importantly, 100 percent of appreciation in the property's value occurring after the term ending date escapes estate and gift tax. This makes a GRIT, GRAT, or GRUT an excellent estate freezing device with respect to post-transfer appreciation, although the GRUT generally will not perform as well as the GRAT or GRIT because it is a "leaky freeze."

6. When the grantor survives the specified term of the trust, no basis adjustment for the property will be allowed. This is because the property was not acquired from a decedent, so Code Section 1014 is inapplicable. The property was acquired by gift when the trust was created. So the basis of the donee/remainder beneficiary generally is the same as in the hands of the grantor/donor (i.e., carryover basis). However, the donee's basis is increased by any gift tax attributable to the gift in the proportion that the net appreciation (fair market value of gift – basis) bears to the value of the gift.[49]

7. If the grantor dies before the specified term of the trust expires, then the date of death value of the property or the value of the corpus necessary to produce the annuity or unitrust, if less, will be included in the grantor's gross estate.[50] If there was an estate tax inclusion: (a) there would be no adjusted taxable gift; and (b) the applicable exclusion amount utilized in making the gift would be restored to the estate.[51] It may be appropriate for a beneficiary to purchase insurance on the life of the grantor and carry that life insurance during the period of time in which the death of the grantor would cause estate tax inclusion. The insurance proceeds, received estate-tax free, could then be used to purchase assets from the grantor's estate and thereby provide the estate with the liquidity to pay the estate tax.

8. If appreciated property is transferred to a GRIT, GRAT, or GRUT, the tax on any gain will eventually be paid by: (a) the grantor (so long as the trust is a grantor trust); (b) the trust (when the trust ceases to be a grantor trust); or (c) the beneficiaries (if the property is distributed outright to them on termination of the trust). Having taxes paid by the grantor may not, however, be a disadvantage, because the purpose of the trust is to defund the grantor's estate and shift as much wealth as possible to the remainder beneficiary with minimal gift taxes.

9. GRITs, GRATs, and GRUTS generally are subject to Code Section 2702. However, Code Section 2702 is inapplicable to GRITs between unrelated parties who are not considered to be members of the same family.

GRATs: DESIGN AND ADMINISTRATION

The following points are very important to consider in GRAT design and administration:

1. Estate planners should back load GRAT payments. By back-loading the GRAT annuity to the greatest extent possible, which is a GRAT with a 20 percent increase in the annuity payment each year,[52] the GRAT often will outperform any other type of GRAT, with the exception of GRATs with a very long term.

2. Two-life GRATs generally cannot be done. Once permitted,[53] the IRS ultimately reversed course and took the position that the annuity would not be fixed and ascertainable, and, therefore, does not count.[54] The Tax Court has agreed with the IRS's more recent view of the two life GRAT that the IRS used to permit.[55] However, the Ninth Circuit does not agree with the Tax Court.[56] In view of the Tax Court jurisprudence, one should avoid the two-life GRAT.

3. Formula GRATs are expressly permissible without drawing the ire of the IRS, as in the defined value gift/sale arena. The Code Section 2702 regulations expressly permit the GRAT annuity to be "[a] fixed fraction or percentage of the initial fair market value of the property transferred to the trust, as finally determined for federal tax purposes."[57] This is how all GRATs should be structured. If the gift tax value of the GRAT property is changed on audit, the GRAT annuity, and the value of the grantor's retained interest, will change proportionately. This means that the taxable gift will remain the same fraction of the total value of the GRAT property. This technique can serve to "audit-proof" a GRAT.

4. There is an issue about the shortest length that a GRAT safely can be. Code Section 2702(b)(1) refers to "fixed amounts payable not less frequently than annually." The regulations provide for amounts "payable periodically, but not less frequently than annually."[58] Court decisions have involved GRATs that have been as short as 366 days, although the length of the GRAT in that case doesn't seem to have been questioned or at issue.[59] However, in view of the language from the Code and Treasury Regulations, out of an abundance of caution, one probably should provide for a minimum GRAT term of at least two years absent extenuating circumstances. Nevertheless, the estate planner must keep abreast of future changes in the law in this regard since there have been proposals to require GRATs to have a ten year minimum term.

5. One of the limitations on a GRAT is that the governing instrument must prohibit additional contributions.[60] This can create logistical problems where a GRAT is being funded with multiple assets, which we do not recommend. See 6 below. The safest way around this issue is to provide that the GRAT is *completely* revocable and amendable until *all* of the property is safely retitled into the name of the trustee of the GRAT. There should be a declaration by the grantor to the trustee of the GRAT that funding is complete to leave no doubt when that is completed.

6. For several reasons, a GRAT probably should be funded with only one asset, e.g., closely-held

interests in Mythico, LLC. If a GRAT is funded with multiple assets, and some of the assets appreciate while others decline in value, the overall investment experience and performance of the GRAT will suffer. On the other hand, significant appreciation by a single asset often will result in a "home run" in a GRAT, transfer of significant appreciation to the GRAT remainder beneficiaries, whereas if the single asset GRAT fails, the asset simply is returned to the grantor in whole, and nothing is lost except the cost of GRAT formation.

7. If it is contemplated that the grantor will create a new GRAT whenever an annuity payment is made back to the grantor, i.e., a rolling GRAT where each annuity payment simply is re-created to a new GRAT, the same trust instrument should not be used in order to avoid estate tax exposure to the grantor. The separation should make it clear that each GRAT is independent and not a part of a "prearrangement" to make sure that the GRATs will not be collapsed via the step transaction doctrine into one long-term GRAT with estate tax exposure through the entire long term. Clients and some estate planners may wish to streamline this process and employ the same documents for the sake of expediency and possibly even cost considerations, but we strongly advise against it.

8. It can be an issue if a GRAT's investment experience exceeds the wildest expectations. In other words, the question might be "What if the GRAT works too well?" It should be possible to cap the amount of value ultimately passing to the remainder beneficiaries of the GRAT, with any excess being returned to the grantor or diverted elsewhere, e.g., to charity. The cap can be an absolute dollar ceiling, or it can be reflected in a proportional sharing in the remainder by the remainder beneficiaries and the grantor, again above a certain dollar amount. For example, Bill Jones might fund a five year GRAT with $1,000,000 of closely-held business interests that are expected to wildly appreciate due to a liquidity event that is expected sometime during the GRAT term. The GRAT instrument might provide that GRAT remainder proceeds in excess of $10,000,000 will revert to Bill. However, the cap can have no effect on the gift tax value of

the remainder, even though it is possible that all of the remainder will not pass to the GRAT remainder beneficiaries and may return, in whole or in part, to the grantor.

9. GRATs must be carefully administered in accordance with the governing instrument and the Treasury Regulations. Otherwise, there is a risk that the GRAT annuity will be held to be an unqualified interest, which would make the original gift a gift of the entire GRAT property and not just of the remainder interest.[61]

10. Where the grantor dies during the GRAT term, it can be challenging to provide that whatever value is included in the grantor's gross estate with respect to the GRAT qualifies for the federal estate tax marital deduction. Simply combining the remaining annuity payments and the remainder at the end of the GRAT and making both payable to the surviving spouse could violate the prohibition on payments to anyone other than the grantor during the GRAT term.[62]

11. Given the recent low interest rate environment (which, of course, can change quickly), many estate planners are considering long-term GRATs, even for ninety-nine years. The longer the GRAT term, the lower will be the annuity required to zero-out the GRAT, i.e., to produce no taxable gift. The regulations under Code Section 2036 provides that where a grantor retained an interest in an annuity the value of the property included in the grantor's estate will be the amount required to produce the annuity using the Code Section 7520 rate in effect at the grantor's death.[63] As a result, if the GRAT substantially appreciates in value or if the applicable federal rate substantially increases, only a small portion of the original GRAT transfer possibly will be included in the grantor's estate. For example, assume that the applicable federal rate at the time of the GRAT creation and funding is 3. percent in February 2019, and the transfer to the GRAT is of assets that have a discounted fair market value of $3,500,000 (undiscounted value of $5,000,000), which are expected to produce 2 percent annual income and 6 percent annual appreciation, it will only take an annual annuity of $117,182.80 (3.34808 percent) to produce a zeroed out GRAT. Assume that the grantor dies in year

thirty of the GRAT, at which point the GRAT is now worth $37,640,181.62, at a time when the applicable federal rate is 6.4 percent, i.e., double what it was when the GRAT was created. The inclusion of the GRAT is governed by Code Section 2036 as stated above. To produce a 6.4 percent annuity (the applicable federal rate at death), considering the $117,182.80 annuity payment, only $1,830,981.25of the GRAT would be includible in the grantor's estate ($117,182.80/.064), and the balance would escape further federal transfer tax. The higher the applicable federal rate at the time of death, the lesser of the GRAT remainder that has to be included in the grantor's estate. However, there also have been legislative proposals to put a cap on the length of a GRAT at the grantor's life expectancy plus ten years, so attention to future law changes in this area is a must.

12. While the GRAT instrument must prohibit commutation, there are several situations during the life of a GRAT where it would be advantageous for the grantor to sell or assign the annuity interest. For this reason, it is critical that the GRAT instrument not contain the traditional spendthrift trust clauses, which prohibit alienation. For example, the GRAT instrument could prohibit involuntary alienation but permit gifts and sales by the beneficiaries.

13. The identity of the remainder beneficiaries of a GRAT must be carefully considered. GRATs don't make for great generation-skipping initial transfers. For example, making grandchildren the remainder beneficiaries of a GRAT – or even making "descendants per stirpes" the remainder beneficiaries of the GRAT so that grandchildren will succeed to the interests of their deceased parents – generally should be avoided, unless the parents are deceased when the GRAT is created.[64] This is because the "ETIP" rule of Code Section 2642(f) prevents allocation of GST tax exemption to such a trust until the expiration of the GRAT term, when the property may have substantially increased in value. As a result, the grantor will not know how much GST tax exemption will be needed or even be available to allocate to the GRAT until its end. Thus, children are the

best recipients of GRAT remainder interests, either as survivors (which would cut out any child who dies during the term of the GRAT) or as vested remainder beneficiaries (which would permit predeceased children to pass on the vested remainder pursuant to the laws of descent and distribution). It may be possible for the children to sell their GRAT remainder interests to dynasty trusts where their GST tax exemption can be safely applied to give the transfers a zero inclusion ratio. Again, care should be taken to not employ a boilerplate spendthrift trust clause that would prohibit such a transaction.

14. GRAT instruments should not prohibit the grantor from purchasing the GRAT assets during the GRAT term (even though QPRT instruments must so prohibit), which can help in a number of situations, including collapsing an underperforming GRAT or swapping the GRAT assets, i.e., low basis assets for high basis assets. If the GRAT is set up as a wholly grantor trust, there will be no gain on such a transaction,[65] even if the purchase is done by the grantor's spouse.[66] Additionally, the GRAT instrument should expressly permit such a transaction to be paid for by a note from the grantor, even though the GRAT instrument must prohibit the GRAT annuity payments from being made with a note.

15. Clearly, the IRS doesn't believe that taxpayers should be able to zero out GRATs. There have been legislative proposals to require a 10 percent minimum remainder gift coming out of a GRAT, so careful attention to future legislative developments is prudent in this arena. How small a gift will be required is a matter up for debate. The Tax Court permitted a zeroed out GRAT in *Walton v. Commissioner*.[67] Nevertheless, the IRS ordinarily will not issue GRAT rulings unless the remainder interest is at least 10 percent.[68] However, the prudent estate planner should counsel the client to consider at least a small gift coming out of the GRAT in order to put the gift on a gift tax return and thereby start the statute of limitations on audit running. While a de minimis gift might draw a challenge on audit, we don't believe that the gift needs to be of a particular minimum size in order to count as a real taxable gift.

FREQUENTLY ASKED QUESTIONS

Question – Assume that a spouse makes a large transfer to a GRAT or GRUT. To reduce the potential gift tax on the value of the remainder beneficiary's interest, the transferor's spouse consents to "split" the gift and use the spouse's applicable exclusion amount against the gift tax to reduce or eliminate the tax. If the husband dies before the specified term expires, will the wife's applicable exclusion amount be restored?

Answer – No. Although the transferor spouse's applicable credit amount is restored if he dies within the specified term, the consenting spouse's applicable credit amount is *not* restored because inclusion is under Code Section 2036, not 2035. A potential solution to this inequity is for the transferor spouse to make a gift to his spouse. The spouse then could make his own actual contribution to the GRAT or GRUT. (Obviously, the IRS could consider this a step transaction, but this logic presumes that the gift to the spouse (assuming the facts indicate it was an outright and unconditional gift) was per se a transfer to an agent of the transferor spouse. This presumption is at odds with the trend of constitutional and even tax law, which recognizes a spouse as an independent person and the trend of antipathy to sexual bias.) For these reasons, one should never elect to split GRAT or GRUT gifts.

Question – What are the best assets to place into a GRIT, GRAT, or GRUT?

Answer – Assets that possess substantial appreciation potential and that throw off some cash flow are the best assets to place into a GRIT, GRAT, or GRUT.

Question – Is there an "escape mechanism" that could redirect the remainder interest if the grantor dies during the term? For instance, is there a way to provide that if the grantor's estate has to include GRIT, GRAT, or GRUT assets, funds in the trust return to the grantor's estate rather than going to the remainder beneficiary?

Answer – A reversion to the grantor (or better yet, to a revocable trust the grantor established during lifetime to avoid probate), conditioned on the grantor's death within the specified term, could be used. However, the value of a contingent reversion will not reduce the value of the taxable gift to the remainder person in the case of a GRAT or GRUT subject to Code Section 2702. However, for GRITs that aren't subject to Code Section 2702 because the transfers aren't to members of the same family, the contingent reversion will reduce the value of the taxable gift.

Question – Is there a cutoff age after which the GRIT, GRAT, or GRUT is no longer mathematically logical?

Answer – Because the GRIT, GRAT, and GRUT are "little to lose – a lot to gain" tools, even clients in their eighties or nineties may want to use such a trust. For instance, assuming a Code Section 7520 rate of 3.2 percent in February 2019, the value of the income interest and contingent reversionary interest retained in a five year GRIT for an 80-year old person is .42053 of the principal. Some elderly clients, especially those who are in very good health, may want to gamble with a GRAT, GRUT, or GRIT. For example, if the eighty-year-old client opted for a ten-year GRIT term, the value of the income interest and contingent reversionary interest jumps to. Of the funds placed in the GRIT (and, therefore, the taxable gift to the remainder person drops accordingly).

For clients with a slightly lower risk tolerance, consider staggered terms. For instance, an eighty-year-old client could transfer some property into a two-year GRIT, GRAT, or GRUT and other property into a three- year GRIT, GRAT, or GRUT.

CHAPTER ENDNOTES

1. I.R.C. Sec. 2704(c)(2); Treas. Reg. Sec. 25.2702-2(a)(1).

2. It is important that the property produce some level of income, or the grantor should be given the right to force the property to be income productive in order to avoid an indirect gift of the foregone income under the principles that the U.S. Supreme Court enunciated in *Dickman v. Comm'r.*, 465 U.S. 330 (1984). See, e.g., PLRs 8801008 and 8642028.

3. I.R.C. Sec. 2702 effectively eliminates GRITs where the remainder interest passes from the transferor or a member of the transferor's family (as defined in I.R.C. Sec 2701 (e)) to a member of the grantor's family, including the grantor's spouse, ancestors and lineal descendants of the grantor and the grantor's spouse, brothers or sisters of the grantor, or any spouses of the above. I.R.C. Sec. 2702(e), which incorporates I.R.C. Sec. 2704(c)(2).

4. Subpart E of Subchapter J of the Internal Revenue Code of 1986, as amended, I.R.C. Secs. 671-678. These rules are known as the grantor trust rules, which have been a part of the tax law in some form or fashion since 1924, so it is difficult for the IRS

to argue that these rules are inapplicable, even though crafty taxpayers are using the grantor trust rules, which were enacted as anti-taxpayer rules, against the IRS. In Rev. Rul. 2004-64, the IRS ruled that the payment by a grantor of the income tax on a grantor trust was not a gift.

5. See, e.g., PLRs 9525032, 9352017, 9416009, 9352007, 9351005, 9345035, 9248016, and 9239015.

6. I.R.C. Sec. 2038.

7. Treas. Reg. Sec. 25.2702-3(d)(6).

8. This risk includes the risk of not properly administering the GRAT or GRUT as such. Cf. *Atkinson Estate v. Commissioner*, 303 F. 3d 1290 (11th Cir. 2002).

9. See, e.g., PLR 9239015; Treas. Reg. Sec. 25.2702-3(e), Example 5.

10. *Walton v. Comm'r.*, 115 T.C. 589 (2000). IRS did not appeal *Walton* and has since acquiesced. Notice 2003-72.

11. This is due to the inability to apply GST tax exemption during the "estate tax inclusion period" (ETIP). This means that no GST tax exemption can be allocated during the term in which the grantor holds an interest. Therefore, the client won't know how much GST tax exemption will be needed to apply to the trust in order to achieve a GST tax applicable fraction of zero until the end of the ETIP, meaning no GST tax is applicable. If the assets have appreciated too much during the ETIP, the client may not have enough GST Tax exemption to ensure a GST tax applicable fraction of zero.

12. Treas. Reg. Sec. 25.2702-3(b)(1)(ii)(B) (for a GRAT) and Treas. Reg. Sec. 25.2702-3(c)(1)(ii).

13. The relief given by I.R.C. Sec. 2001(e) does not cover gift tax paid by a spouse.

14. Treas. Reg. Sec. 25.2702-3(b)(1)(i) (GRATs) and Treas. Reg. Sec. 25.2702-3(c)(1)(i) (GRUTs).

15. Treas. Reg. Sec. 25.2702-3(b)(1)(ii)(A)-(B).

16. Treas. Reg. Sec. 25.2702-1(b).

17. Treas. Reg. Sec. 25.2702-1(c).

18. I.R.C. Secs. 2702(e) and 2704(c)(2).

19. I.R.C. Secs. 2701(e)(2) and 2704(a)(1).

20. Treas. Reg. Sec. 25.2702-(a)(2).

21. Treas. Reg. Sec. 25.2702-2(a)(3).

22. I.R.C. Sec. 2702(b); Treas. Reg. Sec. 25-2702(a)(6).

23. Treas. Reg. Sec. 25.2702-3(b)(1)(i) (GRATs) and Treas. Reg. Sec. 25.2702-3(c)(1)(i) (GRUTs).

24. Treas. Reg. Sec. 25.2702-3(b)(1)(ii).

25. Treas. Reg. Sec. 25.2702-3(b)(1)(iii).

26. Treas. Reg. Sec. 25.2702-3(b)(5). This is a governing instrument requirement.

27. Treas. Reg. Sec. 25.2702-3(b)(2). This is a governing instrument requirement.

28. Treas. Reg. Sec. 25.2702-3(b)(4).

29. Treas. Reg. Sec. 25.2702-3(b)(4).

30. Treas. Reg. Sec. 25.2702-3(b)(1)(ii)(B).

31. Treas. Reg. Sec. 25.2702-3(c)(1)(i).

32. Treas. Reg. Sec. 25.2702-3(d)(1).

33. Treas. Reg. Sec. 25.2702-3(d)(3). This prohibition also applies to GRATs.

34. Treas. Reg. Sec. 25.2702-3(d)(4).

35. Treas. Reg. Sec. 25.2702-3(d)(5).

36. Treas. Reg. Sec. 25.2702-3(e), Ex. 1.

37. Treas. Reg. Sec. 25.2702-3(f)(2).

38. Treas. Reg. Sec. 25.2702-3(f)(1)(iii).

39. Treas. Reg. Sec. 25.2702-3(f)(1)(iv).

40. Treas. Reg. Sec. 25.2702-3(f)(1)(iv).

41. Treas. Reg. Sec. 25.2702-3(f)(2).

42. Treas. Reg. Sec. 25.2702-6(a)(1).

43. Treas. Reg. Sec. 25.2702-6(b)(1).

44. Treas. Reg. Sec. 25.2702-6(a)(2).

45. Treas. Reg. Sec. 25.2702-6(a)(3).

46. Calculations made with NumberCruncher (available at www. leimberg.com).

47. Id.

48. I.R.C. Sec. 677(a)(1).

49. I.R.C. Sec. 1015.

50. I.R.C. Sec. 2036(a)(1); Treas. Reg. Sec. 20.2036-1(c)(2)(i), which recently was held valid in Badgley v. Comm'r., 121 AFTR 2d ¶2018-772 (DC CA 2018).

51. I.R.C. Sec. 2001(b); Treas. Reg. Sec. 25.2702-6(a).

52. Treas. Reg. Sec. 25.2702-3(b)(1)(ii).

53. See PLRs 9352017, 9416009, 9449012, and 9449013, which appeared to approve of the two-life valuation technique.

54. The IRS ruled that the contingent interest of the grantor's spouse is analogous to a reversion in the grantor and must be given a value of zero. See TAMs 9707001, 9717008, 9741001 and 9848004. See also PLRs 199937043 (modifying PLR 9352017),

199951031 (modifying PLR 9449012) and 199951032 (modifying PLR 9449013).

55. Cook v. Comm'r., 115 T.C. 15 (2000); Focardi Estate v. Comm'r., T.C. Memo 2006-56.

56. Schott v. Comm'r., 319 F.3d 1203 (9th Cir. 2003), rev'g and rem'g T.C. Memo 2001-110.

57. Treas. Reg. Sec. 25.2702-3(b)(1)(ii)(B).

58. Treas. Reg. Sec. 25.2702-3(b)(1)(ii).

59. In Kerr v. Comm'r., 113 T.C. 449 (1999), aff'd, 292 F.3d 490 (5th Cir. 2002), there was a GRAT with a term of 366 days. See also Walton v. Comm'r., 115 T.C. 589 (2000), where a zeroed out GRAT had a term of two years.

60. Treas. Reg. Sec. 25.2702-3(b)(5).

61. Cf. Atkinson Estate v. Comm'r., 309 F. 3d 1290 (11th Cir. 2002).

62. Treas. Reg. Sec. 25.2702-3(d)(2). For an excellent discussion of qualifying a GRAT for the marital deduction as well as a roadmap of how to do that, see, Aucutt, Ronald D., Grantor Retained Annuity Trusts (GRATs) and Sales to Grantor Trusts, Sec. 4I (March 11, 2016), accessible at https://www.mcguirewoods.com/news-resources/publications/taxation/grats.pdf .

63. Treas. Reg. Sec. 20.2036-1(c)(2).

64. This is because of the predeceased parent rule of I.R.C. Sec. 2651(e).

65. Rev. Rul. 85-13.

66. I.R.C. Sec. 1041(a).

67. 115 T.C. 589 (2000). The IRS acquiesced in the Walton result. Notice 2003-72.

68. See, e.g., Rev. Proc. 2016-3, Sec. 4.01(58).

CHARITABLE TRUSTS

CHAPTER 13

This chapter discusses the use of three types of charitable trusts:

- Charitable Remainder Annuity Trusts (CRATs)

- Charitable Remainder Unitrusts (CRUTs)

- Charitable Lead Trusts (CLTs)

While CRATs, CRUTs, and CLTs are all split-interest charitable trusts, there are significant differences between charitable lead trusts and charitable remainder trusts. The most obvious difference is that the income and remainder beneficiary roles are reversed. In a lead trust, a charity is entitled to the annuity or unitrust interest and a noncharitable beneficiary is entitled to the remainder. Conversely, in a charitable remainder trust, the noncharitable beneficiary is entitled to the annuity or unitrust interest with a charitable beneficiary receiving the remainder interest.

Aside from the reversed income interest roles, there are other differences. For example, charitable remainder trusts are tax-exempt entities whereas charitable lead trusts are not. Additionally, charitable remainder trusts have minimum and maximum payout rates, as well as maximum term limits. Charitable lead trusts do not have these same requirements.

The major distinction between a CRAT and a CRUT is that the payments from a CRAT are set as a fixed amount or as a fixed percentage of the initial fair market value of the trust's assets at the time the trust is funded. In comparison, the unitrust payments from a CRUT vary in amount from year to year because unitrust payments are a fixed percentage of the annually redetermined fair market value of the trust's assets.

Another important distinction is that no subsequent additions are permitted after the initial contribution for a CRAT, but additions are permitted by the donor (and certain others) for a CRUT. This difference alone frequently serves as a compelling reason for donors to choose a CRUT over a CRAT. Because the amount payable under a CRAT becomes fixed on the date that the trust is created, it is the charity rather than the annuitant(s) that benefits from any increases in value of the trust fund. On the other hand, if the trust does not produce income or does not grow sufficiently, the charity will suffer due to the loss of principal in paying the annuity amount.[1]

The details of all three types of charitable trusts are explored in-depth below.

CHARITABLE REMAINDER ANNUITY TRUSTS

A charitable remainder annuity trust (CRAT) is a form of split-interest trust established between one or more donors and a trustee. (A split-interest trust is a trust that has both charitable and noncharitable beneficiaries.) Typically the donor transfers cash or other property into the trust. The trust then pays a fixed annuity for a term of years or the life (or lives) of one or more individuals. At the end of that specified term (or when the noncharitable annuitants have all died), the trust is continued for, or its assets are distributed to, one or more qualified charities.

Ordinarily, a taxpayer receives a charitable deduction only for a gift of a complete interest in property. A gift of a partial interest does not qualify for a charitable deduction unless a specific provision in the Internal Revenue Code allows for such a partial interest deduction. One such statutory exception to the partial interest rule is the CRAT.

The donor can claim an income and gift tax charitable deduction for the actuarially determined present value of the charity's remainder interest; an estate tax deduction can be taken if the trust is funded by a transfer at death.

HOW ARE CRATS USED?

1. When the donor wishes to make a large charitable gift while retaining a cash flow in the form of an annuity interest in the donated property.

2. When the donor does not anticipate making additions to the trust (see "CRAT Requirements," below).

3. When the donor is risk-averse and would like to "fix" the payments and, thus, avoid a potential decrease in payments should the market value of the charitable remainder unitrust's (CRUT's) assets decline at some point in the future.

4. When the donor wants to make a gift at death while providing an annuity benefit for one or more individuals, with the remainder passing to one or more charities. However, it is not the preferred giving technique if the property being transferred is debt-encumbered.[2]

ADVANTAGES OF A CRAT

1. There is no risk of the reduced cash flow that might result with a CRUT due to a decline in the value of the trust assets.

2. There is no risk of loss of principal as with a charitable gift annuity. The property is in the hands of the trustee of the CRAT until the expiration of the annuity interest.

3. The CRAT can also be an effective way to provide a benefit (i.e., an income stream) to another individual. Of course, if the donor names someone other than the donor or the donor's spouse as an annuitant, a portion of the transfer to the trust is a gift. Depending on the actuarial value of the annuity to be paid to that person other than the donor or the donor's spouse, the donor has made a taxable gift that uses gift tax exemption or results in gift tax if the donor's exemption has already been utilized on prior taxable gifts.

4. Lower administrative burdens because unlike a CRUT, CRATS do not require annual revaluations.

DISADVANTAGES OF A CRAT

1. Once established, no additional contributions may be made to a CRAT. One solution to this problem may be to establish one or more additional CRATs.

2. The set-up costs in a CRAT are higher, and the administrative tasks more burdensome than a charitable gift annuity.

3. Annuity payments are not guaranteed. If the CRAT assets decline in value, the annuity payments decrease even to zero.

4. Charitable remainder trusts are treated as private foundations for various purposes, including the application of the prohibition on self-dealing. As a result, a CRAT may not enter into sales, leases, loans, or certain other transactions with the donor or related parties.[3]

CRAT REQUIREMENTS

Like the other split-interest gifts (i.e., CRUTs, pooled income funds), the CRAT must meet stringent requirements.[4] Foremost among them are:

1. There must be a written trust instrument that is valid under state law. The Internal Revenue Service has promulgated sample forms for CRATs.[5]

2. The trust must provide for: (a) a specific amount; (b) at least annually; (c) to one or more beneficiaries; at least one of which is not a charity; (d) for life or for a term of no more than twenty years; (e) with an irrevocable remainder interest to be held for the benefit of, or paid over to, charity.[6]

3. The trust must be a CRAT from its inception to its termination—it cannot alternate between different types of payments. In other words, a CRAT cannot provide a fixed annuity payment in one year (i.e., as is required with a CRAT), and then provide a percentage of the value of the trust assets in the next year (i.e., as would be the case with a CRUT).[7]

4. The trust must have at least one noncharitable beneficiary and the recipient must be a person other than a charitable organization.[8]

5. The trust must require that the trustee pay the noncharitable beneficiary a fixed dollar amount for life, or for a term of not more than twenty years. This amount may be expressed as either a stated sum or as a percentage of the initial value of the trust assets. For example, the annuity amount could be stated as $20,000, or 5 percent of the trust's initial value ($400,000).[9]

6. The annuity amount must not be less than 5 percent nor more than 50 percent of the initial net fair market value of all property placed into the trust.[10]

7. The present value of the charitable remainder interest must be at least 10 percent of the initial fair market value of the contributed property. This computation is affected by the age(s) of the annuitant(s), the term of the trust, the annuity rate and the section 7520 rate.[11]

8. The trust must be protected from the payment of any estate tax due in the donor's estate (i.e., the CRAT's value will be included in the donor's estate if the donor is the life income beneficiary). If someone other than the donor's spouse is a beneficiary, the value of that interest will be a taxable disposition; consequently, some of the deceased donor's applicable exclusion amount may have to be used, or estate tax may be due (after taking into account the charitable deduction for the remainder value).

9. No additions may be made to a charitable remainder annuity trust after its creation.[12]

10. In a ruling predating the "10 percent remainder interest requirement," described above, the IRS ruled that a gift of a remainder interest through a CRAT must meet the "5 percent probability test." The revenue ruling states that no deduction will be allowed "unless the possibility that the charitable transfer will not become effective is so remote as to be negligible." Essentially, this means that if the actuarial possibility of a charity receiving a remainder interest is less than 5 percent, it is "so remote as to be negligible" and the deduction will be denied. This could happen, for example, where the annuity payout is for the joint life expectancy of a young couple and the trust was drafted before the 10 percent remainder interest requirement went into effect.[13]

Drafting a CRAT

When drafting a charitable remainder trust the term of the annuity interest must be defined as either a fixed number of years *or* the life of the beneficiary. (The lives of the beneficiaries may be used if more than one annuitant is designated.) The trust document must also specify the annuity rate and the identity of the remainder beneficiary, or that the remainder beneficiary must be a "qualified charity." The statutory requirements discussed in the previous paragraphs must also be met.

The drafter may use one of the model forms promulgated by the IRS (see "Frequently Asked Questions" below). However, drafters should be aware that these model forms are incomplete and require insertion of administrative provisions based on applicable state law to create a complete document. Furthermore, it may not be enough to have a properly prepared trust document if the trust is not administered properly. In *Atkinson v. Commissioner*, the failure of the trustee to follow the terms of the trust resulted in the loss of the charitable estate tax deduction.[14]

Example. William, age seventy, desires to provide a benefit to his alma mater. He would also like to receive favorable tax treatment and a fixed level of income for as long as he lives. William transfers appreciated securities to a CRAT, with an annuity payout of 7.5 percent of the initial value of the trust assets to be distributed to him for his lifetime, and the remainder to go to his alma mater.

The stock William places in the trust has a low cost basis and pays dividends annually. Trust distributions to William will be taxed under the four-tier income tax system described below.

TAX IMPLICATIONS OF A CRAT

The use of a CRAT can have important income (including the net investment income tax), gift, and estate tax implications that should be fully considered in light of the client's overall planning objectives.

Ordinary Income Tax

Due to the enactment of Internal Revenue Code section 1411 in the Health Care and Education and Reconciliation Act of 2010, a new complexity of tax reporting applies to CRTs. This section will review the traditional rules and the next section will address the Net Investment Income Tax (NIIT).

Tax implications for trusts. CRATs are not subject to income tax on their general investment income (i.e., dividends, royalties, interest, and gains from the sale or exchange of property) because the trust itself is tax-exempt.[15] However, if the trust has "unrelated business taxable income" (UBTI) during a year, a 100 percent excise tax is imposed on the UBTI. UBTI generally falls into one of two distinct classes of income: (1) income from the regular conduct of an unrelated trade or business; or (2) "unrelated debt financed income."[16] An in-depth explanation of UBTI is beyond the scope of this discussion, but planners should be aware of its application to charitable remainder trusts.

Tax implications for annuity recipients. The recipients of the annuity amounts are subject to income tax on the distributions made to them. The distributions received by the annuitants are taxed under a four-tier income tax reporting rule. Under this four-tier approach, payouts will be taxed in the following order:

1. ordinary income;

2. capital gain;

3. other income (generally tax-exempt income); and

4. return of capital.[17]

Tax implications for donors. The donor receives an immediate income tax charitable deduction for the present value of the remainder interest. The remainder interest is generally the initial fair market value of the trust assets *minus* the present value of the recipient's annuity interest determined using IRS tables issued under section 7520.

Net Investment Income Tax

A 3.8 percent surtax is imposed on net investment income (NII), including income reportable by the annuitant as ordinary income and net gains. This surtax is not imposed on the CRT. In order to ensure compliance, the IRS has issued regulations requiring Trustees of Charitable Remainder Trusts to account for income subject to the NIIT.[18] Under these regulations, NII will be included in amounts paid to annuitants with NII treated as coming out of the trust to the beneficiary first, contrary to the normal tiered distribution rules mentioned in the preceding section.[19]

The 3.8 percent surtax is imposed on net investment income (NII), including amounts otherwise reportable by the annuitant as ordinary income and net gains.

Gift Tax

When the donor and the recipient of the annuity amount are the same, there is a gift of the remainder to charity. This should be reported on a gift tax return (Form 709) by showing the amount of the gift and by taking a corresponding gift tax charitable deduction. Likewise, when the sole recipient of the annuity amount is the donor's spouse, the gift tax marital deduction will be available.

If the recipient of the annuity amount is someone other than the donor (or the donor's spouse), the annuity interest is a separate taxable gift. If there is only one recipient to whom a taxable gift is made, the gift will qualify for the $15,000 (in 2019, subject to inflation adjustments) annual exclusion. If there are successive recipients, only the gift to the first recipient qualifies for the annual exclusion.[20] If there are co-recipients and their percentage interests are not fixed and certain (i.e., as when the trustee can allocate the annuity amount among recipients), no part of the gift will qualify for the annual exclusion.[21] However, the necessity of reporting a taxable transfer can be avoided altogether if the donor retains the right to revoke the recipient's annuity interest.

Estate Tax

If the donor dies prematurely and is the sole recipient (or one of the recipients) of the annuity amount, the donor's estate will include a portion of the value of the CRAT under Code section 2036—specifically, the amount necessary at the specified payout rate to yield the guaranteed annual payment. However, the full value of the CRAT should be includable under Code section 2039. This does not cause a problem if the donor is the only recipient of the annuity amount because a corresponding amount can be deducted from his gross estate. However, if there is a successive noncharitable income recipient, the amount included in the donor's estate for that successive interest is not deductible.[22]

A testamentary bequest or devise of a charitable remainder interest in the form of a CRAT qualifies for the estate tax charitable deduction. An interest left to the donor's spouse qualifies for the marital deduction. Interests left to any recipients other than the donor's spouse are not deductible and will be subject to tax in the donor's estate.

CHARITABLE REMAINDER UNITRUST

A charitable remainder unitrust (CRUT) is an irrevocable, split-interest trust in which the donor or at least one other noncharitable beneficiary receives an unitrust interest, and through which the remainder interest in the property is donated to a qualified charity. The noncharitable unitrust interest term is measured by either (1) the beneficiary's lifetime (or beneficiaries' lifetimes), (2) a term of no more than twenty years, or (3) some combination thereof.

A CRUT resembles a charitable remainder annuity trust, but provides a great deal more flexibility. The primary difference between a CRUT and a CRAT is that the noncharitable interest in a CRAT is a *fixed* annuity (i.e., a fixed dollar amount), whereas the noncharitable interest in a CRUT is a *variable* annuity (i.e., measured as a fixed percentage of the trust value each year). For a detailed explanation of the differences between CRUTs and CRATS, see "Frequently Asked Questions," below.

HOW ARE CRUTS USED?

1. When the client has property that has appreciated or is not producing income, and he or she wishes to convert the property into an income stream.

2. When the client desires to sell an appreciated asset while minimizing current capital gains tax.

3. When the client desires income or transfer tax deductions while retaining some benefit from the assets.

4. When the client wants to give assets to charity but retain some benefit from those assets.

5. When clients do not need an immediate income stream from the CRT, they can use a net-income CRUT (NICRUT) to defer the income until a future date such as retirement.

6. When the donor wants to make a testamentary gift of qualified retirement plan or IRA assets without giving up the lifetime payout for heirs.

7. When clients want some flexibility in changing the ultimate charitable beneficiary.

ADVANTAGES OF CRUTS

1. A charitable remainder trust (CRT) allows the donor to make a currently deductible gift without giving up future income on the donated asset.

2. A properly drafted CRUT is a tax-exempt entity, and the donor can transfer appreciated property to the trust which the trustee may later sell without incurring capital gains tax. Because no taxes are paid on the sale of the asset held by the CRT, the entire net sales proceeds (instead of the net sales proceeds less taxes) are available to provide an income stream to the donor.

3. A CRUT can offer more flexibility with respect to the trust payments as compared to a CRAT. For instance a CRUT can be funded with additional contributions and can be structured to delay or defer payments (through the use of NICRUT, NIMCRUT and flip unitrust designs).

DISADVANTAGES OF CRUTS

1. A gift to a CRUT is irrevocable and the remainder value in the trust passes to charity and not to the donor's heirs. This potentially disinherits the heirs and may not be in line with the client's other estate planning objectives. Other assets including life insurance can be used to replace the inheritance. However, if the donor expects to use life insurance as a means of wealth replacement (see "CRUT with Life Insurance," below), it is important that insurability be ascertained prior to the transfer.

2. The use of a CRUT involves setup and administrative expenses that may not be justified for smaller gifts.

3. While the CRUT provides many benefits, the client is giving up control over the asset in exchange for an income stream that is subject to many rules and restrictions.

CRUT REQUIREMENTS

The requirements for a CRUT are similar to the requirements imposed on a CRAT. In order to qualify for income, estate, and gift tax charitable deductions, the CRUT's structure must meet certain guidelines set forth in the Code, applicable Treasury regulations, and IRS interpretations of the Code.[23] The requirements include:

1. A fixed percentage of the net fair market value of the trust principal—revalued annually—must be payable to one or more noncharitable beneficiaries each year. At least one of the noncharitable beneficiaries must be an individual other than a charitable organization.[24] This interest is sometimes referred to as the "unitrust" interest. The donor may retain this unitrust interest.

2. The fixed percentage payable annually must be between 5 and 50 percent of the trust value.[25] The actual frequency of the payments may be annual, semi-annual, quarterly, or monthly.[26] There is a slight adjustment to the size of the income tax deduction depending upon which payment schedule is selected, and whether the payment is made at the beginning or the end of the time period.[27]

3. The unitrust interest, which is payable to one or more noncharitable beneficiaries, must be made *either* for a term of years (not to exceed twenty) *or*—in the case of individual beneficiaries— for the life or lives of those noncharitable individuals.[28] Unitrust beneficiaries must be alive at the creation of the trust if they are to receive an interest for life. Thus, if a donor wishes to provide for a class of beneficiaries that might be expanded by future births (such as grandchildren), the unitrust interest must be limited to a term of years (not to exceed twenty).[29]

4. The present value of the charitable remainder interest is determined as of the time the CRUT is initially funded and must be equal to at least 10 percent of the initial trust value.[30] Because of this requirement, the intended trust term or payout rate may cause the trust to not qualify. This is particularly true for if the non-charitable beneficiary is fairly young.

A donor can make multiple contributions to a CRUT since it is valued annually (this differs from a CRAT, to which only one contribution can be made). The 10 percent minimum remainder rule applies to the initial contribution *and* to any additional contributions that are made to the unitrust.[31] There is no requirement that a certain amount actually pass to the qualified charity at the termination of the trust. Depending upon trust performance and duration, the actual charitable remainder interest may be more or less than the value of the charitable remainder interest determined at the time of the CRUT's inception.

5. No amount other than the specified unitrust interest can be paid to or for the benefit of any person other than a qualified charitable organization. This requirement means that the *entire* remainder interest must go to a qualified charitable organization.[32]

Net Income Exception CRUT (NICRUT) Requirements

The preceding requirements apply to a "standard" CRUT (sometimes known as a "SCRUT"). With a standard CRUT, the annual unitrust payments are paid regardless of trust income—even if the CRUT does not have sufficient income to make the payment. In other words, the trustee could be forced to sell trust assets or distribute the trust principal. However, some assets do not have an established market and, thus, may be difficult to sell. There are two other types of CRUTs, each of which provides an alternative to the required unitrust payment in the event the CRUT does not have sufficient income to make such payments. These are collectively known as "income exception" CRUTs, meaning that both methods provide that the unitrust beneficiary will receive the lesser of the fixed percentage of the trust's value or the net income earned by the trust.

The first alternative form of CRUT is the "net income CRUT" or "NICRUT." A NICRUT provides that the unitrust beneficiary will receive each year the *lesser of*:

- the unitrust amount specified in the trust instrument (i.e., a fixed percentage of the value of the trust assets); *or*

- the net income earned by the trust during the year.

Example. Assume that a CRUT is established with assets worth $1,000,000, and that it provides an annual payout equal to the lesser of (1) 5 percent of the trust's value (as redetermined annually), or (2) the trust's actual earned income for that year. The trust earns $30,000 in a year in which the trust has a value of $1,000,000. A standard CRUT would require that the unitrust beneficiary receive $50,000—even though that amount exceeds the trust income. However, if the trust instrument is a NICRUT, the unitrust beneficiary receives only $30,000. If the amount of any year's payout to the unitrust beneficiary is less than the stated percentage payout amount, any excess is forfeited for that year and the process repeats for each successive year.

Net Income with Make-up Provision CRUT (NIMCRUT) Requirements

The second alternative CRUT is the "net income with make-up CRUT," or "NIMCRUT." A NIMCRUT resembles a NICRUT in that the unitrust beneficiary will receive the *lesser of* the fixed percentage of the trust's value *or* the net income earned by the trust However, a NIMCRUT differs from a NICRUT in that a "make-up" account accrues in those years when net income is less than the fixed percentage of the trust's value. A make-up account is simply an accounting record of the cumulative net shortfall in the unitrust amounts actually paid out to the unitrust beneficiary each year. In subsequent years, if trust net income is greater than the fixed unitrust percentage, the excess net income after payment of the current year's unitrust percentage will be applied to any balance in the make-up account.

Example. Assume that the NIMCRUT is funded with $1,000,000 on January 1, 2019. The unitrust percentage is 5 percent of the trust's value (measured at the beginning of the year). During 2019, the trust earns income of $30,000. Because $30,000 of income is less than 5 percent of the trust value ($50,000), the unitrust beneficiary receives only $30,000. The $20,000 difference between the fixed percentage

amount and the actual income earned (and distributed) is recorded in the "make-up" account.

Further assume that the trust has a value of $1,100,000 on January 1, 2020. Based upon this revaluation, the unitrust percentage amount is $55,000 for 2017 (5 percent of $1,100,000). If the trust earns $70,000 in 2020, the unitrust beneficiary will receive the entire $70,000. The distribution will be $55,000 for the 2020 unitrust percentage and $15,000 from the make-up account (earned in 2019). At the end of 2020, the make-up account will have a balance of $5,000 (the $20,000 that was not distributed in 2019, *minus* the $15,000 in "excess" earnings distributed in 2020). The make-up account is not adjusted for the time value of money.

The NIMCRUT design can be useful in situations where the client would like to fund a CRUT now (or on an ongoing basis with multiple contributions), but defer receipt of income until a future date (i.e. retirement). The CRT trustee can invest trust assets in a manner that provides for growth and generates little or no trust income through the use of growth stocks, zero coupon bonds or deferred annuities. At some future date, the trustee can begin investing for income and distributions to the income beneficiary from the NIMCRUT can begin. One of the benefits of this design is that the unitrust percentage will be made on a larger trust value since income was not previously distributed and the trust may have grown in value. For example, in a standard 5 percent unitrust funded with $1,000,000, the initial payment would be $50,000. If we assume a NIMCRUT design earning 5 percent per year and no unitrust payments are made to the income beneficiary for ten years, the value of the trust in the eleventh year would be roughly $1,630,000. A 5 percent unitrust payment on the accrued trust value would be $81,500. Thus, the NIMCRUT design can be an effective tool for saving for retirement or other financial goals that have a future date. One caveat: income earned by the trust must be sufficient to pay the unitrust amount and any make-up amounts. Getting the increased payments can be problematic if the trustee cannot generate sufficient income to make the distribution.

Although the use of a NIMCRUT provides numerous planning opportunities, especially for appreciated property, it is important that the donor fully understand that no unitrust payment will be made *until* and *unless* the NIMCRUT earns "income" (as defined for trust accounting).[33]

"FLIP" Unitrust

A NIMCRUT is useful if the contributed assets do not immediately produce income or the need for distributions is not immediate. The trustee need not make distributions-in-kind or undergo a forced sale of contributed property to make the annual unitrust payments to the trust's unitrust beneficiary. Instead, the trustee can sell the trust property at the most opportune time and "make up" payments to the unitrust beneficiary later when the trust receives income. In some instances, NIMCRUT investments are intentionally selected to allow the trustee to postpone the unitrust distributions until income is needed by the beneficiary—in effect making the NIMCRUT a tool for supplemental income at a later time, such as retirement. However, at some point, the unitrust beneficiary may prefer the more predictable distributions that can be obtained with a standard CRUT.

The advantages of a NIMCRUT or NICRUT (income deferral) and a standard CRUT (reliable distributions) are sometimes combined into another type of trust, known as a FLIPCRUT. A FLIPCRUT ordinarily begins as a NIMCRUT, and at some future time flips to a standard CRUT. The flip is permitted to occur only upon the happening of a *triggering event* that cannot be within the control of the donor, unitrust beneficiary, trustee, or any other person.[34] Common triggering events include the sale of illiquid trust assets, such as real estate, the removal of restrictions on Rule 144 stock (i.e., restricted stock), the beneficiary's specific birthday, or the death of the beneficiary's spouse.[35]

A CRUT is allowed to flip only once. The flip must be from a NIMCRUT or NICRUT to a standard CRUT - a reverse flip from a standard CRUT to a NIMCRUT or NICRUT is *not* allowed.[36] Once the triggering event occurs, the change in payout method will occur on January 1 of the year *following* the year in which the triggering event occurred.[37]

Example: Using a CRUT with Life Insurance

One of the first steps in establishing a CRUT is be to determine if the client has a charitable intent. While CRTs provide substantial tax benefits, those reasons alone are not typically sufficient to irrevocably transfer assets. A CRT would be potentially appealing to a donor who wants to meet the following goals: defer capital gains taxes on the appreciated assets; secure a lifetime income stream; create an endowment for the charity of

the donor's choice; and possibly provide for the donor's children. A CRUT provides a donor with a current income tax deduction and an ongoing income stream. Additionally, the donor can use a CRUT to defer paying capital gains taxes on appreciated assets. However, once assets are transferred to a CRUT, and out of the donor's estate, those assets are not available to the donor's heirs after the donor's death. Often, the fact that the assets transferred to the CRT are unavailable for other estate planning purposes (such as the transfer of wealth to the donor's descendants) is a major reason why many donors will not implement a charitable giving plan. Life insurance on the donor's life can complement a CRUT and balance the value of the assets set aside for charity.

Life insurance can be an effective tool for replacing the value of the assets transferred to the CRT. Depending on the size of the donor's estate, the policy can be owned by the donor if estate taxes are not a concern, or held in an irrevocable life insurance trust if the estate exceeds the estate tax threshold ($11,400,000 for single individuals or $22,800,000 for married couples as of 2019). Determining the appropriate amount of life insurance will vary based on the donor's particular estate planning goals. For instance, the donor could choose to have a death benefit equal to the initial value of the assets contributed to the CRT, a death benefit that would approximate the remainder value that charity is expected to receive, an expected remainder value but net of any potential estate taxes that would have been paid by the estate, or any other amount that the donor feels is appropriate.

Example. Donor and donor's spouse are ages sixty-four and sixty-two, respectively. They own $1,000,000 of appreciated stock with a very low basis ($100,000). Although this stock has appreciated greatly, it is not producing much income for donor and donor's spouse. They are charitably inclined and have made substantial cash gifts to charities in the past. They are interested in three things: (1) deferring capital gains taxes on the appreciated assets; (2) securing an income stream for life; and (3) providing for their heirs. A CRUT could be the solution for them.

Donor and donor's spouse decide to donate their stock to a CRUT with an animal rescue organization as the remainder beneficiary. Donor and donor's spouses will receive 7 percent of the trust assets (valued annually each year) as income for as long as either of them is alive. After

Figure 13.1

CHARITABLE REMAINDER UNITRUST INCOME TAX DEDUCTION CALCULATION*	
Table Rate	6.8%
Fair Market Value of Trust	$1,000,000
Rate of Annuity	7%
Payment Periods in Year	1
Number of Months Valuation Date Precedes First Payout	12
Ages	64, 62
Payout Sequence Factor	0.936330
Adjusted Payout Rate	6.554%
Interpolation: Factor at 6.4%	0.23217
Factor at 6.6%	0.22247
Difference: 0.00970	
(6.554% − 6.4%)/0.2% = X/0.00970; Therefore X = 0.00747	
Life Remainder Factor = Factor at 6.4% Minus X:	0.22470
Present Value of Remainder Interest = $1,000,000 × 0.22470:	$224,700
Donors' Deduction:	$224,700
Donors' Deduction as a Percentage of Amount Transferred	22.470%
* Courtesy NumberCruncher Software (http://www.leimberg.com)	

they both die, the charity will receive whatever money is left in the trust.

Donor will receive an immediate income tax deduction based on the remainder value as calculated under IRS guidelines. These guidelines take into account donor's and donor's spouse's ages, the unitrust percentage they will receive each year, the current Section 7520 rate, and their life expectancies. Based upon a Section 7520 rate of 6.8 percent, donor and donor's spouse would receive a total income tax deduction of $224,700 (see Figure 13.1). Assuming they are in a 40 percent marginal tax bracket, this would result in total income tax savings of $89,880. Should their family income not be high enough for them to take the full income tax deduction in the year of donation, they may carry over the remainder of the deduction for up to five years, or until the deduction is completely used.[38]

Figure 13.2

Yr.	Age 1	Age 2	Contribution to Unitrust	Gross Income from Unitrust	Unitrust Value at End of Year
1	64	62	$ 1,000,000	70,000	990,000
5	68	66	0	67,242	950,990
10	73	71	0	63,946	904,382
15	78	76	0	60,812	860,058
20	83	81	0	57,832	817,907
24	87	85	0	55,553	785,678
		Totals:	$1,000,000	$1,500,253	

Figure 13.3

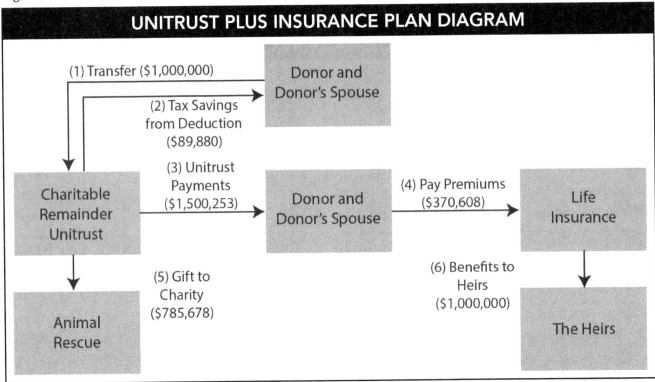

UNITRUST PLUS INSURANCE PLAN DIAGRAM

(1) Transfer ($1,000,000)

Donor and Donor's Spouse

(2) Tax Savings from Deduction ($89,880)

(3) Unitrust Payments ($1,500,253)

Charitable Remainder Unitrust

Donor and Donor's Spouse

(4) Pay Premiums ($370,608)

Life Insurance

(5) Gift to Charity ($785,678)

(6) Benefits to Heirs ($1,000,000)

Animal Rescue

The Heirs

Donor and donor's spouse will also receive income from the CRUT. Every year, the trust assets will be valued at the beginning of the year, and 7 percent of that value will be paid at the end of the year. For instance, in year one they will receive $70,000 from the unitrust. Assuming that the trust assets grow at only 6 percent each year (a declining income stream if the assets are earning 6 percent and the trust has a payout of 7 percent), they will receive a gross income of $1,500,253 over their joint life expectancy of twenty-four years. If the trust grows at more than 6 percent per year, the annual payout to donor and donor's spouse will increase as the value of the CRUT increases.

Donor may decide to use some of this income to create an irrevocable life insurance trust (ILIT) that will buy a survivorship life insurance contract. At their ages and using standard underwriting, assume the premium that would guarantee coverage for donor and donor's spouse joint lives would be $15,000.[39] Over their joint life expectancy of twenty-four years, this would represent total premiums of

$360,000. Every year, donor will give $15,000 cash to the trust, and the trust will pay the insurance premium. Upon the death of the surviving spouse, the proceeds of the ILIT will go to their heirs while the remainder value in the CRT is paid to the animal rescue. Figure 13.3 depicts the CRT coupled with life insurance.

By using the CRUT with life insurance, the donor has satisfied the following goals: secured a current income tax deduction; secured a lifetime annuity stream for the joint life of donor and donor's spouse; created an endowment for the charity of their choice; and provided for their children.

CRUT TAX IMPLICATIONS

Ordinarily, a taxpayer receives a charitable deduction only for a gift of a complete interest in property. Gifts of partial interests do not qualify for charitable deductions unless a specific provision in the Internal Revenue Code allows for such deductions.[40] One such statutory exception to the partial interest rule is the CRUT.[41]

All charitable remainder trusts, including CRUTs, have two distinct tax characteristics. First, the donor is entitled to a deduction for income, gift, and estate tax purposes. The donor's charitable deduction is equal to the present value of the remainder interest to be given to the qualified charity when the income stream terminates. Second, the CRUT itself is exempt from federal income taxes, provided that the CRUT continues to qualify as a charitable remainder trust, and does not engage in certain prohibited activities that give rise to a special type of earnings known as "unrelated business taxable income" (UBTI). The two tax characteristics of a CRUT are discussed in more detail below.

At the time that a donor contributes property to a charitable remainder trust the donor can claim a current income tax charitable deduction for the present value of the remainder interest, which will eventually pass to a qualified charity. Because the assets in the CRUT will ultimately pass to a qualified charity, the CRUT is exempt from federal income taxation. Since the CRUT is exempt from federal income taxation, the trustee may sell the contributed property without incurring capital gains tax. The trustee can reinvest all of the sale proceeds in income-generating assets. However, it is important to note that income tax cannot be completely avoided when using a CRUT. When the unitrust beneficiary of the CRUT receives a payment, income is carried out of the trust and the beneficiary must recognize that income (which may be characterized as ordinary income, capital gains, or other tax-exempt income). See "Taxation of CRUT Income and Payouts" below.

Value of the Charitable Deduction

Income tax charitable deduction. A CRUT may be created during the donor's lifetime (*inter vivos*) or at the donor's death (testamentary). The donor of an *inter vivos* CRUT receives an immediate income tax deduction equal to the present value of the remainder interest that will eventually pass to a qualified charitable remainder beneficiary. The present value of the charitable remainder interest (which determines the amount of the deduction) is determined by multiplying the fair market value of the property transferred to the CRUT by the appropriate unitrust remainder factor.[42] The value of the unitrust remainder interest can be determined from comprehensive tables provided by the IRS or through the use of certain software programs.

The factors considered in determining the value of the charitable remainder interest are as follows:

1. the fair market value of the property being donated to the CRUT;

2. the term of the trust;[43]

3. the form of trust payout to the unitrust beneficiaries (standard payout, net income, or net income with make-up);

4. the stated unitrust payout rate;

5. the frequency of the payments (annually, semi-annually, quarterly, or monthly);

6. the timing of the payments; and

7. the IRS discount rate (i.e., the Section 7520 rate) in effect for the month of the gift, or either of the two months immediately preceding the gift.[44]

While the actual income distribution under a NICRUT or NIMCRUT may be smaller than a standard CRUT, the calculation of the value of the charitable remainder interest (and, thus, the income tax deduction) is the same for all three types of CRUTs. The remainder value is identical because the IRS tables assume that the full unitrust payment will be made at the earliest date under both the NICRUT and NIMCRUT.

The donor's income tax charitable deduction is subject to the same percentage limitations and carryforward rules that apply to outright charitable gifts made during life. Unlike outright charitable gifts, CRT gifts do not require that the donor obtain a contemporaneous written acknowledgement of the contribution by the donee organization.[45]

Gift tax charitable deduction. If the retained unitrust interest is given to anyone other than the donor, the donor has made a gift that must be reported for federal gift tax purposes.[46] The full value of the donated property must be reported on a federal gift tax return (Form 709). However, the donor will be entitled to a gift tax charitable deduction for the value of the remainder interest passing to the qualified charitable organization. Even if no taxable gift is made in connection with the establishment of the CRUT, a federal gift tax return must still be filed for the year of the gift to the CRUT.[47]

Estate tax charitable deduction. If the donor creates an inter vivos CRUT and retains a lifetime unitrust interest in the trust, the full fair market value of the CRUT will be includable in the donor's gross estate. However, an estate tax charitable deduction can be claimed for the amount of the remainder interest donated to charity.[48] For CRUTs established at death (a testamentary CRUT), an estate tax charitable deduction is available. Unlike the income tax deduction, the estate tax charitable deduction is unlimited and not subject to the percentage limitations.

Taxation of CRUT Income and Payouts

Taxation of CRUT income. The CRUT itself is exempt from all federal income taxes unless it has unrelated business taxable income (UBTI). If the CRUT has UBTI, the trust will pay an excise tax equal to the entire amount of the UBTI.[49] Charitable remainder trusts are also exempt from the 3.8 percent NII tax.[50]

Taxation of amounts received by noncharitable beneficiaries. While it appear that ordinary income or capital gains tax can be completely avoided by contributing appreciated property to a CRUT, in reality, it is more appropriate to say that these taxes can be *deferred* (and, at times, reduced) by contributing appreciated property to a CRUT because the donor does not pay income tax until the unitrust payments are made. The tax treatment of income payments to the unitrust income beneficiary is subject to a unique ordering system that is typically called a "four-tier system." The four-tier system characterizes distributions from a CRUT and ensures that any income that escapes taxation at the trust level (due to the tax-exempt status of the trust) will be taxed when received by the noncharitable unitrust beneficiary.[51] Amounts distributed from a CRUT are taxed under the four-tier system in the following order:

1. *Ordinary income.* Distributions to the noncharitable beneficiary are taxable as ordinary income to the extent that the CRUT earned ordinary income in that tax year. If distributions exceed current year ordinary income, the distributions will nevertheless be taxable as ordinary income if the CRUT earned ordinary income in a previous year that was not previously distributed.

2. *Capital gains.* Distributions will be treated as *short-term* capital gain to the extent that the CRUT had short-term capital gains in that year

(or had such gains in a previous year that have not yet been distributed). If the distribution exceeds ordinary income and short-term capital gains (both current year and undistributed gains from previous years), the distribution will be characterized as *long-term* capital gain to the extent that there is current year long-term capital gain (and previously undistributed long-term capital gains).

3. *Other income (e.g., tax-exempt income).* If the distribution exceeds ordinary income (current and past year), short-term capital gains (current and past year), and long-term capital gains (current and past years), the distribution will represent other income to the extent that there is such other income for current and past years. Other income includes income that is tax-exempt for federal income tax purposes.

4. *Return of principal.* Finally, and only after all current year income and all previously undistributed prior year income is deemed to be distributed, a distribution from a CRUT will be characterized as a nontaxable return of principal.[52]

Clearly, the four-tier system makes it impossible for a donor to avoid taxes indefinitely when appreciated property is contributed to a CRUT and later sold by the trustee. Even if the trustee were to invest the proceeds from the sale of the appreciated property entirely in tax-exempt municipal bonds, the distributions to the noncharitable unitrust beneficiary would represent income (either in the form of short-term or long-term capital gain) until the cumulative distributions equaled the total amount of capital gain incurred on the sale of appreciated property. However, while the tax on the gain cannot be avoided, the ability to *defer* the taxation can provide a significant benefit to the grantor.

Application of the 3.8 percent NII Tax. While the NII tax is not applicable to income earned by the CRT, distributions to the income beneficiary may be subject to the tax. Any distributions of income as part of the unitrust payment retain their character as NII, and may be subject to the 3.8 percent tax if the income recipient's modified adjusted gross income exceeds the NII threshold. If there is more than one income beneficiary, the distributed NII is apportioned between the income beneficiaries based on their respective shares.[53]

Determination of Trust Income

For a NICRUT or a NIMCRUT, a distribution can only be made only from trust income. Despite the obvious importance of income determination, the Code provides surprisingly little guidance on what constitutes trust income. Specifically, the Code provides only that trust income is determined by terms of the governing trust instrument or under local (i.e., state) law.[54] In response to adoption of some version of the Uniform Principal and Income Act by most states, the Service has stated that it will respect allocations of amounts between income and principal pursuant to local law.[55] Conversely, definitions of income within a trust document that depart fundamentally from local law will not be respected by the Service.[56] Treasury regulations and IRS rulings provide the following limited guidance about the appropriate classification of capital gain income:

- *Post-contribution capital gains.* Ordinarily, a post-contribution capital gain is considered a return of trust principal, and not trust income. However, the IRS has ruled that a CRUT instrument can specifically classify post-contribution capital gain as income if it does not "represent a fundamental departure from state law." The characterization of post-contribution capital gains as trust income appears to be a commonly accepted practice among practitioners—especially when creating a NIMCRUT.[57]

- *Pre-contribution capital gains.* Treasury regulations make it clear that built in appreciation at the time of contribution is properly treated as principal—regardless of what the trust instrument provides.[58]

CHARITABLE LEAD TRUSTS

A charitable lead trust (CLT) is a form of split-interest charitable trust. Conceptually, the charitable lead trust is the opposite of the charitable remainder trust (CRT) because the charity receives the annuity payments, and the grantor (or the grantor's family) receives the remainder value. Conversely, in a CRT the grantor (or the grantor's family) receives the annuity payments, and the charity receives the remainder value. Technically, CLTs resemble CRTs in some respects, but differ from CRTs in other respects. The differences between

Figure 13.4

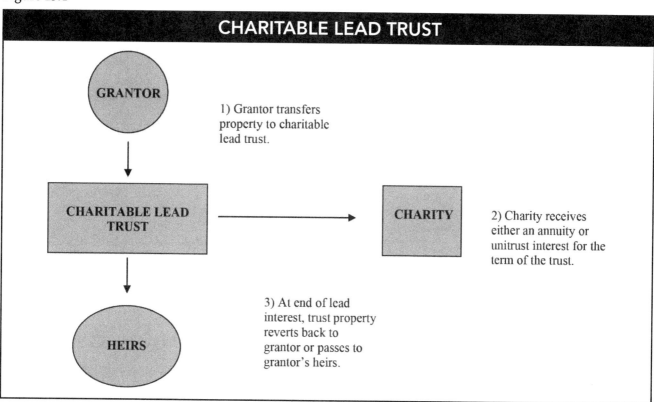

CHARITABLE LEAD TRUST

GRANTOR

1) Grantor transfers property to charitable lead trust.

CHARITABLE LEAD TRUST

CHARITY

2) Charity receives either an annuity or unitrust interest for the term of the trust.

3) At end of lead interest, trust property reverts back to grantor or passes to grantor's heirs.

HEIRS

CLTs and CRTs will be explained below in "Frequently Asked Questions."

Each year's annuity stream can be set up to be paid *either* as a sum certain (i.e., an annuity trust), *or* as a fixed percentage of the trust (i.e., a unitrust). When the charity's income interest ends, the assets in the trust are passed to a noncharity beneficiary (e.g., the grantor's children), or the assets are paid back to the grantor.

Charitable lead trusts can be set up during life or created at death. CLTs may provide income, gift, or estate tax benefits while also meeting the grantor's charitable giving aspirations. Figure 13.4 graphically depicts a CLT.

There are two types of charitable lead trusts, a grantor trust or non-grantor trust. A non-grantor lead trust does not provide an income tax deduction for the grantor, but the grantor is not taxed on the trust income that is provided to the charity. A grantor lead trust does provide an income tax deduction upon funding to the grantor, but the grantor is also taxed on the trust income in all of the following years. These two types of lead trusts are explained in more detail below.

WHEN ARE CLTS USED?

- *When a grantor is charitably inclined and has property that the grantor would like to retain, but does not necessarily need the current income from the property.* The client can provide for a specific charity with annuity payments from a CLT for a period of time and then have the property in the CLT revert back to the grantor for future use.

- *When a grantor would like to distribute assets to the grantor's family in the future with reduced gift or estate tax consequences.* A CLT can be designed so that the assets in the trust pass to the grantor's heirs or other non-charitable beneficiary instead of going back to the grantor when the charitable lead interest terminates.

- *When a grantor would like to create an immediate income tax deduction to offset unusually high taxable income in a particular year.* Using a grantor CLT creates an immediate income tax deduction for the present value of the charitable income interest. This income tax deduction may be used to offset a large taxable income event such as the sale of a business, receipt of a substantial bonus, conversion

of a traditional IRA to a Roth IRA or the exercise of a large block of nonqualified stock options.

The trade-off or cost of obtaining a large, immediate deduction is that beginning with the year following the year the deduction is claimed, and in all future tax years, the income earned by the CLT will be taxed to the grantor as if the grantor owned the assets that are actually held by the CLT. Of course, if the grantor expects an unusually high amount of income in the year the CLT is established, and significantly lower taxable income in later years, the trade-off might be very advantageous.

However, if the grantor retains a reversionary interest in the CLT, the date of death value of the trust is included in the grantor's estate if the grantor dies before the trust terminates.[59] The grantor's estate will receive a charitable deduction for the amount set aside for the charitable beneficiary. If the CLT is set up so that the remainder interest is held or distributed to the grantor's family, the assets do not revert back to the grantor and the value of the CLT is not included in the grantor's estate.

- *When the grantor would like to benefit both charity and the grantor's family upon the grantor's death and would like to accomplish this with reduced estate taxation.* A testamentary CLT can be established to provide for payments to charity for a period of time after the donor's death before ultimately passing the trust remainder value to the donor's heirs. The estate is entitled to an estate tax charitable deduction for the value of the lead interest payable to charity, which will reduce estate taxes.

The testamentary CLT can be an effective tool when the grantor wants to delay inheritance to heirs for a period of time rather than giving them access to a large amount of wealth that they may not be prepared to handle. A series of testamentary CLATs each with different trust termination time frames (for example four CLATs with five, ten, fifteen, and twenty-year trust terms) could be established that would pay the inheritance to heirs over a twenty year time period rather than in one large inheritance.

CLT ADVANTAGES

1. Charitable lead trusts can provide a benefit to charity without having to permanently give away the

asset. The CLT is one of only a few forms of split-interest charitable gifts that qualify for the income, gift, or estate tax charitable deduction.

2. If designed as a grantor lead trust, an income tax charitable deduction is allowed at the date the trust is funded for the actuarial value of the annuity stream payable to the specified charity (or charities). The front loaded deduction for the gift of the income stream can be useful in offsetting a large current income taxable event.

3. Unlike some other wealth transfer techniques (e.g., GRATs or qualified personal residence trusts, "QPRTs"), lead trusts can be created either while the donor is alive (i.e., an *inter vivos* trust) or upon death (i.e., a testamentary trust).

4. It may be possible to create a lead trust that is both a grantor trust for income tax purposes and a completed transfer for gift and estate tax purposes (i.e., a defective grantor trust). This would provide an income tax deduction for the grantor, while also ultimately passing the trust assets to the grantor's heirs thereby reducing the grantor's estate.

5. Unlike charitable remainder trusts (CRTs), which are restricted on the term length that can be used, charitable lead trusts can be for virtually any term length desired by the grantor.

CLT DISADVANTAGES

1. Unlike charitable remainder trusts, lead trusts are *not* tax-exempt entities. If the CLT is a grantor trust, all of the income earned by the trust (including the lead interest paid to charity) will be taxed to the grantor rather than to the trust. On the other hand, a a non-grantor CLT will have to pay income tax on any trust income it receives but it also receives a charitable deduction for the lead interest paid to the charity.[60]

2. Contributions to a CLT do not always generate an income tax deduction. An income tax deduction is allowed only if the lead trust is a grantor trust for income tax purposes.

3. Lead trusts must comply with many of the private foundation rules.[61]

CLT REQUIREMENTS

1. Payments to the charity (i.e., the lead interest) must be paid in the form of:

   - a *guaranteed annuity interest*, which is an irrevocable right to receive payment of a sum certain at least annually (i.e., charitable lead annuity trust or CLAT); or

   - a *unitrust interest*, which is an irrevocable right to receive at least annually a fixed percentage of trust assets, as revalued each year (i.e., charitable lead unitrust or CLUT).[62]

2. The term of the lead interest can be *either* for a specified term of years selected by the donor, *or* for the life of an individual (or individuals) who must be alive at the time the property is transferred to the trust. Only four types of individual(s) may be used as the "measuring life" (or lives): (1) the donor; (2) the donor's spouse; (3) a lineal ancestor of all the remainder beneficiaries; or (4) the spouse of a lineal ancestor of all the remainder beneficiaries.)[63]

   The lead interest (annuity or unitrust) can also be paid for the life of an individual *plus* a term of years.[64] Unlike a charitable remainder trust, which has a "term of years" limit of twenty years, there is no limitation on the term length for a "term of years" CLT. Furthermore, a guaranteed annuity interest may be made to continue for the shorter of (1) a term of years, or (2) lives in being *plus* a term of years.[65]

3. In order to receive an income tax deduction, the grantor of the CLT must be treated as the owner of the trust for income tax purposes (i.e., a grantor trust). In a grantor trust, the trust is ignored for income tax purposes and the grantor pays the income tax on all trust taxable income. The result of this requirement is that the grantor will receive an immediate income tax deduction for the value of the lead interest, but will pay income tax each year on all taxable income generated by the trust (including the income used to pay the lead interest to the specified charity).[66]

4. Charitable lead trusts must comply with many of the private foundation rules. Therefore, the trust document should prohibit certain activities such as engaging in self-dealing, excess business holdings, jeopardy investments, and taxable expenditures.[67]

5. The Internal Revenue Service has published sample declarations of trust which can be used a guide when creating an *inter vivos* or testamentary CLAT.[68]

CLT Example 1:
Reversionary Grantor Lead Trust

Grantor owns a floral and wedding consulting business. Grantor's interest in the business has a fair market value of $1,000,000 with a cost basis of $250,000. Besides this business interest, grantor also owns a sizable portfolio of tax-exempt bonds.

Grantor has received an offer to sell the business. But grantor is concerned about the large capital gains tax that would be generated by the sale. One way for grantor to reduce the potential tax burden on the sale of the business would be to transfer a portion of the tax-exempt bond portfolio to a grantor charitable lead annuity trust for a specified term of years. Grantor would be entitled to an immediate charitable income tax deduction for the calculated value of the charitable lead interest, which could then be used to help offset the taxable income incurred from the sale of the business. At the end of the trust term, the bond portfolio would revert back to grantor.

If grantor contributes $500,000 of tax-exempt bonds to a twelve-year CLAT paying 4 percent, the value of the charitable lead interest for income tax deduction purposes will be $187,702 (assuming that payments would be made at the end and not the beginning of the year, and also assuming a Section 7520 rate of 4.0 percent)[69] a deduction of almost 38 percent of the value of the transfer. In a 39.6 percent income tax bracket, this will save $74,329. Because the maximum income tax deduction allowed in any one year for a contribution to a charitable lead trust is 30 percent of adjusted gross income (AGI), Grantor's AGI would need to exceed $625,673 in order to take full advantage of the tax savings in the current year.[70] If the entire deduction could not be used in the current year, any remaining unused deduction can be carried forward for an additional five years.

Assuming a 20 percent capital gains rate and application of the 3.8 percent NII tax, if grantor sells the business for $1,000,000 and has a cost basis of $250,000, taxes on the sale will be $178,500 ($750,000 gain × 23.8 percent). Therefore, the tax savings of $74,329 generated by creating the lead trust would effectively reduce the taxes due on the sale of the business from $178,500 to $104,171 ($178,500 tax – $74,329 tax savings = $104,171 net tax). The following figures detail the calculation of the income tax deduction allowed for the lead interest.[71]

In addition to the income tax savings provided by creating the lead trust, grantor's favorite charity (or charities) would receive an annuity payment of $20,000 (4% × $500,000) every year for the next twelve years.

Figure 13.5

Trust Type:	Term
§7520 Rate:	4.0%
FMV of Trust:	$500,000
Percentage of Payout:	4.000%
Payment Period:	Annual
Payment Timing:	End
Term:	12
Annual Payout:	$20,000
Term Certain Annuity Factor:	9.3851
Payout Frequency Factor:	1.0000
Present Value of Annuity:	$187,702
Remainder Interest = FMV of Trust less PV of Annuity:	$312,298
Charitable Deduction for Income Interest:	$187,702
Donor's Deduction as Percentage of Amount Transferred:	37.540%

Figure 13.6

Trust Type:	Term
§7520 Rate:	6.2%
FMV of Trust:	$2,000,000
Percentage of Payout:	6.000%
Payment Period:	Annual
Payment Timing:	End
Term:	20
Annual Payout:	120,000
Term Certain Annuity Factor:	11.2860
Payout Frequency Factor:	1.0000
Present Value of Annuity:	$1,354,320
Remainder Interest = FMV of Trust less PV of Annuity:	$645,680
Charitable Deduction for Income Interest:	$1,354,320
Donor's Deduction as Percentage of Amount Transferred:	67.716%

This is attractive to grantor, who is actively involved in several charitable organizations.

Because the lead trust is a grantor trust for income tax purposes, grantor will have to pay income tax on *all* of the income generated by the trust. This includes any income used to make the annuity payment to charity as part of the lead interest. However, since the trust would be funded with tax-exempt bonds, there may be little, if any taxes actually due on the trust income.

Thus, by using a grantor CLT grantor can reduce the taxes incurred from the sale of the business, provide an immediate benefit to the grantor's favorite charities through the lead interest, and enjoy the benefits of the bond portfolio at the end of the trust term.

CLT Example 2:
Family CLAT as an Estate Freeze Tool

Grantor and grantor's spouse (the "grantors") have a net estate of $30,000,000, with a significant portion of the estate consisting of rental real estate. They have four children, , to whom they are currently making yearly gifts equal to the available gift tax annual exclusion ($15,000 in 2019). They have not yet used any of their available gift tax applicable exclusion amount ($11,400,000 per person or $22,800,000 collectively in 2019) but are aware that using the applicable exclusion amount during life will be more beneficial than using it

at death. They make sizable charitable gifts each year, and have considered establishing a private foundation.

Because they are charitably inclined and wish to reduce the potential estate tax bill that may be incurred at the survivor's death, the grantors have decided to create a CLAT and a private foundation. They will fund the CLAT with $2,000,000 of real estate, with the CLAT paying a 5 percent annuity for a term of twenty years. The annuity stream from the CLAT will be paid to their newly established foundation. At the end of the lead interest, the real estate will pass to their children.

Since the assets in the CLAT will not revert back to the grantors, but instead will ultimately pass to their heirs, the transfer to the CLAT will be a completed gift for gift tax purposes. However, the value of that transfer for gift tax purposes will be reduced by the value of the annuity interest paid to the foundation. Assuming a Section 7520 rate of 3.0 percent, the lead interest for a twenty-year annuity of 5 percent will be $1,487,750. Therefore, the value of the taxable gift for gift tax purposes is $512,250 ($2,000,000 – $1,487,750). By implementing the CLAT, the grantors will benefit from a gift tax charitable deduction equal to almost 75 percent of the property transferred to the lead trust. The 25 percent portion of the real estate that is treated as taxable gift can be sheltered from gift taxes by applying a portion of their applicable exclusion amount thus avoiding any gift taxes on the transfer.

Assuming the real estate grows 3 percent per year net of the annuity payments made to charity, it will be worth $3,612,222 at the end of the trust term. Consequently, the grantors will have transferred over $3.6 million of wealth to their children without having incurred any gift or estate taxes while using roughly $500,000 of their applicable exclusion amount. In addition, they will have funded their private foundation with $2,000,000 ($100,000 per year × 20 years) over the term of the CLAT.

Funding a CLT

Almost any type of asset can be transferred to a CLT. However, assets that are both income producing (to pay the lead income interest) and rapidly appreciating (to pass increased wealth to heirs with reduced gift and estate taxes) are preferred. Assets that often work well in a CLT include rental real estate, dividend-paying stock, or a balanced portfolio of securities.

Since the grantor is taxed on all trust income in a grantor lead trust, tax-exempt securities such as municipal bonds are commonly used to fund a grantor lead trust in order to reduce the taxable income the grantor must pay.

Problem Assets

Caution must be used when transferring mortgaged property or closely held business interests to a CLT. Transferring mortgaged property to a CLT can cause problems for the grantor. If the debt on the property exceeds the grantor's basis in the property, the transfer will be treated as part gift/part sale and the grantor may have gain recognition on the transfer. Also, depending on when the debt was placed on the property, the transfer of encumbered property to a CLT may cause unrelated business taxable income (UBTI). If the trust has UBTI, a portion of the trust's deduction for payment of the lead interest to charity may be disallowed.[72]

The transfer of closely-held stock or partnership interests to a CLT may cause problems with the prohibition against "excess business holdings." Charitable lead trusts must comply with the private foundation restriction against excess business holdings. In general, the CLT cannot hold more than 20 percent of the voting interests in a business without running afoul of the excess business holdings restriction. An excise tax is imposed on the value of any excess business holdings that exceed the 20 percent threshold.[73]

There are exceptions to the excess business holdings restriction that may apply to transfers of closely-held business interests to a CLT and allow for a transfer of more than 20 percent of the voting interests:

1. If the CLT receives property through a gift or bequest that may cause an excess business holdings problem, the trust has five years from the date it acquires the holdings to dispose of that property.

2. As long as the value of the charitable lead interest does not exceed 60 percent of the value of the total fair market value of the trust, *and* the entire income interest (but none of the remainder interest) is payable to charity, an exception to the excess business holdings restriction will apply.[74]

CLT TAX IMPLICATIONS

In order to qualify for the income, gift, or estate tax charitable deduction, the lead trust must be structured as either a *guaranteed annuity interest* or a *unitrust interest*. If payments are not made in this manner, charitable income, gift, or estate tax deductions will not be allowed.[75] The present value of the charitable lead interest (i.e., the charity's right to the annuity stream) is deductible for income, gift, or estate tax purposes. In a grantor lead trust, a charitable income tax deduction is allowed. In an *inter vivos* family (non-grantor) lead trust, a charitable gift tax (but no income tax) deduction is allowed. Finally, in a testamentary lead trust, an estate tax charitable deduction is allowed.

Charitable Lead Annuity Trust (CLAT). In a CLAT, the charitable income beneficiary is granted an irrevocable right to a guaranteed sum certain, paid at least annually, for the term of the trust. Unlike the charitable remainder trust however, there are no minimum or maximum percentages that are required to be used to determine the annuity payment.[76] Once the annuity amount is determined, it is guaranteed. Consequently, if the income earned by the trust is insufficient to make the annuity payment, the trustee must invade trust principal to satisfy the annuity interest that has been promised to charity.

Charitable Lead Unitrust (CLUT). In a CLUT, the charitable beneficiary must be paid a fixed percentage of the trust assets each year for the term of the trust. Unlike the charitable remainder trust, there are no specific minimum or maximum unitrust percentages that must be used in a CLUT. So it is possible (at least theoretically) to select any percentage as the payout rate.

Valuing the Charitable Deduction

In general, the value of an income, gift, or estate tax charitable deduction is the present value of the lead (annuity or unitrust) interest payable to charity. The primary factors used in the computation of the present value of the lead interest are: (1) the length of the trust term; (2) the annuity or unitrust rate to be paid to charity; (3) the frequency of payment, and (4) the Section 7520 rate in effect at the time the trust is funded. The Section 7520 rate is 120 percent of the federal applicable midterm rate (rounded to the nearest two-tenths of 1 percent), and is published by the IRS on a monthly basis.

Generally, a larger deduction can be obtained by stretching out the trust term or by increasing the payout rate. The 7520 rate will also have an impact of the charitable deduction. For annuity trusts in particular, a lower 7520 rate yields a larger charitable deduction while a higher Section 7520 rate yields a smaller charitable deduction. The grantor has the choice of using the Section 7520 rate in effect for the month the trust is funded, or the rate in effect for either of the two previous months.[77]

Grantor Lead Trust

Income tax consequences. In order to qualify for the income tax charitable deduction, the grantor must be treated as the owner of the trust for income tax purposes ("a grantor trust").[78] The deductible amount is the present value of the annuity or unitrust lead interest payable to the charitable beneficiary. However, the charitable lead interest is considered a gift "for the use of" charity rather than a gift "to" charity. Therefore, the donor's current charitable deduction will be limited to 30 percent of AGI (20 percent for gifts of appreciated property).[79] Note that the excess is not lost. Any portion of the lead interest that cannot be deducted in the current year due to the deduction limitations can be carried over for an additional five years.[80]

If the trust ceases to be a grantor trust because the grantor dies, or relinquishes grantor trust powers, the charitable income tax deduction is recaptured. The amount recaptured is equal to the initial charitable deduction less the discounted amounts that were

actually paid to the charitable beneficiary up to the time the trust ceased to be a grantor trust.[81]

As explained above, in a grantor trust the grantor is taxed personally on all trust income including the lead interest payable to charity. In essence, a grantor trust is treated as if the trust was nonexistent for income tax purposes. In addition to paying income tax on the income earned by a grantor lead trust, the 3.8 percent net investment income (NII) tax may also be applicable to the trust income earned should the grantor's modified adjusted gross income exceed the NII tax threshold.[82] Because of this tax consequence, grantor lead trusts are commonly funded with tax-exempt assets, such as municipal bonds.

Gift and estate tax consequences. If the grantor retained the remainder interest in the trust, the value of the assets in the CLT will be included in the grantor's estate at death.[83] In addition, where the CLT remainder reverts back to the grantor, the transfer of assets to the CLT is not a completed gift subject to gift taxes.

Non-Grantor Lead Trust

Income tax consequences. The grantor of a non-grantor lead trust is *not* entitled to an income tax deduction and is *not* taxed on trust income because for income tax purposes the trust is a separate entity. Instead, the trust is taxed as a complex trust and the trust receives an income tax deduction for trust income paid to charity as part of the lead interest.[84] All trust income above the annuity or unitrust lead interest paid to charity is taxed to the trust. In addition, the 3.8 percent NII tax could be applicable to trust income that is not paid out as part of the lead interest. The threshold for application of the NII tax to a complex trust is significantly lower than for an individual ($12,150 for trusts and estates in 2018 as compared to $200,000 for single filers).

Gift and estate tax consequences. The transfer of assets to a family lead trust is a completed gift for gift tax purposes. In essence, there are two gifts being made - a gift of the lead interest to charity, and a gift of the remainder interest to the grantor's heirs. When properly structured, a charitable gift tax deduction is allowed for the present value of the lead interest passing to charity. However, the present value of the remainder interest passing to the donor's heirs is a gift subject to gift tax. Because the remainder interest in the trust is a completed gift while the donor is living, the value of the trust is *not* included in the grantor's estate.

For a testamentary lead trust, the donor's estate would be entitled to an estate tax charitable deduction rather than a gift or income tax deduction.

Generation-skipping tax consequences. If the remainder interest in a CLT passes to heirs two generations or lower than the grantor (for example, grandchildren or great-grandchildren), the generation skipping tax (GST) will also apply. Due to the way the GST tax is calculated and the GST exemption is applied with a CLT, use of a CLAT can potentially cause GST tax problems.[85] In general, a CLUT should be considered if a CLT is to be designed as a generation-skipping trust.

FREQUENTLY ASKED QUESTIONS

Question – What factors should be considered when deciding between a charitable remainder annuity trust (CRAT) and a CRUT?

Answer – A CRAT offers the primary benefits of simplicity and certainty. With a CRAT, the retained interest is a fixed dollar amount. Therefore, since the amount is fixed, there is no need for an annual revaluation as with a CRUT. Because no annual revaluation is required, a CRAT will be considerably easier—and less expensive—to administer than a CRUT, especially when hard-to-value assets are contributed to the trust.

A second consideration is the need (or desire) for a fixed return. With a CRAT, the annual payout is fixed. The income interest will not be reduced if the value of the trust decreases, unless the trust is completely liquidated by distributions.

A third consideration is the need for a hedge against inflation. While a CRAT offers the promise of a fixed annual return, the economic value of this fixed annual payout can be a significantly affected by inflation. Assuming assets in the trust grow at a rate higher than the unitrust percentage, the unitrust payment can increase as the trust assets grow. For this reason, younger donors often prefer the flexible unitrust payment that is available with a CRAT, as opposed to the fixed payment guaranteed by a CRAT.

A fourth consideration is whether additional contributions to the trust are contemplated. A donor can make multiple contributions to a single CRUT, but the *initial* contribution is the *only* contribution that can be made to a CRAT.

Finally, the CRUT allows for variations such as the NICRUT, NIMCRUT and FLIP CRUT. Between the ability to make additional contributions, choices in design, and the potential for inflation protection, the CRUT is more flexible than the CRAT. The tradeoff for this flexibility is lack of certainty and variable payments.

Question – Is there any limit to how many annuity beneficiaries may be named by the donor?

Answer – No. Both CRATs and CRUTs are required to have at least one noncharitable beneficiary of the annuity amount or the unitrust amount, respectively, who is a person other than a charitable organization described in Code Section 170(c). There may be multiple noncharitable recipients of the annuity amount to be paid each year. However, the greater the number of income beneficiaries, the smaller the value of the remainder interest, which must be at least 10 percent of the trust's initial fair market value in order for the trust to qualify as a CRUT or a CRAT. Thus, practically speaking, multiple lives may result in the trust failing to qualify under the 10 percent minimum charitable deduction requirement.[86]

An independent trustee can be given the right to allocate the annuity amount among a class of named noncharitable beneficiaries; however, this allocation cannot vary the amount and frequency of payouts to noncharitable beneficiaries otherwise the trust will not qualify.[87] If the annuity amount is to be paid for the joint lives of a group of individuals, all of the individuals must be alive and ascertainable when the trust is created. After-born or after-adopted children may not be added to the trust, nor may new spouses be substituted. This makes practical sense because the addition of such beneficiaries would change the actuarial assumptions upon which the donor's tax deduction is based. For this reason, if the trust is to continue for a fixed number of years (rather than for the specific beneficiaries' lives), the trust may provide for additional beneficiaries who meet the class requirements.

Question – Is there any minimum annuity amount that must be paid to the individual beneficiary?

Answer – Yes. Generally, the annuity amount payable to the noncharitable beneficiary must not be less than 5 percent of the initial trust value. However, there are two safe harbor exceptions to the 5 percent minimum payout rule. The first exception under the Treasury regulations provides that the 5 percent test will not be violated if the reduction in the annuity amount occurs under the following circumstances: (1) the reduction in the annuity amount must occur as a result of the death of the income recipient *or* the expiration of the term of years; (2) the distribution must be made to a "qualified charity" (within the meaning of Code section 170(c)) *either* at the time of the income recipient's death *or* on the termination of a term of years; *and* (3) the total amounts payable each year as the annuity payments "after such distribution are not less than a stated dollar amount which bears the same ratio to 5 percent of the initial net fair market value of the trust immediately after such distribution bears to the net fair market value of the trust assets immediately before such distribution."[88]

Under the second exception to the 5 percent rule, the Treasury regulations also provide relief when the 5 percent minimum payout is violated because of a good faith error in the valuation of the trust assets.[89] If the grantor of an *inter vivos* CRAT establishes a fixed dollar amount in good faith, and later learns that the trust assets are worth a much greater amount, the grantor may enter into an agreement with the IRS consenting to fix the value of the trust, for charitable deduction purposes, at twenty times the value of the annuity.

Question – Is there any maximum payout limit for the annuity of the noncharitable beneficiary?

Answer – Yes. The annuity amount may not be greater than 50 percent of the value of the property, valued at the time of the initial contribution to the trust.[90]

Question – Can the donor name a trust or other entity as the annuity beneficiary?

Answer – Yes. The Code provides that a CRAT must have at least one annuity recipient other than a charity described in Code section 170(c), meaning the grantor (or another person). However, person has a broad meaning and the additional annuity beneficiary may be another trust, estate, partnership, corporation or other entity.[91]

Question – Can amounts be paid to the charitable beneficiaries early?

Answer – Yes. Treasury regulations permit the transfer of trust principal or excess income to the charitable remainderperson prior to the conclusion of the measuring term of the trust. However, a CRAT may distribute the annuity amount, only, to a noncharitable income recipient. Furthermore, no increased or additional deduction is allowed for an early payout.

Question – Can highly appreciated property be used to fund the trust?

Answer – Yes. Charitable remainder trusts are often funded with appreciated property. Typically, the contributed property is sold by the trust at a later date. In fact, the property may have to be sold to provide liquidity for payment of the annuity. However, it is important to make sure that any gain on the sale of appreciated property by the trust will not be attributed to the donor. Thus, the donor should not retain control (either directly or indirectly) over the asset. Nor should there be a prearranged plan for the trustee to sell the property. The IRS has taken the position in some transactions that a charity (or trustee of a charitable trust) may be viewed as the donor's agent in disposing of appreciated assets. These transactions can generally be classified as involving either: (1) the redemption of stock pursuant to a prior binding agreement; (2) the resale of assets by the trust to the grantor pursuant to an understanding; or (3) the sale by the trust of appreciated property, and subsequent reinvestment in tax-exempt bonds.[92]

Question – Can the donor use retirement benefits to fund the CRAT?

Answer – Yes, but grantors and their advisors should be particularly sensitive to the possible tax consequences. If a lifetime gift to charity consists of an individual's qualified plan benefit, the donor will have to include the entire amount of the benefit in his gross income. The same gift using an IRA, however, will expose only the amount of the benefits that were not previously included in his gross income (i.e., the nondeductible portion of the IRA) to income tax. Under both circumstances, the amounts transferred to the trust that represent the remainder interest that will eventually pass to charity should be eligible for the income and gift tax deduction.

If the transfer is made at the grantor's death, however, the adverse income tax consequences do not arise. A donor may designate a charitable remainder trust as the beneficiary of the donor's retirement plan or IRA benefits. Although the IRA or retirement plan payout will be accelerated at death (because the charitable remainder trust is not a "designated beneficiary"), the tax-exempt status of the CRT should protect the retirement benefits from income tax, although a portion of each payment will include some of the retirement benefits subject to income tax on the recipients return. If the surviving spouse is named as the annuity beneficiary, the use of the marital and charitable deductions should protect the retirement benefits from estate tax at the death of the first spouse.[93]

Question – Can the donor use debt-encumbered property to establish the trust?

Answer – Technically such funding is possible, but grantors and their advisors must be particularly sensitive to potential tax issues. The contribution of debt-encumbered property to a charitable remainder trust is treated as part charitable gift, part taxable sale. The transfer is treated as a gift to the extent that the value of the property exceeds the underlying debt. But the same transaction is also treated for income tax purposes as a sale to the extent the debt to which the property is subject exceeds the grantor's basis in the sale portion of the gift.[94] Note that the grantor's basis in the property must be apportioned; consequently, a certain amount of basis is carried away by the gift portion. This results in increasing the grantor's gain on the sale portion.

Example. Grantor owns real estate that has a fair market value of $500,000, an adjusted basis of $100,000, and is subject to a mortgage of $250,000. Grantor creates a CRAT and funds it with the property as a charitable gift, which the trust takes subject to the mortgage. Grantor realizes a gain of $200,000 and is deemed to have made a $250,000 gift to the trust as follows:

Sale Portion

Amount realized	$250,000
Basis allocable to the sale ($250,000/$500,000) × 100,000	– 50,000
Recognized gain	$200,000

Gift Portion

Value of transferred property	$500,000
Amount realized	– 250,000
Gift Element	$250,000

In addition, donors should be aware that several other issues may arise including the creation of "debt financed income"[95] and treatment of the property as a constructive sale to the trust, which in turn may be considered an act of "self-dealing" (which is forbidden under Code section 4911). This problem may be avoided by using a charitable gift annuity.

Question – Can the donor use operating business assets to fund the CRAT?

Answer – While this is possible (although the deduction would be limited to basis), it may cause the CRAT to earn Unrelated Business Taxable Income (UBIT or UBTI as defined in Code section 515). Prior to the enactment of the Tax Relief and Health Care Act of 2006, a CRT would lose its tax exempt status for any year in which UBIT/UBTI was received. This change lessens this burden by providing a 100 percent tax on net UBIT/UBTI, allowing other taxable income to avoid tax under the general exemption available to CRTs.[96]

Question – Can the donor add property to the CRAT after it is established?

Answer – The donor may not add additional property to the trust once it is established.[97]

Question – Can the donor establish the charitable remainder trust at the time of his death?

Answer – Yes, a CRAT created under a will or revocable trust is deemed created at the date of the donor's death even if it is not funded until the end of a reasonable period of estate administration. The payment of the annuity amount may be deferred until the end of the taxable year of the trust in which the trust is fully funded. However, the trust must be obligated to pay the annuity amount from the date of death, and a makeup distribution must be made to adjust for the failure to pay the full amount during the estate administration.[98]

Question – Can the donor reserve the right to change the remainder beneficiary?

Answer – Yes. The donor may reserve the right to change the remainder beneficiary. But that right must be restricted to only "qualified charities" (described in Code section 170(c)).

Question – What types of charities can be named as the remainder beneficiaries of a charitable remainder annuity trust?

Answer – According to the Internal Revenue Code, charities described in section 170(c) may be named as charitable remainder beneficiaries. Trust drafters may also want to include charities described in section 170(b)(1)(A), due to the fact that section 170(c) applies to public charities and private foundations. Use of the public charity category under section 170(b)(1)(A) would increase the income percentage limitation applicable for the donor's charitable deduction.[99]

Question – When must the annuity amount be paid to the beneficiary named in the trust document?

Answer – The annuity amount must be paid at least annually, but may be made more frequently. It must also be paid during the taxable year *or* within a reasonable time after the close of the year. The IRS will treat any payment made before the filing date of the trust tax return (including extensions) as a timely payment for this purpose.[100] The recipient must include the trust distribution in income for the recipient's taxable year in which the trust taxable year ends.[101]

Question – Can the trustee make distributions *other than* the annuity amount to the trust income beneficiaries?

Answer – No, the trustee cannot distribute amounts in excess of the annuity amount to the *income* beneficiaries. However, the trustee may make additional distributions of trust principal to the *charitable* beneficiary (or another qualified charity). Although such payments will not jeopardize the charitable deduction for the donation of the remainder interest, the donor will not receive any additional deduction for contributions to the trust.[102]

Question – May a CRAT make a distribution "in-kind?"

Answer – A CRAT may satisfy the annuity amount by making a distribution "in-kind" instead of a cash payment. However, the trust will be deemed to have sold the asset and, thus, will have to recognize a gain (or loss) on the sale. Furthermore, the resulting capital gain may eventually be taxable to the donor as part of a later annuity payment.

Question – Are there IRS model forms for CRATs?

Answer – Yes. From time to time the IRS has published model forms for creating charitable remainder annuity trusts.[103] In fact, there is a four-part test that ensures IRS recognition of the trust as being qualified under Code section 664. However, the model forms do *not* cover all situations, and additional drafting is generally required to contour the trust clauses to fit each grantor's particular needs.

Question – Can a transfer to a CRAT be subject to the generation-skipping tax?

Answer – Yes. If there is a completed gift to a non-donor annuity beneficiary who is a skip person (i.e., a person who is more than one generation younger than the donor), the value of the interest transferred to that person would be subject to the generation-skipping transfer tax. The donor would need to allocate generation-skipping exemption to exempt the interest from this tax.

Question – Can a holder of a term interest in a CRAT transfer it before the end of the term?

Answer – Yes. It is possible but the tax consequences are complicated. The IRS first addressed a concern about this type of transaction because of contrived step up in basis as to the holder of the term interest in Notice 2008-99.[104] The IRS has issued proposed regulations (effective for transactions that occur on or after January 16, 2014) that will foreclose what it perceives to be an abusive transaction.[105]

Question – Many closely-held businesses are incorporated as S corporations. Can S corporation stock be contributed to a CRUT?

Answer – Yes, technically S corporation stock may be contributed to a CRUT. However, if this happens, the corporation's status as an S corporation will be *automatically terminated*.[106] In some situations, termination of S corporation status may be an acceptable consequence. However, any decision to transfer S corporation stock to a CRUT should be made only after careful consideration. Termination of the S corporation status will affect all shareholders, not just the shareholder contemplating the transfer.

Question – Why is it common for a NIMCRUT to invest in a deferred annuity contract?

Answer – In many instances, the grantor of a NIM-CRUT does not want, or need, an immediate distribution from the CRUT. For instance, a grantor with an irregular income pattern may want to time distributions from the NIMCRUT to occur in years when other income is lower. In fact, this is a primary reason for selecting a NIMCRUT instead of a standard CRUT. (With a standard CRUT, payments must be made from trust principal if income is insufficient.) For a donor who wants to "time" distributions of income from the NIM-CRUT to meet his or her needs, a deferred annuity can provide the desired investment vehicle. By specifying in the trust agreement that distributions of growth from a deferred annuity contract should be treated as trust income, the trustee of a NIMCRUT can virtually "turn on and off" a NIMCRUT's income stream to suit the need of the unitrust beneficiary. This ability to control the recognition of income by the NIMCRUT provides yet another planning opportunity: the trustee can allow the assets in the NIMCRUT to accumulate on a tax-deferred basis for many years, and then control distributions in later years for supplemental retirement benefits.

Question – Has the IRS approved the use of a deferred annuity to control the timing of distributions from a NIMCRUT?

Answer – Although the IRS has addressed this issue on several instances, there is no final, formal guidance on this point.[107] The IRS first addressed this issue in the proposed charitable remainder trust regulations in 1997. At that time, the IRS stated that it was "studying" whether NIMCRUTs that were invested in assets that are used to control the timing of the receipt and taxation of the beneficiary's income could qualify as a valid charitable remainder trust. Furthermore, the IRS has said that it would not issue letter rulings on such trusts.[108] However, in 1998 the IRS issued a Technical Advice Memorandum (TAM)[109] in which it said that a NIMCRUT's purchase of two deferred annuities was not an act of self-dealing and did not disqualify the trust. Recall that a TAM constitutes guidance from the National Office of the IRS to another IRS official in the field, and it cannot be relied upon as authority by a taxpayer other than the taxpayer involved in the specific transaction at issue.[110]

Question – Can the grantor serve as trustee of a CRUT?

Answer – Subject to certain restrictions, the grantor of a CRUT can serve as trustee. However, neither the grantor nor any other person can be given a power that would cause the grantor to be treated as the owner of the trust under the grantor trust rules.[111] Otherwise, the CRUT will fail to satisfy the requirements of a valid charitable remainder trust.[112] In situations where the grantor is not the unitrust beneficiary, the grantor/trustee should *not* be given the sole power to (1) identify the eventual charitable remainder beneficiary, or (2) make discretionary distributions among a class of permissible unitrust beneficiaries. These powers can cause estate tax inclusion where it could otherwise be avoided.[113]

In addition, if the CRUT holds assets that do not have a readily determinable fair market value, the value of those assets should be determined by an independent trustee or by a qualified appraiser.[114]

Question – Can the grantor contribute a personal residence to a CRUT?

Answer – Yes, but the grantor must vacate the property prior to making the contribution, to avoid self-dealing. The grantor's use of the property after the transfer would constitute self-dealing even if the grantor entered into an arm's length lease with the CRUT.[115]

Question – If debt-encumbered appreciated real estate is to be contributed to a charitable remainder trust, does that create any special considerations?

Answer – Yes, several issues must be considered before contributing debt-encumbered real estate to a charitable remainder trust, including a CRUT. In fact, it is generally recommended that the transfer of debt-encumbered real estate be *avoided*. Several issues should be considered before undertaking this risky transaction:

1. If the property is subject to a mortgage and the donor is relieved of the mortgage, the transfer will be treated as a bargain sale, and the donor will recognize income on the sale portion.[116]

2. A transfer of debt-encumbered property could disqualify the charitable remainder trust if the trustee pays the mortgage. If the trustee makes the mortgage payment, it appears that the charitable remainder

trust is a grantor trust for income tax purposes, and cannot qualify as a charitable remainder trust.[117]

3. A transfer of debt-encumbered property may constitute self-dealing for the donor and the trustee.[118] This appears to be the case even if the debt is not assumed by the trust.[119]

4. If the debt was placed on the property within five years of the date of transfer, the charitable remainder trust could be treated as receiving debt-financed income. If a charitable remainder trust realizes any debt-financed income, trust income may be taxable.[120]

Question – Does the charitable remainder beneficiary have to be determined at the time that the CRUT is created?

Answer – No. The selection of the ultimate qualified charitable beneficiary may be left to the trustee, the unitrust beneficiary, the donor, or a third person.[121] However, unless the CRUT instrument mandates that the ultimate charitable beneficiary qualify as a public charity, the grantor's income tax deduction will be treated as a remainder gift to a private foundation. Gifts to a private foundation receive less favorable income tax treatment than gifts to a public charity. Gifts of cash to a private foundation are limited to 30 percent of adjusted gross income, rather than the more favorable 50 percent limitation. Gifts of appreciated property (other than certain marketable securities) are limited to 20 percent of gross adjusted income, and the value of the contributed property is limited to the grantor's adjusted basis.[122] Unless the ultimate charitable beneficiary of a CRUT is intended to be a private foundation, the CRUT instrument should be drafted to explicitly limit the beneficiary of the remainder interest in the CRUT to public charities.

Question – Since a CRUT must have one or more noncharitable beneficiaries, must the noncharitable unitrust beneficiary be an individual?

Answer – No, the noncharitable beneficiary is not required to be an individual. The noncharitable beneficiary of a CRUT can be an individual, trust, estate, partnership, association, company, or corporation. However, the payment to a *non*-individual beneficiary must be limited to a term of no more than twenty years. The IRS has made limited exceptions to this rule for trusts created for the benefit of incapacitated individuals. In a revenue ruling, the IRS approved a charitable remainder trust that provided distributions for the benefit of an incapacitated individual for that person's life.[123]

Question – What are the estate planning opportunities for using ESOPs and CRTs?

Answer – An individual may have a large portion of wealth tied up in the stock of a single corporation and may seek to diversify such holdings. If those shares are highly appreciated, a sale will generally result in the recognition of significant capital gain for federal income tax purposes. However, if such a sale is instead made to the corporation's employee stock ownership plan (ESOP), diversification can be achieved with a concomitant deferral of any capital gain so long as the sale proceeds are reinvested in "qualified replacement property" (generally, securities traded on an established secondary market).[124] If a sale to an ESOP is made, capital gain is recognized only if the qualified replacement property is later sold, and the gain recognized is measured by the difference between the sale price of the qualified replacement property and the owner's original cost basis in the corporate stock. If the individual dies owning qualified replacement property, the individual's capital gain will never be recognized because such property receives a basis adjustment as a result of the individual's death.[125] Thus, after death the individual's estate or beneficiaries may sell the qualified replacement property and invest in other property with little or no gain realized on such later sale.

A sale of stock to an ESOP, and reinvestment of the proceeds in qualified replacement property, can be a useful income and estate tax planning strategy. However, once an individual elects to defer capital gain through the purchase of qualified replacement property, that portfolio of replacement property cannot be adjusted. In other words, the individual cannot reinvest any portion of the qualified replacement property without accelerating the deferred gain. This is a significant drawback of this strategy, as illustrated by the example below:

Example. Assume that grantor (age fifty) owns an interest in a corporation and wishes to diversify this interest. Grantor may elects to sell stock to the corporation's ESOP. Because grantor is relatively young, grantor elects to reinvest the sale proceeds in growth stock that constitutes qualified replacement property. Under IRC Section 1042, grantor will be able to defer the capital gain on the sale of the stock to the ESOP, but only for so long as grantor holds onto the original stock portfolio. When grantor reaches retirement age, it may be desirable to shift the emphasis from growth to current income for supplemental retirement planning needs. However, grantor will not be able to do so without realizing the deferred capital gain.

However, it appears that this problem can be solved with a gift of the qualified replacement property to a charitable remainder trust. Generally, the transfer of highly appreciated, long-term capital gain property to a charitable remainder trust allows the donor to avoid immediate recognition of the gain in such property. This is so because the trust's later sale of the property is not attributed to the donor and, as a tax-exempt entity, the trust does not have to pay tax on the gain. Thus, by transferring the qualified replacement property to a charitable remainder trust, the donor is able to (1) achieve diversification on an ongoing basis through the trust's investment strategy, and (2) receive supplemental retirement income through a retained annuity or unitrust interest. Moreover, if the transfer of the replacement property is made to a NIMCRUT, the donor can achieve maximum planning flexibility.

While the IRS has approved of this approach in several private letter rulings, it has done so with little legal analysis.[126] In those letter rulings, the IRS concluded that the transfer of qualified replacement property to a charitable remainder trust constituted a disposition within the meaning of Code Section 1042(e). Code Section 1042(e) and its legislative history seem to provide for taxation upon disposition of qualified replacement property.[127] Nevertheless, the IRS has consistently determined that recognition of capital gain is avoided on the transfer of qualified replacement property to the trust. Apparently, the IRS views the transfer of qualified replacement property to a charitable remainder trust as a gift that is eligible for the gift exception of Code Section 1042(e). However, in each of the rulings, the IRS noted that the trustee of the charitable remainder

trust in question was under no obligation (express or implied) to sell the qualified replacement property, "nor [could] the trustee be legally bound to sell" such property. In summary, the planner should consider including similar language in any charitable remainder trust that will hold qualified replacement property.

Question – How are CRUTS used in closely-held businesses transfer planning?

Answer – The use of a CRUT to effectuate the transfer of a business from the current owner to the new ownership can benefit the business owner in several ways. By contributing stock to a CRUT, the business owner can take a current income tax charitable deduction for the present value of the charitable remainder interest. In addition, the business owner may also be able to benefit from an increased income stream in the future, as illustrated by the following example:

Example. Grantor owns all of the stock of a corporation and at age sixty, grantor is anxious to implement a plan that will allow the business to pass to grantor's three children. Grantor will complete the transfer through the use of a CRUT with the following steps:

1. Grantor will make gifts of stock to grantor's three children.

2. Grantor will transfer the remaining shares to a CRUT. Grantor will be permitted a current income tax deduction for the value of the remainder interest passing to charity. If grantor structures the CRUT to pay the unitrust interest to grantor for life, there will be no current taxable gift.

3. At some future date, the company will offer to redeem all outstanding shares of the company's stock. Assuming that the CRUT tenders its shares for redemption, but the children do not, the three children will then own all of the remaining outstanding shares of stock. If there are sufficient assets in the corporation, the shares can be redeemed for cash, and the unitrust distribution amount can be used as supplemental retirement income for grantor.

4. Once the company has redeemed all of the stock from grantor, the three children will own all of the remaining outstanding shares.

As discussed earlier in this chapter, a grantor can establish several different types of CRUTs. In the example above, the grantor is likely to choose a NIMCRUT because the closely-held stock owned by the CRUT is unlikely to generate sufficient income to cover the annual unitrust payment. Stated another way, if grantor does not use a NIMCRUT (or NICRUT), the trustee may be forced to sell some of the CRUT assets (i.e., stock) or make in-kind (i.e., stock) distributions to grantor in satisfaction of the annual unitrust interest.

Question – What is a charitable lead "super trust"?

Answer – A "super trust" is a CLT that is considered a grantor lead trust for income tax purposes, but a completed transfer for gift and estate tax purposes. This type of trust design is commonly called a defective grantor trust. By structuring the trust in this manner, the grantor can benefit in the following ways:

- receive an immediate income tax deduction allowed for a grantor lead trust;

- reduce gift taxation on the assets that will ultimately pass to the grantor's family; and

- remove the assets, including future appreciation, from the taxable estate at death.

Designing a "super lead trust" requires careful drafting of the trust document so that provisions are included that will make the trust a grantor trust for income tax purposes, but will not cause the trust proceeds to be included for estate tax purposes. Caution should be used with the charitable lead super trust, and it is not certain that the desired results will be achieved.

CHAPTER ENDNOTES

1. I.R.C. §664(b).
2. I.R.C. §1011; Treas. Reg. §1.1011-2(a)(3).
3. I.R.C. §4947(a)(2); Treas. Reg. §1.664-1(b).
4. See I.R.C. §664(d)(1)(B); Treas. Reg. §1.664-1(a)(2).
5. See Rev. Proc. 2003-54, 2003-31 IRB 236.
6. I.R.C. §664(d)(1).
7. See Treas. Reg. §1.664-1(a)(2).
8. I.R.C. §664(d)(1)(A); Treas. Reg. §1.664-2(a)(3)(i).
9. I.R.C. §664(d)(1)(A); Treas. Reg. §1.664-2(a)(1)(iii).
10. Treas. Reg. §§1.664-2(a)(1)(i), 1.664-2(a)(2)(i). 1.664-2(a)(5)(i).
11. I.R.C. §664(d)(1)(D).
12. Treas. Reg. §1.664-2(b).
13. Rev. Rul. 77-374, 1977-2 CB 329; *Toce, Joseph; Abbin, Byrle; Pace, William; and Vorsatz, Mark. Tax Economics of Charitable Giving* (Thompson Reuters, 2013).
14. *Atkinson v. Comm'r.*, 115 TC 26 (2000).
15. I.R.C. §664(c); *Newhall Unitrust v. Comm'r.*, 104 TC 236 (1995), aff'd, 105 F.3d 482 (9th Cir. 1997).
16. Treas. Reg. §1.664-1(c).
17. Treas. Reg. §1.664-1(d)(1).
18. Treas, Reg, §1.1411-3(c)(2)
19. For a thorough discussion and examples, see Schlesinger, Sanford J. and Goodman, Martin R. "Medicare Contribution Tax on Net Investment Income and Charitable Remainder Trust," *CCH Estate Planning Review*, February 20, 2014, Volume 40, No.2.
20. Treas. Reg. §25.2503-3(c), Example 5.
21. Treas. Reg. §25.2503-2.
22. Rev. Rul. 82-105, 1982-1 CB 133. See also REG-119097-05, 72 Fed. Reg. 31487 (June 7, 2007).
23. I.R.C. §§664(d)(2), 664(d)(3); Treas. Reg. §§1.664-1, 1.664-3.
24. I.R.C. §664(d)(2)(A); Treas. Reg. §1.664-3(a)(1).
25. I.R.C. §664(d)(2)(A); Treas. Reg. §1.664-3(a)(2).
26. Treas. Reg. §1.664-3(a)(1)(i)
27. Treas. Reg. §§1.664-3(c) and 1.665-4.
28. Treas. Reg. §1.664-2(a)(5)(i). I.R.C. §7701(a)(1) defines person as "an individual, trust, estate, association, company corporation or partnership." Therefore, while it is uncommon, the unitrust interest can be payable to a corporation or partnership if limited to a term of no more than twenty years. Priv. Ltr. Rul. 9419021 (May 13, 1994) (limited partnership as beneficiary), Priv. Ltr. Rul. 9205031 (Nov. 5, 1991) (corporation).
29. Rev. Rul. 2002-20, 2002-17 IRB 794 provides an exception to the twenty-year term limitation for a CRUT beneficiary that meets the definition of "financially disabled."
30. See I.R.C. §664(d)(2)(D), Treas. Reg. §1.664-3(b).
31. Treas. Reg. §1.664-3(b).
32. I.R.C. §664(d)(2)(C). A qualified organization is an organization described in I.R.C. §§170(c), 2055(a), or 2522(a).
33. For the rules revising the definition of "income" under Code section 643(b) taking into account changes in the definition of trust accounting income under state laws, see Treas. Reg. §1.643(b)(3).
34. Treas. Reg. §1.664-3(a)(1)(i)(c)(1).
35. Treas. Reg. §1.664-3(a)(1)(i)(d).
36. Treas. Reg. §1.664-3(a)(1)(i)(c)(3).
37. Treas. Reg. §1.664-3(a)(1)(i)(c)(2).
38. I.R.C. §170(d)(1).
39. This is a hypothetical survivor universal life insurance policy for example purposes only, and does not reflect any particular policy or insurance carrier.

40. I.R.C. §170(f)(3)(A).

41. I.R.C. §§664(d)(2), 664(d)(3).

42. In some instances, the value of the property contributed to the CRUT may be limited to the donor's cost basis in that property. See I.R.C. §170(e).

43. The value of a noncharitable beneficiary's life payout (or a payout over the lives of multiple noncharitable unitrust beneficiaries) is ordinarily determined in accordance with the life expectancies provided by the IRS tables. However, an individual who is terminally ill may not use the IRS life expectancy tables. Treas. Reg. §§1.7520-3(b)(3), 20.7520-3(b)(3), and 25.7520-3(b)(3).

44. The IRS discount rate is determined under I.R.C. §7520 and is equal to 120 percent of the applicable federal mid-term rate.

45. Treas. Reg. §1.170A-13(f)(13).

46. I.R.C. §6019(3).

47. Treas. Reg. §25.6019-1(f).

48. I.R.C. §§2036(a)(1), 2039, 2055(e)(2)(A).

49. I.R.C. §664(c)(2)(A)

50. Treas. Reg. §1.411-3(b)(1)(iii).

51. I.R.C. §664(b); Treas Reg. §1.664-1(d)(1).

52. I.R.C. §664(b); Treas. Reg. §1.664-1(d)(1).

53. Treas. Reg, 1.411-3(d)

54. I.R.C. §643(b).

55. Treas. Reg. §1.643(b)-1.

56. Treas. Reg. §1.643(b)-1; see also Priv. Ltr. Rul. 9018015 (Jan. 31, 1990).

57. Treasury Regulations state that with respect to NICRUTs and NIMCRUTs, post-contribution capital gain may be allocated to income pursuant to applicable local law and the terms of the governing instrument, only, but not pursuant to a discretionary power granted to the trustee. See Treas. Reg. §1.664-3(b)(3).

58. Treas. Reg. §1.664-3(a)(1)(i)(b)(4).

59. I.R.C. §2036(a)(1); Prop. Treas. Reg. §20-2036-1; REG-119097-05, 72 Fed. Reg. 31487 (6-7-2007).

60. I.R.C. §§671, 642(c)(1).

61. I.R.C. §§4947(a)(2), 4941, 4943, 4944, 4945.

62. I.R.C. §§170(f)(2)(B), 2055(e)(2)(B), 2522(c)(2)(B).

63. Treas. Reg. §§1.170A-6(c)(2), 20.2055-2(e)(2), 25.2522(c)-3(c)(2).

64. Treas. Reg. §§1.170A-6(c)(2), 20.2055-2(e)(2), 25.2522(c)-3(c)(2).

65. Rev. Rul. 85-49, 1985-1 CB 330; Rev. Proc. 2007-45, 2007-29 IRB 89; Rev. Proc. 2007-46, 2007-29 IRB 102.

66. I.R.C. §170(f)(2)(B); Treas. Reg. §1.170A-6(c)(1).

67. I.R.C. §§4947(a)(2), 4941, 4943, 4944, 4945.

68. Rev. Proc. 2007-45, 2007-29 IRB 89; Rev. Proc. 2007-46, 2007-29 IRB 102.

69. This example assumes a Section 7520 rate of 4.0 percent. Section 7520 rates are issued monthly by the IRS. Donors may use the rate for the month the trust is funded or may "look back" in either of the two prior months and choose the best rate of the three. In fact, by waiting until the IRS releases the next month's rates—typically between the 18th and the 22nd of each month—it is possible to select the best of four month's rates. Section 7520 rates are available at Leimberg.com and taxfactsonline.com.

70. Contributions to a charitable lead trust are considered to be gifts "for the use of" charity rather than as gifts "to" charity. Thus, the donor's contribution is subject to a limitation of 30 percent of adjusted gross income as the maximum deduction that can be taken in one year. I.R.C. §170(b)(1)(B); Treas. Reg. §§1.170A-8(a)(2), 1.170A-8(c).

71. Computation courtesy of NumberCruncher software (Leimberg.com).

72. Treas. Reg. §1.681(a)-2(b).

73. I.R.C. §4943.

74. I.R.C. §4943(c)(6); Treas. Reg. §1.170A-(6)(c)(2)(i)(D).

75. I.R.C. §§170(f)(2)(b), 2055(e)(2)(B), 2522(c)(2)(B).

76. A charitable remainder trust is required to pay an annuity or unitrust amount of not less than 5 percent and not more than 50 percent of the net fair market value of the trust assets. I.R.C. §§664(d)(1), 664(d)(2).

77. I.R.C. §§7520(a).

78. I.R.C. §170(f)(2)(B); Treas. Reg. §1.170A-6(c)(1).

79. I.R.C. §170(b)(1)(B); Treas. Reg. §§1.170A-8(a)(2), 1.170A-8(c).

80. I.R.C. §§170(b)(1)(B), 170(b)(1)(D)(ii).

81. See Treas. Reg. §1.170A-6(c)(4).

82. I.R.C. §1411. The 3.8 percent net investment income or NII tax applies to the lesser of net investment income earned or the excess of adjusted gross income over the threshold which is a modified adjusted income of $200,000 for single filers and $250,000 for joint filers. For trusts and estates the threshold is the amount where the highest income tax bracket begins ($12,150 for 2014).

83. I.R.C. §§2036, 2038.

84. I.R.C. §§641(a), 642(c)(1).

85. Under I.R.C. Section 2642(e), the final determination of the amount of trust exempt from GST is not made until the end of the lead interest. Consequently, there is the possibility that a portion of a CLAT could be subject to GST, or that some of the GST exemption applied could be wasted because the trust remainder value ends up being less than the exemption amount allocated.

86. See I.R.C. §664(d).

87. Rev. Rul. 77-73, 1977-1 CB 175.

88. Treas. Reg. §1.664-2(a)(ii).

89. Treas. Reg. §1.664-2(a)(iii).

90. I.R.C. §664(d)(1)(A).

91. I.R.C. §§664(d)(1)(A), 7701(a).

92. See, Treas. Reg. §1.664-1(e)(2); Rev. Rul. 78-197, 1978-1 CB 83; *Blake v. Commissioner*, 697 F.2d 473 (2d Cir. 1982); Rev. Rul. 60-370, 1960-2 CB 203.

93. I.R.C. §2056(b)(8). See also Let. Rul. 9634019.

94. I.R.C. §1011.

95. I.R.C. §514.

96. I.R.C. §664(c) as revised by Section 424 of the Tax Relief and Health Care Act of 2006.

97. I.R.C. §664(d)(1)(A); Treas. Reg. §1.664-2(b).

98. Treasury regulations §§1.664-1(a)(5)(i) and 1.664-1(a)(5)(ii) provide guidance on calculating the make-up distribution.

99. The IRS has ruled in favor of such a description of the description of the charitable remaindermen in Letter Ruling 903702.

100. Treas. Reg. §1.664-2(a)(1)(i).

101. Treas. Reg. §§1.652(c)-1, 1.662(c)-1.

102. Treas. Reg. §1.664-2(a)(4); Rev. Rul. 82-128, 1982-2 CB 71.

103. The latest iteration of sample forms for CRATs is set forth in Rev. Proc. 2003-54, 2003-31 IRB 236, and Rev. Proc. 2003-54, 2003-31 IRB 236. For an excellent discussion of these forms, see Pusey, J. Michael, "Exploring the New Model Charitable Remainder Trust Forms," *Gift Planner's Digest*, (September 17, 2003), The Planned Giving Design Center, at: www.pdgc.com.

104. 2008-2 CB 1089, 10/30/2008.

105. Treas. Reg. §1.1014-5. For a thorough discussion of this issue by Chuck Rubin see Steve Leimberg's Charitable Planning Email Newsletter-Archive Message #211.

106. Rev. Rul. 92-48, 1992-1 CB 301.

107. See H.R. Rep. No. 91-413, 60 (TRA '69), reprinted in 1969-3 CB 239. In the legislative history to the charitable remainder trust rules, Congress expressed its concern that charitable remainder trusts not be used as a means to manipulate the size of trust distributions for the donor's benefit.

108. Rev. Proc. 2014-3, I.R.B. 111

109. Tech. Adv. Mem. 98-25-001 (June 19, 1998).

110. I.R.C. §6110(k)(3).

111. I.R.C. §§671-8.

112. Treas. Reg. §1.664-1(a)(4).

113. See I.R.C. §2036(a)(2).

114. Treas. Reg. §1.664-1(a)(7). The definitions of "qualified appraisal" and "qualified appraiser" are contained in Code section 170(f)(11)(E).

115. Treas. Reg. §53.4941(d)-(2)(b).

116. I.R.C. §1011(b).

117. Priv. Ltr. Rul. 9015049 (April 13, 1990), citing Treas. Reg. §§1.664-1(a)(4), 1.677(a)-1(d).

118. But see Treas. Reg. §53.4941(d)-1(a).

119. I.R.C. §4941(d)(2)(A).

120. I.R.C. §§664(c), 514(c).

121. Treas. Reg. §1.664-3(a)(4). See also, e.g., Rev. Proc. 2005-52 through Rev. Proc. 2005-58; Rev. Rul. 76-371, 1976-2 CB 305, (trustee); Rev. Rul. 76-8, 1976-1 CB 179 (grantor); Rev. Rul. 76-7, 1976-1 CB 179 (beneficiaries); Priv. Ltr. Rul. 9504012 (Oct. 26, 1994) (grantors); Priv. Ltr. Rul. 9326049 (April 5, 1993) (grantor); Priv. Ltr. Rul. 9014033 (April 6, 1990) (beneficiaries); Priv. Ltr. Rul. 9022014 (Feb. 28, 1990) (beneficiary).

122. I.R.C. §170(e).

123. I.R.C. §7701(a)(1); Rev. Rul. 76-270, 1976-2 CB 194. See Rev. Rul. 2002-20, 2002-17 IRB 794 extending the twenty-year term limitation for a CRUT beneficiary that meets the definition of "financially disabled."

124. See I.R.C. §1042.

125. See I.R.C. §§1042(e), 1014.

126. See Priv. Ltr. Ruls. 9728048 (July 11, 1997), 9547023 (Nov. 24, 1995), 9547022 (Nov. 24, 1995), 9438021 (Sep. 23, 1994), 9438012 (Sep. 23, 1994), and 9234023 (Aug. 21, 1992).

127. Code section 1042(e) provides that: "If a taxpayer disposes of any qualified replacement property, then, notwithstanding any other provision of this title, gain (if any) shall be recognized....." The legislative history provides: "the Act (Section 1042(e)) overrides all other provisions permitting nonrecognition and requires that gain realized upon the disposition of qualified replacement property be recognized at that time." Sen. Rep. 99-313, 1032 (1986), *reprinted in* 1986-3 CB 1032.

INTENTIONALLY DEFECTIVE TRUSTS

CHAPTER 14

INTRODUCTION

This chapter covers two types of irrevocable *inter vivos* trusts for income tax purposes: the *intentionally defective grantor trust* (IDGT) and the *beneficiary defective irrevocable trust* (BDIT).[1] The IDGT and BDIT are similar in that both trusts are irrevocable *inter vivos* trusts for state law purposes, but both are purely income tax constructs. Neither trust pays income tax on its income like regular trusts do: someone else does. In the case of the IDGT, the person who forms the trust, the settlor, is legally responsible for the trust's income tax and must report the income, deductions and credits on the grantor's personal income tax return.[2] In the case of the BDIT, a beneficiary of the trust is legally responsible for the trust's income and must report the income, deductions and credits on the beneficiary's personal income tax return.[3] It should be noted that the grantor trust rules are quite complex and are not the most artfully drafted provisions in the Code. Additionally, the IDGT and BDIT are *very* complicated vehicles that require significant expertise as there remain several unanswered questions and quite a bit of controversy between commentators.[4] In fact, the IRS ordinarily will no longer issue a private letter ruling or determination letter on a trust that could fit the description of a BDIT.[5] Additionally, the IRS will not ordinarily rule on some of the common powers and rights that estate planners often use to create intentional grantor trust status.[6]

In both cases, what makes these people liable for income tax on the trust's income are the rules set forth in Subpart E of Subchapter J of the Internal Revenue Code of 1986, as amended, and set forth in Code Sections 671-679. These rules are referred to as the *grantor trust rules*. The grantor trust rules have been part of the tax law in some form since 1924.[7] Congress originally enacted the grantor trust rules in order to penalize taxpayers who used trusts as separate taxpayers to take advantage of lower marginal income tax brackets where the taxpayers retained significant rights in or control over the trust. Given that since the Tax Reform Act of 1986 significantly compressed the income tax brackets for trusts and estates, query whether the grantor trust rules are even necessary any longer, especially when they are only usually "violated" on purpose for some taxpayer benefit.[8]

Likely due to the fact that the estate tax and the gift tax were each introduced separately and in different years,[9] Congress enacted different rules that caused inclusion of trusts in a taxpayer's estate for federal estate tax purposes than the rules that create grantor trust status for income tax purposes.[10] While, as explained below, there is some overlap between the grantor trust income tax rules and the so-called estate tax "string" provisions of Code Sections 2036-2042, i.e., some rights or powers cause taxation under the grantor trust rules for income tax purposes and includability in the gross estate for federal estate tax purposes, these rules are *not* identical. Crafty taxpayers figured out how to exploit the differences in these two different sets of rules to create trusts that were grantor trusts for *income* tax purposes yet not be includible in the gross estate for federal *estate* tax purposes. These trusts are said to be *intentionally defective* for income tax purposes, i.e., arranged purposefully to run "afoul" of the grantor trust income tax rules.

For several years, there were proposals during President Obama's administration in the so-called "Greenbook" (the President's legislative proposals) to harmonize the grantor trust rules by requiring the inclusion of the value of grantor trust assets in the grantor's gross estate for federal estate tax purposes where the grantor entered into a sales transaction with the grantor trust. While these proposals went nowhere in Congress, and thus far haven't appeared in President Trump's administrative proposals, it is always a good idea to keep a watchful eye for legislative developments in this area.

GRANTOR TRUST RULES

We begin with a comparison of the rules for includability for federal estate tax purposes and the grantor trust rules. In general,[11] an irrevocable inter vivos trust[12] will be a grantor trust with respect to the grantor in any one or more of the following situations:

1. if the grantor holds a reversionary interest that, at the time of the trust's creation, is more than 5 percent of the value of the trust;[13]

2. if the grantor or a nonadverse party[14] has the power to determine the beneficial enjoyment of either corpus or income;[15]

3. if the grantor or a nonadverse party has the power to use the trust income for the benefit of the grantor or the grantor's spouse;[16]

4. if the trust instrument grants certain administrative powers, including:

    (a) the power to deal with trust assets for less than adequate and full consideration;[17]

    (b) the power to borrow trust assets without adequate interest and security;[18]

    (c) actual borrowing of trust assets without adequate interest or security and repayment during the taxable year;[19] and

    (d) certain other administrative powers exercisable in a nonfiduciary capacity,[20] including:

        (i) a power to vote or direct the voting of stock or other securities of a corporation in which the holdings of the grantor and the trust are significant from the viewpoint of voting control;

        (ii) a power to control the investment of the trust funds either by directing investments or reinvestments, or by vetoing proposed investments or reinvestments, to the extent that the trust funds consist of stocks or securities of corporations in which the holdings of the grantor and the trust are significant from the viewpoint of voting control; or

        (iii) a power to reacquire the trust corpus by substituting other property of an equivalent value. Additionally, a person other than the settlor of the trust can be deemed to be an owner of all or a part of the trust under certain circumstances, which is important for the BDIT because this is at the heart of it: that the BDIT is a grantor trust for income tax purposes as to the primary beneficiary.[21]

The following commentary summarizes the major income and estate tax consequences of powers held by various parties in irrevocable inter vivos trusts. It emphasizes that, before naming the grantor or anyone with an interest in the trust as trustee, consideration must be given to these implications. In addition, while consideration is given to having the grantor be trustee of his own irrevocable inter vivos trust, the potential adverse transfer tax consequences generally make it advisable to do so only as a last resort.

The IRS has ruled that transactions between an individual and a wholly grantor trust for income tax purposes are tax nullities, i.e., have no income tax significance.[22] This has created an entire subset of transactions between clients and grantor trusts where the client is legally responsible for the income tax on income that is being paid to someone else simply by intentionally "violating" (more properly, deliberately falling within) the grantor trust rules. This is why certain grantor trusts are often called "intentionally defective grantor trusts." This has the effect of a transfer of wealth that is outside of the gift tax system because the grantor in an IDGT and a beneficiary in a BDIT is legally responsible for the income tax pursuant to the grantor trust rules.[23] This responsibility reduces the income tax grantor's estate and has been called the "tax burn,"[24] all without gift tax consequences because the grantor has a legal obligation to pay the trust's income tax under the grantor trust rules.[25] Grantor trusts also can be very helpful to qualify a trust as a shareholder of an S corporation because the grantor is treated as the shareholder rather than the trust.[26]

The grantor trust rules have proven to be an effective way to delay income tax recognition on transactions that otherwise would be immediately taxable. A good example is a sale of appreciated property to a trust designed to be treated for income tax purposes (but not for federal estate tax purposes) as the alter ego of the grantor. In fact, as has already been noted, many trusts are purposefully set up to fall within the grantor trust rules for *income* tax but not for federal *transfer* tax rules, as the rules are *not* identical. It is important to note that the grantor trust rules can make the grantor or a beneficiary the grantor over only a *part* of the trust, e.g., only over trust income or trust principal, only over certain assets in the trust, or even over only a fraction of the entire trust.[27] Therefore, it is critical to select a power or powers that will make the grantor or a beneficiary the grantor for income tax purposes over the *entire* trust – assuming that grantor trust status is the desired result.

Otherwise, a transaction between an individual and a *partially* grantor trust could have adverse tax consequences.[28] It also is important to realize that a trust might be a grantor trust in one year but not the following year. For example, if the powerholder renounces or otherwise surrenders the right or power that makes the trust a grantor trust for income tax purposes, the trust would no longer be a grantor trust going forward and would become a separate taxpayer. Given the burdens that come with having to pay income tax on income that actually is being paid to someone else, it is always wise to provide a "switch," i.e., a means for terminating grantor trust status within the trust instrument, although that termination might have income tax ramifications in some situations.[29]

Code Section 671 states the general proposition that if the grantor or beneficiary is treated as the owner of trust property under Code Sections 672 through 679, then he or she should include the trust's items of income, deduction and credit that are attributable to that property in computing his or her taxable income and credits. From the words of the statute, it is not clear that a grantor trust is treated as being but one and the same as the grantor, but that is the longstanding position of the IRS, as set forth in Rev. Rul. 85-13, notwithstanding the contrary *Rothstein* decision,[30] which the IRS repudiated in Rev. Rul. 85-13.

Grantor trust status may be desirable for several reasons:

1. the grantor's payment of income taxes on trust income is a "gift" for the benefit of the trust's beneficiaries that is not taxed by the federal transfer tax system;

2. transactions between the grantor and the grantor trust are ignored for federal income tax purposes (such as sales of appreciated property between the grantor and the trust and transactions between different trusts with the same grantor);

3. the grantor may use the trust losses against his or her personal income (subject to all of the limitations on using losses elsewhere set forth in the Code);

4. a grantor trust is an eligible shareholder of a subchapter-S corporation; and

5. a grantor trust can take advantage of the less compressed income tax rates that apply to individuals without having to make distributions of trust property to the individual trust beneficiaries.[31]

We will discuss a series of commonly held powers and their effects for both income tax and transfer tax purposes. For the purposes of this discussion, assume that a grantor has made a gift to an irrevocable inter vivos trust unless the facts indicate otherwise.

I. Powers to affect beneficial enjoyment

A. Power to distribute income to the grantor or the grantor's spouse

1. Grantor as trustee.

   a. Grantor will be taxed on the income of the trust.[32]

   b. Assets in the trust will be includable in the grantor's gross estate.[33]

2. Non-adverse party as trustee.

   a. Grantor will be taxed on the income of the trust.[34] Note that the inclusion of a non-adverse party as Trustee does *not* affect the grantor as being treated as the owner of the Trust (and thereby having the trust being taxed as a grantor trust.)

   b. Assets in the trust will not be includable in the grantor's gross estate unless the grantor retained the power to remove the trustee and appoint himself as successor trustee.[35]

3. Adverse party as trustee.

    a. Grantor will not be taxed on trust income.[36] Note that the inclusion of an adverse party as Trustee removes the grantor as being treated as the owner of the trust (absent other grantor rights or powers) for income tax purposes, even though the trust can distribute income to the grantor or the grantor's spouse.

    b. Assets in the trust will not be includable in grantor's gross estate.[37] Power to distribute or accumulate income to or for the benefit of beneficiaries other than the grantor or the grantor's spouse without a restriction of reasonably definite external standard that is set forth in the trust instrument (should be similar to an ascertainable standard for purposes of the federal transfer tax).

B. Power to distribute income to beneficiaries other than the grantor or the grantor's spouse without the restriction of an ascertainable standard.

1. Grantor as trustee.

    a. Grantor will be taxed on the income of the trust since the grantor will be treated as the owner of the trust or transfers to the trust may be treated as incomplete gifts.[38]

    b. Assets in the trust will be includable in the gross estate of the grantor if the power can be exercised by the grantor alone or with any other party (adverse or not).[39]

2. Non-adverse party as trustee.

    a. Grantor will be taxed on the income of the trust (unless the power is limited to withholding distributions temporarily during legal disability, which is excepted pursuant to Code Section 674(b)(7)).[40]

    b. Assets in the trust will not be includable in the estate of the grantor unless the grantor has retained the right to substitute himself as trustee.[41]

3. Independent party as trustee.

    a. Grantor will not be taxed on the income of the trust.[42]

    b. Assets in the trust generally will not be includable in the grantor's gross estate unless the grantor can substitute himself as beneficiary or as trustee.[43]

C. Power-subject to a reasonably definite external standard that is set forth in the trust instrument (similar to an ascertainable standard for federal transfer tax purposes) to distribute **income** to beneficiaries other than the grantor or the grantor's spouse.

1. Grantor as trustee.

    a. Grantor will not be taxed on the income of the trust (unless the power can be exercised only with the consent of an adverse party).[44]

    b. Assets in the trust generally will not be includable in the grantor's gross estate since the power can only be exercised pursuant to an ascertainable standard.[45] However, a different result occurs if the assets can be used to discharge a legal obligation of support of the Grantor.[46] In this case, the assets will be included in the Grantor's estate pursuant to IRC Secs. 2041(b) or 2036(a)(2).[47]

2. Person other than the grantor (or the grantor's spouse) who are independent of the grantor and the grantor's spouse as trustee.

    a. Grantor will not be taxed on the income of the trust.[48]

    b. Assets in the trust generally will not be includable in the grantor's estate unless the grantor can substitute himself as trustee.[49]

D. Power-subject to an ascertainable standard to distribute *principal* to a beneficiary or class of beneficiaries (and there is no power to add beneficiaries other than after-born or after-adopted children).

1. Grantor as trustee.

    a. Grantor will not be taxed on the *income* of the trust. Note that this section D. relates to distributions of principal; and does not address distributions of income (which is addressed in C., above). With respect to the power to distribute principal based upon an ascertainable standard, the grantor will not be treated as the owner of the principal of the trust (and thereby having the trust not be treated as a grantor trust for the principal) because distributions are based upon a "reasonably definite standard," which essentially means an ascertainable standard.[50] This standard will satisfy the requirement that distributions be limited to a reasonably definite standard under IRC Sec. 674(b)(5).[51] Also, for fiduciary accounting purposes, income consists of interest and dividends, but not capital gains.

    b. Assets in the trust generally will not be included in the grantor's estate because exercise of the power is limited by an ascertainable standard.[52]

2. Person other than grantor as trustee.

    a. The grantor will not be treated as the owner of the principal.[53]

    b. Assets in the trust generally will not be included in the grantor's estate because exercise of the power is limited by an ascertainable standard.[54]

E. Power to distribute *principal* to a current income beneficiary.

1. Grantor as trustee.

    a. Grantor will not be taxable on the *income* of the trust.[55] Note that this section E. relates to distributions of *principal*; it does not address the consequences of distributions of income (which is addressed in section C., above).

    b. Assets in the trust will be includable in the grantor's gross estate unless the power is limited by an ascertainable standard. However, even if the power is limited by an ascertainable standard, the assets will be included in the grantor's estate if the assets can be used to discharge a legal obligation of support of the grantor.[56] In this case, the assets will be included in the Grantor's estate pursuant to Code Section 2036(a)(2).

2. Person other than grantor as trustee.

    a. Grantor is not taxable on the income of the trust.[57]

    b. Assets in the trust will not be includable in the grantor's gross estate unless the grantor can substitute himself as trustee.[58]

F. Power to distribute or accumulate income for a current income beneficiary.

1. Grantor as trustee.

    a. Income of the trust will not be taxable to the grantor.[59]

    b. Assets in the trust will be includable in the grantor's estate.[60] Even if the power is limited by an ascertainable standard, the assets will be included in the grantor's estate if the assets can be used to discharge a legal obligation of support of the grantor.[61] In this case, the assets will be included in the grantor's estate pursuant to Code Sections 2036(a)(2) and 2041(b).

2. Person other than grantor as trustee.

    a. Income of the trust will not be taxable to the grantor.[62]

    b. Assets in the trust will not be includable in the grantor's estate unless the power can be exercised without an ascertainable standard and the grantor can substitute himself as the trustee.[63]

G. Power to make mandatory distributions of income or principal to specified beneficiaries other than the grantor or the grantor's spouse.

1. Grantor as trustee.

    a. Income of the trust will not be taxable to the grantor unless trust income is used to discharge legal obligations.[64]

    b. Assets in the trust will not be included in the grantor's gross estate because the grantor has retained no power to affect beneficial enjoyment of trust property.

2. Person other than grantor as trustee.

   a. Income of the trust is not taxable to the grantor unless trust income is used to discharge legal obligations.[65]

   b. Assets in the trust will not be includable in the grantor's gross estate unless the grantor has the power to remove the trustee and appoint himself as trustee.[66]

H. Power to add beneficiaries generally. The power to add beneficiaries is one that always creates grantor trust status irrespective of who holds that power, with one exception, and that is to provide for after-born or after-adopted children.[67]

   1. Grantor as trustee or power holder.

      a. Income of the trust will be taxable to the grantor, even if the power is only exercisable in conjunction with a non-adverse party or independent trustee.[68]

      b. The trust will be includible in the grantor's gross estate for federal estate tax purposes.[69] Moreover, this will probably prevent the gift from being a completed gift for federal gift tax purposes.[70] For these reasons, a grantor should never hold this power.

   2. Non-adverse party as power holder.

      a. Income of the trust will be taxable to the grantor.[71]

      b. The trust will not be includible in the grantor's gross estate.[72]

   3. Adverse party as power holder. A beneficiary of a trust should not have this power because it could be a taxable gift on exercise and would constitute a general power of appointment.

      a. Grantor will be taxable on the income of the trust.[73]

      b. Assets of the trust will not be includible in the grantor's gross estate for federal estate tax purposes.[74]

   4. Independent trustee as power holder. The fiduciary duty that the trustee owes to the current beneficiaries probably constrains the trustee from ever exercising this power, so it is better to give it to someone like a trust protector, who might not have a fiduciary duty to the beneficiaries. Alternatively, if the trust protector is a fiduciary (and a trust protector might be a fiduciary under applicable state law, notwithstanding what the trust instrument says), then the power to add beneficiaries should be given to someone else.

      a. Grantor will be taxable on the income of the trust.[75]

      b. Assets of the trust will not be includable in the gross estate of the grantor for federal estate tax purposes unless the grantor can replace the trustee with himself.[76]

II. Administrative powers.

A. Power to allocate receipts between principal and income.

   1. Grantor as trustee.

      a. Grantor will not be taxable on the income of the trust.[77]

      b. Assets of the trust will not be includable in the grantor's estate unless the power can be exercised by the grantor in a non-fiduciary capacity either alone or in conjunction with another person.[78]

   2. Person other than grantor as trustee.

      a. Grantor will not be taxable on the income of the trust.[79]

      b. Assets of the trust will not be includable in the grantor's estate.[80]

B. Power to use trust income to pay premiums on insurance insuring the life of the grantor or the grantor's spouse.

   1. Grantor as trustee.

      a. Grantor is taxable on the income of the trust to extent that the income is or may be used for the payment of life insurance premiums without the consent of an adverse party.[81]

b. Assets of the trust will not be includable in the grantor's gross estate, assuming the trust both owns and is beneficiary of the policy proceeds.[82]

2. Non-adverse party as trustee.

    a. Grantor will be taxed on the income of the trust.[83]

    b. Assets of the trust will not be includable in the gross estate of the grantor.[84]

3. Adverse party as trustee.

    a. Grantor will not be taxed on income of the trust.[85]

    b. Assets of the trust will not be includable in the gross estate of the grantor.[86]

C. Power to purchase, exchange or otherwise deal with trust assets for less than adequate consideration.

1. Grantor as trustee.

    a. Grantor will be taxed on income of the trust if he or a non-adverse party (or both) can exercise the power without the consent of an adverse party.[87]

    b. Assets of the trust will be includable in the gross estate of the grantor.[88]

2. Non-adverse party as trustee.

    a. Grantor will be taxable on trust income if the non-adverse party can exercise the power without the consent of an adverse party.[89]

    b. Assets in the trust will not be includable in the estate of the grantor unless the grantor can substitute himself as trustee.[90]

3. Adverse party as trustee.

    a. Grantor will not be taxed on the income of the trust.[91]

    b. Assets in the trust will not be includable in the estate of the grantor unless the grantor can substitute himself as trustee.[92]

D. Power to borrow trust income or principal without adequate interest or adequate security.

1. Grantor as trustee.

    a. Grantor will be taxed on trust income if trust property can be loaned to grantor without adequate interest or security (income will not be taxed to grantor if approval of an adverse party is needed).[93]

    b. Assets in the trust will be includable in the grantor's gross estate.[94]

2. Person other than grantor as trustee.

    a. Grantor will not be taxed on trust income if person other than grantor is trustee and that person has the power to make loans to anyone.[95]

    b. Assets will not be included in grantor's gross estate unless he can substitute himself as trustee.[96]

E. Grantor has borrowed trust funds without adequate interest or security, or both, and has not repaid the loan at the end of the taxable year, including interest.

1. Grantor as trustee.

    a. Grantor will be taxed on the trust income and principal to the extent of the loan.[97]

    b. Trust will be included in the grantor's gross estate.[98]

2. Person other than grantor as trustee.

    a. Grantor will be taxed on trust income and principal to the extent of the loan.[99]

    b. Trust may be included in the grantor's gross estate.[100]

F. Power to vote the securities of a controlled corporation.

1. Grantor as trustee.

    a. Grantor taxed on income of trust if (1) power can be exercised in a non-fiduciary capacity and (2) the stockholdings of the grantor and the trust are significant from the viewpoint of control.[101]

b. Assets in the trust will be included in the grantor's gross estate.[102]

2. Person other than grantor as trustee.

a. Grantor will be taxed on trust income if power to vote securities held by person with non-adverse interest in a non-fiduciary capacity without consent of person in fiduciary capacity, assuming stock holdings of grantor and trust are significant from the viewpoint of control.[103]

b. Assets in the trust will not be included in the grantor's estate unless he has retained the power to substitute himself as trustee.[104]

G. Power to reacquire trust principal by substituting property of equal value.

1. Grantor as trustee.

a. Grantor will be taxed on trust income if the power can be exercised by anyone in a non-fiduciary capacity without the consent of a person in a fiduciary capacity.[105]

b. Assets in the trust probably will not be includable in the gross estate of the grantor.[106]

2. Persons other than the grantor as trustee.

a. Grantor will be taxed on trust income if the power can be exercised by anyone in a non-fiduciary capacity without the consent of a person in a fiduciary capacity.[107]

b. Assets in the trust would not be includable in the grantor's gross estate unless he can substitute himself as trustee.[108]

III. Powers over principal.

A. Power to revoke the trust and revest the principal in the grantor or in grantor's spouse.

1. Grantor as trustee.

a. Grantor will be taxed on trust income unless power can be exercised only with consent of adverse party.[109]

b. Assets in trust will be includable in grantor's gross estate if power exercisable only by grantor alone or with any person, whether or not adverse (unless the power can be exercised only with consent of all persons with a vested or contingent interest in the estate).[110]

2. Non-adverse party as trustee.

a. Grantor will be taxed on trust income unless power can be exercised only with consent of adverse party.[111]

b. Assets in trust will not be includable in grantor's estate unless power is exercisable by trustee and grantor can substitute himself as trustee.[112]

3. Adverse party as trustee.

a. Grantor is not taxed on trust income.[113]

b. Assets in trust will not be includable in grantor's gross estate unless power is exercisable by trustee and grantor can substitute himself as trustee.[114]

B. Power to terminate trust and distribute principal to beneficiaries.

1. Grantor as trustee.

a. Grantor will not be taxed on trust income if principal can be paid out only to income beneficiaries in same proportion as they currently receive income, or if principal can be paid out only with the approval of an adverse party.[115]

b. Assets in the trust will be includable in the grantor's gross estate if the grantor can exercise the power alone or with any other person, whether or not adverse.[116]

2. Adverse party as trustee.

a. Grantor will not be taxed on trust income.[117]

b. Assets in trust will not be includable unless power exercisable by trustee and grantor can substitute himself as trustee.[118]

3. Non-adverse party as trustee.

   a. Grantor will be taxed on trust income unless approval of adverse party required or unless payment must be made to current income beneficiaries in proportion to income receipts.[119]

   b. Assets in trust will not be includable in the grantor's estate unless the power is exercisable by trustee and grantor can substitute himself as trustee.[120]

4. Independent Trustee.

   a. Grantor will not be taxed on trust income if half or more of trustees are independent.[121]

   b. Assets in trust will not be includable unless power exercisable by trustee and grantor can substitute himself as trustee.[122]

IV. Powers to discharge legal obligations.

A. Power to discharge support obligation.

   1. Grantor as trustee.

      a. Grantor will not be taxable on trust income merely because of the existence of the power unless he has the power in a non-fiduciary capacity or the power is to support his or her spouse. But the grantor will be taxed on the income to the extent it in fact is used to discharge the grantor's support obligation.[123]

      b. Assets in the trust will be includable in the grantor's estate if trust assets may be used to discharge the grantor's legal obligation.[124]

   2. Persons other than grantor as trustee.

      a. Grantor will not be taxable on income unless it is in fact used to discharge the grantor's legal obligation.[125]

b. Assets in the trust will not be included unless the grantor could substitute himself for the trustee.[126]

Code Section 678 provides that a person other than the grantor of the trust, e.g., a beneficiary, can be treated as the grantor for income tax purposes. A person other than the grantor shall be treated as the owner of any portion of a trust with respect to which:

1. such person has a power exercisable solely by himself to vest the corpus or the income therefrom in himself, or

2. such person has previously partially released or otherwise modified such a power and after the release or modification retains such control as would, within the principles of Code Sections 671 to 677, inclusive, subject to grantor of a trust to treatment as the owner thereof.[127]

There is an exception to grantor trust treatment under Code Section 678(a) in Code Section 678(b), which provides that if the settlor/grantor of the trust retained any power or right over income[128] that made the trust a grantor trust as to that person pursuant to any provision in Subpart E of Subchapter J, then those provisions prime Code Section 678(a).

INTENTIONALLY DEFECTIVE GRANTOR TRUSTS

The goal in creating an IDGT is to have a trust in which the grantor is treated as the owner of the *entire* trust for federal *income* tax purposes, yet not be includable in the grantor's gross estate for federal *estate* tax purposes. Many of the income tax grantor trust powers also cause inclusion in a grantor's gross estate for federal estate tax purposes, and, as such, can be easily dismissed as estate planning possibilities, e.g., a power to revoke the trust,[129] a reversionary interest[130] and a power in the grantor to add beneficiaries. If the grantor was given the power to add beneficiaries, the grantor would be treated as the owner of the trust for federal income tax purposes[131] and would be includible in the grantor's gross estate for federal estate tax purposes.[132] Moreover, the gift would be incomplete for federal gift tax purposes.[133] Therefore, a grantor should not be given such a power unless the goal was to cause includability in the grantor's gross estate for some reason, e.g., to get a fair market value basis at the grantor's death under Code Section 1014 where the grantor's estate was unlikely to attract any federal estate tax due to its size.

What powers are safest to ensure grantor trust status while not causing includability in the grantor's gross estate for federal estate tax purposes? This question itself foreshadows its answer, which is there is no perfect or perfectly safe power that a grantor can have that will not cause includability in the grantor's gross estate for federal estate tax purposes. However, there are a few powers that practitioners seem to prefer,[134] and those are discussed below:

1. **Power in the hands of a non-adverse party to add charitable beneficiaries.** In general, the power to add beneficiaries makes a trust a grantor trust for income tax purposes irrespective of who holds that power if that powerholder has the power to add beneficiaries without the consent of an adverse party. As noted above, a grantor should not hold this power for several reasons. However, the grantor's spouse can hold this power because powers that a spouse holds are attributed to the grantor,[135] provided that the spouse has not made contributions to the trust[136] and is not an adverse party, i.e., a beneficiary, or if the spouse has any obligation to support the beneficiaries. However, a spouse may not be the best person to hold this power. If the grantor's spouse is given the power to add beneficiaries, grantor trust status will terminate when the spouse dies.[137] Thus, a contingency plan in the form of successor powerholders should be in place in order to continue grantor trust status under Code Section 674(a) if the spouse is given the power to add beneficiaries in the event of the spouse's death. For these reasons, it is probably preferable for tax reasons to give this power to a different non-adverse party, although many clients may not want to give such a power to someone outside of the family. However, it could be a very narrow power to pick between certain charities that the client favors.[138] An adverse party also should not be given a power to add beneficiaries because that power is likely a general power of appointment and its exercise would be a taxable gift by the powerholder. Moreover, there are conceptual fiduciary duty problems if a trustee is given the power to add beneficiaries because the trustee owes a duty to the current beneficiaries, and it is difficult to conjure up a set of facts where the addition of even one new beneficiary would not be harmful to the current beneficiaries' interests.[139] However, those conceptual fiduciary duty problems have not stopped grantors from giving trustees the power to add beneficiaries, so this problem may be more academic than practical. In any event, the powerholder's right could be conditioned on the approval of another non-adverse party without forfeiting grantor trust status, which would provide a check and balance on that power.[140] Moreover, the powerholder and perhaps another non-adverse party should be given the power to terminate the power to add charitable beneficiaries to turn off grantor trust status under IRC Sec. 674(a) to toggle grantor trust status off.

2. **Power to substitute assets held in a non-fiduciary capacity.** A trust will be a grantor trust for income tax purposes if the grantor or any non-adverse party holds a power, acting in a non-fiduciary capacity without the consent of anyone, to *reacquire* trust property by substituting property of *equivalent value*.[141] It is important that the power be exercisable in a non-fiduciary capacity and to not be subject to the consent of a trustee, who, of course, usually is acting in a fiduciary capacity. However, in the opinion of the IRS, the trustee must have a fiduciary obligation (under local law or the trust instrument) to ensure the grantor's compliance with the terms of this power by satisfying itself that the properties acquired and substituted by the grantor are in fact of equivalent value, and further provided that the substitution power cannot be exercised in a manner that can shift benefits among the trust beneficiaries.[142] The trustee's duty to ensure compliance with the equivalent value requirement is different than requiring the trustee's express consent to the swap, which should not be required because that would throw one out of grantor trust status under Code Section 675.[143] The trustee cannot hold a veto power over the swap right because such a power would cause the loss of grantor trust status. The trustee should have an express duty of impartiality and an express power to invest and reinvest trust corpus. As long as the trustee can seek judicial relief if it believes that the swap is not for equivalent value, that satisfies the requirement of the IRS that the trustee have some way of exercising its fiduciary duty to ensure that the asset swap is of

equivalent value. Can the power to swap assets be given to someone other than the grantor? A literal reading of Code Section 675(4)(C) would suggest possibly not because of the word "reacquire" in it. Nevertheless, according to the first sentence of Code Section 675, powers of administration can be held by any person. In fact, the regulations under Code Section 675 reference that the power may be held by any non-adverse party.[144] Most practitioners prefer to give this power to a non-adverse party to avoid any potential estate tax inclusion issues on the part of the grantor.[145] However, if the non-adverse party ever actually exercises the swap power, this will be a taxable exchange, which could have adverse tax consequences to both the grantor and the non-adverse party.[146] This power should not be given to an adverse party because the trust would not then be a grantor trust because of the required consent of an adverse party. The swap power should not be given to the trustee because the trustee probably would only be able to exercise it in a fiduciary capacity, which would be inconsistent with the requirement that the power be exercisable in a non-fiduciary capacity.[147] Like the power to add beneficiaries discussed above, the power to swap assets could be given to the grantor's spouse, but the same risks and caveats discussed above apply here. Additionally, the spouse should not be given the swap power if the spouse also is a beneficiary of the trust.[148] Does the swap power over a trust that holds life insurance on the life of the grantor cause estate tax inclusion under Code Sections 2036, 2038 or 2042? The Tax Court said no as to Code Sections 2038 and 2042 with respect to a situation where the swap power was held by the grantor insured in a fiduciary capacity.[149] The IRS has expressly held that a swap power held by the grantor in a non-fiduciary capacity over life insurance held in trust is not includable under Code Section 2042 as long as the trustee has the same duty and right to ensure that the swap is in fact for equivalent value as the IRS enunciated in Rev. Rul. 2008-22.[150] The grantor should not be given a swap power over closely held corporate stock that is in trust if it would be subject to Code Section 2036(b), which includes the value of stock over which the transferor retained a right to vote said stock of a controlled corporation. If the spouse contributed or is deemed to have contributed the stock to the trust, this power

should be culled out from the spouse too and given to someone else. Like the power to add beneficiaries, the swap power should have a way to toggle the power off by the powerholder being able to surrender it.[151] The problem with the swap power is that one cannot get any real ruling comfort from the IRS because of its position that whether the swap power is held in a non-fiduciary capacity is a question of fact that can only be determined after the fact.[152] For this reason, some commentators suggest that one not rely solely upon the swap power to confer grantor trust status.[153]

3. **Power of the grantor.** or a nonadverse party to allow the grantor or the grantor's spouse to borrow trust funds without adequate security except where a trustee (other than the grantor or the grantor's spouse) is authorized under a general lending power to make loans to any person without regard to interest or security. Note that it is the mere *existence* of the power to borrow that triggers grantor trust status; actual borrowing is *not* required.[154] However, if the trustee can make loans without adequate interest or adequate security to any person under the general powers of the trust, this provision will not trigger grantor trust status, so proper drafting of the power is required; it cannot be a blanket power to lend to anyone without adequate interest or security. This power, which is singled out as a grantor trust power in Code Section 675(2), probably should be given to a non-adverse party other than the grantor in order to avoid an estate tax inclusion issue under Code Section 2036(a)(1) if the IRS was to argue that this right to deal with the trust at less than fair market value was a retained beneficial interest in the trust.[155] Moreover, even though Code Section 675(2) permits a grantor to borrow without adequate interest, this is not advisable, as there could be a stronger argument that borrowing without paying adequate interest would be considered a retained benefit that could cause estate tax includability. Additionally, there is a potential for running afoul of the below market loan rules. The grantor's spouse could be given this power, subject to all of the caveats discussed in the section above pertaining to the power to add charitable beneficiaries. This power also should come with a toggle off switch.[156] It is not unusual to couple this power with a

swap power.[157] There are other examples in the private letter rulings of the power described in Code Section 675(2).[158]

BENEFICIARY DEFECTIVE IRREVOCABLE TRUSTS

The BDIT[159] is an irrevocable inter vivos trust for state law purposes in which someone other than the settlor of the trust is treated as the grantor for income tax purposes over the entire trust pursuant to Code Section 678. In a BDIT, a settlor usually creates a fully discretionary dynastic irrevocable trust in a jurisdiction that has either abrogated the rule against perpetuities or that has a very long perpetuities period for the benefit of a primary beneficiary with up to $5,000, cash.[160] We never recommend that the spouse of the primary beneficiary be the settlor because then the spouse could not then also be a beneficiary of the BDIT due to the estate tax inclusion risks. Most clients want to have a spouse as a discretionary beneficiary, and extra caution must be taken to ensure that the spouse is not considered the grantor for income tax purposes. There also is a practical issue with having the spouse be taxed on all BDIT income yet have no access to the BDIT for help with paying the income tax on the BDIT income, which, in turn, creates a potential client relations/ethical problem for a lawyer who represents the settlor spouse because of the spouse's cash flow exposure. For these reasons, someone other than the spouse of the primary beneficiary should be the settlor of a BDIT.

Typically, the settlor is a parent or other relative of the primary beneficiary. It is critical that the settlor fund this with the settlor's own cash, and that the cash not come directly or indirectly from the primary beneficiary to avoid the primary beneficiary being deemed to be the real transferor and settlor for state law and tax purposes, as this also would create estate tax inclusion pursuant to Code Section 2036(a)(1) as to the primary beneficiary and would lose creditor protection in any jurisdiction that does not protect self-settled trusts from creditors.[161] Query whether there is any real possibility for the IRS to successfully assert the step transaction doctrine to the creation of a BDIT and subsequent sale of assets to the BDIT, which would, if the IRS successfully asserted it, collapse the steps and make the primary beneficiary the true settlor and beneficiary, which would defeat the estate tax planning and creditor-protection planning of the BDIT.[162] There always is a risk that the IRS could assert the step transaction doctrine, but this is a generic risk inherent in every transaction. Therefore, we agree with other commentators, and we do not see application of the step transaction doctrine as a significant risk for a BDIT if the steps are independent of one another and are properly sequenced.[163]

The settlor would file a gift tax return and allocate GST Tax exemption to the entire gift to the BDIT. It is very important that the settlor not have or retain any rights or powers that would cause the trust to be a grantor trust for income tax purposes as to the *settlor*.[164] For example, neither the settlor nor the settlor's spouse can be a beneficiary of the BDIT,[165] neither the settlor nor the settlor's spouse can retain any right or power to deal with BDIT at less than arm's length,[166] neither the settlor nor the settlor's spouse can retain any power to revoke or otherwise amend the trust or change the beneficiaries of the BDIT,[167] and the BDIT instrument probably should prohibit the purchase of life insurance on the life of the settlor and the settlor's spouse.[168] The primary beneficiary must be the grantor for income tax purposes over the *entire* trust.[169] The primary beneficiary alone is given a *Crummey* right to withdraw the entire gift that lapses within thirty-sixty days,[170] as well as broad non-general power of appointment, exercisable during lifetime or at death, which some commentators refer to as the "rewrite power."[171]

The simplest and best way to use a BDIT is opportunity shifting. After the passage of an appropriate period of time, particularly, the lapse of the *Crummey* right of withdrawal, the BDIT trustee[172] would then enter into a purchase of property transaction for full fair market value with the primary beneficiary grantor of the trust, which transaction should be ignored for income tax purposes since the trust is a wholly grantor trust for income tax purposes as to the primary beneficiary.[173] Sales prices and the use of beneficiary guarantee fees, if any,[174] must be determined by qualified appraisers. Out of an abundance of caution, all parties should be represented by independent counsel to prevent the IRS from arguing that the grantor stood on both sides of the transaction. The primary beneficiary can safely serve as administrative and investment trustee without creating estate tax inclusion exposure, but an independent third party must serve as distribution trustee (since the BDIT should provide for wholly discretionary distributions of income and/or principal) as well as trustee over any life insurance policies on the life of the primary beneficiary in order to avoid estate tax inclusion issues with respect to those life insurance policies as to the primary beneficiary.[175] However, the primary beneficiary can have a right to remove an independent trustee and replace it with another independent trustee without creating estate tax inclusion problems.[176] Out of an abundance of caution, a BDIT instrument perhaps should go one step further and prohibit any related or subordinate party from ever serving as distribution or insurance trustee, no matter how selected.[177]

BDIT v. IDGT

While the BDIT and IDGT are both grantor trusts as to trust income and principal if structured properly, they are quite different in terms of design, effect and operation. In an IDGT, the grantor for income tax purposes is the settlor of the trust, who creates a IDGT[178] and who then often sells assets to the IDGT in exchange for an installment note. Therefore, because the grantor is the transferor in an IDGT, Code Sections 2036 and 2038 potentially apply to the sale if the valuation of the sold assets works out to be less than fair market value because the grantor made a gift transfer to the IDGT.[179] Because the primary beneficiary in a BDIT is not a transferor of a gift to the BDIT, it is arguable that Code Sections 2036 and 2038 do not apply because the primary beneficiary transferred nothing to the BDIT. Nevertheless, it is still imperative that the installment sales price be determined by independent qualified appraisers in order to avoid an indirect transfer to the BDIT. Additionally, it also probably is prudent to backstop it all with a defined value sales clause, although the primary beneficiary's non-general power of appointment prevents any gift to the BDIT by the primary beneficiary, which is probably superior protection over a defined value gift/sale clause.[180]

In an IDGT, the grantor cannot retain any interests in or control over the trust, or the grantor risks estate tax inclusion under Code Sections 2036-2038 other than the right to fire and replace independent trustees. This is not the case in a BDIT, where the grantor for income tax purposes is a primary beneficiary and not the settlor, although it is important to ensure that the power of appointment that the primary beneficiary has is not a general power of appointment.[181] Thus, in a BDIT, unlike an IDGT, the primary beneficiary can be a trustee (just not a distribution trustee or trustee over life insurance on the life of the primary beneficiary) and can have a rewrite power to change the *identity* of the beneficiaries of the BDIT, change *when* the beneficiaries receive benefits from the BDIT and *what* benefits the other beneficiaries receive from the BDIT. This is a *significant* advantage of the BDIT over the IDGT.

As was discussed earlier, it also is critical that the primary beneficiary have no control over life insurance on the life of the primary beneficiary that the BDIT owns.[182] Additionally as discussed earlier, the grantor in an IDGT cannot retain any interest in or power over the trust that would cause estate tax inclusion, but the primary beneficiary of the BDIT is a discretionary beneficiary of income and principal, has a non-general power of appointment and can serve as administrative and investment trustee, all without triggering estate tax difficulties.

UNANSWERED QUESTIONS

There are several unanswered questions concerning the BDIT and IDGT, particularly with respect to installment sales that these types of trusts enter into while grantor trusts for income tax purposes. This list is not intended to be an exhaustive discussion of those issues:

Question – Is the income tax grantor in a BDIT or IDGT the grantor over entire trust?

Answer – The answer to this question is it depends upon the selection of the power(s) or right(s) that the tax grantor holds that make the trust a grantor trust for income tax purposes. Some grantor trust powers only affect income or principal only, while other grantor trust powers may only affect certain assets within the trust. Clearly, the goal is for a BDIT or IDGT to be a wholly grantor trust for income tax purposes. Clearly, even a GRAT can be a partially grantor trust for income tax purposes unless the grantor is given additional rights or powers to make it a wholly grantor trust.[183] This issue comes up more often for BDITs because of the breadth of Code Section 678 and its interaction with the Code Section 671 regulations.[184] As was earlier noted, Code Section 678 is not a model of clarity.[185]

There is an unanswered question as to whether a lapse of a *Crummey* right of withdrawal makes the powerholder the grantor over that portion of the trust under Code Section 678(a)(2). Despite the drafting shortcomings of IRC Sec. 678, which several commentators have noted, the IRS private ruling position for a long time has been that a lapse is effectively the same as a partial release or other modification.[186] Some commentators disagree with this position, finding a difference between a lapse and a partial release or other modification.[187]

However, even if the commentators are correct, the primary beneficiary in a BDIT should still be considered the grantor for income tax purposes by virtue of being a discretionary beneficiary where the trustee is an independent, non-adverse party.[188] The IRS has ruled this way for a long time.[189] Therefore, the primary beneficiary in a fully discretionary BDIT will be the grantor over the entire BDIT.

Question – Is a complete lapse of a Crummey right of withdrawal a partial release or other modification for purposes of Code Section 678(a)(2)?

Answer – Even if a lapse is tantamount to a release, is a complete lapse a "partial release or other modification" for purposes of Code Section 678(a)(2)? Again, Code Section 678 suffers from a number of drafting defects, and, in our opinion, this is just another one of them. Notwithstanding the literal language of Code Section 678(a)(2), the IRS has been very consistent in its ruling position that a whole lapse of a Crummey right of withdrawal counts as a "partial release or other modification" in Code Section 678(a)(2).[190] Some commentators have taken issue with that position too.[191] Some of those commentators suggest retention of a non-lapsing right of withdrawal for health, education, maintenance or support (HEMS), citing one private letter ruling that one of the commentators obtained from the IRS National Office.[192] They posit that such a retention would make a release truly a partial release or other modification for purposes of Code Section 678(a)(2). Unfortunately, in the cited private letter ruling, the IRS, despite mentioning the non-lapsing HEMS right in the recitation of the facts, never discusses this right in its legal analysis nor rules on it, leaving reliance upon this ruling (to the extent that any reliance can ever be made on any private letter ruling that is issued to a different taxpayer[193]) for this principle misplaced. One commentator suggests a different approach if one is truly concerned about a partial release, and that is to lapse the Crummey withdrawal right as to all but $1, which would be safer from an asset protection standpoint than retention of a HEMS right and make a release truly partial, if that is a real concern at all, which is debatable.[194] We do not recommend giving the primary beneficiary a HEMS right in a BDIT because it could defeat some of the asset protection benefits of the BDIT as to the primary beneficiary.

Question – Is gain on an unsatisfied note in an installment sale to an IDGT or BDIT recognized at the death of the grantor?

Answer – On this question, commentators are truly split. However, there seems to be some agreement that the termination of the grantor trust status of the IDGT or BDIT may be a transfer of the assets and liabilities by the grantor to the IDGT or BDIT, which, by virtue of the grantor's death, is no longer a grantor trust for income tax purposes and that is now a separate taxpayer.[195] But the debate lies in the type and timing of the transfer. Neither the Code nor the Treasury Regulations address this situation. The commentators disagree on whether the Madorin rationale (loss of grantor trust status during lifetime is a taxable event as to the grantor) applies when the IDIT's or BDIT's loss of grantor trust status is the result of the seller-grantor's death. The commentators also disagree on the effect, if any, of the seller-grantor's death on the income tax basis of the promissory note that the seller-grantor's estate holds at the time of death. Furthermore, commentators disagree as to the effect of the seller's death on the basis of the assets sold to the IDIT or BDIT. We address each of these issues below.

Some commentators take the position that there is no gain realized at death.[196] These commentators view the termination of grantor trust status upon the death of the grantor as in essence a testamentary transfer at the moment of death. This theory recognizes the deemed transfer of all of the assets and all of the liabilities of the trust by the grantor to the trust on the grantor's death, but it states that Code Section 1001 is inapplicable.[197] The final question addressed under this theory is espoused by some of these commentators is what is the basis of the assets in the trust following the death of the grantor? They posit that there are three alternatives: (1) if the transfer is viewed as a bequest or devise, then Code Section 1014 applies to cause the basis to equal the date of death fair market value; (2) if the transfer is viewed as a sale by the grantor to the trust, then the trust's basis will equal the original purchase price under Code Section 1012; or (3) if the transfer is viewed as a gift to the IDGT or BDIT by the decedent grantor, then the basis will be the same as the grantor's basis under Code Section 1015.[198]

The commentators under this theory believe that Code Section 1014 applies, and the assets in the grantor trust should receive a new basis equal to the date of death fair market value of the assets, even though the assets are not included in the grantor's estate for federal estate tax purposes. This new basis approach strikes us as inconsistent with general principles of tax law as well as with the letter and spirit of Code Section 1014.

Another theory espoused by other commentators takes the position that there is no gain recognized at the grantor's death, but there is no new fair market value basis at death.[199] These commentators take the position that, because the cessation of grantor trust status and the resulting deemed transfer occur because of the death of the grantor, the principles that apply to a transfer to the estate should apply.

Some commentators express the view that the sale can be regarded as occurring immediately before the seller's death, with the result that there is gain recognized under a *Madorin* principle.[200] Some commentators take the position that gain will be recognized by the grantor's estate to the extent that the trust's liabilities exceed the estate's basis in the trust's assets.[201] Given that grantor trust status is not lost until the grantor actually *dies*, we fail to see how the transaction could be deemed to have occurred the instant *before* death; the transaction, to the extent that there is one, occurs by reason *of* the grantor's death. In our opinion, it cannot and does not happen *prior* to the grantor's death.

One commentator who argues for gain recognition at death relies on a tax symmetry argument: the rules of recognition during lifetime on conversion of a grantor trust into a non-grantor trust, which have been confirmed,[202] should be the same as the rules for deathtime transfers, which are unknown at the present time.[203] The problem with that position is it neglects to consider that the Code contains a number of different rules for lifetime transfers and deathtime transfers, e.g., the new basis rules for deathtime transfers under Code Section 1014 and the carryover basis general rule of Code Section 1015 for lifetime gift transfers. Therefore, it seems quite plausible and logical that a different rule for deathtime transfers would obtain. In our view, the question answer is unclear, but we lean toward no recognition of gain because the original transaction was ignored for income tax purposes.

Question – What is the basis of the assets of the IDGT or BDIT on the death of the grantor?

Answer – One set of commentators takes the position that the assets inside of the trust receive a new fair market value basis pursuant to Code Section 1014.[204] In our opinion, we see no way for there to be a new fair market value basis under Code Section 1014 without estate tax inclusion in the grantor's estate, as this position just seems too good to be true. The IRS apparently agrees.[205]

Another set of commentators takes the position that the trust gets a cost basis under Code Section 1012, even though no gain is recognized under the principles of *Crane v. Commissioner*.[206] This position cannot be the right answer either because it too seems too good to be true. The right answer on basis must be an unadjusted carryover basis since the original sales transaction was ignored for tax purposes,[207] although it is unclear whether Code Section 1015, which provides for a carryover basis as the general rule for gifts as asserted by other commentators, even applies because there was no gift-it was a full fair market value transaction. Therefore, the question is which Code section applies here. And maybe the answer is that no Code section applies because the sale was ignored under Rev. Rul. 85-13 and that basis simply transfers in the fictitious sale.

Another set of commentators say the gain is recognized to the extent that the liabilities of the IDGT or BDIT exceed the estate's basis in the assets of the IDGT or BDIT.[208] However, these commentators are uncertain between applicability of Code Section 1012 and Code Section 1015. In our view, because the sale was ignored for income tax purposes, the basis that the seller had in the sold assets is simply transferred by operation of tax law to the BDIT or IDGT. No Code section may apply here.

Question – What is the basis of the note in the seller-grantor's estate?

Answer – Commentators are split here too. However, those commenters who believe that gain is recognized on the seller's death believe that the basis of the promissory note in the seller's estate would not be adjusted to its fair market value on date of death or alternate valuation date because it constitutes income in respect of a decedent (IRD). Gain would be recognized to the extent that the balance due on the note exceeded the seller's basis in the sold assets immediately before death, increased by any adjustment allowable under Code Section 691(c) for the estate tax attributable to the IRD.

Commentators who believe that gain is not realized on the seller's death posit that the promissory note is not IRD because no sale occurred during lifetime. Because the IDIT or BDIT is a grantor trust, no payments on the promissory note during the seller's lifetime can constitute taxable income to the seller, including the interest paid on the note as one cannot pay taxable interest to oneself, which strikes us as a correct interpretation of the extension of Rev. Rul. 85-13. The absence of IRD results in the promissory note acquiring a new income tax basis under Code Section 1014 equal to the value at which it is included in the seller's gross estate.

Notwithstanding the question of whether or not gain is recognized at death, it appears to us that this is the easiest of the three questions to answer because the Code actually provides an answer in Code Section 1014 because, unlike the assets in a BDIT or IDGT, the promissory note actually is in the seller's gross estate. Therefore, it should be included at its fair market value as of the date of death or the alternate valuation date under Code Section 1014.

CONCLUSIONS

In light of the unanswered questions about what happens when a seller dies in possession of a promissory note taken back in a sale of appreciated property to a BDIT or IDGT, the split in the commentators and lack of a definitive answer in the law, the safest route is to plan such a transaction to ensure that the seller is fully paid and the promissory note cancelled prior to the seller's demise. Life insurance structured around the amount of the debt could be employed to pay off the debt at the seller's death, thereby reducing or eliminating this problem. If this is not possible, we conclude that the following consequences obtain:

1. No gain is recognized at the seller's death.

2. The basis of the assets inside of the IDGT or BDIT is unchanged by virtue of the seller's death.

3. The promissory note in the seller's estate takes a new fair market value basis under Code Section 1014.

Of the three of these conclusions, we are surest about the third. The only thing that is certain about the first two is that there is no definitive answer as of yet.[209] However, the first two conclusions seem to flow from the logical extension of Rev. Rul. 85-13.

CHAPTER ENDNOTES

1. The terms "Beneficiary Defective Trust" and "Beneficiary Defective Inheritor's Trust" apparently are subject to service mark.

2. I.R.C. Sec. 671.

3. In fact, the grantor's tax year and accounting method apply to the trust. Rev. Rul. 90-55.

4. See, e.g., Blattmachr, Jonathan G. and Zaritsky, Howard M., "Is the BDIT Ready for Primetime?", 24 *Probate Practice Reporter* No. 9 (September 2012) (hereafter, "Prime Time"); Oshins, Richard A., Alexander, Robert G. and Simmons, Kristen E., "The Beneficiary Defective Inheritor's Trust© ("BDIT"): Finessing the Pipe Dream," CCH *Practitioner's Strategies* (November 2008) (hereafter, "Pipe Dream"); Oshins, Richard A., Brody, Lawrence, Hesch, Jerome M., and Rounds, Susan P., "A Gift From Above: Estate Planning On a Higher Plane," *Trusts & Estates* (November 2011) (hereafter, "Higher Plane"); Brown, Edward D., "The Advantages of Beneficiary-Favored Trusts," *The CPA Journal* (January 2014); and McBride, Katarinna, "BDITs and BDON'Ts: Traps to Avoid When Structuring Beneficiary Defective Inheritor's Trusts©," *Trusts & Estates* (March 2012).

5. Rev. Proc. 2016-3, Sec. 4 (44).

6. For example, whether a power exercisable solely in a nonfiduciary capacity to exchange assets of the trust for assets of equivalent value. I.R.C. Sec. 675(4)(C).

7. See Sec. 219(g) and (h), Revenue Act of 1924.

8. See Ascher, Mark L. "The Grantor Trust Rules Should Be Repealed," 96 Iowa Law Review 885 (2011). See also, Ricks, Daniel L. "I Dig It, But Congress Shouldn't Let Me: Closing the IDGT Loophole," 36 ACTEC Law Journal 641 (2010).

9. The federal estate tax was enacted in 1916. There was a gift tax passed in 1924, but it was quickly repealed. However, the gift tax came to stay in 1926.

10. That the three taxes originally were enacted at different times had to have played a role. The income tax came first, in 1913. The federal estate tax was enacted in 1916. The original gift tax and the first grantor trust rules were enacted in 1924, but the gift tax was repealed in 1926, only to return for good in 1932.

11. This analysis does not consider I.R.C. Sec. 679, which pertains to foreign trusts with U.S. beneficiaries where the grantor can be treated as the grantor for federal income tax purposes.

12. A revocable trust will always be a grantor trust for income tax purposes. I.R.C. Sec. 676.

13. I.R.C. Sec. 673.

14. The term "adverse party" is defined by negative implication to be someone other than an adverse party in Code Section 672(b). The term "adverse party" itself is defined in Code Section 672(a) and means any person having a substantial beneficial interest in the trust who would be adversely affected by the exercise or non-exercise of the power.

15. I.R.C. Sec. 674(a).

16. I.R.C. Sec. 677.

17. I.R.C. Sec. 675(1).

18. I.R.C. Sec. 675(2).

19. I.R.C. Sec. 675(3).

20. I.R.C. Sec. 675(4).

21. I.R.C. Sec. 678(a).

22. Rev. Rul. 85-13. In Rev. Rul. 85-13, the IRS repudiated the Second CI.R.C.uit's contrary split decision in *Rothstein v. U.S.*, 735 F. 2d 704 (2d Cir. 1984).

23. Rev. Rul. 2004-64.

24. See, e.g., Pipe Dream, p. 3.

25. Rev. Rul. 2004-64 confirmed this result.

26. I.R.C. Sec. 1361(c)(2)(A)(i).

27. For example, I.R.C. Sec. 674, which governs the control over beneficial enjoyment, can apply to income only, principal only, or both principal and income.

28. Cf. Treas. Reg. Sec. 1.671-3.

29. *Madorin v. Comm'r.*, 84 T.C. 667 (1985). Such a switch would have greatly helped the grantor in *Millstein v. Millstein*. In *Millstein*, the grantor was being reimbursed millions in income tax from another trust, when he was informed that the funding trust had no more liquid assets and therefore could no longer reimburse him for the income tax. The grantor filed a petition in court seeking equitable reimbursement from the grantor trust that the grantor established for the benefit of the trustee, who also was a beneficiary of the trust, who filed a motion to dismiss the petition. The trial court dismissed the petition, concluding that the grantor was hoist by his own petard because he set up the trust to be taxed that way. The appellate court affirmed for similar reasons.

30. *Rothstein v. U.S.*, 735 F. 2d 704 (2d Cir. 1984).

31. I.R.C. Sec. 1.

32. I.R.C. Secs. 674(a) and 677(a)(1); Treas. Reg. Secs. 1.674(a)-1(b) and 1.677(a)-1(b)(2).

33. I.R.C. Sec. 2036(a)(1).

34. I.R.C. Secs. 674(a) and 677(a)(1); Treas. Reg. Secs. 1.674(a)-1(b) and 1.677(a)-1(b)(2).

35. Treas. Reg. Sec. 20.2036-1(b)(3).

36. I.R.C. Secs. 674(a) and 677(a)(1); Treas. Reg. Secs. 1.674(a)-1(a) and 1.677(a)-1(b)(2).

37. I.R.C. Sec. 2036(a)(2).

38. I.R.C. Sec. 674(a); Treas. Reg. Secs. 1.674(a)-1(b) and 1.674(d)-1. Treas. Reg. Sec. 25.2511-2(b).

39. I.R.C. Sec. 2036(a)(2).

40. I.R.C. Sec. 674(a); Treas. Reg. Sec. 1.674(a)-1(b).

41. Treas. Reg. Sec. 20.2036-1(b)(3); Rev. Rul. 95-58.

42. I.R.C. Sec. 674(c); Treas. Reg. Sec. 1.674(c)-1.

43. I.R.C. Secs. 2036(a)(2) and 2038(a); Treas. Reg. Sec. 20.2036-1(b)(3).

44. I.R.C. Sec. 674(d); Treas. Reg. Sec. 1.674(d)-1.

45. Treas. Reg. Sec. 20.2041-1(c)(1).

46. Treas. Reg. Secs. 20.2036-1(b)(2) and 20.2041-1(c1).

47. Treas. Reg. Sec. 20.2041-1(c)(1).

48. I.R.C. Sec. 674(c); Treas. Reg. Sec. 1.674-1(c)(1).

49. *Wall Estate v. Comm'r.*, 101 T.C. 300 (1993); Rev. Rul. 95-58.

50. I.R.C. Sec. 674(b)(5)(A); Treas. Reg. Sec. 1.674(b)-1(b)(5).

51. Treas. Reg. Sec. 1.674(b)-1(b)(5).

52. Treas. Reg. Sec. 20.2041-1(c)(1).

53. Treas. Reg. Secs. 1.674(c)-1 and 1.674(d)-1.

54. Treas. Reg. Sec. 20.2041-1(c)(1).

55. I.R.C. Sec. 674(b)(5)(B); Treas. Reg. Sec. 1.674(b)-1(b)(5).

56. Treas. Reg. Sec. 20.2041-1(c)(1).

57. I.R.C. Sec. 674(c); Treas. Reg. Sec. 1.674.

58. Treas. Reg. Sec. 20.2036-1(b)(3).

59. I.R.C. Sec. 674(b)(6); Treas. Reg. Sec. 1.674(b)-1(b)(6).

60. *United States v. O'Malley*, 383 U.S. 627 (1966).

61. Treas. Reg. Sec. 20.2041-1(c)(1).

62. I.R.C. Sec. 674(c); Treas. Reg. Sec. 1.674(c)-1.

63. Treas. Reg. Sec. 20.2041-1(c)(1).

64. Treas. Reg. Sec. 1.677(b)-1(a).

65. I.R.C. Sec. 677(b).

66. Treas. Reg. Sec. 20.2036-1(b)(3).

67. I.R.C. Secs. 674(b)(5), (b)(6), (b)(7), (c) and (d).

68. I.R.C. Sec. 674(a).

69. I.R.C. Secs. 2036(a)(2) and 2041.

70. Treas. Reg. Sec. 25.2511-2(c), (f); see also *Sanford Estate v. Comm'r.*, 308 U.S. 39 (1939).

71. I.R.C. Sec. 674(a).

72. I.R.C. Secs. 2036(a)(2) and 2038.

73. I.R.C. Sec. 674(a).

74. I.R.C. Secs. 2036(a)(2) and 2038.

75. I.R.C. Sec. 674(a).

76. I.R.C. Secs. 2036(a) and 2038.

77. I.R.C. Sec. 674(b)(8); Treas. Reg. Sec. 1.674(b)-1(b)(8).

78. Treas. Reg. Secs. 20.2041-1(b)(1) and 25.2514-1(b)(1).

79. I.R.C. Sec. 674(b)(8).

80. Treas. Reg. Sec. 20.2041-1(b)(1).

81. I.R.C. Sec. 677(a)(3); Treas. Reg. Sec. 1.677(a)-1(b)(1)(iii).

82. I.R.C. Sec. 2042.

83. I.R.C. Sec. 677(a)(3); Treas. Reg. Sec. 1.677(a)-1(a)(1).

84. I.R.C. Sec. 2042.

85. I.R.C. Sec. 677(a); Treas. Reg. Sec. 1.677(a)-1(a).

86. I.R.C. Sec. 2042.

87. I.R.C. Sec. 675(1); Treas. Reg. Sec. 1.675-1(b)(1).

88. I.R.C. Sec. 2036.

89. I.R.C. Sec. 675(1); Treas. Reg. Sec. 1.675-1(b)(1).

90. Treas. Reg. Sec. 20.2036-1(b)(3).

91. Treas. Reg. Sec. 1.675-1(b)(1).

92. Treas. Reg. Sec. 20.2036-1(b)(3).

93. I.R.C. Sec. 675(2); Treas. Reg. Sec. 1.675-1(b)(2).

94. I.R.C. Sec. 2036(a). See, e.g., *Paxton Estate v. Comm'r.*, 86 T.C. 785 (1986), where a right to borrow trust assets permitted grantor to live off trust assets and relegate his creditors to making claims against a trust was held to have constituted a retained

right to beneficial enjoyment of the entire trust under I.R.C. Sec. 2036(a)(1).

95. I.R.C. Sec. 675(2); Treas. Reg. Sec. 1.675-1(b)(2).

96. Treas. Reg. Sec. 20.2036-1(b)(3).

97. I.R.C. Sec. 675(3); Treas. Reg. Sec. 1.675-1(b)(3).

98. I.R.C. Sec. 2036(a)(1); Treas. Reg. Sec. 20.2036-1(b)(3).

99. I.R.C. Sec. 675(3); Treas. Reg. Sec. 1.675-1(b)(3).

100. I.R.C. Sec. 2036(a)(1); Treas. Reg. Sec. 20.2036-1(b)(3).

101. I.R.C. Sec. 675(4)(A); Treas. Reg. Sec. 1.675-1(b)(4)(i).

102. I.R.C. Sec. 2036(a)(1) and 2036(b).

103. I.R.C. Sec. 675(4)(A); Treas. Reg. Sec. 1.675-1(b)(4)(i).

104. Treas. Reg. Sec. 20.2036-1(b)(3).

105. I.R.C. Sec. 675(4)(C); Treas. Reg. Sec. 1.675-1(b)(4)(iii).

106. Rev. Ruls. 2008-22 and 2011-28; but see *Jordahl Estate v. Comm'r.*, 65 T.C. 92 (1975), acq. in result, 1977–2 C.B. 1.

107. I.R.C. Sec. 675(4)(C); Treas. Reg. Sec. 1.675-1(b)(4)(iii).

108. Treas. Reg Sec. 20.2036-1(b)(3); Rev. Ruls. 2008-22 and 2011-28; but see *Jordahl Estate v. Comm'r.*, 65 T.C. 92 (1975), acq. in result, 1977–2 C.B. 1.

109. I.R.C. Sec. 676(a); Treas. Reg. Sec. 1.676(a)-1.

110. I.R.C. Sec. 2038; Treas. Reg. Sec. 20.2038-1(a).

111. I.R.C. Sec. 676(a); Treas. Reg. Sec. 1.676-1.

112. Treas. Reg. Sec. 20.2036-1(b)(3).

113. I.R.C. Sec. 676(a); Treas. Reg. Sec. 1.676-1.

114. Treas. Reg. Sec. 20.2036-1(b)(3).

115. I.R.C. Sec. 674(b)(5)(B) and 674(a); Treas. Reg. Sec. 1.674(a)-1(b)(2).

116. I.R.C. Secs. 2036(a)(2) and 2038(a); Treas. Sec. 20.2038-1(a)(2).

117. I.R.C. Secs. 2036(a)(2) and 2038.

118. Treas. Reg Sec. 20.2036-1(b)(3).

119. I.R.C. Sec. 674(a); Treas. Reg. Sec. 1.674(b)-1(b)(5)(ii).

120. Treas. Reg. Sec. 20.2036-1(b)(3).

121. I.R.C. Sec. 674(c); Treas. Reg. Sec. 1.674(c)-1.

122. Treas. Reg Sec. 20.2036-1(b)(3).

123. I.R.C. Secs. 674(b)(1) and 677(b); Treas. Reg. Secs. 1.674(b)-1(b)(1) and 1.677(b)-1(a).

124. Treas. Reg. Sec. 20.2036-1(b)(2).

125. I.R.C. Secs. 674(b)(1) and 677(b); Treas. Reg. Secs. 1.674(b)-1(b)(1) and 1.677(b)-1(a).

126. Treas. Reg. Sec. 20.2036-1(b)(3).

127. I.R.C. Sec. 678(a).

128. This only refers to trust income. However, many commentators believe that the limitation to trust income was a drafting oversight. See, e.g., Early, Charles E., "Income Taxation of Lapsed Powers of Withdrawal: Analyzing Their Current Status," 62 *Journal of Taxation* 198 (April 1985) (hereafter, "Early").

129. I.R.C. Sec. 2038.

130. I.R.C. Sec. 2037.

131. I.R.C. Sec. 674(a).

132. I.R.C. Secs. 2036(a)(2) and 2038.

133. Treas. Reg. Sec. 25.2511-2(c).

134. This is not intended to be an exhaustive list of powers that can be safely used.

135. I.R.C. Sec. 672(e)(1).

136. A spouse who made contributions to the trust who holds a power to add beneficiaries would face estate tax inclusion under I.R.C. Secs. 2036(a)(2) and 2038.

137. Grantor trust status for a power that a spouse holds survives the couple's divorce. I.R.C. Sec. 672(e)(1)(A).

138. The power to add charities as beneficiaries in the hands of a nonadverse party, in that case a trustee, was the situation that was accorded grantor trust status under I.R.C. Sec. 674(a) in *Madorin v. Comm'r.*, 84 T.C. 667 (1985). There also have been several private letter rulings that have accorded grantor trust status to situations where the trustee holds the power to add beneficiaries. See, e.g., PLRs199936031 (inter vivos CLAT nonadverse trustees given power to add charitable beneficiaries was sufficient to make CLAT a grantor trust under I.R.C. Sec. 674(a)), 9709001/9710006 (unrelated nonadverse trustee given the power to add charitable or educational beneficiaries was sufficient to accord grantor trust status under I.R.C. Sec. 674(a)), 9010065 (power to add charities as beneficiaries accorded grantor trust status under I.R.C. Sec. 674(a)); 9211006 (power to add charities with the consent of a nonadverse party created a grantor trust under I.R.C. Sec. 674(a)); if the client wants to give the power to add family members other than after-born or after-adopted children as beneficiaries, see PLR 9141037 (power to add family beneficiaries) and 9304017 (power in nonadverse trustee to add grantor's descendants as beneficiaries created a grantor trust under I.R.C. Sec. 674).

139. See Akers, Stephen R., Blattmachr, Jonathan G. and Boyle, F. Ladson, "Creating Intentional Grantor Trusts," 44 *Real Property, Trust and Estate Law Journal* 207 (Summer 2009) at p. 234 (hereafter "Intentional").

140. See, e.g., PLR 9211006.

141. I.R.C. Sec. 675(4) requires a substitution of assets of equivalent value. Query whether a substitution of a promissory note for hard assets is equivalent? The answer seems to depend upon whether the promissory note is secured. In *In re the Matter of The Mark Vance Condiotti Irrevocable GDT Trust*, No. 14CA0969 (Col. App. July 9, 2015), the court rejected an attempt to substitute an unsecured promissory note for hard assets, reasoning that such was a prohibited loan of trust assets. However, in *Benson v. Rosenthal*, No. 15-782, 2016 WL 2855456 (E.D. La. 2016), the court rejected the trustee's attempt to deny the substitution of secured promissory notes and other assets supported by contemporaneous appraisals. In *Benson v. Rosenthal*, the assets that the plaintiff grantor sought to reacquire included interests in the New Orleans Saints of the National Football League and the New Orleans Pelicans of the National Basketball Association, both of which are very unique assets. Query whether an asset can be so unique to preclude a finding of equivalence in value?

142. Rev. Rul. 2008-22.

143. For an example of a post Rev. Rul. 2008-22 private letter ruling, see PLR 201235006.

144. Treas. Reg. Sec. 1.675-1(b)(4).

145. The IRS also believes that this power can be given to someone other than the grantor. See, e.g., Rev. Proc. 2007-45, in which the IRS, in a model form inter vivos CLAT, gave the substitution power to someone other than the grantor, the trustee or any disqualified party to create grantor trust status. See also Rev. Proc. 2008-46. See also PLRs 9548013, 9642039, 9810019 and 199908002 for examples of rulings where the swap power was held by someone other than the grantor.

146. I.R.C. Sec. 1001.

147. Treas. Reg. Sec. 1.675-1(b) (flush language) provides that there is a presumption that any power of administration that is held by a trustee is held in a fiduciary capacity that can only be overcome with clear and convincing evidence that the power is not exercisable in the best interests of the beneficiaries. In our view, it is confusing to give a trustee a power that is not a fiduciary power, and this power should, therefore, not be given to a trustee. And applicable state law might not permit a trustee to hold a power in a non-fiduciary capacity. But see PLRs 8930021 and 9037011, where a trustee beneficiary had the swap power exercisable in a non-fiduciary capacity.

148. However, such a trust would be a grantor trust under I.R.C. Sec. 677.

149. *Jordahl Estate v. Comm'r.*, 65 T.C. 92 (1975), acq. 1977-1 C.B. 1.

150. Rev. Rul. 2011-28.

151. For examples of a situation where a grantor surrendered the swap power, see PLRs200729005 and 200729015. See also, e.g., PLR 9504024 for a situation where the grantor expressly retained the right to surrender the swap power.

152. Treas. Reg. Sec. 1.675-1(b)(flush language). This is so even if the power expressly states that it is only exercisable in a nonfiduciary capacity. See, e.g., PLRs 9335028; 9126015, and 9345035. Nevertheless, the IRS has been inconsistent in its position and has granted some private letter rulings where the swap power was held in a nonfiduciary capacity. See, e.g., PLRs. 9451056, 9352017, 9351005, and 9345035. In other private letter rulings, the IRS has stated while the grantor trust determination depends on the facts and cI.R.C.umstances, if exercise of a swap power is in a nonfiduciary capacity, the trust would be treated as a grantor trust. See, e.g., PLRs 9810019, 200434012 and 200848017.

153. See, e.g., Janes, Craig L. and Kelly Bernadette M., "When Using a Power of Substitution—Take Nothing for Granted," *Estate Planning* (August 2007), at 3; Intentional, at p. 259.

154. Actual borrowing of the trust property will make at least that part of the trust a grantor trust during the pendency of the loan. I.R.C. Sec. 675(3).

155. See, e.g., *Paxton Estate v. Comm'r.*, 86 T.C. 785 (1986).

156. See, e.g., PLRs 9645013 (power included a toggle off switch) and 200840025 (power held by a nonadverse party who had a right to surrender the power).

157. See, e.g., PLRs 9446008 (power to borrow coupled with a swap power), 199942017 (loan power without adequate security coupled with a swap power), and 9525032 (loan without adequate security power coupled with a swap power).

158. PLRs 199942017 (loan power without adequate security coupled with a swap power), 9525032 (loan without adequate security power coupled with a swap power), 9403020 (power to borrow without adequate interest or security) and 8708024 (power to borrow without adequate interest or security).

159. For more on BDITs, see Higher Plane and Pipe Dream.

160. The reason why the gift should be of no more than $5,000 is to come within the "5 or 5 power" exception for lapsed rights not being general powers of appointment under I.R.C. Sec. 2514(e). The gift should be made in cash so that there are absolutely no valuation issues present.

161. Treas. Reg. Sec. 1.671-2(e)(1). The courts have unwound other transactions and gifts to determine the identity of the real donor. See, e.g., *Senda v. Comm'r.*, 433 F.3d 1044 (8th Cir. 2006).

162. See Kestenbaum, Avi Z., Galant, Jeffrey A. and Akhavan, K. Eli, "The Beneficiary Defective Inheritor's Trust: Is it Really Defective?" Steve Leimberg's *Estate Planning* Newsletter No.1730 (December 2010). See also *Pierre v. Comm'r.*, T.C. Memo 2010-106, where the Tax Court applied the step transaction doctrine to a part-gift part-sale that all happened at the same time. However, this article neglects to consider a number of real factors that go into a successful application of the step transaction doctrine, and the article fails to make a convincing case for its application to a BDIT.

163. Higher Plane, pp. 7-8.

164. I.R.C. Sec. 678(b). If the settlor is deemed to be the grantor over the trust pursuant to another provision of Subpart E of Subchapter J, that would prime I.R.C. Sec. 678 grantor trust status as to the primary beneficiary.

165. I.R.C. Sec. 677(a)(1).

166. I.R.C. Sec. 674(a).

167. I.R.C. Secs. 674(a) and 676.

168. I.R.C. Sec. 677(a)(3).

169. You want to avoid the bifurcation rule of Treas. Reg. Sec. 1.671-3(a)(3).

170. Since the gift will be of an amount less than or equal to $5,000, we recommend that the beneficiary's *Crummey* power be over the entire gift so that the beneficiary will be the grantor over the entire trust for income tax purposes, even though there is no real requirement that this gift lapse at all. If the power was limited to a "5 or 5" limitation and the gift was deemed to have been larger than $5,000, which avoids the application of I.R.C. Secs. 2041 and 2514, then there exists a real possibility that the beneficiary would not be the grantor for income tax purposes over the entire trust. Treas. Reg. Sec. 1.671-3(a)(3). There is an unanswered question as to whether a lapse of a *Crummey* right of withdrawal makes the powerholder the grantor over that portion of the trust under I.R.C. Sec. 678(a)(2). Despite the drafting shortcomings of I.R.C. Sec. 678, which several commentators have noted, the IRS private ruling position for a long time has been that the lapse is the effective same as a release or other modification. See, e.g., PLRs 201039010, 200747002, and 200147044. Despite the IRS private ruling position, there is still some uncertainty as to whether a lapse of a right of withdrawal is the same thing as a release or other modification as contemplated by I.R.C. Sec. 678(a)(2). One commentator suggested that the withdrawal right never lapse over the gift, which would ensure grantor trust treatment under I.R.C. Sec. 678(a)(1) without having to reach 678(a)(2). See Pipe Dream, p. 6. If the withdrawal right does not lapse, the primary beneficiary should file a gift tax return and allocate sufficient GST Tax exemption to the gift to give it a zero inclusion ratio. One possible way to avoid this potential problem is to couple a *Crummey* right of withdrawal with a swap power held by the primary beneficiary. See, e.g., PLRs 9311021 and 201216034. However, these private letter rulings appear to be wrong on the issue of whether the swap power held by the primary beneficiary makes the trust a grantor trust as to the primary beneficiary because they conflict with the official IRS published ruling position, which it enunciated in Rev. Procs. 2007-45 and 2008-46, which stand for the proposition that a swap power that a third party holds is nevertheless attributable to the grantor, not to the third party. See also, Prime Time, pp. 3-5. Therefore, we do not recommend giving the primary beneficiary a swap power because it makes the settlor the grantor of the trust for income tax purposes, which defeats the purpose of the BDIT planning.

See also, Gorin, Steven B., Structuring Ownership of Privately Owned Businesses: Tax and Estate Planning Implications (June 28, 2016) (hereafter, "Gorin"), p. 891. Nevertheless, this coupling might also help avoid another unanswered question, which is whether the beneficiary owns the entire trust after lapse of the withdrawal right. Nevertheless, as a discretionary beneficiary over income and principal in a trust that has an independent but non-adverse party as trustee, the primary beneficiary also could be deemed a grantor under I.R.C. Sec. 677(a)(1), which would satisfy I.R.C. Sec. 678(a)(2) as to any lapsed *Crummey* rights.

171. See Higher Plane, p. 2. Retention of the non-general power of appointment renders any gift by the primary beneficiary incomplete for gift tax purposes. Treas. Reg. Sec. 25.2511-2(b)-(d).

172. The BDIT should be represented in the sale by the independent trustee, who must be represented by separate counsel. Otherwise, the primary beneficiary who also serves as investment trustee would stand on both sides of the transaction, which we do not recommend because it would potentially subject the BDIT to IRS scrutiny.

173. Rev. Rul. 85-13. Query whether the initial thin capitalization of the trust may be assuaged with beneficiary guarantees. See Prime Time, pp. 6-9. For more on whether beneficiary guarantees satisfy the informal but unnecessary 9:1 capitalization rule of thumb that the IRS seemed to require in PLR 9535026, see Hatcher, Milford B., Jr. and Manigault, Edward M, "Using Beneficiary Guarantees In Defective Grantor Trusts", *Journal of Taxation* (March 2000). However, there is a real question as to whether a court would ever use this IRS informal rule of thumb funding requirement when the courts have so clearly enunciated the reality-of-sale doctrine. See, e.g., Hesch, Jerome M., Oshins, Richard A. and Magner, Jim, "Note Sales, Economic Substance and the 10% Myth," *Steve Leimberg's Estate Planning Newsletter* No. 2412 (May 2016). Some commentators are hesitant to permit a beneficiary to give a personal guarantee because that could be a deemed contribution to the trust, which, then coupled with the discretionary right over principal and income, could cause estate tax inclusion. See, e.g., Doubts and Gorin, p. 900. However, other commentators seem to have no problem with a guarantee by a beneficiary who is other than the seller. See, e.g., Pipe Dream, p. 6. Given that the transaction will probably be in the best interests of the trust, we see no reason why a beneficiary other than the primary beneficiary seller could not give a guarantee.

174. Payment of a fair market value guarantee fee would avoid a *Dickman* indirect gift argument. See, e.g., PLRs 9113009 and 9409018 (the latter ruling withdrew the former). The fee would be taxable income to the guarantor and probably would not be deductible by the primary beneficiary as grantor of the BDIT. We believe that guarantee payments help deflect any indirect gift argument.

175. I.R.C. Secs. 2036(a)(2), 2038 and 2042. The protection of Rev. Rul. 95-58 would be inapplicable if the primary beneficiary served as distribution trustee because of the absolute discretion over distributions that a BDIT instrument gives to the distribution trustee.

176. One wants to avoid Treas. Reg. Sec. 20.2036-1(b)(3). I.R.C. Sec. 672(c) defines who would be considered related or subordinate as any nonadverse party who is—(1) the grantor's spouse if living with the grantor; (2) any one of the following: The grantor's father, mother, issue, brother or sister; an employee of the grantor; a corporation or any employee of a corporation in which the stock holdings of the grantor and the trust are significant from the viewpoint of voting control; a subordinate employee of

a corporation in which the grantor is an executive. For the estate tax considerations, see Rev. Rul. 95-58, which permits removal and replacement as long as the power only exists as to persons who are not related or subordinate within the meaning of I.R.C. Sec. 672(c). This ruling essentially harmonizes the official IRS position with IRS losses in *Wall Estate v. Comm'r.*, 101 T.C. 300 (1993), and *Vak Estate v. Comm'r.*, 973 F.2d 1409 (8th Cir. 1992), *rev'g* T.C. Memo 1991–503.

177. But see, e.g., *SEC v. Wyly*, 2014 WL 4792229 (S.D.N.Y. September 5, 2014), where the defendants' power over independent trustees was so pervasive to substitute their judgment for that of the independent trustees.

178. Usually with a gift of some size.

179. One way to potentially avoid this is to use a defined value gift/sale clause, which the Tax Court has blessed in *Wandry v. Comm'r.*, T.C. Memo 2012-88. For more on defined value gifts and sales, see Hood, L. Paul, Jr., "Defined Value Gifts and Sales Under the Microscope: What's Possible and What's Not-Revisited," *BNA Tax Management Estates, Gifts and Trusts Journal* (2011).

180. See, e.g., McBride, Katarinna, "BDIT's and BDONT's: Traps to Avoid When Structuring Beneficiary Defective Inheritor's Trusts," *Trusts & Estates* (March 2012), pp. 36-41.

181. Because I.R.C. Sec. 2041 would include the value of the property that is subject to the general power of appointment in the primary beneficiary's estate.

182. I.R.C. Sec. 2042 would include the proceeds of any life insurance policy on the life of the primary beneficiary that the BDIT owns if the primary beneficiary controls those policies because the primary beneficiary would be deemed to hold the incidents of ownership over those policies.

183. See, e.g., PLRs 9525032, 9352017, 9416009, 9352007, 9351005, 9345035, 9248016, and 9239015.

184. Namely, Treas. Reg. Sec. 1.671-3.

185. Query whether I.R.C. Sec. 678(b), which only references trust *income*, also was intended to cover trust *principal*. The legislative history would certainly leave one with that impression, as it states: A person other than the grantor may be treated as a substantial owner of a trust if he has an unrestricted power to take the trust *principal* or income unless the grantor himself is deemed taxable because of such a power. H.R. Rep. No. 1337, 83d Cong., 2d Sess. 63 (1954); S. Rep. No. 1622, 83d Cong., 2d Sess. 87 (1954). [emphasis added] Clearly under I.R.C. Sec. 678(a), a person other than the grantor may be treated as owning all or only a part of a trust for income tax purposes. Therefore, it stands to reason that I.R.C. Sec. 678(b), despite its literal wording, also applies to powers over trust principal.

186. See, e.g., PLRs 201039010, 200747002 and 200147044.

187. See, e.g., Early and Prime Time.

188. I.R.C. Sec. 677(a)(1).

189. See, e.g., PLRs 8342088, 8701007, 9009010, 9320018, 199935047, 199942037, 200011055 and 200147044.

190. See, e.g., PLRs 201216034, 201039010, and 200747002.

191. See, e.g., Prime Time, p. 4; Early; Brattmachr, Jonathan G. and Zeydel, Diana S. C., "PLR 200949012 - Beneficiary Defective Trust(sm) Private Letter Ruling," *Steve Leimberg's Estate Planning Newsletter* No. 1559 (December 10, 2009); and Blattmachr, Jonathan G., Gans, Mitchell M., Alvina H. Lo, "A Beneficiary as Trust Owner: Decoding Section 678," 35 *ACTEC Journal* 106 (Fall 2009).

192. PLR 200949012.

193. I.R.C. Sec. 6110(k)(3).

194. Oshins, Richard A., "PLR 200949012 "Myth" - Now You See It, Now You Don't," *Steve Leimberg's Estate Planning Newsletter* No. 2420 (May 31, 2016).

195. *Madorin v. Comm'r.,* 84 T.C. 667 (1985); Treas. Reg. Sec. 1.1001-2(c), Ex. (5); and Rev. Rul. 77-402.

196. See, e.g., Blattmachr, Jonathan G., Gans, Mitchell M., and Jacobson, Hugh H., "Income Tax Effects of Termination of Grantor Trust Status by Reason of the Grantor's Death," 97 *Journal of Taxation* 149 (2002); Blattmachr, Jonathan G. and Gans, Mitchell M., "No Gain at Death," 149 *Trusts & Estates* No. 2, 34 (2010) (hereafter, "No Gain"); and Peebles, Laura H. "Death of an IDIT Noteholder," *Trusts & Estates* 28 (August 2005).

197. *Crane v. Comm'r.,* 331 U.S. 1 (1947). See also Rev. Rul. 73-183.

198. Another possibility exists that the commentators did not consider, and that is that there is no change in basis under any Code section because the entire transaction is a nullity for income tax purposes, which is what we believe to be the case, if Rev. Rul. 85-13 is carried to its logical conclusion.

199. See Manning, Elliott and Hesch, Jerome M., "Deferred Payment Sales to Grantor Trusts, GRATs and Net Gifts: Income and Transfer Tax Elements," 24 Tax Management Estates, Gifts & Trusts Journal 3 (1999).

200. See, e.g., Covey, Richard B., "Recent Developments Concerning Estate, Gift and Income Taxation - 1996," *31st Annual University of Miami Philip E. Heckerling Institute on Estate Planning,* Sec. 120. 2E (1997). See also, Cantrell, Carol A., "Gain is Realized at Death," 149 *Trusts & Estates* No. 2, 20 (2010) (hereafter, "Gain"). For an immediate rebuttal of that conclusion, see No Gain.

201. Dunn, Deborah V. and Handler, David A., "Tax Consequences of Outstanding Trust Liabilities When Grantor Status Terminates," 95 *Journal of Taxation* No. 1, 49 (2001) (hereafter, "Terminates").

202. *Madorin v. Comm'r.,* 84 T.C. 667 (1985); Treas. Reg. Sec. 1.1001(c), Example (5) and Rev. Rul. 77-402.

203. See Gain.

204. See, e.g., No Gain.

205. CCA 200937028.

206. See Manning, Elliott and Hesch, Jerome M., "Deferred Payment Sales to Grantor Trusts, GRATs and Net Gifts: Income and Transfer Tax Elements," 24 *Tax Management Estates, Gifts & Trusts Journal* 3 (1999).

207. Rev. Rul. 85-13.

208. See Terminates.

209. We did find one commentator whose views are similar to our own: See Mulligan, Michael D., "A 'Reality of Sale' Analysis of Installment Sales to Grantor Trusts: Properly Structured, The Best Transfer Tax Strategy," *41ˢᵗ Annual Notre Dame Tax and Estate Planning Institute* (2015).

QUALIFIED PERSONAL RESIDENCE TRUSTS

CHAPTER 15

INTRODUCTION

For most individuals, a personal residence is their most valuable asset. A Qualified Personal Residence Trust ("QPRT") is an irrevocable trust that is funded with the donor's personal residence. It is an estate planning technique that is expressly authorized and governed by the Internal Revenue Code and the relevant Treasury Regulations. As a result, the QPRT is a "safe harbor" technique, with a detailed road map laid out by the IRS in its own regulations. When such IRS regulations are followed, one can avoid any IRS challenge to the basic plan.

With a QPRT, the owner of a personal residence transfers that property to an irrevocable trust. Under the terms of the trust, the donor retains the exclusive use of the residence free of rent for a term of years (the "QPRT term"). At the end of the QPRT term, the donor's rights to use and occupy the residence terminate. At that time, the residence can remain in trust for beneficiaries named by the donor, or pass outright to them, thus terminating the trust.

Typically, when an individual transfers an interest to a trust and retains the benefit of the transferred property, the full value of the transferred property is treated as a gift.[1] However, an exception applies when the transferred property is a personal residence.[2] The value of the gift to the trust is the fair market value of the personal residence less the donor's retained right to reside in the residence. Due to the donor's retained interest in the QPRT term, a QPRT permits an individual to transfer ownership of the residence at a reduced value for gift tax purposes and removes the value, and the growth in value, from the individual's estate for federal estate tax purposes. Since the value of the gift is determined at the time it is transferred to

the trust, the technique contains elements of an "estate freeze" because it "freezes" the value of the property at the time of the gift, and the growth in value after the date of the gift escapes estate taxation. Therefore, a residence that is expected to appreciate in value is an ideal choice for a QPRT.

If the donor survives the term, the entire value of the property, including appreciation from the date the property is transferred to the trust, is excluded from the federal gross taxable estate. However, if the donor dies during the QPRT term, the property will be included in the donor's gross estate at the date of death value.

Consequently, for the technique to work, the donor must be of sufficiently good health to survive the QPRT term.

In all instances, when considering the use of a QPRT, both the estate tax and income tax considerations must be examined. Because a QPRT transfer is treated as a gift, the beneficiary's basis is generally equal to the donor's basis. Therefore, the potential income taxes due on sale by the beneficiaries must be weighed against the potential estate tax savings.

DEFINITION OF PERSONAL RESIDENCE

In order to take advantage of the favorable special valuation rules of Code section 2702, the QPRT can only hold one personal residence of the donor.[3] The term "personal residence" is not defined in section 2702; instead, the Regulations contain the requirements. There are several tests a property must pass in order to be considered a donor's personal residence for purposes of a QPRT. The first test concerns the primary use of the property. The residence is a "personal residence" only if the primary use is as a residence of the donor when it is occupied by the donor.[4] Second, the residence must be either the "principal residence" or "other residence" of the donor.[5]

Primary Use as a Residence

In order to qualify as a personal residence, the primary use of the residence must be as a residence of the donor when occupied by the donor.[6] A residence is not a personal residence if, during any period when it is not occupied by the donor, its primary purpose is other than as a residence. In most instances, this requirement is not an issue. Satisfying this test generally only becomes an issue when there is some nonresidential use, the property is occupied by tenants, or when the QPRT owns a fractional interest in the property.

Occupancy Shares with Relatives and Guests

The occupancy of the residence by the donor's relatives, guests or servants together with the donor should not have any negative consequence on the status of the residence. These individuals are all considered to be sharing occupancy at the "sufferance" of the donor.[7] This is true so long as the property is the donor's residence and its primary use is as a residence of the donor. Consistent with this reasoning, the presence of an au pair or live- in staff would not impair the status of the property as the donor's residence.

Share Occupancy with Paying Tenants

The use of a portion of the residence as a rental to a third party should not preclude the residence from qualifying as a personal residence. However, the primary use must always be as a residence of the donor when occupied by the donor. Furthermore, the portion of the residence rented to a third party should not constitute a majority of the property. Typically, the use of a portion of the residence as a rental property is permissible if the rental portion cannot be subdivided from the entire property.

The IRS has issued numerous private letter rulings dealing with partially rented residential properties.[8] For example, in one situation, a taxpayer created a QPRT and funded it with a 4,000 square foot building. Approximately 3,500 square feet was occupied by the taxpayer as her residence with the remaining portion being rented to an unrelated third party for dwelling purposes at fair market value. The IRS ruled that the property constituted a personal residence within the meaning of the regulations irrespective of the incidental rental portion.[9]

Under the regulations the primary, but not exclusive, use of the property must be residential.[10] As a result, a secondary nonresidential use should not disqualify the residence unless the residence is for transient lodging with services or the property is divisible. The residence cannot be used as a bed and breakfast or hotel; such use will cause an automatic disqualification as a personal residence regardless of how minor such use may be. If the property is divisible, it is advisable to divide the commercial and residential uses, if at all possible, and leave the nonresidential use out of the gift to the QPRT. However, if the residence has some attendant commercial use that is limited and minor in scope, this should not disqualify the residence.[11]

A portion of the residence may also be used as an office if the use is secondary to the use of the property as a residence.[12] For example, if an individual maintains a principal place of business in one room of the principal residence, the residence will not fail to meet the primary residence test merely because a portion of the residence is used in an activity meeting the requirements of Code section 280A(c)(1) or (4).[13]

Residence Held for Donor's Use

If the donor is forced to move into a nursing home on a temporary or permanent basis, the residence may cease to qualify as the donor's personal residence. The regulations allow the residence to keep its status as a "personal residence" so long as it is "held for use" as a personal residence of the donor. The property is considered "held for use" of the donor so long as the property is not occupied by any other person (except the donor's dependents and spouse) and is available at all times for use by the donor as a personal residence.[14] This allows the donor to move to a nursing home without the trust ceasing to be a QPRT. However, if the property is rented during this time or someone other than the donor's dependents (such as the donor's adult child) or spouse reside on the property, they must move out or the trust will no longer be considered a personal residence.[15]

If the residence is not the donor's principal residence, it can still constitute a personal residence if it is either "used" or "held for use" as the donor's personal residence. Vacation homes are commonly used under this section. A residence is "used" as a personal residence if the donor uses it (actually lives in the residence) more than the greater of:

- fourteen days; or

- 10 percent of the number of days it is rented at a fair rental.

This test should be met in the first year the residence is transferred to the QPRT and every succeeding year of the term. The use of the residence is determined based on the donor's use and not that of the donor's family.

Limitations

There are several numerical limits applicable to QPRTs:

1. A QPRT cannot own more than one residence.[16]

2. The donor cannot be the grantor of more than two QPRTs at the same time. For purposes of this limitation, fractional interests in the same residence are treated as one.[17] However, the donor can be the term holder of more than two QPRTs so long as the donor did not create more than two QPRTs. For example, grantor creates a QPRT for his personal residence and a second QPRT for his vacation home, retaining the right to reside in both for a term of ten years. At the same time, grantor's father creates a QPRT with his vacation home and provides the grantor with a term interest. This results in the grantor being the term holder of three trusts, but only the grantor of two trusts; each of the three trusts qualify as a QPRT. Presumably, the grantor can create more than two QPRTs if they are successive, so long as there are no more than two concurrent QPRTs at one time created by the grantor.

3. A personal residence of the donor is either:

- the principal residence of the donor;[18] or

- one other residence of the donor.[19]

So if the grantor is creating the maximum of two QPRTs at one time, the residences must be one of each.

OTHER PROPERTY HELD BY TRUST

In order for the trust to qualify as a QPRT under Code section 2702, the trust must hold a personal residence only. If property other than the personal residence is transferred to the trust, the entire gift becomes subject to gift tax without discounts for the donor's retained interest. Therefore, great care must be exercised that the personal residence rule is not violated. The Regulations provide that certain property may be considered part of the personal residence, but these should be used cautiously. For example, the trust can hold insurance policies on the residence and a limited amount of cash for mortgage payments and expenses (as discussed below). The personal residence may also include fixtures, land and accompanying structures without violating the rule. The specifics are set forth below.

Appurtenant Structures

A personal residence will not be disqualified by the inclusion of "appurtenant structures" and adjacent land.[20] Examples of "appurtenant structures" are garages, guest homes or a caretaker's home. In order to qualify as part of a personal residence, these appurtenant structures must be used for residential purposes. For example, the IRS has held that a vacation home, consisting of a main residence, separate guest facilities, a caretaker's house and other appurtenant structures, qualified as a personal residence.[21] The main home, appurtenant structures and adjacent land were not in excess of what is reasonably appropriate for residential purposes (taking into consideration the resident's size and location). Furthermore, the ruling confirmed that the occupancy by caretakers and temporary guests during the term, by itself, will not disqualify the property.

Adjacent Land

When the personal residence contributed to a QPRT includes adjacent unimproved property, this may cause the QPRT to be disqualified. A personal residence can include adjacent land provided it is not in excess of what is reasonably appropriate for residential purposes (taking into account the residence's size and location).[22] There is no bright line test for what constitutes a reasonable amount of land for residential purposes. All relevant facts and circumstances must be taken into account. Normally, adjacent land becomes an issue when substantial acreage or multiple lots are transferred to the QPRT. Based on a review of private letter rulings between taxpayers and the IRS, there are five factors which will be considered in determining a reasonably appropriate amount of adjacent land:

1. the combined size in comparison to residences in the same neighborhood;

2. demonstrated use for residential purposes;

3. historical or long-term use as a residence;

4. restrictions prohibiting nonresidential use; and

5. restrictions prohibiting partition or development.

When dealing with the primary residence test, there is a special concern when the property contains multiple lots. Although multiple lots are permissible (even in circumstances when the lots are not connected), the donor will need to demonstrate that the multiple lots constitute one residence. This may be done by showing consistent residential use of the land. For example, the IRS has held that a vacation home on one side of an avenue and two lots on the other side were considered a personal residence.[23] The IRS treated the vacation home and the adjacent land as one personal residence because the two lots were not in excess of what is reasonably appropriate for residential purposes. Similarly, the IRS ruled that three parcels of land shown as one tax lot by the tax assessor constituted a residence and adjacent land that was not in excess of what is reasonably appropriate for residential purposes.[24]

Fixtures

Generally, fixtures are considered part of the personal residence because, by their nature, they are affixed to the property and constitute an irremovable part of the residence. However, furniture contained in the residence is not a fixture and could disqualify the QPRT if it is included in the trust.[25] The Treasury Regulations provide an example where inclusion of other assets disqualifies the property as a personal residence:

Example. An individual owns a 200-acre farm, which includes a house, barns, equipment buildings, a silo and enclosure for confinement of animals and transfers it to an irrevocable trust. The individual retains the use of the farm for twenty years with the remainder to the individual's child. The trust is not considered a QPRT because the farm includes assets that do not meet the requirements of a personal residence. It includes disqualifying personal property.[26]

Fractional Interest in Residence

A QPRT can be funded with less than the entire interest in a residence. The regulations permit funding of a QPRT with an undivided fractional interest in a residence.[27] As a result, the donor can transfer to the QPRT either the entire residence or a fractional interest in the residence.

Trusts holding fractional interests in the same residence are treated as one single trust for purposes of the QPRT numerical restriction. Thus, a grantor can transfer an undivided 25 percent interest in a residence to four separate trusts, one for each child. Doing so will not violate the two-personal-residence-trusts limitation (as discussed above) since the four trusts are treated as one QPRT. If the grantor creates separate trusts, it is generally recommended that the term period of each trust be the same. This avoids the potential problems discussed below resulting from the QPRT being a co-owner of the property with someone else.

The advantage to transferring a fractional interest in a residence rather than the entire interest is to reduce the gift tax cost associated with the transfer. A fractional interest discount results from the concept that the whole is worth more than the sum of its parts. Normally, the value of a gift is based on a hypothetical willing-buyer, willing-seller standard. When transferring less than the whole interest in real estate, the value of each fractional interest will be reduced by application of discounts based upon the risk of incurring costs and legal fees in a partition action, together with other fees associated with the co-ownership of the real estate.

There are risks associated with funding a QPRT with a fractional interest. For starters, valuation discounts are likely to be challenged by the IRS. Discounts must be disclosed on a gift tax return. The risk of audit and reassessment is greatest when the claimed discount exceeds estimated partition costs.

Funding a QPRT with a fractional interest in a residence also creates problems because of the co-ownership of the property. If a fractional interest is transferred, the QPRT will hold title as tenants in common with the other owners. It is unclear how some of the tests required to qualify the QPRT will be applied when only a fractional interest in the property is transferred to the QPRT. There are no rulings dealing with co-ownership of the property when the co-owners are not spouses, so there is a risk of creating a fractional interest for someone other than the grantor's spouse or dependents. One solution to this problem is for the donor to rent the property from the co-owner, thereby having exclusive occupancy rights to the entire property. The rental solution also works well if the property is owned by two QPRTs with different expiration dates. For example, the first QPRT terminates if the beneficiaries exercise their right to possess the property, then the "primary use" requirement of the second QPRT which still has not expired may be jeopardized. The rental by the second QPRT to expire avoids the problem.

When spouses create QPRTs for the same residence, the IRS does not seem to be concerned about the co-occupancy issue discussed above.[28] However, if the QPRTs expire at different times, then the co-occupancy issue can become a problem. If the surviving spouse is the beneficiary of the first QPRT to expire, then the co-occupancy issue is not an issue. However, if the beneficiary is not the spouse, then the rental solution should be considered to avoid the co-occupancy problem.

Residence Subject to Mortgage

Often, a donor wishes to transfer a residence that is encumbered by a mortgage to a QPRT. The status of a personal residence is not affected because of the existence of a mortgage.[29] QPRTs are even permitted to hold cash in a separate account for mortgage payments.[30] A QPRT can hold cash for payments of a mortgage that have been incurred or are reasonably expected to be paid within the next six months.[31]

Notwithstanding that it is permissible for the QPRT to own property encumbered by a mortgage and for it to make mortgage payments, it is generally inadvisable to fund a QPRT with an encumbered property. The problem with a mortgage on a residence owned by a

QPRT is twofold. First, the transfer of an encumbered property is considered a gift of only the donor's equity in the property.[32] Second, each time the donor makes a mortgage payment after the residence is owned by the trust, the principal portion of the payment is considered a gift by the donor to the QPRT. This results in gift tax returns being due each year of the trust term.

One solution to the mortgage issue is to pay off the loan prior to funding the trust. The loan document will have to be reviewed, as some do not permit prepayment without penalty. Another solution is to convert the loan to an interest-only loan with a balloon principal payment due and payable at the end of the trust term. Unlike principal payments, interest payments are not considered additional gifts to the trust. When the trust term ends, the donor can make a gift to the beneficiaries to make the principal balloon payment. If not feasible, the property can be sold or the loan can be refinanced.

Finally, the mortgage payments can be treated as loans to the trust by the donor. This should not cause a gift tax issue if the donor is the beneficiary during the QPRT term because the recipient of the gift is the donor as the beneficiary during the term. Eventually, the donor must be paid the amount due on the loan. This can be satisfied by the beneficiaries directly by forgiveness of the loan by the donor once the term expires or by a sale of the property.

PROVISIONS OF THE TRUST

When drafting the QPRT trust agreement there are certain provisions the trust documents "must" have, some that it "may" have, and others that it "should" have. Each of these are discussed below.

Term of the Trust

The first step in drafting the QPRT agreement is to establish the duration of the term of the trust. There are no requirements dictating how long the QPRT term should last. The term of years selected for a QPRT is typically between five and twenty years. The longer the term, the greater the grantor's retained interest and the smaller the gift. In essence, a longer term provides greater tax benefits. There is a risk, however, with using a longer term.

If the grantor dies during the QPRT term, the entire trust property is included in the grantor's estate. Thus, a practitioner should select a term that provides a high probability that the grantor will survive. For a younger client, a greater discount is provided with a longer QPRT term. For an older client, a greater discount is provided with the retention of a reversionary interest below.

The donor should also choose a term which permits the use of the donor's unified credit. This allows the donor to shield the transfer from gift tax. However, the term selected should not use all of the donor's unified credit. If the IRS establishes upon audit a higher value than originally reported, the donor should have some unified credit available to allocate to the additional amount so that no taxes are due.

Mandatory Trust Terms

In order for a trust to qualify as a QPRT, the Treasury Regulations provide a list of mandatory provisions that the trust instrument must contain.[33] There is little flexibility regarding the trust provisions during the QPRT term. Specifically, there are seven provisions that must be included in the governing instrument and continue in effect during the QPRT term in order to qualify as a QPRT:

1. All income of the trust must be distributed to the donor, at least annually.

2. The QPRT must prohibit the distribution of corpus to any beneficiary other than the donor before the term expires.

3. The trust cannot hold any asset other than one residence to be used or held for use as a personal residence of the donor (with the exception of a limited amount of cash for mortgage payments, expenses and improvements).

4. The trust must prohibit the commutation or prepayment of the donor's interest. Commutation is the termination of the trust and dividing of trust property before the trust term ends among the donor and other trust beneficiaries according to their actuarially determined interests. Commutation is contrary to the basic function of a QPRT, which is to promote the making of a completed gift for gift tax purposes and exclusion of the value of the gifted property from the donor's gross estate.

5. The trust must provide that the trust ceases to be a QPRT if the residence ceases to be "used

or held for use" as a personal residence of the term holder.

6. The trust must provide that, if damage or destruction renders the residence unusable, the trust ceases to be a QPRT upon the earlier of:

    a. two years after the damage occurs; or

    b. termination of the term holder's interest, unless prior to such date, repair or replacement of the residence is completed or a new residence is acquired.

7. A QPRT must prohibit the trust from selling or transferring the residence, directly or indirectly, to the donor, the donor's spouse, or an entity controlled by the donor or the donor's spouse, during the retained term of the trust, or at any time after the retained term.[34]

A controlled entity is a corporation in which the donor or the donor's spouse has at least 50 percent ownership of the voting interests or total fair market value of the equity interests, or a partnership in which the donor or the donor's spouse has at least 50 percent ownership of either the capital or profits interest.[35] A sale or transfer to another grantor trust created by the grantor or the grantor's spouse is considered a sale or transfer to the grantor or the grantor's spouse.[36] However, after expiration of the retained term interest, a distribution without consideration is permitted to another grantor trust of the grantor or the grantor's spouse provided such transferee trust prohibits the sale or transfer of the property to the grantor, the grantor's spouse or an entity controlled by the grantor or the grantor's spouse.[37]

Optional Trust Terms

The regulations also recite provisions that the QPRT may but are not required to contain. The regulations permit the trust to hold cash contributions during the QPRT term in a separate account. However, the Regulations provide an extensive list of the restrictions and limitations imposed on the amounts and manner the funds can be used. The funds may be used as follows:

1. For the payment of trust expenses such as mortgage payments already incurred or reasonably expected to be paid by the trust

within six months from the date the additional funds are contributed;

2. For improvements to the residence to be paid by the trust within six months from the date the additional funds are contributed;[38]

3. For purchase by the trust of the initial residence provided the purchase occurs within three months of the creation of the trust and the trustee must have previously entered into a contract to purchase that residence or acquire a replacement residence.

4. For purchase by the trust of a residence to replace another residence, within three months of the date the additional funds are contributed, provided no additional funds are contributed for this purpose, and the trust may not hold any such additional funds, unless a trustee has previously entered into a contract to purchase that residence.[39]

5. The QPRT may also hold one or more insurance policies on the residence.[40] The trust may make payments for the insurance proceeds payable to the trust resulting from the damage to or destruction of the residence. If included, the trust must require the reinvestment of the insurance proceeds within two years in a replacement residence.

6. The QPRT may permit the sale of the residence (except to the donor, donor's spouse, or certain related entities) and permit the trust to hold the sale proceeds.[41] There are additional limitations which are discussed in section below.

If the trust is permitted to hold cash for purposes (1) through (4) above, the trust must require the trustee to determine at least quarterly the amount of cash held in trust in excess of the amounts permitted and thereafter distribute the excess to the grantor. Upon termination of the QPRT, any excess cash not used must be distributed to the grantor within thirty days of the termination.[42] Any income held by the trust must be distributed to the grantor at least annually.[43]

Although the trust can hold a limited amount for cash to pay expenses, for simplicity purposes, it is recommended that the trust not pay the expenses and instead the donor pay all the expenses directly. The trust may provide that the donor, instead of the trust, will pay all expenses of the property during the term of the trust.[44] From a practical standpoint, most QPRT are administered this way since it avoids the complexity and tedious record keeping described above.

Death of Term Holder and Reversionary Interest

The next step in drafting the QPRT agreement is to determine whether the grantor will or will not retain a reversionary interest in the QPRT. Pursuant to the regulations, the grantor is able to retain a reversionary interest in the transferred property.[45] The reversionary interest means that if the grantor dies during the trust term, the trust property will be returned to the grantor's estate enabling the grantor to dispose of the property as the grantor directs. The donor is considered to have a reversionary interest if either:

1. the trust automatically reverts to the donor's probate estate; or

2. the donor retains the right to direct the trustee to distribute the property to the donor's probate estate or to the donor's creditors.[46]

The grantor's retention of a reversionary interest reduces the value of the gift to the remainder beneficiaries, thereby producing greater tax savings. When a grantor retains a reversionary interest in the residence, the value of the interest retained by the grantor is increased to include the value of the retainer interest. This in turn reduces the value of the interest that passes to the remainder beneficiaries, which is the amount that is subject to gift tax. Consequently, retaining a reversion allows the grantor to dispose of the property and claim a gift tax valuation discount. With respect to estate taxes, there should be no negative estate tax consequences from the retention of a reversion. The trust property is included in the estate of the grantor if the grantor dies during the term whether the grantor retains a reversionary interest or not.

While the donors of most QPRTs retain a reversionary interest because of the increased gift tax savings, there may be a good reason not to have the property revert to the donor. A provision returning the assets to the donor's estate will subject the trust assets to the reach of the deceased donor's creditors. Therefore, if there are creditor concerns, this may not be desirable.

CESSATION OF QPRT STATUS

A trust ceases to qualify as a QPRT if the residence is not used or held for use as a personal residence of the grantor.[47] This normally occurs when the residence is sold, condemned, or there has been casualty damage to it.

Sales of Residence

The QPRT may permit the sale of the residence (except as prohibited in the discussion above).[48] If the residence is sold, the sales proceeds may be held in a separate account. If the governing instrument does not provide for a separate account, the trust ceases to be a QPRT at the time of the sale.[49] If the sales proceeds are permitted to be held in a separate account, the trust continues to have QPRT status until the earlier of either:

- the purchase of a residence;

- the termination of term period; or

- two years from the date of sale.[50]

- In effect, the regulations provide a two year grace period following the sale of a residence to reinvest the proceeds in another replacement residence. The replacement residence must meet all of the requirements of a "personal residence."

If the newly purchased residence is less expensive than the original residence, the reinvested proceeds continue to retain their QPRT status, with the excess proceeds from the sale ceasing to be a QPRT.

If the newly purchased residence is more expensive than the original residence, there are five ways to consummate the purchase:

1. the donor can pay for the difference as a gift to the QPRT;

2. the QPRT and the donor can jointly purchase the residence;

3. the donor can jointly purchase the residence with the QPRT and then gift his interest to the trust;

4. the donor can jointly purchase the residence with the QPRT and then gift his interest to a new QPRT; or

5. the donor can loan the money to the QPRT.

For income tax purposes, if the residence is sold during the term period and the QPRT is entirely a donor trust, the capital gains exclusion for a sale of a primary residence is available.[51]

Condemnation, Casualty and other Reasons

If casualty or fire renders the residence unusable, the QPRT status does not immediately end. Similar to the regulations pertaining to the sale of the residence discussed above, there is a two year grace period following the event for the replacement or repair to be completed. Otherwise, the trust will cease to be a QPRT.[52]

If the residence ceases to be used or held for use as the donor's residence for any reason other than sale, condemnation or casualty, then the QPRT status is terminated instantly and the two year grace period does not apply.

Option upon Cessation

With the cessation of QPRT status, the trust must provide that either:

1. the trust terminates and the trustee must distribute all trust assets outright to the donor;

2. the trust is converted to a Grantor Retained Annuity Trust ("GRAT") with the grantor receiving an annuity interest for the balance of the term (See Chapter 12 on Granter Retained Annuity Trust); or

3. the trustee has discretion to selection one of the two foregoing options.[53]

The trust terms must require that distribution or conversion occur within thirty days of the cessation to qualify as a QPRT.[54]

The first option of termination and outright distribution to the donor is the least desirable option. By distributing the entire trust fund, including all appreciation from the date of transfer, all estate tax savings are negated and the full value of the property will be includible in the donor's gross estate. This option also causes the trust property to be reachable by the donor's creditors.

The third option of providing the trustee with the option to choose between an outright distribution or conversion allows the trustee to make an informed decision based on all the facts as of the date the property ceases to be a QPRT. However if the donor serves as trustee during the QPRT term, the option should not be used as it makes the funding of the trust an incomplete gift, causing estate tax inclusion.

The second option of conversion to a GRAT is the most desirable option and is the one that is included in the IRS's sample QPRT trust agreement. This option allows the donor to retain some of the tax savings even though a portion of the trust property will return to the donor.

Conversion to GRAT

If the terms of the QPRT require a conversion to a GRAT or if the trustee elects this option, the trust pays out an annuity to the donor for the remaining QPRT term. The GRAT portion of the QPRT must then meet the requirements of the GRAT regulations.[55] The right to receive the annuity amount must begin on the "cessation date."[56] The cessation date is the date of the sale, damage or destruction of the residence or when the residence is no longer used or held for use as a personal residence. However, the governing instrument can allow the trustee to defer the payment of the annuity amount until thirty days after the assets are converted to a qualified annuity. All annuity payments, including the deferred payments, are calculated using the §7520 rate. The value of the residence and the mortality rates used are what is in effect upon creation of the QPRT, not at the time of the conversion.[57]

After the Term of the Trust

If the donor survives the QPRT term, the QPRT governing provisions vanish, the interest of the donor terminates and the trust assets pass to the beneficiaries named in the trust. The gift of the residence is then complete.

Identifying the Beneficiaries. The beneficiaries at the time the QPRT term expires can be the donor's issue who can receive their interest either outright or in further trust. The simplest disposition is outright to the children. However, if the donor intends to continue to use the residence by renting it, it is usually better to have the residence remain in trust for the children. This avoids the issue of multiple landlords if there are several children. It also protects the residence from the claims of the children's creditors and spouses.

Before the residence passes to the donor's children or heirs, the donor may want to provide for his or her spouse. The donor can give the spouse a life interest in the trust or a limited power of appointment over the remainder interest. Giving the spouse a life interest in the trust after the QPRT term ends will allow the spouse the right to continue living in the property rent-free.[58] As long as there is no express agreement that the donor has a right to occupy the property together with the spouse, the donor can reside on the property without it being brought back into the donor's estate under Code section 2036. The spouse can also be granted a limited power of appointment. However, the spouse should not be given the right to appoint either income or principal back to the donor as this could result in estate tax inclusion.

Rental of Residence. Often upon termination of the QPRT term, the donor will want to reside in the residence. There are options which permit the donor to reside in the residence:

- rent the residence from the remaindermen

- utilize a reverse-QPRT (as discussed below).

Regardless of the method used, the donor needs to be cautious not to cause the residence to be included in his or her gross estate. The most common method used is for the donor to rent the residence from the remaindermen at fair market value rent. If fair market rent is not paid, the entire trust property will be included in the donor's gross estate.[59] If the donor has not retained the right to rent the residence in the terms of the QPRT, a formal lease agreement is recommended. It is prudent to execute the lease before the QPRT term ends.[60] Furthermore, a professional appraisal should be obtained to establish the fair market value rent for the residence. The rent should be recomputed annually to adjust for any changes in fair market value. There is a risk of estate tax inclusion if the rent is not adjusted annually.

It is also acceptable for the donor to retain the right to lease the residence so that there is no need to negotiate the lease terms after the QPRT expires and to make sure that the house will not be rented to someone else.

Prearranged leases of the residence have been approved in several letter rulings by the IRS and will not cause the inclusion of the property in the donor's gross estate.[61] The terms of such lease must be at arms-length with the payment of fair market value rent.

CHOICE OF TRUSTEE

Selecting the trustee of the QPRT is an important decision. The consequences that flow from this decision are dependent on who serves during the term and after.

During the QPRT Term. The QPRT regulations do not prohibit the donor from serving as trustee during the term. From a tax perspective, there is no disadvantage to serving as trustee. The donor is already the owner of the trust for income tax purposes and its assets will be includible should the donor die before the end of the term. There would be no other penalty to the donor stemming from serving as trustee during the term. However, it is advisable to have an independent party serve as trustee because state or local law could have some bearing on the issue. The trust may be considered a self-settled trust, which will not protect the trust assets from the donor's creditors unless the trust is located in a jurisdiction that permits self-settled trusts.[62]

After the QPRT Term. It is not recommended that the donor serve as trustee after the QPRT term. The donor has survived the term, thus excluding the trust assets from the donor's gross estate. If the donor serves as trustee after the term, this could cause the trust assets to be brought back into the donor's estate. The Code has two provisions, Sections 2036 and 2038, which could cause inclusion. Simply put, if the donor serves as trustee or co-trustee and retains the power to designate who may enjoy the property or the income therefrom, the trust assets will be includible in the donor's estate.[63]

If the donor retains the power to alter, amend, revoke or terminate the trust, the trust assets are includible in the donor's estate.[64] Thus, retaining the power to change beneficial interests or the timing of the enjoyment of trust property will cause inclusion. Notably, if the donor retains the power to remove the trustee and appoint himself or herself, then the donor is treated as holding the trustee's powers, causing inclusion.[65] The prudent approach is for the donor not to serve as trustee after the term. The donor can, however, retain the power to remove and replace the existing trustee with an independent trustee.[66]

Reformation

If the QPRT does not comply with all the regulatory requirements, the trust should be modified.[67] Modification can be accomplished through either judicial modification or non-judicial modification (if available under state law). It is recommended that the QPRT trust instrument permit non-judicial modification or reformation to avoid the cost and delay of initiating a court proceeding. The modification or reformation must be commenced within ninety days after the due date (including extensions) for filing the gift tax return reporting the transfer of the residence to the trust. Completion of reformation must occur within a reasonable time after commencement. If the modification or reformation is not completed by the due date (including extensions) for filing the gift tax return, ninety days is still allowed so long as the donor or donor's spouse attaches a statement of disclosure to the return.

There have also been several private letter rulings which permitted the modification of existing QPRTs prior to the expiration of the QPRT term.[68] The technique used was the modification of the QPRT term prior to its expiration so as to allow the donor to reside in the residence for a longer time period. The QPRTs granted either a power to appoint the trust corpus to the remaindermen or allowed them to extend the donor's term when the original term expired. The remaindermen had exercised their right to extend the donor's term. The IRS ruled that the extension was a taxable gift, not subject to the special valuation rule of Code section 2702, as long as the trusts qualified as QPRTs. However, the IRS refused to express an opinion about the possible tax consequences under Code section 2036.

Reverse QPRTs

In the typical use of a QPRT, the donor is a parent and the remaindermen are the parent's children. Upon the expiration of the QPRT term, the parent may desire to continue to live in the residence but may be unable to afford fair market value rent or be unwilling to pay rent to the remaindermen. The IRS has ruled that at the expiration of the first QPRT, the remaindermen may transfer the residence to a second QPRT (a "reverse QPRT"), and provide the donor (parent) with a term interest in which to reside on the property.[69] The reverse QPRT must meet all the statutory requirements and Treasury Regulations governing a QPRT. At the expiration of the reverse QPRT, the property will be returned to the remaindermen in equal shares as tenants in common.

There are some advantages and disadvantages associated with using a reverse QPRT. Some notable advantages include the ability of the donor to use the residence at the end of the QPRT term. This technique also does not force a parent to rent their own residence from their child or children. However, the remaindermen are treated as making a taxable gift to the donor. Another disadvantage to this technique is that the IRS has not provided guidance as to whether the residence is included in the parent's estate under Code section 2036 should the parent die during the reverse QPRT term. Also, there is a risk that the IRS will attack the transaction with the use of the step transaction doctrine (as discussed below).

TAX CONSIDERATIONS

The principal reasons for using a QPRT are the estate and gift tax savings that can be achieved. Income tax benefits can simultaneously be achieved but caution must be taken to avoid any generation-skipping transfer tax consequences.

Gift Tax

Upon the transfer of the residence to the QPRT, the donor is making a completed gift to the trust beneficiaries for federal gift tax purposes. The value of the gift, however, is not the full fair market value of the transferred property. The gift is the fair market value of the personal residence less the donor's retained right to reside in the residence. This amount is only a fraction of the full amount of the property.

Valuation and Reporting

The value of the retained interest is determined by the interest rate at the time the gift is made (the section 7520 rate for the month of the transfer[70]), the length of the QPRT term and the donor's life expectancy. A higher interest rate equates to a greater retained interest and a smaller gift. Hence, QPRTs are more advantageous when interest rates are high. Also, a longer trust term equates to a greater retained interest and a smaller gift. Thus, the greatest tax benefits are achieved in a high interest rate environment with the selection of a long term.

Gift tax will be due upon the transfer to the trust because the donor is making a completed gift to the remaindermen. A donor can apply the unified credit to protect the transfer from tax or pay the tax if the donor has already exhausted the credit. The gift to the trust does not qualify for the gift tax annual exclusion or the marital deduction.

If the donor dies during the QPRT term, the trust property is includible at its full value in the donor's estate. In theory, because the donor made a taxable gift when the QPRT was created and now the full value is included for estate tax purposes, this results in double taxation. However, in computing the estate tax, gifts which are included in the gross estate of the decedent are not counted. The estate will also be given a credit for gift taxes that were paid on the gift to the QPRT. In sum, either the property is taxed for gift tax purposes at a discounted value or it is taxed for estate tax purposes at its full value, with a credit for gift taxes paid or gift tax exemption used.

The IRS can attack the gift to the QPRT in two ways: (a) by asserting that the gift was undervalued; or (b) by asserting that the special valuation exception for residences[71] does not apply. The gift should be reported on a gift tax return when the property is transferred to the QPRT. The gift should be adequately disclosed to start the clock on the three-year statute of limitations the IRS has to challenge a gift tax return.[72] If there is no adequate disclosure, gift tax may be assessed at any time.

Additionally, it is imperative that the donor make a completed gift of the residence upon the creation of the trust. The donor's retention of the power to control the disposition of the remainder interest will render the gift incomplete.[73] The donor cannot be given the power to add new beneficiaries or change existing interests in the remainder. Moreover, the donor cannot give a power to another that enables the third party to revoke the donor's retained interest.[74] An independent trustee can be given the power to make minor amendments as long as they do not alter the donor's interest in the trust or violate any of the Treasury Regulations.

Married Donors

In addition to numerous tax considerations discussed above upon the creation of a QPRT, there are two additional hurdles that must be overcome: the step transaction doctrine and the reciprocal trust doctrine. These hurdles become more significant when married donors are involved.

The step transaction doctrine is used by the IRS to view a transaction as a whole and disregard intervening steps. In the context of a QPRT, the doctrine could be used to disregard an intervening transaction that the parties thought qualified for the gift tax marital deduction. This would occur, for example, if one spouse transferred their interest in the property to the other spouse who then transferred the entire property to a QPRT. The IRS could combine the steps and disregard the initial transfer that should have qualified for the gift tax marital deduction. There is also a risk of estate tax inclusion if the non-transferring spouse is given a remainder interest in the QPRT. Although the risk of the IRS attacking the transactions with the step transaction doctrine is minimal, caution should be taken. The simplest solution is to permit a certain amount of time to elapse between the intervening steps.

The reciprocal trust doctrine is another judicially created doctrine that can be used to attack the creation of QPRTs by married donors. The doctrine applies when trusts are "interrelated, and that the arrangement, to the extent mutual value leaves the settlors in approximately the same economic position as they would have been in had they created trusts naming themselves as life beneficiaries."[75] If QPRTs are treated as reciprocal, each spouse will be treated as the donor of the other spouse's QPRT. The result is that the QPRTs will fail to remove the properties from their respective estates, thus defeating the principal purpose of using a QPRT. If the married couple owns the property jointly, they have three options:

1. partition the property and have both spouses donate a fractional interest to a QPRT;

2. both contribute to a QPRT without first partitioning the property; or

3. transfer the property into the name of one spouse and then transfer the property to the QPRT.

These options all carry some risk of creditor attachment, unfortunately.

A common technique for a married couple is gift splitting, which allows them to elect to report gifts made by them as made one-half by each.[76] This technique allows one spouse to use the exclusions of the other spouse. Married donors should not split the gift to the QPRT as this has adverse tax consequences. Should the donor die during the QPRT term, the entire gift is included in the donor-spouse's estate under Code section 2036. Importantly, there is no relief provided in the estate tax calculation.[77] The net effect is that the same property will be taxed more than once. It is fully taxable in the donor's estate and half is taxed to the spouse. A married couple should instead either: (a) have both spouses make fractional interest gifts of the residence, with remainders passing to their children (not to each other in order to avoid any implication of reciprocal trusts); or (b) have the healthier spouse make the gift.

Estate Tax

The estate tax consequences of using a QPRT are dependent on whether or not the donor survives the QPRT term. They are also dependent on the existence of a reversionary interest. If the donor survives the QPRT term, the transferred property will be removed from the gross estate. In addition to the transferred property being removed from the donor's estate, any appreciation in the property during the trust term ("post-transfer appreciation") will also be excluded. The one drawback to this is that the beneficiaries will inherit the post-transfer appreciation. Also, there will be no "step-up" in basis for federal income tax purposes upon the donor's death. The loss of a basis step up has become more relevant as the income tax rates can surpass the estate tax rate for some wealthy individuals, making income tax planning more of a priority.

If the donor dies during the QPRT term, the full value of the residence will be included in the donor's gross estate.[78] The amount includible is the date-of-death value of the property. The donor's estate benefits from a credit for any gift tax paid or any unified credit that was applied to the transfer.[79] The net effect is that the donor will not be in a worse position from a transfer tax standpoint (except for the transaction costs). If the inclusion of the assets creates additional estate taxes, the estate will not be able to use them to pay the estate taxes. The donor can hedge the risk of inclusion by creating and funding an irrevocable life insurance trust (ILIT). The term of the ILIT should last as long as the QPRT. Hence, it can provide liquidity to pay any taxes due from the inclusion of the residence. Estate tax inclusion can also be triggered by the donor continuing to reside in the residence after the QPRT term without paying rent. The donor should pay fair-market rental value to the trust if residing the property after the QPRT term.

There is also an estate tax risk which stems from the ability of a donor's creditors to reach the assets of a QPRT. Whether creditors can reach the transferred assets is determined under state law. Generally, a creditor can reach assets up to the amount a trustee can pay to or for the benefit of a donor.[80] If the creditor can reach the trust's assets, the transfer is incomplete for gift tax purposes and thus includible for estate tax purposes. The risk is greatest when the trustee is given the discretion upon the cessation of QPRT status to either distribute the assets outright or convert to a GRAT. The mere existence of this power to return the residence to the donor may cause the trust to be subject to creditor's claims. The net effect is that there is no completed gift until the end of the QPRT term when the donor gives up control of the property. As a result, a valuation discount for the donor's retained interest for gift tax purposes may be disallowed. Thus, it is best to have the QPRT convert to a GRAT and not provide the trustee with the discretion to choose between an outright distribution or conversion.

If the QPRT has converted to a GRAT and the donor dies during the QPRT term, the full value of the residence is not included in the gross estate. Instead, the gross estate will only include the portion of the trust property that is necessary to produce the annuity amount, using the relevant interest rate (the section 7520 rate).

Special consideration should also be given to the estate tax apportionment in the event the QPRT is included in the donor's gross estate for estate tax purposes. Pursuant to Code section 2207B, if a person dies during the QPRT term, causing the QPRT to be included in the donor's gross estate under §2036, the proportionate share of estate taxes attributable to this asset will have to be paid from the QPRT itself unless the donor's will specifically waives the right of recovery. This code provision could upset the estate plan if the donor's intent was for estate taxes attributable to the QPRT to be paid out of other assets of the donor's taxable estate. To avoid this problem, the donor should specifically provide for overcoming the presumption of section 2207B in his or her will.[81]

Generation-Skipping Transfer Tax

In addition to the federal estate and gift taxes consideration relating to a QPRT, generation-skipping transfer (GST) tax[82] issues must also be examined. The GST issues of a QPRT can be tricky and special attention must be given to avoid messy problems. The GST tax is imposed on transfers that "skip" a generation.

The transferee is referred to as a "skip person."[83] The classification as a "skip person" or "non-skip person" depends on the generation assignment of the transferee.[84] There are different generation assignment rules dependent on whether the transferee is related to the transferor, is unrelated to the transferor, or is not an individual (e.g., a business entity or a trust). Additionally, there is a generation assignment rule that may apply if an individual's parent is deceased at the time of the transfer.[85] There are three types of transfers or events to a skip person that trigger GST tax: a direct skip, a taxable termination, and a taxable distribution.

A direct skip occurs when a transfer is made that is subject to gift or estate tax and the transferee is a skip person.[86] Direct skips are rarely an issue with QPRTs because of the donor's retained interest in the trust. Since the donor retains an interest in the trust, the QPRT is not a "skip person" and therefore transfers to the QPRT are not "direct skips." The only time a direct skip[87] is relevant with respect to a QPRT is if the donor dies during the term and the trust assets are distributed to skip persons outright or held in further trust for their benefit.

A taxable termination occurs when the trust beneficiaries are skip persons and non-skip persons and the interests of the non-skip beneficiaries terminate.[88] With a QPRT, a taxable termination can only occur after the QPRT term expires since, prior to the expiration of the term, the donor who is a non-skip person is the beneficiary of the QPRT. A taxable termination would occur at the end of the trust term if the trust assets pass to skip persons.

A taxable distribution occurs when the trustee makes a distribution to a beneficiary who is a skip person and the distribution is neither a direct skip nor a taxable termination.[89]

Similar to taxable terminations, a taxable distribution cannot occur in a QPRT until the QPRT term expires. A taxable distribution occurs if the trust continues after the QPRT term expires and non-exempt distributions are made to skip persons.

Like many other taxes, there are some exceptions and exemptions to the general rule. For GST tax, one exception is the GST annual exclusion.[90] The GST annual exclusion provides that gifts that are nontaxable for gift tax purposes are also nontaxable for GST purposes if the distributions under the trust can be made only to a single individual and the trust is includable in that individual's estate if the individual dies before the trust terminates.[91] The GST annual exclusion[92] does not apply to QPRTs because it only applies to direct skips. As discussed above, transfers to a QPRT cannot be a direct skip because the donor has an interest in the trust, disqualifying it from constituting a skip person.

Once it is determined that GST may be triggered, consideration should be given to allocating the GST exemption to the trust. Every individual is entitled to an exemption for GST tax purposes.[93] In 2017, the GST exemption amount is $5,490,000. The problem with QPRTs and GST is that the time for allocation of the GST exemption is not at the same time that the trust is created and the gift is made.

If the donor's GST exemption is going to be allocated to the QPRT, the allocation cannot be effective until the expiration of the QPRT term. The reason for this is the estate tax inclusion period ("ETIP") rule. The ETIP rule creates one of the most difficult planning problems with a QPRT and makes it unpopular to use as a generation-skipping vehicle.

For gift tax purposes, the donor's gift is complete once the residence is transferred to the QPRT.[94] The gift tax value is fully established as of that date and because of the donor's retained interest in the trust, the value is discounted. The donor allocates his or her gift tax exemption amount at that time. Unfortunately, the same cannot be done for the GST exemption allocation. The ETIP is the period during which, if the donor died, the transferred property would still be includable in the donor's estate.[95] The ETIP rule provides that the allocation of the GST exemption cannot be made before the close of the ETIP period.[96] As a result, for purposes of allocating the GST exemption, the value of the transferred property will be the fair market value at the end of the QPRT term, at which time the valuation discounts caused by the donor's retained interest are no longer available and any appreciation in value of the residence must be included.

The predeceased ancestor rule is also another problematic area for QPRTs and GST. In order to determine whether the GST tax has been triggered and a transfer has been made to a "skip person", each person involved with the transfer must be assigned to a generation. This generation assignment occurs at the time the transfer is subject to gift or estate tax. However, if at the time the gift is complete a descendant of the transferor was already deceased, the issue of that deceased descendant moves up one generation.[97] This is known as the "predeceased ancestor rule".

For example, if the predeceased ancestor rule applies, a grandchild would be assigned to the generation level of a child. If there was a transfer to the grandchild, there would be no generation-skipping transfer because the grandchild is no longer considered a skip person. However, if the child dies after the commencement of the trust, the descendants do not move up a generation since the deceased ancestor rule applies at the time the gift is made. This means that grandchildren remain skip persons. This creates a major problem for any QPRT that distributes to the descendants of a deceased beneficiary which is often the case.

Income Tax

Generally, it is desirable for a QPRT to be treated as a grantor trust. Structuring the trust as a grantor trust has many advantages. During the QPRT term, the grantor trust status allows the grantor to deduct mortgage interest payments and real estate taxes for federal income tax purposes. In the event the residence is sold, the grantor trust status enables the donor to be eligible for the capital gains exclusion for a sale of a primary residence thereby allowing the grantor to exclude gain up to $250,000 from the sale of a residence if it meets the requirement of code section 121.[98]

After the term expires, the grantor trust status ensures that the rental payments made by the grantor to the trustee are free from any income tax. Thus, the payment of rent will not generate income to the trust. There was a risk that if rent is paid to a grantor trust, the IRS may contend that the grantor has retained the economic benefit of the property. However, a recent revenue ruling resolved this issue and there should not be any risk of inclusion under Sections 2036 or 2038 of the Code.[99] Otherwise, if the trust is not a grantor trust, the rental payments to the trust will constitute gross income, but the income can be offset by any depreciation deductions claimed on the property.

- *During the QPRT Term-* A QPRT is generally structured as a "grantor trust" from the outset. This means that the grantor is treated as the owner of the trust for income tax purposes during the QPRT term. A QPRT is automatically structured as a grantor trust as to the income portion of the trust because of grantor's retained interest.[100] However, additional provisions must be included to trigger grantor trust status as to the principal portion of the trust. One such provision would be the inclusion of a reversionary interest in the grantor in the trust property so long as the reversionary interest's value exceeds 5 percent of the value of the trust property upon the trust's creation.[101]

- *After the QPRT Term-* Once the QPRT term expires, the trust will no longer constitute a grantor trust under the qualifying rules above and must qualify otherwise. One way to achieve grantor trust status once the QPRT term expires is to make the grantor's spouse a permissible beneficiary.[102] The downside is that the death of the spouse or divorce will terminate grantor trust status. Therefore, other methods to trigger grantor trust status should be considered. When grantor trust status ends, the grantor is treated as having transferred the trust property to the non- grantor trust or to the remaindermen if the trust also terminates at that time.[103] If the property is not encumbered, there are no income tax consequences for the grantor. If there is a mortgage and its value exceeds the grantor's basis in the property, the grantor will realize gain equal to the excess value.

Income Tax Basis

The value of the residence and its basis (the cost of acquiring the residence, increased by capital expenditures and decreased by depreciation deductions) must be taken into account when deciding whether to pursue the formation of a QPRT. Generally, significant tax savings are achieved by the use of a high-valued property. However, using low basis property can offset any estate tax savings upon a sale of the property after the trust term.

When beneficiaries inherit property, including a residence, the beneficiaries get a basis in that property equal to the estate tax value on date of death.[104] If the value on date of death is higher than the basis the decedent had in the property before death, the beneficiaries get a step up in basis. In contrast, beneficiaries that acquire property by gift get carryover basis, which is the donor's basis in the property.[105]

In order to truly analyze the tax savings of a QPRT, the loss of the step up in basis should always be deducted from the anticipated estate tax savings. Therefore, the increased incomes taxes expected to be due upon sale should be subtracted from the value of the estimated estate tax savings. If the property is not expected to be sold because it is cherished by the family, then the fact that the property may have a low basis should not be an issue. However, if the property is expected to be sold, the analysis should be done. This is especially the case where the property has a low basis, is expected to appreciate significantly during the term, and will likely be sold by the beneficiaries at the end of the term.

Income Tax Exclusion

Code section 121 provides that when a taxpayer sells a principal residence, the taxpayer can exclude gain up to $250,000 from the sale of a residence that was owned and used as the taxpayer's principal residence for at least two of the five years preceding the sale.[106] If the residence is owned by the QPRT and is sold during the term period, provided the QPRT is entirely a grantor trust, the capital gains exclusion for a sale of a primary residence is available.

NONTAX CONSIDERATIONS

In addition to a comprehensive analysis of the tax consequences that result from the use of a QPRT, non-tax factors should also be considered. Non-tax factors may include the costs associated with the creation and administration of the trust as well as the benefits that may be lost or reduced from its use.

Costs

There may also be costs associated with transferring a property into a trust, such as legal fees, appraisal fees and recording fees. Costs may be incurred if the transfer of the residence into trust causes the loss of title insurance protection. A review of the existing homeowner's policy should be conducted to ensure that the policy will not be terminated, or to ensure that there will not be an increase in premium payments upon the transfer of the residence.

Loss of Benefits

When a QPRT is established, a deed must be executed transferring the property to the trust. State or local laws may place restrictions or requirements for the transfer to be completed. Florida, for example, requires a spouse to join in the transfer of homestead property that is owned exclusively by the other spouse.

The transfer of the property to a QPRT may also cause the loss of real estate tax exemptions and/or increase in property taxes. For example, Florida permits a taxpayer to continue to claim the benefits of the homestead exemption for real property tax purposes once the property is transferred to a QPRT. The donor retains beneficial title to the residence because there has not been a change in ownership during the QPRT term.[107] The advantage of homestead status for real property purposes is reduced property taxes. However, at the end of the QPRT term, when the property passes to the remainder beneficiaries, there is a revaluation of the property causing an increase in property taxes. Some practitioners recommend a ninety-eight-year or longer lease be entered into before the end of the trust term between the donor and the beneficiaries to retain the homestead benefits and avoid the revaluation.[108] Although this technique has been approved in certain circuits, there is a concern that such a long term lease will be deemed a retained interest under Code section 2036.

CHAPTER ENDNOTES

1. I.R.C. §2702(a)(1).
2. I.R.C. §2702(a)(3)(ii).
3. Treas. Reg. §25.2702-5(c)(5).
4. Treas. Reg. §25.2702-5(c)(2).
5. Treas. Reg. §25.2702-5(c)(2).
6. Treas. Reg. §25.2702-5(c)(2)(iii).
7. PLR 9328040 and PLR 9249014.
8. PLR 9609015, PLR 9741004, PLR9816003, PLR 9701046, and PLR 1999-06014.
9. PLR 9609015.
10. Treasury Regulations section 25.2702-5(c)(2)(iii).
11. PLRs 9606003, 9739024.
12. Id.
13. Treas. Reg. §25.2702-5(c)(2)(iii).
14. Treas. Reg. §25.2702-5(c)(7)(i). Treasury regulations do not define dependent. The income tax definition of dependent should qualify. See I.R.C. §152(a).
15. Treas. Reg. §25.2702-5(d), Ex. 5.
16. Treas. Reg. §25.2702-5(c)(5)(i).
17. Treas. Reg. §25.2702-5(a)(1).
18. Stock in a co-operative apartment is considered a personal residence. PLR 9151046. If the co-op board of directors do not approve transfer of stock to a QPRT, in PLR 9249014, 9433016 and 199925027, the transfer of beneficial title to the stock and

lease to the QPRT while continuing to hold legal title as nominee for the trust qualifies as a transfer of a personal residence for purposes of the QPRT rules.
19. Treas. Reg. §25.2702-5(c)(2)(i).
20. Treas. Reg. §25.2702-5(c)(2)(ii).
21. PLR 9718007.
22. Id.
23. PLR 9503025.
24. PLR 8529035.
25. Treas. Reg. §1.1034-1(c)(3)(i).
26. Treas. Reg. §25.2702-5(d), Ex. 3.
27. Treas. Reg. §25.2702-5(c)(2)(i)(C).
28. PLR 2000-10013.
29. Treas. Reg. §25.2702-5(c)(2)(ii).
30. Treas. Reg. §25.2702-5(c)(5)(ii)(A-B).
31. Treas. Reg. §25.2702-5(c)(5)(ii)(A)(1). Art. II(A)(3).
32. Treas. Reg. §§20.2053-7, 20.2056(b)-4(b).
33. Treas. Reg. §25.2702-5(c)(1). See Rev. Proc. 2003-42 for a QPRT sample governing instrument that meets the QPRT requirements.
34. Treas. Reg. §§25.2702-5(c)(3)-(7).
35. Treas. Reg. §§25.2701-2(b)(5)(ii) and (iii).
36. Treas. Reg. §25.2702-5(c)(9).
37. Id.
38. Treas. Reg. §25.2702-5(c)(5)(ii)(B).
39. Treas. Reg. §25.2702-5(c)(5)(ii)(A)(1) Art II. (A)(3).
40. Treas. Reg. §25.2702-5(c)(5)(ii)(D).
41. Treas. Reg. §25.2702-5(c)(5)(ii)(C)
42. Treas. Reg. §25.2702-5(c)(9).
43. Treas. Reg. §25.2702-5(c)(3).
44. Treas. Reg. §25.2702-5(b)(1).
45. See Treas. Reg. §25.7520-3(b)(1)(i)(C).
46. Id.
47. Treas. Reg. §25.2702-5(c)(7)(i).
48. Treas. Reg. §25.2702-5(c)(ii)(C).
49. Treas. Reg. §25.2702-5(c)(7)(ii).
50. Treas. Reg. §25.2702-5(c)(7)(ii).
51. I.R.C. §121, PLR 2001-04005, 1999-12026.
52. Treas. Reg. §25.2702-5(c)(7)(iii)(A).
53. Treas. Reg. §25.2702-5(c)(8)(i).
54. Id.
55. See Treas. Reg. §25.2502-3 et al.
56. Treas. Reg. §§25.2702-5(c)(8)(ii)(B).
57. Treas. Reg. §§25.2702-5(c)(8)(ii)(C)(2).
58. PLR 9735035 and PLR 9741004.
59. I.R.C. §2036.
60. Estate of Riese v. Comm'r., TCM 2011-60.
61. PRLs 9827037, 98290020.
62. See The American College of Trust and Estate Counsel (ACTEC), "ACTEC Comparison of the Domestic Asset Protection Trust Statutes", available online at: www.actec.org/assets/1/6/Shaftel-Comparison-of-the-Domestic-Asset-Protection-Trust-Statutes.pdf

QUALIFIED PERSONAL RESIDENCE TRUSTS

63. I.R.C. §2036.

64. I.R.C. §2038.

65. Treas. Reg. §§20.2036-1(b)(3), 20.2038-1(a)(3).

66. Rev. Rul. 95-58.

67. Treas. Reg. §25.2702-5(a)(2).

68. PLRs 201024012, 201019012, 201019007, 201019006.

69. PLRs 200814011, 200848003, 200901019.

70. The section 7520 rate is an interest rate (rounded to the nearest 2/10ths of 1 percent) equal to 120 percent of the Federal midterm rate in effect for the month in which the valuation date (the date the QPRT is created) falls.

71. I.R.C. §2702(a)(3)(A)(ii).

72. I.R.C. §6501(a); Treas. Reg. §201.6501(c)-1(f).

73. Treas. Reg. §25.2511-2(c).

74. Treas. Reg. §25.2511-2(b).

75. *United States v. Estate of Grace,* 395 U.S. 316 (1969).

76. I.R.C. §2513.

77. I.R.C. §2001(e). Adjusted taxable gifts are reduced by gifts made by decedent's spouse that are included in decedent's spouse's gross estate under Section 2035 where gift splitting applied to the transfer. However, inclusion from a QPRT occurs pursuant to Section 2036, hence there is no reduction.

78. I.R.C. §2036.

79. I.R.C. §2001(b).

80. Restatement 2d Trust, §156(2).

81. I.R.C. §2207B(a)(2).

82. I.R.C. §2601.

83. I.R.C. §2613(a).

84. I.R.C. §2651.

85. I.R.C. §2651(e).

86. I.R.C. §2612(c).

87. I.R.C. §2612(c)(1).

88. I.R.C. §2612(a).

89. I.R.C. §2612(b).

90. I.R.C. §2642(c).

91. I.R.C. §2642(c)(2).

92. I.R.C. §2642(c).

93. I.R.C. §2631.

94. Treas. Reg. §25.2511-2(b).

95. I.R.C. §2654(f)(3),(4); Treas. Reg. §26.2632-1(c)(2).

96. I.R.C. §2652(f)(1).

97. I.R.C. §2651(e).

98. I.R.C. §121; PLR 199912026.

99. Rev. Rul. 2004-64.

100. I.R.C. §677(a)(1); Treas. Reg. §25.2702-5(c)(3).

101. I.R.C. §673(a).

102. I.R.C. §677(a).

103. Rev. Rul. 77-402.

104. I.R.C. §1041.

105. I.R.C. §1051(a).

106. I.R.C. §121; PLR 199912026.

107. Fla. Stat. §193.155; *Robbins v. Welbaum,* 664 So. 2d 1 (Fla. 3d DCA 1995); *Nolte v. White,* 784 So. 2d 493 (Fla. 4th DCA 2001).

108. *Higgs v. Warrick,* 994 So.2d 492 (Fla. 3d DCA 2008).

DOMESTIC ASSET PROTECTION TRUSTS

Protecting assets during life and after death is one of the most important objectives of estate planning. In other words, estate planning encompasses not only the accumulation and distribution of an estate but also the conservation of assets and income. Traditional estate planning concentrates on tax reduction and techniques involving the disposition of assets. Estate planning, however, should also consider the litigious nature of society and the potential for the loss of wealth because of an unanticipated (and underinsured or uninsurable) event. Beware of the financial devastation of a lawsuit and its adverse effect on a client's estate, and actively seek an estate planners' assistance to protect assets from such claims. This chapter discusses domestic asset protection trusts (a "**DAPT**" or "**DAPTs**") as a potential solution to the problem of unanticipated loss of wealth.

SELF-SETTLED TRUSTS

A self-settled trust is a trust in which the settlor, *i.e.*, the person who creates the trust, is also a beneficiary of the trust, remaining eligible to receive distributions of income or principal from the trust. The Restatement (Second) of Trusts provides in relevant part, "[w]here a person creates for his own benefit a trust for support or a discretionary trust, his transferee or creditors can reach the maximum amount which the trustee under the terms of the trust could pay to him or apply for his benefit."[1] Restatement (Third) of Trusts provides, "[a] restraint on the voluntary and involuntary alienation of a beneficial interest retained by the settlor of a trust is invalid."[2] This Black Letter rule is commonly referred to as the "**Self-Settled Trust Doctrine**," adopted from old English law.[3] The Self-Settled Trust Doctrine is currently the majority rule in the U.S.; however, the present legislative trend is to reverse this rule.

Under a set of statutes enacted into law in Alaska in 1997, a person can establish a "**self-settled**" perpetual trust (since there is no rule against perpetuities that limits the term of the trust, it can conceivably continue forever), have the assets held in the trust protected from the claims of "**unknown future creditors**," and still remain a discretionary beneficiary of the trust. (Under the law of most states, if a person transfers assets to a trust for his or her own benefit, the transfer can be ignored by both present and future creditors). Alaska was the first state to enact extensive asset protection legislation. Presently, however, at least sixteen states allow a person who settles a trust to remain a as a "**discretionary beneficiary.**"

Proponents claim that DAPTs in those states that have adopted "Alaska-like" laws offer many of the same creditor protection opportunities available from the Cook Islands, Nevis, or other noted offshore trust havens-at less cost, without going offshore, and with the political and economic stability of the U.S. While such position can be questioned, those states that have adopted "Alaska-like" laws have positioned themselves high on the list of jurisdictions in which to establish a trust designed mainly for favorable asset protection. Such a state may be particularly useful for a client who does not want to place the ownership and control of assets in the hands of a person or entity that is offshore or if the size of the estate does not warrant the expense and complexity of an offshore trust. Since some of the states that have adopted legislation favorable for DAPTs also have no income tax, it is possible for such trusts to accumulate income free of state income tax. This absence of income tax on trust income not currently distributed to trust beneficiaries, *vis a vis* most other states, can have a dramatic effect on the net amount received by heirs. Potential advantages of using a DAPT include reduced set-up costs, possible state income tax savings and no extensive tax compliance which is required of foreign trusts. See Chapter 17 for a more detailed discussion of offshore trusts.

Guidelines for Self-settled Trusts

There are guidelines that must be followed for these trusts to achieve the creditor protection that is promised. Such guidelines include:

1. The DAPT must be irrevocable.

2. The DAPT must be created before there is a significant threat by creditors or potential known future creditors against assets or income of the creator. The longer the trust has been in existence before a creditor takes action, the safer the assets will be. A trust created to hinder, delay or defraud a creditor may fail. Depending on state law, some DAPT states will not protect the settlor from alimony or child support obligations.

3. Some (if not all) of the trust assets (many commentators recommend at least $10,000 or more) must actually be held in a bank or brokerage account in the state that is supposed to be the *situs* of the trust and whose DAPT laws the creator seeks to gain benefit. The more significant the amount of stocks, bonds, mutual funds, or bank accounts actually located in the protective state, the stronger the asset protection.

4. The trustee must be either a trust company with its principal place of business in the DAPT state or an individual who is a resident of such state.

5. Some or all of the trust's assets must be deposited in the DAPT state.

6. The trustee must have the power to maintain trust records in the DAPT state and must have the power to file tax returns for the trust.

7. At least some of the trust administration must be performed in the DAPT state.

8. Some proponents recommend that the trust agreement provide that distributions can only be made to the creator's spouse (and not to the creator) "as long as he (she) is alive and married to me" to provide further flexibility and asset protection.

9. The DAPT will not work to hide assets from existing or imminent creditors. A doctor about to be sued for malpractice or someone about to be served with divorce papers or file for divorce will not be able to protect assets by setting up a trust tomorrow because transfers to such trust in contemplation of creditors would be deemed fraudulent transfers.

Pre-existing or imminent creditors may have up to four years in some DAPT states from the date of transfer to the trust (or a year after discovery of the transfer, or such date when discovery was reasonable, depending on state law) to file a fraudulent transfer claim. Compare this with some foreign jurisdictions that allow only a year to prove fraud. Furthermore, the DAPT state will be required under the "full faith and credit" clause of the U.S. Constitution to respect the judgments of courts in other states. Thus, there may be significantly greater creditor protection provided by certain offshore jurisdictions.

With an offshore trust structure, creditors who argue the settlor's transfers were made to defraud them must obtain a judgment against the settlor in that foreign jurisdiction and prove in some cases that the transfers were fraudulent under the criminal standard of "beyond a reasonable doubt." As a result of the rules of most foreign asset protection jurisdictions, the cost (and aggravation) that would be incurred by creditors in the case of a DAPT trust is far less. To this end, in most foreign asset protection jurisdictions the party who loses the claim is required to pay the legal fees and other expenses incurred by the prevailing party. This requirement and the low likelihood of success make an attack on a properly structured foreign asset protection trust far less likely to occur.

INDIVIDUAL STATES

As of November 2016, sixteen states with some form of self-settled asset protection trust legislation include Delaware, Alaska, Utah, Rhode Island, Nevada, Missouri, South Dakota, Tennessee, Wyoming, New Hampshire, Hawaii, Virginia, Ohio, Oklahoma, Mississippi and West Virginia. See Appendices for listing of states along with requirements for each state. Within each DAPT statute, important terms and concepts are defined to clarify who may create a DAPT, how it may be created, who can serve as trustee, what property can be transferred, a list of exception creditors, whether an affidavit of solvency is required and what the statute of limitations is as to present and future creditors. Following is a brief discussion of each of the states, with an introductory focus on Alaska and Delaware, followed by a brief overview of each of the other DAPT states.

Alaska

Alaska became the first state to permit residents and non-residents to create DAPTs.[4] A person who, in writing, makes a "transfer" of "property" in trust may provide that the interest of a beneficiary, including the "settlor," may not be voluntarily or involuntarily transferred before payment or delivery of the interest to the beneficiary by the trustee.[5] The phrase "payment or delivery of the interest to the beneficiary" does not include the beneficiary's use or occupancy of real property or tangible personal property owned by the trust if the use or occupancy is in accordance with the trustee's discretionary authority under the trust.[6] Additionally:

- The term **"property"** means real property, personal property, and interests in real or personal property.[7]

- The term "**transfer**" means any form of transfer, including deed, conveyance or assignment.[8]

- The term "**settlor**" means a person who transfers real property, personal property or an interest in real or personal property, in trust.[9]

A provision in a trust that states the laws of Alaska govern the validity, construction and administration of the trust and that the trust is subject to the jurisdiction of Alaska is valid, effective and conclusive for the trust if:

(1) Some or all of the trust assets are "**deposited in this state**" and are being administered by a "**qualified person**;"

(2) A trustee of the trust is a qualified person who is either designated as trustee under the trust or by a court having jurisdiction over the trust;

(3) The powers of the qualified trustee include or are limited to:

(a) maintaining records for the trust on an exclusive basis or a nonexclusive basis; and

(b) preparing or arranging for the preparation of, on an exclusive basis or a nonexclusive basis, an income tax return that must be filed by the trust; and

(4) Part or all of the administration of the trust occurs in Alaska, including physically maintaining trust records in Alaska.[10]

The term "**deposited in this state**" includes property that is held in a checking account, time deposit, certificate of deposit, brokerage account, trust company fiduciary account, or similar account or deposit that is located in Alaska.[11] The term "**qualified person**" means:

(1) an individual who, except for brief intervals, military service, attendance at an educational or training institution, or for absences for good cause shown:

(a) resides in Alaska;

(b) whose true and permanent home is in Alaska;

(c) who does not have a present intention of moving from Alaska; and

(d) who has the intention of returning to Alaska when absent from the state; or

(2) a trust company that is organized under the Revised Alaska Trust Company Act and has its principal place of business in Alaska; or

(3) a bank that is organized under Alaska Banking Code, or a national banking association that is organized under 12 U.S.C. 21-216d, if the bank or national banking association possesses and exercises trust powers and has its principal place of business in Alaska.[12]

If at least one qualified person serves as trustee of a trust whose Alaska jurisdiction provision is valid, effective and conclusive, any one or more of the following persons may also serve as trustees though not qualified persons:

(1) individuals who do not reside in Alaska;

(2) trust companies that have their principal place of business outside of Alaska and that are not organized under the Revised Alaska Trust Company Act; and

(3) banks that have a principal place of business outside Alaska or that are not organized under Alaska Banking Code.[13]

Notwithstanding any contrary law, a trustee who is not a qualified person is not considered to be engaging in business in Alaska solely by reason of serving as trustee of a trust whose Alaska jurisdiction provision is valid, effective and conclusive.[14]

Transfer Restrictions

If a trust contains a transfer restriction as provided for in Section 34.40.110(a) of the Alaska Statutes, such restriction will preclude an existing creditor or a person who subsequently becomes a creditor from satisfying such claim from the beneficiary's interest in the trust. Notwithstanding the foregoing, a creditor may satisfy his, her or its claim from the beneficiary's interest in the trust if the creditor is a creditor of the settlor and:

(1) the settlor's transfer of property was made with intent to defraud that creditor;

(2) the trust provides that the settlor may "**revoke or terminate**" all or part of the trust without the consent of a person who has a substantial beneficial interest in the trust and the interest would be adversely affected by the exercise of the power held by the settlor to revoke or terminate all or part of the trust. The term "**revoke or terminate**" does not include any one or more of the following rights or powers:

    (a) a power to veto a distribution from the trust;

    (b) a testamentary non-general power of appointment or similar power;

    (c) the right to receive a distribution of income, principal or both in the discretion of a person, including a trustee, other than the settlor;

(3) the trust mandates that all or a part of the trust's income or principal or both, be distributed to the settlor. The foregoing shall not apply to a settlor's right to receive any of the following types of distributions, which remain subject to the restriction provided in section 34.40.110(a) of the Alaska Statutes until such distributions occur:

    (a) income or principal from a charitable remainder annuity trust or charitable remainder unitrust (within the meaning of Section 664 of the Code);

    (b) a percentage of the value of the trust each year as determined form time to time under the trust instrument, but not exceeding the amount that may be defined as income under section 13.38 of the Alaska Statutes or under section 643(b) of the Internal Revenue Code;

    (c) the settlor's potential or actual use of real property under a qualified personal residence trust (within the meaning of section 2702(c) of the Internal Revenue Code); and

    (d) income or principal from a grantor retained annuity trust or grantor retained unitrust that is allowed under section 2702 of the Internal Revenue Code.

(4) when the transfer is made, the settlor is in default by thirty or more days of making a payment due under a child support judgment or order.[15]

The satisfaction of a claim, however, is limited to that part of the trust for which a transfer restriction is not allowed (as described in section 34.40.110(b)(1)-(4), above).[16] An attachment or other order may not be imposed on the trustee with respect to a beneficiary's interest in the trust or against property that is subject to a transfer restriction; however, such an order can be made to the extent that a transfer restriction is not permitted.[17] A transfer restriction permitted under section 34.40.110(a) of the Alaska statutes applies to a settlor-beneficiary of the trust even if the settlor serves as a co-trustee or as an advisor to the trustee so long as the settlor does not possess the power to make discretionary distributions.[18]

A transfer restriction permitted under section 34.40.110(a) of the Alaska Statutes applies to a beneficiary who is not the settlor of the trust even though such beneficiary is the sole trustee, co-trustee or an advisor to the trustee.[19] The restriction still applies if the settlor has the authority under the trust agreement to appoint a trust protector or an advisor to the trustee.[20] A settlor whose beneficial interest in a trust is subject to a transfer restriction permitted under section 34.40.110(a) of the Alaska Statutes may not benefit from, direct a distribution of or use trust property except as provided in the terms of the trust.[21] An express or implied agreement or understanding between the settlor and trustee that purports to grant or permit the retention of greater rights or authority than provided by the terms of the trust is void.[22]

Fraudulent Transfer

A cause of action or claim for relief with respect to a fraudulent transfer of a settlor's assets is extinguished unless the action is filed by a creditor of the settlor who was the settlor's creditor before the settlor transferred assets to the trust and an action to set aside the settlor's transfer of property to the trust with intent to defraud the creditor is filed within the later of:

(1) four years after the transfer is made; or

(2) one year after the transfer is or reasonably could have been discovered by the creditor if the creditor:

    (a) demonstrates, by a preponderance of the evidence, that the creditor asserted a specific claim against the settlor before the transfer; or

    (b) files another action against the settlor in which the creditor assets a claim based on an act or omission of the settlor that occurred prior to the transfer and such action is filed within four years after the transfer; or

    (c) becomes a creditor subsequent to the transfer into trust and an action is filed to set aside the transfer or property because such transfer was made with intent to defraud that creditor.[23]

According to Section 34.40.110(e) of the Alaska Statutes, a trust containing a restriction described in Section 34.40.110(a) prevents anyone from asserting any cause

of action or claim for relief against a trustee or anyone involved in the preparation or funding of the trust for:

(1) conspiracy to commit a fraudulent conveyance;

(2) aiding and abetting a fraudulent conveyance; or

(3) participating in the trust transaction.

(4) the preparation and funding of the trust includes the preparation and funding of a limited partnership or a limited liability company if interests in such entities are transferred to the trust.

A settlor who creates a trust in which the settlor is a beneficiary and the settlor's beneficial interest is subject to a transfer restriction as provided in section 34.40.110(a) shall execute a sworn affidavit prior to the settlor's transfer of assets to such trust.[24]

The affidavit must state that the settlor:

(1) has full right, title and authority to transfer the assets to the trust;

(2) will not be rendered insolvent by the transfer of the assets to the trust;

(3) does not intend to defraud a creditor by transferring the assets to the trust;

(4) does not have any pending or threatened court actions against him or her, except for those identified on an attachment to the affidavit;

(5) is not involved in any administrative proceedings, except for those identified on an attachment to the affidavit;

(6) is not currently in default of a child support obligation by more than thirty (30) days at the time of the transfer of the assets to the trust;

(7) does not contemplate filing for bankruptcy relief; and

(8) did not derive the assets being transferred to the trust from unlawful activities.[25]

No type of action, including an action to enforce a judgment entered by a court or other adjudicative authority, may be filed at law or in equity for attachment or any other remedy against any property of a trust with a transfer restriction as provided in section 34.40.110(a) of the Alaska Statutes or to avoid a transfer of property to a trust with a transfer restriction as provided in Section 34.40.110(a) unless the action is brought pursuant to Section 34.40.110(b)(1) within the limitations period provided in §34.40.110(d).[26]

A court in Alaska has exclusive jurisdiction over a cause of action or claim for relief that is based on a transfer of property to a trust with a transfer restriction as provided in section 34.40.110(a).[27]

If a trust has a transfer restriction as provided in section 34.40.110(a) of the Alaska Statutes and a beneficiary of such trust divorces or dissolves his or her marriage, the beneficiary's interest in the trust will not be considered property subject to division under sections 25.24.160 or 25.24.230 of the Alaska Statutes or a part of a property division under sections 25.24.160 or 25.24.230 of the Alaska Statutes after the settlor's marriage or within thirty days prior to the marriage unless the settlor provides written notice to the other party to the marriage of the transfer.[28]

Unless otherwise agreed in writing by the parties to the marriage, the foregoing shall not apply to a settlor's interest in a self-settled trust with respect to assets transferred to the trust.[29]

Alaska Community Property Law

It should be noted that Alaska has an "**opt-in**" community property law statute.[30] A married couple may establish community property by entering a community property agreement (both must be domiciled) or establishing a community property trust (neither need be domiciled).[31] The Alaska community property establishes a present undivided one-half interest in each spouse.[32] A spouse acting alone may manage community property if owned in such spouse's name, if the property is held "in the alternative" (such as husband or wife), and in other situations.[33] A spouse acting alone may make de minimums gifts, while other gifts require the joint action of the spouses or the consent of the other spouse (including consent on a federal gift tax return).[34] To opt-in, there is no residency requirement.[35]

In re Mortensen

One of the first cases to bring about a national discussion of DAPTs came from an interpretation of Alaska's

self-settled trust statutes which was *In re Mortensen*.[36] *In re Mortensen* was a case of first impression involving an Alaska Bankruptcy Court's interpretation of Section 548(e) of the Bankruptcy Code. In *Mortensen*, Thomas Mortensen ("**D**") was a resident of Alaska and a self-employed project manager who held a master's degree in geology.

In 1994, D and his spouse (now his former spouse) acquired 1.25 acres of real property located in a remote area near Seldovia, Alaska (the "**Seldovia Property**") for $50,000. When D and his former spouse divorced, D received his former spouse's interest in the Seldovia Property. D added some improvements to the Seldovia Property and D deeded his interest in the Seldovia Property to a "self-settled trust," which became the focal point of this case.

Through "casual conversation" D learned about Alaska's laws providing an individual with asset protection with respect to property transferred to a self-settled trust. (The court inappropriately referred to such laws using the derogatory term "scheme.") D investigated the subject further, and using a form he uncovered in his research, drafted a trust document he called the Mortensen Seldovia Trust (the "**Trust**"). D intended the Trust to qualify as an asset protection under Alaska's asset protection trust law. D purportedly asked an attorney to review the Trust and represented that the attorney only suggested "minor changes" be made to the document following the attorney's review.

The court noted:

> The express purpose of the trust was "to maximize the protection of the trust estate or estates from creditors' claims of the Grantor or any beneficiary and to minimize all wealth transfer taxes." The trust beneficiaries were Mortensen and his descendants. Mortensen had three children at the time the trust was created.

As required by Alaska law, the Trust was registered with the state on February 1, 2005 and Mortensen provided an affidavit that stated:

> 1) he was the owner of the property being placed into the trust, 2) he was financially solvent, 3) he had no intent to defraud creditors by creating the trust, 4) no court actions or administrative proceedings were pending or threatened against him, 5) he was not required to pay child support and was not in default

on any child support obligation, 6) he was not contemplating filing for bankruptcy relief, and 7) the trust property was not derived from unlawful activities.

D transferred the Seldovia Property to the Trust by executing a quit claim deed on the same date the Trust was registered with the state. According to the terms of the Trust, the Seldovia Property was "a special family place that should not be sold and should remain in the family."

The Seldovia property was worth approximately "$60,000" when it was deeded into the Trust by D. Interestingly, D's mother sent him checks totaling $100,000 following the transfer of the Seldovia Property into the Trust. D argued that he and his mother had entered into an agreement for him to transfer the Seldovia Property to the Trust to preserve it for his children and that the payment from his mother was made in consideration for the transfer. D's testimony was corroborated by certain notes that D's mother sent to him with two checks sent on February 22, 2005 and April 8, 2005.

D claimed he used some of the funds his mother paid him to pay existing debts and transferred approximately $80,000 to a brokerage account in the name of the Trust as "seed money" for operating expenses related to the property. According to D, he lent the $80,000 to the Trust, however, no promissory note was ever entered into evidence.

According to D, the Seldovia Property was recreational property used by him and his children and sometimes by other family members. Prior to creating and funding the Trust D lived on the property full time and argued that he could have claimed the property was exempt from seizure to satisfy his creditors at that time by claiming the state's homestead exemption.

Following the creation and funding of the Trust D's financial condition deteriorated and his income was "sporadic." According to the court:

> [D] used the cash he received from his mother and his credit cards to make speculative investments in the stock market and to pay living expenses. His credit card debt ballooned after the trust was created. In 2005, total credit card debt ranged from $50,000 to $85,000. When he filed his petition in August of 2009, Mortensen had over $250,000 in credit card debt. The $100,000 he received from his mother has been lost.

Bankruptcy

D claimed that he always had the ability to make the minimum payments required on his credit card debt until he became sick in April of 2009. When D became sick, he required surgery and hospitalization for two weeks followed by a prolonged period of convalescence. D stated that he attempted to return to work following his illness, however, he was on medication that inhibited his cognitive abilities. The cognitive impairment of D resulted in the loss of several contracts.

D filed for bankruptcy on August 18, 2009. D did not list the Seldovia Property as part of his assets. He did list $251,309.16 in debt from twelve separate credit cards. He also listed $8,140.84 in medical debt.

The bankruptcy trustee alleged that D failed to create a valid DAPT because he was not solvent when the Trust was established and funded. After some analysis regarding this issue the court concluded that D was solvent when he established and funded the Trust and therefore recognized the validity of the Trust.

Court's Analysis

The court then turned its analysis to the bankruptcy trustee's claim that the transfer of the Seldovia Property to the Trust violated section 548(e) of the Bankruptcy Code. The fraudulent transfer rule under section 548(a) and (b) of the Bankruptcy Code was modified by section 548(e)(1) in the case of a "**self-settled trust**." Section 548(e) was added to the Bankruptcy Code by the Bankruptcy Abuse Prevention and Consumer Protection Act of 2005 ("**BAPCPA**"). It addresses the transfer of assets to a DAPT providing:

> In addition to any transfer that the trustee may otherwise avoid, the trustee may avoid any transfer of an interest of the debtor in property that was made on or within 10 years before the date of the filing of the petition, if-(A) such transfer was made to a self-settled trust or similar device; (B) such transfer was by the debtor; (C) the debtor is a beneficiary of such trust or similar device; *and* (D) *the debtor made such transfer with actual intent to hinder, delay, or defraud* any entity to which the debtor was or became, on or after the date that such transfer was made, indebted. (Emphasis supplied.)

The court held that D's transfer to the Trust violated the extended ten year fraudulent transfer rule under section 548(e).

Breadth of *In re Mortensen*

Some practitioners have been quick to reach the conclusion that *Mortensen* should be read broadly as enabling a bankruptcy trustee to reach any assets transferred to a self-settled trust during the preceding ten-year period. Caution is warranted reaching such a conclusion for the following reasons:

(1) D's counsel could have argued, with credibility, that D's mother was the grantor of the portion of the trust attributable to the Seldovia Property. This argument is consistent with the record. Of course, had D and his mother sought the advice of competent counsel to assist in originally structuring this transaction, such counsel would have certainly advised D's mother to purchase the land from D and then contribute it to the Trust herself or some variation of this structure. On motion for rehearing in the case D did in fact argue that his mother was the settlor of the Trust, however, the court declined to accept this argument.

(2) The debtor could have argued section 548(e) is unconstitutional because it violates the Tenth Amendment of the Constitution of the United States, which provides "The powers not delegated to the United States by the Constitution, nor prohibited by it to the States, are reserved to the States respectively, or to the people." Until the BAPCPA was enacted, the fraudulent transfer rule in the Bankruptcy Code was only two years and in certain cases the trustee could use the longer period provided by applicable state law. The two year period did not exceed the shortest period provided to question fraudulent transfers under the laws of any state. Defining property rights and how such rights are governed (including rules related to avoiding the transfer of assets) are traditionally considered reserved to the states.

(3) The judge's ruling is too broad. Except for a small portion of D's debt, the creditors in question, that is, under D's twelve credit cards, existed and *were contemplated* when the Trust was created and funded, regardless of whether D was solvent when the Trust was created. This appears to be the most important fact and supports the court's decision under section 548(e). D gave away a substantial portion of his net worth in this case. Such action was certainly odd for someone in his financial

situation who was not contemplating placing such assets beyond the reach of a foreseeable creditor. D does not represent the typical client most estate planning attorneys who specialize in asset protection assist in their practice.

In fact, D did not even retain counsel to assist in structuring this transaction, rather only to review a trust he drafted himself. Section 548(e) should not reach future creditors who are not contemplated when a trust is created and funded. No existing fraudulent transfer statute is that broad nor should any such statute be interpreted that broadly. Accepting such a broad interpretation would bring into question the finality of too many transactions and is not good policy. One would also have to question why Congress would choose to enact a fraudulent transfer rule as opposed to simply enacting a blanket limitation that captures all transfers to a self-settled trust for the ten-year period.

(4) The changes in Section 548(e)(2) of the Bankruptcy Code were spurred by a couple of events around the time of passage of the BAPCPA. Among those events was an article in *The New York Times* that criticized Congress for leaving a so-called "loophole" for the wealthy in that debtors were supposedly avoiding their creditors using self-settled trusts. This led U.S. Senator Charles Schumer, D-N.Y., to propose an amendment that would have limited the use of self-settled trusts by capping their exemption to $125,000. Ultimately, Senator Jim Talent, R-Mo., submitted the eventual amendment that would go on to being Section 548(e)(2) of the Bankruptcy Code whereby the Senators specifically sought to close any sort of "loophole" allowing corporate executives to avoid their creditors using self-settled trusts.[37]

The judge's references in *Mortensen* to Senator Charles Schumer's statement in the legislative history of Section 548(e) are misplaced because they are not relevant to the provision that was ultimately passed by the Senate, especially since Senator Schumer's proposed amendment was defeated and his commentary on the issue was thus rendered completely irrelevant.

(5) Section 522(o) of the Bankruptcy Code contains a substantially similar ten (10) year fraudulent

conversion rule applicable to debtors who convert non-exempt wealth to homestead. This rule provides that if within the ten (10) years prior to filing a petition a debtor converts non-exempt property to homestead with the actual intent to hinder, delay, or defraud a creditor, the value of the homestead is reduced by the value of such converted property. The existing cases involving this rule have not applied it as broadly as some commentators suggest Section 548(e) should be applied.[38] It would seem highly unlikely that Congress intended to pass two substantially similar statutes involving fraudulent transfers and conversions with each statute to be applied in a completely different manner. Arguably, use of a homestead exemption to shelter wealth in this context is significantly more "abusive" than the use of a self-settled trust. The ten (10) year fraudulent transfer rule applicable to the homestead exemption is not interpreted so broadly and neither should the substantially similar rule for self-settled trusts.

Present v. Future Creditors

The law regarding fraudulent transfers generally characterizes a creditor as either a present creditor or a future creditor. Present creditors are those creditors whose claims arose before the transfer. They are also referred to as "existing creditors." A debtor is aware of a present creditor when the debtor effectuates a transfer. A creditor does not have to possess a judgment to constitute a present creditor. In Mortensen, D was clearly aware that he was indebted to certain credit card companies.

Future creditors are those creditors whose claims arose after the transfer. They are also referred to as "subsequent creditors." For clarification, possible future creditors should be further divided into two distinct categories, only one of which is protected:

- *Foreseeable Future Creditors* – Foreseeable future creditors are those creditors whose specific claims did not exist prior to the transfer, but were anticipated or should have been anticipated. Such creditors include a creditor whose rights originated following a transfer where a debtor intended to conduct the debtor's activities or business in a fraudulent way or with reckless disregard for the rights of a potential creditor. In *Mortensen*, D was clearly contemplating that he would continue to be indebted to certain credit card companies and it can be inferred from the facts that he intended to increase such debt following the creation and funding of the Trust. In fact, the court noted that his annual expenses exceeded his annual income.

- *Unforeseeable Future Creditors* – An unforeseeable future creditor is an unidentifiable person or entity who a debtor was not aware existed at the time the debtor effectuated a transfer. An unforeseeable future creditor cannot possess a claim against a debtor. Thus, a transfer made by a debtor should not be avoidable by an unforeseeable future creditor under any existing fraudulent transfer rule including Section 548(e).

One has to question the necessity of a legislative body enacting a fraudulent transfer rule rather than a rule with a blanket limitation if it is to be interpreted so broadly. No other existing fraudulent transfer rule in the United States has been applied in such a broad manner. The result in *Mortensen* can certainly be reconciled with a more appropriate and narrow interpretation of Section 548(e). Section 548(e) should not be applied in a manner that will vitiate the use of DAPTs if such trusts are created and funded under appropriate circumstances.

It is clear that we are in a different period in regards to DAPTs. No longer is a bankruptcy court permitted to dismiss such a trust as a sham when faced with questionable facts. As has been pointed out in prior commentaries, the bankruptcy court is now forced to consider the validity of the trust because of the addition of Section 548(e). This is true regardless of how this provision is ultimately interpreted. We should absolutely counsel our clients to create and fund DAPTs. Our advice to clients should be that DAPTs should be created sooner rather than later given that any funding of the DAPT should be safe from even the reach of a bankruptcy court ten (10) years after the funding.

Also important to the general estate planning community, a broad interpretation of Section 548(e) could have a devastating effect on many new and now commonly used estate planning techniques such as the use of a discretionary tax reimbursement provision that is included in a wholly owned grantor trust and a successor-backend ("**SQIT**"™) self-settled trust used in an *inter vivos* QTIP trust to benefit a donor-spouse who survives the donee-spouse. Many states have laws that specifically provide for a special exception to the self-settled trust doctrine related to these trusts.[39]

Finally, many individuals are contemplating or have established self-settled completed gift dynasty trusts as a vehicle to take advantage of the increased gift tax exemption of $5,490,000. The overwhelming majority of these trusts are taxed as wholly owned grantor trusts. In the same manner as a trust with a discretionary tax reimbursement provision, each payment by a grantor of the income tax liability attributable to the income generated by the assets held in such a trust is arguably an additional contribution and transfer of wealth to the trust. Each such contribution raises the possibility of the application of Section 548(e) to at least a portion of the trust for an additional ten-year period.[40]

In Re Huber

In the case *In re Huber*,[41] the Bankruptcy Court for the Western District of Washington held that a debtor's prepetition transfer of assets to a self-settled Alaska trust for the benefit of himself and his children was void under Washington law.

The debtor, Donald G. Huber ("**D**"), was involved in real estate development and management in Washington for over forty years. In 1968, D founded United Western Development, Inc. ("**UWD**") in Washington. D invested in and developed real estate through UWD. D served as the President of UWD, however, beginning in 2001, D's oldest son, Kevin ("**Kevin**"), served as a Vice President of UWD and had become primarily responsible for the operations of UWD prior to the time that D petitioned for bankruptcy.

Generally, D would own real estate through a corporation or limited liability company separate and apart from UWD, with D owning all, or a portion, of such entity. D was required to sign as guarantor on loans in favor of third party lenders on many projects. Many of the lenders were local banks. All of the real estate held in D's various entities was located in Washington.

D established the Donald Huber Family Trust on September 23, 2008 (the "**Trust**"). The record before the Court demonstrated that the Trust was established to "protect a portion of [D's] assets from [D's] creditors." The beneficiaries of the Trust were D, D's eight children and stepchildren, and D's grandchildren. The Trustees

of the Trust were Kevin, D's stepdaughter, Amber Haines, and the Alaska USA Trust Company ("**AUSA**"). The Trust was created in Alaska and designated Alaska law to govern the Trust.

At the time D established the Trust, UWD was in default on numerous loans of which D was a guarantor. The Court gave four examples of loans that were described by the Court as "fragile at best," which were in existence when D established the Trust. Those loans all came due prior to February 10, 2011, when D petitioned for bankruptcy. At the time of the Court's decision, those loans remained outstanding in the amounts of $1,659,245.46, $1,706,000, $588,250, and $1,101,750, respectively.

D transferred $10,000 in cash and his ownership interests in over twenty-five entities to DGH, LLC ("**DGH**"), an Alaska limited liability company, established on September 4, 2008. D transferred ninety-nine percent (99%) of DGH to the Trust and Kevin owned one percent (1%), and also served as manager of DGH. D also transferred his shares of UWD to the Trust. D's residence in Washington was conveyed to an Alaska corporation, the shares of which were then transferred by D to DGH. D then leased the residence back from the corporation, and the Trust made the mortgage payments for the residence. In summary, most of D's valuable assets were transferred to the Trust.

The Court noted that there was only one asset held in the Trust in Alaska, which was a certificate of deposit of $10,000 transferred by D to a bank account in Alaska held in the name of the Trust. The Court stated that all other assets were located in Washington. *Note*: the Court may have been grossly wrong on this point. D transferred Washington assets to an Alaska corporation and a limited liability company. Generally, the *situs* of intangible assets, such as stock or a membership interest in a limited liability company, is where its owner is. Therefore, when the stock and membership interest were transferred to the trustee of the Trust, the result was that the assets should have had a *situs* in Alaska. The Court ignored any discussion of this question.

The Trust generated $345,248 in net income in 2010, and $360,000 in 2009. The total amount distributed from the Trust to the beneficiaries of the Trust between October 1, 2010, and July 30, 2012, was $571,332.81. From the date of the filing of the petition on February 10, 2011, through July 30, 2012, the amount of the distributions to the beneficiaries of the Trust totaled $406,837.27.

The Bankruptcy Trustee ("**T**") contended that D made requests for disbursements from Kevin, who then prepared a request for a payment, and AUSA approved the disbursement, without any inquiry. D asserted, however, that Kevin at times refused D's requests for disbursements. The Court stated that the record indicated that AUSA did nothing to become involved with the preservation or protection of the assets of the Trust and acted merely as a "**straw man**," approving all distributions of assets.

Court's Analysis

D filed a voluntary petition for bankruptcy on February 10, 2011. The Court examined two principal issues related to whether the assets of the Trust were part of the estate and should be distributable to D's creditors. First, the Court examined whether the Trust should be invalidated under Washington law, and second, whether D's transfer of assets to the Trust should be avoided under 11 U.S.C. section 548(e)(1) and/or under 11 U.S.C section 544(b)(1). The Court could have based its decision solely on a fraudulent transfer analysis.

T contended that D's transfers to the Trust should be invalidated under Washington law. Although the Trust was established under Alaska law, Washington did not recognize the efficacy of a self-settled trust for asset protection purposes.[42] Under Washington law, all transfers made by a person in trust for the use of the transferor are void as to "the existing or subsequent creditors of such person."[43] The Court (inappropriately) examined choice of law rules to determine which state law applied.

The Court examined Section 270 of the Restatement (Second) of Trusts ("**Restatement 270**") to address the validity of the Trust. Restatement 270 states:

> [a]n *inter vivos* trust of interests in movables is valid if valid . . . under the local law of the state designated by the settlor to govern the validity of the trust, provided that this state has a substantial relation to the trust and that the application of its law does not violate a strong public policy of the state with which, as to the matter at issue, the trust has its most significant relationship under the principles stated in §6.

Furthermore, comment b of Restatement 270 provides certain criteria for determining if a state has a substantial relation to the trust. According to comment b:

> A state has a substantial relation to a trust when it is the state, if any, which the settlor designated as that in which the trust is to be administered, or that of the place of business or domicile of the trustee at the time of the creation of the trust, or that of the location of the trust assets at that time, or that of the domicile of the settlor, at that time, or that of the domicile of the beneficiaries.

The Court stated that, under Restatement 270, D's choice of Alaska law designated in the Trust should be upheld if Alaska had a substantial relation to the Trust. The Court noted that D and the Trust beneficiaries were not domiciled in Alaska. The Trust was to be administered in Alaska and the location of one of the trustees, AUSA, was in Alaska, however, the Court noted that, except for a $10,000 certificate of deposit, all of the assets of the Trust were located in Washington. (This contention was at best questionable. See above discussion.) On that basis, the Court held that Alaska did not have a substantial relation to the Trust, applying the standards set forth in Comment b.

The Court also held that Washington had a "strong public policy" against self-settled asset protection trusts.[44] Again, however, the public policy of Washington in regard to a self-settled trust seems rather questionable under the rules set forth in Restatement 270. As a result of the foregoing, the Court disregarded D's choice of Alaska law, and applied Washington law to determine the validity of the transfers to the Trust. Upon application of Washington law, the Court concluded that the assets of the Trust could be reached by D's creditors.[45]

The Court also ruled that D's transfers were fraudulent under 11 U.S.C. section 548(e)(1), which provides that a trustee may avoid any transfer of an interest of a debtor made on or within ten years of the date of the filing of the petition, if (A) such transfer was made to a self-settled trust or similar device; (B) such transfer was by the debtor; (C) the debtor is a beneficiary of such trust or similar device; and (D) the debtor made such transfer with actual intent to hinder, delay, or defraud any entity to which the debtor was or became, on or after the date that such transfer was made, indebted. Under the facts of this case, it seems far more appropriate for the Court to have based its decision under section 548(e)(1) rather than under its alternative choice of law analysis (that rested on dubious grounds).

Under its fraudulent transfer analysis, the Court found that five badges of fraud existed. First, at the time D transferred his assets into the Trust, there was threatened litigation against D. The Court stated that it appeared that "foreclosure of several properties for which D had guaranteed the bank loans was becoming increasingly certain" and D was not making timely payments on those loans. Second, D transferred all or substantially all of his property into the Trust. Third, D was significantly in debt at the time of the transfers to the Trust. Fourth, the Court held that there was a special relationship between D and the trust in that D was both the grantor and a beneficiary of the Trust. Fifth, the Court held that D effectively retained the property transferred into the Trust. Substantially all of D's requests for distributions were granted. On average D received approximately $14,500 per month in distributions from the Trust. The only party to review D's requests for distributions was his son Kevin. The Court stated that, based on the evidence, the only reasonable conclusion was that D continued to use and enjoy the assets of the Trust as he did before the transfers. Based on these badges of fraud, the Court held that D had the actual intent to hinder, delay, or defraud his current or future creditors, and therefore D's transfers to the Trust should be avoided.

Additionally, under section 544(b)(1) of the Bankruptcy Code, T could avoid fraudulent transfers under state law. Under Washington's version of the UFTA, a transfer is fraudulent if the debtor acts with actual intent to hinder, delay, or defraud a creditor, or transfers "[w]ithout receiving a reasonably equivalent value in exchange for the transfer or obligation."[46] The Court held that D had actual fraudulent intent to hinder, delay, or defraud his current or future creditors under UFTA, and therefore D's transfers to the Trust should be avoided based on UFTA.[47]

Toni 1 Trust v. Wacker

In *Toni 1 Trust v. Wacker*,[48] Donald Tangwall ("**Tangwall**") sued William and Barbara Wacker (the "**Wackers**") in state court in Montana. The Wackers counterclaimed against Tangwall, his wife, Barbara Tangwall ("**Barbara**"), his mother-in-law, Margaret "**Toni**" Bertran ("**Toni**") and several of Tangwall's trusts and businesses in 2007. Several default judgments were entered against Tangwall and his family in 2010. Before the last of these judgments were issued Toni and Barbara transferred real property to an Alaska Trust called the "**Toni 1 Trust**." The Wackers filed a fraudulent transfer action in state court in Montana claiming that the transfers were made to avoid the judgments and

should be avoided under Montana fraudulent transfer law. Default judgments were again entered against Barbara, Toni, and the Toni 1 Trust. The Wackers moved to enforce their judgment by levying on a piece of property in Montana that was jointly owned by Barbara and Toni. The Wacker's were able to purchase Barbara's interest in the property at a sheriff's sale; however, Toni, to avoid her half of the property being taken, filed for Chapter 7 bankruptcy in Alaska. Toni's interest in the trust property was therefore subject to the jurisdiction of a federal Bankruptcy Court.

In December 2012, Tangwall, as trustee of the Toni 1 Trust, filed a complaint in the Bankruptcy Court against the Wackers and the bankruptcy trustee, Larry Compton ("**Compton**"). Rather than litigate whether service in Montana was proper, Compton elected to bring a fraudulent transfer claim against Tangwall, and a default judgment was entered against Tangwall. Tangwell next sought relief in the Alaska state court arguing that AS 34.40.110(k) grants Alaska courts "exclusive jurisdiction over an action brought under a cause of action or claim for relief that is based on a transfer of property to a trust" containing such transfer restrictions. The state trial court in Alaska dismissed the complaint and Tangwall appealed.

In *Toni 1 Trust*, the issue was whether Alaska Statute 34.40.110, which purported to grant Alaska exclusive jurisdiction over fraudulent transfer claims against Alaska self-settled spendthrift trusts, could deprive other state and federal courts from exercising jurisdiction over the fraudulent transfer action. Alaska Statute ("**AS**") 40.110(k) states that:

> (B) Alaska courts have "exclusive jurisdiction over an action brought under a cause of action or claim for relief that is based on a transfer of property to a [self-settled spendthrift] trust."

Tangwall claimed that this deprived the bankruptcy court and the state court in Montana of jurisdiction. While the statute as written attempts to restrict jurisdiction to a state court in Alaska, the Supreme Court of Alaska concluded that based on the United States Constitution and case law, it could not.

The court considered the Full Faith and Credit Clause of the United States Constitution which requires states to give "Full Faith and Credit" to "the Public Acts, Records and Judicial Proceedings of every other state."[49] The court also reviewed at *Tennessee Coal, Iron & R. Co. v. George*,[50] where the court held that the Full Faith and Credit Clause does not compel one state to follow another the statute of another state claiming exclusive jurisdiction over suits based on a cause of action *"even though* [the other state] created the right of action."[51] *Tennessee Coal* also provided that "a state cannot create a *transitory* cause of action and at the same time destroy the right to sue on that transitory cause of action in any court having jurisdiction" which suggested that states are not barred from asserting exclusive jurisdiction when the cause of action is *local* rather than transitory. Fraudulent transfer actions are, however, transitory actions. See *Toni 1 Trust v. Wacker*, at Footnote (20). The court also noted that "an Alaska statute cannot prevent Montana courts from applying Montana fraudulent transfer law." See *Toni 1 Trust v. Wacker*, at Footnote (21). Additionally, the Supreme Court of Alaska stated, "Delaware… cannot unilaterally preclude a sister state from hearing claims under [that state's] law."[52] "We agree with the Court of Chancery and with those courts that have reached similar conclusions…As applied to this case, it means that AS 34.40.110(k)'s assertion of exclusive jurisdiction does not render a fraudulent transfer judgment against an Alaska trust from a Montana court void for lack of subject matter jurisdiction."

That court also refused to grant Tangwall relief from the federal judgment. In *Marshall v. Marshall*,[53] the United Stated Supreme Court noted that efforts to limit federal jurisdiction in such a manner were invalid "even though [the state] created the right of action" giving rise to the suit. *Marshall v. Marshall*[54]. This was supported in 2006 by the Sixth Circuit in *Superior Beverage Co. v. Schieffelin & Co.*,[55] providing "a state may not deprive a federal court of jurisdiction merely by declaring in a statute that it holds exclusive jurisdiction" and in 1982 by the Ninth Circuit in *Begay v. Kerr McGee Corp.*,[56] where the court held "states… have no power to enlarge or contract the federal jurisdiction." Additionally, several courts, including *In re Daniel Kloiber Dynasty Trust*,[57] have concluded that the Supremacy Clause of the United States Constitution precludes states from limiting federal jurisdiction.[58] Thus, the judgment from the superior court was confirmed by the Alaska Supreme Court.

Toni 1 Trust provides a prime example of the inherent dangers and uncertainty for those who desire to use domestic asset protection trusts. The risks are high and the state statutes enabling the use of such trusts may contain many such mines buried in their fields. Jurisdictional and numerous other issues may

cause such trusts to fail to protect the wealth that is transferred into such trusts. This uncertainty will remain for many decades to come and quite possibly may never end.[59]

Delaware

Delaware permits residents and non-residents to create wealth protection trusts under its "**Qualified Dispositions in Trust Act**" (the "QDTA").[60] According to the QDTA, a "**qualified disposition**" is a disposition by a donor to one or more "**qualified trustees**" through the use of a "**trust instrument**."[61] The disposition can be made *with or without* consideration.[62] Under §3570(4) of the QDTA a "**disposition**" is:

> a transfer, conveyance or assignment of "**property**" (that includes a change in legal ownership of property that occurs if a trustee is substituted for another trustee or one or more new trustees are added); or the exercise of a power that causes a transfer of property to one or more trustees.

The term disposition does not include the release or relinquishment of an interest in property that was previously the subject of a qualified disposition.[63]

The term "**property**" means and includes real property, personal property, and interests in either.[64] A "**transferor**" is any "**person**" who is:

(1) an owner of property;

(2) a holder of a power of appointment that authorizes the donee of the power to appoint property subject to the power in his or her favor, to his or her creditors, to his or her estate or to the creditors of his or her estate; or

(3) a trustee - directly or indirectly - makes or causes a disposition to be made.[65]

The term "**qualified trustee**" means:

(1) an individual who is a resident of Delaware (except for a transferor); or

(2) a person who is authorized under the law of Delaware to act as a trustee if such person's activities are subject to supervision by the Delaware Bank Commissioner ("**DBC**"),

the Federal Deposit Insurance Corporation ("**FDIC**"), the Comptroller of the Currency ("**CC**"), or the Office of Thrift Supervision ("**OTS**").[66]

Furthermore, to be a qualified trustee the foregoing individual or person *must maintain or arrange for the custody of some or all of the property that is the subject of a qualified disposition in Delaware, maintain records for the trust on an exclusive or nonexclusive basis, prepare or arrange for the preparation of fiduciary income tax returns for the trust, or otherwise materially participate in the administration of the trust.*[67]

Any individual who is not a resident of Delaware, and any entity that is not authorized under Delaware law to act as a trustee or whose activities are not supervised by the DBC, the FDIC, the CC, or the OTS can be considered a qualified trustee.[68] Nonetheless, §3570(8) of the QDTA specifically permits a donor to appoint one or more advisers for the donor's Delaware wealth protection trust who:

(1) can remove and appoint qualified trustees and trust advisors;

(2) can direct the trustee to make distributions from the trust;

(3) must consent to or approve any distributions made by the trustee from the trust; and

(4) direct the investment decisions of the trust. (For this purpose, an investment decision includes the power to direct a trustee to retain, purchase, sell or exchange property held in the trust or to engage in any other transaction affecting the ownership or rights over such property.)[69]

The term "**adviser**" encompasses a "**trust protector**" or any other person who is given one or more trust powers.[70] If a trustee ceases to qualify as a qualified trustee, such trustee is deemed to have resigned at that time and is replaced with a successor trustee appointed in the trust instrument or by court order.[71] The QDTA also permits a donor-settlor to appoint one or more trustees of a Delaware wealth protection trust who are not qualified trustees.[72]

The term "**trust instrument**" refers to an agreement that appoints one or more qualified trustees to hold property that is the subject of a qualified disposition.[73] The agreement must:

(1) expressly incorporate Delaware law to govern the validity, construction and administration of the trust;

(2) be irrevocable; and

(3) provide that the interest of a donor-settlor or other beneficiary in the trust income and assets may not be transferred, assigned, pledged or mortgaged, whether voluntarily or involuntarily, before it is actually distributed by a qualified trustee to a beneficiary.[74]

The QDTA specifically provides that such a spendthrift provision in a trust agreement is deemed a restriction on the transfer of the donor-settlor's beneficial interest in the trust that is enforceable under applicable non-bankruptcy law (within the meaning of Section 541(c)(2) of the Bankruptcy Code).[75]

Irrevocable Trust

A trust instrument (or agreement) is considered irrevocable under the QDTA even though it includes one or more of the following provisions:

(1) a provision permitting the donor-settlor to veto a distribution from the trust;

(2) a provision providing that the donor-settlor retains a power of appointment exercisable by will or other written instrument, *however, the power can be effective only upon the donor-settlor's death.* Furthermore, the power of appointment cannot be exercisable by the donor-settlor in his or her favor or in favor of his or her creditors, his or her estate or the creditors of his or her estate;

(3) a provision permitting a donor-settlor's potential or actual receipt of trust income, *including a retained right to receive such income*;

(4) a provision permitting a donor-settlor's potential or actual receipt of income or principal from a charitable remainder unitrust or charitable remainder annuity trust (as such trusts are defined in Section 664 of the Code);

(5) a provision permitting a donor-settlor's potential or actual receipt of income or principal from a grantor-retained annuity

trust or grantor-retained unitrust as defined in Section 2702 of the Code or the donor-settlor's receipt each year of no greater than 5 percent of the initial value of the trust or its value determined from time to time under the trust agreement;

(6) a provision permitting a donor-settlor's potential or actual receipt or use of trust assets if such would be the result of a qualified trustee acting in its own discretion; pursuant to a standard governing such distribution that does not confer upon the donor-settlor a substantially unfettered right to the receipt or use of the principal; or is at the direction of an advisor;

(7) a provision permitting a donor-settlor to remove a trustee or adviser and appoint a successor or replacement trustee or adviser, except such successor or replacement trustee must be a person who is not related or subordinate to the donor-settlor (within the meaning of Section 672(c) of the Code;

(8) a provision permitting a donor-settlor to potentially or actually use a residence held in a qualified personal residence trust (within the meaning of Section 2702(c) of the Code);

(9) a provision providing for the transferor's potential or actual receipt of income or principal to pay, in whole or in part, income taxes due on income of the trust if such potential or actual receipt of income or principal is pursuant to a provision in the trust instrument that provides for the payment of such taxes and if such potential or actual receipt of income or principal would be the result of the exercise of a qualified trustee's discretion, pursuant to a mandatory direction in the trust instrument or qualified trustee acting at the direction of an adviser or trust protector; and

(10) a provision giving a qualified trustee the ability, whether pursuant to discretion, direction or the grantor's exercise of a testamentary power of appointment, to pay, after the death of the transferor, all or any portion of the debts of the transferor outstanding at the transferor's death, the expenses of administering the transferor's estate, or any estate or inheritance tax imposed on or with respect to the transferor's estate.[76]

Under section 302 of the Delaware Code, the term "**person**" includes an individual, a corporation, company, association, firm, partnership, society or joint-stock company. Under this definition it should be possible for a business entity to establish a wealth protection trust under the QDTA.[77]

A donor-settlor has no right or authority with respect to assets that are the subject of a qualified disposition and any agreement or understanding that purports to grant or permit the retention of any greater rights or authority is void.[78] The foregoing does not prevent the donor from retaining the right to veto distributions from a Delaware wealth protection trust or from serving as an investment advisor to the trust. Additionally, Section 3572 of the QDTA applies to a qualified disposition even if a transferor retains any or all of the powers and rights described in section 3570(11)b. of the QDTA and a transferor serves as investment adviser.

Section 3573 of the QDTA provides that the limitations on creditor actions for qualified dispositions under the QDTA do not apply to any person to whom a donor-settlor owes a debt because of an agreement or a court order for the payment of support or alimony to such donor's spouse, former spouse or children, or for a division or distribution of property in favor of a donor-settlor's spouse or former spouse (but only to the extent of such debt).[79] Furthermore, the provisions of the QDTA do not apply to any person who suffers death, personal injury or property damage on or before the date of a qualified disposition by a donor-settlor if such death, injury or damage is at any time determined to have been caused in whole or in part by the actions or an omission of either a donor-settlor or another person for whom a donor is or was vicariously liable (but only to the extent of such claim).[80] Notwithstanding the foregoing, the provisions of Section 3573 of the QDTA do not apply to a claim for forced heirship or legitimacy. That is the limitations on creditor actions do apply to such claims.

Fraudulent Transfers

No type of action, including an action to enforce a judgment entered by a court or other adjudicative authority, may be filed at law or in equity for attachment or any other remedy against any asset that is the subject of a qualified disposition unless such action is filed pursuant to Delaware's fraudulent transfer laws set forth in Sections 1304 and 1305 of Title 6 of the Delaware Code and, in the case of a creditor whose claim originated after a qualified disposition, unless the qualified disposition was made with actual intent to *defraud* such creditor.[81] This includes an action to avoid a qualified disposition.[82] The Delaware Court of Chancery is vested with exclusive jurisdiction over any such action.[83]

A creditor's claim is extinguished unless it accrued: prior to the qualified disposition and the action is filed within the period set forth in Section 1309 of Title 6 of the Delaware Code to avoid fraudulent transfers, that is, within four years after the transfer or the obligation was incurred; concurrently or subsequently to the qualified disposition and the action is filed within four years after the qualified disposition, despite the provisions of Section 1309 of Title 6 of the Delaware Code.[84]

Burden of Proof

In any action filed under Section 3572(a) of the QDTA the burden of proof is on the creditor to prove its case **by clear and convincing evidence**. If the *situs* of a wealth protection trust in another jurisdiction is moved to Delaware, for purposes of the Delaware fraudulent transfer rule, the transfer will be considered made when assets were originally transferred to such trust.[85] That is, if a transfer was made before the trust was moved to Delaware, the time from when the transfer was made until the time the trust was moved to Delaware will count toward the Delaware statute of limitations.

Limitations on Creditor Rights

A creditor's rights with respect to a qualified disposition are limited to the rights granted under sections 3572, 3573 and 3574 of the QDTA. Furthermore, a creditor has no claim or cause of action against:

(1) a trustee or trust advisor of a trust that is the subject of a qualified disposition; or

(2) any person who counsels, drafts, prepares or assists with the execution or funding of a trust that is the subject of a qualified disposition.[86]

Additionally, all actions involving a qualified disposition to a trust are barred unless filed against a trustee, advisor or any other person involved with counseling, drafting, preparing, executing or funding the trust

within the period permitted under Section 3572 of the QDTA. Delaware appears to have its own statutory version of a duress provision:

> If, in any action brought against a trustee of a trust that is the result of a qualified disposition, a court takes any action whereby such court declines to apply the law of this State in determining the validity, construction or administration of such trust, or the effect of a spendthrift provision thereof, such trustee shall immediately upon such court's action and without the further order of any court, cease in all respects to be trustee of such trust and a successor trustee shall thereupon succeed as trustee in accordance with the terms of the trust instrument or, if the trust instrument does not provide for a successor trustee and the trust would otherwise be without a trustee, the Court of Chancery, upon the application of any beneficiary of such trust, shall appoint a successor trustee upon such terms and conditions as it determines to be consistent with the purposes of such trust and this statute. Upon such trustee's ceasing to be trustee, such trustee shall have no power or authority other than to convey the trust property to the successor trustee named in the trust instrument in accordance with this section.[87]

The QDTA provides that a qualified disposition will be avoided only to the extent necessary to satisfy a donor-settlor's debt to a creditor (plus any costs, including legal fees, permitted by a court) who successfully filed an action to have the qualified disposition avoided.[88]

If a qualified disposition is avoided and a court concludes that a qualified trustee did not act in bad faith in accepting or administering property that is the subject of the qualified disposition, such trustee will be given a first lien against the property that is the subject of the qualified disposition equal to the amount of the costs (including attorneys' fees) properly incurred in defending the action or proceedings to avoid the qualified disposition. Furthermore, the disposition will be avoided subject to the proper fees, costs, preexisting rights, claims and interests of the qualified trustee (and any predecessor qualified trustee that did not act in bad faith). It is presumed that a qualified trustee did not act in bad faith by merely accepting property that is the subject of a qualified disposition.[89]

If a qualified disposition is avoided and a court determines that a beneficiary of a trust did not act in bad faith, the beneficiary will be permitted to retain any distribution received by him, her or it as a result of the exercise of discretion granted to the qualified trustee provided such power or discretion was properly exercised before the creditor commenced an action to avoid the qualified disposition. It is presumed that a beneficiary (including a donor-settlor) did not act in bad faith in settling the trust or accepting a distribution permitted by the trust.[90]

Tenants by the Entireties

When two spouses make a qualified disposition of property and, immediately before such qualified disposition, such property or any part thereof or any accumulation thereto was, pursuant to applicable law, owned by them as tenants by the entireties, then notwithstanding such qualified disposition and except where the provisions of the trust instrument may expressly provide to the contrary, that property and any accumulation thereto shall, while held in trust during the lifetime of both spouses, be treated as though it were tenancy by the entireties property and be dealt with in a manner consistent with that applicable law but in every other respect shall be dealt with in accordance with the terms of the trust instrument. Furthermore, in any action concerning whether a creditor of either or both spouses may recover the debt from the trust, upon avoidance of the qualified disposition, the sole remedy available to the creditor with respect to the trust property treated as though it were tenancy by the entireties property shall be an order directing the trustee to transfer the property to both spouses as tenants by the entireties.[91]

Delaware also has two statutes that appear to provide substantial flexibility in dealing with tenancy by the entireties property ("**T by E**") in the context of asset protection planning. In many instances Jonathan E. Gopman has met and advised a number of married couples who were resident or owned property in states that recognize T by E as a form of ownership. The conversation in many of these meetings included an extensive discussion of the fundamental principles of ownership of property in T by E. The discussion also included the potential pitfalls of continuing to own property in T by E and relying on this form of ownership as an asset protection strategy. Although the unexpected loss of the protection provided by ownership of property in T by E could be disastrous, for example, as the result of an untimely death, many of these couples desired

to continue to use T by E as their primary asset protection strategy. Often, only one spouse would resist the changes we would recommend in structuring the ownership of assets held in T by E. The reasons for not moving forward varied in many cases.

As an asset protection strategy, T by E has its limitations and it is important for planners to understand these limitations. The limitations include the following: divorce severs the T by E estate; and death severs the T by E estate.

In many instances the solutions to the potential creditor protection problems of owning property T by E are not acceptable to one or both spouses. For example, the cost of insurance might be expensive, one spouse might be concerned that transferring ownership of such spouse's interest to the other spouse could be the impetus for a surprise divorce or the other spouse might not be cooperative with further planning with the property after such spouse is given full ownership.

Statutory Tenancy by the Entireties (STET)

Through an idea propounded by Jonathan E. Gopman and the efforts of Thomas R. Pulsifer, an attorney with Morris, Nichols, Arsht & Tunnell LLP in Wilmington, Delaware, Delaware law now provides an additional and perhaps more flexible solution to this problem. Delaware provides this new strategy through an innovative type of trust known as a statutory tenancy by the entireties trust (or a "**STET**").[92] Section 3574(f) of the Delaware Code provides:

> Where a husband and wife make a qualified disposition of property to 1 or more trusts and, immediately before such qualified disposition, such property or any part thereof or any accumulation thereto was, pursuant to applicable law, owned by them as tenants by the entireties, then notwithstanding such qualified disposition and except where the provisions of the trust instrument may expressly provide to the contrary, that property and any accumulation thereto shall, while held in trust during the lifetime of both spouses, be treated as though it were tenancy by the entireties property to the extent that, in any action concerning whether a creditor of either or both spouses may recover the debt from the trust, upon avoidance of the qualified disposition, the sole remedy available to the creditor with respect to trust property

that is treated as though it were tenancy by the entireties property shall be an order directing the trustee to transfer the property to both spouses as tenants by the entireties.[93]

The Delaware Civil Union and Equality Act of 2011 (the "2011 Act")[94] provides that parties to a civil union shall have the same rights, protections and benefits under Delaware law that are provided to spouses in a traditional marriage. Under the 2011 Act, a party to a civil union is included in any definition or use of the terms "husband and wife," "spouse," "tenants by the entireties" and any other terms that denote a spousal relationship as these terms are used throughout the Delaware Code or in judicial decisions. Furthermore, the 2011 Act provides that a same-sex union formed under the laws of another jurisdiction shall be recognized as a validly established civil union for all purposes under Delaware law.

The Civil Marriage Equality and Religious Freedom Act of 2013 (the "2013 Act"), signed into law on May 7, 2013 and effective as of July 1, 2013:

- legalized same-sex marriage in Delaware;

- gave parties to an existing civil union the ability to convert the civil union to a marriage by petition;

- provided that same-sex unions formed under the laws of another jurisdiction shall be recognized for all purposes under Delaware law as a marriage;

- provided that all laws of Delaware applicable to married couples shall apply equally to same gender married couples; and

- stipulated that on July 1, 2014 all remaining Delaware civil unions will automatically convert to marriages.

As a result of the 2011 Act and the 2013 Act, a Delaware STET is an asset protection option for not only parties to a civil union and same-sex married couples in Delaware, however, also for parties to same-sex unions and same-sex marriages performed in other jurisdictions.

The STET provides an additional weapon in an estate planner's arsenal to deal with the pitfalls of T by E ownership as an asset protection strategy. Of course,

the client must be domiciled or own property in a jurisdiction that recognizes T by E as a form of ownership and also recognizes it in regards to the ownership of personal property. Furthermore, in the jurisdictions that recognize this extended form of T by E ownership such as Florida, it should be possible to use a STET even though there is an existing creditor with a claim or a judgment against one spouse. This is because the UFTA specifically exempts the transfer of property held in T by E that cannot be reached by a creditor of only one spouse from the application of the fraudulent transfer rules. UFTA provides that "[a]n interest in property that is owned in tenancy by the entireties to the extent such property is not subject to process by a creditor who possesses a claim against only one tenant" is not subject to the application of the statute.

TrustCo Bank v. Mathews

In *TrustCo Bank v. Mathews*, C.A.,[95] the parties disputed which state's law and which state's statute of limitations applied in regards to alleged fraudulent transfers to tree purported Delaware asset protection trusts. The plaintiffs asserted that New York's six-year or two-years-from-discovery statute of limitations governed the plaintiffs's claims. The defendants argued that either Delaware or Florida law controlled, and that most of the plaintiffs' claims were barred by the identical four-year or one-year-from-notice statutes of limitations adopted by both of those states.

TrustCo Bank ("TrustCo") had its principal place of business in New York. TrustCo provided a construction loan to StoreSmart of North Ft. Pierce, LLC ("StoreSmart"), a Florida limited liability company. Plaintiff ORE Property Two, Inc. ("ORE," and together with TrustCo, the "Plaintiffs") was a Florida corporation and the assignee of TrustCo's rights, title, and interest in the StoreSmart loan and related agreements.

Defendant Susan M. Mathews ("Mathews") was a manager and member of StoreSmart and she personally guaranteed the loan from TrustCo to StoreSmart. Mathews created three Delaware trusts (the "Trusts") on December 21, 2006. Mathews and her children were the discretionary beneficiaries of the Trusts. RBC Trust Company ("RBC"), a Delaware corporation was the trustee of the Trusts (RBC, together with Mathews, the "Defendants").

TrustCo loaned $9,300,000 to StoreSmart in July 2006 for the purpose of constructing a self-storage facility in St. Lucie, Florida (the "**StoreSmart Loan**"). The StoreSmart Loan was secured by StoreSmart's real estate and other assets. Mathews also executed a personal guaranty of the StoreSmart Loan. StoreSmart defaulted on the loan in April 2011. On April 25, 2011, TrustCo filed a foreclosure action against StoreSmart and Mathews in state court in Florida. That case resulted in a judgment on July 12, 2011, in favor of TrustCo of roughly $8.2 million plus post-judgment interest (the "**Foreclosure Judgment**").

TrustCo assigned its rights, title, and interest in the StoreSmart Loan, including the related security agreements, and the Foreclosure Judgment to ORE in August 2012. The Plaintiffs, StoreSmart, and Mathews agreed to entry of a deficiency judgment of about $2.3 million and submitted a stipulation to that effect to the Florida court in February 2013, which the court approved (the "**Deficiency Judgment**").

The Plaintiffs alleged that various transfers to the Trusts constituted fraudulent transfers. The Defendants contended that Mathews created the Trusts as part of her estate planning, which was underway before she guaranteed the StoreSmart Loan. For purposes of the pending motion for summary judgment, the court considered only the statute of limitations defense, and the court assumed, without deciding, that the challenged transfers were fraudulent.

The Plaintiffs' complaint challenged several transfers. The most important of these were the transfers of ITRAX stock. Mathews co-founded a company called Corporate Health Dimensions ("**CHD**"). Mathews retired from CHD in 1999. CHD was purchased by ITRAX in 2004. Walgreens later purchased ITRAX in 2008. In two sets of transfers that occurred on January 9 and 22, 2007, Mathews transferred her ITRAX stock to two of the Trusts (generally, the "**ITRAX Transfers**").

Mathews also held an interest in Terra Optima Ventures, LLC ("**TOV**"). TOV was an investment vehicle for a business owned by her son. Mathews sold her interest in TOV to one of the Trusts in March 2010 for $63,000 (generally, the "**TOV Transfer**"). The TOV interest had been valued at $500,000 only a year earlier, therefore, the Plaintiffs contended that the TOV sale was a fraudulent transfer. The Plaintiffs argued that they did not have legally sufficient notice of the ITRAX transfers such that the statute of limitations would begin to run until July 19, 2011. The Defendants contended that the Plaintiffs had: (1) inquiry notice in March and April of 2008; (2) inquiry notice on May 6, 2008; (3) inquiry notice on June 27,

2008; and (4) both inquiry notice and actual notice of the alleged fraudulent ITRAX Transfers in May 2010.

The Plaintiffs filed their initial complaint on March 1, 2013, along with a motion to expedite and a motion for a preliminary injunction. That complaint specifically alleged violations of Delaware's fraudulent transfer statute. On May 28, 2013, the Plaintiffs amended their complaint to remove all references to substantive Delaware law. In an effort to halt all distributions from the Trusts, the Plaintiffs renewed their motion for a preliminary injunction on July 2, 2013.

The parties framed the dispute as whether the Plaintiffs' claims were subject to the statute of limitations under Delaware law or New York law. The Defendants requested that the court treat its submissions on the preliminary injunction as the equivalent of a motion for partial summary judgment on the statute of limitations issue.

The general rule of following the forum state's relevant statute of limitations arguably may be modified by either Delaware's borrowing statute or Delaware's Qualified Dispositions in Trust Act (the "**QDTA**").[96] The court concluded that the applicable statute of limitations should be determinative as to whether the Plaintiffs delayed unreasonably in filing suit more than six years after the allegedly fraudulent transfers took place.

The Defendants sought partial summary judgment that the Plaintiffs' claims for fraudulent transfer as to the ITRAX Transfers were barred by the relevant statute of limitations and laches. The ITRAX transfers occurred in January 2007. An additional disputed transfer, the TOV Transfer, occurred in March 2010. As such, regardless of which statute of limitations applied, the TOV Transfer was not barred by laches and was not subject to the Defendants' motion for partial summary judgment. The Plaintiffs initially filed suit in March 2013. The Plaintiffs also admitted that they discovered the potentially fraudulent ITRAX Transfers by July 19, 2011. Accordingly, the court relied upon the July 19, 2011 date as the date by which the Plaintiffs had discovered the fraudulent transfers under the various statutes of limitations.

The Plaintiffs argued that New York's statute of limitations applied to their fraudulent transfer claims. Under New York law, an action to avoid a fraudulent transfer must be brought within "the greater of six years from the date the cause of action accrued or two years from the time the plaintiff or the person under whom the plaintiff claims discovered the fraud, or could with reasonable diligence have discovered it."[97] The Defendants contended that Delaware's statute of limitations governed. Under Delaware law, an action to avoid a fraudulent transfer must be brought "within four years after the transfer was made or the obligation was incurred or, if later, within one year after the transfer or obligation was or could reasonably have been discovered by the claimant."[98]

The Plaintiffs filed their initial complaint more than six years after the January 2007 ITRAX Transfers occurred. Even under New York law, therefore, the Plaintiffs were required to file within two years of discovery of the allegedly fraudulent transfer. Assuming the undisputed July 19, 2011 discovery date, the Plaintiffs' filing of their claims to avoid the ITRAX Transfers in March 2013 would be sufficiently timely to survive summary judgment if New York law governed. If the Delaware or Florida statutes of limitations applied, the Plaintiffs' fraudulent transfer claims as to the ITRAX Transfers would be substantially outside the relevant limitations period, which would have run by July 19, 2012.

The Delaware Legislature has altered the usual rule of applying the forum state's statute of limitations through 10 Del. C. §8121 (the "**Borrowing Statute**"), which provides:

> Where a cause of action arises outside of this State, an action cannot be brought in a court of this State to enforce such cause of action after the expiration of whichever is shorter, the time limited by the law of this State, or the time limited by the law of the state or country where the cause of action arose, for bringing an action upon such cause of action. Where the cause of action originally accrued in favor of a person who at the time of such accrual was a resident of this State, the time limited by the law of this State shall apply.

The court concluded that the Borrowing Statute presumptively applied. To determine where the causes of action arose in this case, the court looked to Delaware's conflict of law rules.

According to the court, "Delaware conflict of law rules direct that the Court determine where a plaintiff's claims arose by application of the 'most significant relationship test', as set forth in the Restatement (Second) Conflict of Laws ("**Restatement**")."[99] The Defendants

argued that Delaware or, alternatively, Florida had the greatest connection. The Plaintiffs maintained that New York had the most significant relationship. The Restatement factors differ slightly depending on whether the alleged wrong sounds in tort or contract.

The court determined that fraudulent transfers bear some resemblance to both tort and contract claims, so the court addressed both the Restatement's tort and contract factors. The court concluded that the contract factors were either in equipoise between New York and Florida, or only weakly favored New York, and that that the tort factors from the Restatement moderately favored Florida. Delaware had the next strongest connection to the case, with New York having the weakest relationship to it. The court found that Florida had the most significant relationship to this case and that Florida's four year statute of limitations should apply.

Alternatively, the court concluded that Delaware had the next most significant relationship and had essentially an identical statute of limitations. Under either of those scenarios, the Borrowing Statute was held to be inapplicable. As a third alternative, even if New York did have the most significant relationship, the court held that its contacts were not sufficient to make this case a "special circumstance" where application of the Borrowing Statute to preclude use of New York's longer statute of limitations would be inequitable. As such, if New York did have the most significant relationship, the Borrowing Statute would be triggered and Delaware's statute of limitations nevertheless would have applied. Regardless of which of these three states had the most significant relationship with this case, the court concluded that the Plaintiffs would be subject to a statute of limitations equivalent to Delaware's of four years from the time the transfer was made or one year from when discovery of the transfer occurred or reasonably should have occurred, whichever was longer. The Plaintiffs did not file this action relating to the ITRAX Transfers until after the expiration of that period. Therefore, the court held that the Plaintiffs' claims regarding the ITRAX Transfers were barred by laches.

The Defendants further argued that Delaware's statute of limitations applied for the independent reason that the **QDTA** controlled the dispute. The QDTA limits a creditor's available remedies when attempting to avoid a "**qualified disposition**." A qualified disposition is a "disposition by or from a transferor . . . to one or more trustees, at least one of which is a qualified trustee, with or without consideration, by means of a trust instrument."[100] The Defendants contended that the case involved such qualified dispositions. In that regard, the Defendants argued that (1) Mathews was a "transferor" in that she owned property and disposed of that property, (2) that RBC satisfied the definition of a qualified trustee, and (3) the Trusts each were governed by a "trust instrument."[101] The QDTA requires that any claim by a creditor, to avoid a qualified disposition, must be brought pursuant to 6 Del. C. §§1304 or 1305, Delaware's fraudulent transfer statutes. The QDTA also specifically provides that a creditor's claim will be extinguished unless it is brought within the time constraints of 6 Del. C. §1309, Delaware's statute of limitations for fraudulent transfers.[102] Finally, the QDTA stated that "The Court of Chancery shall have exclusive jurisdiction over any action brought with respect to a qualified disposition."[103] The Defendants argued that the QDTA is a statutory command requiring both that the Plaintiffs file their suit in Delaware, specifically in the Court of Chancery, and that the court apply Delaware's statute of limitations in Section 1309 without regard to any most significant relationship analysis. The Plaintiffs contended, primarily, that the QDTA was substantive law and that, under the most significant relationship test, the court should apply New York law. However, the Court rejected the proposition that New York had the most significant relationship with the case.

The Plaintiffs further argued that the restrictions of the QDTA were inapplicable because Mathews maintained impermissible control over the property transferred to the Trusts.[104] The court concluded that the Plaintiffs' claims relating to the ITRAX Transfers were barred because of either the most significant relationship choice of law analysis, which pointed to the use of Florida or, perhaps, Delaware law, or Delaware's Borrowing Statute, which required the application of Delaware's statute of limitations even if New York had been found to have the most significant relationship to the instant case. As a result, the court did not resolve the question of whether the QDTA required application of Delaware's fraudulent transfer statute of limitations without regard to the normal choice of law analysis or the Borrowing Statute. However, the court noted that (1) little case law interpreting the QDTA existed, and some of the issues implicated appeared to be issues of first impression, (2) the Court of Chancery had rejected the argument that the QDTA requires suits to avoid a qualified disposition to be brought exclusively in Delaware, and (3) whether or not Mathews maintained impermissible control over the assets transferred to the Trusts such that the QDTA's restrictions would not apply presented a material question of disputed fact not appropriate for summary resolution. For the foregoing reasons, the court declined to reach the question of whether the QDTA required the application of 6 Del. C. §1309 (the Delaware statute of limitations for fraudulent transfers).

Ultimately, the court concluded that the Plaintiffs were on inquiry notice of the ITRAX Transfers by July 2010, and that the statute of limitations began running at that time. The Plaintiffs filed suit in March 2013, and thus, the Plaintiff's claims relating to the ITRAX Transfers were untimely even under New York's statute of limitations. The court therefore granted the Defendants' motion for partial summary judgment, holding that the ITRAX Transfers were brought after the expiration of the applicable statute of limitations and were barred by laches.[105]

Nevada

Nevada law permits both residents and non-residents to create asset protection trusts.[106] Nevada boasts the shortest applicable period for a creditor to challenge a transfer to an asset protection as a fraudulent conveyance among states with DAPT legislation.[107] Some commentators view Nevada as the strongest DAPT jurisdiction and trust jurisdiction in the U.S.[108]; others have pointed out its flaws.[109]

A creditor may not bring an action with respect to a transfer of property to a spendthrift trust:

1. if the creditor is a creditor when the transfer is made, unless such action is brought within:

2. two years after the transfer is made; or

3. six months after the creditor discovers or reasonably should have discovered the transfer, whichever is later; or

4. if the creditor becomes a creditor subsequent to the transfer to the spendthrift trust, unless the action is brought within two years after the transfer is made to the spendthrift trust.[110]

Dahl v. Dahl

In *Dahl v. Dahl*,[111] a Utah trial court in Provo, Utah denied a spouse's request to consider the assets of a DAPT (the "**Trust**"), established in Nevada and created by her husband, in the division of marital assets.

Dr. Charles F. Dahl ("**Charles**") and Kim Dahl ("**Kim**") married in 1992 and were living in Utah during their marriage. In 2002, Charles created the Trust, naming his brother, C. Robert Dahl, as investment trustee (the "**Trustee**"). The discretionary beneficiaries of the Trust were Charles, Kim, their issue and organizations to be designated by Charles. Shortly after the Trust was created, Charles transferred 97 percent of a Utah LLC to the Trust, retaining a 1 percent interest for himself and 1 percent for each of his two children. The LLC owned brokerage accounts valued at just under $1 million. In 2003, Charles and Kim transferred their primary residence to the Trust.

Beginning in 2006, Charles and Kim became embroiled in a highly-contested divorce. While the divorce was still pending, Kim brought an action in the Fourth Judicial District Court, Appellate Court in Utah County (the "**Court**") seeking to attack the Trust on a number of grounds. In her petition, Kim sought the following determinations from the Court with regard to the Trust:

1. that the trust should be null and void;

2. that Kim had an immediate interest in the trust; and

3. a determination that the Trust was revocable.

The Court granted Charles' Motion for Summary Judgment on all three issues.

On the first claim, the Court ruled that "null and void" is not a formal cause of action. The Court noted that under the law set out in *Ockey v. Lehmer*,[112] contracts that offend an individual, such as those arising from fraud, misrepresentation, or mistake, are voidable, and only contracts that offend public policy or harm the public are void ab initio. Kim failed to accuse Charles of anything actionable under *Ockey*. Therefore, the Court found no basis on which to find the Trust "null and void."

With regard to the second claim, the Court noted that Trust distributions could only be made in the absolute discretion of the Trustee and, additionally, were subject to Charles' veto power. Kim was merely a discretionary beneficiary. Therefore, the Court found that Kim had no immediate interest in the Trust corpus.

Regarding the third claim, the Court ruled that the language used in the Trust reserved a statutory right

to amend with the consent of all beneficiaries and did not, as Kim argued, create a general right to amend or alter the terms of the Trust. On the contrary, the Court noted that the Trust clearly reflected Charles' intention that it be irrevocable. The Court pointed out that the "most compelling" counter-argument was based on the relevant Nevada statute,[113] which provided that a trust explicitly declared to be irrevocable is irrevocable for all purposes. The Court noted that under *Innerlight, Inc. v. Matrix Group, LLC*,[114] choice of law and choice of forum provisions in contracts and legal document are enforceable. The Court upheld Charles' choice of Nevada law and found that it was irrevocable.

Kim appealed ruling on August 7, 2012, making the following arguments:

(1) The Trust was revocable under Utah law;

(2) The Court erred in resorting to Nevada law as an alternative basis to find the Trust irrevocable because the application of Nevada law leads to a result that violates Utah's public policy;

(3) The Court abused its discretion in entering summary judgment on Kim's alter ego theory without allowing her to conduct discovery; and

(4) The Court erred in issuing a hypothetical ruling that cause of action not before him would have been barred by the state of limitations.

Upon Kim's appeal to the Supreme Court of Utah, the court held that Utah law applies, that the Trust was revocable as a matter of law, and that Kim was entitled to withdraw her share of the marital property she contributed to the Trust as a settlor. In reversing the district court, the Supreme Court of Utah determined that Utah law applied because of Utah's strong public policy interest in the equitable division of marital assets, and that Utah state law should apply to the trust even though the stated choice of law in the trust was Nevada. The Court's opinion cited to *Waddoups v. Amalgamated Sugar Co.*,[115] for the authority that Utah choice-of-law rules apply whereby although Utah will generally enforce a choice-of-law provision contained in a trust document, it would not do so if such a reading would undermine a strong public policy of the State of Utah.[116] Thus, the court refused to enforce a settlor's choice-of-law since doing so undermined Utah's strong public policy goals.

Kim argued that the Trust was revocable under Utah law, despite the Trust stating "Trust Irrevocable," because

Charles reserved in the Trust an unrestricted power to amend the Trust as the Trust stated "Settlor reserves *any power whatsoever* to alter or amend *any* of the terms or provisions hereof. Emphasis added)." Charles argued that the stated Trust language did not give him a right to unilaterally amend, alter or terminate the trust without consent from all beneficiaries. Charles did not argue that there may have been a typographical error (i.e., using the term "any" instead of the term "no"); which may have been the better argument. The Supreme Court of Utah was unpersuaded, analyzing secondary sources (Restatement (Second) of Trusts and The Law of Trusts and Trustees) and citing to Utah law[117] for the proposition that an unrestricted power to amend any and all provisions of a trust renders a trust revocable under Utah Law.

After holding that the Trust was revocable under Utah law, the Supreme Court of Utah dismissed Charles' argument that Kim had no enforceable interest in the trust because Utah law prohibited her from withdrawing her assets from an irrevocable trust.[118] Charles argued that Kim could not revoke the Trust with regards to the portion of Trust property attributable to her separate property or any marital property. The Supreme Court of Utah concluded that Kim was a settlor of the Trust, despite having nothing to do with the preparation of the Trust and not signing the Trust or related documents. A trust under Utah law is created by the transfer of property by the owner to another person acting as trustee.[119] It was indisputable that Kim contributed property to the Trust. Kim neither knowingly nor intentionally forfeited her status as a settlor. As a settlor of the Trust, Kim could revoke that portion of the Trust funded with either her marital or separate property.[120] This case now falls into the category of cases where DAPT cases have not fared well in domestic courts.[121]

Klabacka v. Nelson

In *Klabacka v. Nelson*,[122] after ten years of marriage, in 1993, Eric Nelson ("**Eric**") and Lynita Nelson ("**Lynita**"), who were still married, entered into a separate property agreement ("**SPA**") to convert the family's community assets into the parties' respective separate property, equally dividing the parties assets into two separate property trusts ("**SPT**"s). Eight years later, in 2001, Eric and Lynita converted their SPTs into self-settled spendthrift trusts (collectively, "**SSST**"s, individually "**Eric's SSST**" and "**Lynita's SSST**") and funded the SSSTs with the separate property contained within the SPTs. In 2009, Eric filed for divorce. On June 3, 2013, the district court issued the decree of divorce. In addition

to the dissolution of marriage, the district court ordered: (1) an equalization of $8.7 million in total trust assets to remain in or be transferred into each trust, (2) and (3) jointly held real estate property (the "Russell Road" and "Lindell" properties) be divided equally between the trusts, (4) Eric's SSST to use the distribution of $1.5 million from a previously enjoined trust account to pay Lynita spousal support in a lump sum of $800,000, (5) Eric's SSST to pay: Lynita child support arrears, (6) Lynita's attorney fees, (7) Lynita's expert fees, and (8) child support for each child and half of the private school tuition for his daughter. The district court equalized the marital property, including the property in the SPAs, and reached into Eric's SSST to pay child support, alimony, and other expenses.

The appellate court held that the SPA and SSSTs were signed, written agreements, and are all valid and the terms therein unambiguous. Nevada Revised Statutes 123.220(1) provides that:

> "[a]ll property, other than [separate property outline] in NRS 123,130, acquired after marriage by either husband or wife, or both, is community property *unless otherwise provided by ... [a]n agreement in writing between the spouses.*" (Emphasis added). Additionally, "[w]here a written contract is clear and unambiguous on its face, extraneous evidence cannot be introduced to explain its meaning."[123]

The terms of the SPA were clear and unambiguous as the parties agreed "to split the community estate into the sole and separate property of each spouse." The parties' community property was, thus, converted into separate property and should not have been considered otherwise. Furthermore, the SSSTs were validly formed and funded with the separate property in the SPTs, and are, therefore, afforded the statutory protections against court-ordered distribution. The court would have to trace the assets in the trusts to determine which assets are community property and subject to equal distribution, and which assets are separate property and not subject to distribution.

The appellate court also held that the lower court erred in equalizing the trust and ordering Eric's personal obligations to be paid by Eric's SSST. Nevada Revised Statutes chapters 163 and 166 evince a clear intention to protect spendthrift trust assets against court orders. Such distributions from Eric's SSST would be outside the scope of the trust agreement and would run afoul of NRS 166.120(2), which prohibits payments made pursuant to or by virtue of any legal process.

Additionally, Nevada statutes explicitly protect spendthrift trust assets from the personal obligations of the beneficiaries, including child-support and alimony, unless the debts were known at the time the trust was created. Indeed, the "key difference" among Nevada's self-settled spendthrift statutes and statues of other states with SSSTs, including Florida, South Dakota, and Wyoming, "is that Nevada abandoned the interest of child- and spousal-support creditors, as well as involuntary tort creditors," seemingly in an effort to "attract the trust business of those individuals seeking maximum asset protection." Michael Sjuggerud,[124] Therefore, the court erred in ordering Eric's personal obligations to be paid by Eric's SSST. Furthermore, the court erred in placing constructive trusts and imposing equitable remedies over assets held in valid SSSTs; the Russell Road and Lindell properties. The constructive trust would violate the statutory protections shielding spendthrift trusts from court order, specifically the trust's prohibition on assignment or alienation of assets.[125]

Utah

Utah allows for the creation of asset protection trusts by both residents and non-residents. However, compared to the other asset protection states, Utah's law is more limited in application and contains numerous exceptions to the protection provided in the wealth protection legislation.[126]

Oklahoma

Oklahoma passed the Family Wealth Preservation Trust Act (the "**FWPTA**").[127] According to the FWPTA, the income and corpus of a "**preservation trust**" will be exempt from the claims of creditors of a "**grantor**" up to an amount equal to **$1,000,000** in value.[128] Furthermore, any "**incremental growth derived from income retained by the trustee**" of such a trust in excess of the $1,000,000 amount is also considered exempt from the claims of the grantor's creditors.[129] Of extraordinary interest, the preservation trust can be *revocable* by the grantor, however, the grantor would forfeit the exemption if the grantor revokes the trust.[130]

Restrictions

For a trust to qualify as a preservation trust it must be established by the grantor under Oklahoma law and at "all times" must have an Oklahoma-based bank that maintains a trust department or an Oklahoma-based trust company" serving as its trustee.[131] The preservation trust can designate only certain individuals and charities as beneficiaries, who are referred to as "qualified beneficiaries."[132] Additionally, the corpus of the trust must consist solely of "Oklahoma assets," and the terms of the trust must provide that the income produced by its corpus is subject to tax under the income tax laws of Oklahoma.[133] The FWPTA contains many similar provisions to the states previously described, above.[134]

Interestingly, the FWPTA refers to the protection afforded to the assets held in the preservation trust as an "**exemption**."[135] *Note that this appears fundamentally different from the self-settled asset protection trust acts in states such as Alaska, Delaware, Nevada, Rhode Island and Utah.* It is probably not yet time to run to Oklahoma to assist with the formation of a preservation trust. There appear to be numerous interpretation questions that cause uncertainty in the application of the provisions of the FWPTA. There is no significant benefit available to a grantor who creates an irrevocable trust under the Act that is not available in any other common law jurisdiction.[136]

South Dakota

South Dakota law enables residents and non-residents to create asset protection trusts under sections 55-16-1, *et. seq.* of the South Dakota Codified Laws ("**SDCL**"). South Dakota is often touted by commentators as one of the top three jurisdictions in the U.S. to form a DAPT.[137]

Under South Dakota law, no type of action, including an action to enforce a judgment entered by a court or other adjudicative authority, may be filed at law or in equity for attachment or any other remedy against any property that is the subject of a qualified disposition or for the avoidance of a qualified disposition unless the action is filed pursuant to chapter 54-8A of the UFTA.[138] Notwithstanding sections 55-16-9 to 55-16-14, the following persons may bring an action against a trust subject to a qualified disposition:

- a person who is owed alimony or child support payments to the extent of such debt; and

- any person who suffers death, personal injury or property damage on or before the date of a qualified disposition by a transferor and such death, personal injury or property damage is determined to be caused by the transferor's act or omission or the transferor is vicariously liable.[139]

Fraudulent Transfers

A claim for relief with respect to a fraudulent transfer of a settlor's assets is extinguished unless the action is brought by a creditor of the settlor meeting one of the following requirements:

1. two years after the transfer is made; or

2. six months after the transfer is or reasonably could have been discovered by the creditor if the creditor:

    a. demonstrates that the creditor asserted a specific claim against the settlor before the transfer;

    b. files another action, other than an action under section 55-16-9, against the settlor that asserts a claim based on an act or omission of the settlor that occurred before the transfer, and the action is filed within two years after the transfer; or

    c. becomes a creditor subsequent to the transfer into the trust, and the action under section 55-16-9 is brought within two years after the transfer is made.[140]

The creditor has the burden to prove the matter by clear and convincing evidence.[141]

A qualified disposition will be avoided only to the extent necessary to satisfy a transferor's debt to a creditor (including any costs if authorized by a court) who successfully filed an action to have the qualified disposition avoided.[142] If a qualified disposition is avoided and a court concludes that a qualified trustee did not act in bad faith in accepting or administering property that is the subject of the qualified disposition, such trustee will be given a first lien against the property that is the subject of the qualified disposition equal to the amount of the costs (including attorney's fees) properly incurred in defending the action or proceedings to avoid the qualified disposition.[143] Additionally,

the qualified disposition will be avoided subject to the proper fees, costs, pre-existing rights, claims and interests of the qualified trustee (and any predecessor qualified trustee that did not act in bad faith).[144] It is presumed that a qualified trustee did not act in bad faith by merely accepting property that is subject of a qualified disposition.[145] If a qualified transfer is avoided and a court concludes that a beneficiary of a trust did not act in bad faith, the beneficiary will be permitted to retain any distribution received by the beneficiary as a result of the exercise of discretion granted to the qualified trustee provided such power or discretion was properly exercised before the creditor commenced an action to avoid the qualified disposition.[146] It is presumed that a beneficiary (including the transferor) did not act in bad faith in settling the trust or accepting a distribution permitted by the trust.[147]

Like Alaska and Tennessee, South Dakota allows the elective creation of community property trusts (a "South Dakota special spousal trust").[148]

Wyoming

Both residents and not residents can create "**qualified spendthrift trusts**." In Wyoming.[149] Although Wyoming's DAPT statute falls short in terms of being as advantageous as Nevada or South Dakota, Wyoming has other ancillary advantages.[150]

Tennessee

Tennessee permits a resident and non-resident to create an "**Investment Services Trust**" under the Tennessee Investment Services Act of 2007 ("**TISA**").[151] Besides DAPT legislation, Tennessee law includes the ability to create joint revocable trusts[152] and broad decanting power.[153]

New Hampshire

New Hampshire law permits residents and non-residents to create asset protection trusts under the New Hampshire Qualified Dispositions in Trust Act ("**NHQDTA**").[154] While not featuring any groundbreaking variations to its DAPT statute, New Hampshire repealed its Rule against Perpetuities[155] law and provides that income of a non-grantor trust, without New Hampshire based beneficiaries, is not subject to New Hampshire state income tax.[156]

Hawaii

Residents and non-residents can create asset protection trusts in Hawaii under the Permitted Transfers in Trust Act ("**PTTA**").[157] Hawaii's DAPT statute was initially best known for requiring a one-time 1 percent excise tax on the funding of the trust, a narrow definition of "**permitted property**" and a 25 percent net worth limitation on the transfer of permitted property to a trustee.[158]

Fortunately on June 23, 2011, Hawaii passed an amendment repealing the excise tax, expanding the definition of permitted property and removing the net worth limitation. Additionally, Hawaii eliminated its rule against perpetuities as it applies to a trust created pursuant to the PTTA.[159]

Virginia

Virginia law permits residents and non-residents to create an asset protection trust, called a qualified self-settled spendthrift trust (**QSSST**).[160] Only trusts that comply with sections 64.2-745.1 and 64.2-745.2 are eligible to receive protection from the settlor's creditors. Virginia law has one of the more creditor-friendly statutes of limitation in the amount of five years.[161] Even if the administration of a trust migrates from another *situs* to Virginia, the statute of limitations for purposes of the five-year look back period begins to run as of the date the trust meets all of the requirements for a QSSST under Virginia Law.[162]

However, the settlor of a QSSST is permitted to make an initial and subsequent transfers to a QSSST whereby a subsequent transfer to a QSSST does not recommence the statute of limitations as to the initial transfer or any other prior transfer.[163] Therefore, multiple transfers to a QSSST may have multiple statute of limitation periods running simultaneously. Any distribution from the trust to a beneficiary is deemed to come from the most recent property transferred to the trust first.

Ohio

Ohio law permits an individual to establish an asset protection trust under the "**Ohio Legacy Trust Act**" (the "**Ohio Act**").[164] The Ohio Revised Code contains many of the same definitions that are common to forming a DAPT in other jurisdictions.[165] Ohio's special features include its unique approach on Ohio's UFTA,[166] statute

of limitations on avoidance claims[167] and limitations on exception creditors.[168]

Mississippi

Mississippi permits residents and non-residents to create a "**qualified disposition trust**" under the Mississippi Qualified Disposition in Trust Act (the "**MQDTA**"), Title 91, Chapter 9, Article 15.[169] The MQDTA is modeled after the Delaware Qualified Disposition in Trust Act, and borrowed heavily from the language of the Tennessee Investment Services Trust Act.[170]

One of the most important aspect of the MQDTA is the authorization of spendthrift clauses that are effective against the settlor's own creditors, provided the transfer of property into a "**qualified disposition trust**" does not violate the Mississippi Uniform Fraudulent Transfer Act.[171] However, the limitations on actions by creditors in law or equity shall not apply and the creditors' claims shall not be extinguished if the transferor is indebted on account of an agreement, judgment, or order of a court for the payments enumerated in Miss. Code Ann. §91-9-707(i)(1).[172]

Although the MQDTA may be similar to the Delaware Qualified Disposition in Trust Act and the Tennessee Investment Services Trust Act, there are several factors that will generally render Mississippi an undesirable *situs* for non-residents to establish a DAPT, including issues related to an insurance requirement,[173] exception creditors,[174] state income taxation,[175] lack of directed trust legislation,[176] lack of decanting legislation[177] and use of the common law rule against perpetuities.[178]

West Virginia

West Virginia enables its citizens and persons residing outside of West Virginia to establish a DAPT; the "qualified self-settled spendthrift trust," under the West Virginia Uniform Trust Code (the "WVUTC").[179]

Unlike the handful of jurisdictions that established legislation that invites those from outside the state to have the strongest protection available for transfers to trusts, West Virginia's statute requires that there be no creditors existing that would be expected to be able to pursue the assets of the trust upon funding, and requires an extensive affidavit to be executed when any contribution is made to the trust that such contribution does not constitute a fraudulent transfer or other inappropriate arrangement.

OBSERVATION: This statute may provide West Virginia residents who have or will establish DAPTs in other jurisdictions some confidence that their local law may be applied in a challenge to such a trust structure in a supportive manner if the requirements of the West Virginia statutes are met (or close thereto).

West Virginia law contains many similar provisions to the other DAPT states. It should be noted that in considering West Virginia to create a DAPT, West Virginia has not repealed the statutory rule against perpetuities and instead follows the Uniform Statutory Rule Against Perpetuities.[180]

The major issues to address with the West Virginia legislation are the ability of a grantor to retain powers that will cause the grantor's gifts to the trust to be considered incomplete under what appears to be the current position of the Service and the ability of the grantor to use certain types of trusts that are common in the estate planning process such as grantor retained annuity trusts and qualified personal residence trusts while benefiting from the asset protection features otherwise provided to a grantor under the act. Other less salient issues are present as well such as the state income that will apply to non-grantor trusts in West Virginia and the potential change in the taxpayer who is considered the grantor of the trust under the grantor trust rules when a *Crummy* power is granted to a beneficiary and after it lapses and the original grantor retained certain powers or interests over or in the trust that would otherwise cause grantor trust status to the original grantor.

Additionally, West Virginia has a directed trust statute, albeit limited.[181]

Colorado

Colorado is not included as one of the sixteen states with DAPT law, as its law does not contain extensive statutory provisions permitting wealth protection trusts. However, section 38-10-111 of the Colorado Revised Statutes provides:

All deeds of gift, all conveyances, and all transfers or assignments, verbal or written, of goods,

chattels, or things in action, or real property, made in trust for the use of the person making the same shall be void as against the creditors existing of such person.

It is possible that this provision condones the creation of self-settled wealth protection trusts under certain circumstances in Colorado.[182]

Missouri

While Missouri law permits residents and non-residents to create DAPTs, the legislation is limited in scope.[183]

Rhode Island

While Rhode Island law permits residents and non-residents to create DAPTs, the legislation is limited in scope.[184]

CONCLUSION

Since 1997, when Alaska and Delaware revised their trust laws, the use of DAPTs has become a popular planning technique. Except for the cases featuring egregious facts as cited above, the efficacy of using such a trust for asset protection purposes has yet to be tested. With legislators in many states moving to enact the Uniform Voidable Transactions Act which, it is argued, will curtail the use of DAPTs,[185] it will be interesting to see whether DAPTs continue their popularity.

CHAPTER ENDNOTES

1. Restatement (Second) of Trusts §156(2) (1959). See also Restatement (Third) of Trusts §25.
2. Restatement (Third) of Trusts §58(2) (2003).
3. *See e.g.*, Stat. 3 Hen. VII, c.4. (1487), providing, "[a]ll deeds of gift of goods and chattels, made or to be made in trust to the use of that person or persons that made the same deed or gift, be void and of none effect."
4. Alaska Stat. §34.40.110.
5. Alaska Stat. §34.40.110(a).
6. *Id.*
7. *Id.*
8. *Id.*
9. Alaska Stat. §34.40.110(n)(2).
10. Alaska Stat. §13.36.035(c).

11. *Id.*

12. Alaska Stat. §13.36.390(3).

13. Alaska Stat. §13.36.320.

14. *Id.*

15. Alaska Stat. §34.40.110(b)(1)-(4).

16. Alaska Stat. §34.40.110(c).

17. *Id.*

18. Alaska Stat. §34.40.110(f).

19. Alaska Stat. §34.40.110(g).

20. Alaska Stat. §34.40.110(h).

21. Alaska Stat. §34.40.110(i).

22. *Id.*

23. Alaska Stat. §34.40.110(d).

24. Alaska Stat. §34.40.110(j).

25. *Id.*

26. Alaska Stat. §34.40.110(k).

27. *Id.*

28. Alaska Stat. §34.40.110(l).

29. *Id.*

30. *See* Alaska Community Property Act, effective May 23, 1998; Alaska Stat. §34.77.060.

31. *Id.*

32. Alaska Stat. §34.77.030(c).

33. Alaska Stat. §34.77.040.

34. Alaska Stat. §34.77.050.

35. Alaska Stat. §34.777.060(b).

36. *Battley v. Mortensen, et al., (In re Mortensen)*, 2011 WL 5025249 (Bankr. D. Alaska).

37. For a discussion of the background behind the closing of the so-called "loophole" of the self-settled trust, see Rothschild, "Did Bankruptcy Reform Act Close the 'Loophole' for the Wealthy?," Tax Notes (Apr. 25, 2005).

38. *See e.g., In re Addison*, 8th Cir., Nos. 07-2064, 07-2727, 8/7/08; *In re Osejo*, U.S. Bankruptcy Court, S.Dist. Florida, Case No. 10-31218-BKC-JKO, Chapter 7, 22 Fla. L. Weekly Fed. B727a (2011).

39. *See e.g.,* Fla. Stat. §§736.0505(1)(c), (3).

40. For an excellent analysis of *Mortensen*, see Shaftel, "*Court Finds Fraudulent Transfer to Alaska Asset Protection Trust,* 39 Est. Plan. 15 (Apr. 2012); Sulivan, Merric, Gillen, Bove & Nenno, *Fraudulent Transfer Claims,* * Trusts & Estates 43 (Dec. 2011); and Gopman & Rubin, *Further Analysis on In re Mortensen*, LISI Asset Protection Newsletter #187 (Nov. 7, 2011). See also Oshins & Keebler, *Mortensen: No, the Sky Isn't Falling for DAPTs!*, LISI Asset Protection Newsletter #186 (Oct. 31, 2011); and Adkisson & Riser, *Mortensen: Alaska Asset Protection Trust Fails To Protect Future Assets in Bankruptcy under New Section 548(e) Against Future Creditors,* LISI Asset Protection Newsletter #185 (Oct. 20, 2011).

41. 493 B.R. 798 (Bankr. W.D. Wash 2013).

42. Wash. Rev. Code §19.36.020.

43. *Id.*

44. *See e.g., id.*

45. *Id.*

46. Wash. Rev. Code §19.40.041(a)(1)–(2).

47. For a discussion of the *Huber* case see, Blattmachr, *In re Huber: Alaska Self-Settled Trust Held Subject to Claims of Creditors of Grantor-Beneficiary"* LISI Asset Protection Newsletter #225 (May 22, 2013); and Riser & Adkisson, *In re Huber*, LISI Asset Protection Newsletter #226 (June 18, 2013).

48. 413 P.3d 1199 (2018),

49. U.S. Const. Art. IV, §1.

50. 233 U.S. 354 (1914).

51. *Tennessee Coal, Iron & R. Co. v. George* 233 U.S. 354, at 360 (1914).

52. *In re IMO Daniel Kloiber Dynasty Trust*, 98 A.3d 924 (Del. Ch. 2014).

53. 547 U.S. 293 (2006),

54. 547 U.S. 293 at 314 (2006).

55. 448 F.3d 910 at 917 (6th Cir. 2006).

56. 682 F.2d 1311 at 1315 (9th Cir. 1982).

57. 98 A.3d 924 (Del. Ch. 2014),

58. *See e.g., Allstate Ins. Co. v. Gammon* 838 F.2d 73 (3rd Cir. 1988).

59. For further discussion and commentary of the *Toni I Trust* case and domestic asset protection trusts see, Blattmachr, Blattmachr, Shenkman and Gassman, *"Toni 1 Trust v. Wacker*: Reports of the Death of DAPTs for Non-DAPT Residents Is Exaggerated" (March 19, 2018) in the LISI Asset Protection Planning Newsletter #362, at http://www.leimbergservices.com; and Gassman and Tobergte, "Good Reasons that Domestic Asset Protection Trusts Are Still a Viable Strategy" (March 26, 2018) in the LISI Asset Protection Planning Newsletter #363 at http://www.leimbergservices.com.

60. *See* Del. Code Ann. tit. 12, part V, chap. 35, subchap. VI.

61. Del. Code Ann. tit. 12 §3570(7).

62. *Id.*

63. Del. Code Ann. tit. 12 §3570(4).

64. Del. Code Ann. tit. 12 §3570(6).

65. Del. Code Ann. tit. 12 §3570(8).

66. Del. Code Ann. tit. 12 §3570(10).

67. Del. Code Ann. tit. 12 §3570(8).

68. *Id.*

69. Del. Code Ann. tit. 12 §3313(d).

70. Del. Code Ann. tit. 12 §3570(8).

71. *Id.*

72. *Id.*

73. Del. Code Ann. tit. 12 §3570(11).

74. *Id.*

75. *Id.*

76. Del. Code Ann. tit. 12 §3570(11)b.

77. Del. Code Ann. tit. 1 §302(15).

78. Del. Code Ann. tit. 12 §3571.

79. Del. Code Ann. tit. 12 §3573(1).

80. Del. Code Ann. tit. 12 §3573(2).

81. Del. Code Ann. tit. 12 §3572(a).

82. *Id.*

83. *Id.*

84. Del. Code Ann. tit. 12 §3572(b).

85. Del. Code Ann. tit. 12 §3572(c).

86. Del. Code Ann. tit. 12 §3572(c).

87. Del. Code Ann. tit. 12 §3572(g).

88. Del. Code Ann. tit. 12 §3574(a).

89. Del. Code Ann. tit. 12 §3574.

90. *Id.*

91. Del. Code Ann. tit. 12 §3574(f).

92. Del. Code Ann. tit. 12 §3574(f) (for T by E property contributed to an asset protection trust); §3334 of (for T by E property contributed to a revocable trust).

93. *See* Del. Code Ann. tit. 12 §3334 (providing substantially similar rules regarding creditor rights with respect to T by E property contributed to a revocable trust).

94. Del. Code Ann. tit.13, chap. 2.

95. No. 8374-VCP (Del. Ch. Jan. 22, 2015).

96. (12 Del. C. §§3570-3576).

97. N.Y. C.P.L.R. §213(8).

98. 6 Del. C. §1309.

99. *TL of Fla.*, 2014 WL 3362367, at *5 (citing *Travelers Indem. Co. v. Lake*, 594 A.2d 38, 47 (Del. 1991)).

100. 12 Del. C. §3570(7).

101. 12 Del. C. §§3570 (8),(10),(11).

102. 12 Del. C. §3572(b)(2).

103. 12 Del. C. §3572(a).

104. *See* 12 Del. C. §3571.

105. For an excellent summary of this case, see "Alan Gassman & Travis Arango on *Trustco Bank v. Mathews*: Self-Settled, Spendthrift Trust Debtor Victory Involving Delaware Trusts, Allegations of Impermissible Control & Statute of Limitations Analysis," LISI Asset Protection Planning Newsletter #288 (Mar. 31, 2015) at http://www.leimbergservices.com.

106. Nev. Rev. Stat. §§166.010-166.170.

107. Nev. Rev. Stat. §166.170.

108. *See* Oshins, supra note 33.

109. *See* Sitkoff & Horowitz, *Unconstitutional Perpetual Trusts*, 67 Vand. L. Rev. 1769 (2014); Borowsky & Wallace, *In re Garretson*, LISI Asset Protection Newsletter #221 (Feb. 28, 2013). *But see* Oshins, *Bullion Monarch Mining, Inc. v. Barrick Goldstrike Mines: Unconstitutional Perpetual Trusts - Not So Fast Says the Nevada Supreme Court!* LISI Asset Protection Newsletter #2297 (Apr. 6, 2015).

110. Nev. Rev. Stat. §166.170.

111. 345 P.3d 566, 2015 UT 23, 2015 WL 404521 (Jan. 30, 2015), rehearing dened (Mar. 23, 2015), *opinion amended & superseded by* –P.3d— (Utah, Aug. 27, 2015), *cert.denied*, 136 S.Ct. 239 (Utah, Oct. 5, 2015).

112. 189 P.3d 51 (Utah 2008).

113. Nev. Rev. Stat. §163.560.

114. 2009 UT 31, 214 P.3d 854 (2009).

115. 2002 UT 69, ¶ 14, 54 P.3d 1054 (2002).

116. *See* Utah Code Ann. §75-7-107 & cmt. ("This section does not attempt to specify the strong public policies sufficient to invalidate a settlor's choice of governing law."); *see also Jacobsen Constr. Co. v. Teton Builders*, 2005 UT 4, ¶ 19, 106 P.3d 719 (2005)

(refusing to allow parties to "employ choice of law provisions to force forum states to enforce contractual terms wholly repugnant to local public policy").

117. Utah Code Ann. §75-7-605.

118. Utah Code Ann. §75-7-605(2).

119. Utah Code Ann. §75-7-401(1)(a).

120. *See* Utah Code Ann. §75-7-605(2).

121. *See e.g., Battley v. Mortensen, et al., (In re Mortensen)*, 2011 WL 5025249 (Bankr. D. Alaska); *Parrott v. Sasaki*, Del. Ch., C.A. No. 7227-VCL (Filed Feb. 7, 2012); & *In re Huber*, 493 B.R. 798 (Bankr. W.D. Wash 2013). For additional background on the Utah Supreme Court case, see Oshins & Spackman, *Dahl v. Dahl: Utah Supreme Court Rules Trust Not a Domestic Asset Protection Trust!*, LISI Asset Protection Newsletter #283 (Feb. 12, 2015). *See also* Adkisson, *Dahl v. Dahl*, LISI Asset Protection Newsletter #291 (Apr. 16, 2015).

122. 394 P.3d 940 (Supreme Court of Nevada 2017),

123. *Kaldi v. Farmers Inc. Exch.*, 117 Nev. 273, 281, 21 P.3d 16, 21 (2001).

124. Defeating the Self-Settled Spendthrift Trust in Bankruptcy, 28 Fla. St. U. L. Rev. 977, 986 (2001).

125. For additional commentary see: James Kane, "Augmening the 2017 Nevada Trust Win in Klabacka" in LISI Asset Protection Newsletter #358 (February 15, 2018) at http://www.leimbergservices.com.

126. *See* Utah Code Ann. §25-6-14.

127. *See* Okla. Stat. tit. 31, §10.

128. *Id.*

129. *Id.*

130. Okla. Stat. tit. 31, §13.

131. Okla. Stat. tit. 31, §11.5.a., b.

132. Okla. Stat. tit. 31, §11.5.c.

133. Okla. Stat. tit. 31, §11.5.d., e.

134. *See* Okla. Stat. tit. 31, §11.1., 11.2., 11.3. and 11.6.

135. Okla. Stat. tit. 31, §§12, 14.

136. Can a resident of another state create a preservation trust in Oklahoma? It is not specifically permitted in the FWPTA, however, it is not prohibited either? FWPTA §11.1. Under general trust law principals, non-residents should be able to establish such a trust, however, specific legislation inviting non-residents to establish such trusts would be comforting. It is also worth noting that the other exemptions under Title 31 of the Oklahoma Statutes appear to apply only to residents of Oklahoma. FWPTA §§1-3, 7. Additionally, drafting a preservation trust could also be tricky. For example, use of generic language permitting the trustee to make distributions to the grantor's "descendants" may disqualify the trust under the FWPTA. See FWPTA §11.6.a.

137. Oshins, 7th Annual Domestic Asset Protection Trust State Rankings Chart...with Links to Statutes!, LISI Asset Protection Newsletter (Apr. 5, 2016), chart available at http://www.oshins.com/images/DAPT_Rankings.pdf.

138. S.D. Codified Laws §55-16-9.

139. S.D. Codified Laws §55-16-15.

140. S.D. Codified Laws §55-16-10.

141. *Id.*

142. S.D. Codified Laws §55-16-16.

143. *Id.*

144. *Id.*

145. *Id.*

146. *Id.*

147. *Id.*

148. *See* South Dakota Codified Laws (SDCL) Ch. 55-17 "Special Spousal Trusts" effective July 1, 2016. Sections 29-42 of South Dakota Session Law 231—2016.

149. Wyo. Stat. Ann. §4-10-510.

150. *See* Leonard, *Wyoming Self-Settled Asset Protection Trusts*, LISI Asset Protection Newsletter #281 (Feb. 10, 2015).

151. Tenn. Code Ann. §35-15-505(1).

152. Tenn. Code Ann. §35-15-510.

153. Tenn. Code Ann. §35-15-816(b)(27).

154. N.H. Rev. Stat. Ann. §564-D:1, *et. seq.*

155. N.H. Rev. Stat. Ann. §564:24.

156. N.H. Rev. Stat. Ann. §77:10. *See* Burke, Brassard, Sanborn & Shields, *Why the Granite State Rocks at Trust Administration*, 43 Est. Pl. J. 3 (June 2016).

157. Haw. Rev. Stat. §554G-1, *et. seq.*

158. *See* Bove & Langa, *The Hawaiian Asset Protection Trust Law*, LISI Asset Protection Newsletter #165 (Oct. 26, 2010).

159. Haw. Rev. Stat. §525-4.

160. *See* VA Code §64.2-745.1-§64.2-745.2.

161. VA Code §64.2-745.1.

162. VA Code §64.2-745.1(G).

163. VA Code §64.2-745.1(F)(2).

164. Ohio Rev. Code §5816.14.

165. Ohio Rev. Code §5816.02.

166. Uniform Fraudulent Transfer Act (1984), §§4, 5; Ohio Rev. Code §§1336.04-.05, 5816.07(A) & (C).

167. Ohio Rev. Code §5816.07(B).

168. Ohio Rev. Code §5816.03(C). Additionally, a Legacy Trust is not subject to a spouse's marital property claim. *See* Ohio Rev. Code §5816.03(E).

169. Mississippi may have borrowed language from the Tennessee Act to a fault. Miss. Code Ann. §91-9-707(a) may be inconsistent with Miss. Code Ann. §91-9-707(b)(2)(B)—the former provision requires proof of "actual intent to defraud the creditor" only if the creditor's claim arose after a qualified disposition, while the latter provision requires proof of "intent to defraud that specific creditor" without any distinction as to when the claim arose.

170. *See* Mississippi Trust Reform Package Proposal, Report of the 2013 Secretary of State.

171. Sec. 15-3-101 *et seq.*, Miss. Code of 1972.

172. Miss. Code Ann. §91-9-707(i).

173. Miss. Code Ann. §91-9-707(i)(1)(D).

174. Miss. Code Ann. §91-9-707(i)(1)(B).

175. *Compare* Mississippi (Miss. Code Ann. §27-7-5(1); instructions to 2012 Miss. Form 81-110 at 1, 2), *with* Delaware, Hawaii, Missouri, New Hampshire, Ohio and Tennessee (states which do not tax asset protection trusts of nonresident settlors).

176. *See* Mississippi Trust Reform Package Proposal, Report of the 2013 Secretary of State.

177. *Id.*

178. *See Matter of Estate of Anderson*, 541 So.2d 423 (Miss. 1989); *Gill v. Gipson*, 982 So.2d 415 (Miss. App. 2007); *McCorkle v. Loumiss Timber Co.*, 760 So.2d 845 (Miss. App., 2000); *Weeks v. Mississippi College*, 749 So.2d 1082 (Miss. App. 1999).

179. See Title 91, Chapter 9, Article 15. Code of W.V. §§44D-5-503a, 44D-5-503b and §44D-5-503c (and amending and reenacting §44D-5-505).

180. *See* Code of W.V. §36-1A-1(a).

181. *See* Code of W.V. §44D-8-808. *See also* Nenno, Directed Trusts: Making Them Work, 38 Est. Gifts & Tr. J. 159 (Mar. 14, 2013).

182. *See e.g., In re: Baum*, 22 F.3d 1014 (1994). See, however, Sitkoff, "State Competition for Trust Funds," Ch. 12 University of Miami Heckerling Institute on Estate Planning 40, fn. #69 (2008) providing, "Some commentators have read an older statute in Colorado as authorizing APTs as to future creditors, see Colo. Rev. Stat. Ann. §38-10-111, but in *dicta* the Colorado Supreme Court has rejected that interpretation. *In re Cohen*, 8 P.3d 429, 432-34 (Colo. 1999)."

183. M.O. Rev. Stat. §456.5-505.

184. *See* R.I. Gen. L. §18-9.2-1, *et. seq.*

185. *See* Nenno & Rubin, *Uniform Voidable Transactions Act: Are Transfers to Self-Settled Spendthrift Trusts by Settlors in Non-APT States Voidable Transfers Per Se?*, LISI Asset Protection Newsletter #327 (Aug. 15, 2016), www.leimbergservices.com; Karibjanian, Wehle & Lancaster, *History Has Its Eyes on UVTA—A Response to Asset Protection Newsletter #319*, LISI Asset Protection Newsletter #320 (Apr. 18, 2016), www.leimbergservices.com.

OFFSHORE ASSET PROTECTION TRUSTS

CHAPTER 17

Trusts give clients an opportunity to "**forum shop**;" that is, to select the jurisdiction based on the laws that are most advantageous to protect assets. Just as real estate is governed by the laws of the location in which it is situated, a trust is usually governed by the laws of its situs, or "**home**." Grantors can even use a foreign country with laws more favorable to debtors.

A trust established in a foreign country is often called an **offshore trust.** Some foreign countries have a more protective statute of fraudulent conveyances for debtors. A trust in one of those countries can place a substantial practical barrier to debt collection because a creditor must first win in a United States court and then sue successfully in the foreign jurisdiction to be able to reach assets.

Nevertheless, offshore trusts have their own costs and limitations, which include the following:

- U.S. residents who establish offshore trusts remain within reach and jurisdiction of United States courts.

- A United States court that finds a debtor/ trustee liable to a creditor may hold the trustee in contempt if the trustee doesn't exercise retained powers to distribute trust assets back to himself or herself—and therefore back to the hands of creditors. Therefore, grantors can't have the use of the trust assets and protection too.

- If an independent foreign individual or corporate fiduciary (a more common technique) is a trustee, grantors may be giving up control of the trust assets and incurring significant administrative expenses.

- Few lawyers or accountants fully understand offshore trusts and the tax complexities that surround them, so the costs of sound advice is high (and there is a great potential for poor advice, which can turn out to be more expensive than good advice).

- The political stability and the security of cash and other assets sent abroad can be concerning, depending on the jurisdiction. It is a common practice to retain the power to change the situs of the trust and the power to remove and replace the trustee so, if there is a political change or other instability, grantors can quickly change the situs of the trust. Note that there is a problem only if the assets and the trust are in the same country.

Most offshore asset protection trusts are grantor trusts for federal income tax purposes (a result that is difficult to avoid). When a trust is a grantor trust, the grantor continues to be considered the owner of trust assets for income tax purposes and continues to be taxed on the trust income as it is produced. Thus, offshore asset protection trusts are not income tax savings devices. Because most asset-protection trusts are structured to avoid a current gift tax (by having the grantor retain certain powers or interests strong enough to classify the transfer of assets to the trust as something less than a completed and therefore taxable gift), the trust assets will still be included in the grantor's gross estate for estate tax purposes.

As a result, offshore asset protection trusts are not estate or generation-skipping transfer tax savings devices. Claims that offshore trusts can save taxes are almost always founded upon a scheme involving multiple trusts, corporations, and other parties, such as the creation of a Panamanian corporation to create a Bahamian trust that will invest in Swiss bank accounts for the benefit of a Cayman Islands corporation that will be the beneficiary of the trust, the stock of the corporation to be held by another trust created by another corporation of which family members will be the beneficiaries. The assumption is that the introduction of enough layers of trusts and corporations will keep the IRS from figuring out what is really happening. Such a structure is fraud, not tax planning.

The following sections discuss the laws of the relevant jurisdictions which offer offshore asset protection: Nevis, the Cook Islands, Belize, Bermuda and the Bahamas, with a particular focus on Nevis and the Cook Islands.

NEVIS TRUST LAW

The law of Nevis (officially known as the Federation of St. Christopher and Nevis; the island of St. Christopher is often referred to as "**St. Kitts**") contains specific legislation permitting the establishment of a self-settled trust. The legislation in Nevis contains all of the "**bells and whistles**" that a lawyer trained in the United States legal system should want included in a trust act of this type.

On May 27, 2015, the Nevis Island Assembly enacted the Nevis International Exempt Trust (Amendments) Ordinance, 2015 (the "**Trust Amendments**"). The Trust Amendments became effective July 1, 2015. The Nevis International Exempt Trust (Amendment) Ordinance, 2015 (the "**Ordinance**"), modernized the Nevis International Exempt Trust Ordinance, 1994 (the "**Original Ordinance**") and made it more competitive in the trust services market. Selected portions of the Ordinance are reproduced at the back of this chapter

Section 2 includes various definitions.[1] The terms *charitable remainder annuity trust* ("**CRAT**"), *charitable remainder unitrust* ("**CRUT**"; CRATs and CRUTs may collectively be referred to as charitable remainder trusts, or "**CRTs**"), *grantor retained annuity trust* ("**GRAT**"), and *grantor retained unitrust* ("**GRUT**") are defined to clarify that such trusts can be formed in Nevis with the settlor's retained interest in such trusts also being protected under Nevis law. Section 32(5) provides an expansive list of beneficiaries of an international trust:

> **(5)** A Nevis Company, a corporation, a limited liability company or a multiform foundation may also be a beneficiary of the trust.[2]

International Trust

The definition of *international trusts* requires that at least one of the trustees should be a Nevis LLC, a Nevis law firm, or a Nevis multiform foundation. The definition of non-residents is broad enough to include:

- a natural person who obtains citizenship in St. Kitts and Nevis by way of the citizenship investment program;

- a Nevis Business Corporation;

- a Nevis LLC; and

- a business entity incorporated, formed or established under the laws of any jurisdiction other than St. Kitts and Nevis, and which does not ordinarily engage in any trade or business within St. Kitts and Nevis.

Code Section 679 Issues

It should be noted that despite the specific reference to CRTs under Nevis trust law, a U.S. citizen would want to consider creating a CRT in the U.S. as opposed to Nevis. The settlor of a CRT would generally fund such trust with property that he or she expects to appreciate, with the goal of not paying tax on the gain. Under Section 679(a)(1) of the Internal Revenue Code, for each tax year, a U.S. person who directly or indirectly transfers property to a foreign trust is treated as the owner of the portion of the trust attributable to such property if for such taxable year there is a U.S. beneficiary of any portion of the trust. Since the charitable beneficiaries of a CRT must be U.S. charities, a Nevis CRT established by a U.S. settlor with a U.S. charitable remainder beneficiary would be subject to the provisions of section 679 because the domestic charity is a U.S. person with an interest in the trust. This would cause unnecessary tax consequences to the U.S. citizen settlor. The exception to the application of section 679 for foreign charitable trusts only applies to trusts that are exclusively devoted to charitable purposes under Code section 501(c)(3), not to CRTs that gain their U.S. tax exemption under section 664(c).[3] According to the applicable regulation:

> In order for a trust to be a charitable remainder trust, it must meet the definition of and function exclusively as a charitable remainder trust from the creation of the trust. Solely for the purposes

of section 664 and the regulations thereunder, the trust will be deemed to be created at the earliest time that neither the grantor nor any other person is treated as the owner of the entire trust under subpart E, part 1, subchapter J, chapter 1, subtitle A of the Code (relating to grantors and others treated as substantial owners), but in no event prior to the time property is first transferred to the trust. For purposes of the preceding sentence, neither the grantor nor his spouse shall be treated as the owner of the trust under such subpart E merely because the grantor or spouse is named as a recipient.[4]

While this provision prevents the interest of the U.S. settlor or settlor's spouse from causing a foreign trust to fail to qualify as a CRT, the requirement that the charitable beneficiary be domestic would cause any otherwise eligible CRT to fail to qualify if the CRT were set up as a foreign trust because section 679 would still apply.[5]

Code Section 684 Issues

An additional consideration for foreign CRTs is warranted under Code section 684, which is an income recognition provision for a taxpayer who transfers appreciated property to certain foreign trusts. Absent section 684, appreciated property could be transferred to a foreign nongrantor trust without any gain recognition, and the asset subsequently sold without any U.S. income taxation being imposed on that asset's built-in gain at the time of transfer. Section 684(a) provides that a transfer of appreciated property by a U.S. person to a foreign nongrantor trust is not subject to gain recognition. The transferor must recognize a capital gain with respect to the transferred property, which is then included on the transferor's U.S. income tax return for the year of the transfer and subject to U.S. income taxation.

Under section 684(b), section 684(a) does not apply to the extent a U.S. person is treated as the owner of such trust under Code section 671. As previously discussed, section 679 specifically applies to foreign trusts, which have one or more U.S. beneficiaries. If section 679 ceases to apply due to a change in circumstances, then section 684 could apply at the change in circumstances, even if the change occurred years later.

If section 679 were to apply and the appreciated property contributed to the foreign trust were subsequently sold, any built-in gain with respect to the appreciated property contributed to the foreign trust would be recognized and subject to U.S. income taxation. Consequently, the income recognition provision of section 684(a) would not be necessary. In this case, there is no reason to accelerate the taxation of the built-in gain in those cases where section 679 applies.[6] Under the applicable regulations, if the settlor ceases to be treated as the section 679 owner because of the settlor's death but the trust is includible in the settlor's taxable estate, making it eligible for a step-up in basis, section 684 is not triggered.[7] Also, section 684 is not triggered if property is transferred to a foreign trust devoted exclusively to charitable purposes as described in section 501(c)(3), even if the trust has not applied for recognition of its exempt status or given notice of its intent to do so.[8] Section 3 provides that an international trust registered under the Ordinance is valid and enforceable even if it is invalid according to the law of settlor's domicile, residence, place of current incorporation, place of formation or establishment.[9] This section is helpful since most trusts are formed or established in jurisdictions other than a settlor's domicile or residence.

Rule Against Perpetuities

For many years, Nevis' Rule Against Perpetuities (RAP) was a restrictive one hundred years.[10] Section 5(1) eliminates the RAP and permits a trust to continue forever if the terms of the trust provide that the trustee has the unlimited power to sell all trust assets or if one or more persons (one of whom may be the trustee) has the unlimited power to terminate the trust, and Sections 5(3) and 5(4) eliminate the Rule Against Accumulations.

Creditor Claims

Section 8A greatly limits the rights of a creditor to reach a beneficiary's interest in such a trust. In the absence of such a provision, a creditor of a beneficiary might attempt to obtain a court order to garnish future distributions made to or for the benefit of a beneficiary. Such garnishment could result in a trustee being unable to make any distributions for the benefit of a beneficiary. This section also specifically permits a trustee to make payments to third parties on behalf of the beneficiary without incurring any liability to a creditor and prevents even the remote possibility of any such attachment, garnishment or interference.

Section 9(3) allows a trust protector to be granted the authority to direct a trustee to make distributions; approve distributions made by a trustee; and direct the trustee to make investments. By giving a protector authority to direct the trustee to make distributions and investments, in conjunction with giving trustees an indemnity for following the directions of the protector, a trustee has the ability to administer trusts it might not otherwise be willing to administer and it will facilitate the administration of a trust because the trustee is exonerated from liability for acting at the direction of a protector. Section 45(1) coincides with Section 9 by providing an expanded list of authorized trust investments to include such assets approved by the protector.

Section 9A of the Ordinance clarifies that creditors will only have a right to a beneficiary's interest in a trust if that beneficiary has either a lifetime or testamentary general power of appointment, that is, a power to appoint the trust property to the beneficiary, the beneficiary's estate, the beneficiary's creditors, or the creditors of the beneficiary's estate, however, only to the extent that the beneficiary exercises such power of appointment. This provision codifies the common law rule regarding general powers of appointment and further provides that the amount subject to a creditor's reach could never exceed the amount subject to the exercise of the beneficiary's power.

Additionally, Section 9B clarifies that creditors only have a right to a settlor's interest in a trust if the settlor retains a power to revoke the trust and to appoint the trust property to the settlor, the settlor's estate, the settlor's creditors, or the creditors of the settlor's estate, however, only to the extent the settlor exercises such power. Section 9B enhances the asset protection provided by an international trust by giving creditors the right to a settlor's interest only in the limited circumstances where the settlor has unfettered control of the trust property and exercises such control, however, only to the extent of such exercise.

The additions of Sections 9A and 9B were in direct response to the holding in *Tasarruf Mevduati Sigorta Fonu v. Merrill Lynch Bank and Trust Company, et al.*[11] In *Tasarruf*, the Privy Council held that a power to revoke retained by the settlor of two trusts established and funded in the Cayman Islands was tantamount to a property interest because it was a personal power, not a fiduciary power, *i.e.*, the settlor owed no duty of trust or confidence to any other person, and no act personal to the settlor was required to be performed. Therefore, the

power could be delegated and/or assigned by the settlor to another person. Thus, the court in *Tasarruf* allowed the settlor's creditors to reach the assets held in two revocable trusts. The holding in *Tasarruf* was in direct conflict with existing Cayman law and represented a rare instance where the Privy Council overturned the holding of the trial court and the Eastern Caribbean Court of Appeals where underlying common law in the jurisdiction was clear.

The codification of this rule should preclude a creditor of the settlor of an international trust who has retained a power of revocation from reaching the assets held in such trust and subject to the power of revocation notwithstanding the holding in *Tasarruf*. Likewise, Section 9A should preclude creditors of a beneficiary possessing a power of withdrawal from attaching the trust property. Even though the Ordinance contains these specific provisions, it is recommended that U.S. clients refrain from including such powers in an international trust as a U.S. court would almost certainly have serious problems with a settlor's unfettered control of the trust property.

Section 13 provides that any person granted the power under the terms of a trust to demand or request any act on the part of a settlor, beneficiary, trustee, protector, or other person, or who has the authority to approve, veto or compel any action or exercise any power that could affect an international trust, may ignore demands or requests given by or as the result of persons acting under duress, including pursuant to any legal process, court, administrative body, etc. This Section prevents a claimant from circumventing the limitations on remedies contained elsewhere in the Ordinance, such as under Section 24 concerning creditor claims.

The main purpose of an asset protection trust is to protect its settlor in a time of great need. In *Federal Trade Commission v. Affordable Media, LLC*,[12] the court in the Cook Islands issued a *Mareva* injunction freezing the assets of the trust (i.e., cash in a bank account at a bank in the Cook Islands). Then, while frozen, such funds were not available for use by the settlors to pay their basic living expenses. Such action frustrated the purpose of the trust until the creditors settled. Section 22 clarifies that the Court may not issue a *Mareva* injunction, Anton Piller order, or any similar remedy.

Section 35A automatically removes a trustee or protector of an international trust that is subject to any other court's jurisdiction, except the High Court of

St. Christopher and Nevis. This statutory duress provision is unique among jurisdictions. The provision has its origins in the section 3327 of the Delaware Trust Code. However, it is a vastly improved provision. Together, Sections 13, 22 and 35A of the Ordinance make Nevis the strongest jurisdiction in the world to establish an asset protection trust.

Section 17(1) allows the *terms* of an international trust to indemnify the trustee against liability.

> A beneficiary may relieve a trustee of liability for a breach of trust or indemnify a trustee against liability for a breach of trust and the terms of the trust may relieve a trustee of liability for a breach of trust or indemnify a trustee against liability for a breach of trust.

This is an expansion from many offshore jurisdictions which typically only permitted a *beneficiary* to indemnify the trustee.

Fraudulent Transfers[13]

The original text was modeled after Section 13B(3) and (4) of the Cook Islands International Trusts Act ("**ITA**"). The ITA deems a transfer in trust not to be fraudulent as against a creditor if the transfer takes place two years from when the creditor's cause of action accrues. If the transfer takes place within two years of the cause of action accruing, the ITA deems the transfer to be not fraudulent if the creditor fails to commence a court action within one year. Similarly, the ITA deems a transfer in trust to be not fraudulent as against a creditor if the transfer takes place before the creditor's cause of action accrues.

Section 24(3) differs from other jurisdictions by eliminating what arguably had previously given a creditor a three-year window to file a fraudulent transfer claim against an international trust. This "**sliding window**" was introduced in section 13B(3) of the Cook Islands ITA, after which subsection (3) of Section 24 was modeled. While paragraph 13B(3)(a) of the ITA is intended to protect a transfer in trust made more than two years after a creditor's cause of action accrues, paragraph (b) gives the creditor one more year to bring a claim if the creditor's claim happens to arise right before the expiration of the two year period referenced in paragraph (a). The revision to section 24(3) implements a fixed one-year window beginning with the date on which the creditor's cause of action accrues.

Further, section 24(5)(b) expands the list of powers that a settlor can retain without having an intent to defraud a creditor imputed to the settlor.

Other Notable Sections

Bankruptcy. Section 46 clarifies that an international trust may be void or voidable in the event of a settlor's bankruptcy, insolvency or liquidation, including if a corporation or limited liability company is in liquidation.

Combination and division of trusts. Section 35B allows the trustee of an international trust to combine two or more separate trusts into a single trust or divide a single trust into two or more separate trusts provided that such action does not impair the rights of any beneficiary or adversely affect the purpose of the trust or trusts. This provision permits the trustee to segregate the assets of a trust for greater protection and liability purposes, and to combine the assets of separate trusts where administratively more convenient or efficient. It also provides rules governing any such combination or severance. Section 36 allows a trustee to act pursuant to a resolution and to appoint an agent to act on its behalf.[14]

Effect of provisions of instrument. Section 35C(1) provides that the terms of a trust deed may expand, restrict, eliminate, or otherwise vary the rights and interests of beneficiaries, including the right of beneficiaries to be informed of their interests in the trust for any period, the grounds for removal of a trustee, the circumstances, if any, in which the trustee must diversify investments, and a trustee's powers, duties, standard of care, rights of indemnification and liability to persons who are granted interests under the trust instrument. Section 35C(1) provides that a trustee has no duty to account and differs from a longstanding rule under English law.[15] In *Armitage v Nurse*,[16] the court provided in *dicta*:

> The respondents submit that the policy to which section 21(3) of the Act of 1980 gives effect is that it would be unfair to bar a plaintiff from bringing a claim unless and until he is of full age and entitled to see the trust documents and so has the means of discovering the injury to his beneficial interest. The difficulty with this argument, in my judgment, is that it proves too much. Every beneficiary is entitled to see the trust accounts, whether his interest is in possession or not.

The rationale of section 21(3) appears to me to be different. It is not that a beneficiary with a future interest has not the means of discovery, but that he should not be compelled to litigate (at considerable personal expense) in respect of an injury to an interest which he may never live to enjoy. Similar reasoning would apply to exclude a person who is merely the object of a discretionary trust or power which may never be exercised in his favor.

Registered office. Section 42(1) includes limited liability companies and multiform foundations on a list of entities where an international trustee may have its registered office: "(1) The registered office of an international trust shall be the office of the Nevis Company, attorney-at-law, corporation, limited liability company or multiform foundation which is the trustee."

Retention of control by Settlor. Section 47 provides a list of interests and powers that a settlor can retain over an international trust without a trust being declared invalid. The list incorporates many of the types of trusts used in the United States for estate planning purposes, such as GRATs and GRUTs which are permitted under the statutes of most of the states that allow self-settled asset protection trusts.[17]

The revisions broaden the circumstances where the validity of an international trust will be upheld. Thus, the settlor can retain various rights and/or benefits over the trust and from the income and/or principal of the trust and the terms of a trust deed can provide for an expanded array of powers to be granted to a protector.

Power to establish the Nevis International Exempt Trust Ordinance Advisory Committee. Section 54 clarifies that the Minister (as defined in Section 2) may establish an advisory body for matters affecting the Ordinance.

Bond requirement to bring action. Section 55 is the amount of the bond required by a creditor before the creditor is permitted to bring an action governed by the Ordinance.[18] The bond requirement is 270,000 Eastern Caribbean Dollars. As a comparison, the previous bond requirement was only 100,000 Eastern Caribbean Dollars.[19] This increase was made to eliminate frivolous or nuisance claims against the trustees of international trusts. The bond requires that a creditor will pay the trustee's legal fees expended to defend and protect the assets held in a trust.

Community property and tenancy by the entireties property. Section 56 deals with concepts familiar to most United States attorneys: community property and tenants by the entireties. A new Section 56(2) was added permitting married settlors of an international trust to establish a STET. Following funding the settlors' interest in such trust with tenancy by the entireties property, the underlying property of the international trust will remain tenancy by the entireties property.

COOK ISLANDS

The law of the Cook Islands contains specific legislation permitting the establishment of a self-settled trust. The legislation in the Cook Islands contains all of the "bells and whistles" that a lawyer trained in the United States legal system should want included in a trust act of this type. The act is referred to as the International Trusts Act 1984 (the "Cook Islands Act").

Section 13F(1) of the Cook Islands Act contains a provision specifically recognizing the validity and enforceability of a spendthrift provision in the trust.[20] Section 13C(g) of the Cooks Islands Act provides that a settlor may also be a beneficiary of the trust and the settlor's interest will not affect the validity of the trust. The settlor can be either the sole beneficiary of the trust or one of multiple beneficiaries.[21] Under Section 13C of the Cook Islands Act, an international trust will not be declared invalid or otherwise be affected in any manner if the settlor retains, possesses or acquires:

- the power to revoke the trust;

- the power to amend the trust;

- any benefit, interest or property from the trust;

- the power to remove or appoint a trustee or protector; and

- the power to direct a trustee or protector on any matter.[22]

Further, Section 13C(g) of the Cook Islands Act provides that an international trust is not invalid even though the settlor may be the only beneficiary of the trust or the settlor is one of multiple beneficiaries. Although the Cook Islands Act permits a settlor to retain the right to revoke and/or amend the trust, it is not recommended that the settlor retain such authority. Such a power might cause even a court in the United

Kingdom to rule against the efficacy of such trust for asset protection purposes.[23]

Under Section 13D of the Cook Islands Act, foreign judgments against settlors, donors, trustees, protectors or beneficiaries of international trusts will not be recognized.[24]

Section 14 of the Cook Islands Act provides that a trust established under the act must be registered with the Registrar of International Trusts within forty-five days after it is established.[25]

The Cook Islands is viewed as one of the most difficult jurisdictions for a creditor to attack a trust and gain access to its assets.[26] More than one recent article has described the potential creditor protection benefits of a Cook Islands Trust.[27]

International Trust

Section 2 of the Cook Islands Act defines the term "International Trust." Under this section an International Trust is a trust registered under the Cook Islands Act that has at least one trustee that is either a registered foreign company, an international company or a trustee company.[28] Furthermore, all beneficiaries of the trust must be "nonresident." According to Section 2 of the Cook Islands Act, "nonresident" means an individual who is not domiciled in the Cook Islands and is not ordinarily resident in the Cook Islands.

Fraudulent Transfers

The issue of what constitutes a fraudulent transfer is addressed in Section 13B of the Cook Islands Act:

- The burden of proof is on the creditor.

- The standard of proof is "beyond a reasonable doubt" (the highest standard in a common law system).

- A creditor must meet a conjunctive test to prove a transfer was fraudulent:

  o The creditor must prove that the trust was settled, established or disposed of by the settlor with the principal intent to defraud the particular creditor questioning the transfer; and

  o The creditor must prove that the transfer rendered the settlor insolvent or without assets that such creditor's claim (if successful) could have been satisfied.

Assuming a creditor is successful in proving a fraudulent transfer it is important to note that the trust is *not* void or voidable.

If immediately following the transfer of property to the trust the settlor retained property with a fair market value that exceeded the value of the creditor's claim, the transfer to the trust shall be deemed not to have been made with the principal intent of the settlor to defraud his creditor.

There is a two-year/one-year statute of limitations. A transfer to a trust is not fraudulent if settled, established or the disposition occurs after the expiration of two years from the date such creditor's cause of action accrued. (This time limit will not apply, however, in situations where a creditor has already commenced proceedings in respect of his cause of action.) Furthermore, a transfer to a trust is not fraudulent if settled, established or a disposition occurs before the expiration of two years from the date that a creditor's cause of action accrued and that creditor fails to commence such action before the expiration of one year from the date that such settlement, establishment or disposition occurs.[29]

Under Section 13K of the Cook Islands Act, no action may be brought in the Cook Islands to set aside an international trust or a transfer to an international trust or to seek relief under Section 13B of the act (for fraudulent transfers) unless the action is brought within two years of the date of the settlement or disposition.[30]

Confidentiality

Section 23(1) of Cook Islands Act contains a privacy provision that mandates that matters related to an International Trust must kept confidential and not be disclosed. It provides:

Except where the provisions of this Act require and subject to this section, it shall be an offence under this Act for a person to divulge or communicate to any other person information relating to the establishment, constitution, business undertaking or affairs of an international trust.[31]

Section 23(2) of the Cook Islands Act contains limited exceptions to this privacy rule providing that it will not apply if disclosure is required or authorized by the "**Court**," is made to discharge any duty, perform any function or exercise any power under the Act or is required by a search warrant.[32] (The term "Court" refers to the High Court of the Cook Islands. See Section 2 of the Cook Islands Act.)

Section 23(5) of the Cook Islands Act also contains a limited exception to this privacy rule permitting disclosure for administrative purposes and when the trustee needs to seek the advice of legal counsel in administering the trust.[33]

Section 28 of the Cook Islands Act provides penalties for any person who violates this privacy rule, including the imposition of a fine not to exceed $10,000 or imprisonment for up to one (1) year.[34]

BELIZE

Belize has enacted the "Belize Trusts Act of 2000." The act was amended by the Trusts (Amendment) Act, 2007 (collectively the "Belize Acts").

International Trust

Part XA, Section 64 of the Belize Acts defines the term "international trust" or "offshore trust." Under this section an international trust or offshore trust means a trust where the settlor is not a resident in Belize, none of the beneficiaries are residents of Belize, the trust property does not include land situated in Belize, the trust is governed by the law of Belize and in the case of a purpose trust, the purpose or object of the trust is to be performed or pursued outside of Belize.[35]

Under Section 65C of the Belize Acts, trusts registered in the "International Trusts Registry" shall not be open for public inspection except that the trustee or the trust agent of a trust may in writing authorize a person to inspect the entry of that trust on the Register.[36] Under Section 65D of the Belize Acts, where an international trust is duly registered, the trust shall be exempt from taxes and duties.[37]

Rule Against Perpetuities

Under Section 6 of the Belize Acts, the maximum duration of a non-charitable trust is 120 years from the date of the trust's creation and a trust shall terminate on the 120th anniversary of the date of the trust's creation.[38] However, under section 6(3), the rule against perpetuities shall not apply to any trust.[39]

Foreign Claims

Under Section 7 of the Belize Acts, without any waiting period, the Belizian Court cannot set aside a trust created under its laws, recognize any claim against the assets of the trust, or the order of a court of another jurisdiction respecting the trust, with regard to marriage, divorce, forced heirship, and creditor claims in the event of a settlor's insolvency.[40] This applies notwithstanding Belizian fraudulent transfer laws, bankruptcy laws, and international reciprocity laws according to the Law of Property Act Section 149, the Belizian Bankruptcy Act Section 42 and the Belizian Reciprocal Enforcement of Judgments Act.[41]

Spendthrift Provision

Section 12 of the Belize Acts contains a provision specifically recognizing the validity and enforceability of a spendthrift provision in the trust.[42] Section 9(2), Part II of the Belize Acts provides that a settlor may also be a beneficiary, trustee or protector of the trust.[43]

Fraudulent Transfers

Under section 149(1) of the Belize Law of Property Act, every transfer of property made, whether before or after the commencement of Section 149, with intent to defraud creditors, shall be voidable, at the instance of any person thereby prejudiced. There are two exceptions: the operation of a disentailing assurance, or the law of bankruptcy for the time being in force; and any estate or interest in property transferred for valuable consideration and in good faith or upon consideration and in good faith to any person not having, at the time of the transfer, notice of the intent to defraud creditors.[44]

Under section 7(2) of the Belize Acts, a trust shall be invalid and unenforceable if:

(i) it purports to do anything contrary to the law of Belize; or

(ii) it purports to confer any right or power or impose any obligation the exercise of which or the carrying out of which is contrary to the law of Belize; or

(iii) it has no beneficiary identifiable or ascertainable (unless the trust was created for a valid charitable or non-charitable purpose).[45]

Additionally, a trust shall be invalid and unenforceable to the extent that the Court declares that—

(i) the trust was established by duress, fraud, mistake, undue influence or misrepresentation; or

(ii) the trust is immoral or contrary to public policy; or

(iii) the terms of the trust are so uncertain that its performance is rendered impossible (provided that a charitable purpose shall be deemed always to be capable of performance); or

(iv) the settlor was, at the time of its creation, incapable under the law in force in Belize of creating such a trust.[46]

Breach of Trust

Under Section 50 of the Belize Acts, a trustee who commits or concurs in a breach of trust is liable for any loss or depreciation in value of the trust property resulting from the breach and any profit which would have accrued to the trust had there been no breach.[47] Where trustees are liable for a breach of trust, they are joint and severally liable.[48] However, under Section 54 of the Belize Acts, the court may relieve a trustee of liability for a breach of trust where it appears that the trustee acted honestly and reasonably and ought fairly to be excused for the breach of trust.[49]

Under Section 55 of the Belize Acts, where a trustee commits a breach of trust at the instigation, at the request or with the concurrence of a beneficiary, the Court may impound all or part of the interest by way of indemnity to the trustee or any person claiming through him.[50] Section 56 provides:

(1) no period of limitation or prescription applies to an action brought against a trustee-

(a) in respect of any fraud to which the trustee was a party or was privy; or

(b) to recover from the trustee trust property or the proceeds thereof-

(i) held by or vested in the trustee or otherwise in the trustee's possession or under control; or

(ii) previously received by the trustee and converted to the trustee's use.[51]

Also under Section 56 of the Belize Acts, the period to bring an action founded on breach of trust may be brought against a trustee within three years from delivery of the final accounts of the trust or three years from the date on which the plaintiff first has knowledge of the breach of trust, whichever period begins to run first.[52]

BERMUDA TRUST LAW

Unlike the Cook Islands or Nevis, Bermuda's trust laws are not contained in one act. Laws governing Bermuda trusts are The Trusts (Special Provisions) Act 1989 (as amended by the 1998 and 2004 Amending Acts, collectively the "Bermuda Special Provisions Act"); Perpetuities and Accumulations Act 1989 (as amended by the Perpetuities and Accumulations Act of 2009); Bankruptcy Act of 1989; Judgment (Reciprocal enforcements) 1976; Bermuda Conveyancing Act of 1983 and the Trustee Act (as amended by the 1999 Amending Act).

Under Section 2 of the Bermuda Special Provisions Act, the expressions "trust" and "trustee" extend to cases where the trustee has a beneficial interest in the trust property.[53] Section 12A of the Bermuda Special Provisions Act defines a purpose trust as a trust created for a non-charitable purpose or purposes provided that the following conditions are that the purpose or purposes are:

• sufficiently certain to allow the trust to be carried out;

• lawful; and

• not contrary to public policy.[54]

Under Section 11 of the Bermuda Special Provisions Act, a Bermuda trust shall not be varied or set aside (neither shall the capacity of any settlor be questioned nor shall any trustee, beneficiary or other person be subject to any liability or deprived of any rights) by reason that:

(a) the law of any another jurisdiction prohibits or does not recognize the concept of a trust;

(b) the trust or disposition avoids or defeats rights, claims or interests conferred by the law of another jurisdiction upon any person by reason of a personal relationship to the settlor or any beneficiary or by way of heirship rights; or

(c) the trust or disposition avoids or defeats rights, claims or interests conferred by the law of another jurisdiction upon any person in respect of the protection of creditors in matters of insolvency.[55]

Rule Against Perpetuities

The Perpetuities and Accumulations Act of 2009 repealed Section 12A(5) of the Trusts (Special Provisions) Act of 1989 (which applied the rule against perpetuities to a purpose trust).[56] Under Section 3 of the Perpetuities and Accumulations Act of 2009, the rule against perpetuities applies to each of the estate or interests only to the extent that the property is *land* in Bermuda.[57]

Creditor Claims

Under Section 36A of the Conveyancing Act of 1983, a "disposition" means any disposition of property including the exercise of a power of appointment, any trust, gift, transfer, sale, exchange, etc; an "eligible creditor" is a person to whom:

(a) On, or within two years after, the material date the transferor owed an obligation and on the date of the action or proceeding to set aside the relevant disposition that obligation remains unsatisfied;

(b) On the material date the transferor owed a contingent liability and since that date the contingency giving rise to the obligation has occurred and on the date of the action or proceeding to set aside the relevant disposition that obligation remains unsatisfied; or

(c) On the date of the action or proceeding to set aside the relevant disposition, the transferor owes an obligation in consequence of a claim, made by that person against the transferor, arising from a cause of action which accrued prior to, or within two years after, the material date.[58]

The "material date" means the date on which a relevant disposition is made, and the "obligation" means any obligation or liability, other than a contingent liability, to pay a sum of money or to transfer property.[59] Property includes money goods, things in action, land and every description of property wherever situated and every description of interest, whether present or future or vested or contingent, arising out of, or incidental to, property.[60]

Requisite intention means an intention of a transferor to make a disposition the dominant purpose of which is to put the property which is the subject of that disposition beyond the reach of a person or a class of persons who is making, or may at some time make, a claim against him.[61]

Under Section 36C of the Conveyancing Act of 1983, every disposition of property made with the requisite intention and at an undervalue shall be voidable at the instance of an eligible creditor; where a person seeking to set aside a relevant disposition was not, on the material date, a person to whom an obligation was owed by the transferor, the Court shall not set aside that disposition unless the Court is satisfied that the person was, on the material date, reasonably foreseeable by the transferor as a person to whom an obligation might become owed by him.[62] Section 36C(3) of the Conveyancing Act of 1983 provides that no action or proceeding to set aside a disposition shall be commenced *unless* such action or proceeding is commenced:

(1) in the case of an eligible creditor, within six years after the material date or within 6 years after the date when the obligation became owed, which is the later date;

(2) in the case of an eligible creditor, within six years after the material date;

(3) in the case of eligible creditor, within six years after the material date, or within 6 years after the date when the cause of action accrued, whichever is the later date.[63]

Under section 36D(2) of the Conveyancing Act of 1983, the burden of proving that a transferee or any person through whom the transferee claims has not acted in good faith shall be upon the person making the allegation.[64]

However, Section 36G of the Conveyancing Act of 1983 states that nothing in Section 36 shall be construed as creating or enable any right, claim or interest on behalf of a creditor or person which right, claim or interest would be avoided or defeated by Section 11 of the Bermuda Special Provisions Act.[65]

The United States and Bermuda have a treaty providing for an exchange of information and assistance in collection issues against non-Bermuda residents with regard to both criminal and civil tax cases.[66]

Foreign Claims

Under section 11(2) of the Bermuda Special Provisions Act, a foreign judgment shall not be recognized, enforced or give rise to any estoppels.[67]

Section 12B of the Bermuda Special Provisions Act provides that the Supreme Court may make such order as it considers expedient for the enforcement of a purpose trust, provided that under subsection (3), the Supreme Court, with regards to costs incurred in connection with any application under Section 12B, may make such order as it considers just as to payment of any costs incurred.[68]

Breach of Trust

Under section 22(1) of the Trustee Act, a trustee is not liable for loss except where arising through deliberate, reckless or negligent breach of an equitable duty.[69]

BAHAMAS TRUST LAW

The law governing trusts in the Bahamas is referred to as the Trustee Act, 1998 (the "Bahamian Act").

Section 2(i) of the Bahamian Act provides that the term "trust" shall not include the duties incident to property subject to a mortgage but with this exception "trust" and "trustee" extend to implied, constructive and resulting trusts.[70] Section 3(1) of the Act provides, however, that

the retention, possession or acquisition by the settlor of any one or more powers and provisions referred to in section 3(2) shall not invalidate a trust or the trust instrument or cause a trust created *inter vivos* to be a testamentary trust or disposition or the trust instrument creating it to be a testamentary document, including:

- power to revoke the trust or withdraw property from the trust;

- powers of appointment or disposition over any of the trust property;

- powers to amend the trust;

- powers to appoint, add or remove trustees, protectors or beneficiaries;

- powers to give directions to trustees in connection with said trustee's exercise of any of the trustee's powers or discretions;

- any provisions requiring the consent of the settlor to any act or abstention of trustees;

- the appointment of the settlor as protector of the trust;

- any beneficial interests of the settlor; and

- any interests of the settlor in any companies or assets underlying the trust property.[71]

Section 40(1) of the Bahamian Act provides that it shall be lawful for an instrument or disposition to provide that any estate or interest in any property given or to be given to any individual as a beneficiary shall not during the life of the beneficiary, or such lesser period as may be specified in the instrument or disposition, be alienated or pass by bankruptcy, insolvency or liquidation or be liable to be seized, sold, attached, or taken in execution by process of law and where so provided such provision shall take effect accordingly.[72] However, section 40(5) of the Bahamian Act provides that Subsection 1 does *not* apply to the settlor nor to any other person donating property to a Bahamian trust.[73]

Rule Against Perpetuities

Section 6 of the Bahamian Perpetuities Act of 1995 and Section 2 of the Perpetuities Act of 2004 provides that trusts are limited in duration to a period measured by the lives of persons alive at the time when the perpetuity period beings to run, plus twenty-one years or, alternatively, a period of years not to exceed 150 years.[74]

Note that the Bahamas has entered into mutual assistance agreements regarding disclosure of information in connection with suspected criminal activities, including a tax information exchange with the United States.[75]

Spendthrift Provision

Section 40(5) of the Bahamian Act, taken in conjunction, with section 3(1) and section 2(i), indicate that although a settlor may be a beneficiary of a Bahamian trust, said settlor may not benefit from a spendthrift provision of such Bahamian Trust.[76]

Fraudulent Transfers

Under Section 4 of the Bahamian Fraudulent Disposition Act of 1991, a two year statute of limitations is placed on the commencement of any action related to a fraudulent transfer. The burden of establishing a settlor's fraudulent intent is on the creditor seeking to set aside the transfer.[77]

Taxation

Section 93 of the Bahamian Act exempts non-Bahamian trust beneficiaries from taxes, including income tax, capital gains tax, estate tax, or inheritance tax.[78]

Registration

Section 94 of the Bahamian Act exempts trusts and other deeds executed by the trustees, settlors, beneficiaries or protectors of a trust from registration under the provisions of the Bahamian Registration of Records Act.[79]

Section 90(16) (First Schedule) of the Bahamian Act provides that the trustees of a Bahamian trust shall not be required to give a bond or security for the administration of a "Trust Fund" or for the discharge of a Bahamian trust.[80]

Choice of Law

Under Section 5 of the Trusts (Choice of Governing Law) Act of 1989, a Bahamian trust may be moved from the jurisdiction of the Bahamas or moved to the jurisdiction of the Bahamas; the governing law being Bahamas (moving to) or the law of the new jurisdiction (moving from).[81]

Under Section 8 of the Trusts (Choice of Governing Law) Act of 1989, no trust governed by Bahamian law and no disposition of property to be held by a Bahamian trust is void, voidable, liable to be set aside or defective in any manner by reference to a foreign law; nor is the capacity of any settlor to be questioned nor is the trustee or any beneficiary or any other person to be subjected to any liability or deprived of any right by reason that:

(a) the laws of any foreign jurisdiction prohibit or do not recognize the concept of a trust; or

(b) the trust or disposition avoids or defeats rights, claims or interest conferred by foreign law upon any person by reason of a personal relationship to the settlor or by way of heirship rights or contravenes any rule of foreign law or any foreign, judicial or administrative order or action intended to recognize, protect, enforce or give affect to any such rights, claims or interest.[82]

Confidentiality

Section 83(7) of the Bahamian Act provides that when disclosing any documents or information to any beneficiary or other person the trustees shall, if other beneficiaries have requested confidentiality or if the trustees in their absolute discretion determine confidentiality to be in the best interest of such other beneficiaries, take all reasonable steps to secure the right to confidentiality of the other beneficiaries by providing such beneficiary or other person only with such documents or information as shall enable that beneficiary's own true entitlement and actual interest or benefits under the trust to be determined.[83]

Additionally, section 83(8) provides that trustees shall not be bound or compelled by any process of discovery or inspection or under any equitable rule or principle to disclose or produce to any beneficiary or other person any of the following documents:

(a) any memorandum or letter of wishes issued by the settlor or any other person to the trustees, or any other document recording any wishes of the settlor;

(b) any document disclosing any deliberations of the trustees as to the manner in which the trustees

(c) should exercise any discretion of theirs or disclosing the reasons for any particular exercise of any such discretion or the material upon which such reasons were or might have been based; or

(d) any other document relating to the exercise or proposed exercise of any discretion of the trustees (including legal advice obtained by them in connection with the exercise by them of any discretion).[84]

CHAPTER ENDNOTES

1. Nevis Int'l Exempt Tr. Ordinance §2.

2. Nevis Int'l Exempt Tr. Ordinance §32(5).

3. *See* discussion in Galligan, "International Charitable Giving and Planning Under U.S. Tax Law," 29 Est., Gft. & Tr. J. 151 (May 13, 2004).

4. Treas. Reg. §1.664-1(a)(4).

5. *See* Rev. Rul. 77-285, 1977-2 C.B. 213.

6. *See* Levin, "Transfers to Foreign Trusts Could Trigger Gain Recognition," 37 Est. Plan J. 14 (Oct. 2010).

7. Treas. Reg. §1.684-3(c).

8. Treas. Reg. §1.684-3(b).

9. Nevis Int'l Exempt Tr. Ordinance §3.

10. *See* Nevis International Exempt Trust Ordinance, 1994 at §5.

11. Privy Council of the Cayman Islands, Appeal No. 0036 of 2010, decided June 21, 2010. *Fonu v Merrill Lynch Bank and Trust Company (Cayman) Ltd & Ors (Cayman Islands)*, [2012] 1 WLR 1721, [2011] 4 All ER 704, 14 ITELR 102, [2011] UKPC 17, [2011] BPIR 1743, [2011] WTLR 1249.

12. 179 F.3d 1228 (9th Cir. 1999).

13. Nevis Int'l Exempt Tr. Ordinance §24.

14. Nevis Int'l Exempt Tr. Ordinance §36.

15. See *e.g., Armitage v. Nurse* [1997] EWCA Civ 1279, [1998] Ch 241, [1997] 3 WLR 1046, [1997] 2 All ER 705.

16. 1998 Ch. 241 at 261.

17. Nevis Int'l Exempt Tr. Ordinance §47.

18. Nevis Int'l Exempt Tr. Ordinance §55.

19. *See* Nevis International Exempt Trust Ordinance, 1994 at §55.

20. Int'l Tr. Act §13F(1).

21. Int'l Tr. Act §13C(g).

22. Int'l Tr. Act §13C.

23. *See e.g., Fonu v. Merrill Lynch Bank and Trust Company (Cayman) Limited,* Privy Council Appeal No 0036 of 2010 (Lord Collins, June 2011); *JSC VTB Bank v. Skurikhin,* EWHC 2131 (Comm) (21 July 2015); *JSC Mezhdunarodniy Promyshlenniy Bank v. Pugachev,* EWCA Civ 139 (27 February 2015).

24. Int'l Tr. Act §13D.

25. Int'l Tr. Act §14.

26. *See* Brooke Harrington, "Inside the Secretive World of Tax-Avoidance Experts", *The Atlantic* (Oct. 26, 2015) available at http://www.theatlantic.com/business/archive/2015/10/elite-wealth-management/410842 ("No litigant on earth has been able to break a Cook Islands trust, including the U.S. government, which has repeatedly been unable to collect on multi-million-dollar judgments against fraudsters convicted in federal court.")

27. For a non-law review level article on the Cook Islands as a trust jurisdiction, see Leslie Wayne, "Cook Islands, a Paradise of Untouchable Assets", *New York Times* (Dec. 14, 2013), available online at http://www.nytimes.com/2013/12/15/business/international/paradise-of-untouchable-assets.html. For a discussion of Cook Islands law, see Patricia Donlevy-Rosen, "Offshore Trusts: Why They Work Well", *LISI Asset Protection Planning Newsletter* #306 (September 16, 2015), availbale online at http://www.leimbergservices.com.

28. Int'l Tr. Act §2.

29. Int'l Tr. Act §13B.

30. Int'l Tr. Act §13K.

31. Int'l Tr. Act §23(1).

32. Int'l Tr. Act §23(2).

33. Int'l Tr. Act §23(5).

34. Int'l Tr. Act §28.

35. Belize Tr. Act §64.

36. Belize Tr. Act §65(C).

37. Belize Tr. Act §65(D).

38. Belize Tr. Act §6.

39. *Id.*

40. Belize Tr. Act §7.

41. *Id.*

42. Belize Tr. Act §12.

43. Belize Tr. Act §9(2).

44. Belize L. of Prop. Act Ch. 190, §149.

45. Belize Tr. Act §7(2).

46. *Id.*

47. Belize Tr. Act §50.

48. *Id.*

49. Belize Tr. Act §54.

50. Belize Tr. Act §55.

51. Belize Tr. Act §56.

52. *Id.*

53. Bm. Spec. Prov. Act §2.

54. Bm. Spec. Prov. Act §12A.

55. Bm. Spec. Prov. Act §11.

56. Perp. & Accum. Act §11.

57. Perp. & Accum. Act §3.

58. Convey. Act §36A.

59. *Id.*

60. *Id.*

61. *Id.*

62. Convey. Act §36C.

63. Convey. Act. §36C(3).

64. Convey. Act §36D.

65. Convey. Act §36G.

66. *See* U.S. – Bermuda Income Tax Treaty 1986, art. 5; *see also* "Agreement between the Government of the U.S.A. and the Government of Bermuda for Cooperation to Facilitate the Implementation of FATCA", Dec. 19, 2013, available at http://www.treasury.gov/resource-center/tax-policy/treaties/Documents/FATCA-AgreementBermuda-12-19-2013.pdf (illustrating the intergovernmental agreement between the U.S. Treasury Department and Bermuda that will require financial institutions in Bermuda to report on the holdings of U.S. taxpayers to the IRS or face penalties).

67. Bm. Spec. Prov. Act §11(2).

68. Bm. Spec. Prov. Act §12B.

69. Bm. Tr. Act §22(1).

70. Bs. Tr. Act §2(i).

71. Bs. Tr. Act §3(1).

72. Bs. Tr. Act §40(1).

73. Bs. Tr. Act §40(5).

74. Bahamian Perp. Act §2, §6.

75. *See Agreement for the Provision of Information with Respect to Taxes,* U.S.-Bah., Jan. 25, 2002, *available at* http://www.oecd.org/unitedstates/ 35514646.pdf.

76. *See* discussion at Rothschild & Rubin, "Asset Protection Planning", *BNA Estate, Gift & Tax Portfolio.* 810-3d at §VII, B.5 (2013).

77. Bahamian Fraud. Disp. Act §4.

78. Bs. Tr. Act §93.

79. Bs. Tr. Act §94.

80. Bs. Tr. Act §90(16).

81. Choice of Gov. L. Act §5.

82. Choice of Gov. L. Act §8.

83. Bs. Tr. Act §83.

84. Bs. Tr. Act §83(8).

NEVIS INT'L EXEMPT TR. ORDINANCE

§3. Validity of international trusts-

(1) An international trust registered under this Ordinance shall be valid and enforceable notwithstanding that it may be invalid according to the law of the settlor's domicile or residence or place of current incorporation, formation or establishment.

(2) An international trust shall be invalid and unenforceable to the extent that:

    (a) it purports to do anything contrary to the laws of St. Christopher and Nevis;

    (b) it purports to confer any right or power or impose any obligation the exercise of which or the carrying out of which is contrary to the laws of St. Christopher and Nevis; or

    (c) the property of the trust, or any part thereof, are the proceeds of a crime for which the settlor has been convicted.

§5(1) No rule of law against perpetuities or suspension of the power of alienation of the title to property, any other existing law against perpetuities, or any law restricting or limiting the duration of an international trust shall apply with respect to any interest in real or personal property held in trust if the terms of an international trust specifically state that the trustee of the trust has the unlimited power to sell all trust assets or if one or more persons, one (1) of whom may be the trustee, has the unlimited power to terminate the entire trust.

(2) The rule of law known as the rule against perpetuities shall not apply to an international trust and unless otherwise provided in its terms, an international trust shall have an unlimited duration.[1]

(3) Notwithstanding any rule of law or equity to the contrary, where a trust instrument empowers a trustee to accumulate income, or to refrain from making any distribution of capital or income until a specified date or event, or where any provision of the instrument otherwise prevents the making of any distribution of capital or income, notwithstanding that a beneficiary may, but for this section, otherwise be entitled to that accumulation or distribution, the trustee may, in his absolute discretion, subject to any other terms of the instrument, give effect to that direction as he thinks fit notwithstanding that a beneficiary shall request the trustee to immediately distribute the accumulation or distribution and will give a valid discharge to the trustee for such distribution.

(4) The income arising from any international trust may be accumulated in accordance with the terms of the trust for as long a time as is necessary to accomplish the purposes for which the trust was created, notwithstanding any law limiting the period during which trust income may be accumulated.[2]

§8A. Discretionary interests in international trusts

(1) This section applies to a creditor's claim with respect to a discretionary interest of any beneficiary (including a settlor) in an international trust unless the trust deed provides explicitly otherwise.

(2) A discretionary interest in an international trust is not a property interest or an enforceable right rather is a mere expectancy that a creditor of a beneficiary (including the settlor) may not attach, garnish or otherwise reach.

(3) A creditor of a beneficiary (including the settlor) may not compel or force a distribution with regard to a discretionary interest in an international trust, nor compel or force a trustee to exercise the trustee's discretion to make a distribution with regard to a discretionary interest in an international trust.

(4) A creditor of a beneficiary (including the settlor) may not compel or force a protector to exercise a power to direct a trustee to make a distribution to any beneficiary of an international trust.

(5) In the case of a discretionary interest in an international trust, a trustee who has the authority to pay income or principal to a beneficiary (including the settlor) may pay it to a third party if the payment is for the benefit of the beneficiary (including the settlor), and the trustee of an

international trust shall not be liable to any creditor of a beneficiary (including the settlor) for paying income or principal on behalf of such beneficiary.

(6) A creditor of a beneficiary (including the settlor) may not maintain an action or a proceeding in Court that interferes with the trustee's discretion to apply income or principal on behalf of the beneficiary of an international trust.

(7) A creditor of a beneficiary (including the settlor) may not obtain an order of attachment, garnishment or similar relief that would prevent a trustee from making a discretionary payment to a third party on behalf of the beneficiary (including the settlor) of an international trust.

(8) In this section, a beneficiary's entitlement (or lack thereof) to a distribution is within the discretion of a trustee, whether or not the trust deed states the purposes for the distribution, is expressed in the form of a standard of distribution or uses the terms 'may,' 'shall,' 'sole and absolute,' 'uncontrolled,' 'unfettered,' or similar words and whether or not the trustee has abused the discretion.

(9) Regardless of whether a beneficiary of an international trust has any outstanding creditor, a trustee of a discretionary interest may directly pay any expense on behalf of such beneficiary and may exhaust the income and principal of the trust for the benefit of such beneficiary. No trustee is liable to any creditor for paying the expenses of a beneficiary (including the settlor) who holds a discretionary interest.

(10) (a) In this section, 'discretionary interest' means a beneficiary's interest in an international trust if the beneficiary's entitlement to a distribution is within the discretion of the trustee."

(b) This section shall not prevent a creditor from obtaining relief from under Section 23 of this Ordinance that is not inconsistent with this Section 8A.

§9. Protector of a trust

(1) The terms of an international trust may provide for the office of protector of the trust. Where a person is given authority by the terms of an international trust to direct, consent to or disapprove a trustee's actual or proposed investment decisions, distribution decisions or other decision of the trustee, such person shall be considered to be a protector when exercising such authority (unless the terms of the trust shall otherwise provide).

(2) The protector of an international trust shall have the power to:

(a) (unless the terms of the trust shall otherwise provide) remove a trustee and appoint a new or additional trustee; and

(b) exercise such further powers as are conferred on the protector by the terms of the international trust or by the provisions of this Ordinance.

(3) The terms of an international trust may grant the protector the power to:

(a) direct the trustee to make distributions from the trust;

(b) consent to or approve any distributions made by the trustee from the trust; and

(c) direct the trustee regarding any or all investment decisions of the trust, which includes the power to direct a trustee to retain, purchase, sell or exchange property held in the trust or to engage in any other transaction affecting the ownership or rights over such property. [*emphasis added*]

(4) If the terms of an international trust provide that a trustee shall follow the direction of the protector and the trustee acts in accordance with such a direction, then except in cases of willful misconduct on the part of the trustee so directed, the trustee shall not be liable for any loss resulting directly or indirectly from any such act.

(5) If the terms of an international trust provide that a trustee shall make decisions with the consent of the protector, then except in cases of willful misconduct or gross negligence on the part of the trustee, the trustee shall not be liable for any loss resulting directly or indirectly from any act taken or omitted as a result of such protector's failure to provide such consent after having been requested to do so by the trustee.

(6) Whenever the terms of an international trust provide that a trustee shall follow the direction of the protector with respect to investment decisions of the trustee, then, except to the extent that the

international trust provides otherwise, the trustee shall have no duty to:

(a) monitor the conduct of the protector;

(b) provide advice to the protector or consult with the protector; or

(c) communicate with or warn or apprise any beneficiary or third party concerning instances in which the trustee would or might have exercised the trustee's own discretion in a manner different from the manner directed by the protector.

Absent clear and convincing evidence to the contrary, the actions of the trustee pertaining to matters within the scope of the protector's authority (such as confirming that the protector's directions have been carried out and recording and reporting actions taken at the protector's direction), shall be presumed to be administrative actions taken by the trustee solely to allow the trustee to perform those duties assigned to the trustee under the governing instrument and such administrative actions shall not be deemed to constitute an undertaking by the trustee to monitor the protector or otherwise participate in actions within the scope of the protector's authority.

(7) Unless the terms of the trust shall otherwise provide the protector of an international trust may also be a settlor or a beneficiary of the trust.

(8) Subject to the terms of the international trust, in the exercise of his office a protector shall owe a fiduciary duty to the beneficiaries of the trust or to the purpose for which the trust is created.

(9) Where there is more than one (1) protector of a trust then, subject to the terms of the trust, any functions conferred on the protectors may be exercised if a majority of the protectors for the time being agree on its exercise.

(10) A protector who dissents from a decision of the majority of protectors may require his dissent to be recorded in writing.

(11) (a) A protector may delegate duties and powers with regard to investment decisions. The protector shall exercise reasonable care, skill, and caution in:

(i) selecting an agent such as an investment advisor;

(ii) establishing the scope and terms of the delegation, consistent with the purposes and terms of the trust; and

(iii) reviewing the agent's actions periodically to monitor the agent's performance and compliance with the terms of the delegation.

(b) In performing a delegated function, an agent owes a duty to the protector/trustee/beneficiary or purpose for which the trust was created to exercise reasonable care to comply with the terms of the delegation.

(c) A protector who complies with subsection (a) and, when investment functions are delegated, is not liable to the beneficiaries or to the trust for an action of the agent to whom the function was delegated.[3]

Section 9A. General power of appointment granted to a beneficiary

A creditor shall have no right against the interest of a beneficiary of an international trust or against the beneficiary or trustee of the trust with respect to such interest unless.

(1) The beneficiary (other than the settlor) has a power to appoint all or part of the trust property to the beneficiary, the beneficiary's estate, the beneficiary's creditors, or the creditors of the beneficiary's estate by will or other instrument such that the appointment would take effect only upon the beneficiary's death and the beneficiary actually exercises such power in favor of the beneficiary, the beneficiary's creditors, the beneficiary's estate, or the creditors of the beneficiary's estate but then only to the extent of such exercise.

(2) The beneficiary (other than the settlor) has a power, including a power of withdrawal, to appoint all or part of the trust property to the beneficiary, the beneficiary's creditors, the beneficiary's estate, or the creditors of the beneficiary's estate during the beneficiary's lifetime and the beneficiary actually exercises such power in favor of the beneficiary, the beneficiary's creditors, the beneficiary's estate, or the creditors of the beneficiary's estate but then only to the extent of such exercise.[4]

Section 9B. Right of revocation retained by settlor

A creditor shall have no right against the interest of a beneficiary of an international trust who is the settlor or against the settlor or trustee of the trust with respect to such interest unless the settlor has a power to revoke the trust and appoint all or part of the trust property to the settlor, the settlor's creditors, the settlor's estate, or the creditors of the settlor's estate during the settlor's lifetime and the settlor actually exercises such power in favor of the settlor, the settlor's creditors, the settlor's estate, or the creditors of the settlor's estate but then only to the extent of such exercise.[5]

Section 13. Duress; Termination by beneficiaries

To the extent any person is granted the power under the terms of a trust to demand or request any act on the part of a settlor, beneficiary, trustee, protector, or other person, or has the authority to approve, veto, or compel any action or exercise any power which affects or will affect an international trust or any interest therein, each such person is directed, to the extent such person would not be subject to personal liability or personal exposure:

(1) to accept or recognize only demands or requests, or the effects of any approval, veto, or compelled action or the exercise of any power, which are given by or are the result of persons acting of their own free will and not under compulsion or pursuant to any legal process, directive, order, or like decree of any court, administrative body, or other tribunal or like authority; and

(2) to ignore any demands or requests, or the effects of any approval, veto, or compelled action or the exercise of any power, where the person attempting to demand, request, approve, veto, compel the act, or exercise the power is not a person either appointed or so authorized pursuant to the terms of such trust.

§22(4) No action or proceeding (whether substantive or interlocutory in nature) shall be heard, and no injunction, order of any kind, or any other relief or remedy, whether legal or equitable, shall be made, issued, granted or ordered, by the Court concerning an international trust where the purpose of such action or proceeding would be to detain, inspect, garnish, attach or otherwise interfere in any manner whatsoever or possible with:

(a) any trust property wherever situated whether in St. Christopher and Nevis or elsewhere, or

(b) any right, duty, discretion, obligation or power which a trustee may have in respect of any trust property.

Section 24. Avoidance of fraud

(1) Where it is proven beyond reasonable doubt by a creditor that a trust settled or established, or property disposed or transferred to a trust-

(a) was so settled established or disposed by or on behalf of the settlor with principal intent to defraud that creditor of the settlor; and

(b) did at the time such settlement establishment or disposition took place render the settlor insolvent or without property by which that creditors claim (if successful) could have been satisfied, then such settlement establishment or disposition shall not be void or voidable and the international trust shall be liable to satisfy the creditor's claim and such liability shall only be to the extent of the interest that the settlor had in the property prior to settlement establishment or disposition and any accumulation to the property (if any) subsequent thereto.

(2) In determining whether a trust, settled or established or a disposition, has rendered the settlor insolvent or without property by which a creditor's claim (if successful) may be satisfied, regard shall be had to the fair market value of the settlor's property, (not being property of or relating to the trust) at the time immediately after the settlement establishment or the disposition referred to in subsection (1) (b) and if the fair market value of such property exceeded the value of the creditor's claim, at that time, after the settlement establishment or disposition, then the trust so settled or established or the disposition shall for the purposes of this Ordinance be deemed not to have been so settled or established or the property disposed of with intent to defraud the creditor.

(3) A trust settled or established, or a disposition or transfer of property to such trust, shall not be fraudulent as against a creditor of a settlor if such settlement, establishment, disposition or transfer occurs after the expiration of one year from the date that such creditor's cause of action accrued or originated.

(4) A trust settled or established, or a disposition of property to such trust, shall not be fraudulent as

against a creditor of a settlor if such settlement, establishment or disposition took place before the creditor's cause of action against the settlor had accrued or had arisen.

(5) A settlor shall not have imputed to him an intent to defraud a creditor, solely by reason that the settlor-

    (a) has settled or established a trust or has disposed of property to such trust within two years from the date of that creditors cause of action accruing;

    (b) has retained, possesses or acquires any of the powers or benefits referred to in Subsections (a) to (i) of Section 47;

    (c) is a beneficiary.

(6) Where a trust is liable to satisfy a creditor's claim in the manner provided for in subsection (1), that creditors right to recovery shall be limited to the property referred to in subsection (1), or to the proceeds of that property, to the exclusion of any claim right or action against any trustee or any other property of the trust.

(7) The burden of proof regarding the settlor's intent to defraud the creditor shall be borne by the creditor.

(8) For the purpose of this section-

    (a) the date of the cause of action accruing shall be, the date of that act or omission which shall be relied upon to either partly or wholly establish the cause of action, and if there is more than one act or the omission shall be a continuing one, the date of the first act or the date that the omission shall have first occurred, as the case may be, shall be the date that the cause of action shall have accrued;

    (b) the term "cause of action" means the earliest cause of action capable of assertion by a creditor against the settlor of a trust or, as the case may be against the settlor of property upon a trust by which that creditor has established (or may establish) an enforceable claim against that settlor;

    (c) the entry of judgment in any action or proceeding shall not constitute a separate cause of action.

(9) The provisions of this section shall apply to all actions and proceedings brought into the Court, however described, against the person (whether a party to the action or proceedings or not) with regard to the settlement of an international trust or the disposition of property to such a trust, or receipt of property by or for such a trust and the remedy conferred by subsection (1) shall be the sole remedy available in such an action or proceedings to the exclusion of any other relief or remedy against any party to the action or proceeding.

(10) Failure by a creditor to present all claims arising out of any controversy and join all parties with a material interest shall prevent that creditor from presenting such claims and bringing an action against such parties in a subsequent proceeding.

(11) For the purposes of this section the term "creditor" means a creditor of the settlor, including a judgment creditor and an assignee from such creditor of any claim and includes any person who alleges a cause of action against a settlor.

Section 35A. Removal of trustee and protectors

(1) If, in any action is brought against a trustee of an international trust in a foreign court, such foreign court fails to dismiss such action, or orders such trustee to take any action in regards to such trust, such trustee shall immediately upon such court's action and without the further order of any court, cease in all respects to be trustee of such trust and a successor trustee shall thereupon succeed as trustee in accordance with the terms of the trust instrument or, if the trust instrument does not provide for a successor trustee and the trust would otherwise be without a trustee, the Court, upon the application of any beneficiary of such trust, shall appoint a successor trustee upon such terms and conditions as it determines to be consistent with the purposes of such trust and this statute.

    Upon such trustee ceasing to be trustee, such trustee shall have no power or authority other than to convey the trust property to the successor trustee named in the trust instrument or appointed by the Court in accordance with this section. The trustee shall, within fourteen (14) days of its removal, give notice in writing to the Registrar of such removal.

(2) If, in any action is brought against a protector of an international trust in a foreign court, such foreign

court fails to dismiss such action, or orders such protector to take any action in regards to such trust, such protector shall immediately upon such court's action and without the further order of any court, cease in all respects to be a protector of such trust. Upon such protector ceasing to be a protector, such protector shall have no power or authority in regards to the trust. The protector shall, immediately following its removal hereunder, give notice in writing to the trustee of the international trust of such removal.

Section 35B. Combination and division of trusts

(1) Unless otherwise provided in the trust instrument, after notice to the beneficiaries, a trustee may combine two or more trusts into a single trust or divide a trust into two or more separate trusts, if the result does not impair rights of any beneficiary or adversely affect achievement of the purposes of the trusts or trust, respectively.

(2) Subject to the terms of the trust instrument, the trustee may take into consideration the difference in tax attributes and other pertinent factors in administering the trust property of any separate trust, in making applicable tax elections, and in making applications or distributions.

(3) A separate trust created by severance must be treated as a separate trust for all purposes from the date on which the severance is effective, including, but not limited to any and all issues related to the liability of a trustee or the trust assets pursuant to a contract, in tort or otherwise.

(4) The effective date of the severance may be retroactive to a date before the date on which the trustee exercises such power and any such action under this provision shall be made only pursuant to a written instrument filed with the records of the trust.

(5) In dividing a trust into two (2) or more separate trusts, a trustee shall accomplish the division by severing the trusts on a fractional basis and funding the separate trusts either (a) with a pro rata portion of each asset held by the undivided trust; or (b) on a non-pro rata basis based on either the fair market value of the assets on the date of funding or in a manner that fairly reflects the net appreciation or depreciation in the value of the assets measured from the valuation date to the date of funding.

(6) An international trust may be established to simultaneously benefit beneficiaries and to fulfill a purpose.[6]

Section 35C. Effect of provisions of instrument

(1) Notwithstanding any other provision of this Ordinance or other law, the terms of a governing instrument may expand, restrict, eliminate, or otherwise vary the rights and interests of beneficiaries, including, but not limited to, the right to be informed of the beneficiary's interest for any period, the grounds for removal of a trustee, the circumstances, if any, in which the trustee must diversify investments, and a trustee's powers, duties, standard of care, rights of indemnification and liability to persons whose interests arise from that instrument.[7]

(2) Nothing contained in this section shall be construed to permit the exculpation or indemnification of a trustee for the trustee's own willful misconduct or preclude the Court from removing a trustee on account of the trustee's willful misconduct.

(3) The rule that statutes in derogation of the common law are to be strictly construed shall have no application to this provision.

This section shall give maximum effect to the principle of freedom of disposition and to the enforceability of governing instruments.[8]

Section 36. Trustee resolutions

A trustee which is a either a Nevis trust company, a corporation, a limited liability company or a multiform foundation, may–

(a) act in connection with a trust pursuant to its board of directors, board of managers, management board or other governing body; and

(b) appoint an officer, employee or agent to act on its behalf in connection with the trust.

§45(1) A trustee shall not invest any of the trust funds other than in securities, assets, or property authorized expressly or by necessary implication for the investment of the trust funds by and under the instrument by which the trust is established or created or in such securities, assets, or property authorized and approved by the protector pursuant to Section 9 (2) and (6) of this Ordinance.[9]

Section 47. Retention of control by settlor

(1) An international trust shall not be declared invalid or otherwise be affected in any manner if the settlor, and if more than one (1), any of them either retains, possesses or acquires -

(a) the power to revoke the trust;

(b) the power to veto a distribution of income or principal by the trustee;

(c) the power to amend the trust;

(d) any benefit, interest or property from the trust, including, but not limited to the following:

    (i) the settlor's potential or actual receipt of income or principal from the trust, including rights to such income or principal retained in the trust deed;

    (ii) the settlor's potential or actual receipt of income or principal from a charitable remainder unitrust or charitable remainder annuity trust and the settlor's right, at any time and from time to time by written instrument delivered to the trustee, to release such settlor's retained interest in such a trust, in whole or in part, in favor of a charity that has or charities that have a succeeding beneficial interest in such trust;

    (iii) the settlor's potential or actual receipt of income or principal from a grantor retained annuity trust or grantor retained unitrust;

    (iv) the settlor's receipt each year of a percentage (as specified in the trust deed) of the initial value of the trust assets (which may be described either as a percentage or a fixed amount) or the value determined from time to time pursuant to the trust deed;

    (v) the settlor's potential or actual receipt or use of principal if such potential or actual receipt or use of principal would be the result of a trustee acting:

        A. in such trustee's discretion;

        B. pursuant to a standard that governs the distribution of principal and does not confer upon the settlor a substantially unfettered right to the receipt or use of the principal; or

        C. at the direction of a protector who is acting:

            1. in such protector's discretion; or

            2. pursuant to a standard that governs the distribution of principal and does not confer upon the settlor a substantially unfettered right to the receipt of or use of principal;

    (vi) a settlor's potential or actual use of real property, chattels or tangible assets held either directly or indirectly in the trust;

    (vii) the settlor's potential or actual receipt of income or principal to pay, in whole or in part, income taxes or other levies due on income or principal of the trust to any taxing authority located in any jurisdiction if such potential or actual receipt of income or principal is pursuant to a provision in the trust deed that expressly provides for the payment of such taxes and if such potential or actual receipt of income or principal would be the result of a trustee acting in such trustee's discretion or pursuant to a mandatory direction in the trust deed; or at the direction of a protector who is acting in such protector's discretion. Distributions to pay income taxes made under a discretionary or mandatory provision included in a settlement establishing an international trust may be made by direct payment to a taxing authority;

(e) the power to remove or appoint a trustee or protector;

(f) the power to direct a trustee or protector on any matter;

(g) except as provided in subsection (1)(h), an inter vivos or testamentary power of appointment (other than a power to appoint to the settlor, the settlor's creditors, the settlor's estate or the creditors of the settlor's estate) exercisable by will or other written instrument of the settlor;

(h) the ability, whether pursuant to discretion granted to the trustee, a direction in the trust deed or the settlor's exercise of a testamentary power of appointment, of a trustee to pay, after the death of the settlor, all or any part of the debts of the settlor outstanding at the settlor's death, the expenses of administering the settlor's estate, or any estate or inheritance tax or other levies imposed on or with respect to the settlor's estate; and

(i) the ability to serve as investment adviser to the trust.

(2) An international trust is not invalid even though the settlor may be the only beneficiary of the trust or the settlor is one of multiple beneficiaries. Except as provided in this Section, a settlor shall have no other rights or authority with respect to property held in an international trust or the income therefrom, and any agreement or understanding purporting to grant or permit the retention of any greater rights or authority shall be void and of no effect.

Section 54. Power to establish the Nevis International Exempt Trust Ordinance Advisory Committee.

(1) The Minister may establish an advisory body for matters affecting this Ordinance; and such body so established, shall consist of such members as the Minister may from time to time appoint.

(2) In establishing the body under sub-section (1) above, the Minister shall have regard to the desirability of having members who have the expertise and knowledge of the Ordinance and the law of trusts.

(3) It shall be the duty of the Nevis International Exempt Trust Ordinance Advisory Committee established under this section to:

(a) advise the Minister on any matter that the Nevis International Exempt Trust Ordinance Advisory Committee believes that the Minister should be aware of, on an annual basis by September 30th or on such more frequent occasions as may be necessary;

(b) provide recommendation regarding possible amendments to this Ordinance; and

(c) advise the Minister on any matter which is referred to it by the Minister.

(4) The Minister may defray or contribute towards the expenses of an advisory body established under this section."[10]

Section 56. Community property and tenancy by the entireties property

(1) Where spouses transfer property to one or more trusts established under an international trust or a trust that subsequently becomes an international trust and, immediately before being transferred, such property or any part thereof or any accumulation thereto is, pursuant to the law of its location or the law of either of the transferring spouses' domicile or residence, determined to be community property, then notwithstanding such transfer and except where the provisions of the trust deed may provide to the contrary, that property and any accumulation thereto shall, for the purpose of giving effect to that law, be deemed to be community property and be dealt with in a manner consistent with that law but in every other respect shall be dealt with in accordance with the trust deed and the governing law of that deed.[11]

(2) Where spouses transfer property to one or more trusts established under an international trust or a trust that subsequently becomes an international trust and, immediately before such transfer, such property or any part thereof or any accumulation thereto was, pursuant to applicable law, owned by them as tenants by the entireties, then notwithstanding such transfer and except where the provisions of the trust deed may expressly provide to the contrary, that property and any accumulation thereto shall be tenancy by the entireties property while held in trust during the lifetime of both spouses and shall be dealt with in a manner consistent with that applicable law however in every other respect shall be dealt with in accordance with the terms of the trust deed. Furthermore, in any action concerning whether a creditor of either or both spouses may recover the debt from the trust, upon avoidance of the transfer, if at all, the sole remedy available to the creditor with respect to trust property that is tenancy by the entireties property shall be an order directing the trustee to transfer the property to both spouses as tenants by the entireties."

ENDNOTES

1. Nevis Int'l Exempt Tr. Ordinance §5(1).

2. Nevis Int'l Exempt Tr. Ordinance §5(3)-(4).

3. Nevis Int'l Exempt Tr. Ordinance §9.

4. Nevis Int'l Exempt Tr. Ordinance §9(A).

5. Nevis Int'l Exempt Tr. Ordinance §9(B).

6. Nevis Int'l Exempt Tr. Ordinance §35B.

7. Nevis Int'l Exempt Tr. Ordinance §35(C).

8. Nevis Int'l Exempt Tr. Ordinance §35C(2)-(4).

9. Nevis Int'l Exempt Tr. Ordinance §45(1).

10. Nevis Int'l Exempt Tr. Ordinance §54.

11. Nevis Int'l Exempt Tr. Ordinance §56.

FEDERAL TAX ISSUES WITH ASSET PROTECTION TRUSTS

Generally, gratuitous transfers to wealth protection trusts are structured to qualify as incomplete gifts for Federal gift tax purposes because most individuals who establish and fund such trusts plan to transfer assets to the trust in excess of the $11,400,000 (for 2019)) lifetime gift tax exemption amount available under Section 2505 of the Code.[1] A number of techniques can be used to design a trust to cause gifts to the trust to be deemed as incomplete gifts for gift tax purposes, however, not incomplete for property law purposes.

Section 2501 imposes a tax "on the transfer of property by gift." The gift tax imposed under Section 2501 applies whether the transfer is in trust or otherwise, whether the transfer is direct or indirect, and regardless of the property transferred.[2] Nonetheless, the gift tax under Section 2501 is imposed only if a donor parts with such dominion and control over the property in a manner that renders the gift complete.[3] If, upon a transfer of property, the donor reserves any power over its disposition, the gift may be wholly incomplete, or it may be partially complete and partially incomplete, depending upon all the facts in the particular case.[4] Accordingly, in every case of a transfer of property subject to a retained power, the terms of the power must be examined and the scope of such retained power determined.[5] Regulation §25.2511-2(b) provides in part:

> if a donor transfers property to another in trust to pay the income to the donor or accumulate it in the discretion of the trustee, and the donor retains a testamentary power to appoint the remainder among his descendants, no portion of the transfer is a completed gift.

A gift is incomplete if and to the extent that a donor reserves the power to name new beneficiaries or to change the interests of the beneficiaries as between themselves unless the power is a fiduciary power limited by a fixed or ascertainable standard.[6] A gift is not considered incomplete, however, merely because the donor reserves the power to change the manner or time of enjoyment of the gift, *i.e.*, change the timing of the beneficiary's enjoyment.[7]

Where a donor retains the power to change or modify the beneficial interests in a trust, the retention of such power will result in the gratuitous transfer of property by the donor to the trust to be incomplete for gift tax purposes, even if the exercise of such power can be defeated by the actions of other parties.[8] If the donor-settlor is the sole current beneficiary of a trust and retains a testamentary special power of appointment over trust property, any gratuitous transfers by the donor to the trust will constitute incomplete gifts for Federal gift tax purposes.

A donor-settlor should also be able to avoid a taxable gift by retaining a testamentary special power of appointment over the trust even though the settlor may be one of a class of permissible beneficiaries to whom an independent trustee may at any time make distributions of income and principal in such trustee's sole, absolute and uncontrolled discretion (that is, a "pot trust").[9] The foregoing concept is similar to the gift tax rule set forth in Treasury Regulations section 25.2511-1(h)(4) which provides:

> If A creates a joint bank account for himself and B (or a similar type of ownership by which A can regain the entire fund without B's consent) there is a gift to B when B draws upon the account for his own benefit, to the extent of the amount drawn without any obligation to account for a part of the proceeds to A. Similarly, if A purchases a United States savings

bond, registered as payable to "A or B," there is a gift to B when B surrenders the bond for cash without any obligation to account for a part of the proceeds to A. [10]

Chief Counsel Memorandum 201208026. Nevertheless, use of a testamentary special power of appointment as the sole mechanism to cause a gift to be incomplete for Federal gift tax purposes was called into question when two settlors created an irrevocable trust and gratuitously transferred property to it. The trustee of the trust was a child of the settlors who was also a current beneficiary (that is, an adverse party for tax purposes), and the beneficiaries during the lifetime of the settlors were the settlors' children, other descendants, and their spouses. The only power the settlors retained was a testamentary limited power of appointment. The trust was to terminate when both settlors died. The ruling held that transfers to the trust were completed gifts because during the term of the trust the settlors retained no dominion or control over trust assets. The fact that the settlors retained a limited testamentary power of appointment was insufficient to treat the transfers as incomplete gifts. The terms of the trust in IRM 201208026 can be distinguished from the terms of the trusts in the other authority discussed above in that neither settlor was a current beneficiary of the trust, that is, the trustee could not make any distribution of trust property to either settlor. [11]

Regulation §25.2511-2(e). A donor is considered as possessing a power if the power is exercisable by the donor in conjunction with any person who does not have a substantial adverse interest in the disposition of the transferred property or the income from such property. A person who serves as a trustee is not considered as possessing an adverse interest in the disposition of such property or its income merely by reason of such person's position as a trustee. [12]

COMPLETE GIFTS

Discretionary Trust. In Revenue Ruling 76-103, [13] a settlor established an *inter vivos* trust with the terms of the trust providing that the trustee could distribute income or principal to the settlor in the trustee's "absolute discretion." Upon the death, of the settlor any remaining principal was payable to the descendants of the settlor. The circumstances surrounding the creation of the trust indicated that the trust had not been created primarily for the settlor's benefit. The trustee was given the absolute discretion to change the *situs* of the trust

to another state. The trust was considered a "discretionary trust" in the state where it was established and administered. Furthermore, under the law of the state where the trust was created and administered, all of the property in a discretionary trust "may be subjected to the claims of the grantor's creditors, whenever such claims may arise."

The ruling addressed whether the transfer to the trust was an incomplete gift for federal gift tax purposes because all of the assets transferred to the trust were subject to the claims of the grantor's creditors. In this ruling, the Service held that the gift was incomplete because both "prior and subsequent creditors" of the settlor could reach the maximum amount of trust property the trustees could in their discretion distribute to the settlor. The Service noted that the settlor could enjoy all trust property "by relegating [his] creditors to the trust for settlement of their claims." [14]

The Service reached the opposite result in Revenue Ruling 77-378, [15] where the settlor's creditors could not compel distributions under state law. In this ruling, a settlor contributed one-half of his "income-producing property" to a trust with a corporate trustee. The trustee was given the power to distribute trust income and principal to the settlor in its "absolute and uncontrolled discretion." Upon the settlor's death, the trustee was directed to terminate the trust and distribute the assets to the settlor's spouse and children. Unlike the facts in Revenue Ruling 76-103, "under applicable state law the trustee's decision whether to distribute trust assets to the grantor [was] entirely voluntary." The settlor could not require any trust property be distributed to him. Additionally, the settlor's creditors could not reach any of the assets in the trust.

The Blackletter law appears to be that a gift is incomplete when a trustee has an unrestricted power to distribute income or principal to a settlor, if the settlor's creditors can reach the trust assets under the self-settled trust doctrine. [16] However, if the settlor's creditors cannot reach trust assets because the self-settled trust doctrine is not applicable, a gratuitous transfer to such a trust should be a completed gift for Federal gift tax purposes provided the settlor has not retained a power over the trust that would cause gifts to be incomplete or includible in the settlor's estate. [17] Thus, it is important to determine the exact nature of the settlor's retained rights.

If it is not possible to ensure that anything of value would pass to the other beneficiaries of the trust, the settlor's transfers to the trust will constitute incomplete gifts. Importantly, in a string of private letter rulings, it is apparent that the IRS will respect the *situs* issues related to the settlement of self-settled trusts for tax planning purposes.[18] Thus, although a grantor is resident in a jurisdiction that recognizes the self-settled trust doctrine, the grantor can establish and transfer assets to a trust in another jurisdiction that does not recognize the doctrine. If the trust is drafted properly, gifts to such a trust will be treated as completed gifts for federal gift tax purposes.

Importantly, the trust in PLR 201510001 was presumably established in Nevada in accordance with the Spendthrift Trust Act of Nevada.[19] This is because the Spendthrift Trust Act of Nevada permits a settlor to retain an *inter vivos* special power of appointment like the one included in the trust agreement in the facts of this private letter ruling.[20] This type of trust (commonly referred to as a "NING Trust" or a "Nevada Income Non-Grantor Trust") is established by a resident of a state that imposes a state income tax to shift certain income from the settlor's state of residence to Nevada which does not impose an income tax. The only possible way for the Internal Revenue Service (the "**Service**") to conclude that the trust in this ruling qualified as a non-grantor trust for federal income tax purposes was for the Service to respect the *situs* issue, that is, that a non-resident of Nevada could establish a trust in Nevada and obtain the benefits of Nevada legislation applicable to self-settled asset protection trusts.

Section 2036 provides: The value of the gross estate shall include the value of all property to the extent of any interest therein of which the decedent has at any time made a transfer...by trust or otherwise, under which he has retained for his life or for any period which does not in fact end before his death—(1) the possession or enjoyment of, or the right to the income from, the property, or (2) the right, either alone or in conjunction with any person, to designate the persons who shall possess or enjoy the property or the income therefrom.

Section 2038 provides in pertinent part that:

> The value of the gross estate shall include the value of all property to the extent of any interest therein of which the decedent has at any time made a transfer...by trust or otherwise, where the enjoyment thereof was subject at the date of his death to any change through the exercise of a power (in whatever capacity exercisable) by the decedent alone or by the

decedent in conjunction with any other person...to alter, amend, revoke, or terminate, or where any such power is relinquished during the three-year period ending on the date of the decedent's death.

If the settlor is a discretionary beneficiary and his or her creditors, either existing or future, may reach the trust assets in satisfaction of claims under applicable state law, the trust property will be includible in the settlor's gross estate under Section 2038 because of the settlor's power to "terminate the trust by relegating his or her creditors to the entire property of the trust."[21]

Making a revocable trust irrevocable. PLR 7833062, May 18, 1978, concerns the federal gift tax consequences of making a revocable trust irrevocable.

On February 11, 1966, a settlor transferred corporate stock to a revocable trust executed by the settlor on that date. The trust provided that the net income from the trust would be distributed quarterly or monthly to, or used for the benefit of, the settlor and the settlor's wife during the settlor's life. The trust further provided that the trustee shall distribute to the settlor as much of the principal of the trust as the settlor requested. If the settlor was unable to request a distribution of principal, the trustee was authorized to distribute such amounts from the principal as the trustee deemed "advisable for the (settlor's) comfortable maintenance, support and welfare or for that of his wife."

On the death of the settlor, the trust principal was to be distributed to the settlor's wife and children. On October 19, 1977, the settlor modified the trust agreement to release his power to alter, amend or revoke the trust. The settlor further released his power to invade the principal or demand distribution of principal to himself. The modification did not, however, affect the authority of the trustee, in the trustee's discretion, to invade principal for the settlor's benefit.

Generally, if a trustee is given a broad discretionary power to invade the trust corpus on behalf of the settlor, and the power is not limited by a definite standard, the settlor has parted with dominion and control over the property and the entire transfer is complete and subject to the gift tax.[22] If the power of the trustee to invade on behalf of the settlor is subject to a fixed and ascertainable standard, which makes it possible to value the maximum amount to which the settlor might be entitled, the transfer is incomplete to that extent.[23] If the trustee's power, although governed by some ascertainable standard, permits the settlor to demand the return of the entire trust corpus, the gift may be wholly incomplete, or partially incomplete and partially complete, depending upon all the facts in the particular case.[24] The gift is normally wholly incomplete, however, only where, under the facts and circumstances of the case, substantial invasion is probable and there is no assurance that anything of value will pass to anyone other than the settlor.[25]

Treasury Regulation §25.2511-1(g)(2) provides that an ascertainable standard is a clearly measurable standard under which the holder of a power is legally accountable. Thus, if under the standard provided in the trust agreement and applicable state law, the settlor can compel the trustee to return trust property to the settlor, the standard is ascertainable.

Additionally, the gift may be incomplete, irrespective of whether the trustee's discretion is subject to an ascertainable standard, if the settlor can indirectly recapture the trust property under applicable state law by borrowing money and relegating his creditors to the trustee for satisfaction of their debts.[26]

Gift Splitting, Discretionary Trusts and Self-Settled Completed Gift Trusts

Generally, "[a] gift made by one spouse to a person other than his (or her) spouse may, for the purpose of the gift tax, be considered as made one-half (1/2) by his spouse. . . ."[27] Both spouses must signify their consent to gift splitting. This consent, if signified during any calendar period, is effective for all gifts made to a beneficiary, however, there are five exceptions:

(1) If the consenting spouses were not married to each other during a portion of the calendar period, the consent is not effective with respect to any gifts made during such portion of the calendar period. . . .

(2) If either spouse was a nonresident not a citizen of the United States during any portion of the calendar period, the consent is not effective with respect to any gift made during that portion of the calendar period. . . .

(3) The consent is not effective with respect to a gift by one spouse of a property interest over which he created in his spouse a general

power of appointment (as defined in section 2514(c)) . . . .

(4) If one spouse transferred property in part to his spouse and in part to third parties, the consent is effective with respect to the interest transferred to third parties only insofar as such interest is ascertainable at the time of the gift and hence severable from the interest transferred to his spouse. . . .

(5) The consent applies alike to gifts made by one spouse alone and to gifts made partly by each spouse, provided such gifts were to third parties and do not fall within any of the exceptions set forth in subparagraphs (1) through (4) of this paragraph. The consent may not be applied only to a portion of the property interest constituting such gifts. . . .[28]

Under Regulation Section 25.2513-1(b)(4), if a donor gifts property in part to the donor's spouse and in part to others, gift splitting may only be elected with respect to the interest given to third parties if such interest is ascertainable when the gift is made and thus severable from the interest given to the donor's spouse. Where the donor is a discretionary beneficiary of a self-settled completed gift trust, under the same principles, gift splitting may not be elected as it is not possible to determine how much will be severable to third parties, and it cannot be determined if it will be distributed to the donor or the donor's spouse. There is authority in three tax court cases that carves out a limited exception to allow gift splitting where a spouse is not likely to ever receive a distribution under a standard because, for instance, she is exceedingly wealthy.[29] In these cases, the court considered the non-donor spouse's financial condition and incorporated that analysis into its opinions.[30]

Crummey Powers

In *Crummey v. Commissioner*,[31] the grantors executed an irrevocable trust in 1962 for the benefit of their four children, ages twenty-two, twenty, fifteen, and eleven. The trust was divided into separate equal shares for each child. Under the terms of the trust, income of a minor's share was to be accumulated until the minor attained the age of twenty-one unless the trustee in his discretion thought that a distribution should be made to a "needy beneficiary." From ages twenty-one to thirty-five a child was entitled to all income from his or her share. Thereafter, all distributions were within the trustee's discretion. Except for the foregoing, the only way a child could receive a benefit from his or her trust was by exercising the withdrawal right. In the year that the trust was established, the grantors gifted $53,867.77 to it and each grantor claimed a $3,000 gift tax annual exclusion per beneficiary.

The Service determined that each grantor was entitled to only one gift tax annual exclusion because the portion of the gifts in trust for the grantors' minor children were future interests. However, the court held that the grantors were allowed all of the claimed exclusions because the minors had a "right to enjoy" the property. The court noted that it is only necessary to find that the demand could not be resisted, *i.e.,* legally resisted.

Crummey was not the first case where a trust granted a beneficiary a power of withdrawal over contributions to qualify transfers for the annual exclusion. However, it is the seminal case involving qualifying transfers to a trust for the annual exclusion and it lent its name to withdrawal rights granted to a beneficiary as a result of a gift to a trust (a "*Crummey* Power"). A *Crummey* Power permits a beneficiary to demand that the trustee distribute the gift (or cash or other assets of equivalent value in the trust) to the beneficiary.[32] Usually, a *Crummey* Power may be exercised for a limited period, such as thirty days following, or until the end of the year in which, the gift creating the *Crummey* Power is made to the trust. Upon the expiration of the withdrawal period, the property (or value) that was subject to the power continues to be administered and disposed of as provided in the trust agreement. The gift that qualifies for the annual exclusion is the withdrawal right.[33] A *Crummey* Power is probably the most common withdrawal power included in trust agreements.

Gift Splitting and *Crummey* Trusts

In many *Crummey* Trusts, the spouse may be a discretionary beneficiary. Thus, a trustee might be given the discretionary power to distribute income and principal to the donor's spouse. As previously noted, if such a trust did not contain *Crummey* Power provisions, the donor should not be able to split a gift to the trust with his or her spouse under Section 2513 and Reg. §25.2513-1(b)(4). The same would be the case with a completed gift asset protection trusts where the donor is also a current discretionary beneficiary. However, if such a

trust contains *Crummey* Power provisions granting withdrawal rights to third parties such as the donor's descendants, the donor should be able to split the portion of each gift to the trust that is subject to withdrawal rights in the third parties.[34]

Effect of *Crummey* Powers on Gift Splitting

Crummey provisions should take into account the possibility that a donor and his or her spouse could elect to gift split a gift to a *Crummey* trust under Section 2513. The amount subject to withdrawal by a powerholder should not be contingent upon a donor and a donor's spouse electing to gift split. The election to gift split is made on a gift tax return. A gift tax return is generally not filed until the year following the year of the gift because it is not due until April 15 of the year following the year of the gift.[35] If the amount subject to a powerholder's *Crummey* Power is contingent upon the donor's spouse electing to gift split, the powerholder's interest will not qualify as a present interest for the portion of a gift that is not withdrawable until the donor's spouse consents to gift split. This is because the withdrawal right is contingent upon the occurrence of a future event. For example, in PLR 8022048, a *Crummey* Trust contained the following *Crummey* Power provisions:

(a) In any calendar year, the beneficiary shall have the power to withdraw from the corpus the lesser of:

   (i)   all amounts added to the trust during such year by the grantor and by any additional grantors; or

   (ii) the sum of the following amounts:

        (A) the product of Three Thousand Dollars ($3,000) multiplied by the number of grantors who have made gifts totaling $3,000 or more during such year to the trust and have not elected to have such gifts treated as being made one-half by the donor's spouse pursuant to Section 2513 of the Internal Revenue Code.

        (B) the product of Six Thousand Dollars ($6,000) multiplied by the number of grantors who have made gifts totaling $6,000 or more during such year to the trust and have elected to have such gifts treated as being made one-half by the donor's spouse pursuant to Section 2513; and

(C) the sum of all gifts to the trust from all donors whose aggregate gifts to the trust during such year are less than $3,000. Such power of withdrawal may be exercised by the beneficiary at any time, and from time to time, during the year up to and including midnight of December 31. The power is not cumulative; it lapses if, or to the extent, it is not exercised by delivery to any trustee of written notice of exercise of the power signed by the beneficiary or by any person lawfully empowered to act for the beneficiary. The trustee shall immediately satisfy the withdrawal in cash or, if additions to the trust have been made during such year in kind, by delivery in kind of such property.

In the ruling, the Service recognized that the election to gift split might not be made until the due date for filing the donor's gift tax return. Such due date could be several months following a donor's gift to the trust. Thus, under the foregoing *Crummey* Power provision, the trustee could not be required to make an immediate distribution in excess of $3,000 to a powerholder based on a married donor's gift. According to the ruling, "[s]uch a delay on the right of withdrawal … would render the gift a future interest."

Crummey Provisions should be drafted to automatically increase the amount that a powerholder may withdraw if the donor is married at the time of the gift. Such a provision should be operative regardless of whether the donor and the donor's spouse eventually elect to gift split. For example, if the donor is not married, a *Crummey* Power provision should grant a powerholder the right to withdraw up to the amount of the annual exclusion (currently $15,000) of any gift to the trust, however, if the donor is married, the *Crummey* Power provision should grant a powerholder the right to withdraw up to twice the amount of the annual exclusion (currently $30,000) of any gift to the trust.

Gift Splitting With Regard to Preceding Calendar Periods

In PLR 201523003, the Service ruled that otherwise ineffective gift splitting by a husband ("Husband")

and wife ("Wife"), for tax years where the period of limitations under Section 6501 for the gift tax return had expired, was irrevocable; however, the husband could file amended gift tax returns reporting gifts as made only by him for tax years that were not yet closed. Additionally, Husband and Wife's allocation of GST exemption based upon the otherwise invalid gift splitting was likewise held to be effective.

During Year 1, Husband created and funded a trust for the benefit of Wife and their descendants (the "Family Trust"). The independent trustee of the Family Trust had the power to pay to or use for the benefit of any one or more of Wife, Husband's descendants and the spouses of such descendants so much or all of the income and principal of the Family Trust for their respective welfare and best interests. Also during Year 1, Husband established and funded two grantor retained annuity trusts (GRATs; "Trust 1" and "Trust 2"). Trust 1's annuity term ended during Year 2 and Trust 2's annuity term ended during Year 3. Upon termination of the annuity terms, the property of Trusts 1 and 2 was distributable to the Family Trust.

Husband and Wife filed gift tax returns for Year 1 and consented to gift split under Section 2513. On the gift tax returns, Husband and Wife opted out of the GST automatic allocation rules with respect to the gift to the Family Trust. However, both Husband and Wife affirmatively allocated GST exemption to a portion of the property transferred to the Family Trust. Husband and Wife did not allocate GST exemption to the transfers to Trust 1 and Trust 2 because the estate tax inclusion periods ("ETIP") had not closed with respect to those trusts. Husband filed a gift tax return for Year 2 reporting the transfer of property from Trust 1 to the Family Trust, but he did not allocate GST exemption to this transfer. Wife did not file a gift tax return for Year 2.

During Year 3, Husband established and funded two additional GRATs ("Trust 3" and "Trust 4"). Both Trust 3 and Trust 4's annuity terms ended during Year 4 and at that time, the property of Trust 3 and Trust 4 became distributable to the Family Trust. Husband and Wife both filed a gift tax return for Year 3. They again consented to gift split made in Year 3 under Section 2513. Neither Husband nor Wife allocated GST exemption to Trust 3 or Trust 4 because of the ETIP, however, they both affirmatively allocated GST exemption to Trust 2 because the ETIP for that trust ended. Additionally, they took the position on the Year 3 gift tax returns that their respective GST exemptions had been automatically allocated in Year 2 to the transfer of property from Trust 1 to the Family Trust.

At the time of the ruling request, Husband and Wife had not filed gift tax returns for Year 4. Further, the period of limitations under Section 6501 had expired for Year 1 and Year 2, so those tax years were closed. Husband and Wife requested the following rulings:

(1) The election to split gifts in Year 1 is effective with respect to the Family Trust, Trust 1, and Trust 2.

(2) Husband and Wife's allocation of his and her GST exemption equal to $b to the Year 1 transfer to the Family Trust is effective.

(3) At the close of the ETIP in Year 2, Husband's and Wife's GST exemption was automatically allocated to one-half of the transfer of property from Trust 1 to the Family Trust.

(4) At the close of the ETIP in Year 3, Husband's and Wife's GST exemption was affirmatively allocated to one-half the transfer of property from Trust 2 to the Family Trust.

(5) The election to split gifts in Year 3 is ineffective with respect to the transfers to Trust 3 and Trust 4.

(6) Husband may file a Form 709 to allocate his remaining GST exemption to the Year 4 transfers of property from Trust 3 and Trust 4 to the Family Trust.

The PLR stated that because Wife was a permissible beneficiary of the Family Trust and her interests were not susceptible of determination and, consequently, were not severable from the interests of other beneficiaries, Husband's gifts to the Family Trust, Trust 1, Trust 2, Trust 3, and Trust 4 should not have been eligible for gift splitting. However, because the period of limitations had expired for Year 1 and Year 2, gift split treatment for Husband's transfer to the Family Trust and the transfers from Trust 1 and Trust 2 to the Family Trust were irrevocable and thus determined to be effective. Since the period of limitations had not yet expired for Year 3, Husband could file an amended return reporting the gifts to Trust 3 and Trust 4 as being made solely by him. The ruling also stated that gift splitting was effective for GST purposes so Husband's and Wife's allocation

of GST exemption to the Family Trust and automatic allocation to Trust 1 was irrevocable. Although Husband and Wife's allocation of GST exemption to the transfer of property from Trust 2 to the Family Trust was effective, it could be modified by Husband filing an amended gift tax return for Year 3.

INCOME TAX ISSUES

When "violated," the grantor trust rules attribute income earned by a trust and items of deduction and credits to the grantor.[36] In general, much of the income tax attributes of foreign and domestic asset protection trusts overlap. Nonetheless, there are some important differences to consider. The grantor trust rules are set forth in Sections 671 through 679. For purposes of this chapter, references to a "grantor trust" refer to a trust that is treated as owned entirely by the grantor for income tax purposes under Section 671, *et seq.*

Domestic Asset Protection Trusts

The grantor will be treated as the owner of a trust under Section 677(a)(1) and (2) if a nonadverse party has the power to distribute income to the grantor or the grantor's spouse. A "nonadverse party" is any person who is not an adverse party.[37] For purposes of the grantor trust rules, adversity is measured on the basis of an individual's interest in the trust and not whether an individual is adverse to the grantor or other deemed owner.[38] A trustee is not an adverse party merely because of the interest as a trustee.[39] An individual's interest in a trust is substantial "if its value in relation to the total value of the property subject to the power is not insignificant."[40] According to one commentator, "use of the double negative [in the quoted language in the text] implies that the standard [of substantiality] is rather low; the interest need only be 'not insignificant'" to be substantial.[41] A beneficiary will ordinarily be an adverse party.[42] Nonetheless, if a beneficiary's right to share in the income or corpus of a trust is limited to only a portion, the beneficiary may be only an adverse party as to that portion.[43]

Unlike a foreign asset protection trust, a domestic asset protection trust can be designed to be a nongrantor trust or separate taxpayer. Of course, in states with high income tax rates it may be possible to remove certain income from a taxpayer's state tax base by transferring the assets that generate such income to a trust having a *situs* and administered in a state with no income tax that would apply to such trust income. Thus, a popular technique known as a Delaware Income Non-Grantor Trust (DING) or a Nevada Income Non-Grantor Trust (NING) was born from the minds of practitioners seeking to help their clients reduce state income tax liability. A string of private letters rulings over the years have been issued demonstrating how a DING and then a NING should be designed to obtain the proper income and estate and gift tax result.[44]

The DING was not without controversy on the estate and gift tax side. In calendar year 2007, the Service took a particular interest in issues related to general powers of appointment in DING type trusts and to the methods that could be used to cause transfers to the trust to constitute incomplete gifts for Federal gift tax purposes. The Service publicly stated that it was studying such issues closely and requested comments.[45] The Estate and Gift Tax Committee of the Trust and Estate Division of the ABA's Section of Real Property Trust and Estate Law Section submitted comments in response to IR-2007-127 on September 26, 2007.[46] Between PLR 200715005 and PLRs 201310002-201310006, no DING Trust rulings were issued. Further, CCA 201208026 concluded that testamentary powers of appointment retained by grantors over a trust under which the grantors were not beneficiaries caused the remainder interest to be an incomplete gift. However, the testamentary powers of appointment related only to the remainder interest. This had the effect of raising concerns that merely reserving a testamentary limited power of appointment in the grantor could have been insufficient by itself to cause the transfer to a DING trust to be an incomplete gift by the grantor.[47]

Some see the use of DING and NINGs as a mechanism to avoid taxes, "[t]he only purpose of setting up these trusts, near as far as we can tell, is avoiding state tax. . . ."[48] One commentator went as far as to analogize the use of DING trusts by residents from high tax states such as New York to stealing with a pen: "another example of how those who steal with a pen get richer, while those who steal at the point of a gun get jail."[49]

On March 31, 2014, Governor Andrew Cuomo signed into law the 2014-2015 Executive Budget for the state of New York.[50] Under the legislation, income non-grantor trusts (such as NINGs and DINGs) created by New York residents are deemed to be "grantor trusts" for New York income tax purposes, which results in the trust's income being included in the New York grantor's income whether or not the income is distributed to the grantor.[51] This provision is effective for income earned

on or after January 1, 2014. However, not for trusts that were liquidated before June 1, 2014. Additionally, the legislation provides that distributions from Exempt New York Resident Trusts (trusts established by New York residents that have no New York trustees, no New York tangible property or real estate, and no New York source income) to a New York resident beneficiary after 2014 are subject to New York income taxes with respect to certain accumulations of trust income. This "throwback" tax, similar to the tax imposed by the state of California, will not apply to income that was accumulated in the trust either (A) before 2014, or (B) before the beneficiary first became a New York resident. There is no interest charge on the throwback tax. Capital gains are not typically considered income for these purposes (if the capital gains are not included in distributable net income).[52]

Foreign Asset Protection Trusts

In general, under Section 679, a "United States person" who directly or indirectly contributes property to a foreign trust will be treated as the owner of the portion of the foreign trust attributable to such contribution if there is a United States beneficiary of any portion of the trust. The definition of a foreign trust is set forth in Sections 7701(a)(30) and (31). Thus, in addition to the numerous ways a trust can violate the grantor trust rules under Sections 671-677, almost any foreign trust with a United States beneficiary that is established and funded by a citizen or resident of the United States will violate the grantor trust rules while the grantor is living.

Generally, the transfer of property to a foreign trust by a citizen or resident of the United States will be treated as a taxable sale for the fair market value of the property transferred.[53] Nevertheless, this rule does not apply if the transfer is made to a foreign trust to the extent that the grantor-donor is treated as the owner of the trust under the grantor trust rules.[54] In addition to the numerous ways a trust can violate the grantor trust rules, as previously mentioned, almost any foreign trust with a United States beneficiary that is established and funded by a citizen or resident of the United States will violate the grantor trust rules while the grantor is living.

The tax imposed under Section 684 could also apply to a foreign trust upon cessation of grantor trust status. Grantor trust status can cease upon the death of the grantor of a trust. Nevertheless, the tax imposed under Section 684 will not apply to assets in a grantor trust if such assets are includable in the estate of the grantor for estate tax purposes because "the basis of the property in the hands of the foreign trust is determined under" Section 1014(a). The assets in an incomplete gift trust should be includable in the grantor's estate for estate tax purposes at the grantor's death.

When a foreign grantor trust that is not included in the United States grantor's estate for Federal estate tax purposes ceases to be treated as a grantor trust as to its United States grantor, under Section 684, the grantor-donor is *"treated as having transferred, immediately before (but on the same date that) the trust is no longer"* a grantor trust, the assets of the former grantor trust to a foreign trust.[55] Grantor trust status ceases at the grantor's death. Therefore, upon his death the grantor is treated as having transferred assets to a foreign trust immediately before, but on the same date that the trust ceases to be a grantor trust. Illustrating the application of this rule Example (2) of Regulation §1.684-2(e)(2) provides in relevant part:

> On July 1, 2003, A dies, and as of that date no other person is treated as the owner of [Foreign Trust]. On that date, the fair market value of the property is 1200X, and its adjusted basis equals 350X…*A is treated as having transferred the property to* [Foreign Trust] *immediately before his death, and generally is required to recognize 850X of gain at that time*. [Emphasis added.]

Thus, the Section 684 income tax liability generated because of a deemed transfer of assets to a foreign trust when a grantor dies is deemed to be incurred by the grantor while living and not following his death. This is important because Section 2053 generally permits an estate tax deduction for the amount of claims against the estate if such claims are allowable under the laws of the jurisdiction where the estate is administered. Unpaid income taxes are deductible as a claim against an estate under Section 2053 provided such taxes are attributable to income properly includible in an income tax return of a decedent for a period prior to the decedent's death.[56] Any income taxes on income received after a decedent's death are not deductible on a decedent's estate tax return.[57] Section 2053(c)(1)(B) provides in relevant part "Any income taxes on income received after the death of the decedent…shall not be deductible under this section." The legal obligation for payment of the Section 684 tax is imposed on the grantor. Therefore, similar to the liability imposed on the grantor for the tax on the income of a grantor trust, payment of the Section 684 tax by the grantor's estate should not constitute a taxable gift to the foreign trust

even though an economic benefit is being passed to the trust and its beneficiaries.

In several private letter rulings, the Service takes the position under Sections 678(a)(1) and (a)(2) that an individual possessing a *Crummey* withdrawal power (a "Powerholder") is treated as the owner for income tax purposes of all or a portion of a trust since the Powerholder possesses or possessed a *Crummey* Power over such property.[58]

Under Section 678(a), an individual who is not the grantor is treated as the owner of any portion of a trust if such individual has a power exercisable solely by the individual to withdraw trust corpus or the income therefrom. Additionally, if that person previously released or modified his or her withdrawal power and thereafter retains such control over the trust which would otherwise make the grantor the owner under Sections 671 to 677 of the grantor trust rules, then Section 678(a) will continue to treat the Powerholder as the owner. Use of the term "control" in Section 678 should be read in light of the grantor trust rules and viewed with an expansive meaning (*i.e.*, "within the principles of Sections 671 to 677").

Section 678(a)(2) uses the terms "release" and "modify," which seem to indicate the need for an overt act on the part of the Powerholder for the statute to apply. Conversely, most *Crummey* Powers generally lapse by operation of the terms of the trust instrument. Compare also, Sections 2041(b)(2) and 2514(e) (the 5 and 5 exemption), provisions which specifically use the term "lapse." Under these provisions it would seem *inaction* may be necessary to claim the desired tax benefits.

Section 678(b) provides that the general rule of Section 678(a) shall not apply with respect to a power over income if the grantor of the trust is otherwise treated as the owner under any other provision in the grantor trust rules. Consequently, Section 678(b) resolves any potential overlap in favor of treating the grantor, rather than a beneficiary, as owner of the trust income. Thus, assuming any other provision of the grantor trust rules initially causes the grantor to be treated as the owner of a trust, the existence of a *Crummey* Power in one or more beneficiaries should not change this treatment due to the ordering rule of Section 678(b).

However, the holding of two earlier private letter rulings, P.L.R. 8142061 and P.L.R. 8545076, may be based on a different theory from the rulings cited above. Some commentators believe these earlier rulings could be read to hold that a Powerholder who allows a *Crummey* Power to lapse is treated as having withdrawn the assets subject to the withdrawal right and to have recontributed such assets to the trust.[59] Under this theory, a Powerholder is treated as the new grantor of the trust upon the lapse of the *Crummey* Power. Furthermore, the original grantor cannot be taxed on the income earned by a grantor trust after the lapse because he is no longer considered the grantor of the trust. From an economic standpoint, this "recontribution" theory has merit.[60] If followed, however, the recontribution theory would render Section 678(b) nugatory in all but the rarest of circumstances. From a tax perspective, it is unlikely that Congress intended such a result.

The law regarding the taxation of items relating to trust principal over which a powerholder possesses or possessed a *Crummey* Power may also be unclear because of the peculiar language used in Section 678(b). Section 678(b) refers to competing powers "over income" whereas Section 678(a)(1) refers to a power to vest "corpus or the income therefrom." The Code is silent on this issue. Some commentators suggest that this was merely an oversight in drafting the statute.[61] The holdings of Private Letter Rulings 9321050, 9309023, 9140127, 8308033, 8326074, 8142061, 8103074, and 7909031 seem to reach the same conclusion. In these private letter rulings, the Service takes the position that the grantor is treated as the owner of the corpus (whenever possible) despite the existence of a Section 678 power held by a beneficiary. These rulings also suggest that the Service agrees that the language in Section 678(b) referring only to income and not corpus was an error in drafting and should be ignored. The expansive definition of the term "income" under Reg. §1.671-3(b) also supports this interpretation of the statute.[62] Additionally, the Congressional committee reports support the interpretation of Section 678(b) set forth in the foregoing private letter rulings.[63]

Grantor trust status must cease either through the lapse or suspension of the power which violates the grantor trust rules or because of the death of the grantor. Consideration should be given to the income tax consequences of a trust with *Crummey* Power provisions following cessation of grantor trust status. In PLR 9321050, a powerholder was granted a *Crummey* Power for a period of thirty (30) days over a contribution of property to a trust. After the lapse of the *Crummey* Power, the Powerholder retained an interest in the trust which would have caused him to be treated as the owner for income tax purposes of the portion of the trust previously subject to his *Crummey* Power. Nonetheless,

the trust also contained provisions which triggered grantor trust treatment as to the grantor. Thus, it was determined that the grantor would be treated as the owner of the income and corpus of the trust under the grantor trust rules during her lifetime. Following the grantor's death, however, the ruling held that the Powerholder who formerly possessed the lapsed *Crummey* Power would not be treated as the owner of the income or corpus of the trust related to his lapsed *Crummey* Power. The Service cited no authority to support its position in PLR. 9321050. Additionally, PLR 9026036, a ruling involving the same facts, reached the opposite conclusion. It held that following the grantor's death, the Powerholder who formerly possessed the lapsed *Crummey* Power right would be treated as the owner of the income or corpus of the trust related to that right. PLR 9026036 was withdrawn by the Service on February 25, 1993 and replaced by PLR 9321050.

In the holding in PLR 9321050, it would seem that Section 684(b) would be inapplicable upon the grantor's death as the trust would continue to be treated as owned by one or more of the PowerholderS assuming such PowerholderS are all US persons.

Generally, under the law of US income taxation of trusts the amounts of income required to be distributed to a trust beneficiary or the discretionary amounts actually distributed to a trust beneficiary are taxed to such beneficiary, while all other amounts of income not distributed are taxable to the trust. For a wholly discretionary non-grantor trust, US income tax is only imposed when US beneficiaries receive a distribution from the trust.[64] When such beneficiary receives a discretionary distribution from the trust (which can occur up to sixty-five days after the end of the tax year), the trust receives an income tax deduction for such amounts distributed, limited by the Distributable Net Income (DNI) of the trust, which is a trust's taxable income subject to certain statutory modifications.[65] To the extent distributions are not made to US beneficiaries, the income earned by such trust is not subject to income taxation currently in the US unless, as mentioned above, it is US source income or effectively connected with a trade or business.[66]

However, foreign non-grantor trusts also must consider the "Undistributed Net Income" (UNI) of such trust. The UNI of a foreign non-grantor trust is any income and gains that have accrued in a current year and not distributed to any one or more of the beneficiaries that same year. The treatment of the UNI of a foreign non-grantor trust is subject to certain throwback rules under Sections 665 through 668, which are designed to impose on the beneficiaries of a foreign non-grantor trust with UNI the same income taxes that would have been imposed had the trust distributed its income currently. Unfortunately, the UNI receives draconian treatment under these rules.

The throwback rules compute the tax on an accumulation distribution to a US beneficiary in a five (5) step process, after which an "interest" charge is imposed. This process includes:

a. The number of preceding taxable years of the trust to which the distribution is attributable is determined.[67] (The years to which the distribution is attributable are the earliest years of the trust in which the trust had UNI.)[68]

b. The average taxable income years are determined. (These are the US beneficiary's five (5) immediately preceding taxable years, ignoring the years with the highest and lowest total taxable incomes.)[69]

c. The average annual accumulation is computed by dividing the total accumulation distribution, which includes the amount of any taxes paid by the trust on the distribution by the number of years in which it was accumulated. (This average annual accumulation is then added to the US beneficiary's taxable income in each of the three base years.[70] Additionally, the US beneficiary's income includes any amounts added to the taxable income from prior accumulation distributions.)[71]

d. The increase in the beneficiary's tax caused by the addition of the average annual accumulation in each of the three base years is computed and averaged.[72]

e. The "partial tax" on the accumulation distribution is computed by multiplying the average of the annual additional tax by the number of years of accumulation and subtracting the credit for taxes paid by the trust on the distribution.[73] A foreign non-grantor trust makes an accumulation distribution in any year in which the trust distributes more than its current year's DNI, if it has UNI.[74]

When capital gains are accumulated in a foreign non-grantor trust, the US beneficiaries of such a trust receive disparate tax treatment from the treatment that is applicable to US beneficiaries of a non-grantor domestic trust. Generally, capital gains recognized by a domestic trust are allocated to corpus so that the trust itself is taxed on such gains and if later distributed to the beneficiaries such gain is distributed tax free to them. However, a foreign non-grantor trust allocates all of its capital gains to DNI and if the trust's capital gains are not currently distributed, such capital gains become a part of the trust's UNI.[75] When such UNI is distributed to US beneficiaries **the gains lose their character as capital gains and are taxed to the beneficiaries as ordinary income**.[76] Under Section 667(a), only tax-exempt interest retains its character. Note that, with respect to capital gains realized by a domestic trust, such loss of characterization would normally have no effect because such income is not generally included in DNI; however, as mentioned, DNI of a foreign trust includes capital gains.

Furthermore, Section 668 imposes a nondeductible "interest" charge on a US beneficiary's tax on an accumulation distribution from a foreign non-grantor trust for each year of accumulation beginning after December 31, 1976. The interest charge is levied on the amount of the additional tax imposed on the US beneficiary on account of the accumulation distribution, after the credit for any taxes paid by the trust on the distributed income.[77] The interest charge on accumulations after December 21, 1995 is based on a compound interest rate determined in the same manner as the interest imposed on underpayments of income tax under Section 6621(a)(2).[78]

The interest charge on distributions of income accumulated over a period of years will be based on the average number of years of accumulation.[79] The interest rate is determined by multiplying the charge by a fraction, the numerator is the sum of the taxable years between each year of accumulation and the year of distribution and the denominator is the number of taxable years to which the distribution is attributable.[80]

Interest is calculated annually and there is no proration for partial years. As a result, if income is deemed distributed in one year and actually distributed in the following year, the tax on the distribution is subject to a full year's interest charge, regardless of when during the first year the income was earned by the trust.[81] However, the interest charge plus the tax incurred on the accumulation distribution *cannot* exceed the amount of the distribution itself but it may equal one hundred percent (100%) of the distribution.[82]

The interest charge is computed without regard to the age of the UNI of a foreign non-grantor trust. For example, it is irrelevant how much of the total accumulation distribution was accumulated five (5) years ago and how much was accumulated two years ago.

For the foregoing reasons and the reasons that follow, as a result of the draconian tax treatment of a foreign non-grantor trust, if the beneficiaries of the Trust are US persons at the death of the settlor, it may be advisable to take one of the following actions upon the settlor's death:

1. Migrate the Trust to the US on or shortly after it becomes a foreign non-grantor trust, thereby transforming it into a domestic non-grantor trust. After a trust is migrated to the US, the throwback rules would no longer apply because the trust would no longer be considered a foreign trust.[83] Therefore, a US-resident trustee may be appointed after the settlor's death to avoid the application of the throwback rules, so long as the *situs* and administration of the Trust are also moved to a domestic jurisdiction. However, the migration of a trust to the US would need to be completed before the accumulation of UNI by the trust to avoid the application of the throwback rules.[84]

2. Instead of migrating the trust to the US, another strategy would be for the trustee to make a decanting distribution from the trust to a separate domestic trust. However, this decanting distribution would also need to be made before UNI is accumulated in the trust to avoid the application of the throwback rules.

3. Other options include:

   a. Merging the foreign trust with a domestic trust;

   b. Distributing all DNI out to beneficiaries on an annual basis, thus avoiding accumulation of income under the throwback rules;

   c. Distributing all DNI to a domestic trust via annual decanting distributions (however, this would include distributing all capital gains in this manner);

   d. Distributing UNI to beneficiaries under the averaging rules mentioned above to escape the interest charge penalty;

   e. Retaining all income and build up UNI for years adding it to principal and then never distribute principal and contain UNI problem by investing the trust corpus in an annuity or bond that produces income to be distributed annually forever thereafter; and

   f. Distributing appreciated property to a US beneficiary with capital gains payable by the recipient beneficiary upon the sale of the distributed appreciated property. A distribution in kind, other than a distribution of appreciated assets in satisfaction of a fixed dollar amount, carries out DNI equal to the lesser of the trust's tax basis in the property or the property's fair market value.

CHAPTER ENDNOTES

1. ll references to the "**Code**" found herein are to the Internal Revenue Code of 1986 as amended and all references to sections ("§") are to sections of the Code unless otherwise provided herein.

2. I.R.C. §2511(a).

3. Treas. Reg. §25.2511-2. All references to the "Regulations" or the "Treas. Reg." are to the Treasury Regulations promulgated under the Code.

4. Treas. Reg. §25.2511-2(b).

5. Treas. Reg. §25.2511-2(b).

6. Treas. Reg. §25.2511-2(c). See also e.g., PLR 201507008.

7. Treas. Reg. §25.2511(d).

8. *See Estate of Goelet v. Com'r.*, 51 T.C. 352 (1968); *Goldstein v. Com'r.*, 37 T.C. 897 (1962).

9. *See e.g.*, Treas. Reg. §25.2511-2(b); PLRs 9030005, 200148028, 200247013, 200502014, 200612002, 200647001, 200715005, 200729025, 200731019 and 200731019. *See also* Wells, *Domestic Asset Protection Trusts-A Viable Estate and Wealth Preservation Alternative*, 77 Fla. Bar J. 44 (May 2003); & Fox & Huft, *Asset Protection and Dynasty Trusts*, 37 Real Prop. Prob. & Tr. J. 287 (Summer 2002).

10. *See* also PLRs 201410001, 201410002, 201410003, 201410004, 201410005, 201410006, 201410007, 201410008, 201410009 and 201410010 all providing:

    Further, Grantor retained Grantor's Testamentary Power to appoint the property in Trust to any person or persons or entity or entities, other than Grantor's estate, Grantor's creditors, or the creditors of Grantor's estate. Under §25.2511-2(b) the retention of a testamentary power to appoint the remainder of a trust is considered a retention of dominion and control over the remainder. Accordingly, the retention of this power causes the transfer of property to Trust to be incomplete with respect to the remainder in Trust for federal gift tax purposes.

11. For an additional discussion of some of the practical issues created by this memorandum and some revisions to the trust

agreement which may have allowed the settlors to achieve their goals in establishing the trust, see Freda, *Chief Counsel Memorandum Switches IRS Position on Completed Gifts*, 54 DTR G-6 (Mar. 21, 2012); Zaritsky, Gans & Blattmachr, *Chief Counsel Advisory 201208026*, LISI Estate Planning Newsletter #1936 (Mar. 6, 2012). *See also* Rubin, *CCM 201208026: Using Testamentary Powers of Appointment to Create Incomplete Gifts-The IRS Throws Down the Gauntlet*, LISI Estate Planning Newsletter #1959 (May 8, 2012); Aucutt, *Ron Aucutt's Top Ten Estate Planning and Estate Tax Developments of 2012*, LISI Estate Planning Newsletter #2043 (Dec. 31, 2012); *and* Gassman, *et. al*, *Planning After IRS Memo 201208026: How Foreign Can Creditor Protection Trust Laws Get?*, LISI Asset Protection Newsletter #207 (Sept. 11, 2012).

12. Treas. Reg. §25.2511-2(e). See *e.g.*, PLR 201507008 providing, "Trustor also retained a Lifetime Limited Power of Appointment to appoint income and principal to the issue of Trustor's father or Foundation. Trustor's Lifetime Limited Power of Appointment can only be exercised in conjunction with the Trust Protector. Under Sections 25.2511-2(e) and 25.2514-3(b)(2), Trustor is considered to solely possess the power to exercise Trustor's Lifetime Limited Power of Appointment because the Trust Protector (who is merely a coholder of Trustor's Lifetime Limited Power of Appointment) has no substantial adverse interest in the disposition of the assets transferred by the Trustor to Trust because (i) the Trust Protector may not have any beneficial interest in any trust (whether before or after the Trustor's death), (ii) the Trust Protector is not a permissible appointee of the Trustor's Lifetime Limited Power of Appointment, and (iii) the Trust Protector is not a taker in default of the exercise of the Trustor's Lifetime Limited Power of Appointment." See PLR 201525002 and PLR 201525003 both providing:

    because the CDA, either Spouse or the LLC, or in default, the Trust Protector, does not have a substantial adverse interest to Grantor's Consent Veto Power, under §25.2511-2(e), Grantor is considered as having himself the power to veto any Charitable Quarterly Distribution to Grantor's Charities for any reason and for no reason. Accordingly, based upon the facts submitted and representations made, we conclude that the Proposed Transfer of property to Trust will be an incomplete gift, assuming Grantor retains Grantor's Consent Veto Power, Grantor's Sole Discretionary Veto Power, and Grantor's Testamentary Power.

13. 1976-1 C.B. 293.

14. See *e.g.*, *Outwin v. Com'r*, 76 T.C. 153 (1981); *Paolozzi v. Com'r*, 23 T.C. 182 (1954). See also *Estate of Paxton v. Com'r*, 86 T.C. 785 (1986) (Estate tax inclusion based on creditor's rights doctrine).

15. 1977-2 C.B. 347.

16. *Com'r. v. Vander Weele*, 254 F.2d 895 (6th Cir. 1958); *Outwin v. Com'r*, 76 T.C. 153 (1981), *acq.*, 1981-1 C.B. 2; *Hambleton v. Com'r.*, 60 T.C. 558 (1973), *acq. in result*, 1974-1 C.B. 1; *Paolozzi v. Com'r.*, 23 T.C. 182 (1954), *acq.* 1962-1 C.B. 4.

17. *See e.g.*, PLR 200944002; PLR 9837007; PLR 9332006.

18. *See e.g.*, PLR 201628010 (Service deferred ruling on income tax status of trust); PLR 201614008; PLR 201614007; PLR 201614006; PLR 201613009; PLR 201550005 PLR 201550006 PLR 201550007; PLR 201550008; PLR 201550009; PLR 201550010; PLR 201550011; PLR 201550012; PLR 201550005 PLR 201550006 PLR 201550007; PLR 201550008; PLR 201550009; PLR 201550010; PLR 201550011; PLR 201550012; PLR 201510008; PLR 201510007; PLR 201510006; PLR 201510005; PLR 201510004; PLR 201510003; PLR 201510002; PLR 201510001; PLR 201440012; PLR 201440011; PLR 201440010; PLR 201440009; PLR 201440008; PLR 201436032; PLR 201436031;

PLR 201436030; PLR 201436029; PLR 201436028; PLR 201436027; PLR 201436026; PLR 201436025; PLR 201436024; PLR 201436023; PLR 201436022; PLR 201436021; PLR 201436020; PLR 201436019; PLR 201436018; PLR 201436017; PLR 201436016; PLR 201436015; PLR 201436014; PLR 201436013; PLR 201436012; PLR 201436011; PLR 201436010; PLR 201436009; PLR 201436008; PLR 201430007; PLR 201430006; PLR 201430005; PLR 201430004; PLR 201430003; PLR 201426014; PLR 201410001, PLR 201410002, PLR 201410003, PLR 201410004, PLR 201410005, PLR 201410006, PLR 201410007, PLR 201410008, PLR 201410009, PLR 201410010, PLR 200148028, PLR 200247013, PLR 200502014, PLR 200612002, PLR 200647001, PLR 200715005, PLR 200729025, PLR 200731019, PLR 200731019, PLR 201310002, PLR 201310003, PLR 201310004, PLR 201310005 and PLR 201310006.

19. *See* Nev. Rev. Stat. §166.010, *et. seq.*

20. *See* N.R.S. 166.040.2(b).

21. Rev. Rul. 76-103, 1976-1 C.B. 293; see also, *Outwin v. Com'r*, 76 T.C. 153 (1981), *acq.*, 1981-1 C.B. 2.

22. *Herzog v. Commissioner*, 41 B.T.A. 509 (1940), aff'd, 116 F.2d 591 (2d. Cir. 1941); *Higgins v. Commissioner*, 129 F.2d 237 (1st Cir. 1942); Rev. Rul. 77-378, 1977-42 IRB 10.

23. Treas. Reg. §25.2511-2(b); Rev. Rul. 62-13, 1962-1 C.B. 181.

24. Treas. Reg. §25.2511-2(b).

25. *Gramm v. Commissioner*, 17 T.C. 1063 (1951); *Estate of Holtz v. Commissioner*, 38 T.C. 37 (1962).

26. *Paolozzi v. Commissioner*, 23 T.C. 182 (1954); *Commissioner v. Vander Weele*, 254 F.2d 895 (6th Cir. 1958); Rev. Rul. 62-13, 1962-1 C.B. 181, Rev. Rul. 76-103, 1976-1 C.B. 292.

27. Treas. Reg. §25.2513-1(a).

28. Regs. §§25.2513-1(b)(1)-(5).

29. *See Robertson v. Commissioner*, 26 T.C.M. 246, 251-52 (1956); *Kass v. Commissioner*, TC Memo 1957-227, 876; and *Falk v. Commissioner*, T.C.M. 86, 93 (1965).

30. *Id.*

31. 397 F.2d 82 (9th Cir. 1968).

32. *See e.g., id.; Halsted v. Com'r.*, 28 T.C. 1069 (1957), *acq.*, 1958-1 CB 5; *Perkins v. Com'r.*, 27 T.C. 601 (1956); *Gilmore v. Com'r.*, 213 F.2d 520 (6th Cir. 1954); *Kieckhefer v. Com'r.*, 189 F.2d 118 (7th Cir. 1951).

33. *See* Fiore & Ramsbacher, *IRS Takes Tougher Position on Crummey Trusts in TAM*, 413 Est. Plan 23 (Nov. 1996).

34. *See*, e.g., PLRs 8143045, 8015133, 8008040 and 8044080.

35. *See* I.R.C. §§6019 and 6075.

36. *See* I.R.C. §671; Treas. Reg. §1.671-2(b).

37. Section 672(a).

38. *See* 819 T.M., Grantor Trusts: Income Taxation Under Subpart E, IV, A, 1.

39. Treas. Reg. §1.672(a)-1 (a).

40. *Id.*

41. *See* 860 T.M., Revocable Inter Vivos Trusts, V, B, 1, c.

42. Treas. Reg. 1.672(a)-1(b).

43. *Id.*

44. *See e.g.*, PLR 201628010 (Service deferred ruling on income tax status of trust); PLR 201614008; PLR 201614007; PLR 201614006; PLR 201613009; PLR 201550005 PLR 201550006 PLR 201550007; PLR 201550008; PLR 201550009; PLR 201550010; PLR 201550011;

PLR 201550012; PLR 201550005 PLR 201550006; PLR 201550007; PLR 201550008; PLR 201550009; PLR 201550010; PLR 201550011; PLR 201550012; PLR 201510008; PLR 201510007; PLR 201510006; PLR 201510005; PLR 201510004; PLR 201510003; PLR 201510002; PLR 201510001; PLR 201440012; PLR 201440011; PLR 201440010; PLR 201440009; PLR 201440008; PLR 201436032; PLR 201436031; PLR 201436030; PLR 201436029; PLR 201436028; PLR 201436027; PLR 201436026; PLR 201436025; PLR 201436024; PLR 201436023; PLR 201436022; PLR 201436021; PLR 201436020; PLR 201436019; PLR 201436018; PLR 201436017; PLR 201436016; PLR 201436015; PLR 201436014; PLR 201436013; PLR 201436012; PLR 201436011; PLR 201436010; PLR 201436009; PLR 201436008; PLR 201430007; PLR 201430006; PLR 201430005; PLR 201430004; PLR 201430003; PLR 201426014; PLR 201410001, PLR 201410002, PLR 201410003, PLR 201410004, PLR 201410005, PLR 201410006, PLR 201410007, PLR 201410008, PLR 201410009, PLR 201410010, PLR 200148028, PLR 200247013, PLR 200502014, PLR 200612002, PLR 200647001, PLR 200715005, PLR 200729025, PLR 200731019, PLR 200731019, PLR 201310002, PLR 201310003, PLR 201310004, PLR 201310005 and PLR 201310006. PLR 201510008; PLR 201510007; PLR 201510006; PLR 201510005; PLR 201510004; PLR 201510003; PLR 201510002; PLR 201510001; PLR 201440012; PLR 201440011; PLR 201440010; PLR 201440009; PLR 201440008; PLR 201436032; PLR 201436031; PLR 201436030; PLR 201436029; PLR 201436028; PLR 201436027; PLR 201436026; PLR 201436025; PLR 201436024; PLR 201436023; PLR 201436022; PLR 201436021; PLR 201436020; PLR 201436019; PLR 201436018; PLR 201436017; PLR 201436016; PLR 201436015; PLR 201436014; PLR 201436013; PLR 201436012; PLR 201436011; PLR 201436010; PLR 201436009; PLR 201436008; PLR 201430007; PLR 201430006; PLR 201430005; PLR 201430004; PLR 201430003; PLR 201426014; PLR 201410001, PLR 201410002, PLR 201410003, PLR 201410004, PLR 201410005, PLR 201410006, PLR 201410007, PLR 201410008, PLR 201410009, PLR 201410010, PLR 200148028, PLR 200247013, PLR 200502014, PLR 200612002, PLR 200647001, PLR 200715005, PLR 200729025, PLR 200731019, PLR 200731019, PLR 201310002, PLR 201310003, PLR 201310004, PLR 201310005 and PLR 201310006.

45. *See* IR-2007-127.

46. *See* ABA Section of Real Property, Trust and Estate Law, Letter to Internal Revenue Service dated September 26, 2007.

47. *See* Akers, *Private Letter Rulings 201310002-201310006 (March 8, 2013): Favorable "DING Trust" Letter Rulings; Confirmation of IRS's Position That Settlor's Retention of Testamentary Power of Appointment Does Not Necessarily Cause Full Transfer to Trust to be Incomplete Gift*, Bessemer Trust (Mar. 2013).

48. Rubin, *Wealthy N.Y. Residents Escape Tax With Trusts in Nevada*, Bloomberg (Dec. 18, 2013) (*quoting* James Wetzler, former New York state tax commissioner).

49. *See* David Cay Johnston, *Getting Dinged by the DING*, 2010 TNT 59-8, 1655 (Mar. 29, 2010).

50. *See* N.Y. Laws 2014, ch. 59.

51. N.Y. Tax Law §612(b)(41).

52. *See* Montesano, *New York Enacts Significant Changes to Its Estate, Gift, GST and Trust Income Tax Laws*, 39 Est. Gift & Tr. J. 165 (July 10, 2014).

53. I.R.C. §684(a).

54. I.R.C. §684(b).

55. Treas. Reg. §1.684-2(e)(1).

56. Treas. Reg. §20.2053-6(f).

57. *See* also Regulation §2053-6(a) providing in relevant part "Taxes are deductible in computing a decedent's gross estate only as claims against the estate…and only to the extent not disallowed by section 2053(c)(1)(B)."

58. *See e.g.*, PLRs 201216034, 201039010, 200747002, 200238012, 200238011, 200238010, 200238009, 200238008, 200238007, 200238006, 200238005, 200238004, 200235009, 200235008, 200235007, 200147044, 200022035, 200011054, 200011055, 200011056, 200011058, 9812006, 9810008, 9810007, 9810006, 9809004, 9809005, 9809006, 9809007, 9809008, 9801025, 9745010, 9739026, 9625031, 9541029, 8142061, 8521060, 8545076, 8809043, 8805032, 8701007, 9034004, 9320018 and 9311021. See also Rev. Rul. 67-241, 1967-2 CB 225.

59. *See* Early, *Income Taxation of Lapsed Powers of Withdrawal: Analyzing their Current Status*, 62 J.Tax'n 198 (Apr. 1985); Mulligan, *Defective Grantor Trusts Offer Many Tax Advantages*, 19 Est. Plan 131 (May/June 1992).

60. Support for the application of the recontribution theory can also be found in *Jalkut v. Com'r*, 96 T.C. 675 (1991).

61. *See* Early, *Income Taxation on Lapsed Powers of Withdrawal: Analyzing their Current Status*, 62 J.Tax'n 198 (Apr. 1985); Wark, *IRS Rulings Hint "Super" Life Insurance Trust Okay for Gift, Income and Estate Tax Savings*, 54 J.Tax'n 162 (Mar. 1981); Dye, *Several Routes Exist to Avoid IRS' Income Tax Roadblock to Use of Crummey Trust*, 9 Est. Plan 220 (July 1983); Adams, *Irrevocable Life-Insurance Trusts, What are the Current Tax Considerations?*, 120 Tr. Est. 6 (July 1981).

62. *See* Davis, *Interaction of the Grantor Trust Rules and Life Insurance*, 26 Est. Plan 418 (Nov. 1999)

63. *See* H.R. Rep. No. 1337, 83d Cong., 2d Sess. (1954); S. Rep. No. 1622, 83d Cong., 2d Sess. (1954).

64. I.R.C. §662(a)(2).

65. I.R.C. §643(a).

66. I.R.C. §871.

67. I.R.C. §67(b)(1)(A).

68. I.R.C. §666(a).

69. I.R.C. §667(b)(1)(B).

70. I.R.C. §667(b)(1)(C).

71. I.R.C. §667(b)(4).

72. I.R.C. §665(b)(1)(D).

73. I.R.C. §667(b)(1).

74. I.R.C. §665(b).

75. I.R.C. §643(a)(6)(C).

76. I.R.C. §667(a); S. Rep. No. 938, 94th Cong., 2d Sess. 222 (1976).

77. *See e.g.*, I.R.C. §§667(d)(1), 667(d)(1)(C) for the application of the foreign tax credit limitation rules and the retention of the income tax character of the particular income, deduction, or credit item for this purpose.

78. I.R.C. §668(a)(1).

79. I.R.C. §668(a)(3).

80. I.R.C. §668(a)(3).

81. I.R.C. §667(a).

82. I.R.C. §668(b).

83. *See* I.R.C. §665(c); Revenue Ruling 91-6, 1991-1 CB 89.

84. Revenue Ruling 91-6, 1991-1 CB 89.

RETURNS, COMPLIANCE AND BEST PRACTICES FOR ASSET PROTECTION TRUSTS

CHAPTER 19

All of the asset protection trust arrangements described in the other chapters of this book, including domestic asset protection trusts (DAPT), *inter vivos* QTIP trusts (the "QTIP trust") and offshore asset protection trusts (the "offshore trust"), are legitimate tax and personal financial planning techniques. Although the IRS has announced a program to investigate abusive trusts and to vigorously attack their promoters and participants, the IRS announcement also clearly states that there should no concerns about the legitimate uses of trusts, including the proper use of trusts in estate planning. They are based on full compliance with the rules and regulations under the Internal Revenue Code. The problem is often not the trust itself, however, the use to which the trust has been put or the tax treatment claimed for the trust. Even some of the abusive trusts identified by the IRS may be perfectly valid trusts under state law. The trusts simply will not produce the tax results claimed for the trust. Any of the trusts described in this book could be used as part of a fraudulent or abusive arrangement. That is why you need to understand what trusts can—and cannot—do and work only with advisors who are knowledgeable, experienced, and highly ethical.

MODEL RULES OF PROFESSIONAL CONDUCT

The following are the Model Rules of Professional Conduct that may be applied by a state bar committee in analyzing whether an attorney's conduct was unethical for assisting or counseling a client in a transaction deemed to be a fraudulent transfer.

Model Rule 1.2(d) provides:

> "A lawyer shall not counsel a client to engage, or assist a client, in conduct that the lawyer knows is criminal or fraudulent, but a lawyer may discuss the legal consequences of any proposed course of conduct with a client and may counsel or assist a client to make a good faith effort to determine the validity, scope, meaning or application of the law."

Model Rule 4.4(a) provides:

> "In representing a client, a lawyer shall not use means that have no substantial purpose other than to embarrass, delay, or burden a third person, or use methods of obtaining evidence that violate the legal rights of such a person."

Model Rule 8.4(c) provides:

> "It is professional misconduct for a lawyer to:
>
> (a) violate or attempt to violate the Rules of Professional Conduct, knowingly assist or induce another to do so, or do so through the acts of another;
>
> (b) commit a criminal act that reflects adversely on the lawyer's honesty, trustworthiness or fitness as a lawyer in other respects;
>
> (c) engage in conduct involving dishonesty, fraud, deceit or misrepresentation;
>
> (d) engage in conduct that is prejudicial to the administration of justice;
>
> (e) state or imply an ability to influence improperly a government agency or

official or to achieve results by means that violate the Rules of Professional Conduct or other law; or

(f) knowingly assist a judge or judicial officer in conduct that is a violation of applicable rules of judicial conduct or other law."

STATE ETHICS OPINIONS

Connecticut

In Connecticut Informal Opinion 91-23, a lawyer sought an opinion on whether the lawyer could ethically recommend and/or assist a client in making a transfer of the client's jointly owned residence to the client's wife while the client was insolvent. Based on the Model Rules of Professional Responsibility, the Connecticut Bar Association's Committee on Professional Ethics stated that:

"A lawyer may not counsel or assist a client to engage in a fraudulent transfer that the lawyer knows is either intended to deceive creditors or that has no substantial purpose other than to delay or burden creditors."

The committee further stated:

"[W]hether or not a particular transaction is a fraudulent transfer as a matter of substantive law is not the decisive factor in applying the Rules. The decisive factors are whether the lawyer knows that the transfer constitutes conduct having a purpose to deceive (see Rule 1.2(d)) or whether in counseling or assisting the client the lawyer is using means that have no substantial purpose other than to embarrass, delay or burden third parties (see Rule 4.4)."

The committee concluded that although all fraudulent transfers are thought of as illegal, the Model Rules do not apply to all illegal conduct and only apply to conduct that is "known" to be criminal or fraudulent. As a result, following the reasoning in Connecticut Informal Opinion 91-23, if a lawyer assists or counsels a client in a transaction "known" to be a fraudulent transfer, the attorney's conduct would be unethical.

South Carolina

In South Carolina Bar Ethics Advisory Opinion 84-02, the ethics committee considered whether the model code prohibited a lawyer from transferring a client's property from the client's name to the client's spouse's name in anticipation of the possibility that an adverse judgment would be rendered against the client. The committee held that "a lawyer may not transfer a client's property from the client's name to the client's spouse's name in order to avoid the likely possibility that the client's creditors could recover the property if a judgment were rendered against the client." The committee held that this conduct would be prohibited because it violates DR 7-102(A)(7) which states that "in his representation of a client, a lawyer shall not counsel or assist his client in conduct that the lawyer knows to be illegal or fraudulent." The committee further stated:

"The critical issue would be whether or not the transfer took place with a reasonable prospect that a judgment would be obtained against the client, or whether or not the transfer took place to avoid some possibility in the distant future. If the transfer was solely for the purpose of avoiding creditors, it could not be done by an attorney for a client. If, however, there does not exist the immediate reasonable prospect of a judgment being entered against the client, the transfer merely to avoid the possibility of an action by a creditor or creditors would not be in violation of DR 7-102(A)(7)."

Based on South Carolina Bar Ethics Advisory Opinion 84-02, if a transfer is only for the purpose of avoiding the "possibility" of a judgment against the client, it would probably not be a violation of the canons; however, if the transfer is made with the sole purpose to avoid the "likely probability" of a judgment, then such a transfer would be a violation.

California

In Ethics Opinion 1993-1 of the Legal Ethics and Unlawful Practice Committee of the San Diego County Bar Association the issue of the extent an attorney may advise or assist a client with respect to an avoidance of existing and identifiable creditors' rights and a protection of the client's assets. A potential client sought advice to protect the client's personal assets from existing and identifiable creditors. The client expressed an intent to transfer the assets beyond the reach of the client's creditors to the attorney and requested that the attorney advise, prepare and assist in the implementation of an asset protection plan, which may include trusts, family limited partnerships and similar techniques. The committee cited Rule 3-210 of the State Bar of California Rules of Professional Conduct:

> "A member shall not advise the violation of any law, rule, or ruling of a tribunal unless the member believes in good faith that such law, rule or ruling is invalid. A member may take appropriate steps in good faith to test the validity of any law, rule, or ruling of a tribunal."

The Uniform Fraudulent Transfer Act provides a remedy to creditors to whom its provisions apply for transfers deemed fraudulent. Section 3439.04(a) of the California Civil Code sets forth that a transfer made or obligation incurred by a debtor is fraudulent as to a creditor whether the creditor's claim arose before or after the transfer was made or the obligation was incurred if the debtor made the transfer or incurred the obligation with the actual intent to hinder, delay or defraud the creditor. The committee viewed an attorney's "knowing" assistance in fraudulent transfers as contrary to civil law and would subject an attorney to discipline.

Furthermore, to the extent that the attorney participates in the transfer, the attorney and the client may be subject to criminal sanctions under section 154 of the California Penal Code. It imposes a criminal misdemeanor on a debtor's fraudulently transferring property out of state or transferring with the "intent to defraud, hinder or delay creditors." Section 531 of the Penal Code provides:

> "Every person who is a party to a fraudulent conveyance of any lands, tenements, or hereditaments, goods, or chattels, or any rights or interest issuing out of the same, or to any bond, suit, judgment, or execution, contract or conveyance, had, made or contrived with intent to deceive and default others, or to defeat, hinder or delay creditors or others or their just debts, damages, or demands; or who, being a party as aforesaid, at any time wittingly and willingly puts in, uses, avows, maintains, justifies, or defend the same, or any of them, as true, and done, had, or made in good faith, or upon good consideration, or aliens, assigns or sells any of the lands, tenements, hereditaments, goods, chattels, or other things before mentioned, to him or them

conveyed as aforesaid, or any part thereof, is guilty of a misdemeanor."

Section 6128 of the California Business and Professions Code also indicates that an attorney is guilty of a misdemeanor if the attorney engages in any deceit or collusion or consents to any deceit or collusion with an intent to deceive the court or any party. Based on the foregoing statutes, the committee concluded that if the attorney assisted the client in the fraudulent transfer, such conduct would also result in criminal sanctions relative to the client and the attorney.

Iowa

In *Iowa Supreme Court Attorney Disciplinary Board v. Ouderkirk*,[1] the Iowa Supreme Court determined that an attorney did not commit an ethical violation in assisting a client (who was accused of murder and ultimately convicted of manslaughter) with transactions that were determined by a court to be fraudulent transfers. While the ruling was based on the Iowa Code of Professional Responsibility, which has been replaced by the Iowa Rules of Professional Conduct, the rules considered in the case are retained in the current rules.

The court discussed whether a fraudulent transfer is fraud for purposes of the rules of professional responsibility and concluded that fraud is not presumed. The court distinguished between an attorney drafting documents knowing that a transaction is a fraud and an attorney drafting documents for a transaction that is later determined to be a fraudulent transfer. If the attorney does know that the client is engaging in a fraudulent transfer, then the attorney's assistance in preparing documents does cross ethical lines.

AIDING AND ABETTING LIABILITY FOR A FRAUDULENT TRANSFER

Some states may not recognize an action for aiding and abetting a fraudulent transfer by third-party non-transferees of the property in question.[2] As an example, Florida does not recognize such an action.[3] In the case of *Yusem v. South Florida Water Management District*,[4] South Florida Water Management District (SWFWMD) obtained a judgment against Henry Yusem ("D") in the amount of $224,695.42. D failed to make any payment on the judgment. In April 1998, D's attorneys settled a legal malpractice action for D receiving $244,701.11. D directed his attorneys to wire the funds into a tenancy by the entireties bank account of D and his wife ("W"). D then initiated a wire transfer of $210,000 to an offshore trust account which D held in his name. This money was lost in a foreign currency investment. SWFWMD filed a suit against D and W, alleging that D engaged in a fraudulent asset conversion in violation of section 222.30 of the Florida Statutes.

The court reasoned that D was the debtor and D's offshore trust account was the transferee. W was not a debtor because the judgment was not entered against W. W was also not a transferee because the funds were only momentarily transferred into the tenancy by entireties account without her knowledge and there was no evidence that W benefited from the transfer in any way. As a result, the court held that there was no basis in the law to hold W liable for the fraudulent conversion made by D. The court further stated:

"The trial court misapprehended the purpose and scope of a fraudulent conveyance action. A fraudulent conveyance action is simply another creditors' remedy. It is either an action by a creditor against a transferee directed against a particular transaction, which, if declared fraudulent, is set aside thus leaving the creditor free to pursue the asset, or it is an action against a transferee who has received an asset by means of a fraudulent conveyance and should be required to either return the asset or pay for the asset (by way of judgment and execution). A fraudulent conveyance action, under section 726.108, is not an action against a debtor for failure to pay an amount owing from a prior judgment."

In the Florida Supreme Court case of *Freeman v. First Union National Bank*,[5] First Union (the "Defendant") was sued by investors (the "Plaintiffs") in Unique Gems International Corp. ("Unique Gems"). Unique Gems conducted a Ponzi scheme involving jewelry assembly. The Plaintiffs alleged that the Defendant, as a banking institution servicing Unique Gems' financial transactions, aided and abetted Unique Gems in the fraudulent transfers of money causing harm to the Plaintiffs. The Eleventh Circuit Court of Appeals certified the following question for the Florida Supreme Court: Under Florida law, is there a cause of action for aiding and abetting a fraudulent transfer when the alleged aider-abettor is not a transferee?

The Plaintiffs argued that the Florida Uniform Fraudulent Transfer Act (FUFTA) encompasses a separate tort for aiding and abetting a fraudulent transfer by including the words "[a]ny other relief the circumstances may require" in the language of the statute. The Plaintiffs contended that FUFTA is broad enough to allow a claim for money damages against the Defendant, which allegedly facilitated the fraudulent transfers. The Defendant responded that FUFTA is strictly limited to relief against a "transferee" and the Defendant was not a transferee. The court reasoned:

"On the face of the statute, there is no ambiguity with respect to whether FUFTA creates an independent cause of action for aiding-abetting liability. There simply is no language in FUFTA that suggests the creation of a distinct cause of action for aiding-abetting claims against non-transferees. Rather, it appears that FUFTA was intended to codify an existing but imprecise system whereby transfers that were intended to defraud creditors could be set aside."

The Florida Supreme Court held that FUFTA was not intended to create a cause of action against a non-transferee party for monetary damages arising from the non-transferee's alleged aiding-abetting of a fraudulent transfer and the court answered the certified question in the negative.

ADDITIONAL CASES ILLUSTRATING ETHICAL CONCEPTS

In *Grupo Mexicano de Desarrollo, S.A. de C.V. v Alliance Bond*,[6] during February 1994, Grupo Mexicano de Desarrollo, S.A. (GMD), a Mexican holding company issued $250 million of 8.25 percent unsecured guaranteed notes due in 2001. Interest payments were due in February and August of every year. Four GMD subsidiaries guaranteed the notes. Several investment funds invested approximately $75 million in the notes (the "Investors"). Due to the downturn in the Mexican economy, in mid-1997 GMD was in serious financial trouble and missed its interest payments in August 1997. GMD attempted to restructure its debt between August and December 1997. On October 28, 1997, GMD announced that it was placing in trust its right to receive $17 million of Toll Road Notes to cover employee compensation payments and that it had transferred its right to receive $100 million of Toll Road Notes to the Mexican government.

On December 11, 1997, the Investors accelerated the principal amount of the notes and on December 12, 1997 filed suit for the amount due. The Investors' complaint alleged:

"GMD is at risk of insolvency, if not insolvent already; that GMD was dissipating its most significant asset, the Toll Road Notes, and was preferring its Mexican creditors by its planned allocation of Toll Road Notes to the payment of their claims, and by its transfer to them of Toll Road Receivables; and that these actions would frustrate any judgment respondents could obtain."

The Investors requested a preliminary injunction restraining GMD from transferring the Toll Road Notes or Receivables. The Investors contended that the preliminary injunction issued was analogous to a creditors bill. GMD argued that a creditors bill could only be brought after a creditor has a judgment. The United States Supreme Court held that the courts had no authority to issue a preliminary injunction preventing GMD from disposing of its assets pending the adjudication of the contract claim for money damages. The Court stated: "[t]he requirement that the creditor obtain a prior judgment is a fundamental protection in a debtor-creditor law-rendered all the more important in our federal system by the debtor's right to a jury trial on the legal claim (emphasis added)." The Court further stated:

"There are other factors which likewise give us pause: The remedy sought here could render Federal Rule of Civil Procedure 64, which authorizes use of state prejudgment remedies, a virtual irrelevance. Why go through the trouble of complying with local attachment and garnishment statutes when this all-purpose prejudgment injunction is available? More, importantly, by adding, through judicial fiat, a new and powerful weapon to the creditor's arsenal, the new rule could radically alter the balance between debtor's and creditor's rights which has been developed over centuries through many laws-including those relating to bankruptcy, fraudulent conveyances, and preferences. Because any rational creditor would want to protect his investment, such a remedy might induce creditors to engage in a "race to the courthouse" in cases involving insolvent or near-insolvent debtors, which might prove financially fatal to the struggling debtor."

In *Morganroth & Morganroth v. Norris, McLaughlin & Marcus, P.C.,*[7] the Third Circuit allowed a Michigan law firm ("P") to pursue its claims against a New Jersey law firm and two other attorneys ("D") for engaging in acts of fraud to hinder P's ability to collect a judgment in excess of $6 million against John DeLorean and a corporation controlled by him. More than one year after P filed its suit against DeLorean, D assisted DeLorean in the formation of a corporation, Genesis, and conveying his New Jersey farm to it. Soon thereafter the transfer was set aside as a fraudulent conveyance. Two years after bringing its suit against DeLorean, P obtained its judgment against DeLorean. Almost immediately, D took a series of actions impeding P's ability to collect. First, D prepared and recorded a confirmatory deed that purported to transfer the farm to Genesis the prior year.

Two months later, D prepared a Memorandum of Life Lease having Genesis acknowledge the purported existence of a 1987 lease of the farm between DeLorean, as lessor, and DeLorean as guardian for his children, as lessee. After recording the memorandum, D prepared and recorded a corrective deed purporting to transfer the farm to Genesis. In addition, D sent a deceptive letter to the clerk of courts in the county where the farm was located. The face of the letter indicated that the judge had dissolved an injunction order, which resulted in the clerk indicating such in the records. Finally, D asked the attorney of a company owned by DeLorean's brother not to communicate with P about DeLorean moving some furniture to that company's warehouse to avoid a writ of execution. The court held that the plaintiff stated a viable claim against an attorney who knowingly and intentionally participated in a client's unlawful conduct to hinder, delay, and/or fraudulently obstruct the enforcement of a judgment, regardless of whether the attorney made a misrepresentation with or without detrimental reliance on such misrepresentation.

In Florida, based on *Yusem* and *Freeman* it is clear a third party non-transferee may not be held liable under the FUFTA for assisting a client in making a fraudulent transfer; however, an attorney may separately be subject to Bar discipline depending on how the Florida Bar (or any other state bar) interprets and applies the Rules of Professional Conduct 1.2(d), 4.4(1) and/or 8.4(c) in a fraudulent transfer situation. Based on the state ethics opinions discussed above, it appears that there exists a reasonable basis that a state bar may subject an attorney to discipline if the attorney "knows" he is assisting a client in making a fraudulent transfer.[8]

In *In re Niroomand,*[9] debtor, Akram Niroomand ("D"), was being pursued by Great American Insurance Company ("C"), which commenced a bond indemnity action on June 8, 2007 in the Southern District of Florida. Nearly a year later in May of 2008, C obtained a judgment against D in the amount of $2,930,899.97 (the "Judgment").

Approximately one year prior to the Judgment and eighteen months prior to filing for bankruptcy protection, D engaged a law firm ("Firm") to create and fund an offshore asset protection trust structure. According to D, Firm advised her to establish the Niroomand Family Trust, dated July 6, 2007 (the "Trust"), in the Cook Islands to protect her assets. The pending claim was disclosed to Firm.

After establishing the Trust, D transferred $500,000 to the trust, however, following the initial transfer D requested the trustee to return approximately $325,000. D used the funds that were distributed to her to pay down mortgages on her home in Florida. (Applying funds to pay down a mortgage on a primary residence is a common asset protection technique used in Florida when a debtor has an existing outstanding claim.)[10]

Following receipt of the first distribution D then requested the trustee in the Cook Islands to terminate the Trust and repatriate the funds to the United States. The trustee complied with D's request. Presumably, D made this request because she was concerned that a court would eventually order her to repatriate such funds and then hold her in contempt if she failed to comply with such order.[11]

Based on the foregoing, the bankruptcy trustee ("T") in the Chapter 7 bankruptcy of D, in furtherance of his statutory duties as bankruptcy trustee, alleged D's payment of legal fees constituted a fraudulent transfer to Firm (such transfers alleged to be both actually and constructively fraudulent). According to T, the payment of legal fees for Firm's advice, which T claimed was negligent, was not justified and did not constitute reasonably equivalent value. Under section 548 of the Bankruptcy Code, such transfers would be avoidable by T. T also alleged Firm committed malpractice in assisting D in establishing the Trust and was unjustly enriched from the payment of legal fees. According to T, D was insolvent when she paid for such legal services.[12]

The only evidence T presented to the bankruptcy court to prove his case was D's testimony. According to T's Initial Brief, "extensive documentary evidence was introduced, for the most part, by stipulation." T further stated, "the Bankruptcy Court made manifest error by not considering the documentary evidence that establishes that the Debtor made the transfers to the Appellees in exchange for less than reasonably equivalent value…" Notwithstanding T's objections, the Eleventh Circuit did not find any support in the record for T's claim that the bankruptcy court did not consider the documentary evidence in reaching its conclusions. D testified she was insolvent when she transferred assets to the trust. T did not present any expert testimony regarding the alleged malpractice claim. Firm, however, presented "voluminous documentary and testimonial evidence" that D was solvent when she transferred assets to the Trust. This evidence included D's affidavit of solvency in which D testified she was solvent and could pay her anticipated debts, including any judgment that might be incurred in a lawsuit. The affidavit of solvency was used to impeach D's testimony and the court found her testimony lacked credibility. As a result of D's lack of credibility, the court found T's case "woefully lacking" any evidence to support its allegations. The credible evidence supported finding D was solvent when she transferred assets to the Trust. The court found no fraudulent transfer and no evidence of malpractice or unjust enrichment. According to the Bankruptcy Court:

> The plaintiff's case consisted of one witness, which in the first place the Court did not find credible, but, in addition, the evidence presented is rather clear.

> While, I never found any evidence about legal malpractice, I'm looking for what could possibly be argued as unjust enrichment. As to the constructive fraud, fraudulent transfer, the Court thinks it's abundantly clear that there's been no establishment of insolvency.

> In fact, the record is abundant with records of solvency. The witness signed a solvency affidavit, which she said she did not read, *but the Court notes-noted that the witness could remember some things in the way of financial numbers of a rather complicated structure down to the penny, and other things, she couldn't remember at all.* (Emphasis added.)

On appeal, the district court upheld the bankruptcy court's findings. The Eleventh Circuit affirmed these decisions on Oct. 17, 2012. The court found no error in the bankruptcy court's findings. The bankruptcy court heard D's testimony and discredited it, which left

T without any credible evidence to support his case. The bankruptcy court was entitled to find D was solvent at the time of the transfers because the credible evidence supported that finding. There was no indication that the Bankruptcy Court looked beyond the solvency badge to other indicia that established fraudulent intent. T's unwillingness to stop litigating after the Bankruptcy Court's dismissal apparently fueled a significant amount of animosity between Firm and T. T's rationale for his appeals is set forth below by cause of action.

Negligence & Unjust Enrichment

Firm cited *Grupo Mexicano de Desarrollo S.A. v. Alliance Bond Fund, Inc.*,[13] to justify its willingness to assist D with this planning. T disagreed with Firm's reliance on this case. T's Civil Appeal Statement indicated that the determination of the appeal would turn on the interpretation of *Grupo*. Indeed, Firm engaged in planning based on his interpretation of *Grupo*, which was articulated in the pleadings that stated:

> I have sort of a general feeling about it, that once there's a judgment, there probably are restrictions on how you can transfer property, okay, that don't exist pre-judgment, at least according to the U.S. Supreme Court in *Groupo* [sic] *Mexicano*, so that's sort of been like the guideline for us…

However, T correctly countered that *Grupo*'s holding did *not* evaporate remedies available to creditors prior to obtaining a judgment providing:

> Although *Grupo* held there was no common law authority entitling a plaintiff the right to a pre-judgment injunction preventing a debtor from transferring their property as they see fit, it specifically noted there may be one or more statutory basis that may nevertheless preclude a debtor from doing so, but that was not before the Court.

Indeed, the Supreme Court acknowledged pre-judgment remedies available to creditors under UFCA and UFTA. "Several States have adopted the Uniform Fraudulent Conveyance Act (or its successor the Uniform Fraudulent Transfers Act), which has been interpreted as conferring on a nonjudgment creditor the right to bring a fraudulent conveyance claim.[14] Insofar as Rule 18(b) applies to such an action, the state statute eliminating the need for a judgment may have altered the common-law rule that a general contract creditor has no interest in his debtor's property. Because this case does not involve a claim of fraudulent conveyance, we express no opinion on the point."[15]

T argued that Firm's advice, which grossly misinterpreted *Grupo*, was negligent, resulted in a fraudulent transfer of fees paid to Firm, and allowed Firm to be unjustly enriched. D's planning resulted in legal fees paid to Firm totaling $41,000 and accomplishing nothing (and according to T, could have subjected D to civil contempt). T argued that such fees should have been part of the bankruptcy estate. T felt Firm should have known a creditor has remedies that involve reversing transfers pre-judgment and refusal to comply with a court order could result in D being held in civil contempt.

Firm also argued that their inclusion of a "loophole" (commonly referred to as a "Jones Clause") negated liability on his part for alleged negligence in providing advice to create the Trust.[16] It should be noted, however, that the Jones Clause included in the Trust would have required T to file a law suit in a court in the Cook Islands and obtain a determination that T was entitled to a remedy. The Cook Islands does not give full faith and credit to judgments entered by a court in the United States. Thus, any ruling issued by a court in the United States would not be respected under the law of the Cook Islands. As a result, it would seem strained to argue that the Jones Clause in the Trust assuaged a fraudulent transfer concern. To the contrary, it seems clear that it had the effect of hindering or delaying T from collecting on its debt.

T also disagreed with Firm's view on the application the "impossibility defense" if D became subject to a court order involving Firm's planning. T cited Firm's memorandum to file which included the note, "I told her that the law in the US is such that one cannot be incarcerated for failing to do that which is [im]possible to do, even if one has created the impossibility, no matter how reprehensible the conduct…"[17]

Fraudulent Transfer

The court's ruling on the fraudulent transfer issue rendered the negligence argument asserted by T nugatory. As previously mentioned, T argued that the Supreme Court did not intend to eviscerate creditor remedies under the Uniform Fraudulent Transfer Act (UFTA) in its holding in *Grupo Mexicano*. While the authors firmly believe this position is correct, the Eleventh Circuit accepted the Bankruptcy Court's findings that a fraudulent transfer simply *did not* exist in this case. Thus, the issue of whether *Grupo Mexicano* applied to UFTA became immaterial.

T also cited *Martinez v. Hutton (In re Harwell)*,[18] in his Initial Brief for his Eleventh Circuit appeal and asserted a similar course of conduct between Firm and the attorney in *Harwell*.[19] However, in *Harwell*, the issue before the Eleventh Circuit was whether the attorney (who the court determined was an initial transferee) was entitled to use the conduit defense while failing to meet a good faith standard. In *Niroomand*, Firm avoided transferee status due to D's solvency. Furthermore, D did not use the Firm's trust account as a vehicle to orchestrate fraudulent transfers. Instead, D paid Firm for services rendered which would normally constitute "reasonably equivalent value" in a fraudulent transfer analysis. T's argument was essentially that the fees could not be reasonably equivalent value because the advice was negligent. According to T in his pleadings, "It is inconceivable that the Debtor received any value from Appellees when the facts are that Debtor could have been held in contempt for hiding behind the Trust in an attempt to avoid payment of her debts. Obviously, the Debtor realized such and repatriated the balance of the funds, after incurring substantial losses related to the creation and termination of the Trust."[20] As noted, however, the Bankruptcy Court dismissed the fraudulent transfer argument based on D's solvency.

In re Niroomand does represent an important victory for attorneys who assist clients with asset protection planning. It also teaches planners a valuable lesson, attorneys considering helping clients with asset protection planning should engage in an appropriate level of due diligence in relation to clients to ensure that the attorney is advising clients to engage in appropriate planning (see discussion, *infra*).

We believe it would be unwise to view the *In re Niroomand* case (or *Grupo Mexicano* for that matter) as permitting free transferability of assets in disregard of existing or foreseeable claims that have not been reduced to judgment. Such reliance could place an attorney in a difficult position. This case also fires a warning shot at aggressive creditors counsel and bankruptcy trustees to proceed with caution and ensure that they have a strong basis for asserting claims against other professionals.

Good practitioners understand full well that we do not collect due diligence on the theory that it will later be used to impeach a client's credibility. Quite the contrary, due diligence is collected to protect a client's interest

and prove why a structure and sound planning should be respected. What transpired in *Niroomand* regarding the use of the affidavit of solvency to discredit D is no different than a tax lawyer providing a letter that explained the risks of a transaction that is later being questioned by a client. Asset protection planning, when done properly, helps the client *and* the attorney. In this case, it only helped the attorney.

PRE-PLANNING INVOLVING ASSET PROTECTION TRUSTS

From a moral and legal perspective it is acceptable to protect wealth using a properly implemented foreign wealth protection structure, a domestic asset protection trust, a QTIP trust or other similar strategy. When properly structured and implemented under appropriate circumstances, an Offshore Trust is one of the most effective and versatile wealth protection strategies available. In a mobile world where professional and business opportunities require clients to move from one jurisdiction to another, such trusts enable a client to protect wealth without relying on arbitrary local law exemptions that differ from one jurisdiction to the next. Additionally, for the sophisticated investor an Offshore Trust will be far more attractive as a wealth protection vehicle in comparison to most other strategies such as investment in annuities and insurance contracts (investment vehicles that are potentially exempt in one form or another from the claims of creditors under laws of many states). The cost and limitations of using such vehicles will not be palatable to many sophisticated clients.

To avoid assisting clients in making fraudulent transfers in a manner that will subject the attorney to liability for the transfer or ethical issues, it is crucial to have sufficient procedures for due diligence in place. Such procedures should be adhered to so that you can readily identify existing and/or potential claims or sources of liability prior to counseling and assisting clients transfer assets into asset protection structures. The following are best practices for counseling clients on asset protection strategies.

1. First, timing is a critical aspect of effective asset protection planning. If a claim against a grantor exists, the creation and funding of a DAPT, QTIP Trust or Offshore Trust is not appropriate. Clients should plan only at appropriate times and under appropriate circumstances and attorneys should only assist clients under such conditions. Many people seek advice

about wealth protection strategies because they are involved or concerned that they are about to become involved in serious litigation. Once litigation is in process or soon to be is the wrong time to start an asset protection plan. Starting an asset protection plan at the wrong time will result in valuable opportunities being foreclosed and may raise serious fraudulent transfer issues. As a general rule, if assisting a client with a particular strategy raises an issue as to a fraudulent transfer, do not proceed or proceed with a great caution. Bad things can happen to good people if planning is done under inappropriate circumstances. This does not mean that we cannot ethically assist clients who are involved in litigation (or concerned that litigation is imminent). It does however mean that you should exercise discretion.

2. Second, as a result of the jurisdiction where a client resides or may want to reside, the manner in which a client owns certain property interests (for example, homestead or tenancy by the entirety), may result in the ability to achieve significant wealth protection for a client involved in litigation or concerned that litigation is imminent. For example, in *In re Niroomand*,[21] it was only after tens of thousands of dollars were wasted on an offshore trust structure that the defendant eventually followed advice to pay down her mortgage – which ultimately may have been a much safer strategy for the defendant as well as far less expansive.

3. Third, carefully consider the consequences of using a Jones clause in an asset protection trust.[22] If the clause is substantially similar to the one used in *In re Niroomand*, that is, it creates substantial hurdles for a creditor, it probably will not work to protect the client (or the attorney).[23]

4. Fourth, following the creation and funding of an Offshore Trust or any other wealth protection strategy, filing bankruptcy should be viewed as an option of last resort notwithstanding that the planning may have been completed under appropriate circumstances. This is not to say that a properly implemented Offshore Trust structure or other wealth protection strategy cannot survive a challenge in a bankruptcy proceeding; however, it is clear from a few bad fact cases that the present environment in

the Bankruptcy Court system is hostile toward certain wealth protection strategies. Unfortunately, bankruptcy judges typically have the pleasure of reviewing bad fact cases involving Offshore Trusts. Experience demonstrates that judges in bad fact cases usually reach the proper result; however, the legal analysis is faulty. This faulty analysis has significantly damaged public perception regarding legitimate wealth protection planning. It is clear, however, that section 548(e)(1) of the Bankruptcy Code (that is, the ten-year fraudulent transfer rule that applies to self-settled or classic asset protection trusts) mandates that bankruptcy courts respect the validity of such trust structures. Gone are the days when bankruptcy judges could wrongfully dismiss such trust structures as shams. Instead, the court must now engage in an analysis of whether a debtor's transfer of assets to such a trust constituted a fraudulent transfer.[24] The importance of obtaining an affidavit of solvency should not be ignored in this context. If a debtor's financial situation and affidavit is such that a transfer would not render the debtor insolvent, it would seem difficult for a creditor to argue that a debtor possesses the *actual* intent to hinder, delay or defraud such creditor from collecting on its judgment.

5. Fifth, reliance on a line of cases, such as *Grupo Mexicano*,[25] for the proposition that a creditor has no pre-judgment remedies seems misplaced. Clearly, a creditor does have pre-judgment rights and can exercise such rights to a client's detriment. These rights should be disclosed to a client prior to assisting a client with making any transfers. Additionally, the issue of civil contempt should be discussed in these situations emphasizing that a judge may order incarceration in certain circumstances. It is important to advise a client in the context of using an Offshore Trust that it is likely that the client will remain in the United States within the jurisdiction of a court here. It is just as important, however, to recognize that honest people seek legitimate wealth protection by using Offshore Trusts that are created and funded under appropriate circumstances. When properly structured and established under appropriate circumstances, Offshore Trusts are one of the most (if not the most) effective wealth protection strategies available. It is also important to recognize that the law permits individuals,

businesses and other organizations to plan to protect assets and income from the claims *of future unforeseen creditors*. It is equally important to recognize that lawyers have a duty to zealously represent their clients, including lawyers who practice in the estate planning area. Zealous representation mandates that practitioners discuss all available planning wealth protection strategies and convey sufficient accurate information regarding such strategies so clients can make informed decisions. In determining the scope of zealous representation, an attorney should note that in *Ouderkirk*, the court determined that in conjunction with the duty of zealous representation, the attorney has a concurrent duty to avoid inflicting harm on others. Assisting a client knowingly engaging in a fraud would result in unnecessary infliction of harm on another.

6. Finally, collection of due diligence should never be viewed primarily as a method of impeaching a client's testimony as addressed by the court. Properly collecting due diligence to ensure that an attorney is not assisting a client with a fraudulent transfer should not only protect the attorney by proving the planning was done under appropriate circumstances, it should also protect the client by enabling the attorney, as the client's advocate, to prove to the court that such planning should be respected and accepted by the court.

In assisting a client with the implementation of an effective wealth protection plan a firm should have due diligence-client intake procedures (know your client, or "KYC", procedures) in force that are used as a matter of common business practice in all cases.

An individual should be prepared to answer questions candidly and produce any documentation related to a wealth protection plan that may be required in a court proceeding. This does not mean that it is necessary to disclose such information if it is not required in a legal proceeding, however, a quality wealth protection plan will withstand scrutiny and should not require or be based upon any concealment.

Know your client and document the reasons your client is establishing an offshore structure or other wealth protection structure. Reputable banks, trust companies and other financial institutions in quality foreign jurisdictions are required to conduct extensive due diligence

before accepting a new client relationship. This process is generally far more extensive and impressive than the due diligence required by domestic institutions. A client may be required to prove source of wealth and substantiate that funding the structure will not result in a fraudulent transfer issue. Collect extensive financial information on a client who is engaging you to provide wealth protection advice, including a financial statement prepared by a reputable accounting firm that has extensive knowledge of the client's financial condition, individual and entity tax returns for at least the past three tax years and extensive information regarding the source of the client's wealth and employment or business history. Demand reference letters from professionals who have worked with the client such as attorneys, accountants, bankers and financial advisors. Finally, conduct an extensive background check on the client using Lexis-Nexis, WorldCheck, Google and any one or more of the deep web search engines available. Properly using these data bases should enable a planner to uncover civil and criminal cases involving the client as well as any tax liens, administrative proceedings and civil penalties that may have been imposed against the client.

A properly drafted engagement letter is a very important tool for the wealth protection plan. The scope of the engagement should be clearly defined, particularly if the scope is limited. The engagement letter should indicate that the client shall disclose all relevant information to the attorney and that the attorney is entitled to rely on the client's representations. The letter should state that failure on the part of the client to fully and properly disclose is grounds for the attorney to terminate the relationship (or fail to commence if failure to disclose occurs before services commence).

TAX COMPLIANCE FOR DOMESTIC ASSET PROTECTION TRUSTS

Form 709

A settlor must report a transfer to his or her DAPT on a Form 709 United States Gift (and Generation-Skipping Transfer) Tax Return (a "Gift Tax Return").[26] A gift tax return will need to be filed even though the gift is designed as an incomplete gift.[27]

When reporting gifts by a grantor to an incomplete gift trust on Schedule A of a Gift Tax Return, the gifts should be reported at a value of zero and a statement similar to the following should be included on the return:

The donor has retained such dominion and control (within the meaning of Treasury Regulations §25.2511-2) over the assets transferred to this trust as to render the gift incomplete for federal gift tax purposes. The donor has retained an *inter vivos* and a testamentary special power of appointment over the trust assets.

The foregoing statement alerts the Service of the grantor's position that the gift is not a taxable transfer. According to Treasury Regulations section 25.6019-3(a):

> If a donor contends that his retained power over property renders the gift incomplete . . . and hence not subject to tax as of the . . . calendar year of the initial transfer, the transaction should be disclosed in the return for the . . . calendar year of the initial transfer and evidence showing all relevant facts, *including* a copy of the instrument of transfer, shall be submitted with the return. [Emphasis added.]

Although the gift should be reported at a value of zero on the return for purposes of circulating the donor's gift tax liability, the full value of the transfer should be disclosed on an appropriate attachment to the return.

Any transfer to a completed gift DAPT must also be reported on a Form 709. The grantor is the only person who should transfer assets to the DAPT. The Gift Tax Return must be filed in each year following the year in which the grantor makes a gift to the DAPT. The gift must be reported at its fair market value at the time of the gift. In the case of a completed gift, working with a qualified appraiser is essential to ensure that the value of the gift is properly substantiated.

Form 1041

The DAPT should also file its own Form 1041.[28] The trustee of the DAPT is required to file a statement referred to as a grantor trust information letter. This statement must be attached to the Form 1041 to report the income of the trust. The form and attached statement should be filed with the appropriate IRS Service Center by the fifteenth day of the fourth month following the close of the taxable year of the trust. If the trust is a grantor trust, this will correspond to the grantor's taxable year. The person preparing this return for the asset protection trust should check the box in the upper left corner of the return to indicate that the return is for a grantor-type trust or for a complex type trust, as

the case may be. No income should be reported by the DAPT on its Form 1041 if the trust is a wholly owned grantor trust. Instead, the return for the DAPT should include a statement which identifies its grantor as the person to whom the income, deductions, and credits of the trust are taxable.

TAX COMPLIANCE FOR INTER VIVOS QTIP TRUSTS

Form 709

The transfer of any assets to an *inter vivos* QTIP trust (the "QTIP Trust") by the grantor is a completed gift. The grantor is the only person who should transfer assets to the QTIP Trust. Any gift by the grantor should qualify for the unlimited gift tax marital deduction for gift tax purposes, provided a qualified terminable interest property ("QTIP") election is made on a timely filed gift tax return. For purposes of state law and to accomplish the objectives of using this type of trust, it is imperative that an election to qualify the grantor's entire gift to the QTIP Trust for QTIP treatment be made on a timely filed Gift Tax Return. If the grantor does not file a timely Gift Tax Return, he or she will have made a taxable gift, which would cause him or her to use part of his or her gift tax exemption to the extent not previously exhausted, and, if exhausted, cause him or her to incur a gift tax liability. Failure to file could also cause the QTIP Trust to fail to achieve its creditor protection objectives should the grantor survive the spouse-beneficiary and could frustrate the estate and gift tax planning objectives in such a case.

The QTIP Trust should not be considered a "GST Trust" within the meaning of section 2632(c)(3)(B) of the Code. Normally, an "indirect skip" transfer triggers an automatic allocation of GST exemption. However, section 2632(c)(3)(B)(iv) of the Code provides an exception to the automatic allocation of GST exemption for trusts any portion of which would be included in the gross estate of a non-skip person, other than the transferor, if such non-skip person died immediately after the transfer. The grantor is a non-skip persons. If the beneficiary-spouse died immediately after the transfer to the QTIP Trust, the entire corpus of the QTIP Trust should be included in the beneficiary-spouse's gross estate for estate tax purposes, provided a Gift Tax Return electing "QTIP" treatment for the QTIP Trust was timely filed. Thus, the QTIP Trust should fall within the exception to automatic allocation of GST exemption, and should not be considered a "GST trust" within the meaning of section 2632(c)(3)(B) of the Code.

The grantor should not be deemed to automatically allocate any GST exemption upon making a gift to the QTIP Trust. However, it is recommended that the grantor elect out of GST allocation any time he or she makes a gift of property to the QTIP Trust. The grantor should make such an election out on his or her Gift Tax Return. This will avoid any problems related to the inclusion ratio of the QTIP Trusts. To make such an election, a statement similar to the following should be included on the gift tax return:

Pursuant to Internal Revenue Code section 2632(c)(5)(A)(i)(II) and Treasury Regulations section 26.2632-1(b)(2)(iii)(A)(2), the donor elects that the automatic generation-skipping transfer tax exemption allocation rules will not apply to all current-year transfers to this trust.

Form 1041

As previously noted, the trustee of a domestic trust that is a grantor trust for US income tax purposes must file a grantor trust information letter attached to Form 1041 to report the income of the trust. The form and attached letter should be filed with the IRS by the fifteenth day of the fourth month following the close of the trust's taxable year. (In the case of a grantor trust, this will correspond to the grantor's taxable year.)

The person preparing the return for the QTIP Trust should check the box in the upper left corner of the Form 1041 return to indicate that the return is for a grantor type trust. No income should be reported by the QTIP Trust on the 1041. The Form 1041 for the QTIP Trust should include a statement which identifies the grantor as the person to whom the income, deductions, and credits of the QTIP Trust are taxable.

TAX COMPLIANCE FOR OFFSHORE TRUSTS

Under Code section 679 a "United States person" who directly or indirectly contributes property to a foreign trust will be treated as the owner of the portion of the foreign trust attributable to such contribution if there is a United States beneficiary of any portion of the trust. The definition of a foreign trust is set forth in Code sections 7701(a)(30) and (31) and is discussed *infra*. Thus, in addition to the numerous ways a trust can violate the grantor trust rules under Code sections 671-677, almost any foreign trust with a United States beneficiary that is established and funded by a citizen or resident of the United States will violate the grantor trust rules while the grantor is living.

Definition of Foreign Trust

Section 7701(a)(31)(B) of the Code contains the definition of a "foreign trust" stating that it is "any trust other than a trust described in subparagraph (E) of paragraph (30)" of the same section.[29] Section 7701(a)(30) defines the term "United States person" and subsection (E) of such section includes in that definition:

- any trust provided a court within the United States is able to exercise primary supervision over the administration of the trust (the "court test"); *and*

- one or more United States persons possess the authority to control *all substantial decisions* of the trust (the "control test").

Additionally, the term United States person includes a citizen or resident of the United States, a domestic partnership, a domestic corporation and any estate other than a foreign estate, as defined in Code section 7701(a)(31)(A).[30]

A trust must meet both the court test and the control test to constitute a domestic trust.[31] With limited exception a trust will fail the court test if it contains a migration provision.[32] Treasury Regulations section 301.7701-7(d)(ii) provides that "substantial decisions" are those decisions that persons are permitted or mandated to make under a trust instrument and applicable law and that are not ministerial. Ministerial decisions include decisions regarding details related to bookkeeping, collection of rents, the execution of investment decisions and similar decisions.[33]

According to Treasury Regulations section 301.7701-7(d)(ii)(A)-(J), substantial decisions include, however, are not limited to, decisions regarding:

- if and when to distribute income and principal and the amount of any such distribution

- selecting a beneficiary

- allocating receipts to income or principal

- terminating a trust

- compromising, arbitrating or abandoning claims for or against a trust

- suing or defending suits for or against a trust; removing, adding or replacing a trustee

- appointing a successor trustee to succeed a trustee who resigns, dies, or otherwise ceases to act as a trustee even though the authority to make such a decision is not accompanied by an unrestricted power to remove a trustee, unless such authority is restricted so that it cannot be exercised in a way that would alter the residency of the trust from a foreign jurisdiction to a domestic jurisdiction or from a domestic jurisdiction to a foreign jurisdiction; and making investment decisions.

If a United States person retains an investment advisor for a trust, investment decisions made by the advisor will be considered substantial decisions controlled by the United States person if such person can terminate the advisor's authority to make investment decisions at will.

Cessation of Grantor Trust Status of a Foreign Trust

To fully understand the tax consequences of the cessation of grantor trust status for a foreign trust, it is important to have an understanding of some basic tax consequences of non-grantor trusts. The basic principles of non-grantor trust taxation include the following steps:

Step 1: The Trust's Tax Liability

A non-grantor trust's taxable income (before the deduction for distributions to beneficiaries, discussed at Step 3, below) is computed in the same way as the taxable income of an individual, subject to modifications prescribed by section 642 of the Code. The trust's distributable net income (DNI) is computed under section 643 of the Code. The concept of DNI plays a central role in separating distributions of income, which are taxed to beneficiaries and allowed as deductions in determining trust taxable income, from distributions of corpus, which beneficiaries receive tax-free and do not affect the trust's taxable income. The trust's deduction for distributions to beneficiaries is computed under sections 651 or 661 of the Code as the lesser of:

- DNI (adjusted to exclude tax-exempt income and any deductions allocable thereto); or

- the sum of income required to be distributed currently (whether distributed or not) and the trust's other distributions during the taxable year.

Step 2: The Trust's Taxable Income

The trust's taxable income (that is, the amount computed in Step 1 less its deduction for distributions in Step 3) is taxed at the rates prescribed by section 1(e) of the Code. The tax rates under 1(e) are highly compressed, and the highest marginal rate of 39.6 percent is reached at just $7,500 of income, adjusted for inflation. For the year 2016, a trust's taxable income in excess of $12,400 will be taxed at the maximum 39.6 percent tax rate.[34] Additionally, the Net Investment Income Tax (NIIT) is imposed by section 1411 of the Code. The NIIT applies at a rate of 3.8 percent to non-grantor trusts if they have undistributed "net investment income" and also have adjusted gross income over the dollar amount at which the highest tax bracket for a trust begins for such taxable year under section 1(e) of the Code.

Step 3: The Beneficiaries' Tax Liabilities

If trust distributions made during the taxable year do not exceed DNI for the year (discussed at Step 2, above), beneficiaries must include all distributions in gross income, except for any portion attributable to tax-exempt items.[35]

If distributions exceed DNI, DNI is first distributed to first-tier beneficiaries (recipients of mandatory distributions of current trust income), and if any DNI is left over, to other beneficiaries (second-tier beneficiaries).[36] Beneficiaries' gross incomes include their allocable shares of current DNI (Step 5 or 6, as the case may be), except for any portion consisting of tax-exempt items.[37]

If a foreign trust makes a distribution exceeding DNI:

a. section 666 of the Code allocates any DNI left over from past years to the recipient;

b. the recipient is taxed on such an "accumulation distribution" under the "throwback rules" at section 667 of the Code; and

c. an interest charge is added under section 668 of the Code. These rules are discussed in further detail below.

Distributions not taxed to beneficiaries under the foregoing rules are tax-free receipts of trust corpus. Subchapter J of the Internal Revenue Code distinguishes between two types of trusts:

- those that are required to distribute all income currently, do not provide for charitable contributions, and distribute nothing except fiduciary accounting income in the current year ("simple trusts"); and

- trusts not satisfying these conditions ("complex trusts").

The income taxation of simple trusts is governed under sections 651 and 652 of the Code, while complex trusts are governed by the provisions of sections 661 and 662.

Step 4: Compliance Related to Foreign Trust

Under section 6048 of the Code, a donor-settlor of (or other transferor to) a foreign trust must report a "reportable event"[38] and information required to be reported under section 6048(a) of the Code.[39]

Under section 6048 of the Code, a reportable event is: the establishment of any foreign trust by a United States person; the transfer of any funds or property to a foreign trust by a United States person; the death of a United States person who was treated as the owner of the foreign trust under the grantor trust rules (sections 671-679 of the Code) or if any portion of the foreign trust is included in the estate of the United States person.

Exceptions to reporting requirements include: transfers for fair market value and transfers to deferred compensation arrangements under sections 402(b), 404(a)(4) or 404A of the Code or transfers to charitable trusts described in section 501(c)(3) of the Code.

The "responsible party" must report the information required to be reported by section 6048 of the Code. Under section 6048(a)(4) of the Code the responsible party is the settlor who established an *inter vivos* foreign trust. In the case of a reportable event the responsible party is the transferor, except in the case of a transfer at death, in which case the personal representative of the transferor's estate is the responsible party.

Annual reporting by the trustee of a foreign trust is also required when any United States person is treated as the owner of any portion of a foreign trust under the grantor trust rules (sections 671-679 of the Code).[40] The return must be filed by the trustee of the foreign trust, however, the requirement to ensure the return is filed is imposed on the settlor (or the person treated as the owner of any portion of the trust under the grantor trust rules).[41]

There is a requirement that a foreign trust appoint a United States Agent.[42] If the trust does not appoint a United States Agent, the Service may compute the tax liability of the owner of the trust under the grantor trust rules.[43] Additionally, the supplementary documentation which must accompany annual reporting for a foreign trust becomes more cumbersome if a United States Agent is not appointed. The United States Agent is appointed solely for the limited purpose of complying with any requests by the IRS to examine trust records, produce testimony related to the trust, or to respond to any summons by the IRS for such records or testimony.

Step 5: Reporting Requirements of the Settlor and Beneficiaries of a Foreign Trust[44]

A number of returns may be required to be filed by the settlor and the trustee to report transfers to a foreign trust, assets held by such a trust, distributions and/or transactions between the trust and the settlor or another beneficiary.

a. **Form 709.** A settlor must report a transfer to his or her Offshore Trust on a Form 709 United States Gift (and Generation-Skipping Transfer) Tax Return (a "Gift Tax Return").[45] Like a DAPT, a gift tax return will need to be filed for a transfer to an Offshore Trust even though the gift is designed as an incomplete gift.[46] When reporting gifts by a grantor to an incomplete gift Offshore Trust on Schedule A of a Gift Tax Return, the gifts should be reported at a value of zero and a statement similar to the following should be included on the return:

> The donor has retained such dominion and control (within the meaning of Treasury Regulations §25.2511-2) over the assets transferred to this trust as to render the gift incomplete for federal gift tax purposes. The donor has retained an *inter vivos* and a

testamentary special power of appointment over the trust assets.

The foregoing statement alerts the Service of the grantor's position that the gift is not a taxable transfer. According to Treasury Regulations section 25.6019-3(a):

> If a donor contends that his retained power over property renders the gift incomplete . . . and hence not subject to tax as of the . . . calendar year of the initial transfer, the transaction should be disclosed in the return for the . . . calendar year of the initial transfer and evidence showing all relevant facts, including a copy of the instrument of transfer, shall be submitted with the return.

> Although the gift should be reported at a value of zero (0) on the return for purposes of calculating the donor's gift tax liability, the full value of the transfer should be disclosed on an appropriate attachment to the return.

b. **Form 3520.**[47] Form 3520, "Annual Return to Report Transactions with Foreign Trusts and Receipt of Certain Foreign Gifts" is used to report the information required by section 6048 of the Code. A United States person who establishes an Offshore Trust or transfers assets to an Offshore Trust must report the establishment of the trust or the transfer of assets to such trust on a Form 3520. The Form 3520 is also required to be filed on an annual basis by the grantor of an Offshore Trust. The return is required to be filed even if the grantor did not make any transfers to the trust during the applicable period. The return must be filed annually with the IRS Service Center located in Ogden, Utah. The minimum penalty for failure to file Form 3520 is the greater of ten thousand dollars ($10,000) or the following (as applicable): (i) 35 percent of the gross value of any property transferred to the foreign trust; (ii) 35 percent of the gross value of the distributions received from the foreign trust; or (iii) 5 percent of the gross value of the portion of the foreign trust's assets treated as owned by a US person under the grantor trust rules.[48] Furthermore, additional $10,000 penalties will be imposed each thirty-day period (or

fraction thereof) for continued failure to file such a return after notice is received from the Service.[49] The Form 3520 is due to be filed on the date that the personal income tax return is due for the grantor.

c. **Form 3520A.**[50] A Form 3520-A is used to report the information required by section §6048(b) of the Code. A United States person who is treated as the owner of an Offshore Trust under the grantor trust rules is responsible for ensuring that the trustee of an Offshore Trust files a Form 3520-A annually. The trustee of the Offshore Trust is responsible for filing this return, however, the penalty for failing to file this return is enforced against the grantor of the trust.[51] The US owner is subject to an initial penalty equal to the greater of $10,000 or 5 percent of the gross value of the portion of the trust's assets treated as owned by the US person at the close of that tax year, if the foreign trust (i) fails to file a timely Form 3520-A, or (ii) does not furnish all of the required information or includes incorrect information.[52] Furthermore, additional $10,000 penalties will be imposed each thirty-day period (or fraction thereof) for persisting in failing to file after receipt of notice from the IRS.[53] Form 3520-A must be filed annually by the trustee with the IRS Service Center in Ogden, Utah. It is important to note that this return is due by the fifteenth day of the third month following the close of the grantor's tax year (unless the return is extended pursuant to Form 7004). In practice, many return preparers fail to recognize that the due date for this return is one month before the due date of the grantor's personal income tax return. The trustee of an Offshore Trust that is a grantor trust is required to provide a Foreign Grantor Trust Owner Statement to the United States grantor when the trustee files Form 3520-A. (This form is included on page 3 of Form 3520-A.) No noncompliance penalty is applicable for failure to comply with this rule. It is important to note that a taxpayer should notify the IRS of any inconsistency between the taxpayer's income tax return and the information contained in the Foreign Grantor Trust Owner Statement.[54]

d. **Form 1041.** The trust should also file its own Form 1041.[55] The trustee of the Offshore Trust is required to file a statement referred to as a grantor trust information letter. This statement must be attached to the Form 1041 to report the income of the trust. The form and attached statement should be filed with the IRS Service Center in Ogden, Utah, by the fifteenth day of the fourth month following the close of the taxable year of the trust. If the trust is a grantor trust, this will correspond to the grantor's taxable year. The person preparing this return for the Offshore Trust should check the box in the upper left corner of the return to indicate that the return is for a grantor-type trust. No income should be reported by the Offshore Trust on its Form 1041. Instead, the return for the Offshore Trust should include a statement which identifies its grantor as the person to whom the income, deductions, and credits of the trust are taxable.

e. **Form 1040NR.** The Service has intimated that it will issue a Form 1041NR for use by foreign trusts filing United States tax returns. As of the date of the last revision to this chapter, the Service has not yet published this form. When this form is published by the Service it will probably be the most appropriate form for an Offshore Trust to file annually. As of the date of this chapter, a joint project between the Service and the AICPA Foreign Trust Task Force is currently underway to develop a Form 1041NR.[56] It should also be noted that the instructions to Form 1040NR currently provide that it should be used to report the income of a foreign trust. The first page of Form 1040NR also provides a box for the taxpayer to check indicating whether the taxpayer is an individual or an estate *or trust*. Until Form 1041NR is issued, it is appropriate to file Form 1040NR *in addition* to Form 1041.

f. **Authorization of Agent Agreement.** An Authorization of Agent Agreement should be filed to notify the Service regarding the identity of the United States agent appointed for the trust. The agent is appointed pursuant to this agreement, and the agreement should be filed with the IRS Service Center in Ogden, Utah, when the initial Form 3520 is due to be filed. The name, address, and taxpayer identification number of the United States agent must be included on Forms 3520 and 3520-A.

g. **FinCEN Form 114.** FinCEN Form 114, Report of Foreign Bank and Financial Accounts (FBAR) is used to report a financial interest in or signature authority over a foreign financial account. A US person that has a financial interest in or signature authority over foreign financial accounts must file an FBAR if the aggregate value of the foreign financial accounts exceeds $10,000 at any time during the calendar year. With regard to trusts, a grantor has a financial interest in a foreign financial account for which the owner of record or holder of legal title is: (i) a trust of which the US person is the trust grantor and has an ownership interest in the trust for US federal tax purposes (*i.e.*, under Code sections 671-679); or (ii) a trust in which the US person has a greater than 50 percent present beneficial interest in the assets or income of the trust for the calendar year. Special rules apply in the case of joint accounts.

Any other foreign financial accounts in which a grantor of a foreign trust has a financial interest or signature authority must be aggregated for purposes of applying the $10,000 threshold and must be reported accordingly. The FBAR is an annual report and must be filed on or before April 15th of the year following the calendar year being reported. An automatic sixth month extension to October 15th is granted to filers without a requirement for a separate extension request. The FBAR must be filed electronically through FinCEN's Bank Secrecy Act E-Filing System. For FBAR reporting purposes, a financial account includes, however, is not limited to, a securities, brokerage, savings, demand, checking, or other account maintained with a financial institution, and a foreign financial account is a financial account located outside of the US. Failure to file an FBAR may give rise to a civil penalty of up to $10,000, and for willful failures, the penalty is increased to the greater of $100,000 or 50 percent of the account balance at the time of the violation. Willful failures may also involve criminal penalties.

h. **Form 8938, Statement of Specified Foreign Financial Assets.** A "specified individual" that has an interest in "specified foreign financial assets" must file Form 8938 if the value of those assets is more than the applicable reporting threshold. A "specified individual" includes a US citizen and a US resident. A "specified foreign financial asset" includes, among other types of assets, financial accounts with foreign financial institutions. A specified person that is treated as the owner of a trust or any portion of a trust under Code §§671 through 679 is generally treated as having an interest in any specified foreign financial assets held by the trust or the portion of the trust. US beneficiaries of a foreign grantor trust may have to file Form 8938 as well.[57] Special valuation rules apply in valuing beneficial interests in foreign trusts.

In the case of a specified individual living in the US, Form 8938 reporting is generally triggered if such person's interest in one or more specified foreign financial assets during the relevant year exceeds, in the aggregate, $50,000 on the last day of the taxable year or $75,000 at any time during the taxable year. Married taxpayers filing joint returns are obligated to file Form 8938 if the total value of specified foreign financial assets is greater than $100,000 on the last day of the taxable year or more than $150,000 at any time during the taxable year. The foregoing threshold amounts are increased in certain cases for certain specified individuals who live outside of the US. Form 8938 must be attached to the specified individual's US income tax return and is due by the due date for the income tax return (including extensions).

Duplicative reporting rules exist for certain assets. In particular, a specified individual that is treated as an owner of a foreign trust or any portion of a foreign trust under Code sections 671 through 679 is not required to report any specified foreign financial assets held by the foreign trust on Form 8938, provided the following conditions are satisfied:

1. the specified individual reports the trust on a timely filed Form 3520 for the taxable year;

2. the trust timely files Form 3520-A for the taxable year; and

3. the Form 8938 filed by the specified individual for the taxable year reports the filing of the Form 3520 and Form 3520-A (see Part IV of Form 8938).[58]

Additionally, a specified individual is not required to report ownership of an interest in a foreign corporation on Form 8938, provided the following conditions are satisfied: (i) the specified individual reports the interest in the foreign corporation on a timely filed Form 5471; and (ii) the Form 8938 filed by the specified individual for the taxable year reports the filing of the Form 5471 (see Part IV of Form 8938).[59]

Specified individuals who fail to file a complete and timely file Form 8938 for the taxable year may be subject to a penalty of $10,000. Additional penalties may apply for continued noncompliance.

i. **Interests in Foreign Companies.** Various information reporting requirements also apply to US persons who own interests in foreign companies. These reporting requirements may include, however, are not limited to, Form 5471, *Information Return of US Persons With Respect To Certain Foreign Corporations*, Form 8621, *Information Return by a Shareholder of a Passive Foreign Investment Company or Qualified Electing Fund*, and Form 8858, *Information Return of US Persons With Respect to Foreign Disregarded Entities*. If a grantor establishes a foreign trust which owns interests in any other foreign companies, it will be necessary to determine the reporting specific requirements that will apply to the grantor with respect to such ownership interests.

Step 6: Foreign Bank Account Reporting

If a US person has a financial interest in or signature authority over a foreign financial account, including a bank account, brokerage account, mutual fund, trust, or other type of foreign financial account, exceeding certain thresholds (discussed below), that person may be required to file an FBAR. For this purpose a financial account includes any bank, securities, derivatives, or other financial instruments account. Prior to this e-filing mandate, US persons could file an FBAR by mailing in the paper form to the Department of the Treasury in Detroit, Michigan.[60] Section 7701(a)(30) of the Internal Revenue Code provides a general overview of what constitutes a US person. Nevertheless, the Treasury Regulations and the instructions to the FBAR provide great detail with respect to specific situations. In accordance with section 7701(a)(30) of the Internal Revenue Code a US person is: a citizen or resident of the United States, a domestic partnership, a domestic corporation, any estate (other than a foreign estate (the term "foreign estate" is defined in paragraph (31) of Code section 7701(a)), and a trust if a court within the United States can exercise primary supervision over the administration of the trust (referred to as the "court test.")[61]

US persons are required to file an FBAR if:

a. the U.S. person had a financial interest in or signature authority over at least one financial account located outside of the United States; and

b. the aggregate value of all foreign financial accounts exceeded $10,000 at *any time* during the calendar year to be reported.[62]

Filing exceptions exist for certain foreign financial accounts jointly owned by spouses, U.S. persons included in a consolidated FBAR, correspondent/*nostro* accounts (*i.e.*, an account at a foreign bank in which a domestic bank keeps a reserve of foreign currency), foreign financial accounts owned by a governmental entity, foreign financial accounts owned by an international financial institution, Individual Retirement Account owners and beneficiaries, participants in and beneficiaries of tax-qualified retirement plans, certain individuals with signature authority over, however, no financial interest in a foreign financial account, trust beneficiaries (however only if a US person reports the account on an FBAR filed on behalf of the trust), and foreign financial accounts maintained on a US military banking facility.[63] Failure to properly file a complete and correct FBAR may subject you to a civil penalty of up to $10,000 per violation for violations that are not due to reasonable cause.[64] (One has to wonder how many wealthy individuals who are valued taxpayers will choose to expatriate rather than become subject to such intrusive rules.)[65]

The grantor of an Offshore Trust must file an FBAR annually to report any foreign financial accounts held in the trust.[66] Furthermore, a US beneficiary of an Offshore Trust who has a beneficial interest in more than 50 percent of the assets or income of a trust that owns foreign financial accounts must file an annual FBAR.[67] A US beneficiary of a foreign grantor trust is not required to file an FBAR if the trust, trustee of the trust, or agent of the trust is a US person that files an FBAR.[68]

Failure to properly file a complete and correct FBAR may subject a taxpayer to a civil penalty of up to $10,000 per violation for violations that are not due to reasonable cause.[69] Where a person willfully violates or willfully causes any violation of 31 USC section 5314, the maximum penalty is increased to the greater of $100,000

or 50 percent of the amount determined under 31 USC section 5314(D).[70] A person who willfully violates the FBAR reporting requirements may also be prosecuted criminally and upon conviction, fined up to $250,000, imprisoned for not more than five years, or both.[71] "A civil [monetary] penalty may be imposed . . . notwithstanding the fact that a criminal penalty is imposed [for] the same [FBAR reporting] violation."[72]

Step 7: Foreign Account Tax Compliance Act

Enacted in 2010 as part of the HIRE Act,[73] the Foreign Account Tax Compliance Act (FATCA)[74] seeks to prevent US taxpayers from evading tax by hiding wealth in foreign financial accounts. FATCA requires foreign financial institutions (FFIs) to report to the Service certain information about financial accounts owned by US taxpayers or by foreign entities in which US taxpayers have substantial ownership interests.[75] Foreign entities that are not financial institutions are non-financial foreign entities (NFFEs) and must identify United States persons' substantial ownership interests, if any, to avoid FATCA withholding.[76]

If an FFI fails to comply with the requirements imposed by FATCA, a 30 percent withholding tax is applied on any "withholdable payment" made to the FFI unless the United States withholding agent can reasonably rely on documentation that the payment is exempt from withholding.[77] A withholdable payment means a payment of US source fixed or determinable annual or periodical income and gross proceeds from sale of property which can produce US source interest or dividends.[78] FATCA withholding applies regardless of whether the FFI receives a withholdable payment as a qualified intermediary or beneficial owner.[79]

A foreign entity will be an FFI if it comes within one or more of the categories of FFI contained in the Regulations under FATCA.[80] In the case of an entity that is resident in a jurisdiction that has in effect a Model 1 or Model 2 Intergovernmental Agreement (IGA) with the US that entity is treated as an FFI according to the Model 1 or Model 2 IGA and has reporting alternatives and modified withholding obligations.[81]

In the context of an Offshore Trust, an FFI includes an investment entity that:

- "primarily conducts as a business" specified activities "for or on behalf of a customer"[82];

- whose gross income is "primarily attributable" to specified investment activities and that is "managed by" an FFI[83]; and

- a collective investment vehicle or one of several different types of funds.[84]

Specified activities that can trigger FFI status include financial trading and portfolio management activities, and "otherwise investing, administering, or managing funds, money, or financial assets on behalf of other persons."[85]

Most corporate trustees will be classified as investment entity FFIs because trustees manage and administer the funds or money, or financial assets of a trust according to the mandates in such trusts.[86] The Final Treasury Regulations provide examples that demonstrate the Service considers a trust with primarily investment income that is professionally managed by a corporate trustee to be an investment entity.[87] A trust primarily has investment income if its gross income attributable to investing, reinvesting, or trading in financial assets equals or exceeds 50 percent of its gross income during the stated period.[88] The definition of an investment entity in the Model IGA does not require the entity to primarily have investment income.[89]

A trust is "professionally managed" if the managing entity performs, directly or through a third party, any financial trading, portfolio management, or "otherwise investing, administering, or managing funds, money, or financial assets on the trust's behalf."[90] This "professionally managed" test can be satisfied for either the trust itself or the trust's assets.[91] Trusts with individual trustees and individual asset managers are not FFIs.[92] Under an IGA, however, not under the Regulations, the "professionally managed" test can be satisfied although the trust's assets are managed by a US investment management firm because the managing entity need not be a non-US financial institution.[93]

If an entity is classified as an FFI, it must meet the reporting requirements under FATCA to avoid withholding.[94] An FFI can meet the reporting requirements by entering into an agreement with the Service to become a participating FFI and provide the required information.[95] Generally, a participating FFI must: identify US accounts it maintains in accordance with certain verification and due diligence procedures; report certain information to the Service regarding the US accounts and accounts held by a US person who is unwilling to provide the required information (recalcitrant account holder); and deduct a withholding tax on any payment

of US source income by the FFI to a recalcitrant account holder or nonparticipating FFI.[96]

Additionally, an FFI can avoid withholding if it is treated as a deemed-compliant FFI.[97] A trust can become a registered deemed-compliant FFI if the trustee, which is also an FFI, agrees to sponsor the trust.[98] As the trust's sponsoring FFI, the trustee handles the reporting obligations for the trust.[99] A trust that is not resident in a FATCA partner jurisdiction can also avoid withholding by becoming a certified deemed-compliant FFI.[100] For example, an owner-documented trust must identify both US and non-US beneficiaries to the "designated withholding agent" that in turn reports the information about the US beneficiaries to the Service.[101] To certify its status to the withholding agent, the trust can either provide an owner's report or obtain an auditor's letter from an auditor or US licensed attorney certifying the trust qualifies as an owner-documented FFI.[102]

Trusts resident in a jurisdiction that has in effect a Model 1 or Model 2 IGA with the US are treated as FFIs pursuant to the Model IGAs. Under a Model 1 IGA FFIs are treated as registered deemed compliant FFIs and report to the tax authorities in the partner jurisdiction instead of the Service.[103] A Model 1 IGA also alters the reporting requirements and eliminates the withholding responsibilities of financial institutions resident in that jurisdiction.[104] Financial institutions resident in a Model 2 IGA jurisdiction must enter agreements with the Service to become participating FFIs as described above.

If the non-US trust does not fall within the definition of an FFI, it will be an NFFE.[105] If an NFFE is the beneficial owner of a withholdable payment, it must report certain information to the withholding agent.[106] An NFFE meets this reporting requirement if the NFFE provides identifying information for each of its substantial US owners or certifies that it has no such owners. A substantial US owner is in the case of a trust, a US person treated as an owner of any portion of the trust under the grantor trust rules[107] and any US person holding more than 10 percent of the beneficial interests.[108]

If the NFFE fails to meet the reporting requirement, the withholding agent must deduct and withhold 30 percent from the withholdable payment.[109] However, a withholding agent is not required to withhold on a payment treated as beneficially owned by an excepted NFFE.[110] An excepted NFFE includes an Active NFFE, meaning any NFFE if less than 50 percent of its gross income for the preceding tax year is passive income, and less than 50 percent of its assets produce or are held for the production of interest, dividends, rents or royalties (other than those derived in the active conduct of a trade or business), annuities, or other passive income.[111]

TAX REIMBURSEMENT PROVISIONS

Drafting irrevocable trusts as "wholly-owned grantor trusts" for federal income tax purposes is a common technique used by estate planners to enhance the benefits of such trusts by effectively permitting tax-free gifts when the grantor pays income taxes attributable to trust assets. Still, it may be desirable to grant the trustee a discretionary power to pay such taxes or reimburse the settlor. Although not found in the UTC, the FTC ensures that such discretionary power will not subject an irrevocable trust to the claims of creditors under the general rule established in section 736.0505(1)(b) of the Florida Statutes.[112] This provision provides in relevant part:

> "the assets of an *irrevocable* trust may not be subject to the claims of an existing or subsequent creditor or assignee of the settlor, in whole or in part, solely because of the existence of a discretionary power granted to the trustee by the terms of the trust, or any other provision of law, to pay directly to the taxing authorities or to reimburse the settlor for any tax on trust income or principal which is payable by the settlor under the law imposing such tax."

As a result of this provision, the state legislature may have unwittingly added Florida to the list of asset protection states. Normally such a decision is made with substantially more consideration. Issues related to this provision include:

There is no time limit on reimbursement. Thus, in theory a trustee can accrue a reimbursement account for several decades and reimburse the settlor for a tax liability incurred many years in the past. While policy arguments can be made to permit reimbursement for a tax liability incurred within the statute of limitations for a tax return, permitting reimbursement for tax liability incurred beyond that point is ridiculous unless the state has made a conscientious decision to become an asset protection trust jurisdiction. This certainly has not occurred in this instance.

As a result of the issue identified above, Florida has unwittingly added a new exemption to its laws. Practitioners are certainly obligated to discuss the use of this potentially substantial exemption with their clients.

The provision could have been drafted to prevent abuse by mandating the formula for determining the maximum amount that the trustee could distribute to the settlor. Some methods of constructing such a formula might have been to mandate that the trustee can pay up to:

- the highest marginal rate of tax. Thus, the income generated by the assets in the trust is assumed to be taxed at the highest rate applicable to the settlor.

- its proportional share of the tax liability. Thus, all income generated by the assets in the trust is assumed to be taxed at the settlor's average tax rate.

- the lowest possible tax rate applicable. Thus, the settlor's remaining income from sources other than the assets in the trust is assumed to be taxed at the higher rates applicable to the settlor.

Although potentially difficult under certain circumstances, the provision could have prevented abuse by directing that any tax payments be made directly to the appropriate taxing authority rather than reimbursing the settlor for such amounts. Of course, one could argue that such a provision would be too restrictive.

Is the payment by the settlor of the settlor's tax liability subject to the fraudulent transfer statute? The funds could one day be returned to the settlor pursuant to a discretionary distribution. At first blush it would seem that such payment should not be a fraudulent transfer, however, inequitable results will be caused to a creditor because of this provision if the fraudulent transfer statute is not applicable. How will the bankruptcy law (discussed *infra*) treat this provision?

Can distributions be made from the reimbursement account *for the benefit of* the grantor rather than having to be distributed directly to him. The statute provides no guidance in this respect.

Is the trustee permitted to offset the tax benefits that accrue to the settlor as a result of grantor trust status, such as deductions and tax credits, against the reimbursement account?

Example. Trust ("T") contains a discretionary tax reimbursement provision. T holds interests in limited liability companies that own substantial real estate investments. T was established and funded by A and T is a wholly owned grantor trust as to A. In calendar year x T's real estate generates $2,000,000 of taxable income and it also generates $1,000,000 of depreciation. In the same year A has $2,000,000 of taxable income. Assume a 35 percent income tax rate applies. A includes the $2,000,000 of taxable income from T on his personal income tax return with his $2,000,000 of personal taxable income. He also includes the $1,000,000 of deduction provided by the depreciation on the assets held in T. Assume the trustee does not reimburse T for any income tax liability in year x. How much should be allocated to the reimbursement account? The answer is unknown. The statute does not appear to mandate the $1,000,000 of depreciation be used to offset the trust income specifically. It would seem logical to assume that it should, however, the answer remains unclear. The provision applies even though the grantor trust may be designed to receive gifts that are incomplete for federal gift tax purposes. This can lead to serious abuse of the statute.

Caution: A tax reimbursement provision is not appropriate for use in every type of grantor trust. For instance, such a provision should never be used in a general power of appointment marital trust,[113] a QTIP trust,[114] a section 2642(c) trust or a section 2503(c) trust. Additionally, if it is necessary for a trust to qualify as a skip person for GST tax purposes, a tax reimbursement provision should not be included in the trust agreement.[115]

CHAPTER ENDNOTES

1. *Iowa Supreme Court Attorney Disciplinary Board v Ouderkirk*, 845 N.W. 2d 321 (Supreme Court of Iowa Mar. 28, 2014).

2. For example, Alaska and Delaware specifically negate the potential for attorney liability to a client's creditors in certain instances, see, e.g., Alaska Stat. §34.40.110(f); Del. Code tit. 12 §3572(e), which do not permit a creditor or any other person from asserting a cause of action for conspiracy to commit a fraudulent conveyance or aiding and abetting a fraudulent conveyance against a person involved in the preparation or funding of an "asset protection" trust.

3. *See Freeman v. First Union National Bank*, 865 So.2d 1272 (Fla. 2004); *Danzas Taiwan, Ltd. v. Freeman*, 28 Fla. L. Weekly D 1163 (3d DCA 2003); *BankFirst v. UBS Paine Webber*, 842 So 2d 155 (5th DCA 2003); *Yusem v. South Florida Water Management District*, 770 So. 2d 746 (4th DCA 2000).

4. 770 So. 2d 746 (4th DCA 2000).

5. 865 So.2d 1272 (Fla. 2004).

6. 527 U.S. 308 (1999).

7. 331 F.3d 406 (3rd Cir. 2003).

8. For examples of other potential liability, see e.g., *Elie v. Smith*, 2011 WL 9349985 (Cal. Super. Napa, Oct. 13, 2011); *In re Cutuli*, 2013 WL 5236711 (S.D. Fla., Sept. 16, 2013); *Cevdet Aksut v. Cavusoglu*, 2015 WL 4318131 (D.N.J., Unpublished, July 14, 2015), *Trustee v. Rupprecht, Trustee's Second Amended Complaint* (Cal.Super. Napa., Feb. 6, 2013). For a discussion of this group of cases see *Adkisson & Slenn*, "*In re Cutuli*: $10 Million in Punitive Damages Result After Financially-Distressed Clients Seek Asset Protection Advice," LISI Asset Protection Planning Newsletter #229 (Oct. 10, 2013); & Gassman & Lawrence, "Imposing Punitive Damages on Fraudulent Transfer," LISI Asset Protection Planning Newsletter #235 (Jan. 15, 2014).

9. 11th Cir. No. 12-11231 (Oct. 17, 2012).

10. Under section 4 of Article X of the Florida Constitution a debtor can shelter such wealth even though such act represents a fraudulent conversion or transfer as to an existing creditor. See e.g., *Havoco of America, Ltd. v. Hill*, 790 So.2d 1018 (Fla. 2001), *Republic Credit Corporation, Inc. v. Upshaw*, 4th Dist. Case No. 4D08-1591 (March 25, 2009); *Palm Beach Savings & Loan Ass'n. v. Fishbein*, 619 So.2d 267 (Fla. 1993); *Jones v. Carpenter*, 106 So. 127 (Fla. 1925); *Craven v. Hartley*, 135 So. 899 (Fla. 1931); *LeMar v. Lechlider*, 185 So. 833 (Fla. 1939); *Sonneman v. Tuszynski*, 191 So. 18 (Fla. 1939); *In re: Gosman*, 382 B.R. 826 (S.D.Fla. 2007). Of course, following the enactment of the Bankruptcy Reform Act of 2005 the ability to shelter such wealth using this strategy was greatly reduced by the addition of several new statutes specifically designed to prevent the use of an unlimited homestead exemption to shelter such wealth immediately prior to filing for bankruptcy. See §522(b)(3)(A) (730 day residency rule), §522(p) (the value of the homestead of a debtor (other than farmers) in excess of $146,450 (as adjusted for inflation pursuant to §104(b)(1) and (2) of the Bankruptcy Code) is no longer exempt until 1,215 days (that is, three (3) years and four (4) months) after the debtor *acquired an interest* in the home) and §522(o) (if within the ten (10) years prior to filing a petition a debtor converts non-exempt property to homestead with the actual intent to hinder, delay, or defraud a creditor, the value of the homestead is reduced by the value of such converted property).

11. In some cases involving egregious fact patterns where such orders have been issued to debtors courts have order such debtors incarcerated for failing to comply with such orders. See *e.g.*, *In re Lawrence*, 279 F.3d 1294 (11th Cir. 2002) and *Federal Trade Commission v. Affordable Media*, 179 F. 2nd 1228 (9th Cir. 1999). The authors strongly urge readers to review such cases carefully to understand the reasons such debtors were incarcerated. In each such case no debtor *was ever* incarcerated for creating and funding such a trust. Incarceration was ordered to remedy what the court deemed to be serious problems in the design or timing of the funding of such trusts.

12. Interestingly, T was also the bankruptcy trustee in *In re Lawrence*, 279 F.3d 1294 (11th Cir. 2002), another famous "bad" fact case involving an Offshore Trust.

13. 527 U.S. 308 (1999).

14. *See* generally P. Alces, Law of Fraudulent Transactions & ¶ 5.04[3], p. 5–116 (1989).

15. *See* also, *American Surety Co. v. Conner*, 251 N.Y. 1, 166 N.E. 783, 65 A.L.R. 244 (1929), "We think the effect of these provisions is

to abrogate the ancient rule whereby a judgment and a lien were essential preliminaries to equitable relief against a fraudulent conveyance. The Uniform Act has been so read in other states."

16. For a discussion of Jones Clauses see LISI Asset Protection Planning Newsletter #212 (Oct. 30, 2012).

17. *See* page 27 of T's Notice of Appeal to the United States Court of Appeals for the Eleventh CI.R.Cuit, citing Defendants' Exhibit Register, Bankruptcy Court, ECF 99, Exhibit "L."

18. 628 F.3d 1312, (11th Cir. 2010).

19. For a discussion of *Harwell*, see LISI Asset Protection Planning Newsletter #168 (Jan. 13, 2011). See also, Gassman, "In re Harwell: Years of Bankruptcy Court Litigation End Badly for Lawyer Who Allowed His Trust Account to be Used for Transfers to Avoid Creditors," LISI Asset Protection Planning Newsletter #243 (Apr. 24, 2014).

20. *See* page 22 of T's Notice of Appeal to the United States Court of Appeals for the Eleventh CI.R.Cuit, filed March 7, 2012.

21. *Id.*

22. *See* Bove & Langa, "Special Drafting Considerations for Asset Protection Trusts – The Offspring of Offshore Trusts," Mass. Law. Wkly. (Sept. 6, 2004)

   To give the client and the lawyer, and often the trustee, peace of mind, a 'contingent payment clause' – sometimes cryptically referred to within the asset protection bar as a 'Jones clause' – should be included within the FAPT. Simply stated, the clause tells the trustee 'If this creditor obtains a judgment and comes knocking, pay him.

23. *Id.*

24. *See* e.g., *Battley v. Mortensen, et al.*, (*In re Mortensen*), 2011 WL 5025249 (Bankr. D. Alaska). For an excellent discussion of Mortensen see Shaffel, "Court Finds Fraudulent Transfer to Alaska Asset Protection Trust," 39 EP 15 (April 2012); Sulivan, Merric, Gillen, Bove & Nenno, "Fraudulent Transfer Claims," 150 Trusts & Estates 43 (Dec. 2011); and "Gopman & Rubin: Further Analysis on *In re Mortensen*," LISI Asset Protection Planning Newsletter #187 (Nov. 7, 2011). See also, "Oshins & Keebler on Mortensen: No, the Sky Isn't Falling for DAPTs!," LISI Asset Protection Planning Newsletter #186 (Oct. 31, 2011); "Adkisson & Riser on Mortensen: Alaska Asset Protection Trust Fails To Protect Future Assets in Bankruptcy under New Section 548(e) Against Future Creditors," LISI Asset Protection Planning Newsletter #185 (Oct. 20, 2011).

25. *Grupo Mexicano de Desarrollo, S.A. de C.V. v Alliance Bond*, 527 U.S. 308 (1999).

26. *See* I.R.C §6019.

27. *See* Treas. Regs. §§25.2511-2(j) and 25.6019-3.

28. Treas. Regs. §1.671-4.

29. *See* also, CCA 201509035.

30. *See* I.R.C §7701(a)(30).

31. Treas. Regs. §301.7701-7(a)(2). See also, CCA 201509035.

32. *See* Treas. Reg. §301.7701-7(c)(4)(ii), providing:

   A court within the United States is not considered to have primary supervision over the administration of the trust if the trust instrument provides that a United States court's attempt to assert jurisdiction or otherwise supervise the administration of the trust directly or indirectly would cause the trust to migrate from the United States. However, this paragraph (c)(4)(ii) will not apply if the trust instrument provides that the trust will migrate

from the United States only in the case of foreign invasion of the United States or widespread confiscation or nationalization of property in the United States.
See also, CCA 201509035.

33. Treas. Reg. §301.7701-7(d)(ii).

34. Revenue Procedure 2015-53.

35. I.R.C §§652(b) and 662(b).

36. I.R.C §§662(a)(1) (first tier) and 662(a)(2) (second tier).

37. I.R.C §§662(a)(1), 662(a)(2).

38. I.R.C §6048(a)(1).

39. See I.R.C §6048(a)(2).

40. I.R.C §6048(b)(1).

41. *Id.*

42. *See* I.R.C §6048(b)(2)(B).

43. I.R.C §6048(b)(2)(A).

44. *See* I.R.C §6048(c).

45. *See* I.R.C §6019.

46. *See* Treas. Reg. §§25.2511-2(j) and 25.6019-3.

47. *See* I.R.C §6048.

48. I.R.C §6677(a).

49. *Id.*

50. I.R.C §6048(b)(2)(B).

51. I.R.C §6677(b)(1).

52. I.R.C §§6677(a), (b)(2).

53. *Id.*

54. I.R.C §§6048(d)(5), 6034A(c).

55. Treas. Reg. §1.671-4

56. *See* McNamara, "New Foreign Trust Tax Form Project: 1041NR," 38 The Tax Adviser 516 (Sept. 2007).

57. Treas. Reg. §1.6038D-3(c) provides in pertinent part: "An interest in a foreign trust…is not a specified foreign financial asset of a specified person unless the person knows, or has reason to know based on readily accessible information, of the interest. Receipt of a distribution from the foreign trust…constitutes actual knowledge for this purpose."

58. Treas. Reg. §1.6038D-7(a)(2).

59. Treas. Reg. §1.6038D-7(a)(1)(i)(B).

60. *See* Instructions to Form TD F 90-22.1, p.7.

61. *See* also Treasury Regulation §301.7701-7(c)(4)(ii)), and one or more U.S. persons have the authority to control all substantial decisions of the trust. (The definition of "**substantial decisions**" is set forth in Treasury Regulation §301.7701-7(d).)

62. 31 CFR §§1010.350(a) and 1010.306(c).

63. 31 CFR §1010.350.

64. 31 USC §5321(a)(5)(B).

65. For an excellent discussion of the new FinCen Form 114 see Gopman, Morgan & Simmons, "Electronic Filing Requirement for FBAR," LISI Income Tax Planning Newsletter #52 (August 29, 2013). See also, Bowers, "U.S. Tax Reporting Obligations of Foreign Trusts," 39 Estates, Gifts & Tr. J. 136 (May-June 2014).

66. 31 CFR §§1010.350(a) and (e)(2)(iii).

67. 31 CFR §§1010.350(a) and (e)(2)(iv).

68. 31 CFR 1010.350(g)(5).

69. 31 USC §5321(a)(5)(B).

70. 31 USC §5321(a)(5)(C).

71. 31 USC §5322(a).

72. 31 U.S.C. §5321(d). For an excellent discussion of penalities related to failure to file FBARs see Rubin, "IRS Telegraphs What It Expects Will Be "Normal" FBAR Failure To File Penalties," LISI Asset Protection Planning Newsletter #300, (June 24, 2015).

73. Hiring Incentives to Restore Employment Act of 2010 (P.L. 111-147) (Mar. 18, 2010).

74. I.R.C §§1471 and 1472.

75. See I.R.C §1471.

76. See I.R.C §1472.

77. I.R.C §1471(a); Treas. Regs. §1.1471-2T(a)(1).

78. I.R.C §1473(1).

79. Treas. Reg. §1.1471-2T(a)(1).

80. Treas. Reg. §1.1471-5(d).

81. *Id.*

82. *See* Treas. Reg. §1.1471-5(e)(4)(i)(A).

83. *See* Treas. Reg. §1.1471-5(e)(4)(i)(B).

84. *See* Treas. Reg. §1.1471-5(e)(4)(i)(C).

85. Treas. Reg. §1.1471-5(e)(4)(i)(A)(1)-(3).

86. Treas. Reg. §1.1471-5(e)(4)(i)(A).

87. Treas. Reg. §1.1471-5(e)(4)(v), Ex. 6.

88. Treas. Reg. §1.1471-5(e)(4)(iv).

89. *See Model Intergovernmental Agreement to Improve Tax Compliance and to Implement FATCA*, Article 1(j).

90. Treas. Reg. §1.1471-5(e)(4)(i)(B).

91. Treas. Reg. §1.1471-5(e)(4)(iv), Ex. 5 and Ex. 6.

92. Treas. Reg. §1.1471-5(e)(4)(iv), Ex. 5.

93. *See Model Intergovernmental Agreement to Improve Tax Compliance and to Implement FATCA (Model 1 IGA), Article 1, para. (j).*

94. I.R.C §1471(b).

95. *Id.*

96. I.R.C §1471(b); Treas. Reg. §§1.1471-4(a) and 1.1471-4T(a).

97. I.R.C §1471(b)(2); Treas. Reg. §1.1471-5(f).

98. Treas. Reg. §1.1471-5(f)(1)(i)(F).

99. *Id.*

100. Treas. Reg. §§1.1471-5(f)(2)(iii) and 1.1471-5(f)(3).

101. Treas. Reg. §1.1471-3(d)(6)(iv).

102. Treas. Reg. §1.1471-3(d)(6)(ii).

103. *See e.g.,* Model 1 IGA, Article 4, para. 1.

104. Model 1 IGA, Article 4, para. 1(e).

105. I.R.C §1472(d).

106. I.R.C §1472(b); Treas. Reg. §§1.1472-1; and 1.1472-1T.

107. *See* I.R.C §§671-679.

108. I.R.C §1473(2); Treas. Reg. §1.1473-1(b).

109. I.R.C §1472(a).

110. I.R.C §1472(c).

111. Treas. Reg. §1.1472-1T(c)(1)(iv).

112. Fla. Stat. §736.0505(1)(c).

113. I.R.C §2523(e)

114. I.R.C §§2056(b)(7) & 2523(f).

115. *See* I.R.C §2613. For a further discussion of tax reimbursement clauses, see Durkin, *Understanding Tax Payment/Reimbursement Clauses for Sales to Intentionally Defective Grantor Trusts,* 29 Prob. & Prop. 45 (Sept./Oct. 2015).

POWER OF APPOINTMENT SUPPORT TRUSTS (POAST)

CHAPTER 20

INTRODUCTION

Since the passage of the American Taxpayer Relief Act of 2012 ("ATRA"),[1] it is fair to say that the focus for many clients has broadened from estate tax to income tax reduction. Two of the primary reasons for this shift are the majority of wealthier individuals are no longer subject to the Federal estate tax[2] and income tax rates have increased for those with higher incomes.[3] This combination has the wealthy searching for ways to minimize the impact of income taxes, while accomplishing other non-tax planning objectives.

Properly structured, the power of appointment support trust (or "POAST")[4] can potentially accomplish stepping-up the income tax basis of appreciated assets during the donor's lifetime, while providing benefits to the grantor's ancestors (i.e., parents, grandparents, aunts, uncles, etc.) and descendants (i.e., children, grandchildren, and more remote descendants) and taking advantage of such ancestors transfer tax benefits (i.e., otherwise unused[5] applicable exclusion amount ("AEA")[6] and otherwise unused GST exemption).[7]

WHAT IS A POWER OF APPOINTMENT SUPPORT TRUST (POAST)?

A POAST is an irrevocable trust:

- typically created by a wealthy individual (whom we refer to as "G2");

- for the benefit of children, grandchildren, etc. (G3);[8] and

- parents, grandparents, aunts, uncles, etc., (G1).[9]

The POAST is generally structured as a dynastic trust (i.e., a trust that can last beyond the traditional common law rule against perpetuities ("RAP").[10] Additionally, the POAST is often structured as a grantor trust[11] for income tax purposes. We discuss all of the POAST's attributes below.

Some may wonder whether the POAST is a new concept. It is, and it is not! The idea is new, in that it is an idea that would now work well as a favorable tax planning strategy after ATRA, but the concepts that are implemented are well established.[12] The POAST is "an amalgam of old concepts used in an innovative way, which can potentially yield tremendous new tax benefits."[13] Simply put, the POAST uses old concepts and incorporates them innovatively to achieve better tax and non-tax planning results.

WHO MAY BENEFIT FROM THE POAST?

The POAST strategy may be an ideal income and estate tax and asset protection strategy for the so called "sandwich-generation." The sandwich generation, whom we refer to as "G2", is the generation of individuals who are both (a) planning for their children, grandchildren, and more remote descendants, whom we refer to as "G3", and (b) planning for the contingency that parents, grandparents, aunts, uncles, and more senior generations, whom we refer to as "G1", may need financial assistance in the future.

The POAST is not strictly for the sandwich generation. Because of its collateral benefit as a transfer tax planning tool, the POAST strategy may be used to simply take advantage of any otherwise unused "AEA" ("OU-AEA") or otherwise unused GST exemption

("OU-GST exemption) that G1 may "waste" at death. Additionally, because the POAST may also be used as a mechanism to achieve a basis 'step-up' for appreciated assets during G2's lifetime, it may be used by those G2s who may not have an immediate need to plan to assist their parents, grandparents, etc., but can be used proactively as an income tax planning tool.

We explore other ways in which a POAST can be used to enhance planning for current and future generations throughout this chapter.

WHY USE A POAST?

There are two questions to answer:

1. Why use a POAST?

2. Why won't other irrevocable trusts work?

We will answer the questions in reverse order. Let's first examine the benefits and limitations of other irrevocable trusts and then examine how the POAST, because of the changes in ATRA, brings to light new benefits, typically not seen in traditional irrevocable trusts.

Why Won't Any Other Irrevocable Trusts Work?

The typical irrevocable trust that one creates for long-term estate planning is designed for a multitude of reasons, including but not limited to the following:

- Removing transferred assets (and appreciation) from G2's estate; and

- Placing those transferred assets into asset-protected vehicles (i.e., trusts).[14]

Typically, these are multi-generational trusts; therefore, if the donor's GST exemption is allocated to the trust, depending upon the trust's terms, an added benefit is:

- Removing transferred assets (and appreciation) from the Federal transfer tax[15] system.

Before ATRA, planners would generally limit a beneficiary's rights so that the assets in the trust would not be included in the beneficiary's estate. With the POAST, however, the trust is specifically designed to include a

portion or all of such trust in the senior generation's (G1's) estate, for the purpose of using G1's OU-AEA and/or OU-GST exemption. Thus, another benefit of the POAST is that it removes assets (and appreciation) from the Federal transfer tax system for the donor (G2) and more junior generations (G3).

Further, if the trust is created as a grantor trust for income tax purposes, during the period that it remains a grantor trust (i.e., generally during the grantor's lifetime), a further benefit is having the grantor pay the income tax on the taxable income earned by the trust.[16]

Those are the upsides of the traditional irrevocable grantor dynastic trust. There are limitations, however. For instance, before ATRA, planners cautioned clients that recipients of *inter-vivos* gifts take a transferred basis (and such transferred assets generally do not receive a basis adjustment at the donor's death).[17] However, the cautionary income tax rule was generally not a significant factor, because, at that time, the benefits of the estate tax savings generally outweighed any potential income tax burden. After ATRA's passage, the contrary may be true (i.e., the income tax burden may outweigh the transfer tax benefit, if any). Thus, today, planners emphasize the potential downside of giving the assets away during life (i.e., the trust takes the donor's basis in the assets at the time of the gift[18] and there may be no basis adjustment at death).[19] Thus, if the donated asset is highly appreciated at the time of the gift, or appreciates during the donor's lifetime, then the unrealized gains are a detriment when the asset is eventually sold.[20] Thus, the traditional trust would not accomplish the income and transfer tax planning goals of basis step-up and fully utilize the senior generation's (G1's) OU-AEA and/or OU-GST exemption.

Advantages of the POAST

Like the traditional irrevocable dynastic grantor trust, the POAST:

1. is irrevocable;

2. can be a dynastic trust; and

3. can be structured as a grantor trust.

Unlike the traditional irrevocable dynastic grantor trust, where the trust is intentionally structured to be excluded from a beneficiary's gross estate, the POAST (in whole or in part, depending upon the circumstances) is intentionally structured to be included in the senior generation's (G1's) gross estate.

The goal is to cause inclusion in G1's gross estate to the extent that the estate tax burden (if any) is significantly outweighed by the income tax benefit of a basis adjustment at G1's death. The added bonus is G1 will be able to allocate any part or all of G1's OU-GST exemption to the POAST's assets that were included in G1's estate. Thus, to the extent that the inclusion is limited to G1's OU-AEA, the included assets effectively obtain a date of death basis adjustment (without G1's estate having been subject to an estate tax liability). This is a very compelling reason to create and fund the POAST.

An additional non-tax benefit of the POAST over the traditional trust would is that G2 will be able to financially assist G1, through the POAST, if future needs arise.

WHO ARE THE PARTIES TO THE POAST?

- *The Trust* – In general, the POAST is an irrevocable dynastic grantor trust.[21]

- *The Grantor* – G2 is the grantor. If G2 is married, we suggest that each G2 create a separate POAST. If there are two POASTs, we advise against the split gift election,[22] and instead each G2 makes a separate gift and files separate Federal gift tax returns.

- *The Beneficiaries* – All trusts have current beneficiaries and remaindermen. For most irrevocable dynastic trusts, the current beneficiaries are generally G2's descendants (G3). For the POAST, we include G2's parents, grandparents, etc., (G1) as beneficiaries.[23] If there are multiple G1s, we suggest a separate POAST for each G1, since the allocation of such G1's OU-GST exemption and utilizing each separate G1's OU-AEA would be important.

- *Trustee* – As is the case with all trusts, there is a trustee. Depending upon the circumstances, it is possible for a beneficiary or a spouse of a grantor to be a trustee. However, we suggest that in cases where there is a need to have an "independent trustee" that a corporate trustee and/or a non-family, non-beneficiary be nominated as an independent trustee.

- *The Trust Protector* – As is discussed in Chapter 2 of this book, appointing a trust protector may be prudent. The Trust protector would be given the power to deal with unanticipated challenges or take advantage of future opportunities. For example, the trust protector may have the power to add or remove beneficiaries, or to add certain powers where one may be able to take advantage of a GST taxable event or a new basis adjustment opportunity.

Specifically, the trust protector may be given the ability to provide a beneficiary with a general power of appointment ("GPOA"), which may be contingent, testamentary and/or inter-vivos, depending on the circumstances, to enhance income or transfer tax benefits.

WHAT ARE THE POAST'S DISPOSITIVE PROVISIONS?

Provisions for Descendants – G3

The POAST's dispositive provisions for G3 will be similar to what they would have been for any irrevocable dynastic trust. Generally, during G2's lifetime, G3 would be discretionary income and principal beneficiaries. Upon G2's death, the POAST would distribute assets in the manner that is typically provided for under G2's testamentary instruments (e.g., last will and testament and/or revocable trust). It is beyond the scope of this chapter to discuss the variations of dispositive provisions that are typical under these circumstances.

G3s are given a power of appointment upon death. Typically, the power of appointment is not a general power of appointment (as such term is defined under Code section 2041) rather the power would be generally limited in favor of spouses, descendants, and/or spouses of descendants (and perhaps charity).[24]

Provisions for Ancestors- G1

As stated above, POASTs have two primary goals: First, POASTs are designed to provide financial assistance to G1, if needed. Second, POASTs are designed to take advantage of G1's OU-AEA and/or OU-GST exemption, while obtaining a basis adjustment for some or all of the assets in the POAST. To accomplish these two goals, the dispositive provisions for G1 will be different than that for G3.

To accomplish the support goal, the trustee has the discretion to distribute income and/or principal to G1 for G1's health, maintenance and/or support. Additionally, an independent trustee should have the discretion to distribute income and/or principal for G1's best interest. This allows the trustee to make distributions if needed.

To utilize G1's OU-AEA and OU-GST exemption, G1 is given a testamentary general power of appointment (GPOA). We suggest limiting the testamentary GPOA as to its scope and amount to the extent possible. For instance, the GPOA should be limited only to the creditor of G1's estate. To the extent that any of the POAST's assets are included in G1's estate, the income tax basis of those assets would be adjusted to the date of death value.[25]

Below we discuss how to structure and limit the GPOA to avoid triggering estate taxes (while obtaining a basis adjustment at G1's death) and how to maximize the potential benefit of G1's OU-GST exemption.

Provisions for Spouse of G2

It is possible to give G2's spouse a beneficial interest in the trust, so that during G2's spouse's lifetime, the trustee would have discretion to distribute funds to the spouse as may be needed. If G2's spouse wants to create a POAST and also give the other spouse a beneficial interest, the drafter of the trusts would have to be very careful not to trigger the reciprocal trust doctrine, which may cause inclusion of both POASTs in each of the spouse's estates.[26]

THE POAST'S STRUCTURE

The POAST is generally structured as follows:

- G2 will be the grantor.

- G1 and G3 will be the beneficiaries.

- G2's spouse could possibly be a beneficiary.

- The following could be potential trustees,[27] depending upon the circumstances:

  o G2's spouse;

  o G1;

  o G1's spouse;

  o G3;

  o G3's spouse;

  o other trusted individuals (who are not the grantor, nor a beneficiary); and/or

  o a corporate trustee.

- The trust's duration should be the longest possible allowable by state law.

- G1 should be given a general power of appointment.

- G3 should be given a non-general power of appointment.

- If G2's spouse is a beneficiary, G2's spouse should be given a non-general power of appointment.

- At G1's death, the trust is then held for the benefit of G3 and G2's spouse, if G2's spouse was a beneficiary.[28] If G2 predeceases G1, the trust continues for G1, G3 and G2's spouse, if G2's spouse was a beneficiary.

G1's Power of Appointment

In general, G1 should be given a power of appointment that would be as limited as possible to achieve the goal of being able to use G1's OU-AEA and OU-GST exemption, while at the same time not opening the assets in the trust to any exposure as a result of the power of the power of appointment.

If G1 is given a testamentary GPOA over the POAST, at the time of G1's death, the entire value of the POAST would be included in G1's gross estate.[29] This could cause unintended consequences (i.e., it may cause a Federal estate tax, where one was not anticipated). To eliminate this contingency, G1's testamentary GPOA should be structured as a contingent testamentary GPOA (or a "CT-GPOA").[30] In general, the CT-GPOA should be limited to the lesser of G1's (a) OU-AEA, and (b) OU-GST exemption.[31] We discuss limiting the CT-GPOA in more detail below.

To limit the exposure, the GPOA should only be exercisable at G1's death and limited only to the creditors of G1's estate. This would likely be the least intrusive GPOA. As discussed below, if G1 has creditor issues, or if the planner believes that there would be creditor issues, the POAST may not be a suitable estate planning vehicle.

WHAT ARE THE TAX IMPLICATIONS?

There are income and transfer tax implications to all of the parties.

- *During G1's Lifetime* – the most senior generation, will generally be a discretionary beneficiary during his/her lifetime. Upon death, G1 will have a CT-GPOA.

- *Gift and GST Tax Implications* – During G1's lifetime, there should be no gift and GST tax implications to G1.

- *Income Tax Implications* – In general there should be no income tax implications to G1 during G1's lifetime, because the POAST is structured to be a grantor trust as to G2.[32] However, should the trust cease to be a grantor trust as to G2 during G1's lifetime (e.g., because G2 predeceased G1 or G2 opted for the trust to no longer be a grantor trust), any trust distributions made from the POAST to G1 may be subject to income tax to G1, based on the POAST's distributable net income.[33]

- *Estate and GST Tax Implications* – Upon G1's death, to the extent of G1's CT-GPOA, assets will be includable in G1's gross estate.[34] G1's GPOA should be a CT-GPOA limited to the lesser of G1's: (a) OU-AEA; or (b) OU-GST exemption, which would thus trigger the minimum adverse estate and/or GST tax. We use a few examples to explain why the CT-GPOA should be so limited, and discuss some planning options.

Examples

For the following examples, assume the following:

- The basic exclusion amount is $5 million and has no cost-of-living-adjustment (COLA).[35]

- The estate and gift tax rates are 40 percent. The GST exemption is $5 million (and has no COLA).[36] The GST tax rate is 40 percent.

- Grandmother, "GP" (who is assigned to the G1 generation) is unmarried. GP has no deceased spousal unused exemption. GP is the parent of C (who is assigned to the G2 generation).

- GP is the grandparent of a number of grandchildren, collectively GC (who are assigned to the G3 generation).

- The value of GP's gross estate (not including assets from the POAST) will be $1million.

- GP will have no debts or expenses at death (for simplicity purposes).

- C creates a POAST that is valued at $12 million at GP's death.

- The POAST is for the benefit of GP and GC (unless otherwise stated).

- GP is given a GPOA limited to creditors of GP's estate (unless otherwise stated). (Note: The GPOA may be limited in amount depending upon the example).

- C is married.

- C's spouse is not a beneficiary of the POAST.

- Corporate Trustee is the trustee of the POAST.

Example 1. GP dies in 20XX, having made no taxable gifts, and having used no GST exemption as of death. GP is not a beneficiary of a POAST. GP leaves her entire estate outright and free of trust to her grandchildren, GC. As a result of her death, GP's OU-AEA would be $4 million (i.e., $5 million basic exclusion amount less the $1 million net taxable estate), and OU-GST exemption would also be $4 million (i.e., $5 million GST exemption reduced by the generation-skipping transfer to G1's grandchildren).

In Example 1, we demonstrate that if GP is not the beneficiary of a POAST, GP will waste $4 million of her AEA and GST exemption.

Example 2. Assume the same facts as Example 1, however, GP is not a beneficiary of a POAST and GP is given an unlimited GPOA, and GC will be the only other beneficiaries.

This example demonstrates the POAST's tax benefits and disadvantages (if not properly structured). One of the benefits is that all of the assets in the POAST will obtain a basis adjustment; the downside is all of the assets will also be included in GP's gross estate which will cause an estate tax liability, and there will also be a GST tax liability. Because GP's GPOA is not limited, the entire value $12 million (i.e., the POAST's value at GP's date of death) would be included in GP's gross estate.[37] GP's gross estate would be $13 million (i.e., $1 million of GP's assets plus the $12 POAST trust). Assuming the estate tax rate of 40 percent, the tax would be $3.2 million ($13 million less the AEA of $5 million = $8 million × 0.40 = $3.2 million).

In addition to the estate tax, a GST tax would be due. At GP's death, the POAST will only have skip persons as beneficiaries;[38] therefore, a taxable termination would occur.[39] GP's executor could allocate GP's OU-GST exemption to the POAST, which would then reduce the tax burden.[40] Assuming that GP's OU-GST exemption (of $4 million) is allocated, that amount would be GST exempt; however, the balance of $8 million (i.e., $12 million less $4 million) would be subject to the GST tax.[41] Since this is a taxable termination, the POAST's trustee would be liable for the tax.[42]

Example 3. Assume the same facts as Example 2, however, assume that GP made no taxable gifts, but had used $500,000 of her GST exemption during life, so that GP's OU-AEA was $4 million and her OU-GST exemption was $3.5 million.

In this case, the estate tax liability would be the same; however, the GST tax liability would increase as a result of the OU-GST exemption begin $500,000 less. At a tax rate of 40 percent, this would translate to a $200,000 increase in GST tax.

Example 4. Assume the same facts as Example 2, however, assume that GP's GPOA is a CT-GPOA limited to the lesser of (a) GP's OU-AEA or (b) OU-GST Exemption.

In this case, at the time of GP's death, there would be no estate or GST tax liability. In this case, the OU-AEA or OU-GST exemption is the same (i.e., $4 million), thus, the amount that is included in GP's gross estate is $4 million, and her taxable estate would be $5 million (i.e., her $1 million of assets plus GP's CT-GPOA of $ 4 million). Because GP's AEA[43] immediately before death is $5 million, there will be no estate tax. For GST tax purposes, GP will be considered the transferor as to $4 million of the POAST. GP's executor could allocate her GST exemption to that portion of the trust and the trust would be wholly GST exempt (as to that portion).[44] Thus, there would be no GST tax liability.

Example 5. Assume the same facts as Example 3, however, assume that GP's GPOA is a CT-GPOA limited to the lesser of GP's OU-AEA or OU-GST Exemption.

Recall that in Example 3, GP's OU-AEA was $4 million and her OU-GST exemption was $3.5 million. The amount included in GP's taxable estate would only be $3.5 million (i.e., the lesser amount), thus, the taxable estate would be $4.5 million (i.e., $1 million of GP's assets plus GP's CT-GPOA of $3.5 million). In this example, $500,000 of GP's OU-AEA is wasted, because her AEA (of $5 million) exceeds her taxable estate (of $4.5 million). However, for GST tax purposes; there will be no GST tax liability. In this case, since GP is the transferor of $3.5 million, and GP's executor can allocate all $3.5 million of her OU-GST exemption to the portion of the POAST that was included in GP's estate, such portion of the trust (or if the trust was severed, the entire severed trust over which GP had the CT-GPOA) would be tax exempt, and thus there will be no GST tax liability.

Example 6. Assume the same facts as Example 5, however, assume that GP's GPOA is a CT-GPOA limited to the greater of GP's OU-AEA or OU-GST exemption.

In Example 6, we illustrate that if the CT-GPOA is not limited to the lesser of the OU-AEA or OU-GST exemption, but is instead limited to the greater of GP's OU-AEA and OU-GST exemption, it could potentially trigger the GST tax (which is generally an undesirable result). Example 6 is based on Examples 3 and 5. In this example, the value of GP's CT-GPOA would be $4 million (i.e., the greater of $4 million or $3.5 million). GP's estate will not suffer an estate tax liability; because GP's taxable estate would be $5 million (i.e., $1 million of her assets plus $4 million of the CT-GPOA over the POAST) which is offset by her $5 million AEA. However, there will be a generation-skipping transfer that will be considered a taxable termination as to $500,000 (i.e., the difference between the $4 million CT-GPOA over the amount of GP's OU-GST exemption of $3.5 million), which would trigger a GST tax liability. Assuming a 40 percent GST tax, the liability would be $200,000.

The question for the planner is whether it is worth paying the GST tax to obtain the income tax basis adjustment in cases where it is anticipated that the OU-AEA will be larger than the OU-GST exemption.

In cases where the OU-GST exemption will be larger than the OU-AEA, a decision should be made by G2 (i.e., the grantor of the POAST) to determine whether it makes sense to trigger an estate tax to accomplish two goals: (1) a basis step up as to the amount of the taxable estate in excess of G1's AEA, and (2) full utilization of G1's GST exemption. We illustrate this in the next example.

Example 7. Assume the same facts as Example 5. Assume GP's GPOA is a CT-GPOA limited to the greater of GP's OU-AEA or OU-GST exemption. And, assume further that at the time of GP's death, her OU-AEA is $3 million and her OU-GST exemption is $4 million.

In this example, if GP is given a CT-GPOA which is valued at $4 million (i.e., the greater of GP's OU-AEA (of $3 million) or GP's OU-GST exemption (of $4 million). In this case the $4 million additional inclusion in GP's gross estate will trigger an estate tax on the difference between such addition and the OU-AEA of $3 million. At a 40 percent estate tax rate, this would be a $400,000 liability (i.e., $4 million – $3 million = $1 million × 0.40 tax rate = $400,000).

In comparing Example 7 and 6, the analysis is slightly different. In Example 6, the question is whether it is worth triggering an estate tax for two perceived benefits: (a) income tax basis adjustment; and (b) full utilization of the GST exemption. In Example 5, the analysis was whether paying the GST tax was beneficial to get the income tax basis adjustment. On balance, it appears that in Example 7, since you get two benefits (i.e., income tax basis adjustment and full utilization of GST tax) it is worth it. We are not sure about whether it is worth it for Example 6. One would have to run the numbers and determine if there is a net after tax benefit.

Basis Adjustment

To the extent that the POAST's assets are included in GP's gross estate (due to the CT-GPOA), the included assets receive a basis adjustment.[45] Some may wonder whether grantor trust status ends after G1's death. The answer is, "it depends!" The rule is if GP exercises the CT-GPOA, GP becomes the grantor. If not then C continues as the grantor for income tax purposes.[46] It is important to note, for estate tax inclusion, it is not necessary for GP to exercise the CT-GPOA; GP need only be possessed of the power.[47] Thus, the goal would be to have GP possessed of the power, but not exercise the power at death.

Depending on how the POAST is structured, there may be income and transfer tax implications during G2's life and at G2's death.

Tax Implications during G2's Lifetime

- *Income Tax* – If the POAST is structured as a grantor trust[48] for Federal income tax purposes, the transfer of the assets to the trust would not be a taxable event. In fact, under Revenue Ruling 85-13,[49] it is deemed as if G2 never transferred the assets to the POAST. Rather G2 continues to own the property for Federal income tax purposes. Thus, there is no recognition event for income tax purposes. The tax basis of the assets in the POAST will be G2's tax basis immediately before the gift.[50] If the POAST is structured as a non-grantor trust for Federal income tax purposes, the transfer of the assets would not be a taxable event. The basis of the assets will be a transferred basis, subject to the rules under Code section 1015.

- After the transfer, while G1 is alive, if the trust is a grantor trust, all items of income, deduction, credits, etc., are reported on G2's personal income tax return. If the trust is a non-grantor trust then the trust, the beneficiaries, and/or both will be subject to income tax, based on the distributable net income of the beneficiaries.[51] When G1 dies, to the extent that any portion of the trust is included in G1's estate as a result of G1's GPOA, the basis of those assets will receive a basis adjustment under Code sections 1014(a) and (b)(9). The grantor trust status should continue after G1's death.[52]

Planning Pointer: From a planning perspective, when the basis of the assets are adjusted (as a result of G1's death), it may be a good time to consider diversifying the trust's assets, since the basis and fair market value would be roughly the same[53] when the assets are finally sold.

- *Gift and GST Tax* – Generally, if G2 makes a transfer to the POAST, it will be considered a completed gift.[54] At the time of the transfer, G2 has the ability to allocate G2's GST exemption to the trust. However, since the goal is to utilize G1's GST exemption (when G1 dies), it would be imprudent for G2 to allocate any of his/her GST exemption at the time of the transfer. Rather, it would be better for G2 to wait until after G1 dies before determining if G2 wants to allocate his/her GST exemption.[55]

- *Estate Tax* – Upon G1's death, to the extent assets are included in G1's estate (as a result of the GPOA), depending upon the limitations of the GPOA, there may or may not be a Federal estate tax.[56] Upon G1's death, to the extent that G1 is the 'transferor' (as such term is defined in Code section 2652(a) for GST tax purposes), part or all of G1's OU-GST exemption should be allocated to the POAST.

Planning Pointer: It may be better if the trustee severs the trust[57] so that the part of the trust over which G1 is a transferor is a separate trust and G1's executor can then allocate G1's OU-GST exemption to that portion of the trust (with the intention that the trust would have in inclusion ratio[58] of zero (0) and be fully GST exempt). If G1's OU-GST exemption is less

than the value of the severed trust, then a subsequent severance would be generally better to have trusts with inclusion ratios of zero (0) and one (1).[59]

After the allocation of G1's OU-GST exemption, G2 should determine whether G2 wishes to allocate any of his/her unused GST exemption to the POAST (that is not otherwise GST exempt as a result of the allocation of G1's OU-GST exemption). If so, G2 can make a late allocation.[60]

Tax Implications at G2's Death

- *Income Tax* – Conventional wisdom is that the income tax basis of the assets in the POAST is unaffected by G2's death. However, well-versed, highly-respected estate planners argue that, read literally, there should be a basis adjustment at G2's death.[61] We leave it to the reader to determine which approach is appropriate for his/her client.

  - If the trust was a grantor trust during G2's lifetime, generally at the time of G2's death, the trust would cease to be a grantor trust (i.e., it would become a non-grantor trust). However, if G2's spouse was a beneficiary of the trust, depending upon her interest in the trust, the trust may continue to be a grantor trust until her death (or other event that would cause grantor trust status to cease).[62] If the trust was a non-grantor trust before G2's death, there will be no change as a result of G2's death.

- *Estate and GST Tax* – Upon G2's death, the assets are excluded from G2's gross estate; therefore, there are no estate tax implications. To the extent of G2's OU-GST exemption and G2 is deemed to be a transferor of any part of the POAST, G2's executor could make a late allocation of G2's OU-GST exemption to that portion of the POAST.

Tax Implications during G3's Lifetime

- *Income Tax* – During G3's lifetime, if the trust is a grantor trust and distributions are made to G3, those distributions would be tax free to G3. If the trust is a non-grantor trust, G3, the trust, or both, will be subject to income tax, depending on the trust's distributable net income.[63] When G3 dies, there should be no income tax implications to the POAST or any of the beneficiaries. Gift and GST Tax Implications- In general, there will be no gift and/or GST tax implications to G3. There should also be no estate or GST tax implications because the POAST is designed to be excluded from G3's estate at his/her death. These benefits should continue as long as the trust remains in existence.

FUNDING THE POAST

Traditional Funding

The POAST is created in the same manner that any other irrevocable trust is created. One would look to one's state laws to determine the legal formalities in creating an irrevocable trust. Generally, there are generally two ways to fund a POAST: (1) G2 can transfer his / her assets to the POAST's trustee; or (2) existing trusts can pour assets into the POAST.

- *Annual Exclusion Gifts* – If G2 decides to contribute assets to a POAST, G2 can do so by making annual exclusion or *Crummey*[64] gifts. Annual exclusion gifts avoid any gift tax liability.

- *Taxable Gifts* – To the extent that the transfers to the POAST exceed G2's annual exclusion amounts, the gifts would be taxable gifts, which, depending upon G2's available AEA, may or may not trigger a gift tax liability.

The decision on how much to fund the trust would be left to G2 and his/her advisors to determine what would make the most sense, based upon G2's financial situation and G1's anticipated OU-AEA and OU-GST exemption.

Innovative Funding

One of the major goals of the POAST is to utilize G1's OU-AEA and OU-GST exemption, by causing part or all of the assets in the POAST to be included in G1's gross estate. A goal, not explicitly stated before, is to try to fund the POAST with assets, but to do so without using too much of G2's AEA. Funding by using G2's annual exclusion amounts accomplishes that goal; however, it is very limited.[65] Thus, in the following paragraphs we suggest a number of other planning ideas where assets could fund the POAST during G1's lifetime, yet use little or none of G2's available AEA.

- *Grantor Retained Annuity Trust ("GRAT") Pour-over* – Using zeroed-out GRATs are generally a good planning tool in low interest rate environments. One of the benefits is that there is minimal use of G2's AEA, and if the GRAT is successful, the assets remaining in the GRAT after payment of the final annuity to G2 could be used to fund the POAST. This is an ideal way to fund the POAST, because of the low use of G2's AEA, and because the assets that come from the GRAT will not be GST exempt.

  o The downside of this type of mechanism is that G2 could die and thus the GRAT would not pour over to the POAST, or the investments in the GRAT may not outperform the GRAT's hurdle rate (i.e., the Code section 7520 rate on date of funding). To mitigate those issues, the planner should have other mechanism to fund the POAST.

- *Charitable Lead Annuity Trust ("CLAT") Pour-over* – CLATs, like GRATs, are also a good estate planning tool to use in low interest rate environments. Like GRATs, if the investments inside of the CLAT exceed the hurdle rate, the remainder generally passes to non-charitable beneficiaries. If there is a POAST, consider leaving the remainder to the POAST.

- *Make an Existing Trust a POAST* – Although not technically a way to "fund" a POAST, consider turning an existing irrevocable trust into a POAST. There are a few possible ways to do this, depending upon the governing law of the existing trust. First, the parties could consider a judicial modification of an existing trust. For instance, the grantor, beneficiaries and trustee could petition a court to add G1 as a discretionary income and principal beneficiary (providing G1 with a CT-GPOA). Second, if state law permits, it may be possible to accomplish the same (i.e., adding G1 as a beneficiary) through non-judicial modification. Third, again, depending on state law, if there is a trust protector, and the trust protector can add beneficiaries, it may be possible to simply add G1 as a beneficiary and provide G1 with a CT-GPOA. Finally, again, depending on state law, perhaps the trustee of the existing trust could decant the trust and have G1 added as a beneficiary (with a CT-GPOA).

- *Life Insurance on G1's Life* – Depending upon G1's insurability and the cost of insurance, another way to increase the value of the POAST at G1's death is to have the trust purchase a life insurance policy on G1's life.

- *Selling Assets to the POAST* – Finally, another way to add value to the POAST is to sell assets such as closely-held businesses at a discounted value to the POAST and take back a promissory note with a favorable interest rate. If the assets outperform the interest rate on the promissory note, the appreciation will increase the net value of the POAST.

OTHER IMPORTANT ISSUES TO THINK ABOUT

Premature Death of G2

Some may posit that it is possible that G2 predeceases G1 (i.e., the child predeceases the parent). We agree. Although death, like taxes, is certain, its timing is not nearly so certain. Thus, we should analyze the impact of this contingency.

If G2 predeceased G1, the basis of the transferred assets will likely not receive a basis adjustment[66] upon G2's death (i.e., the opposite income tax result then if G2 had done nothing). When that happens, we won't obtain a basis adjustment until some future date when G1 dies.

We must put the issue of G2's premature death into perspective, however. If the death was foreseeable (i.e., G2 was ill at the time of the planning), the POAST should not have been a suggested planning tool. Conversely, if death was not foreseeable, the statistical likelihood of G2 predeceasing G1 would have been small, and thus likely ignored. Also remember, premature death simply delays the income tax benefit of the basis adjustment (unless you take the position that the basis can be adjusted at G1's death).[67] "Additionally, if the trust is a grantor trust, it is likely that there would be a 'swap power' under Code section 675(4)(C).[68] This swap power would allow G2 to swap G2's higher-basis assets with the POAST's lower-basis assets during G2's lifetime to reduce the impact of waiting for the lower-basis assets to be adjusted when G1 dies. Finally, it is important to remember the income tax benefit (i.e., basis adjustment) is only one of the benefits, the other benefits include the

allocation of G1's OU-GST exemption and the ability to care financially for G1, should the need arise.

If there is concern about G2's premature death, then consider two options:

1. have the POAST purchase a life insurance policy on G2's life; and

2. do not use the POAST, if basis adjustment is the primary goal.

Creditor Issues of G1

We suggest giving G1 a general power of appointment in favor of creditors of G1's estate to cause the inclusion of the POAST assets (in whole or in part, depending upon the extent of the CT-GPOA and the POAST's value). If G1 has creditor issues, we suggest that the advisor examine state law to determine if the POASTs assets could be reached by G1's creditors. What appears to be clear is that state laws vary and the state of the law in this particular area is not clear. Thus, we suggest that the advisor determine whether the POASTs assets will be well-protected, and if not, the POAST should not be used as a planning vehicle.

G1 Redirecting Assets

Another issue that may arise is the fact that G1 may either want to redirect assets in the POAST or may be persuaded to do same. If the CT-GPOA is limited to creditors of G1's estate, then the risk of redirection is limited. However, one should be mindful of this issue.

CONCLUSION

The POAST is not just an income tax planning vehicle to obtain a basis adjustment during the grantor's life. The POAST is not just a trust instrument that can be used to support the grantor's parents, grandparents, etc. The POAST is not just a vehicle that can utilize a senior generation's otherwise unused GST exemption to benefit the family. The POAST is not just an irrevocable grantor trust that can benefit future generations. The POAST is not just another irrevocable trust that can be the ultimate recipient of assets that pour over from GRATs and CLATs. The POAST is not just an irrevocable grantor trust. The POAST is all of these things, and, importantly should be considered in estate planning today.

CHAPTER ENDNOTES

1. Pub.L. 112-240, H.R. 8, 126 Stat. 2313, enacted Jan. 2, 2013.

2. According to the Joint Committee on Taxation, based on 2013 data, less than 0.2 percent of decedents will have to file a Federal estate tax return and pay estate tax. Thus, 99.8 percent of the population is not subject to Federal estate taxes. We acknowledge that for those living in states that have a state estate tax, the percentage of the population subject to an estate tax may be higher than that those who are exclusively subject to the Federal estate tax.

3. For instance, the highest marginal capital gains rates for most sales pre-ATRA were 15 percent, whereas, post-ATRA, this rate is 20 percent. This increased rate combined with the so-called 3.8 percent Medicare surtax (as provided for under Internal Revenue Code of 1986, as amended, Code section 1411, means a 43 percent increase in capital gains taxes for the higher income earners, who are, for the most part, the group of taxpayers who are no longer subject to the Federal estate tax.

4. We borrow this term from the co-author's earlier paper, Austin *et al.*, *Introducing the Power of Appointment Support Trust.* See Note 1, *supra.*

5. We use the term "otherwise unused" to denote the amount of tax benefit that would go unused if the individual opted not to utilize the particular tax planning strategy (i.e., the POAST in this case).

6. I.R.C. §2010(c)(2). An individual's AEA is the combination of his or her basic exclusion amount (as such term is defined in I.R.C. §2010(c)(3)) and any deceased spousal unused exclusion amount (as such term is defined in I.R.C. §2010(c)(4)).

7. I.R.C. §2631.

8. For purposes of this chapter, G3 will refer collectively to any of G2's living descendants (i.e., persons who are at least one generation below G2 (e.g., children, grandchildren, great-grandchildren, etc.)).

9. For purposes of this chapter, G1 will refer collectively to any of G2's living ancestors (i.e., persons who are at least one generation above G2 (e.g., G2's parents, aunts, uncles, grandparents, great-grandparents, etc.)).

10. Thus, the POAST would generally be created in jurisdictions that have a substantially extended RAP period (e.g., Florida (that has a RAP of 360 years), or a jurisdiction that has eliminated the RAP (e.g., Alaska, Delaware, Illinois, South Dakota, New Hampshire).

11. For purposes of this chapter, the term "grantor trust" refers to a trust where the items of income, gain, loss, deductions, credits, etc., are reportable by "grantor" of such trust under I.R.C. §671 *et seq.*

12. As is the case with most estate planning concepts, one borrows liberally from others' thoughts and writings. The concept of the POAST was based on thoughts presented in the following articles: Davis, *Planning for new Basis at Death*, American Bar Association, Fiduciary Income Tax Committee Meeting (Jan. 31 2015); Berry, *Powers of Appointment in the Current Planning Environment*, 49 U. Miami Heckerling Inst. on Est. Plan (2015); Bergner, *Waste Not Want Not, Creative Use of General Powers of Appointment to Fund Tax-Advantaged Trusts*, 2006 ACTEC Annual Meeting Presentation; Franklin and Law, *Clinical Trials with Portability*, 48 U. Miami Heckerling Inst. on Est. Plan (2014); and Morrow,

The Optimal Basis Increase Trust (OBIT), LISI Estate Planning Newsletter #2080 (March 20, 2013) at www.leimbergservices.com.

13. Austin, *et al.*, *Introducing the Power of Appointment Support Trust.*

14. It is beyond the scope of this chapter to discuss the asset protection nuances that irrevocable trusts offer. Suffice it to say, properly structured (which includes such issues as choice of governing law, dispositive terms, selection of assets, selection of trustee's, etc.), many, if not most, irrevocable trusts today offer asset protection for the grantors and beneficiaries.

15. For purposes of this chapter, the term "transfer tax" refers to the Federal estate, gift and generation-skipping transfer (GST) taxes.

16. In Rev. Rul. 2004-64, 2004-2 CB 7 (2004), after much reticence, the IRS finally acquiesced that a grantor does not make a taxable gift by paying the income tax attributable to the income earned by the grantor trust. Effectively, this ruling allows G2s to enhance the G3s wealth by having G2 pay the income tax on the trust, rather than having the trust (which ultimately benefits G3) bear that burden.

17. I.R.C. §1014. For a good discussion of income tax basis for estate planners, see, Zaritsky and Law, *Basis, Banal? Basic? Benign? Bewildering?*, 49th U. Miami Heckerling Inst. on Est. Plan, 2015.

18. *See, e.g.*, Lee, Venn Diagrams, Meet me at the Intersection of Estate and Income Tax, 48th U. Miami Heckerling Inst. on Est. Plan, 2014. See also, Franklin and Law, Never Pay Estate Taxes: The Annual Taxable Gifts Approach with a CLAT Remainder, ABA-RPTE 2016 Spring Symposia, May, 2016. See, Notes 24 and 25, supra, for a citation to another article that discusses the possibility that there is an argument that there could be a basis adjustment at death.

19. *See* Notes 24 and 25, *supra*, for a discussion about the possibility of a basis adjustment at the grantor's death.

20. We acknowledge that if the trust is a grantor trust (i.e., a trust what is taxed to the grantor under Code Section 671 *et seq.*,) the recognition of gain will be generally imposed on the donor, and, thus, is not as big a concern. However, if the asset is not sold until after the donor's death, the asset is worth less to the beneficiaries because of the future income tax liability associated with the built in gain. There is some discussion among well-respected planners that there may be a possibility that the basis of the assets given during lifetime to an irrevocable grantor trust may be eligible for a basis adjustment at the donor's death. See, Zaritsky *et al.*, *Basis, Banal? Basic? Benign? Bewildering?* and Blattmachr, Gans & Jacobson, *Income Tax Effects of Termination of Grantor Trust Status by Reason of the Grantor's Death*, 96 Journal of Taxation (Sept. 2002).

21. To ensure that transfers to the POAST are completed gifts for Federal transfer tax purposes, it must be an irrevocable trust. Additionally, because another goal is to have the trust last for generations, it should have dynastic type terms and be in a state where the governing law allows for multi-generational trusts. Finally, to take advantage of the benefits of having the grantor pay the income tax on the POAST's income, it is structured as a grantor trust.

22. I.R.C. §2513.

23. G1 would likely be a discretionary current beneficiary as to income and/or principal, if support is needed.

24. The reason for not giving G3 a general power of appointment is because under I.R.C. §2041, assets subject to such general power

of appointment are included in the beneficiary's gross estate. Because it is anticipated that the trust would be outside of the Federal transfer tax system, to give the descendant-beneficiary (i.e., G3) flexibility, yet avoid inclusion in such beneficiary's gross estate, one would give G3 a non-general power of appointment, if any.

25. I.R.C. §§1014(a) and (b)(9).

26. Much has been written about giving the spouse lifetime access to a trust; hence, the term "Spousal Lifetime Access Trust" or "SLAT". The authors first remember reading about this in US Trust's publication, Practical Drafting over 20 years ago. The SLAT concept became popular recently with the increase of the basic exclusion amount. There are numerous articles written about SLATs. *See, e.g.*, Merric and Goodwin, *Spousal Lifetime Access Trusts – The Good, The Bad and The Ugly*, Part I, LISI Estate Planning Newsletter # 1334 (August 20, 2008) at www.leimbergservices.com/; Merric *et al., Part II*, LISI Estate Planning Newsletter # 1368 (November 12, 2008) at www.leimbergservices.com/; and Merric *et al., Part III*, LISI Estate Planning Newsletter # 1379 (December 2, 2008) at www.leimbergservices.com/. Not only are the articles written by well-respected attorneys, but the concept has reached mainstream media. See, e.g., Garcia, *Spousal Lifetime Access Trusts – Use Your Gift Tax Exemption Without Giving It all Away*, Forbes, August 9, 2012, and Willis, *Spousal Lifetime Access Trusts Save Clients Millions*, Wall Street Journal, December 3, 2012.

27. To avoid adverse estate tax consequences (such as including of the POAST in G2's gross estate), G2 should not be trustee.

28. If G2's spouse was a beneficiary, after G2's death, the trust would be held for G2's lifetime and thereafter for G3's benefit (i.e., a dynastic trust for the maximum duration permitted under law). If G2's spouse was not a beneficiary, the trust would be held for G3's benefit.

29. I.R.C. §2041.

30. The CT-GPOA is not a new concept. It has been used for over 30 years (i.e., since the inception of the 1986 version of the GST tax) to minimize the impact of such tax. The drafter should be careful in structuring the CT-GPOA to minimize risking the IRS raising the step transaction / implied agreement doctrine.

31. We do not discuss the state estate tax implications for those individuals living in states that are subject to a state estate tax. However, such taxes should be considered, analyzed and the implications discussed with the grantor and the donee of the power when drafting the CT-GPOA.

32. Statistically, G2 (i.e., the child of G1) would outlive G1.

33. For a leading treatise on how income is taxed for non-grantor trusts, *see*, Bittker & Lokken, *Federal Taxation of Income, Estates and Gifts*, Thompson Reuters / Tax & Accounting, 2d/3d ed. 1993-2016, Supp. 2., Chapter 81.

34. I.R.C. §2041.

35. For simplicity we assume that the GST exemption is not adjusted by a COLA factor, even though the law so provides (I.R.C. §2010(c)(3)(B)).

36. For simplicity we assume that the GST exemption is not adjusted by a COLA factor, even though the law so provides (I.R.C. §2631(c)).

37. I.R.C. §2041.

38. I.R.C. §2613; Treasury Regulations ("Treas. Reg.") §26.2612-1(d).

39. I.R.C. §§2611(a)(2) and 2612(a); Treas. Reg. §§26.2612-1(b) and -1(f)(Example 6). The taxable termination is a generation-skipping transfer under I.R.C. §2611(a)(2); thus, it potentially triggers the GST tax. Note: because the POAST's assets are included in GP's gross estate, GP will become the transferor. I.R.C. §2652(a)(1)(A); Treas. Reg. §26.2652-1(a).

40. I.R.C. §2631(a); Treas. Reg. §26.2632-1(a).

41. At a 40% GST tax rate, the GST tax liability would be $3.2 million (i.e., $8 million × 40%).

42. I.R.C. §2603(a)(2).

43. Recall that one's AEA is the combination of one's basic exclusion amount (in this example $5 million) and one's deceased spousal unused exclusion amount (in this example $0).

44. Arguably, the Trustee of the POAST should sever the trust, so that as to the portion that GP is the transferor, there would be a wholly-GST exempt trust and as to the other portion, C would remain the transferor. As to that portion which is not included in GP's estate, C remains the transferor. Recall that GC are C's children, thus, as to that portion where C is the transferor, there has been no GST transfer, since GC's are not skip persons (relative to C).

45. I.R.C. §§1014(a) and (b)(9). It should be noted that under I.R.C. §1014(b)(9) it is not necessary for the estate to pay an estate tax liability. All that is required is that the assets have to be included in GP's gross estate as a result of GP having a GPOA.

46. I.R.C. §671; Treas. Reg. §§1.671-2(e)(1); -2(e)(5); and -2(e)(6) (Example 9).

47. I.R.C. §§2041(a) and (b).

48. See Note 14.

49. Rev. Rul. 85-13,1985-1 C.B. 184.

50. An interesting question arises in the case where a gift is made to an irrevocable grantor trust, whether the basis of the property should be adjusted for any gift tax paid on the transferred property's appreciation pursuant to I.R.C. §1015(d)(6). For a discussion of this issue, s*ee*, Franklin, et al., *Never Pay Estate Taxes: The Annual Taxable Gifts Approach with a CLAT Remainder.*

51. *See*, Note 38 and accompanying text.

52. *See*, Notes 51and 52 and accompanying text.

53. Generally, at date of death, if assets are included in G2's estate, I.R.C. §1014(a) and 1014(b)(9) provide that basis will be the date of death value. Obviously, it would almost be impossible, if not impractical, to sell the assets on that day, thus, by the time the assets are sold (especially if they are sold on an open market), it is likely that the value on the date of sale will be different than the date of death value. Thus, there will generally be a modest gain or loss recognized on the sale.

54. *See* generally, I.R.C. §2511; Treas. Reg. §25.2511-2.

55. *See* "planning pointer" discussion below in Section VI.B.1.b)(2) (b)(ii) of this chapter.

56. For donees of the GPOA who live in states that impose a state estate tax, see, Note 36 for our discussion about the same.

57. For trust severances, *see generally*, I.R.C. §2642(a)(3); Treas. Reg. §26.2642-6.

58. I.R.C. §2642.

59. I.R.C. §2642(a)(3); Treas. Reg. §26.2642-6.

60. For rules on late allocations, see generally Treas. Reg. §26.2642-2(a)(2).

61. *See*, Blattmachr, *et al., Income Tax Effects of Termination of Grantor Trust Status by Reason of the Grantor's Death,* and Zaritsky *et al., Basis, Banal? Basic? Benign? Bewildering?*

62. I.R.C. §§677(a)(1) and (2); Treas. Reg. §§1.677-1(a) and -1(b).

63. *See* Notes 51and 52 and accompanying text.

64. *Crummey v. Comm'r.,* 397 F.2d 82 (9th Cir. 1968)

65. G2 can fund the POAST by using *Crummey* gifts. However, this is limited to the extent of the number of beneficiaries in the trust and the dollar amount of the annual exclusion. For instance, if there are 5 beneficiaries (who are G1 and G3s), in 2016 the total amount of annual exclusion gifts will be $70,000 (i.e., $14,000 × 5).

66. However, *see* Note 68 and accompanying text.

67. *See* Note 68 and accompanying text.

68. The POAST would be a grantor trust as to G2 during G2's lifetime. It should be noted that if G2 were married and G2's spouse was a beneficiary of the POAST for such spouse's lifetime, and should G2's spouse survive G2, that, depending upon G2's spouse's beneficial interest, the trust would be a grantor trust as to G2's spouse for such spouse's lifetime, too.

TRUSTS FOR UNIQUE ASSETS AND DIFFICULT SITUATIONS

CHAPTER 21

INTRODUCTION

What follows is a discussion on trusts for unique assets, with some discussion on difficult situations posed on trust administration. These issues include using trusts when beneficiaries have unique issues, such as financial problems or a history of addiction, as well as trusts that deal with unusual types of property, including animals and firearms. As the author of this chapter is licensed to practice law in Florida, some specific emphasis will be placed on Florida law. However, practitioners should consult their local laws before relying on some of the suggested planning described in this chapter.

BENEFICIARIES FACING UNIQUE ISSUES

This book is full with examples of ways to try to make sure that loved ones are provided for after death. Practitioners make specific provisions for the care of a client's children, parents, and favorite charities. Clients have the right to spell out in detail upon what terms and when their children will receive their money and who has the responsibility of making decisions for them. Clients can make a gift to charity and request that it be used to establish a scholarship for a specific class of individuals. Additionally, clients can even make provisions for payments to grandchildren that will be effective many years following his death.

Be aware, however, that if trust provisions attempt to unreasonably modify or control the lives of intended beneficiaries, these gifts may not be legally enforceable, depending on the laws of the state, how the courts interpret public policy, and the degree of control. Some questionable trust provisions include a gift to a public college to be used only for scholarships for a specific religious group; a gift to a child but only if he renounces all contact with the cult with which he is presently associated; and a gift in trust for a grandchild but only if she marries someone of the grantor's faith (compare that with a gift to a grandchild who is being raised in a different faith from that of the grantor, providing that the grandchild take at least one college course on the grantor's religion). If clients have strong feelings about a particular provision that he or she would like to place in trust, practitioners should strongly recommend that said provisions be researched for ease of use and applicability. The practitioner needs to understand the validity and enforceability of such provision in the governing law state of the trust.

Some clients have specific ideas and goals that go beyond these situations. Many of these ideas find their way into trusts, even though their enforcement may, in certain instances, be quite difficult. For example, leaving money to children or grandchildren, providing they do not smoke or use drugs or leave money to persons depending on their marital status. Many people may want to provide for a son-in-law or daughter-in-law, for example, especially if there has been a long and happy marriage, however, not if the son-in-law or daughter-in-law is not living with and married to their child at the time the gift becomes effective. In that case, a husband and wife could make a gift in trust to their daughter-in-law, providing that she is married to and living with their son when the second of them dies.

Unfortunately, many clients face serious day-to-day problem situations. One concern is how these situations will be handled after death. Chapter 10 discussed some of the ways that trusts can help solve the problems of caring for special needs children. Similar problems could arise in caring for children or other relatives who are dependent on drugs. Additionally, often clients have a brother or sister in serious financial difficulty whom the client has been giving financial assistance during his lifetime. The client might have a child who has joined a religious or political cult that would confiscate any funds given directly or for the benefit of the child in trust. The client might have a child or other relative who has broken the law or may very well do so in the near future. The client might have a son or daughter who is in the process of going through a second or third contested divorce with all of its inherent financial problems.

Although these problems will obviously not disappear after death—and no trustee will be able to deal with them with the same knowledge and background that the client has, oftentimes after years of practice—a trust may be the only plan that can be established to handle the problem situation in the best possible way when the grantor is no longer able to do so. The reason a trust is the preferable solution is that only through a trust can the grantor set money aside for the beneficiary, while at the same time give the trustee as much flexibility as possible to deal with whatever may arise.

Spendthrift Provisions

As a further precaution, the trust should contain a spendthrift provision, which prohibits the assignment of any interest or distributions from the trust to creditors of the beneficiary. That means a beneficiary could not go to Las Vegas and use his or interest in a trust as collateral. In most states, this will prevent general creditors from reaching any of the trust assets, and, in some states, it can bar a beneficiary's spouse from attacking the trust assets or claiming that they are marital property and therefore subject to the spouse's claim against the trust beneficiary's assets. An example of a spendthrift provision might resemble the following:

> The interest of any beneficiary of a trust created under this instrument is held pursuant to a spendthrift provision. A beneficiary may not transfer an interest in a trust created under this instrument in violation of the spendthrift provision, and a creditor or assignee of the beneficiary may not reach the interest or a distribution by the trustee before receipt of the interest or distribution by the beneficiary.[1]

Substance Abuse Issues

If the child in question has an alcohol or substance abuse problem, the trust might provide that only funds necessary for food, clothing, and shelter be disbursed—and that payments be made directly and only to the people providing the food, clothing, and shelter, not to the child. The trust can be set up to withhold trust assets until and unless two doctors are willing to certify that the child has been drug free for a specified period of time. Incentives could be provided in return for documenting that they have met specified "drug free periods" or for meeting other accomplishments important to the client. The issue with these types of trusts though is that the smart drug addict beneficiary could always find two doctors willing to certify such specific period of time as such "doctor shopping" has become commonplace. Additionally, unless the trustee is a corporate fiduciary, many individual trustees do not have the time or resources to follow a beneficiary's every move.

Family Disharmony

Chapters 16 and 17 discussed domestic asset protection trusts and offshore asset protection trusts. In the case of an unsettled marriage, the trust could provide only income for the child and specify in the event of a divorce that all income is to be paid to or for the benefit of the couple's children or to another child. This may prevent the divorcing spouse from reaching trust principal.

The possible solutions to difficult problems are almost endless if the practitioner is creative. For example, trustees can be instructed to reward or discourage behavior, such as:

- Achieving grades in school that are appropriate to the abilities of the beneficiary.

- Gainful full-time employment.

- Entrepreneurial endeavors in starting new businesses.

- charitable or volunteer work.

- Thrift and financial responsibility, such as regular savings and the avoidance of unnecessary debt.

- Regular religious worship (but see below).

- Abstinence from alcohol, drug, or other substance abuse, or promiscuous sexual behavior (although this may be difficult for the trustees to monitor and enforce).

Limits to Control

As previously noted, there are limits on "dead hand control," and there are some conditions that courts will not enforce on the grounds that the conditions violate public policy. These policy considerations will vary from state to state, however, courts will usually not enforce provisions which could disrupt or restrict family relationships (such as encouraging a divorce or discouraging marriages with persons of different religious, racial, or ethnic backgrounds) or restrict freedom of religion (such as encouraging or discouraging particular religious affiliations). A recent case is most illustrative of the outer limits of "dead hand control." In *In the Matter of the Estate of Kenneth E. Jameson, Deceased*,[2] the decedent's will provided the following statement in disinheriting his only living child:

> As an extremely loving and devoted parent, I found that the love, care and concern which I lavished on my daughter was not acknowledged or returned in any way by my daughter. Instead, she acted toward me with selfishness, manipulation, cruelty, and with abusiveness. My daughter . . . blatantly lied to and about me, acted with hatefulness and vindictiveness towards me, and was abusive and physically violent towards me. [Stacy's] shameful and hateful behavior towards me and her mother has brought me to my carefully considered decision that [Stacy] is to receive absolutely nothing from my estate.[3]

The decedent (along with his wife) had a non-existent relationship with their daughter after she married a man of the Jewish faith. They had no contact with their grandchildren. They left all of their money to charity. Mother predeceased father. On her father's death, the daughter received a copy of the will and subsequently filed suit against her father's estate. In her complaint, the daughter claimed that the statements contained in her father's will were incorrect and fabricated. She alleged that she was disowned solely because at that time, she was dating her future husband, who happened to be Jewish. She alleged that the statements in the will were completely untrue. Her cause of action in the complaint alleged that the will was invalid because it was the product of undue influence, religious discrimination, did not contain a clear intent to disinherit grandchildren and was libelous to the plaintiff. The daughter's complaint was dismissed and the court's dismissal was upheld on appeal.

Key to the discussion in this chapter is the case's commentary on the testator's testamentary intent. The court indicated that under New Jersey law, the motivation of a testator is not relevant to the validity of a decision to disinherit.[4] In New Jersey, an unreasonable and discriminatory purposes for disinheritance is not a reason to set aside a will. The key to this case is the absence of a statement of discriminatory reasoning and intent. The court noted that the will did not impose "any conditions related to [daughter's] disinheritance or upon the bequest to [charity] that violate public policy."[5]

It is the author's view that had the will in the *Jameson* case stated "I disinherit my daughter because she married someone Jewish," the daughter would have had a better ground on which to challenge. This case is applicable to the discussion of trusts. For example, in Florida, a trust can only be created for purposes that are lawful and not contrary to public policy. Thus, a trust with the clause "I make no provisions in this trust agreement for my daughter because she married someone Jewish" could be challenged. However, it should be noted in Canada that decisions have varied based on whether the disposition was in a testator's will as opposed to a grantor's trust.[6]

GUN TRUSTS

The disposition of a firearm at death is not as easy as putting the firearm on a statement of tangible personal property or leaving the firearm to a traditional terminating revocable trust. Traditional methods of transferring unique assets to an irrevocable may not be sufficient for a firearm. An additional caveat is that by typing in the words "gun" and combining it with "trust" in any online search engine, a typical search results in numerous confusing hits: create your own gun trust; safe gun trusts; frequently asked questions on guns; and probably the best hit of them all, "how attorneys lie to get money."[7] What is fact and what is fiction? What can an attorney do to dispose of a client's firearm during such client's lifetime and upon his death? What this section of the chapter is not a primer on the "right to bear arms" and the Second Amendment, a position piece on whether or not clients should own firearms, or an opinion piece on firearms. There are plenty of resources available on the internet which discuss the morality and use of firearms. There are even better scholarly articles on the second amendment, including some articles which discuss gun trusts and their evolution.[8]

The Uniform Trust Code does not specifically address assets such as firearms.[9] Additionally, state's trust laws are silent on the ownership of firearms. However, state's laws are not silent on the overall position and ownership of firearms. For example, Chapter 790, Florida Statutes, deals with weapons and firearms. Within Chapter 790 are various laws governing the regulation, possession and laws applicable to firearms and other weapons. Each state will have such statutes on its books. For those looking into basic gun and firearm ownership laws, it might seem a daunting task to review such a numerous collection of legal text. What is the everyday firearm owner or prospective owner to do?

Federal Laws Regarding Ownership and Transfer of Firearms

There are two major federal laws regulating firearms. Under the first major federal law, the National Firearms Act ("NFA"),[10] Congress sought to impose a tax on the making and transfer of specifically enumerated firearms, as well as those engaged in the sale, manufacturing and importing of such firearms.[11]

The NFA requires registration of all firearms with the Secretary of Treasury by "[e]ach manufacturer, importer, and maker shall register each firearm he manufactures, imports, or makes. Each firearm transferred shall be registered to the transferee by the transferor."[12] The NFA mandates that each person possessing a registered firearm must retain proof of registration, available to the Secretary of Treasury upon request.[13]

In addition to the NFA, the second major federal law, the Gun Control Act of 1968 (the "Act"),[14] regulates the interstate transportation of firearms.[15] A destructive device is defined TO include an exhaustive list of things including: bombs, grenades, rockets, missiles, mines, and other types of weapons either designed or intended for use in converting such device into a destructive device.[16] Additional terms, such as "shotgun," "rifle," "short-barreled rifle," and "antique firearm" are also defined with specificity within this Act.[17] The Act regulates unlawful, acts, licensing, penalties, remedies, concealed firearms, possession and prohibitions by certain individuals of firearms.[18] However, the Act indicates that it is not intent on taking away a State's right to regulate firearms, "unless there is a direct and positive conflict between such provision and the law of the State so that the two cannot be reconciled or consistently stand together."[19] The Act gives the U.S. Attorney General the right to "prescribe only such rules and regulations as are necessary

to carry out the provisions of this chapter. . . ."[20] As the other sections of the Act define certain terms and discuss particular situations, Section 922 of the Act is its teeth, declaring unlawful various actions pertaining to the sale of firearms within interstate commerce.[21] The penalties for violation of the unlawful acts in Section 922 of the Act are set out in Section 924 of the Act.[22]

The NFA is referred to as Title II, and the Act is referred to as Title I.[23] While the tax imposed by the NFA of $200 on the making and transfer of firearms has not changed since its inception, the substance of the NFA is "virtually unenforceable."[24] In 1968, the decision in *Haynes v. U.S.*[25] held that the Fifth Amendment privilege against self-incrimination was a full defense to prosecutions ". . . either for failure to register under §5841 or for possession of an unregistered firearm under §5851."[26] As such, the Act was passed to rectify the problematic system set out in the NFA to regulate firearms.[27] Today, the Bureau of Alcohol, Tobacco, Firearms and Explosives ("ATF") "issues firearms licenses and conducts firearms licensee qualification and compliance inspections," including "compliance inspections of existing licensees focus on assisting law enforcement to identify and apprehend criminals who illegally purchase firearms,"[28] while the Act (incorporating the Firearms Owners' Protection Act of 1986, the Brady Handgun Violence Prevention Act of 1993 and the NICS Improvement Act of 2008) regulates "interstate and foreign commerce in firearms, including importation, "prohibited persons", and licensing provisions.[29]

The Department of Justice published revisions, a "final rule," under 27 CFR part 479 applicable to machine guns, destructive devices and certain other firearms.[30] The revisions, effective July 13, 2016, are referred to as Rule 41F and discuss background checks for "Responsible Persons."[31] These revisions closed the so-called "gun show loophole." Rule 41F is important because it closed what effectively amounted to a "loophole" that allowed individuals, under the disguise of a trust, to purchase a firearm without the identification and background check requirements.[32]

There are two key definitions: a "person" and a "responsible person." A person is any "partnership, company, association, trust, corporation, including each responsible person associated with such an entity; an estate; or an individual."[33] A responsible person is:

In the case of an unlicensed entity, including any trust, partnership, association, company (including any Limited Liability Company (LLC)), or corporation, any individual who possesses, directly or indirectly, the power or authority to direct the management and policies of the trust or entity to receive, possess, ship, transport, deliver, transfer, or otherwise dispose of a firearm for, or on behalf of, the trust or legal entity. In the case of a trust, those persons with the power or authority to direct the management and policies of the trust include any person who has the capability to exercise such power and possesses, directly or indirectly, the power or authority under any trust instrument, or under State law, to receive, possess, ship, transport, deliver, transfer, or otherwise dispose of a firearm for, or on behalf of, the trust. Examples of who may be considered a responsible person include settlors/ grantors, trustees, partners, members, officers, directors, board members, or owners. An example of who may be excluded from this definition of responsible person is the beneficiary of a trust, if the beneficiary does not have the capability to exercise the powers or authorities enumerated in this section.[34]

Rule 41F requires responsible persons, of trusts or legal entities, to:

1. complete ATF form 5320.23 (the National Firearms Act Responsible Person Questionnaire); and

2. submit photographs and fingerprints when the trust or legal entity:

    a. files an application to make an NFA firearm; or

    b. is listed as the transferee on an application to transfer an NFA firearm.[35]

Additionally, all applications to make or transfer a firearm are required to be copied and "forwarded to the chief law enforcement officer (CLEO) of the locality in which the applicant/transferee or responsible person resides."[36]

Most importantly, section 479.90a has been newly created to guide executors through the disposition of firearms process from a decedent's estate:

The executor. . . may possess a firearm registered to a decedent during the term of probate without such possession being treated as a "transfer" as defined in §479.11. No later than the close of probate, the executor must submit an application to transfer the firearm to beneficiaries or other transferees in accordance with this section. If the transfer is to a beneficiary, the executor shall file an ATF Form 5 (5320.5), Application for Tax Exempt Transfer and Registration of Firearm, to register a firearm to any beneficiary of an estate in accordance with §479.90. The executor will identify the estate as the transferor, and will sign the form on behalf of the decedent, showing the executor's title (e.g., executor, administrator, personal representative, etc.) and the date of filing. The executor must also provide the documentation prescribed in paragraph (c) of this section.[37]

The Act, including newly enacted Rule 41F, is a crucial study for attorneys creating trusts for their clients, as well as attorneys whose clients express a desire to leave guns to certain persons at death. Under the Act, it is unlawful for a person to knowingly, or having reasonable cause to have known, sell a firearm or ammunition to certain persons, including, but not limited to: persons convicted of specific crimes such as stalking or domestic violence; fugitives; persons renouncing their U.S. citizenship; persons committed or adjudicated mentally incompetent; illegal aliens; drug addicts; or persons who are "under indictment for, or has been convicted in any court of, a crime punishable by imprisonment for a term exceeding one year (i.e., a felon).[38]

On the other hand, it is unlawful for certain persons "to ship or transport in interstate or foreign commerce, or possess in or affecting commerce, any firearm or ammunition; or to receive any firearm or ammunition which has been shipped or transported in interstate or foreign commerce" including, but not limited to: persons convicted of specific crimes such as stalking or domestic violence; fugitives; persons renouncing their U.S. citizenship; persons committed or adjudicated mentally incompetent; illegal aliens; drug addicts; or persons who are "under indictment for, or have been convicted in any court of, a crime punishable by imprisonment for a term exceeding one year (i.e., a felon).[39] Additionally, it is "unlawful for a person to purchase, own, or possess body armor, if that person has been convicted of a felony. . . ."[40]

The statutes combined make it particularly difficult to summarily leave assets in trust to just any person. We often hardly know ourselves, let alone those friends and loved ones whom we do not have minute to minute contact with, *i.e.*, the potential heirs and beneficiaries of a client's estate or trust. How would your client know if his best friend that he hunts with annually had been convicted of any of the aforementioned crimes unless the client actively sought out this information or was told by the friend? If a friend knows that he is going to be left firearms and would otherwise have no reason of knowing that he could not own a firearm, then what is the incentive to disclose the felony? Additionally, if you have inadvertently left a firearm in trust to an otherwise disallowed person, what duty does your executor or trustee have once it becomes time to transfer the firearm from the trust or estate to the beneficiary outright? While above we went over the specific laws: what effect do the laws have on creation of a trust; the beneficiary of a trust; and the trustee of the trust?

One case illustrates the problems associated with firearms where a trust was not used. In *Henderson v. U.S.*,[41] Henderson, a U.S. Border Patrol agent, was charged with the felony of distributing marijuana. The judge required Henderson to surrender all of his guns as a condition of his release on bail. Henderson complied with judge's requirement and the FBI took custody of his guns. Henderson was convicted of the felony offense of distributing marijuana. As a result of his conviction, Henderson was prevented from legally repossessing his firearms.

Henderson asked the FBI to transfer the guns to a friend who had agreed to purchase them for an unspecified price. The FBI denied his request. The FBI explained that the release of the firearms to the buyer would place Henderson in violation of Section 922(g) of the Act as it would amount to "constructive possession" of the guns. Henderson sought release of his firearms. The district court and 11th Circuit Court of Appeals ruled for the government.

On appeal to the Supreme Court, the issue was whether Section 922(g) of the Act categorically prohibits a court from approving a convicted felon's request to transfer his firearms to another person. The court indicated that the government's theory of constructive possession by Henderson wrongly conflated the right to possess a gun with another incident of ownership. The Court noted that the government's construction would prevent someone like Henderson from disposing of firearms even in ways that guarantee he never uses them again, solely since he played a part in selecting their transferee. The Court ruled 9-0 in favor of Henderson. But the moral of the story is had Henderson used a gun

trust, the trustee of the gun trust could have sold his guns without FBI or court involvement. So how does one create a gun trust?

Creation of a Gun Trust

How can your client safely and legally dispose of a firearm, in trust, to a beneficiary during the client's (grantor's) lifetime? How can the client safely and legally dispose of the firearm to a beneficiary at death? Or, to think of it another way, how can a client safely and legally dispose of [any] asset, in trust? The contents of a typical gun trust are no different than any other revocable trust, except for references and terms related to firearms and the Act.[42]

The grantor or gun owner creates a trust during his lifetime for his benefit, naming himself as a trustee.[43] The trust should make specific references to an intent of complying with not only the Gun Control Act, but also the National Firearms Act. It is also important to note in the trust's statement of intent that the trust is created specifically to comply with local, state and federal law on firearms in its administration and interpretation.

In order to properly accomplish its purposes, the gun trust should have successor trustees listed whom are eligible to own firearms themselves, in accordance with the Act. Since the grantor cannot predict the future, the trust should contain automatic removal language that indicates if a successor trustee, who, at the time he is to become trustee, is an ineligible trustee in accordance with the provisions of the Act, he is deemed to have predeceased the grantor. It is recommended that at least two qualifying successor trustees be named. Instead of naming successor trustees, a trust protector or trustee selector could be named in the trust to select successor trustees who are eligible to serve in accordance with the Act. It is the author's experience that corporate fiduciaries are unwilling to serve as trustee of a gun trust.

During the grantor's lifetime, the gun trust's benefit is that the grantor has a vehicle to own title to his firearms in case of incapacity, and also aids in inventorying the grantor's collection during life (using a "firearm schedule"). Often, the grantor will prepare a list of his firearms to accompany the creation of the gun trust.[44] During his lifetime, the grantor will leave himself with the power to amend the trust and add and/or remove additional property from the trust.

The gun trust gives the successor trustee broad language in order to deal with the grantor's firearms. This may include filling out the requisite transfer forms to transfer the firearms, reimbursement for shipping costs and/or reimbursement for travel costs to transport such firearms. The trustee should be given discretion to transfer firearms to beneficiaries, in accordance with local, state and federal law. If the grantor is going to name specific beneficiaries during his lifetime, he should ascertain that such beneficiary(ies) is able to own a firearm. The trust will give the trustee authority to ascertain whether such beneficiary can receive the firearm upon the grantor's death. The trust should make an alternate disposition of the firearm(s) in case a certain beneficiary is unable to own a firearm. If the trust has only one beneficiary, a charitable remainder beneficiary should be utilized.[45] The gun trust can leave the firearms in further trust for the ultimate beneficiary(ies), or provide an outright distribution of the firearms. However, if the firearms are of historical value, it would be recommended to utilize the gun trust in a dynastic trust type manner, thereby preserving the firearms for generations to come (bearing in mind the applicable law for the relevant jurisdiction regarding the rule against perpetuities).

A gun trust has limits. In *U.S. v. One (1) Palmetto State Armory PA-15 Machinegun Receiver/Frame*,[46] a trustee of a gun trust was banned from the possession of a machine gun. The trustee submitted applications on behalf of a trust for permission to make and register an M-16-style machine gun. The ATF explained in a letter to the trustee that his application was denied because he was prohibited by law from possessing a machine gun. The trustee claimed to be exempt from the prohibition on possessing machine guns because he had applied on behalf of a trust, which he argued was not a "person" covered by the Act. ATF explained that although a trust is not a "person" under the Act, a trust cannot legally make or hold property. Therefore, ATF considers the individual acting on behalf of the trust to be the proposed maker and possessor of the machine gun.

The appellate court ruled for the government. It opined that irrespective of whether the appellant was a trustee (as opposed to applying in his individual capacity), he is also a natural person and therefore prohibited from performing any of the acts forbidden of natural persons under the Act. The court noted that its holding is necessarily correct because to interpret the Act as the trustee suggests would allow any party—including convicted felons, who are expressly prohibited from

possessing firearms under Section 922(g)(1) of the Act—to avoid liability simply by placing a machine gun "in trust." It noted that had the trustee's argument been believed, any "individual, company, association, firm, partnership, society, or joint stock company" could lawfully possess a machine gun using this method. It added that all U.S. courts are in agreement on this issue: governments may restrict the possession of machine guns.

Expatriation

A final contingency is what to do with a gun trust where the grantor is considering expatriation? Transfers of firearms to a gun trust should be made before the grantor becomes a "prohibited person," *i.e.*, an expatriate. The gun trust would be drafted to ensure that if the grantor became a prohibited person under 18 U.S.C. section 922(g), the grantor would immediately cease to be a trustee and/or a beneficiary of the trust, and the trust would contain language prohibiting distributions of firearms to any prohibited person under any circumstances. Beneficiaries of such a gun trust who were not prohibited persons could still use the firearms held in the trust.

ANIMAL TRUSTS

If a client owns a dog, cat, or any domesticated animal for whom he or she cares a lot, such client may be concerned about what will happen to the pet after his death. Generally, a grantor cannot name a dog, cat, or any domesticated animal as a beneficiary of a trust, because an animal cannot own property or sue in court, and so cannot receive money from the trust or sue in court to enforce the trust. However, the grantor can name an individual as a beneficiary with the request that the money from the trust used to take care of the pet. Referred to as an "honorary" trust, this is an excellent solution—perhaps the only solution. Through a trust, the grantor can leave a friend (or even a veterinarian or a home that cares for pets) a specific sum of money that is to be used for his pet's care, comfort and room and board during its lifetime and to pay for its burial when the animal dies.

The grantor can go into as much detail as he or she wishes concerning the particulars of the pet's care. However, in establishing a trust for his pets—as in most trust situations—the client must be sure to explain plans with the proposed trustee to be certain that the trustee will accept the responsibility of caring for the pet and complying with the trust provisions. There are companies which offer services for a fixed rate that include the preparation of a trust documents, customized lifestyle considerations, the identification of appropriate caregivers, and monitoring the pet's care once the trust is funded. The trust arrangement is transferable to various animals throughout the owner's lifetime to include all pets in the owner's household. The company claims trust fund monies are used solely to fund the care of the pet and are maintained in an FDIC-insured bank account for the life of the pet.

Previously, it was thought that honorary trust provisions were not legally binding on the trustee. Now, almost all states have legislation authorizing the creation of trusts for the care of animals.[47] For example, under Florida law:

1) A trust may be created to provide for the care of an animal alive during the settlor's lifetime. The trust terminates on the death of the animal or, if the trust was created to provide for the care of more than one animal alive during the settlor's lifetime, on the death of the last surviving animal.

2) A trust authorized by this section may be enforced by a person appointed in the terms of the trust or, if no person is appointed, by a person appointed by the court. A person having an interest in the welfare of the animal may request the court to appoint a person to enforce the trust or to remove a person appointed.

3) Property of a trust authorized by this section may be applied only to the intended use of the property, except to the extent the court determines that the value of the trust property exceeds the amount required for the intended use. Except as otherwise provided in the terms of the trust, property not required for the intended use must be distributed to the settlor, if then living, otherwise as part of the settlor's estate.[48]

Florida's statute, like many states with trust legislation for the care of animals, is based on the Uniform Trust Code ("UTC").[49] In the Comments to Section 408 of the UTC, the drafters of the UTC note that unlike common law honorary trusts, a trust for the care of animal is valid and enforceable.[50] The Comments go on to break down each subsection of Section 408.

One of the key issues is what happens if an animal is pregnant? The Comments to Section 408 indicate that:

A trust for the care of an animal may last for the life of the animal. While the animal will ordinarily be alive on the date the trust is created, an animal may be added as a beneficiary after that date as long as the addition is made prior to the settlor's death. Animals in gestation but not yet born at the time of the trust's creation may also be covered by its terms.[51]

Thus, under Section 408, the grantor could specifically identify the animal beneficiary in order to avoid providing for other animals which could potentially be born following the grantor's death (i.e., if the grantor has no benefit or enjoyment from the specific animal, then why provide for its costs).[52]

It is important that the grantor have a charity, continuing trust or beneficiary in mind to leave the animal trust property to upon the animal's death. The issue is that under the default statutory framework, if no beneficiary is named, the money would be devised to the grantor-decedent's estate (which may or may not be what the grantor intended).[53]

It should be noted that this area of the law is rife with abuse. If an improper or morally bankrupt person is appointed as trustee of the trust or animal caretaker for the animal, the animal may never come into contact with the money.[54] However, as with any trust, the trustee is subject to a fiduciary duty (which varies on a state-by-state basis).[55] In Florida for example, the trustee will be expected to administer the trust impartially, prudently, and solely in the interests of the beneficiaries.[56]

A pet trust should not be used for every type of animal. For certain animals, such as cattle, certain horses, racing dogs and other types of animals involved in a business (such as a circus), a pet trust is not the ideal vehicle for disbursing funds for an animal's care upon the owner's death. For example, a horse involved in thoroughbred racing may have multiple owners or necessitate a sale upon the owner's death due to multiple factors unavailable to the grantor at the time of trust creation: when should the horse be sold; when should the horse be retired; should the horse have a different trainer, etc. A limited liability company, corporation or some other ownership structure should be sought during the grantor's lifetime.

TAX IMPLICATIONS

An additional consideration for a pet trust is its federal tax treatment. While states recognize pet trusts and pets as beneficiaries, the Internal Revenue Service does not.[57] In Revenue Ruling 76-486, advice was requested whether a deduction was allowed with respect to a charitable remainder interest in three different situations. Of note:

> By the terms of the decedent's will, executed January 1, 1977, the decedent devised and bequeathed the residuary estate in trust. The trust provides that the trustee is to pay monthly a sum certain in the amount of 10x dollars (which is not less than 5 percent of the initial fair market value of all the property placed in trust) for the care of the decedent's pet animal. At the death of the pet animal, the trust is to terminate and the remainder is to be transferred to or for the use of a specified charitable institution, as described in sections 170(c), 2055(a), and 2522(a) of the Code. The trust otherwise qualifies as a charitable remainder annuity trust described in section 664(d) of the Code. The decedent was a resident of State X. The laws of State X specifically permit a bequest in trust for the lifetime of a pet animal where the funds are to be used for the care of a pet animal.[58]

The IRS ruled that although the trust was valid and enforceable under state law, the care of the decedent's animal did not meet the requirements of the Internal Revenue Code specific to the definition of a "person," which would control whether the animal could have been defined as a "beneficiary" for purposes of the trust qualifying for the deduction for a charitable remainder interest.[59]

Another point to note from Revenue Ruling 76-486 is the discussion in Situation 3:

> The facts are the same as those of Situation 1, except that the decedent was a resident of State Z instead of State X. In State Z, the interest of an animal in a trust is void at its inception and a vested remainder designated to succeed the trust will be accelerated to a present interest. Under the laws of State Z, the accelerated present interest is deemed to have passed from the decedent directly to charity.[60]

In its ruling, the IRS noted:

> Since the trust for the decedent's pet animal is void under the laws of State Z because the duration of the trust is measured by the life of an animal, the remainder interest is accelerated and a present interest is vested. The present interest, acquired under the laws of State Z, constitutes an interest inherited from the decedent for Federal tax purposes. Cf. Bel v. United States, 452 F.2d 603 (5th Cir. 1971). Inasmuch as the interest passing to the charitable beneficiary at the death of the decedent is a present interest rather than a remainder interest, the requirements of section 2055(e)(2) are not applicable. Therefore, the value of the interest that passed directly from the decedent to the charity at the time of the decedent's death is allowed as a deduction under section 2055(a) of the Code.[61]

The key to this particular part of the Ruling is the discussion of state law as it pertains to the measuring life of an animal. As previously noted, most states allow for the creation of a pet trust. However, care should be taken in moving the *situs* of a pet trust to another jurisdiction to avoid an argument that the pet trust is void, particularly with reference to the measuring life of such animal.

Since its issuance, Revenue Ruling 76-486 is cited every time an article on pet trusts is published.[62] When drafting a lifetime or testamentary pet trust, care must be taken in explaining the federal tax implications to the grantor.

CHAPTER ENDNOTES

1. *See e.g.*, Fla. Stat. §736.0502(2)-(3)

2. *In the Matter of Estate of Kenneth E. Jameson, Deceased*, unpublished (NJ App., Aug. 12, 2016).

3. *Id.*

4. *Id.* (citing In re Blake's Will, 21 N.J. 50, 57 (1956) ("If capacity, formal execution, and volition appear, the will of the most impious man must stand, unless there is something not in the motives which led to the disposition, but in the actual disposition, against good morals or against public policy." (quoting Den d. Trumbull v. Gibbons, 22 N.J.L. 117, 153 (Sup. Ct. 1849))).

5. *Id.*

6. *Compare Canada Trust Co. v Ontario Human Rights Commission* (1990), 69 DLR (4th) 321, *with Spence v BMO Trust Company*, 2016 ONCA 196.

7. *See e.g.*, Firearm Concierge, "The Truth About Gun Trusts – and How Attorneys Lie to Get your Money," Jan. 26, 2014, available at www.thetruthaboutguns.com/2014/01/firearmconcierge/truth-gun-trusts-attorneys-lie-get-money/ (last visited Sept. 17, 2016).

8. *See e.g.*, Tritt, "Dispatches from the Trenches of America's Great Gun Trust Wars, 108 Nw. U. L. Rev. 743 (2014); Kopel, "Does the Second Amendment Protect Firearms Commerce?" 127 Harv. L.

Rev. F. 230 (Apr. 11, 2014); Johnson, *et. all*, "Firearms Law and the Second Amendment: Regulations, Rights, and Policy" (2012).

9. *See* National Conference of Commissioners on Uniform State Laws, "Uniform Trust Code," Jan. 15, 2013, available at www.uniformlaws.org/shared/docs/trust_code/utc_final_rev2010.pdf.

10. Pub. L. No. 73-474, 48 Stat. 1236 (codified at I.R.C. ch. 53) (June 26, 1934).

11. *See* ATF, "National Firearms Act," June 23, 2016, available online at: www.atf.gov/rules-and-regulations/national-firearms-act (last visited Sept. 18, 2016).

12. 26 U.S.C. §5841.

13. *See* 26 U.S.C. §5841(e).

14. Pub. L. No. 90-618, 82 Stat. 1213 (codified as amended at 18 U.S.C. §§921–931 (2012)).

15. *See* 18 U.S.C. §926A.

16. *See* 18 U.S.C. §921(a)(4)(A)-(C).

17. *See* 18 U.S.C. §921(a).

18. *See* 18 U.S.C. Chap. 44, *et. seq.*

19. 18 U.S.C. §927.

20. 18 U.S.C. §926.

21. *See* 18 U.S.C. §922.

22. *See* 18 U.S.C. §924.

23. *See* ATF, *supra note* ____.

24. *Id.*

25. 390 U.S. 85 (1968).

26. *Id.* at 95-100.

27. *See* ATF, *supra note* ____.

28. ATF, "Firearms," www.atf.gov/firearms (last visited Sept. 18, 2016).

29. ATF, "Gun Control Act of 1968," www.atf.gov/rules-and-regulations/gun-control-act (last visited Sept. 18, 2016).

30. *See* 27 CFR Part 479 (Jan. 15, 2016), available at www.gpo.gov/fdsys/pkg/FR-2016-01-15/pdf/2016-00192.pdf.

31. *See* e.g., ATF, "FINAL Rule 41F – Background Checks for Responsible Persons – Effective July 13 2016," Sept. 22, 2016, www.atf.gov/rules-and-regulations/final-rule-41f-background-checks-responsible-persons-effective-july-13#Who%20is%20a%20Responsible%20Person (last visited Oct. 31, 2016) ["ATF on 41"].

32. *Id.*

33. 27 CFR part 479; §479.11.

34. *Id.*

35. *See* ATF on 41, *supra note* ____.

36. *Id.*

37. 27 CFR part 479; §479.90a(a).

38. 18 U.S.C. §922(d).

39. 18 U.S.C. §922(g).

40. 18 U.S.C. §931(a).

41. 575 U.S. ___, 135 S. Ct. 1780; 191 L. Ed. 2d 874 (2015).

42. *See* Chapter ____ for a discussion on revocable trusts in general.

43. *See* Tritt, *supra note* ____ at 743 (indicating that the grantor cannot be the sole trustee and sole beneficiary which would otherwise merge the interests, thereby terminating the trust and frustrating the trust's purposes). It should be noted that if the trust is not transferring firearms during the grantor's lifetime and is merely used to hold title to an owner's firearms until his or her death, arguably the doctrine should not be present and is analogous to transferring assets into a revocable trust during the client's lifetime.

44. This is analogous to completing a Schedule "A" upon creation of a revocable trust or simultaneously executing a statement of tangible personal property when creating a will.

45. Ideally a beneficiary such as the National Rifle Association, *i.e.*, an organization that can properly dispose of the firearm.

46. 822 F.3d 136 (3d Cir. 2016).

47. "Pet trusts: Caring for a pet that outlives its owner," AVMA (March 2014), available online at: www.avma.org/Advocacy/StateAndLocal/Pages/sr-pet-trusts.aspx (last visited Aug. 31, 2016).

48. Fla. Stat. §736.0408.

49. Unif. Tr. Code §408.

50. Unif. Tr. Code §408, cmt.

51. *Id.*

52. Fla. Stat. §736.0408(1).

53. *See e.g.*, Fla. Stat. §736.0408(3)

54. *See e.g.*, Marsh, *Dachsund robbed of $100k trust fund: lawsuit*, N.Y. Post, July 28, 2016, *available online at:* nypost.com/2016/07/28/dachsunds-100k-trust-fund-stolen-by-late-owners-friend-suit/ (last visited Aug. 31, 2016); Buckley, *Cosseted Life and Secret End of a Millionaire Maltese*, N.Y. Times, June 9, 2011, *available online at:* www.nytimes.com/2011/06/10/nyregion/leona-helmsleys-millionaire-dog-trouble-is-dead.html?_r=0 (last visited Aug. 31, 2016). *See also* Suzdaltsev, *Why Rich People Set Up Trust Funds for Their Pets*, Vice, Aug. 1, 2016, *available online at:* www.vice.com/read/why-rich-people-set-up-trust-funds-for-their-pets (last visited Aug. 31, 2016).

55. *See e.g.*, Fla Stat. §§736.0801-.0804.

56. *Id.*

57. Rev. Rul. 76-486, 1976-2 C.B. 192.

58. *Id.* All reference to the Code are to the Internal Revenue Code of 1954.

59. *Id.*

60. *Id.*

61. *Id.*

62. *See* Hoyt & AuMiller, "Can You Trust Your Pet? A Primer on Florida Pet Trusts," 88 Fla. Bar J. 12 (Nov. 2014); Hirschfeld, "Protect Your Pet's Future: Pet Trusts and Pet Protection Agreements," NAEPC J. of Est. & Tax Planning (3d Q., 2014), *available online at:* www.naepc.org/journal/issue19f.pdf; Zenov & Ruiz-Gonzalez, "Trusts for Pets," 79 Fla. Bar. J. 22 (Dec. 2005); J. Alan Jensen, "Tax and Estate Planning Involving Pets: Stupid Pet Tricks for the IRS and FIDO, Aug. 1, 2000 *available online at:* www.hklaw.com/publications/Tax-and-Estate-Planning-Involving-Pets-Stupid-Pet-Tricks-for-the-IRS-and-FIDO-08-01-2000/.

PLANNING FOR BLENDED FAMILIES

CHAPTER 22

INTRODUCTION

There are many similarities and significant differences in the planning for traditional first marriage couples than planning for unmarried couples, remarried couples without children, and remarried couples with children from prior relationships (hereafter sometimes referred to as "blended" families). Usually estate planners tend to focus on planning for the traditional couple with children born from a first marriage. When blended families seek advice, many professionals approach the planning for these couples and families from the perspective of their experience with traditional couples and families. Treating blended families the same as first married couples may produce an estate plan that does not address the blended family's unique issues and may ultimately result in missed tax planning opportunities and contention among family members and heirs. With the changing demographics, blended families may soon far outnumber traditional couples. For this reason, you need to become much more familiar with the planning opportunities and pitfalls that exist regarding planning for blended families. Most importantly, with the uncertainty regarding the continued existence of the estate tax, the non- tax planning required for these blended families may produce a client development opportunity. While trusts are integral in planning for blended families, this chapter will also discuss the overall planning process where a blended family is your client.

PLANNING FOR TRADITIONAL AND BLENDED FAMILIES

Most couples, whether traditional or blended, have similar trust planning goals. An individual first and foremost will want his or her dispositive wishes fulfilled. Secondary goals will generally include reducing estate taxes and avoiding probate. Estate planners, especially in trust planning for blended families, must keep these goals, particularly the satisfaction of the client's dispositive wishes, upper most in his or her mind. Estate planners sometimes tend to let the tax issues drive a trust plan to the detriment of the client's other goals, the achievement of which may in fact be more important than reducing estate taxes.

Traditional and Remarried Couples vs. Other Blended Families

Traditional couples and remarried couples have distinct advantages over other couples. The institution of marriage has always been highly regarded by American society. In the 1888 case of *Maynard v. Hill*,[1] Justice Field defined marriage as "creating the most important relationship in life, as having more to do with the morals and civilization of people than any other institution." Due to society's reverence for the institution of marriage, the law confers many rights and benefits on married couples that are unavailable to other couples (other than the Federal Income Tax "marriage penalty"). Rarely does the law distinguish between first married couples and remarried couples in bestowing these rights and benefits.

Rights and Benefits.

WHICH MARRIAGES ARE RECOGNIZED

The legislature of each state has the right to prescribe what constitutes a valid marriage and thereby who will marry.

State legislatures also have the power to decide if a "Common Law" or "Informal" Marriage should be recognized as a legal marriage. Mere cohabitation by an opposite-sex couple does not constitute a common law marriage. Generally, to be recognized as a common law marriage, in a state that recognizes common law marriages, the couple must:

- be over eighteen years of age;

- have manifested an intent to be husband and wife (own joint property, filed a joint income tax return); and

- hold themselves out to the public as husband and wife.[2]

Due to the increased cohabitation by unmarried opposite-sex couples, several states have changed the existing statutes recognizing common law marriages. Most statutes "grandfather" common law marriages that existed on the date of the statutory change, but deny recognition to relationships that would have qualified for common law marriage treatment, where such qualifications were met, after that effective date of the change to the law.

Conflicts of Law

First Restatement (Second) of Conflict of Law, 283, states that "a marriage is valid everywhere if the requirements of the marriage laws of the state where the marriage takes place are met, except in rare instances."[3] These rare instances include situations where recognition of the marriage would go against strong public policy.

IRS Position

The current position of the IRS is that it will recognize a relationship as a valid marriage, if the applicable state does so. Following Revenue Ruling 2013-17,[4] the IRS makes no distinction between same-sex or opposite-sex marriages.

PLANNING FOR REMARRIED COUPLES

For purposes of this discussion, a remarried couple is one where at least one of the partners has at least one child prior to the marriage, whose natural parent is not the other partner. This classification of remarried couples may include couples, where neither couple has actually ever been married and may not include remarried couples where neither party has had a child or children in his or her previous marriage. The following discussion of planning for remarried couples may also apply to marriages where both partners have no children and desire to have their respective assets left to their respective families.

Relying on simple wills (so called "I love you wills" or "he who lives longest wins") is insufficient in 2019 where a remarried couple is involved. Often remarried couples may sign a prenuptial agreement (also called an antenuptial agreement) where the parties predetermine estate planning outcomes such as the minimum amount of money each spouse will receive upon death. Important for trust planning is that oftentimes remarried couples, where one spouse is wealthier than the other, will contract that the wealthier spouse shall create a testamentary marital trust for the benefit of the less wealthy spouse, with the wealthier spouse's children as the remainder beneficiaries of this marital trust. This can be done using the wealthier spouse's revocable trust. The issue can become what happens if the spouses divorce; does the wealthier spouse have to change his or her revocable trust? The short answer is yes, the revocable trust should be revised to remove the divorced spouse. But if properly drafted, a revocable (and even irrevocable) trust will not have to be revised if the definition of the term "spouse" is revised to provide that a spouse shall have predeceased in the event of a filing for divorce or prolonged separation (not caused by medical or incapacity reasons).

Assets Subject to Probate vs. Assets Includible in Taxable Estate

An asset may be included in the decedent's estate for death tax purposes, but not be includible in the probate estate. For example, the decedent's assets held in joint tenancy, in a bank account, or in a funded revocable living trust will be included in the decedent's estate for tax purposes, but are not subject to probate. Moreover, if the decedent retained any of the incidents of ownership in a life insurance policy on the decedent's life, or transferred such ownership within three years of death, the proceeds will be includible in the decedent's estate for tax purposes,[5] but if payable to a beneficiary other than the decedent's estate, the proceeds will not be subject to probate. Assets which have been gifted by the decedent in such a way that the decedent retained a prohibited right or power will also be includible in the taxable estate, but not in the probate estate.[6] It is important to keep in mind that avoiding probate does not necessarily avoid estate taxes. It is also important to keep in mind that these techniques should not be utilized without thorough evaluation, especially by blended families, as they may produce unintended results.

Other Methods of Avoiding Probate

Trusts are not the only way to avoid probate. There are a number of methods for planning an estate that will avoid the probate process and the disadvantages regularly associated with such process, without causing any great risk that the asset or proceeds will not be distributed as the decedent desired. The remainder of this section reviews those important alternatives.

Joint Ownership with Rights of Survivorship. Ownership of real and personal property in joint tenancy is the most common method of avoiding probate. Joint tenancy is an estate in real or personal property held by two or more persons jointly with rights to share in its enjoyment. Upon the death of a joint tenant, the entire estate passes immediately to the surviving joint tenant or tenants. The survivor(s) automatically own(s) the entire asset without the need for probate or any other form of court intervention. The death certificate of the deceased joint owner is all that is necessary to establish the title of the surviving joint tenant(s). Often there is a presumption against the creation of a joint tenancy in real or personal property other than bank accounts, unless the legal instrument transferring the property states that the property is conveyed or transferred in joint tenancy. The safest way to establish joint tenancy is to state clearly on the deed, assignment, or other document creating title, "in joint tenancy," "as joint tenants," or "as joint tenants with right of survivorship and not as tenants in common." The absence of such language will ordinarily create a tenancy in common, which does not have the survivorship feature. A joint tenant's share of the estate may be conveyed by a joint tenant at any time, thereby terminating the joint tenancy. If the joint tenants cannot agree on how to divide the property, either may bring a partition suit and ask the court to divide the property. No one can destroy or affect the joint tenancy or prevent the entire interest owned by the deceased joint tenant from passing to the survivor.

Joint Tenancy. The following summarizes the advantages and disadvantages of joint tenancies:

Advantages

- Joint tenancies are easily understood.

- Joint tenancy can be used to avoid probate, although joint tenancy property is required to be included in the estate tax return.

- Joint tenancy property is often free from the claims of creditors of the deceased joint tenant if no prior lien was attached.

Disadvantages

- Joint tenancy property cannot be passed by the will of the joint tenant dying first; instead, the property passes to, and is subject to disposition by, the surviving tenant. The estate may be deprived of liquid funds necessary to pay death costs, claims, and taxes.

- Joint tenancy property may be caught up in discord between spouses because of the inability to reach agreement on management of the property and the right of noncontributing spouse to acquire one-half of the property through partition or severance.

- If the joint tenancy property is subject to a mortgage, the property will pass to the surviving joint tenant, but the estate may be required to pay the mortgage out of the residue, thus frustrating the decedent's family giving plan.

- Creditors of either joint tenant may attach the person's interest in the property during life.

- There may be unfavorable gift and estate tax consequences depending on the specific facts of each case.

Tax Issues

There are many tax issues and traps for the unwary that develop from joint ownership with rights of survivorship, including the following:

- The creation of a joint tenancy between spouses does not create a taxable gift because of the unlimited marital deduction.

- The creation of a joint tenancy with a non-spouse creates a taxable gift when the contributions are unequal. When a donor conveys to himself or herself and a donee as joint tenants and either party has the right to sever the interest, there is a gift to the donee in the amount of one- half of the value of the property. The gift usually occurs when the non-contributor claims or takes a portion of the joint interest.

- In the case of the property held in joint tenancy between spouses, only one-half of the value is included in a deceased joint tenant's estate. The deceased's one-half interest acquires a stepped-up basis. Compare this with states recognizing community property where both halves acquire a stepped-up basis. This adjustment to the surviving spouse's basis is a major incentive for classifying property as community property, and creates complex tax issues when moving from a community property state. All of Wisconsin, Washington, Texas, New Mexico, Nevada, Louisiana, Idaho, California and Arizona are community property states. Alaska has an opt-in community property statute.[7] Currently Alaska, South Dakota and Tennessee permit married couples to create a community property trust.[8] For an in-depth discussion on community property trusts see Chapter 4.

- In the case of property held in joint tenancy with a non-spouse, termination may trigger gift tax consequences. The entire interest of the property is included in the estate of the joint tenant who dies first, unless the estate is able to prove the amount of consideration furnished by the survivor.

- The contribution of the survivor must not be traceable to the decedent. There is an exception where the property was acquired by the decedent through inheritance.

Additionally, use of joint tenancy may frustrate other tax planning. For example, use of joint tenancy can result in over-qualification of the marital deduction, resulting in property being taxed a second time.

INSURANCE, SAVINGS, AND RETIREMENT PLANS AND ANNUITIES

Insurance policies, annuity contracts, profit-sharing and pension plan accounts, Keogh plans, and individual retirement accounts (IRAs) are just some examples of assets that may be passed by contract, agreement, or beneficiary designation and avoid probate. Contingent beneficiaries should be named in the event the primary beneficiary named does not survive to receive the benefit. Mistake and neglect in properly designating and changing beneficiaries result in many problems in estate administration. Many beneficiary designations are made and forgotten in the files of insurance companies and banks. Later marriages, divorce, births, deaths, financial needs, and estate planning goals are not taken into consideration. Imagine the surprise when a former spouse turns up as the beneficiary after a bitter divorce (In many states divorce acts to treat the former spouse as predeceased in any existing will or trust agreement, however this does not usually remove the former spouse as a beneficiary on non-probate assets) or an after-born child is forgotten. Beneficiary designations should always be signed and reviewed when any family or planning changes occur. If no beneficiary designation exists, most policies, plans, or accounts have an automatic designation. If your estate is large enough to be subject to federal estate taxes, coordinate the designation with tax planning.

Payable on Death Accounts

In most states an individual may enter into a contract with a bank or other institution authorized to receive money whereby the proceeds of the owner's account may be payable to another person upon the owner's death, notwithstanding the provisions of his or her will. Such accounts as "payable on death" or "payable on the death of" may be abbreviated to "P.O.D." During the depositor's lifetime, he or she has the sole control of the account and may withdraw it or change the beneficiary at will. From a tax and estate planning point of view, this form of holding title is similar to a bank account in joint tenancy created with one tenant's separate funds. The outstanding difference is that the non-contributing party (and his or her creditors) has no right of withdrawal during the depositor's lifetime. If the P.O.D. trust is not revoked during the depositor's lifetime, the beneficiary will receive the proceeds on the death of the depositor.

Transfer-on-Death Deed

Some states have enacted legislation to provide for a transfer-on-death deed (in Florida, an "enhanced life estate deed" or "lady bird" deed), adding to the selection of methods to avoid probate administration of estates, which include payable-on-death bank accounts, joint ownership of personal and real property with rights of survivorship, transfer on death designation for securities, and beneficiary designation for life insurance and qualified retirement plans. The most important advantage of a transfer-on-death (TOD) deed is that the beneficiary or beneficiaries have no interest in the property during the lifetime of the owner of the interest.

The interest of the named transfer- on-death beneficiary is not subject to attachment by such beneficiary's creditors, is not transferable through the estate of the named transfer-on- death beneficiary if such beneficiary precedes the owner's death, and the spouse of the named transfer-on-death beneficiary has no interest in the property during the life of the owner of the interest. The owners of the interest may change or revoke the deed, and may sell or do anything with the property during the owner's life without the consent or signature of the designated transfer-on-death beneficiary.

To change the designated transfer-on-death beneficiary or add a new beneficiary, the owner need only execute another deed in which a new or no transfer-on-death beneficiary is named. Generally, the owner of real property may create a transfer-on-death interest in either the entire or any separate interest in the property. Such interest may be designated to one or more individuals including the owner (grantor).

Finally, such deed need not be supported by consideration and need not be delivered to the transfer-on-death beneficiary to be effective.

TRUSTS

QTIP Trusts

Remarried couples have the perfect tool, as opposed to other blended families, for planning their estates. A Qualified Terminal Interest Property Trust ("QTIP") allows an individual to provide for his or her surviving spouse, while still controlling the ultimate distribution of the assets contained in the trust. While an in depth discussion on QTIP trusts can be found in Chapter 8, briefly QTIP also qualifies for the unlimited marital deduction, if requirements are met.

The basic requirements are that the surviving spouse must be the only beneficiary of the trust during his or her lifetime and the spouse must receive at least all the income from the trust for life. In most states income is defined as interest and dividends but not capital gains. Due to the manipulation of income that may be possible, the choice of Trustee should be carefully considered. One option is to have the surviving spouse and one of the decedents children act as Co-Trustees. The client may wish to structure the trust as an "income only" trust, particularly if the surviving spouse is likely to enter a nursing home.

Note that placing all assets in trust for the surviving spouse, where the trust allows for principal distributions for the surviving spouse's health, maintenance and support, may deprive the children of any inheritance.

QTIP Trusts also can be used during life to equalize assets, in order not to waste a "poorer spouse's" credit. An in depth discussion on inter vivos QTIP trusts can be found in Chapter 9.

Credit Shelter - QTIP Trust Plan

Generally, a client's estate plan is structured as a credit shelter trust, so as to take advantage of both the Unified Credit Amount and the unlimited marital deduction. In the case of a remarried couple, the first trust to be funded on the predeceased spouse's death should be structured as a QTIP. Many times it turns out the first trust to be funded on the predeceased spouse's death has been structured as an Outright Marital Trust or a Power of Appointment Trust, thereby giving the surviving spouse complete control. This mistake is usually made by either an inexperienced estate planner or an estate planner who is only focusing on obtaining tax saving and not on the family situation.

In structuring a credit shelter-QTIP trust plan, consideration should be given to either distributing the trust assets to the decedent's children (subject to any state elective share law) or holding it for the children's benefit, even if the spouse survives. The needs of the surviving spouse should be considered, but so should the age of the spouse in relation to the ages of the children. The client may wish to only give a portion of the trust assets to the children, or on the other hand, especially in a larger estate, the client may not want to maximize the marital deduction. With the changing Unified Credit Amount, careful drafting is necessary to avoid unintended results

Life Insurance and IRAs in Trusts

In some situations so as not to complicate the drafting of the client's trust agreement, life insurance and/or Individual Retirement Accounts (IRAs) can be left directly to the children or to a trust for their benefit. Careful consideration should be given to both the income and estate tax consequence of such an arrangement. If the client has a taxable estate, the life insurance should be owned by an irrevocable trust to minimize and/or eliminate the transfer tax consequence. An Irrevocable Life Insurance Trust (referred to as an "ILIT") can leave a much greater amount of money to the children, while still maximizing the marital deduction. Leaving an IRA directly to the children generally will result in continued income tax deferral, and may attain income tax savings, if the children are in lower brackets. (Qualified Plans at many companies will make only deferred payments over the life of the surviving spouse, therefore naming the children as beneficiaries of such plans may result in income tax acceleration. In addition, in order to name children as beneficiaries of such a plan may require the spouse's consent.)

One benefit of designating the children as beneficiaries of the client's IRA or as beneficiaries of the client's life insurance (not owned by an ILIT), is that the client can change the beneficiary without the expense of redrafting the estate planning documents. However, the client should keep you informed to avoid any unintended results.

Anticipating Conflicts Using "Anti-hovering" Money

Whether a client leaves a portion of the credit shelter trust or other assets to his or her children, or makes them the beneficiaries of life insurance or other non-probate assets, it is a good idea to leave something to the children, even if the spouse survives. This gesture may minimize potential conflict between the spouse and the children. It may keep the children from "hovering", (i.e., waiting for the spouse to die to inherit what they feel is rightfully theirs).

Funded Trusts

In some states it is possible to disinherit a spouse. Normally the statutory spousal election only applies to probate assets. Anything that passes outside of probate is not subject to that election. Making sure that all assets avoid probate will, in effect, disinherit a spouse. It may be difficult to transfer real estate to a trust without the knowledge of the other spouse, even if the real estate is only held in the trust grantor's name due to dower, homestead and/or community property rights which exist in some states. A fully funded trust may be an alternative to a prenuptial agreement (only for death not divorce) in these states, especially if the trust is fully funded prior to the marriage.

PLANNING FOR NON-MARRIED COUPLES

Some opposite-sex and same-sex couples choose not to marry for a number of reasons. Previously divorced clients may be marriage shy. Older individuals may not want to risk their assets should the other spouse enter a nursing home. They may not want to lose social security or other benefits that may result should they remarry. The couple may not want to be subject to the income tax "Marriage Penalty." Same-sex couples were previously prevented from marrying. The estate planning for these couples can be very similar to the estate planning for married couples, except that the tax benefits and priority rights do not exist. These couples may resemble traditional couples in the fact that they have children together and there are no children outside this relationship. They may resemble remarried couples in that one or both have children from prior marriages.

Using simple wills and/or revocable trust structure that pour outright in these situations may leave the estate plan subject to attack by the natural objects of the decedent's bounty, those who would have inherited had the decedent died without a will. The surviving partner will not have any statutory protection. (If there are only children from this union, this probably will not be an issue.) A partner's will may be subject to claims, by family members, of undue influence by the other partner. Caution must be used in following all formalities regarding the execution of the will. Heirs-at-law should be specifically mentioned in the will and disinherited.

Some commentators suggest including heirs in the will, who would potentially contest the will and also include a "no-contest" clause. Such "no-contest" clauses are not valid in all states.[9] This may not work because, if the will is declared invalid, so is the clause. It may, however, deter some uninformed heirs. Unmarried opposite-sex and same-sex couples should update their wills regularly to demonstrate their continued desire to benefit each other. All prior wills should be retained and marked as superseded. A client may also want to include funeral instructions in the will. Although the will is not admitted to probate until after the funeral, it demonstrates the decedent's intent. Prepaid funeral arrangements also should be considered to prevent biological family members from taking control of the situation.

Probate Avoidance Techniques

As discussed above, joint and survivorship and other non-probate estate planning strategies are very risky due to their unintended tax and legal consequences. If these mechanisms are used, the client should clearly document his or her intent to avoid any challenge after death. The advantage of using these probate avoidance techniques, including fully funded living trusts, are that they are usually more difficult to challenge and the transfers are not a matter of public record. However, in some cases, appearing secretive can make other heirs, particularly children, more suspicious of the situation leading to increased legal action. Again clearly documenting the client's intent should reduce these risks.

Trusts

Much the same as in the case of a married couple, a trust can be used to support a partner while leaving the ultimate distribution of the assets in the control of the grantor. Sometimes there is no desire to control the ultimate distribution of the assets. In such an instance, the easiest course of action would be an outright distribution to the other partner. Unless the estates are modest this will result in double taxation of the transferred assets and the loss of one partner's Unified Credit Amount. These trusts, however, are not eligible to defer estate tax on assets in excess of the Unified Credit Amount, until the surviving partner's death. The advantage non-married couples have over married couples is that these trusts do not have to be structured as QTIP Trusts. The trust may have more than one beneficiary, does not have to pay all income and may terminate at a desired event such as the marriage of the surviving partner. Other types of trusts beyond the scope of this chapter may be used to leverage one partner's Unified Credit Amount and annual gift tax exclusions to provide greater income to the other partner. Such trusts may include Charitable Remainder Trusts, Charitable Lead Trusts (see Chapter 13 for a discussion of charitable trusts), and Grantor Retained Annuity Trusts (see Chapter 12).

Gifting

The ability of these couples to equalize assets, to take advantage of both partners' Unified Credit Amounts, is severely restricted due to the unavailability of the unlimited marital exclusion. In addition, gifts between these partners may be reclassified as taxable income, subject to both regular income tax and self-employment tax, to the partner receiving the gifts. This may happen in a situation where one partner works and the other partner provides domestic duties. Also, if one partner owns the home and the other lives there rent free and is the one who provides domestic services, half the rental value of the home may be deemed taxable income to the non-owner partner.

Life Insurance

As long as a partner is still insurable, life insurance can be used to provide for the other partner. In cases where it is likely that disinherited relatives are likely to enter into litigation, a client can chose to leave all his assets to his heirs-at-law, while providing for the partner through life insurance (including by making such partner as a beneficiary of an ILIT). In order to minimize the tax consequences, the insurance should either be owned by the other partner or by an ILIT. If the partner owns the insurance to the extent the proceeds are not consumed during the surviving partner's life, they will be taxable on his or her death. If the non-insured partner should predecease the other partner, any cash surrender value would be taxable in his or her estate and the disposition of the policy would be governed by such partner's estate plan. In these situations, there also may be an issue of whether or not the partner has an insurable interest with regard to the other partner's life.

NON-ESTATE PLANNING REMEDIES AVAILABLE TO UNMARRIED COUPLES

Cohabitation Agreement

Where marriage is not an option, a blended family can enter into a cohabitation agreement. Such an agreement fulfills the same function that a prenuptial agreement does in a marriage. Such an agreement may address the following issues:

- The treatment of income earned by either party during the relationship.

- What property was owned and what debts are owed prior to the relationship.

- The rights with regard to property acquired during the relationship by purchase, gift and inheritance.

- How different debts incurred during the relationship should be handled.

- What any change in ownership or the purchase of joint property during the relationship means.

- How living expenses and household responsibilities are to be shared. (Income tax consequences must be considered.)

- How property is to be divided if the relationship terminates. Agreement to transfer property on death and/or option to purchase property from the other's estate.

- If arbitration is to apply to the agreement.

Remedies at Law

Even if no formal planning is undertaken, at the termination of a relationship, either during life or at death, a partner may still recover some benefit from the other partner or such partner's estate. *Marvin v. Marvin*,[10] established contractual rights and equitable remedies for individuals involved in an intimate cohabiting relationship. Other actions have been brought in these situations based on the theories of quantum meruit, unjust enrichment and the theories of constructive and resulting trust.

IMPORTANT CONSIDERATIONS

Who is Your Client?

When either a traditional couple or a blended family approaches an estate planner for legal advice there is always a question of who is the client and can you ethically represent both partners. Although this issue

is obvious in the case of a blended family, this issue is sometimes ignored in the case of the traditional first marriage, husband and wife, couple, but should never be ignored in any other type of couple. Even in situations involving first married couples, not addressing this issue can cause serious consequences. Even these couples can have different goals. One partner may disclose information to you, which he or she says should not be shared with the other partner. Such a situation would put you in an ethical dilemma. If you represent both partners, it is essential that a clear engagement letter be used which should contain a waiver of conflicts and confidentiality of communications between each individual partner and you, however, not a waiver of confidentiality between the couple and you. You should be cautious in agreeing to represent both partners, even if a waiver is obtained. If it appears that an actual conflict exists between the partners, despite their representations to the contrary, you should refer one of the partners to another planner. In practice, attorneys typically strive to represent the wealthier spouse, however that is not always the case.

Information Gathering

It is essential in all situations that a complete listing of all of your clients' assets, including the exact titling of such assets, be obtained prior to initiating the actual plan itself. You must also obtain a thorough knowledge of the clients' heirs-at-law, especially in the case of a blended family. It is generally a good practice to have this information contained in a completed client questionnaire that the clients sign off on, which states that the information provided is a clear and complete representation to the best of the clients' knowledge (although it is the author's opinion that such signature is self-serving at best for an estate planning attorney in the event of a legal malpractice challenge). The big issue in cases of blended family members is making sure that you do not have any conflicts with any of the other family members. If your law firm does not perform a comprehensive conflict check then you should implement one. Otherwise, a conflict of interest may prevent you from continuing representing one or more family members.

Fee Payment

In the case of a blended family, a planner should be wary of one partner's children paying the fee, as this may give the appearance of undue influence. What could happen is that the non-wealthy spouse's children desire to be part of the wealthy spouse's estate planning and pay legal fees for an attorney that will draft such a plan. Be wary of the over zealous step-son or daughter. As a best practice you should always meet your blended family married couple without children.

CONCLUSION

Estate planning for blended families can be interesting and lead to creative engagements. These couples share many of the issues and concerns of traditional couples and other issues and concerns that are unique to them. Working with these couples can be rewarding for you if you are sensitive to these couples' needs and fully aware of the planning options available.

CHAPTER ENDNOTES

1. 125 U.S. 190, 205 (1888).

2. *See* Tex. Fam. Code §2.401.

3. Restatement (Second) of the Conflicts of Laws §283(2) (1971).

4. Rev. Rul. 2013-17, 2013-2 C.B. 201, 2013-38 I.R.B. 201 (I.R.S. Aug. 29, 2013).

5. *See* I.R.C. §§2035 and 2042.

6. *See* I.R.C. §§2036-2038.

7. *See* Alaska Stat §34.77.10 et seq. (The Alaska Community Property Act effective May 23, 1998.)

8. Alaska Stat. §34.77.100; Tenn. Code Ann. §35-17-101, et seq.; and S.D. Codified Laws ch. 55-17.

9. For example, see Fla. Stat. §732.517.

10. 18 Cal. 3d 660 (1976).

TRUST AMENDMENTS

CHAPTER 23

REVOCABLE TRUSTS

A trust is a legal arrangement created by a grantor (also known as settlor) wherein a trustee holds legal title to property as a fiduciary for the benefit of one or more beneficiaries who are the equitable owners of the trust property. A revocable trust (also known as a living trust) is a trust in which the grantor reserves the right to amend or terminate the trust during his or her lifetime. The right of amendment provides a grantor with the comfort of knowing that as circumstances change, he or she has retained the power to make corresponding changes to the trust agreement.

Revocable trusts are often promoted as will substitutes because they serve as an alternative to a last will and testament by passing assets to the grantor's heirs upon death, but they have the added advantage of allowing avoidance of the probate process to pass such assets. Even in states where the probate process is simple and inexpensive, many people seek an even quicker, easier, and often less expensive mechanism for transferring the assets of a deceased person to the beneficiaries of that person. Revocable living trusts often serve this purpose. As a result, a revocable trust is typically designed with distribution provisions which apply during the grantor's lifetime and after the grantor's death.

In certain jurisdictions, revocable trusts have also gained popularity because along with probate avoidance, revocable trusts allow for the confidential distribution of the decedent's assets without subjecting the terms to public exposure as in most states' probate process. Finally, the transfer of title to a revocable trust of property located in a state other than the state of the decedent's domicile usually avoids an ancillary administration proceeding in that state.

Due to the rise in popularity of the use of a revocable trust, it is critical to understand the circumstances surrounding the amendment of such trust to ensure that the amendment is properly effectuated.

TYPES OF REVOCABLE TRUST

Revocable trusts are commonly created by either a single grantor or by two (or possibly more) joint grantors. The grantors are typically the individuals that retain the power to amend and revoke the trust. Therefore, in order to properly amend a trust, it is critical that the trust instrument be examined to establish that the person seeking to amend the trust does in fact have the right to amend.

Single Grantor Revocable Trust

A revocable trust with a single grantor is most often used by grantors residing in a common law jurisdiction who want to have sole control over the disposition of their assets. In the case of married couples, a single grantor revocable trust is also used when a couple desires to create two separate and independent revocable trusts, which will allow each grantor to include provisions specific to his or her goals and intentions. If a married couple has sufficient assets to subject them to estate taxation, separate trusts are often simpler to administer and will avoid some of the potential risks created by a joint trust.

The amendment of a single grantor revocable trust is usually simple and is accomplished by the powerholder (the individual having the power to amend) executing a written trust amendment which modifies the existing document. As with any trust amendment, the powerholder must have the requisite mental capacity to execute the amendment and the execution formalities required in the applicable jurisdiction, if any, should be strictly followed.

Joint Grantor Revocable Trust

When planning with the assets of married and unmarried person, joint revocable trusts are a frequently used instrument. In non-community property states,[1] joint trusts are used for married couples as a mechanism for them to combine assets and control their disposition in a uniform manner. Many married couples consider a joint trust to be easier to understand and administer than the creation of two separate and independent revocable trusts since they are already accustomed to holding their assets jointly. However, when the married couple has complicated assets and are subject to estate taxation, a joint revocable trust can cause significant gift and estate tax problems.

Joint trusts are frequently used for couples residing in a community property states and couples that move from a community property state to a non-community property state and want their property to retain its community property character. The joint revocable trust is routinely drafted to take advantage of the unique "double basis" benefit of community property on the death of the first spouse which "steps up" the basis of the entire property, even though only one-half of the property is included in the predeceasing spouse's estate for estate tax purposes.[2]

The amendment of joint trusts is more complex than the amendment of single grantor revocable trusts. When dealing with amendment of a joint trust, the important issues to consider and resolve are:

1. who should have the power of revocation during the lifetime of the joint grantors and after the death of the first grantor; and

2. should the power to amend apply to the entire trust or only portions of the trust. Therefore, a well drafted joint revocable trust should clearly address the revocation power at the death of each grantor.

There are various options for structuring the power to revoke and amend in joint trusts which are discussed below.

Outright Power

The first option is to give the power to amend and revoke to either grantor during their joint lifetimes and, after the death of the first grantor, have the trust continue to be revocable by the surviving grantor. This is sometimes referred to as the "outright approach". This will give each grantor the independent right to revoke or amend the entire trust, even after one grantor has died. Upon the death of the first grantor, the right to amend the entire trust is still permitted by the surviving grantor.

This outright approach option is extremely useful where both grantors want the other to have full and complete access over the entire trust, much like a joint bank account. It is generally used for smaller, typically non-taxable estates where the primary purpose for creating a trust is probate avoidance. This approach is most effectively used where the interests of the grantors in the trust property are not segregated upon the first death or where neither grantor is concerned that the surviving grantor might change the disposition of the other grantor's share of the trust after his or her death. Many spouses use the outright approach because it is simple and the surviving spouse may not have fiduciary duties to other beneficiaries that are imposed upon a trustee of an irrevocable trust. Nevertheless, a variety of other factors are relevant in making the decision to employ the outright approach.

Joint Power

The second option is to give the grantors the ability to jointly amend or revoke the trust during their joint lifetime and to have the surviving spouse alone hold a power to revoke the trust after the death of the first grantor. This approach allows the amendment and revocation of the trust upon the joint consent of both grantors, or by the surviving grantor, as to the entire trust. Although infrequent, some clients will want any amendment during their joint lifetimes to be joined in and signed by both of them, but have no problem with the trust being completely revocable and amendable by the survivor upon the death of the first grantor.

Joint Power until First Death

The third option is to give the grantors the ability to jointly amend or revoke the trust during their joint lifetime but render the trust irrevocable at the death of the first grantor. This option is useful to effectuate a joint dispositive scheme and is often suitable in second marriage situations, particularly where one or both of the grantors has children from a prior marriage. The purpose of this approach is to allow both spouses together to consent to the change in the dispositive plan of the trust during their joint lifetime, but after the death of the first spouse, the surviving spouse will not be able to alter the dispositive scheme. The problem with this arrangement is that the surviving spouse may be deemed to have made a gift of the remainder in his or her beneficial interest in the trust.[3] To avoid this result, the trust should provide that the trust may be revoked by either grantor, acting alone, as to any separate property, but only jointly by both grantors as to any community property. Thus, in the case of a revocable trust funded with community property, a right to modify the trust as to the rights and interest in community property during the marriage must be exercised only with the joinder and consent of both spouses in order to preserve the character of community property in the trust. The usual practice is to provide that after the death of the first grantor, the trust becomes irrevocable as to all or part of the deceased grantor's interest. The trust remains revocable as to the interest of the surviving grantor. Although this would enable the surviving spouse to alter the any joint scheme that the couple may have envisioned, the potential gift tax consequences would be avoided.

PRESUMPTION OF REVOCABILITY

A well-drafted revocable trust instrument will specify whether the trust is revocable and the method that must be used to accomplish a revocation or amendment. It is never good practice to rely upon the state law presumption and fail to include an express statement of revocability in the trust instrument. Failing to include express revocability provisions becomes especially problematic when the trust *situs* is moved to another state where the law regarding the presumption of revocability may differ from the original jurisdiction. Even if the *situs* of the trust is not moved, it is still not wise to rely on a statutory presumption as it may differ from the client's intent, and the law may be amended by the state's legislature or modified by case law.

In the event the trust instrument is silent as to revocability, state law of the state governing the trust instrument must be examined to determine whether the trust is presumed to be revocable or not. The most recent version of the Restatement of Trusts does not provide a presumption of revocability or irrevocability if the trust instrument is silent.[4] Instead, the question is one of interpretation and depends on whether the settlor has retained an interest in the trust.[5] Pursuant to the Restatement of Trusts, if the settlor has retained no interest in the trust, there is a rebuttable presumption that the trust is irrevocable. On the other hand, where the settlor has retained an interest in the trust, the presumption is that the trust is revocable.

Certain states such as New York have the presumption that a trust is considered irrevocable unless the power to amend or revoke is expressly or impliedly reserved in the trust.[6] Yet other states and the UTC presume a trust is revocable unless the trust expressly provides that it is irrevocable.[7] This latter view is adopted by states such as California, Florida, and Montana.[8]

State law presumptions may also apply to joint trusts. In California for example, a joint revocable trust containing community property is presumed to be revocable by either spouse acting alone as to the community property unless the trust instrument provides otherwise.[9] Because of the potential tax and nontax problems that sometimes arise with the presumption of revocability, the draftsman should not rely on the statutory presumption of revocability, but should specify in the trust instrument whether and under what circumstances the trust is revocable.

MENTAL CAPACITY TO AMEND

In order for a revocable trust to be amended, the individual holding the power to revoke must have sufficient mental capacity to do so. The requisite mental capacity may differ from one jurisdiction to the next. Under the UTC[10] and the Restatement (Third) of Trusts,[11] the capacity required to create, amend, revoke or add property to a revocable trust is testamentary capacity, the same as is required to create a last will and testament.[12] Testamentary capacity generally means the ability to recognize the natural objects of one's bounty (i.e., the people who would normally inherit), general knowledge of the nature and extent of one's assets, and a basic understanding that one is making a plan to dispose of one's assets or estate after death. Testamentary capacity is the standard imposed by most states, and is said to be one of the lowest capacity standards existing in the law.

Some states, like California, may require that a grantor has contractual capacity when amending or revoking a document other than a last will and testament. Contractual capacity is a higher standard than testamentary capacity and requires that the individual be able to "communicate verbally, or by any other means, the decision, and to understand and appreciate, to the extent relevant, all of the following:

1. the rights, duties, and responsibilities created by, or affected by the decision;

2. the probable consequences for the decision maker and, where appropriate, the persons affected by the decision; and

3. the significant risks, benefits, and reasonable alternatives involved in the decision."[13]

This disparity between testamentary capacity and contractual capacity is not uncommon and has resulted in case law in various states about the standard that should apply when amending a revocable trust. Therefore, the applicable law and requisite mental capacity of the governing jurisdiction must be examined.

The powerholder's lack of requisite mental capacity to amend a trust does not necessarily prevent the exercise of the power to amend. The power to amend may still be possible with the exercise by the agent of the powerholder under a power of attorney or the conservator or a guardian of the powerholder. Alternatively, the grantor of the trust may want the trust to become irrevocable in the event of the grantor's incapacity. To this end, the trust instrument can provide that the right to amend or revoke is personal to the grantor, and cannot be exercised on the grantor's behalf by an agent, conservator or guardian, or other fiduciary.

AMENDMENT BY AGENT UNDER A POWER OF ATTORNEY

A power of attorney is an instrument by which a person (the principal) grants someone the authority to act as an agent on his or her behalf, thus conferring authority on the agent to perform certain acts or functions on behalf of the principal. At times, the agent is granted authority to amend a trust. An agent under a power of attorney may have the right to exercise a grantor's power of amendment, revocation or distribution of trust property if authorized by the trust or power of attorney instrument.[14] By way of

example, California permits a revocable trust to be modified or terminated by an agent or attorney-in-fact so long as the trust instrument does not prohibit it.[15] Other jurisdictions, such as Florida, require that both the trust instrument and the power of attorney provide this authority to the agent.[16]

The benefit of granting an attorney-in-fact or agent the authority to revoke or amend a trust is that the terms can be spelled out in detail in the document as opposed to defaulting to other authority. Limitations and conditions can be placed on the extent of the exercise of the amendment, such as allowing modification to the extent it does not substantially alter the provisions effective upon the grantor's death, or as long as amendment does not result in any adverse tax consequences to the grantor's estate.

AMENDMENT BY GUARDIAN

In the event that the settlor of a revocable trust is determined to be incapacitated, a guardian or conservator may obtain court permission to exercise the settlor's power to amend or revoke the trust.[17] This can create numerous issues, however, and can cause litigation among interested persons with different agendas.

In New York, the Supreme Court, Appellate Division, determined that the court had statutory authority to permit an incapacitated settlor's guardian to exercise the settlor's right to amend the trust by naming additional co-trustees.[18] In a case of first impression, the Supreme Court of Nebraska determined that Nebraska statutes empowered courts (after a hearing and based upon clear and convincing evidence) to allow conservators to exercise settlors' reserved rights to revise or revoke their trusts, unless the trust at issue expressly provided otherwise.[19]

Although some courts will allow a conservator or guardian to amend a revocable trust, courts are exceedingly cautious in exercising their authority to approve the request. For example, in Florida, a court-appointed guardian petitioned a court to amend the trust to change the nominated successor trustee in the settlor's revocable trust.[20] The court granted the request, but in so doing, required proof that the change was in the "ward's best interests" even though there was no evidence of wrongdoing by the nominated successor trustee.[21] The court also refused to allow the guardian to amend the trust in any other manner.

A Nebraska court required that a conservator had to prove by clear and convincing evidence that the request to amend the trust to change successor trustees and remove beneficiaries were in the settlor's best interests.[22] In New Jersey, a court reiterated the importance of a hearing and court approval in holding that a state public guardian did not have the power to revoke a revocable trust established by the ward without the court's permission.[23]

EXECUTION OF TRUST AMENDMENTS

In order to amend a revocable trust, the trust amendment must be executed properly to be effective. The laws of the state governing the trust instrument imposes the execution requirements that must be followed. The trust instrument may also contain additional requirements by which the trust can be modified. In all cases, the method set forth in the trust agreement and under state law should be followed closely.

Jurisdiction of Trust Amendment

Americans have become increasingly mobile. With this increase in mobility, it is often difficult to determine which state's law applies to the requirements for execution of a trust amendment or revocation. This should not be confused with "jurisdiction" which is used to refer to the place whose law will govern the trust,[24] or used to refer to the trust's principal place of administration,[25] also commonly referred to as "*situs*."

The UTC validates trusts (other than testamentary trusts) executed in compliance with the law of a variety of places in which the settlor or the trustee had significant contact.[26] Pursuant to section 403 of the UTC, a trust not created by will is validly created if its creation complies with the law of the jurisdiction in which:

1. the trust instrument was executed;

2. the settlor was domiciled;

3. the trustee was domiciled or had a place of business; or

4. any trust property was located.

These provisions govern not only the effective creation of trusts, but also their modification, reformation, and amendment.

Most states that have adopted the UTC have implemented section 403 in whole.[27] Other jurisdictions, such as Virginia, have no execution requirements. Yet other jurisdictions have implemented a modified and more restrictive version of section 403. For example, Florida provides that a trust, not created by will, is validly created if the creation complies with the law of the jurisdiction in which the trust instrument was executed or the law of the jurisdiction in which, at the time of creation, the settlor was domiciled.[28]

Manner of Amendment

The manner of amending or revoking a trust depends on the method provided in the trust instrument and the nature of the trust property, such as whether the trust consists of real property or personal property. Most states require trusts holding real property to be executed in accordance with the statute of frauds, which necessitates a writing and a signature from the party to be charged.[29] Most states do not require any trust formalities for a trust consisting of personal property.

Most revocable trust agreements contain provisions concerning revocation of the trust. If the terms of the trust do not provide a method to revoke or amend a revocable trust, or the method provided in the trust terms is not exclusive, then revocation or amendment may be accomplished in some jurisdictions by either:

- a later will or codicil that expressly refers to the trust or specifically devises property that would otherwise have passed according to the terms of the trust; or

- another method which evidences clear and convincing evidence of the settlor's intent.[30]

Amendment by Written Instrument

A written amendment is the recommended method of revoking or amending a revocable trust. Some jurisdictions go so far as to make it the exclusive method. The Restatement (Third) of Trusts considers a revocation ineffective if there is no written instrument delivered to the trustee.[31] States like New York follow this rule by requiring that the creation, amendment and revocation of a revocable trust must be evidenced by a writing.[32] Georgia also requires that a revocation or modification of a revocable trust be in writing and signed by the settlor.[33]

Normally, the amendment or revocation is accomplished by a separate instrument specifically drafted for the purpose of amending or revoking the existing trust. However, revocation or amendment by will is another acceptable method recognized in some jurisdictions, even though the amendment does not become effective until probate of the will following the settlor's death.[34] Usually, to be effective, the provision in the will must expressly refer to the trust or the will must dispose of specific assets that would otherwise have passed pursuant to the trust terms (a residuary clause alone is insufficient). The Third District Court of Appeal of Florida in a recent case held that a will can revoke a trust where the language in the will stated that all prior wills, codicils and trusts are revoked, even though the trust is not specifically identified, if the proponent proves the settlor's intent by clear and convincing evidence including extrinsic evidence.[35]

Certain jurisdictions do not allow a revocable trust to be revoked by a will. California, for example, only permits revocation under the following methods:

- compliance with a method provided in the trust; or

- by a writing signed by the settlor or a person holding the power of revocation and delivered to the trustee or the person holding the power of revocation.[36]

Other Methods of Amendment

While revocation of a trust generally will require a signed and written declaration be delivered to the trustee, other methods, such as a physical act or an oral statement coupled with a withdrawal of the property, might demonstrate the necessary intent of the settlor to revoke. For example, a Florida court upheld the settlor's revocation of her revocable trust during her lifetime where the settlor transferred cash and securities to an account that was jointly titled in the settlor's and her sister's names.[37] In another example, the South Carolina Trust Code, a version of the UTC, provides that the settlor may revoke or amend an oral trust by making an oral statement of that intent to the trustee.[38]

Although methods other than a written instrument may be legally acceptable in certain jurisdictions, it is ill advised to rely on these methods because of the evidentiary problems in proving their existence and terms. Less formal methods may not evidence the settlor's

intent as clearly as a signed and delivered writing, and they could be challenging to prove.[39] The importance of a written declaration of revocation is illustrated by the Fourth District Court of Appeal in California in Heaps v. Heaps, where the court held that under terms of a trust agreement between the settlor and his first wife, removing an asset from the trust required something more than merely taking title in one's own name.[40] Courts are more inclined to rely on written instruments as the primary guide for ascertaining a settlor's intent. A revocation or amendment may be challenged by a third party on the grounds that the settlor lacked capacity, the amendment was procured by fraud, duress, or undue influence, or on other grounds. Therefore, it is advisable that the amendment or revocation be accomplished by a method which most clearly demonstrates and shows the highest level of intent. That method is usually a writing.

Order of Execution

A revocable trust is customarily used as a will substitute. A pour over will which transfers money or property to an existing trust is commonly used in conjunction with a revocable trust as a means of ensuring that the entire probate estate is transferred to the revocable trust. This assures that property that the grantor was not able or neglected to transfer to the trust during his or her life is combined with those assets the grantor was able to transfer. Thereafter, the assets will be held, administered and distributed in accordance with the terms of the revocable trust. The Uniform Testamentary Addition to Trusts Act and the section 2-511 of the Uniform Probate Code state that a will may validly devise property to the trustee of a trust established or to be established during the testator's lifetime by the testator, by the testator and some other person, or by some other person. Most jurisdictions, such as Florida, require that the trust be in existence at the time of making the will, or executed contemporaneously with the will.[41] In some jurisdictions, the trust does not have to be signed and validity of the trust does not have to be established in order for the trust to be "in existence."[42]

Substantial Compliance

Some jurisdictions require strict compliance with the stated formalities.[43] Other jurisdictions, recognizing that the formalities were inserted primarily for the trustee's benefit and not the settlor's benefit, will accept other methods of revocation as long as the settlor's intent is clear.[44] For example, a Hawaii court found that by signing a letter sent by his attorney to confirm his plans to amend trust, a decedent sufficiently manifested his intent to amend the trust, even though the subsequent execution of a more formal document was contemplated.[45]

Under the UTC, a grantor may amend or revoke a trust by substantial compliance with a method prescribed by the trust instrument or by a later will or codicil or any other method manifesting clear and convincing evidence of the settlor's intent to revoke.[46] Only if the method specified in the terms of the trust is made exclusive is use of the other methods prohibited. A well-drafted revocable trust instrument will specify the method that is to be used to accomplish a revocation or amendment. If the trust instrument does this, the provision in the instrument is exclusive in the sense that the trust can be revoked or amended only by substantially complying with the method stated in the instrument. Even then, a failure to comply with a technical requirement, such as required notarization, may be excused as long as there is substantial compliance with the method specified in the terms of the trust. A settlor's trust was effectively revoked by his later will under New Mexico's modified version of section 602(c) of the UTC because the terms of the trust did not provide an exclusive method of revocation of its provisions, and the will executed during the settlor's lifetime constituted substantial compliance with the terms of the trust relating to revocation.[47]

Tax Implications of Power to Revoke

During the time the grantor retains the power to revoke a trust, the grantor will be deemed the owner of the trust for income tax purposes and all income from the trust property will be taxed to the grantor.[48] If the grantor is serving as a trustee, either alone or with a co-trustee, the grantor will report trust income on the grantor's individual income tax return (Form 1040) and a separate fiduciary income tax return (Form 1041) is not needed.

As a result, the amendment of a revocable trust should not have an income tax effect unless the grantor will no longer be serving as trustee. When the grantor transfers property to a trust and the grantor has a power to revoke the trust, the transfer will not be treated as a completed gift for gift tax purposes, since the grantor will have the right to revest beneficial title in himself or herself.[49] Upon the death of the grantor, if the grantor dies still holding the power to revoke the trust, all property subject to the power of revocation will be included in the grantor's gross estate for estate tax

purposes.[50] In the case of joint revocable trusts, there are possible adverse gift tax consequences which may be caused by certain revocability provisions contained in the trust (see section above regarding joint trusts).

IRREVOCABLE TRUSTS

As the name indicates, an irrevocable trust is a trust the terms and provisions of which cannot be revoked or terminated. Irrevocable trusts are used to accomplish a client's tax and personal objectives. With most states having abolished the common law rule against perpetuities, there has been a movement towards longer and, if permitted by the governing jurisdiction, perpetual "dynasty" trusts.[51] Given that trusts can have such a long duration, circumstances may arise over the course of the duration of trust that may prevent or hinder an irrevocable trust from accomplishing the grantor's intent or from serving a material purpose. Flexible trust provisions and expansive trust statutes are important tools available to practitioners that enable irrevocable trusts to be amended. These tools are detailed below.

Governing Law of Trusts

Trusts are creatures of state law. Accordingly, state law (both statutory and common law) dictates how the terms of trusts can be changed, and it governs reformation, division, termination and modification of trusts. The requirements for each modification technique vary from state to state. Consequently, there is a threshold question of which state law applies. Usually, the law of the trust's principal place of administration will govern administrative matters and the law of the place having the most significant relationship to the trust's creation will govern the dispositive provisions.[52] In some cases, only one jurisdiction governs all aspects of a trust. In other cases, there are multiple jurisdictions to consider because the law governing construction and the law governing administration of a trust may be different.[53]

The governing law of a trust, which applies to issues regarding the meaning and effect of the terms of the trust, is the jurisdiction designated in the trust instrument.[54] Examples of items that fall within the category of "governing law" include trust execution, capacity or competency of grantor upon trust execution, identity and determination of beneficiaries and heirs, effect of class gifts, meaning of terms, effect of premature death, and determination of vested or contingent interest, spousal rights and rule against perpetuities.

Generally, the governing law provision in the trust instrument applies[55] and the grantor of a trust is free to designate the governing law of any state for matters of construction. The jurisdiction selected need not have any other connection to the trust.

Pursuant to the UTC and Restatement of Trusts, the construction or "meaning and effect" of the terms of an instrument are governed by the law designated in the instrument unless the designation of that jurisdiction's law is contrary to a strong public policy of the jurisdiction having the most significant relationship to the matter at issue. If the trust is silent as to the governing law, one should look to laws of the state that the grantor would probably have desired to be applicable. Section 107 of the UTC refers to this as "place having the most significant relationship" to the matter at issue.

Trust Administration

Generally, the trust will contain a provision designating the principal place of administration of the trust which governs administrative matters relating to the trust. Administrative matters of a trust include issues such as dividing or merging a trust, change of trustee, trustee power, duties and liabilities, creditor's rights and spendthrift protections, notice requirements, termination, modification or division of trusts, and principal and income determinations. Pursuant to the UTC, a trust provision designating the place of administration will govern if the trustee resides in or has a principal place of business in the jurisdiction, or all or part of the trust administration occurs in the jurisdiction.[56]

If the trust agreement is silent with respect to the *situs* of administration, pursuant to the Restatement (Second) of Conflicts of Laws and the UTC, one should look to the law of the trust's principal place of administration.[57] According to the UTC, the principal place of administration is ordinarily the place where the trustee is located. In states that have not adopted the UTC[58] or a variation of it, a conflict of law analysis applies. Generally, in that instance, the law of the testator's domicile upon death will apply for testamentary trusts unless the trust is to be administered in another state, in which case that other state's law governs. For *inter vivos* trusts, the law of the state to which administration is most substantially related will govern. Finally, for a trust which holds title to land, the law of the state where the land is located will govern.

Exercise of Trust Powers

Ideally, a trust is drafted with the flexibility to account for change in circumstances. A well drafted trust will contain provisions that enable changes to be made to the trust terms, frequently by giving certain powers to certain individuals. Some examples of the powers enabling changes include:

- giving a trustee, individual or trust protector a power to add beneficiaries

- a power of appointment

- a power to modify or suspend distributions

- a power to change the *situs* of the trust or its governing law

- a power to divide a trust into two or more trusts, combine or merge two or more trusts

- a power to decant the trust.

Powers Given to Trustee

The power to add charitable beneficiaries and the power to change the *situs* or governing law of a trust are two powers that are often given to someone to provide trusts with flexibility to account for change in circumstances. To avoid adverse tax consequences to the grantor, the power is usually given to the trustee of the trust – preferably, an independent trustee.

Power to Add Beneficiaries

Granting someone the power to add beneficiaries to a trust can be a good mechanism to make adjustments to the trust. For example, the trust can permit an independent trustee to add a beneficiary to whom distributions can be made or modify the ultimate distributions so that the new beneficiary gets a share. Sometimes the settlor's spouse can be added as a discretionary beneficiary or someone who was not an initial beneficiary of the trust.

Although a provision to add beneficiaries can add a great deal of flexibility to the documents, it is most often used for tax reasons, specifically as a means of triggering "grantor trust" status for a trust. A grantor trust is a trust over which the grantor or other owner retains the power to control or direct the trust's income or assets. If a grantor retains certain powers over the benefits in a trust, the income of the trust will be taxed to the grantor, rather than to the trust.

Generally, any power exercisable by the grantor or a nonadverse party to control beneficial enjoyment of trust property without the consent of an adverse party will render the grantor the deemed owner of the trust for income tax purposes.[59] But most powers that affect beneficial enjoyment of trust property will also trigger inclusion in the grantor's gross estate under either or both Section 2036 and 2038. One important exception is a power to add one or more charitable beneficiaries held by a "nonadverse party". A *nonadverse* party is anyone who is not an "adverse party".[60]

An *adverse* party is a person with a substantial beneficial interest in the trust that will be adversely affected by the exercise or nonexercise of a power possessed by such party.[61] An interest in the trust is substantial if "its value in relation to the total value of the property subject to the power is not insignificant."[62] If a nonadverse party trustee has the power to add one or more 501(c)(3) organizations as beneficiaries to the trust, grantor is treated as the owner of the trust for federal income tax purposes.[63] If the grantor has no retained interest in the trust and no direct power to alter or amend the terms of the trust, no portion of the trust will be included in the grantor's estate.

Change of *Situs* and/or Governing Law

Another provision commonly found in irrevocable trusts is the ability to change the *situs* or governing law of the trust from one state to another. Section 108(b) of the UTC provides that a trustee is under a continuing duty to administer the trust at a place appropriate to its purposes, its administration, and the interests of the beneficiaries. Commonly, there are three reasons why it is desirable to change the *situs* of a trust from one state to another:

1. to avoid state income tax;

2. to take advantage of favorable state trust laws in the transferee state; or

3. convenience and efficiency.

For example, one might change trust *situs* to a new state to reduce or eliminate entirely the trust's exposure to state income tax. The laws of another state may be

more favorable for dynasty trusts because of that state's extended rule against perpetuities. Asset protection laws may also be more favorable in another jurisdiction. Finally, it may be more convenient to administer a trust in a new state because of the relocation of the trustee or beneficiaries, the appointment of a new trustee, or the change in underlying trust assets.

To change the administration or governing law *situs* of a trust, the first step is to review the trust instrument to determine if there is a controlling provision. If the trust is silent, the next step is to review the applicable laws of the original jurisdiction and the new jurisdiction which may require the need to initiate a court proceeding in the transferor state (and possibly the transferee state as well) so that the *situs* of the transferee state will govern.

Sections 108(c)-(f) of the UTC provide the procedure for changing the trust's principal place of administration to another state or to a jurisdiction outside of the United States, without court involvement. However, this procedure only applies in the absence of a contrary provision in the terms of the trust. A trustee may transfer a trust's principal place of administration without court approval if (i) the trustee provides notice to all qualified beneficiaries[64] of the proposed transfer and (ii) no qualified beneficiary objects to the transfer within sixty days of the notice.[65] If a qualified beneficiary objects, the trustee must seek court approval to transfer a trust's principal place of administration.

Changing the *situs* of the trust for administration does not automatically change the governing law of the trust.[66] The Comment to Section 108 explains that the transfer of the principal place of administration will usually change the governing law with respect to administrative matters, but does not normally alter the controlling law with respect to the validity of the trust and the construction of its dispositive provisions. Thus, it is imperative to review the trust instrument to see whether there is a mechanism for changing *situs* and whether a change of *situs* has an effect on the governing law of the trust instrument. If the trust instrument provides that the validity, construction and administration of the trust will be governed by the laws of a specific state, changing the *situs* for administrative matters will not change the governing law. If the trust instrument is silent as to the trustee's ability to change the governing law, a court proceeding generally must be initiated. A court will normally consider the settlor's intent, the benefits generated from the change and whether there is a nexus with the new state in considering the change of governing law.

Powers of Appointment

Powers of appointment are one of the most flexible estate and tax planning tools available. A properly drafted power of appointment can be used to build flexibility into a trust by altering the ultimate disposition of some or all of the property within a trust. However, practitioners must be aware of the complicated tax ramifications of powers of appointment in order to realize their optimum use.

A power of appointment is the authority vested in a person (the "holder" or "powerholder"), either during lifetime (*inter vivos*) or at the person's death (testamentary), to direct who will become the beneficial owner of property (the "appointee").[67] The person who creates the power of appointment is called the "donor." The powerholder is the only person that has the ability to exercise the power and is constrained by the inability to transfer the power to another person.[68] A power of appointment cannot be exercised by the personal representative of the powerholder's estate or by the powerholder's successors in interest.[69] However, during the life of a powerholder, the powerholder's agent, guardian, conservator, or custodian may (depending on applicable state law) be able to exercise a power of appointment on behalf of the powerholder.[70] The nonexercise of the power causes it to expire or lapse.

For state law purposes, powers of appointment are considered "general" or "non-general" (also known as "limited" or "special" powers of appointment). A power is classified as "general" if it can be exercised in favor of the powerholder, his or her creditors, his or her estate, or the creditors of his or her estate.[71] All other powers are classified as "non-general." From a federal tax perspective, the same designations (i.e., limited or general) are used.[72] One looks at the substance and effect of the power, and not to either the terminology used in creating the power or local property law implications, to determine whether there is, in fact, a "power of appointment."[73] The instrument creating a power of appointment must satisfy three requirements:

1. it must be valid under applicable state law;

2. it must transfer the appointive property; and

3. the instrument must manifest the donor's intent to create the power of appointment.[74]

A power of appointment may be exercisable presently, at death, at some future date, or upon the occurrence of a future event. If the instrument is silent as to when the power of appointment may be exercised, it may be exercised both presently and upon death.[75] A power of appointment created by an *inter vivos* trust is considered as created on the date the trust takes effect, and not on some future date. This is the case even if the power of appointment is not exercisable on the date the trust takes effect, or it is revocable, or the identity of its holders is not ascertainable until after the date the trust takes effect.[76] However, if the holder of a power exercises it by creating a second power, the second power is considered as created at the time of the exercise of the first power.

General Powers of Appointment

A general power of appointment is a broad power, which, subject to certain exceptions, may be exercised in favor of any one of the following appointees: (i) the donee; (ii) the donee's estate; (iii) the donee's creditors; or (iv) the creditors of the donee's estate. Code section 2041 recites the appointees in the alternative, so the inclusion of any one of them will make the power a general power. There are three exceptions to the definition of a general power of appointment:

1. First, a power of appointment will not be considered a general power if exercise of the power is limited by an ascertainable standard relating to health, education, support or maintenance.[77]

2. Second, a power of appointment will not be considered a general power if it may be exercised by the powerholder only in conjunction with the donor.[78]

3. Third, a power of appointment will not be considered a general power if it may be exercised by the powerholder only in conjunction with another person who has a substantial interest in the property subject to the power of appointment that is adverse to the exercise of the power.[79]

The definition extends to powers held in a fiduciary capacity, and to joint powers (other than joint powers held with either the creator of the power or a party whose interest would be adversely affected by an exercise of the power, which are exceptions (2) and (3) above). The powers of a trustee to make discretionary distributions to the beneficiaries can be a general power if the trustee is also a beneficiary and therefore can make unrestricted distributions to himself. Also, where a beneficiary and two other persons hold the power, as trustees, to terminate and distribute the trust property to the beneficiary, the property is includible in the beneficiary's estate.[80] A beneficiary will not be deemed to have a general power if the beneficiary is given the right to remove the trustee and to appoint an individual or successor trustee, so long as the successor is not related to or subordinate to the beneficiary.[81]

General powers of appointment are usually avoided because of their potentially adverse income, gift and estate tax consequences for the holder. The income from property subject to a presently exercisable general power is taxable to the holder unless the grantor is treated as the owner of the trust.[82] The exercise or lapse of a general power may result in a taxable gift under Code section 2514. The mere possession of a general power, even without knowledge of possession, will cause inclusion in the holder's estate.[83] Also, the grantor may not want to confer a broad power to dispose of trust property on another person. In those cases, a limited power of appointment may provide sufficient flexibility.

In some cases, the tax benefits of a conferral of a general power may outweigh the potential disadvantages. For example, allowing the trustee the power to grant a general power of appointment to a beneficiary can be utilized to change the transferor of the trust for GST tax purposes from the grantor to the powerholder. Giving a beneficiary a general power that will require the trust to be included in the beneficiary's estate may also be utilized to support an increase in basis of the trust assets under Code section 1014. For gift tax purposes, beneficiaries of an irrevocable trust may be given *Crummey* withdrawal powers so the gift tax annual exclusion will be available for property transferred to the trust.[84] A "five or five" power, when a donee's power is limited to the greater of 5 percent or $5,000, non- cumulative, each year, is another common power granted to the donee which is exempt from gift tax consequences.[85] The benefit of this power is that it gives the donee a general power of appointment over a portion of the property while limiting the exposure to gift tax consequences if the power is not exercised.

Limited Powers of Appointment

A power of appointment can be structured as a limited to special power of appointment over the trust income or principal. A limited power of appointment is any power that is not general power, i.e., a power that falls within one of the aforementioned exceptions to a general power or is either:

- exercisable only in favor of one or more designated persons or classes other than the powerholder, his or her creditors, the powerholder's estate or the creditors of his or her estate; or

- expressly not exercisable in favor of the powerholder, his her creditors, the powerholder's estate or the creditors of his or her estate.[86]

The flexibility of the trust can be increased without significant adverse gift or estate tax consequences by giving a beneficiary a power to withdraw trust property limited to an ascertainable standard.[87] The other two exceptions to a general power of appointment, a power exercisable in conjunction with the creator of the power and a power that is only exercisable in conjunction with a person having an adverse interest, are of little use for planning purposes to allow additional flexibility to trusts.

The ascertainable standard exception to the general power rule is the most challenging of the general power exceptions. It is commonly given to the surviving spouse to be his or her own trustee of the credit shelter trust. The use of any standard other than "health, education, maintenance and support" presents the risk that the power may be viewed as a general power. Thus, the use of any standard relating to "comfort," "happiness," "well-being," and "welfare" may result in the power being viewed and general power, which will result in inclusion in the powerholder's gross estate.[88] A state court, however, may apply its laws or point to other language in the trust to hold that a power is subject to an ascertainable standard.[89] The safest course is to use the language of the examples in the Treasury Regulations when crafting the power to withdraw.

A testamentary power of appointment granted to the son of the trust's settlors, to appoint the principal and accrued, undistributed income to a class consisting of the "Settler's issue," was properly viewed by the

IRS as a non-general power of appointment within the meaning of Code section 2041(b)(1) and will not cause the value of the trust property to be included in the son's gross estate.[90] A number of states have enacted savings statutes that automatically convert what would be general powers of appointment held be trustees into limited powers of appointment.[91] Similarly, state statutes prohibit a trustee from exercising the trust powers to discharge the trustee's support obligation.[92]

STATUTORY MODIFICATION

Just because an irrevocable trust cannot be revoked or terminated under the terms of the document does not mean that the trust cannot be modified. In the event the trust document cannot facilitate the amendment or the method is inadequate, there are various state law strategies to modify an irrevocable trust. Such judicial and non-judicial methods include but are not limited to:

- judicial modification;

- non-judicial modification;

- decanting; and

- unitrust conversion.

Judicial Modification

There are several judicial methods that may be employed to modify an irrevocable trust. These judicial methods require court approval. Some practitioners dislike court involvement due to the uncertainty of the outcome and court ruling, while others prefer it because of the comfort and certainty for all parties when court approval is obtained. Either way, certain methods are require judicial consent, such as reformation, combination or division of trusts, termination of an uneconomic trust and modification. This subpart and the next discusses the provisions of the UTC for illustrative purposes and to show the potential scope of state law authority for changes to trusts for judicial and non-judicial modification.

Trust reformation is a judicial action in which a trust document that is unambiguous is amended to correct a mistake in order to reflect the settlor's actual intent. There are two types of reformation actions: reformation to correct a scrivener's error and reformation to correct

a mistake of law or fact. Trust reformation is a deviation from the common law rule that no remedy exists to correct mistakes and that extrinsic evidence of intent is not admissible absent an ambiguity in the trust. Many states have changed the old common law rule by state statute.

Reformation to correct a scrivener's error may include actions to correct the drafting attorney's misstatement of the settlor's intent, or to add a term or provision that the settlor intended to include, or to nullify a term that the settlor did not intent to include. It is accomplished through the addition or replacement of language instead of interpretation of existing language. Reformation to correct a mistake of law or fact is utilized to modify terms when the settlor was unaware of facts or law at the time the trust document was created, or when the settlor could not have predicted a change in facts or law after the trust document was created.

Reformation requires that a judicial action or proceeding be instituted with the court having jurisdiction over the trust. The presiding court will examine the trust document and, if the petitioner is successful, the court will make a corresponding correction (either the addition or deletion of language). Both the UTC and the Restatement of Trusts provide that the settlor's intent must be proven by clear and convincing evidence and extrinsic evidence may be introduced.[93] Generally, all affected beneficiaries must either be parties to the action or receive notice thereof. If living, the settlor must typically be a party to the reformation action and provide an affidavit attesting to the fact that the reformation is essential to effectuate his or her intent. If the reformation action is initiated because of a scrivener's error, the scrivener must provide an affidavit as well. The key advantage of a reformation proceeding is that the effectuated changes relate back to the creation of a trust.

Termination of an Uneconomic Trust

Section 411 of the UTC provides that a trustee may terminate a trust that is no longer economical to administer. Many states have adopted similar statutes. Usually, the trust property must have a value of less than $50,000 and the Trustee must provide notice to the qualified beneficiaries. A settlor can set a higher or lower threshold, can specify different termination procedures, or can altogether prohibit trust termination without court order.[94]

Furthermore, whether or not the trust has a value of more or less than $50,000, a court may modify or terminate a trust or remove the trustee and appoint a new one if it determines that it is no longer economical to administer the trust without such action.[95] If a trust is terminated pursuant to this section, the trustee is required to distribute the trust assets consistent with the purposes of the trust. The inclusion of a spendthrift provision in a trust does not preclude termination.[96]

Modification of Charitable Trusts

Section 413 of the UTC codifies a court's power to apply *cy pres,* which is an equitable doctrine used to modify a trust where the grantor's charitable purpose cannot be accomplished as expressed in the instrument. If a trust's charitable purpose becomes unlawful, impracticable, impossible to achieve or wasteful, the trust does not fail. Instead, the court may apply *cy pres* by either modifying the trust's terms or distributing the trust property in a manner consistent with the settlor's charitable purposes.[97] The settlor of any trust, with the exception of a charitable lead trust, may require the distribution of trust property to a noncharitable beneficiary upon the failure of a particular charitable purpose.[98]

Modification Due to Unanticipated Circumstances

One of the broadest sources of authority for modification is contained under Section 412 of the UTC. This section permits termination or modification of a trust by a court upon a showing that changed circumstances not anticipated by the grantor suggest that a termination or modification furthers the purposes of the trust, and distribution would be in a manner consistent with the purpose of the trust. To the extent practicable, modification must be made in accordance with the settlor's probable intention.[99]

Modification to Achieve Settlor's Tax Objectives

Section 416 of the UTC allows a court to modify the terms of a trust in a manner that is not contrary to the settlor's probable intent in order to achieve the settlor's tax objectives. The trust terms are modified to align with the settlor's tax objectives in a way that is consistent with the settlor's probable intent.[100] The court may provide that the modification has retroactive

effect but, as discussed above, this may not be binding on federal authorities.[101]

Non-Judicial Modification

The UTC and many states have provisions that allow a trust to be modified without the need for court involvement. This provides the parties with greater latitude to implement a desired goal. Under the UTC, the nonjudicial methods that may be available are dependent on whether the settlor consents to the modification. Some states have modified this rule by eliminating this requirement.[102]

Settlement Agreements. An alternative to the aforementioned judicial modification options is a non-judicial modification in which "interested persons" enter into a binding non-judicial settlement agreement regarding a trust. An interested person is an individual or entity "whose consent would be required in order to achieve a binding settlement were the settlement to be approved by the court."[103] If the interested person is a minor, incapacitated, unborn or unascertained, or under a disability, the virtual representation rules can be used. The settlor's consent is not required. A non-judicial settlement agreement can be entered into regarding any matter involving a trust so long as the following two requirements are satisfied:

1. it must not violate a material purpose of the trust;[104] and

2. its terms and conditions must not be contrary to applicable law.[105]

The use of a settlement agreement avoids the intervention of a court and associated fees and costs. Nevertheless, the UTC provides an avenue for ensuring the validity of a non-judicial settlement agreement by allowing interested persons to request court approval of the settlement agreement.[106] This would be done to establish that representation was adequate and to determine whether the agreement contains terms and conditions the court may approve.

Consent Agreements. If the settlor is alive, then the settlor together with all trust beneficiaries can consent to non-judicial modification even if inconsistent with a material purpose of the trust.[107] If a beneficiary refuses to consent, then modification by consent is unavailable. Modification on consent is broader than a non-judicial settlement agreement because the settlor must also consent. If the settlor is not legally competent, then modification can be accomplished by an agent under a power of attorney or by a court appointed guardian. Generally, the consent of the trustee is not required. However, under section 410(b) of the UTC, a trustee would have standing to object to the proposed modification.

Combination and Division of Trusts

The division of a trust is the split of a trust into two or more separate trusts. A trust may be divided for many reasons which range from tax planning, simplified administration, litigation avoidance or resolution, and economics or state income tax savings.

The ability to divide a trust creates a great planning opportunity to solve many tax issues. The division of a trust is frequently tax motivated. A division is useful where there is a desire to treat one trust as a grantor trust and the other as a non-grantor trust, or to utilize the GST tax exemption (e.g., qualified severance) of marital deduction. It is also helpful to qualify a trust for QSST treatment or to obtain the marital or charitable deduction. There are also nontax reasons for division of a trust; it enables the trustee to more effectively respond to the needs and expectations of a much smaller group of beneficiaries and attend to their different investment goals, and it even allows for appointment of difference trustees to the separate trusts. When beneficiaries do not get along and do not agree on aspects of trust administration, dividing a trust can avoid or resolve litigation and save fees, costs and the emotional toll of litigation.

Various states and the UTC authorize a trustee to divide a trust into separate trusts provided the division does not impair the rights of a beneficiary or adversely affect achievement of the purposes of the trust.[108] The statutes do not require that the separate trust be identical to the original trust, but the beneficial interests of any beneficiary cannot be impaired in any manner. Some states do not require approval from either the court or the beneficiaries, but require only notice to the beneficiaries.[109] Other states require court approval.[110] At a minimum, the division should be memorialized in a division agreement which lays out how the trust is to be divided and the terms that will govern the separate trusts. Upon division, the trustee can make distributions in divided or undivided interests, allocate particular assets in proportionate or disproportionate shares, value the trust property for those purposes, and adjust for resulting differences in valuation.[111]

A trustee may also combine two or more trusts into a single trust pursuant to terms in the trust instrument, state statute, or Section 417 of the UTC. Typically, a combination of trusts is done to reduce administrative costs such as trustee's fees or income tax filings, or for investment reasons. Notice to qualified beneficiaries is required and the combination of trusts cannot impair the rights of a beneficiary or adversely affect achievement of the purposes of the trust. As with a division of trusts, a combination or merger of trusts should be memorialized in a merger document.

TAX IMPLICATIONS AND BINDING THE IRS

Practitioners needs to exercise great care when employing any of the options discussed above so as not to trigger any unintended tax consequences. Often, the foregoing strategies are tax motivated. In those circumstances, one must always consider the tax consequences and whether the desired tax motivated changes to the trust will be binding for federal tax purposes. Some of the tax consequences that could be an issue are as follows:

1. Creation of a gift by the beneficiary thereby triggering a gift tax;

2. Altering of the GST inclusion ratio on the trust;

3. Causing inclusion in the gross estate of the beneficiary;

4. Realization of income, gain or loss to the trust or beneficiaries;

5. Whether income tax basis will be altered;

6. How the trusts will be treated for income tax reporting purposes;

7. Self-dealing concerns with changes to a charitable trust; and

8. Loss of the marital deduction.

Completed Transaction Doctrine and the Bosch Decision

There are two reasons why the modification procedures discussed above may not have the desired federal tax result: the Bosch rule and the completed transaction role. In cases where the transaction has already been completed, an attempt to undo the action giving rise to the tax consequences may fail. The "completed transaction" doctrine provides that one cannot unwind the tax consequences of a transaction that has already taken place.[112] As a result, any of the foregoing strategies will not change the tax consequences of the transaction that has already been completed. Such retroactive changes to the document do not have retroactive effect for federal tax purposes. Nevertheless, in certain limited circumstances, the IRS has allowed the amendment of an irrevocable trust to have retroactive effect.[113] In these cases, the taxpayers established that due to a mistake of law or fact, the transaction had a tax effect that the taxpayer did not intend at the time of the transaction.

Furthermore, in *Commissioner v. Estate of Bosch*,[114] the Supreme Court held that the IRS is not conclusively bound by a state court decision regarding property rights unless the matter has been decided by the highest state court.[115] If the highest court in the state does not consider the issue, the federal tax authorities (e.g. IRS, the Tax Court or federal court) are then free to give "proper regard" to the state court's determination and to relevant rulings of other courts of the state.[116] In this respect, the federal agency may be said, in effect, to be sitting as a state court.

Although it would be clearly desirable to bind the IRS to the modification transaction, making the IRS a party to the state court proceeding is not the answer. Due to the doctrine of sovereign immunity, the government will be dismissed as a party in a state court action unless Congress has specifically waived sovereign immunity, which it has done in very limited instances in the tax arena. If the client wants assurance that the change will be given effect by the IRS, one possibility is to arrange for a determination by the highest court of the state. The other alternative is to request a private letter ruling[117] from the IRS. A practitioner should review Revenue Procedure 2016-1 to determine the specific requirements for obtaining a private letter ruling and whether the tax issue is one upon which the IRS will render an opinion.

Pre-Transaction Construction Action and Revenue Ruling 73-142

Where a change or amendment to the trust is contemplated but has not yet occurred, the *Bosch* principals discussed above do not apply. In Revenue Ruling 73-142,[118] the state court determination occurred before the taxing event. After the applicable period for

appeal, the IRS (and everyone in the world) was the bound by the decision. As a result, if the determination of rights and interests is prospective and is settled by local adjudication before the federal tax question occurred, res judicata applies, and such determination will be binding for federal tax purposes. Therefore, when modifying an irrevocable trust, it is recommended that one obtain a final order from the court before the taxing event, wait for the appeals period to expire, and thereafter complete the transaction, for which the federal tax authorities will be bound.

Decanting

Decanting is a method by which a trustee can effectively change one or more terms of an irrevocable trust by distributing the trust principal from the original trust (the "Distributing Trust") to another trust which is almost always a newly drafted trust (the "Receiving Trust") containing the preferred provisions. A trustee's power to decant derives from state law and can be based on an express provision in the trust document, common law, or state statute. Decanting is frequently used to correct a scrivener's error, to provide the trustee with more to allocate between principal and income, to change the trust *situs*, to extend the trust's duration (and attendant tax benefits), or, perhaps most controversially, to remove one or more beneficiaries. Decanting is a relatively new but increasingly popular amendment strategy; there is a great variance among states as to what is permitted, and states' laws are being revised to accommodate more decanting with fewer restrictions. Because of the lack of established authority governing the tax consequences of decanting, it should be employed with caution.

With the rise in popularity of decanting over the last decade or so, many practitioners are now including decanting provisions into their trust documents when decanting is permitted under that state's law. A trustee seeking to decant should first examine the trust for an express provision, and if found, the trustee must ensure that the provision is compliant with that state's requirements and follow the procedures set forth in the provision or other state-required mandates. In all cases, a trustee seeking to decant must carefully review that state's trust statutes relating to decanting (if any), and also review that state's common law which may provide for greater decanting flexibility or which may supplement or interpret the state's statute. Florida, for example, has broader decanting authority under case law than under that state's current decanting statute. If the jurisdiction does not have any statute authorizing decanting, the only authority for decanting would exist under the state's common law.

Some practitioners seeking to decant a trust in a jurisdiction which does not allow for decanting, either at all or under the particular circumstances the trustee is facing, may change the *situs* of the trust to a jurisdiction which does allow for the proposed decanting. The trust may contain a provision allowing for a change in *situs*, it may authorize a trust protector to change *situs*, or the change of *situs* may be accomplished under applicable law. A concern about forum shopping has caused some states to adopt favorable decanting statutes.

Authority. The authority to decant a trust is usually found in common law or state statute unless a provision in drafted into the trust document.

1. *Common Law Authority* – There are only few definitive cases on decanting. Instead, there is a patchwork of cases spread over seventy-six years and numerous states. Currently, the common law basis for decanting is recognized under court decisions in Florida, New Jersey, Iowa and Massachusetts, and is also supported under the Second and Third Restatements of Property.[119] The common law basis for decanting follows the logic that a trustee with discretionary authority to distribute assets has, in effect, a power of appointment to transfer the assets into a new trust.[120]

2. *Statutory Authority* – In 1992, New York became the first state to codify decanting legislation.[121] Currently, twenty-nine states (including New York) have enacted decanting statutes and that number is increasing.[122] The state decanting statutes generally allow a trustee who has discretionary authority to distribute assets under the terms of the trust to transfer the trust assets into a new trust for the benefit one or more of the same beneficiaries. However, state statutes then impose differing requirements. The majority of decanting statutes provide the trustee authority to decant without obtaining beneficiary consent and without court intervention. A minority of decanting statutes require judicial approval. Decanting generally cannot be used to add beneficiaries to the Receiving Trust that were not beneficiaries of the Distributing Trust. Some decanting statutes allow for the elimination of beneficiaries under the Distributing Trust. In early 2013,

the Uniform Law Commission formed a Trust Decanting Committee. In July 2015, the National Conference of Commissions on Uniform State Law released the Uniform Decanting Act in an effort to bring some uniformity in this area of the law.

Method of Exercise. The general principle of decanting statutes is that if the trustee has the authority under the trust document to invade principal for a beneficiary even to the extent of completely emptying the trust, the trustee may instead appoint the principal to a Receiving Trust for the benefit of some or all of the beneficiaries of the Distributing Trust. Therefore, it is the trustee who is responsible for decanting the trust.

Many states limit the scope of the changes that the decanting can effectuate. For example, some states require that the same distribution standard be included in the second trust, and some require that it be exercisable in favor of the same beneficiaries as the first trust.[123] Several states also provide that the trustee's discretionary power to distribute must apply to trust income, not just principal.[124] Some states will allow limited changes when the standard of distribution is subject to an ascertainable standard, but will permit greater changes when the standard of distribution is broader.[125]

Notice. The majority of decanting statutes require some form of notice to interested parties (beneficiaries or other persons) before decanting. These jurisdictions require that notice be provided in a range from twenty to sixty-three days in advance of decanting. For example, Alaska, California, Michigan and Ohio require notice for a trust to be decanted.[126] Yet, in Nevada notice is not required, but may be given, making it optional.[127] Delaware does not require any notice at all.

State statutes also differ as to which interested persons must receive notice. Some states only require current beneficiaries to receive notice. In other states, both current beneficiaries and presumptive remaindermen must receive notice. Some states also require notice to the state's attorney general where the trust has a current or future charitable beneficiary.

Many statutes permit the beneficiaries to waive the notice period. This allows the decanting to be effective prior to the expiration of the notice period.[128] Missouri, Texas and Virginia permit the beneficiaries to waive notice itself.

Beneficiary Consent and/or Court Approval. The majority of decanting statutes provide the trustee with the sole and absolute discretion to decant without obtaining beneficiary consent. This is preferable because beneficiary consent can cause adverse gift and GST issues.

A minority of decanting statutes give the trustee the ability to obtain judicial approval before decanting. These states include Arizona and Nevada.[129] However, only Ohio requires court approval and only in cases where the first trust is a testamentary trust created by an Ohio domiciliary. New York has a court filing requirement for testamentary trusts and for *inter vivos* trusts that were the subject of a prior court proceeding, but court approval is not required.

Mechanics of Exercise. Most state statutes require a written instrument to be signed and acknowledged by the trustee and filed with the records of the first trust (and in some cases the second trust) for the decanting to be valid. Yet some states like New Hampshire, Arizona and Missouri are silent on the method of exercise. Some state like Alaska and South Dakota specifically require that a new governing instrument be created. Other statutes specifically authorize the trustee to establish the second trust under the first trust or to create a new governing instrument.[130]

Beneficiaries of the Second Trust. One of most challenging issues with trust decanting is determining the identity of the permissible beneficiaries of the second trust and to what extent the beneficiary provisions of the first trust may be varied in the second trust.

The requirements to decant vary from state to state but there are commonalities among decanting jurisdictions. Under all state statutes, the addition of beneficiaries in the second trust is not permitted, and the majority specifically provide that the beneficiaries of the second trust may include only persons who are beneficiaries of the first trust. All state statutes also provide that where the trustee has absolute discretion, the current beneficiaries of the first trust can be eliminated in the second trust. If the trustee does not have absolute discretion, then most states provide that the current beneficiaries cannot be eliminated.[131] Texas takes it one step further and does not permit the current and presumptive remainder beneficiaries to be eliminated when the trustee does not have full discretion.

Only a handful of states has a provision addressing the elimination of remainder beneficiaries of the first trust in the second trust. Alaska, Illinois, Michigan, New York, Ohio and Texas statutes specifically provide that

remainder interests can be eliminated but only when the trustee of the first trust has absolute discretion in distribution. Delaware, on the other hand, does not permit the interests of remainder beneficiaries to be eliminated in the second trust regardless of the level of the trustee's discretion to make distributions.

The grant of a power of appointment not provided for under the first trust is also a consideration in some jurisdictions. Illinois, Ohio and Texas allow the addition of a power of appointment under the second trust provided the trustee has absolute discretion to distribute trust principal. New York provides the additional restriction of requiring the beneficiary of the first trust to have been able to receive the entire principal of the first trust outright and the power granted in the second trust must be unlimited. Most of the other states are more lenient and permit the second trust to grant a power of appointment not provided for in the first trust to a beneficiary of the second trust. The potential appointees under the power do not have to be beneficiaries of either the first trust or the second trust, thus providing a method for adding beneficiaries.[132]

Limitation of Power. Despite all the differences in the various state decanting statutes, all states place some form of limitation on the exercise of the power to decant. Most of the limitations are to protect certain fixed or mandatory rights and tax benefits.

All of the decanting statutes prohibit the reduction or elimination of a beneficiary's fixed or mandatory income interests under the first trust. In some cases, the scope of the prohibition is limited. Delaware and South Dakota, for example, apply the restriction only to marital trusts. Alaska, Illinois, Nevada, New Hampshire, New York, Ohio and Texas, apply the restriction to all trusts, but only to current income interests, not future income interests. Kentucky protects both current and future fixed income interests.

Many statutes also prohibit the reduction or elimination of an annuity or unitrust interest.[133] This is most commonly encountered with marital or charitable trusts. The intent is to preserve the specific tax benefits of the first trust. However, only Delaware, Michigan, Missouri, and South Dakota limit the prohibition to marital and charitable trusts.

Due to gift tax concerns, many states have prohibitions on decanting if the trustee is a beneficiary of the first trust. In Alaska, New York, North Carolina and Virginia, a beneficiary-trustee is not authorized to decant a trust. In cases where the beneficiary-trustee has an absolute discretion for distribution, the action of decanting by the beneficiary-trustee would be tantamount to the exercise of a general power of appointment. As a result, states have placed restrictions or prohibition in this instance. For example, in Arizona, the beneficiary-trustee cannot act if decanting would have an adverse tax impact on the beneficiary-trustee. In Missouri, Michigan, Nevada, New Hampshire, and South Dakota, the beneficiary-trustee is prohibited from acting unless the trust contains certain safeguards that would prevent adverse tax consequences to the beneficiary, or where beneficiaries have the right to remove and replace trustees or are not prohibited from using trust assets to discharge their legal support obligations.

Finally, there is a potpourri of prohibited acts that vary among the state statutes aimed at protecting tax benefits or property rights. Some of these prohibitions include altering qualification for the gift tax annual exclusion, qualification for subchapter S election, presently exercisable right of withdrawal, extension of rule against perpetuities or the term of the trust, or reduction of a trustee's standard of care.

Tax Issues of Decanting. A practitioner contemplating the use of decanting should be cautious to not trigger any negative gift, estate, generation-skipping transfer (GST) or income tax consequences. Although decanting is a current trend, guidance on the tax consequences associated with it have not yet been clearly established. Adding further to the uncertainty of the tax consequences associated with decanting, in 2011, the IRS placed decanting on its no-ruling list when it issued Revenue Procedure 2011-3. The IRS included decanting among the "areas under study in which rulings or determination letters will not be issued until the Service resolves the issue through publication of a revenue ruling, revenue procedure, regulations or otherwise."[134] The specific list of matters that the IRS will not rule on are:

- Does decanting gives rise to a Code section 661 deduction or inclusion in gross income under section 662?

- Does decanting results in a taxable gift?

- Does decanting cause the loss of GST exempt status or a taxable event under Code section 2612?[135]

Currently, the IRS is working on these tax issues. In the meantime, the tax consequences relating to the exercise of a decanting power are discussed below.

Gift. Under Code section 2512, a gift arises when property is transferred for less than adequate and full consideration in money or money's worth. In order for a gift tax to be imposed, there must be an intentional act of transfer.[136] In most cases, a trust decanting effectuated by a trustee who does not have a beneficial interest in the first or second trust should not raise any gift tax issues.

1. *Beneficiary Consent* – If beneficiary consent to the decanting is required and the decanting reduces or eliminates a beneficiary's interest in the first trust, then the beneficiary may be deemed to have made a transfer subject to gift tax. Treasury Regulations section 25.2512-8 suggests that when a beneficiary consents to or acquiesces in a decanting that reduces the beneficiary's interest, the beneficiary has made a taxable gift. This conclusion is consistent with Revenue Ruling 81-264, which holds that a taxable gift can occur when a taxpayer allows legal rights to expire.

   This issue should rarely arise because, except in some very limited circumstances, the decanting statutes do not require beneficiary consent. If possible, a trustee should consider dispensing with beneficiary consent when the decanting changes a beneficiary's interests in the first trust. If the decanting is being made pursuant to the terms contained in a trust instrument, the trust should not require beneficiary consent. Where a decanting changes only the administrative provisions of the first trust without altering a beneficiary's interest, no gift tax consequences should arise regardless of whether or not beneficiary consent is required.

2. *Notice to Beneficiaries* – Many decanting statutes require notice to trust beneficiaries in advance of decanting a trust. A beneficiary's mere receipt of notice should not give rise to adverse gift tax consequences. If the notice does not give the beneficiary a legal right to oppose a decanting that is undertaken in accordance with state law or the trust instrument, acquiescence of the notice should not result in a taxable gift by the beneficiary. However, if the beneficiary has a legal right to object to the trustee's exercise, waiving the right to do so could be deemed a taxable

gift. The prospect of objecting is generally very narrow because the ability to decant lies with the discretionary power of the trustee. Generally, courts do not interfere with a trustee's discretion unless there has been an abuse of discretion.[137]

3. *Trustee-Beneficiary* – Special gift tax problems can arise where a trustee-beneficiary participates in a decanting that reduces or eliminates the beneficial interest in the first trust. For example, if a trustee-beneficiary's life income interest in a trust is eliminated by a decanting, a taxable gift equal to the actuarial value of the life income interest could occur. If the trustee has absolute discretion to distribute to himself, he would be treated as having a general power of appointment under Code sections 2514 and 2041. If decanting reduces the trustee-beneficiary's presently exercisable general power of appointment, it could cause the beneficiary to incur gift tax.[138]

4. Some statutes prevent unintended gift tax consequences from arising by expressly prohibiting a trustee-beneficiary from participating in a decanting.[139] Moreover, the statement in the decanting statutes that the power to decant must be construed as a nongeneral power of appointment[140] should be enough to prohibit a trustee-beneficiary from participating in a decanting that would give the trustee-beneficiary an interest in the trust tantamount to a general power of appointment. Other states statutes allow a trustee with a beneficial interest to act only when distributions to the beneficiary are subject to an ascertainable standard and the same standard is included in the second trust. The limitation by a reasonably fixed or ascertainable standard does not make it a taxable transfer.[141] In all cases, when the decanting by the trustee- beneficiary only changes administrative provisions, there should be no adverse gift tax consequences.

GENERAL POWER OF APPOINTMENT

In the event the decanting of a trust results in the lapse of a general power of appointment, a gift results under Code section 2514(b). An example of this is when

a beneficiary's presently exercisable right of withdrawal in excess of a 5-and-5 power is eliminated. All of the state decanting statutes contain provisions that prevent such a lapse from occurring. However, when decanting is done in accordance with the terms of a trust, it may be an issue.

Delaware Tax Trap

Code section 2514(d), commonly referred to as the "Delaware tax trap," provides that the exercise of a power of appointment will be considered a transfer for transfer tax purposes if:

1. the powerholder, in exercising the power of appointment, grants another person the right to exercise a power of appointment; and

2. under applicable local law, the new powerholder can exercise his or her power of appointment to postpone the vesting of any trust interest or suspend the absolute ownership or power of alienation of such property for a period ascertainable without regard to the date that the first power was created.

The Delaware tax trap applies whether or not the second powerholder exercises the power in the prohibited manner. If a person exercises a power of appointment as provided in Code section 2514(d) during his or her lifetime, then such exercise is treated as a taxable gift. If the person exercises his or her power at death, then such exercise will result in estate inclusion under section 2041(a)(3). The overwhelming majority of the state decanting statutes characterize a decanting as the exercise of special power of appointment. If the second trust can extend beyond the first trust's perpetuities period, then the Delaware tax trap may be triggered.

However, the Delaware tax trap should not apply to a trust decanting when:

1. it is prohibited by a state's decanting statute;[142]

2. an independent trustee with no beneficial interest in the trust initiates the decanting; or

3. the second trust includes a provision that prohibits the exercise of a power of appointment in such a manner that extends the vesting period or suspends the ownership or alienation of any interest in the first trust.

Estate

Generally, there should be no adverse estate tax consequences as a result of decanting a trust. When a trust is decanted, the transferor of the property of the first trust is deemed to be the transferor of the property of the second trust. This is the case whether the second trust is created by the trustee of the first trust or by its grantor. If the property held in the first trust was not included in the transferor's gross estate for federal estate tax purposes, the property held in the second trust should not be included in the transferor's gross estate unless the second trust contains a provision that causes estate tax inclusion. This could arise when the second trust gives the transferor a general power of appointment or a dispositive power over trust property that triggers inclusion under Code section 2038, or when the second trust holds a life insurance policy on the life of the transferor and gives the transferor an incident of ownership with respect to the property (causing estate tax inclusion under Code section 2042(2)).

Decanting could result in estate tax inclusion if a beneficiary was deemed to make a gift but the gift was incomplete (e.g., the beneficiary retained a limited power of appointment). If the power was not exercised during life, the gift would be completed at death and the property included in the gross estate under Code sections 2036(a)(2) or 2038. However, the beneficiary would likely need to have the ability to object to the decanting as discussed above in the gift tax section. The ability to object is seldom present.

GST

The GST tax implications of decanting a trust must be examined in cases when the first trust is GST exempt. The GST tax is imposed when any one of the following three types of transfers occurs:

1. direct skip – this is a transfer made to a skip person that is subject either to gift or estate tax. A skip person is a person who is assigned to the generation of the transferor's grandchildren or to any generation below that;

2. taxable termination – when a person's interest in a trust terminates and there is no non-skip person who has an interest in the trust; and

3. taxable distribution – when a distribution is made from a trust to a person who is a skip person.

A trust can be considered GST exempt either because it became irrevocable on or before September 25, 1985 (a "grandfathered trust") or because sufficient GST exemption has been allocated to the trust. A taxpayer can allocate GST tax exemption to a trust in order to shelter future distributions to skip persons from the GST tax.

Regulations provide that a grandfathered GST exempt trust retains its exempt status following a decanting if it qualifies under either one of two safe harbors: (1) a discretionary distribution safe harbor; or (2) a trust modification safe harbor. A trust qualifies for the discretionary distribution safe harbor if three requirements are met:

- when the trust became irrevocable, either the terms of the trust instrument or local law (i.e., common law or state statute) authorized the trustee to make distributions to a new trust;

- neither beneficiary consent nor court approval is required for the decanting; and

- the new trust will not suspend or delay the vesting of an interest in trust beyond the federal perpetuities period, which is any life in being at the time (measured from the date the grandfathered trust became irrevocable) plus a period of twenty-one years.

No state had a decanting statute in effect prior to 1992, so to meet the first prong of this test, either the trust instrument itself must have authorized the decanting or state common law in effect at the date of the trust's creation must have permitted decanting.

A trust qualifies for the trust modification safe harbor if: (1) the modification does not shift a beneficial interest in the trust to a beneficiary occupying a lower generation than the person holding the interest under the original trust; and (2) the modification does not extend the time for vesting of any beneficial interest in the trust beyond the period provided in the original trust.[143] As a result, if using the trust modification safe harbor, the term of the trust cannot be extended because any postponement of the vesting of interest would violate the second prong of the safe harbor.

No guidance has been issued on trusts created after September 25, 1985, that are considered GST exempt because they have been allocated sufficient GST exemption so that they have a zero-inclusion ratio for

GST tax purposes. The safe harbors under the Regulations do not specifically apply to post September 25, 1985 trusts. However, in private letter rulings (PLRs), the IRS has suggested that the same two safe harbor tests described above should apply.[144] These PLRs have applied the trust modification safe harbor to post September 25, 1985 trusts and found that when there was no shift of beneficial interest and no extension of the time for vesting, the trust did not lose any of its GST exemption.

Income

One of the key questions of decanting a trust is whether decanting from one trust to another results in gain recognition by either the first trust or the beneficiaries of the first trust. The answers depend on the income tax status of the two trusts and the change in interest of the beneficiaries after decanting.

When determining whether there will be a recognition of gain for federal income tax purposes by the first trust upon decanting, it is important to determine the income tax status of both the first trust and the second trust before decanting occurs. To do so, the identity of the grantor of the second trust for income tax purposes must be established. If the second trust is viewed as a continuation of the first trust, then the same person should be considered to be the grantor of both trusts. This result is consistent with Treasury Regulations section 1.671- 2(e)(5), which generally provides that if a trust transfers assets to another trust, the grantor of the first trust will be treated as the grantor of the second trust.

An exception arises when property is distributed from one trust to another pursuant to the exercise of a general power of appointment. In such a case, the person exercising the power of appointment is treated as the grantor of the second trust. Thus, when a trustee-beneficiary participates in a decanting that results in the beneficiary making a taxable gift, or when a beneficiary's consent to a decanting is deemed to result in a taxable gift, the beneficiary should be treated as the grantor of the second trust.

If both the first trust and the second trust are grantor trusts deemed owned by the same person, then no gain should be recognized. Transactions between two grantor trusts are deemed to have the same owner and are treated as non- events for federal income tax purposes.[145] If the first trust is a non-grantor trust, but

the second trust is not, there is no deemed transfer and no income recognition on decanting.[146]

If both trusts are non-grantor trusts, decanting generally does not result in a realization event under Code section 1001 for the first trust when the decanting is authorized by either the trust's governing instrument or state law.[147] If the decanting is non-pro rata, the governing instrument or state law must authorize decanting on a non-pro rata basis to avoid gain recognition.[148] However, there are exceptions to the general rule. First, decanting could be a taxable exchange if it is not decanting authorized by the governing instrument or applicable state law.[149]

Also, gain is recognized on a transfer of negative basis assets, such as property with debt in excess of basis or a partnership or LLC interest with a negative capital account. In such case, gain may be triggered under *Crane v. Commissioner*,[150] which held that when a taxpayer sells or exchanges property and is discharged from liability, the taxpayer's amount realized includes any debt that is discharged. Based on Crane, the IRS has concluded that the termination of grantor trust status results in gain recognition if the trust holds properties having liabilities in excess of basis or partnership interests with negative capital accounts.[151] It is not clear if *Crane* applies to a distribution from a non-grantor trust. Code section 643(e) provides that gain generally is not recognized on a distribution of appreciated property from a non-grantor trust and it is not clear whether *Crane* trumps section 643(e). As a result, practitioners have requested that the IRS issue guidance on this issue. However, even if *Crane* does trump section 643(e), if all of the assets of the first trust are distributed to a second trust that is viewed as a continuation of the first trust, no gain should be recognized on a decanting distribution.

If the first trust is a grantor trust, but the second trust is not, upon the decanting, the grantor trust status terminates causing a deemed disposition of the trust assets from a grantor trust to a non-grantor trust. Gain is then recognized to the extent that the liabilities of the transferred assets exceed the trust's basis in the assets.[152]

Gain Recognition by Beneficiaries

The basic rule under Code section 1001 is that an exchange of property is a disposition of property and results in the recognition of gain or loss only if the exchanged properties are "materially different" in either kind or extent.[153] In *Cottage Savings v. Commissioner*,[154] the Supreme Court adopted a test for determining when property received in an exchange is considered to be materially different from the property transferred. Under Cottage Savings, two properties are materially different if its owners have legal entitlements that differ in kind or extent. Several PLRs issued after *Cottage Savings* suggest that a distribution of assets from one trust to another results in gain to the beneficiary if the interests of the beneficiaries under the second trust differ materially from their interests under the first trust.[155]

In *Cottage Savings* and the PLRs that followed, the taxpayers voluntarily exchanged their assets. However, when a trust is decanted, the changes in the beneficiary's interests under the trust result from the trustee's decision to decant, not the beneficiary's actions. Trust beneficiaries rarely participate in the decanting and under most state statutes are prohibited from doing so. Therefore, the exercise by the trustee of a decanting power, whether conferred under the instrument itself or pursuant to state law, seems to result in no recognition of gain or loss to a beneficiary. Several IRS private letter rulings are consistent with this view.[156] These PLRs are also consistent with Treasury Regulations section 1.1001-1(h), which provides that a non-pro rata severance of a trust does not constitute an exchange of property for other property differing materially in either kind or extent if applicable state law or the trust instrument authorize the severance and non-pro rata funding. It seems critical to this conclusion that the beneficiary's consent, and possibly the court's approval, is not required for the trustee to decant.

Application of Subchapter J

Under the rules of Subchapter J, a distribution from a complex trust carries out a share of the trust's distributable net income (DNI) to the beneficiary who receives the distribution. The trust receives a distribution deduction under Code section 661 and the beneficiary includes in gross income an amount equal to his share of the trust's DNI under section 662. It is not clear whether the Subchapter J rules apply to a trust decanting, but the Treasury regulations and case law indicate that a trust can be a beneficiary of another trust, with the Subchapter J rules applicable to a distribution to the second trust.[157]

Decanting could be considered either a continuation or modification of an existing trust. If the terms of the second trust are essentially the same as the terms of the first trust, the decanting should be treated as a continuation. The trusts will have substantially similar terms if the trusts have the same beneficiaries, the same standards for distribution and the same timing for payments. The first trust and the second trust would then be treated as the same trust for income tax purposes. The distribution from the first trust would be tax neutral and no DNI would be carried out.[158] This should be the case even if the property is encumbered with debt in excess of basis or negative capital account property is decanted. Since the second trust is viewed as a continuation of the first trust, the second trust should be able to use the same EIN as the first trust.

If the terms of the new trust were significantly different, the decanting should be treated as a modification. The transfer of assets should carry out DNI, resulting in income to the receiving trust under Code section 662(a). However, there would be a corresponding distribution deduction for the distributing trust under section 661(a).

Credits and Capital Loss Carryover

The Code and Regulations specifically provide that in a trust's final year, any unused NOL and capital loss carryovers on termination are passed out to the trust beneficiaries and allowed as deductions by them.[159]

There is no specific authority on whether beneficiaries succeed to a terminated trust's other tax attributes. However, if all of the assets of the first trust are distributed to a second trust with substantially similar terms so that the second trust is viewed as a continuation of the first trust, the second trust should succeed to the first trust's tax attributes and carryover should apply.[160] Even if there are significant differences, the tax attributes might carry over under general tax principles which consistent with other areas of the law, including the private foundation rules and the rules for corporate reorganizations.[161]

CHAPTER ENDNOTES

1. Arizona, California, Idaho, Louisiana, Nevada, New Mexico, Texas, Washington, and Wisconsin are community property states.

2. I.R.C. §1014(b)(6).

3. Treas. Reg. §25.2511-2(b); *Moran Trust v Comm'r.*, 259 F.2d. 231, 5th CCA 1958; Priv. Ltr. Rul. 8617006.

4. Restatement (3d) Trusts §63.

5. *Id*. See Comment C regarding presumptions regarding revocability.

6. Restatement (2d) Trusts §330 (1959); NY EPTL §7-1.16; O.C.G.A. §53-12-40(a).

7. UTC §602(a).

8. 10 Cal. Probate Code §15400; Fla. Stat. §736.0602(1); Montana Code Ann. §72-33-401; Ohio Rev. Code §5806.02; Utah §75-7-605(1); N.C. Gen. Stat. §36C-6-602; Va. Code §64.2-751; Alabama §19-3B-602; Arizona Rev. Stat. §14-10602; Arkansas Trust Code §28-73-602; Colorado §15-16-702.

9. Fam. Code §761(b).

10. Comment to UTC §601.

11. Restatement (3d) of Trusts, §11.

12. UTC §601.

13. Cal. Probate Code §812.

14. UTC §602(e).

15. Cal. Probate Code §15401(c).

16. Fla. Stat. §736.0602(5).

17. UTC §602(f).

18. See *In re Elsie B.*, 707 N.Y.S.2d 695 (N.Y. App. Div. 2000).

19. See *In re Guardianship and Conservatorship of Garcia*, 262 Neb. 205 (2001).

20. See *Rene v. Sykes-Kennedy*, 156 So. 3d 518 (Fla. Dist. Ct. App. 2015).

21. *Id.* at 519.

22. See *In re Guardianship and Conservatorship of Garcia*, 262 Neb. 205 (2001).

23. *In re Chandler*, 767 A2d 1036 (NJ Super. Ct. App. Div. 2001).

24. See UTC §§107 and 403.

25. See UTC §108.

26. Comment to UTC §403. The validity of a trust created by will is ordinarily determined by the law of the decedent's domicile.

27. See, e.g., Ala. Code 19-3B-407 (2016); D.C. Code 19-1304.03 (2014); S.C. Code 62-7-403 (2016).

28. Fla. Stat. §736.0403(1).

29. See Restatement (3d) Trusts §22.

30. UTC §602(c)(2).

31. Restatement (3d) Trusts §63, Comment i.

32. NY EPTL §7-1.17.

33. O.C.G.A. §53-12-40 (2016).

34. Comment to UTC §602.

35. See *Bernal v. Marin*, 41 Fla. L. Weekly D1428 (Fla. 3d DCA 2016).

36. Cal. Probate Code §15401(a). California allows initialed post-execution interlineations or additions to constitute valid amendments to a trust. See Cal. Prob. Code §15402(a)(2); see also *Estate of Williams* (2007) 155 Cal. App. 4th 197, 217 (2007).

37. See *MacIntyre v. Wedell*, 12 So. 3d 273 (Fla. 4th DCA 2009).

38. See S.C. Code Ann. 62-7-602(c).

39. See, e.g., *Monell v. College of Physicians and Surgeons*, 17 Cal. Rptr.744 (Cal. Ct. App. 1961) (invalid oral trust of money).

40. *Heaps v. Heaps*, 124 Cal. App. 4th 286 (2004).

41. See Fla. Stat. §732.513.

42. See *Estate of Phelan v. Baskin*, 375 Ill. App. 3d 875 (2007) (the will's execution prior to signing the trust did not bar incorporation of the trust by reference into the will, because no law required the trust to be signed before the will in order to be in existence).

43. See comment to UTC §602.

44. *Id.* citing Restatement (Third) of Trusts §63 Reporter's Notes to comments h-j.

45. See *In re Trust Estate of Daoang*, 953 P. 2d 959 (Haw. Ct. App. 1998).

46. UTC §602(c).

47. See *Barlow v. Olguin (In re Estate of Schlicht)*, 2014 WL 1600914 (N.M. App. 2014).

48. I.R.C. §676.

49. Treas. Reg. §25.2511-2(c).

50. I.R.C. §2038.

51. A dynasty trust is a trust that is designed to last more than two generations.

52. *Id.*

53. See Restatement (Second) Conflicts of Laws §§268, 277; UTC §107 (2010 rev.).

54. Comment to UTC §107.

55. The Restatement (Second) Conflicts of Laws: Trusts §§268(1), 272(a) (1971).

56. Comment to UTC §108.

57. See Restatement (Second) Conflicts of Laws §§268, 277; Uniform Trust Code §107 (2010 rev.).

58. Twenty-nine states including Virginia, the District of Columbia, and Florida have enacted various forms of the UTC.

59. I.R.C. §674(a).

60. I.R.C. §672(b).

61. I.R.C. §672(a).

62. Treas. Reg. §1.672(a)-1(a).

63. *Madorin v. Comm'r.*, 84 T.C. 667 (1985).

64. "Qualified beneficiary" means a beneficiary who, on the date the beneficiary's qualification is determined: (A) is a distributee or permissible distributee of trust income or principal; (B) would be a distributee or permissible distributee of trust income or principal if the interests of the distributees described in subparagraph (A) terminated on that date without causing the trust to terminate; or (C) would be a distributee or permissible distributee of trust income or principal if the trust terminated on that date. UTC §103(13).

65. UTC §§108(c)-(f).

66. UTC §107.

67. A. Casner, 5 *American Law of Property* §23.1 (Little, Brown 1952); Pertham, "A Look at the Principles and Uses of Powers of Appointment," 132 Tr. & Est. 38 (Aug. 1993).

68. The powerholder can cI.R.C.umvent this rule by exercising the power to give another person a new power of appointment over the same assets.

69. §11.1, comment b (2011).

70. *Id.* at §19.13, comment g.

71. *Id.* at §17.3.

72. The taw law with respect to powers of appointment changed significantly on October 21, 1942, and powers of appointment created before that date were grandfathered under the pre-existing law. This chapter only discusses powers of appointment created after October 21, 1942.

73. Treas. Reg. §20.2041-1(b)(1).

74. Restatement (3d) Property §§18.1, 18.2.

75. *Id*. at §19.9, comment. g. So long as a trust remains revocable on the decedent's death, a testamentary power of appointment may be exercised by a provision in decedent's revocable trust.

76. See Treas. Reg. §20.2041-1(e).

77. I.R.C. §2041(b)(1)(A).

78. I.R.C. §2041(b)(1)(C)(i).

79. I.R.C. §2041(b)(1)(C)(ii).

80. *Maytag v. United States*, 493 F.2d 995 (10th Cir. 1974).

81. See Rev. Rul. 95-58.

82. I.R.C. §678.

83. I.R.C. §2041.

84. *Crummey v. Comm'r.*, 347 F. 2d 82 (9th Cir. 1968); Rev. Rul. 73-405, 1973-2 C.B. 721.

85. I.R.C. §§2041(b)(2) and 2514(c).

86. Treas. Reg. §20.2041-1(c)(1).

87. I.R.C. §2041(b)(1)(A).

88. See Treas. Reg. §20.2041-1(c)(2).

89. See Estate of *Vissering v. Comm'r.*, 990 F. 2d 578 (10th Cir. 1991).

90. Priv. Ltr. Rul. 201229005.

91. See Rev. Rul. 54-153.

92. See, e.g., Va. Code. Ann. §64.2-776.

93. UTC §§411 and 415; Restatement Third of Law of Property §12.1.

94. Comment to UTC §411.

95. UTC §411(b).

96. UTC §411.

97. Comment to UTC §413.

98. UTC §413(b).

99. UTC §412(a).

100. Comment to UTC §416.

101. UTC §416; *Comm'r. v. Estate of Bosch*, 387 US 456.

102. F.S. 726.0412.

103. UTC §111(a).

104. Some states have eliminated this requirement. See Del. §3338(c).

105. UTC §111(c).

106. UTC §111(e).

107. UTC §411(a).

108. UTC §417; e.g. Fla. Stat. 736.0417 and Tex. Prop Code 112.057(a).

109. *Id*.

110. Cal. Probate Code §15412.

111. UTC §816(22).

112. *Van Den Wymelenberg v. U.S.*, 397 F.2d 443. 97th Cir. 1968).

113. Priv. Ltr. Ruls. 200219012, 200106008, and 200144018.

114. *Comm'r. v. Estate of Bosch*, 387 U.S. 456 (1967).

115. The IRS honors some amendment that do not fall within the Bosch decision, because they are authorized by the Internal Revenue Code or the regulations. For example, amending a trust to qualify it as a "qualified domestic trust under Treas. Reg. §20.2056A-4.

116. Priv. Ltr. Rul. 201243001.

117. A written statement explaining the tax implications of a particular transaction.

118. Rev. Rul. 73-142, 1973-1 C.B. 405.

119. Restatement (2d) Property §11.1 (1986); Restatement (3d) Property §19.14 (Tentative Draft No. 5, 2006).

120. The first case to recognize a trustee's decanting power was Phipps v. Palm Beach Trust Co., 142 Fla. 782 (Fla. 1940) (a trustee could invade trust property by transferring it to another trust so long as one or more of the beneficiaries of the original trust are also beneficiaries of the new trust). After *Phipps* came *Wiedenmayer v. Johnson*, 106 N. J. Super 161 (1969); *In re Estate of Spencer*, 232 N.W.2d 491, 493–95 (Iowa 1975); *Morse v. Kraft*, 992 N.E.2d 1021 (Mass. 2013); and *Ferri v. Powell-Ferri*, 2013 WL 5289955in Connecticut (applying Massachusetts law).

121. NY EPTL §10-6.6.

122. Alabama (H.B. 163) Alaska (Alaska Stat. §13.36.157), Arizona (Ariz. Rev. Stat. §14-10819), Delaware (12 Del. Code §3528), Florida (Fla. Stat. §736.04117), California (§19501-19530), Colorado (C.R.S. 15-16-901-930), Georgia (O.C.G.A. §53-12-62 Illinois (760 ILCS 5/16.4), Indiana (Ind. Code 30-4-3-36), Kentucky (Ky. Rev. Stat. §386.175), Michigan (Mich. Comp. Laws §700.7820a; M.C.L.A. 556.115a), Minnesota (Minn. Stat. §503.851), Missouri (Mo. Rev. Stat. §456.4-419), Nevada (Nev. Rev. Stat. §163.556), New Hampshire (NH Rev. Stat. Ann. §564-B:4-418), New Mexico (§46-12-101-129, New York (NY EPTL §10-6.6), North Carolina (N.C. Gen. Stat. §36C-8-816.1), Ohio (Ohio Rev. Code §5808.18), Rhode Island (R.I. Gen. Laws §18-4-31), South Carolina (S.C. Code §62-7-816A), South Dakota (S.D. Codified Law §55-2-15), Tennessee (Tenn. Code Ann. §35-15-816(27)), Texas (Texas Prop. Code §§112.071–112.087), Virginia (Va. Code §64.2-778.1), Washington (RCW §11.107), Wisconsin (Wisconsin Trust Code §701.0418), and Wyoming (W.S. 4-10-816(a)(xxviii)).

123. Alaska, Illinois, Missouri, New York, North Carolina and Texas.

124. Arizona and New Hampshire.

125. Florida, Michigan, New York.

126. Alaska Stat. §13.36.159, Cal. Stat. §19507, M.C.L.C. §700.7820A(7),-and Ohio Rev. Code Ann. §5808.18(F).;.

127. Nev. Rev. Stat. §163.556(7).

128. Florida, Indiana, Kentucky, Michigan, Nevada, North Carolina, Ohio, Rhode Island and South Dakota.

129. Ariz. Rev. Stat. Ann. §14-10819(D); Nev. Rev. Stat. §163.556(7)..

130. Arizona, Delaware, Florida, Indiana, Michigan, Missouri, North Carolina, Ohio and Tennessee.

131. Alaska, Florida, Illinois, Michigan, New York, North Carolina, Ohio and Virginia.

132. Alaska, Delaware, Illinois, Kentucky, Michigan, Nevada, New York, North Carolina, Ohio, South Dakota, Tennessee, Texas and Virginia.

133. Alaska, Arizona, Florida, Indiana, Illinois, Michigan, Nevada, Kentucky, New Hampshire, New York, North Carolina, Ohio, Rhode Island, Texas and Virginia.

134. This designation has continued under Rev. Proc. 2019-3, §§5.01(7), (12) & (13).

135. *Id*.

136. See Treas. Reg. §25.2511-1(c)(1).

137. See Section 50 of the Restatement (Third) of Trusts.

138. I.R.C. §2514(b), (e); Regs. §§25.2514-3(a), (c)(4).

139. New York and New Hampshire.

140. See. F.S. §736.0814(4).

141. Treas. Reg. §25.2511-1(g)(2).

142. See, e.g., N.C. Gen. Stat. §36C-8-816.1(c)(8), (e)(2).

143. Treas. Reg. §26-2601-1(b)(4)(i)(D).

144. Priv. Ltr. Ruls. 201134017 and 200839025.

145. Rev. Rul. 85-13; Priv. Ltr. Rul. 200228019.

146. CCA 20092303.

147. Treas. Reg. §1.1001-1(h); Priv. Ltr. Rul. 200743022.

148. Priv. Ltr. Rul. 200810019.

149. Rev. Rul. 69-486.

150. *Crane v. Comm'r.*, 331 U.S. 1 (1947).

151. See Treas. Reg. §1.1001-1(e), Example 5, TAM 200010010 (March 13, 2000), *Madorin v. Comm'r.*, 84 T.C. 667 (1985).

152. *Madorin v. Comm'r.*, 84 T.C. 667 (1985); rev. Rul. 77-402; Reg. §1.1001-2(c), Example 5; *Crane v.Comm'r.*, 331 U.S. 1 (1947).

153. Treas. Reg. §1.1001-1(a).

154. 499 U.S. 504 (1991).

155. Priv. Ltr. Ruls. 2012207001, 201136014 and 199951028.

156. See Priv. Ltr. Ruls. 201204001, 201133007, and 201134017.

157. See Treas. Reg. §1.643(c)-1; *Duke v. Comm'r.*, 38 BTA 1264, 1269 (1938); *Comm'r v. Bishop Trust Co.*, 136 F2d 390 (9th Cir. 1943), aff'g. 42 BTA 1309 (1940); *Harwood Estate v. Comm'r.*, 3 TC 1104 (1945); *White Estate v. Comm'r.*, 41 BTA 525 (1939); *Lynchburg Tr. & Sav. Bank v. Comm'r.*, 68 F2d 356 (4th Cir. 1934).

158. See Priv. Ltr. Ruls. 200527007, 200607015, and 200723014.

159. I.R.C. §642(h) and Treas. Reg. §1.642(h)-3(d).

160. Priv. Ltr. Rul. 200607015.

161. See I.R.C. §381.

INCOME TAX TABLES

The American Taxpayer Relief Act of 2012 (ATRA) made the income tax brackets put into place under the Economic Growth and Tax Relief Reconciliation Act (EGTRRA) permanent and added a new top tax bracket for certain high income taxpayers. The permanence of the ATRA provisions eliminated much of the uncertainty faced by taxpayers in previous years.

Under ATRA, for tax years beginning after 2012, individual income tax rates are set at 10 percent, 15 percent, 25 percent, 28 percent, 33 percent, 35 percent and 39.6 percent.

INDIVIDUAL 2019 TAX RATES

		Taxable Income		
Tax Rate	Single	Married Filing Jointly Including Qualifying Widow(er) with Dependent Child	Married Filing Separately	Head of Household
10%	$0 to $9,700	$0 to $19,400	$0 to $9,700	$0 to $13,850
12%	$9,700-$39,475	$19,400-$78,950	$9,700-$39,475	$13,850-$52,850
22%	$39,475-$84,200	$78,950-$168,400	$39,475-$84,200	$52,850-$84,200
24%	$84,200-$160,725	$168,400-$321,450	$84,200-$160,725	$84,200-$160,700
32%	$160,725-$204,100	$321,450-$408,200	$160,725-$204,100	$160,700-$204,100
35%	$204,100-$510,300	$408,200-$612,350	$204,100-$306,175	$204,100-$510,300
37%	Over $510,300	Over $612,350	Over $306,175	Over $510,300

ESTATE AND TRUSTS 2019 TAX RATES

Tax Rate	Trusts and Estate Income
10%	$0 to $2,600
$260 plus 24% of the excess over $2,600	$2,600-$9,300
$1,868 plus 35% of the excess over $9,300	$9,300-$12,750
$3,075.50 plus 37% of the excess over $12,750	Over $12,750

INDIVIDUAL 2018 TAX RATES

	Taxable Income			
Tax Rate	Single	Married Filing Jointly Including Qualifying Widow(er) with Dependent Child	Married Filing Separately	Head of Household
10%	$0 to $9,525	$0 to $19,050	$0 to $9,525	$0 to $13,600
12%	$9,525-$38,700	$19,050-$77,400	$9,525-$38,700	$13,600-$51,800
22%	$38,700-$82,500	$77,400-$165,000	$38,700-$82,500	$51,800-$82,500
24%	$82,500-$157,500	$165,000-$315,000	$82,500-$157,500	$82,500-$157,500
32%	$157,500-$200,000	$315,000-$400,000	$157,500-$200,000	$157,500-$200,000
35%	$200,000-$500,000	$400,000-$600,000	$200,000-$300,000	$200,000-$500,000
37%	Over $500,000	Over $600,000	Over $300,000	Over $500,000

ESTATE AND TRUSTS 2018 TAX RATES

Tax Rate	Trusts and Estate Income
10%	$0 to $2,550
$255 plus 24% of the excess over $2,550	$2,550-$9,150
$1,839 plus 35% of the excess over $9,150	$9,150-$12,500
$3,011.50 plus 37% of the excess over $12,500	Over $12,500

INDIVIDUAL 2017 TAX RATES

	Taxable Income			
Tax Rate	Single	Married Filing Jointly	Married Filing Separately	Head of Household
10%	$0 to $9,325	$0 to $18,650	$0 to $9,325	$0 to $13,350
15%	$9,325 - $37,950	$18,650-$75,900	$9,325-$37,950	$13,350-$50,800
25%	$37,950 - $91,900	$75,900-$153,100	$37,950-$76,550	$50,800-$131,200
28%	$91,900 -$191,650	$153,100-$233,350	$76,550-$116,675	$131,200-$212,500
33%	$191,650 -$416,700	$233,350-$416,700	$116,675-$208,350	$212,500-$416,700
35%	$416,700-$418,400	$416,700-$470,700	$208,350-$235,350	$416,700-$444,550
39.6%	Over $418,400	Over $470,700	Over $235,350	Over $444,550

ESTATES AND TRUSTS 2017 TAX RATES

Tax Rate	Trusts and Estate Income
15%	$0 to $2,550
25%	$2,550-$6,000
28%	$6,000-$9,150
33%	$9,150-$12,500
39.6%	Over $12,500

INDIVIDUAL 2016 TAX RATES

Tax Rate	Single	Married Filing Jointly	Married Filing Separately	Head of Household
		Taxable Income		
10%	$0 to $9,275	$0 to $18,550	$0 to $9,275	$0 to $13,250
15%	$9,275-$37,650	$18,550-$75,300	$9,275-$37,650	$13,250-$50,400
25%	$37,650-$91,150	$75,300-$151,900	$37,650-$75,950	$50,400-$130,150
28%	$91,150-$190,150	$151,900-$231,450	$75,950-$115,725	$130,150-$210,800
33%	$190,150-$413,350	$231,450-$413,350	$115,725-$206,675	$210,800-$413,350
35%	$413,350-$415,050	$413,350-$466,950	$206,675-$233,475	$413,350-$441,000
39.6%	Over $415,050	Over $466,950	Over $233,475	Over $441,000

ESTATES AND TRUSTS 2016 TAX RATES

Tax Rate	Trust sand Estate Income
15%	$0 to $2,550
25%	$2,550-$5,950
28%	$5,950-$9,050
33%	$9,050-$12,400
39.6%	Over $12,400

CORPORATIONS

Beginning in 2018, all corporations have a 21percent tax.

2019 INFLATION INDEXED AMOUNTS

In April, 2018, the IRS announced, in Revenue Procedure 2018-30, these 2019 inflation indexed amounts:

Health Savings Accounts. An HDHP has annual deductible of not less than $1,350 for self-only coverage, $2,700 for family coverage, annual out-of-pocket expenses not exceeding $6,750 for self-only coverage, or $13,500 for family coverage. The maximum annual HSA contribution is $3,500 for self-only coverage and $7,000 for family coverage.

TRANSFER TAX TABLES

2010 ESTATE AND GIFT TAX TABLE

Taxable Gift/Estate		Tax on Col. 1	Rate on Excess
From	To		
$0	$10,000	$0	18%
10,001	20,000	1,800	20%
20,001	40,000	3,800	22%
40,001	60,000	8,200	24%
60,001	80,000	13,000	26%
80,001	100,000	18,200	28%
100,001	150,000	23,800	30%
150,001	250,000	38,800	32%
250,001	500,000	70,800	34%
500,001	....	155,800	35%

2011-2012 GIFT AND ESTATE TAX TABLE

Taxable Gift/Estate		Tax on Col. 1	Rate on Excess
From	To		
$0	$10,000	$0	18%
10,001	20,000	1,800	20%
20,001	40,000	3,800	22%
40,001	60,000	8,200	24%
60,001	80,000	13,000	26%
80,001	100,000	18,200	28%
100,001	150,000	23,800	30%
150,001	250,000	38,800	32%
250,001	500,000	70,800	34%
500,001	750,000	155,800	35%

IRC Secs. 2001(c), 2502(a), 2210, as amended by EGTRRA 2001.

2013-2018 GIFT AND ESTATE TAX TABLE

Taxable Gift/Estate		Tax on Col. 1	Rate on Excess
From	To		
$0	$10,000	$0	18%
10,001	20,000	1,800	20%
20,001	40,000	3,800	22%
40,001	60,000	8,200	24%
60,001	80,000	13,000	26%
80,001	100,000	18,200	28%
100,001	150,000	23,800	30%
150,001	250,000	38,800	32%
250,001	500,000	70,800	34%
500,001	750,000	155,800	37%
750,000	1,000,000	248,300	39%
1,000,000		345,800	40%
IRC Secs. 2001(c), 2502(a), 2210, as amended by EGTRRA 2001 and ATRA.			

2018 STATE ESTATE AND INHERITANCE TAX TABLE

State	Estate Tax (Rate)	Inheritance Tax (Rate)	Exemption
Alabama	None	None	
Alaska	None	None	
Arizona	None	None	
Arkansas	None	None	
California	None	None	
Colorado	None	None	
Connecticut	7.2%-12%	None	$2 million
Delaware	0.8%-16%	None	$5.49 million
District of Columbia	0.8%-16%	None	$1 million
Florida	None	None	
Georgia	None	None	
Hawaii	0.8%-16%	None	$5.49 million
Idaho	None	None	
Illinois	0.8%-16%	None	$4 million
Indiana	None	None	
Iowa[1]	None	0%-15%	$25,000
Kansas	None	None	
Kentucky[2]	None	0%-16%	$1,000
Louisiana	None	None	
Maine	8%-12%	None	$5.49 million
Maryland[3]	0%-16%	0%-10%	$3 million (estate)
Massachusetts	0.8%-16%	None	$1 million
Michigan	None	None	
Minnesota[4]	9%-16%	None	$1.6 million
Mississippi	None	None	
Missouri	None	None	
Montana	None	None	

State	Estate Tax (Rate)	Inheritance Tax (Rate)	Exemption
Nebraska[5]	None	1%-18%	$40,000/$15,000/$10,000
Nevada	None	None	
New Hampshire	None	None	
New Jersey[6]	0.8%-16%	0%-16%	$675,000 (estate) $25,000 (inheritance for certain relatives only)
New Mexico	None	None	
New York[7]	5%-16%	None	$5.25 million
North Carolina	None	None	
North Dakota	None	None	
Ohio	None	None	
Oklahoma	None	None	
Oregon	0.8%-16%	None	$1 million
Pennsylvania[8]	None	0%-15%	
Rhode Island[9]	0.8%-16%	None	$1.5 million
South Carolina	None	None	
South Dakota	None	None	
Tennessee[10]	None	None	
Texas	None	None	
Utah	None	None	
Vermont	0.8%-16%	None	$2.75 million
Virginia	None	None	
Washington[11]	10%-20%	None	$2.129 million
West Virginia	None	None	
Wisconsin	None	None	
Wyoming	None	None	

[1] Most states that impose an inheritance tax distinguish the applicable tax rate or exemption based upon the person who inherits. In Iowa, a surviving spouse, parents, grandparents, children, grandchildren and certain charitable organizations are exempt from the inheritance tax regardless of the size of the estate. All others who inherit are entitled to the $25,000 exemption.

[2] In Kentucky, a surviving spouse, parents, children, grandchildren, brothers, and sisters are exempt from the state inheritance tax.

[3] Maryland passed a new law in 2014 that will gradually increase the estate tax exemption. The exemption will increase to $2 million (2016), $3 million (2017), $4 million (2018) and by 2019, the exemption will be equal to the federal exemption amount. Maryland's inheritance tax does not apply to surviving spouses, children, grandchildren, parents, grandparents, brothers or sisters of the decedent, among others.

[4] The Minnesota state estate tax exemption will rise by $200,000 each year until it reaches $2 million in 2018.

[5] A surviving spouse is exempt from the inheritance tax in Nebraska no matter how large the estate. The $40,000 exemption applies only to close family members, including parents, grandparents, children, and grandchildren. The $15,000 exemption applies to more distant relatives, including aunts, uncles, nieces, nephews, and the lineal descendants or spouses of these relatives. Any other heir receives the $10,000 exemption.

[6] Spouses, domestic partners, civil union partners, parents, grandparents, children (including stepchildren), grandchildren (but not step grandchildren) are exempt from the inheritance tax. The $25,000 inheritance tax exemption applies to brothers, sisters, spouses or civil union partners of the decedent's child, and surviving spouses or civil union partners of the decedent's child. There is no exemption for any other person who inherits.

[7] The New York exemption amount will increase by $1.0625 million on April 1 of each year until it reaches $5.25 million in 2017. On January 1, 2019, it will jump to the federal estate tax exemption amount.

[8] In Pennsylvania, the inheritance tax does not apply to surviving spouses, parents, stepparents (if the decedent was 21 or younger), charitable organizations and government entities that inherit. The Pennsylvania inheritance tax rates differ depending upon who inherits (children, grandchildren and spouses of children pay a 4.5% rate, while brothers and sisters pay a 12% rate, and all others pay a 15% rate).

[9] The Rhode Island exemption is indexed annually for inflation beginning in 2016.

[10] The Tennessee estate tax is scheduled to be eliminated for 2016 and beyond.

[11] The Washington exemption amount is indexed annually for inflation.

ESTATE TAX UNIFIED CREDIT

Year	Exclusion Equivalent	Unified Credit
2000-2001	$675,000	$220,550
2002-2003	$1,000,000	$345,800
2004-2005	$1,500,000	$555,800
2006-2008	$2,000,000	$780,800
2009	$3,500,000	$1,455,800
2010	$5,000,000	$1,730,800
2011	$5,000,000	$1,730,800
2012	$5,120,000	$1,772,800
2013	$5,250,000	$2,045,800
2014	$5,340,000	$2,081,800
2015	$5,430,000	$2,117,800
2016	$5,450,000	$2,125,800
2017	$5,490,000	$2,141,800
2018	$11,180,000	$4,371,600
2019	$11,400,000	

IRC Sec. 2010(c), as amended by EGTRRA 2001 and ATRA. Pub. Law No. 115-97 (2017 Tax Act).

GIFT TAX UNIFIED CREDIT

Year	Exclusion Equivalent	Unified Credit
1977 (1-1 to 6-30)	$30,000	$6,000
1977 (7-1 to 12-31)	120,667	30,000
1978	134,000	34,000
1979	147,333	38,000
1980	161,563	42,500
1981	175,625	47,000
1982	225,000	62,800
1983	275,000	79,300
1984	325,000	96,300
1985	400,000	121,800
1986	500,000	155,800
1987-1997	600,000	192,800
1998	625,000	202,050
1999	650,000	211,300
2000-2001	675,000	220,550
2002-2009	1,000,000	345,800
2010	$5,000,000	$1,730,800
2011	$5,000,000	$1,730,800
2012	$5,120,000	$1,772,800
2013	$5,250,000	$2,045,800
2014	$5,340,000	$2,081,800
2015	$5,430,000	$2,117,800

Year	Exclusion Equivalent	Unified Credit
2016	$5,450,000	$2,125,800
2017	$5,490,000	$2,141,800
2018	$11,180,000	$4,371,600
2019	$11,400,000	
IRC Secs. 2505(a), 2010(c), as amended by EGTRRA 2001 and ATRA. Pub. Law No. 115-97 (2017 Tax Act).		

MAXIMUM STATE DEATH TAX CREDIT (SDTC)

Adjusted Taxable Estate		Credit on Col. 1	Rate on Excess
From	To		
$40,000	$90,000	$0	0.8%
90,001	140,000	400	1.6%
140,001	240,000	1,200	2.4%
240,001	440,000	3,600	3.2%
440,001	640,000	10,000	4.0%
640,001	840,000	18,000	4.8%
840,001	1,040,000	27,600	5.6%
1,040,001	1,540,000	38,800	6.4%
1,540,001	2,040,000	70,800	7.2%
2,040,001	2,540,000	106,800	8.0%
2,540,001	3,040,000	146,800	8.8%
3,040,001	3,540,000	190,800	9.6%
3,540,001	4,040,000	238,800	10.4%
4,040,001	5,040,000	290,800	11.2%
5,040,001	6,040,000	402,800	12.0%
6,040,001	7,040,000	522,800	12.8%
7,040,001	8,040,000	650,800	13.6%
8,040,001	9,040,000	786,800	14.4%
9,040,001	10,040,000	930,800	15.2%
10,040,001	....	1,082,800	16.0%
For this purpose, the term "adjusted taxable estate" means the taxable estate reduced by $60,000.			

REDUCTION IN MAXIMUM SDTC

Year	Multiply Maximum SDTC Above By
2002	75%
2003	50%
2004	25%
2005-2009	NA*
2010	NA*
2011-2018	NA*
*deduction for state death taxes paid replaces credit	
IRC Secs. 2011(b), 2011(g), 2058, as amended by EGTRRA 2001 and ATRA.	

QUALIFIED FAMILY-OWNED BUSINESS DEDUCTION

Year	Deduction Limitation
1998-2003	$675,000
2004-2018	NA
IRC Secs. 2057(a)(2), 2057(j), as amended by EGTRRA 2001 and ATRA.	

ESTATE TAX DEFERRAL: CLOSELY HELD BUSINESS

Year	2% Interest Limitation
1998	$410,000
1999	$416,500
2000	$427,500
2001	$441,000
2002	$484,000
2003	$493,800
2004	$532,200
2005	$539,900
2006	$552,000
2007	$562,500
2008	$576,000
2009	$598,500
2010	($603,000)
2011	$601,600
2012	$486,500
2013	$572,000
2014	$580,000
2015	$588,000
2016	$592,000
2017	$596,000
2018	$608,000

SPECIAL USE VALUATION LIMITATION

Year	Limitation
1997-1998	$750,000
1999	$760,000
2000	$770,000
2001	$800,000
2002	$820,000
2003	$840,000

Year	Limitation
2004	$850,000
2005	$870,000
2006	$900,000
2007	$940,000
2008	$960,000
2009	$1,000,000
2010	$1,000,000
2011	$1,020,000
2012	$1,040,000
2013	$1,070,000
2014	$1,090,000
2015	$1,100,000
2016	$1,110,000
2017	$1,120,000
2018	$1,140,000
2019	$1,160,000
IRC Sec. 2032A(a). As updated by Rev. Proc. 2017-58.	

QUALIFIED CONSERVATION EASEMENT EXCLUSION

Year	Exclusion Limitation
1998	$100,000
1999	$200,000
2000	$300,000
2001	$400,000
2002 and thereafter	$500,000
IRC Sec. 2031(c)(3).	

GIFT (AND GST) TAX ANNUAL EXCLUSION

Year	Annual Exclusion
1997-2001	$10,000
2002-2005	$11,000
2006-2008	$12,000
2009-2010	$13,000
2011-2012	$13,000
2013-2017	$14,000
2018	$15,000
2019	$15,000
IRC Sec. 2503(b). As updated by Rev. Proc. 2017-58.	

GIFT TAX ANNUAL EXCLUSION

(Donee Spouse not U.S. Citizen)

Year	Annual Exclusion
1997-1998	$100,000
1999	$101,000
2000	$103,000
2001	$106,000
2002	$110,000
2003	$112,000
2004	$114,000
2005	$117,000
2006	$120,000
2007	$125,000
2008	$128,000
2009	$133,000
2010	$134,000
2011	$136,000
2012	$139,000
2013	$143,000
2014	$145,000
2015	$147,000
2016	$148,000
2017	$149,000
2018	$152,000
2019	$155,000
IRC Sec. 2523(i). As updated by Rev. Proc. 2017-58.	

GENERATION-SKIPPING TRANSFER TAX TABLE

Year	Tax Rate
2001	55%
2002	50%
2003	49%
2004	48%
2005	47%
2006	46%
2007-2009	45%
2010	0%
2011-2012	35%
2013-2018	40%
IRC Secs. 2641, 2001(c), 2664, as amended by EGTRRA 2001 and ATRA.	

GENERATION-SKIPPING TRANSFER TAX EXEMPTION

Year	GST Exemption
1997-1998	$1,000,000
1999	$1,010,000
2000	$1,030,000
2001	$1,060,000
2002	$1,100,000
2003	$1,120,000
2004-2005	$1,500,000
2006-2008	$2,000,000
2009	$3,500,000
2010-2011	$5,000,000
2012	$5,120,000
2013	$5,250,000
2014	$5,340,000
2015	$5,430,000
2016	$5,450,000
2017	$5,490,000
2018	$11,180,000
2019	$11,400,000

*Plus increases for indexing for inflation after 2012.

IRC Secs. 2631, 2010(c), as amended by EGTRRA 2001 and ATRA, Rev. Proc. 2017-58, Pub. Law No. 115-97 (2017 Tax Act).

INDEXED AMOUNTS SOURCE

Year	Rev. Proc.
1999	98-61, 1998-2 CB 811
2000	99-42, 1999-46 IRB 568
2001	2001-13, 2001-3 IRB 337
2002	2001-59, 2001-52 IRB 623
2003	2002-70, 2002-46 IRB 845
2004	2003-85, 2003-49 IRB 1184
2005	2004-71, 2004-50 IRB 970
2006	2005-70, 2005-47 IRB 979
2007	2006-53, 2006-48 IRB 996
2008	2007-66, 2007-45 IRB 970
2009	2008-66, 2008-45 IRB 1107
2010	2009-50, 2009-45 IRB 617
2011	2010-40, 2010-46 IRB 663
2012	2011-52, 2011-45 IRB 701
2013	2013-15, 2013-5 IRB 444
2014	2013-35, 2013 -47 IRB 537
2015	2014-61,2014-47 IRB 860
2016	2015-53, 2015-44 IRB 1
2017	2016-55, 2016-45 IRB 1
2018	2017-58, 2017-42 IRB 1; Pub. Law No. 115-97 (2017 Tax Act)

REQUIRED MINIMUM DISTRIBUTION (RMD) TABLES

APPENDIX C

RMD Uniform Lifetime Table - Distribution Period					
Age	Factor	Age	Factor	Age	Factor
10	86.2	45	51.5	80	18.7
11	85.2	46	50.5	81	17.9
12	84.2	47	49.5	82	17.1
13	83.2	48	48.5	83	16.3
14	82.2	49	47.5	84	15.5
15	81.2	50	46.5	85	14.8
16	80.2	51	45.5	86	14.1
17	79.2	52	44.6	87	13.4
18	78.2	53	43.6	88	12.7
19	77.3	54	42.6	89	12.0
20	76.3	55	41.6	90	11.4
21	75.3	56	40.7	91	10.8
22	74.3	57	39.7	92	10.2
23	73.3	58	38.7	93	9.6
24	72.3	59	37.8	94	9.1
25	71.3	60	36.8	95	8.6
26	70.3	61	35.8	96	8.1
27	69.3	62	34.9	97	7.6
28	68.3	63	33.9	98	7.1
29	67.3	64	33.0	99	6.7
30	66.3	65	32.0	100	6.3
31	65.3	66	31.1	101	5.9
32	64.3	67	30.2	102	5.5
33	63.3	68	29.2	103	5.2
34	62.3	69	28.3	104	4.9
35	61.4	70	27.4	105	4.5
36	60.4	71	26.5	106	4.2
37	59.4	72	25.6	107	3.9
38	58.4	73	24.7	108	3.7
39	57.4	74	23.8	109	3.4
40	56.4	75	22.9	110	3.1
41	55.4	76	22.0	111	2.9
42	54.4	77	21.2	112	2.6
43	53.4	78	20.3	113	2.4
44	52.4	79	19.5	114	2.1
				115	1.9

Treas. Reg. Sec. 1.401(a)(9)-9

THE TOOLS & TECHNIQUES OF TRUST PLANNING

RMD Single Life Table - Life Expectancy					
Age	Factor	Age	Factor	Age	Factor
0	82.4	38	45.6	76	12.7
1	81.6	39	44.6	77	12.1
2	80.6	40	43.6	78	11.4
3	79.7	41	42.7	79	10.8
4	78.7	42	41.7	80	10.2
5	77.7	43	40.7	81	9.7
6	76.7	44	39.8	82	9.1
7	75.8	45	38.8	83	8.6
8	74.8	46	37.9	84	8.1
9	73.8	47	37.0	85	7.6
10	72.8	48	36.0	86	7.1
11	71.8	49	35.1	87	6.7
12	70.8	50	34.2	88	6.3
13	69.9	51	33.3	89	5.9
14	68.9	52	32.3	90	5.5
15	67.9	53	31.4	91	5.2
16	66.9	54	30.5	92	4.9
17	66.0	55	29.6	93	4.6
18	65.0	56	28.7	94	4.3
19	64.0	57	27.9	95	4.1
20	63.0	58	27.0	96	3.8
21	62.1	59	26.1	97	3.6
22	61.1	60	25.2	98	3.4
23	60.1	61	24.4	99	3.1
24	59.1	62	23.5	100	2.9
25	58.2	63	22.7	101	2.7
26	57.2	64	21.8	102	2.5
27	56.2	65	21.0	103	2.3
28	55.3	66	20.2	104	2.1
29	54.3	67	19.4	105	1.9
30	53.3	68	18.6	106	1.7
31	52.4	69	17.8	107	1.5
32	51.4	70	17.0	108	1.4
33	50.4	71	16.3	109	1.2
34	49.4	72	15.5	110	1.1
35	48.5	73	14.8	111	1.0
36	47.5	74	14.1		
37	46.5	75	13.4		

Treas. Reg. Sec. 1.401(a)(9)-9

Ages	35	36	37	38	39	40	41	42	43	44	45	46
35	55.2	54.7	54.3	53.8	53.4	53.0	52.7	52.3	52.0	51.7	51.5	51.2
36	54.7	54.2	53.7	53.3	52.8	52.4	52.0	51.7	51.3	51.0	50.7	50.5
37	54.3	53.7	53.2	52.7	52.3	51.8	51.4	51.1	50.7	50.4	50.0	49.8
38	53.8	53.3	52.7	52.2	51.7	51.3	50.9	50.4	50.1	49.7	49.4	49.1
39	53.4	52.8	52.3	51.7	51.2	50.8	50.3	49.9	49.5	49.1	48.7	48.4
40	53.0	52.4	51.8	51.3	50.8	50.2	49.8	49.3	48.9	48.5	48.1	47.7
41	52.7	52.0	51.4	50.9	50.3	49.8	49.3	48.8	48.3	47.9	47.5	47.1
42	52.3	51.7	51.1	50.4	49.9	49.3	48.8	48.3	47.8	47.3	46.9	46.5
43	52.0	51.3	50.7	50.1	49.5	48.9	48.3	47.8	47.3	46.8	46.3	45.9
44	51.7	51.0	50.4	49.7	49.1	48.5	47.9	47.3	46.8	46.3	45.8	45.4
45	51.5	50.7	50.0	49.4	48.7	48.1	47.5	46.9	46.3	45.8	45.3	44.8
46	51.2	50.5	49.8	49.1	48.4	47.7	47.1	46.5	45.9	45.4	44.8	44.3
47	51.0	50.2	49.5	48.8	48.1	47.4	46.7	46.1	45.5	44.9	44.4	43.9
48	50.8	50.0	49.2	48.5	47.8	47.1	46.4	45.8	45.1	44.5	44.0	43.4
49	50.6	49.8	49.0	48.2	47.5	46.8	46.1	45.4	44.8	44.2	43.6	43.0
50	50.4	49.6	48.8	48.0	47.3	46.5	45.8	45.1	44.4	43.8	43.2	42.6
51	50.2	49.4	48.6	47.8	47.0	46.3	45.5	44.8	44.1	43.5	42.8	42.2
52	50.0	49.2	48.4	47.6	46.8	46.0	45.3	44.6	43.8	43.2	42.5	41.8
53	49.9	49.1	48.2	47.4	46.6	45.8	45.1	44.3	43.6	42.9	42.2	41.5
54	49.8	48.9	48.1	47.2	46.4	45.6	44.8	44.1	43.3	42.6	41.9	41.2
55	49.7	48.8	47.9	47.1	46.3	45.5	44.7	43.9	43.1	42.4	41.6	40.9
56	49.5	48.7	47.8	47.0	46.1	45.3	44.5	43.7	42.9	42.1	41.4	40.7
57	49.4	48.6	47.7	46.8	46.0	45.1	44.3	43.5	42.7	41.9	41.2	40.4
58	49.4	48.5	47.6	46.7	45.8	45.0	44.2	43.3	42.5	41.7	40.9	40.2
59	49.3	48.4	47.5	46.6	45.7	44.9	44.0	43.2	42.4	41.5	40.7	40.0
60	49.2	48.3	47.4	46.5	45.6	44.7	43.9	43.0	42.2	41.4	40.6	39.8
61	49.1	48.2	47.3	46.4	45.5	44.6	43.8	42.9	42.1	41.2	40.4	39.6
62	49.1	48.1	47.2	46.3	45.4	44.5	43.7	42.8	41.9	41.1	40.3	39.4
63	49.0	48.1	47.2	46.3	45.3	44.5	43.6	42.7	41.8	41.0	40.1	39.3
64	48.9	48.0	47.1	46.2	45.3	44.4	43.5	42.6	41.7	40.8	40.0	39.2
65	48.9	48.0	47.0	46.1	45.2	44.3	43.4	42.5	41.6	40.7	39.9	39.0
66	48.9	47.9	47.0	46.1	45.1	44.2	43.3	42.4	41.5	40.6	39.8	38.9
67	48.8	47.9	46.9	46.0	45.1	44.2	43.3	42.3	41.4	40.6	39.7	38.8
68	48.8	47.8	46.9	46.0	45.0	44.1	43.2	42.3	41.4	40.5	39.6	38.7
69	48.7	47.8	46.9	45.9	45.0	44.1	43.1	42.2	41.3	40.4	39.5	38.6
70	48.7	47.8	46.8	45.9	44.9	44.0	43.1	42.2	41.3	40.3	39.4	38.6
71	48.7	47.7	46.8	45.9	44.9	44.0	43.0	42.1	41.2	40.3	39.4	38.5
72	48.7	47.7	46.8	45.8	44.9	43.9	43.0	42.1	41.1	40.2	39.3	38.4
73	48.6	47.7	46.7	45.8	44.8	43.9	43.0	42.0	41.1	40.2	39.3	38.4
74	48.6	47.7	46.7	45.8	44.8	43.9	42.9	42.0	41.1	40.1	39.2	38.3

RMD Joint and Last Survivor Table - Life Expectancy

Ages	35	36	37	38	39	40	41	42	43	44	45	46
75	48.6	47.7	46.7	45.7	44.8	43.8	42.9	42.0	41.0	40.1	39.2	38.3
76	48.6	47.6	46.7	45.7	44.8	43.8	42.9	41.9	41.0	40.1	39.1	38.2
77	48.6	47.6	46.7	45.7	44.8	43.8	42.9	41.9	41.0	40.0	39.1	38.2
78	48.6	47.6	46.6	45.7	44.7	43.8	42.8	41.9	40.9	40.0	39.1	38.2
79	48.6	47.6	46.6	45.7	44.7	43.8	42.8	41.9	40.9	40.0	39.1	38.1
80	48.5	47.6	46.6	45.7	44.7	43.7	42.8	41.8	40.9	40.0	39.0	38.1
81	48.5	47.6	46.6	45.7	44.7	43.7	42.8	41.8	40.9	39.9	39.0	38.1
82	48.5	47.6	46.6	45.6	44.7	43.7	42.8	41.8	40.9	39.9	39.0	38.1
83	48.5	47.6	46.6	45.6	44.7	43.7	42.8	41.8	40.9	39.9	39.0	38.0
84	48.5	47.6	46.6	45.6	44.7	43.7	42.7	41.8	40.8	39.9	39.0	38.0
85	48.5	47.5	46.6	45.6	44.7	43.7	42.7	41.8	40.8	39.9	38.9	38.0
86	48.5	47.5	46.6	45.6	44.6	43.7	42.7	41.8	40.8	39.9	38.9	38.0
87	48.5	47.5	46.6	45.6	44.6	43.7	42.7	41.8	40.8	39.9	38.9	38.0
88	48.5	47.5	46.6	45.6	44.6	43.7	42.7	41.8	40.8	39.9	38.9	38.0
89	48.5	47.5	46.6	45.6	44.6	43.7	42.7	41.7	40.8	39.8	38.9	38.0
90	48.5	47.5	46.6	45.6	44.6	43.7	42.7	41.7	40.8	39.8	38.9	38.0

RMD Joint and Last Survivor Table - Life Expectancy

Ages	47	48	49	50	51	52	53	54	55	56	57	58
47	43.4	42.9	42.4	42.0	41.6	41.2	40.9	40.5	40.2	40.0	39.7	39.4
48	42.9	42.4	41.9	41.5	41.0	40.6	40.3	39.9	39.6	39.3	39.0	38.7
49	42.4	41.9	41.4	40.9	40.5	40.1	39.7	39.3	38.9	38.6	38.3	38.0
50	42.0	41.5	40.9	40.4	40.0	39.5	39.1	38.7	38.3	38.0	37.6	37.3
51	41.6	41.0	40.5	40.0	39.5	39.0	38.5	38.1	37.7	37.4	37.0	36.7
52	41.2	40.6	40.1	39.5	39.0	38.5	38.0	37.6	37.2	36.8	36.4	36.0
53	40.9	40.3	39.7	39.1	38.5	38.0	37.5	37.1	36.6	36.2	35.8	35.4
54	40.5	39.9	39.3	38.7	38.1	37.6	37.1	36.6	36.1	35.7	35.2	34.8
55	40.2	39.6	38.9	38.3	37.7	37.2	36.6	36.1	35.6	35.1	34.7	34.3
56	40.0	39.3	38.6	38.0	37.4	36.8	36.2	35.7	35.1	34.7	34.2	33.7
57	39.7	39.0	38.3	37.6	37.0	36.4	35.8	35.2	34.7	34.2	33.7	33.2
58	39.4	38.7	38.0	37.3	36.7	36.0	35.4	34.8	34.3	33.7	33.2	32.8
59	39.2	38.5	37.8	37.1	36.4	35.7	35.1	34.5	33.9	33.3	32.8	32.3
60	39.0	38.2	37.5	36.8	36.1	35.4	34.8	34.1	33.5	32.9	32.4	31.9
61	38.8	38.0	37.3	36.6	35.8	35.1	34.5	33.8	33.2	32.6	32.0	31.4
62	38.6	37.8	37.1	36.3	35.6	34.9	34.2	33.5	32.9	32.2	31.6	31.1
63	38.5	37.7	36.9	36.1	35.4	34.6	33.9	33.2	32.6	31.9	31.3	30.7
64	38.3	37.5	36.7	35.9	35.2	34.4	33.7	33.0	32.3	31.6	31.0	30.4
65	38.2	37.4	36.6	35.8	35.0	34.2	33.5	32.7	32.0	31.4	30.7	30.0
66	38.1	37.2	36.4	35.6	34.8	34.0	33.3	32.5	31.8	31.1	30.4	29.8

Ages	47	48	49	50	51	52	53	54	55	56	57	58
67	38.0	37.1	36.3	35.5	34.7	33.9	33.1	32.3	31.6	30.9	30.2	29.5
68	37.9	37.0	36.2	35.3	34.5	33.7	32.9	32.1	31.4	30.7	29.9	29.2
69	37.8	36.9	36.0	35.2	34.4	33.6	32.8	32.0	31.2	30.5	29.7	29.0
70	37.7	36.8	35.9	35.1	34.3	33.4	32.6	31.8	31.1	30.3	29.5	28.8
71	37.6	36.7	35.9	35.0	34.2	33.3	32.5	31.7	30.9	30.1	29.4	28.6
72	37.5	36.6	35.8	34.9	34.1	33.2	32.4	31.6	30.8	30.0	29.2	28.4
73	37.5	36.6	35.7	34.8	34.0	33.1	32.3	31.5	30.6	29.8	29.1	28.3
74	37.4	36.5	35.6	34.8	33.9	33.0	32.2	31.4	30.5	29.7	28.9	28.1
75	37.4	36.5	35.6	34.7	33.8	33.0	32.1	31.3	30.4	29.6	28.8	28.0
76	37.3	36.4	35.5	34.6	33.8	32.9	32.0	31.2	30.3	29.5	28.7	27.9
77	37.3	36.4	35.5	34.6	33.7	32.8	32.0	31.1	30.3	29.4	28.6	27.8
78	37.2	36.3	35.4	34.5	33.6	32.8	31.9	31.0	30.2	29.3	28.5	27.7
79	37.2	36.3	35.4	34.5	33.6	32.7	31.8	31.0	30.1	29.3	28.4	27.6
80	37.2	36.3	35.4	34.5	33.6	32.7	31.8	30.9	30.1	29.2	28.4	27.5
81	37.2	36.2	35.3	34.4	33.5	32.6	31.8	30.9	30.0	29.2	28.3	27.5
82	37.1	36.2	35.3	34.4	33.5	32.6	31.7	30.8	30.0	29.1	28.3	27.4
83	37.1	36.2	35.3	34.4	33.5	32.6	31.7	30.8	29.9	29.1	28.2	27.4
84	37.1	36.2	35.3	34.3	33.4	32.5	31.7	30.8	29.9	29.0	28.2	27.3
85	37.1	36.2	35.2	34.3	33.4	32.5	31.6	30.7	29.9	29.0	28.1	27.3
86	37.1	36.1	35.2	34.3	33.4	32.5	31.6	30.7	29.8	29.0	28.1	27.2
87	37.0	36.1	35.2	34.3	33.4	32.5	31.6	30.7	29.8	28.9	28.1	27.2
88	37.0	36.1	35.2	34.3	33.4	32.5	31.6	30.7	29.8	28.9	28.0	27.2
89	37.0	36.1	35.2	34.3	33.3	32.4	31.5	30.7	29.8	28.9	28.0	27.2
90	37.0	36.1	35.2	34.2	33.3	32.4	31.5	30.6	29.8	28.9	28.0	27.1

RMD Joint and Last Survivor Table - Life Expectancy

Ages	59	60	61	62	63	64	65	66	67	68	69	70
59	31.8	31.3	30.9	30.5	30.1	29.8	29.4	29.1	28.8	28.6	28.3	28.1
60	31.3	30.9	30.4	30.0	29.6	29.2	28.8	28.5	28.2	27.9	27.6	27.4
61	30.9	30.4	29.9	29.5	29.0	28.6	28.3	27.9	27.6	27.3	27.0	26.7
62	30.5	30.0	29.5	29.0	28.5	28.1	27.7	27.3	27.0	26.7	26.4	26.1
63	30.1	29.6	29.0	28.5	28.1	27.6	27.2	26.8	26.4	26.1	25.7	25.4
64	29.8	29.2	28.6	28.1	27.6	27.1	26.7	26.3	25.9	25.5	25.2	24.8
65	29.4	28.8	28.3	27.7	27.2	26.7	26.2	25.8	25.4	25.0	24.6	24.3
66	29.1	28.5	27.9	27.3	26.8	26.3	25.8	25.3	24.9	24.5	24.1	23.7
67	28.8	28.2	27.6	27.0	26.4	25.9	25.4	24.9	24.4	24.0	23.6	23.2
68	28.6	27.9	27.3	26.7	26.1	25.5	25.0	24.5	24.0	23.5	23.1	22.7
69	28.3	27.6	27.0	26.4	25.7	25.2	24.6	24.1	23.6	23.1	22.6	22.2
70	28.1	27.4	26.7	26.1	25.4	24.8	24.3	23.7	23.2	22.7	22.2	21.8

RMD Joint and Last Survivor Table - Life Expectancy											
Ages	59	60	61	62	63	64	65	66	67	68	69	70
71	27.9	27.2	26.5	25.8	25.2	24.5	23.9	23.4	22.8	22.3	21.8	21.3
72	27.7	27.0	26.3	25.6	24.9	24.3	23.7	23.1	22.5	22.0	21.4	20.9
73	27.5	26.8	26.1	25.4	24.7	24.0	23.4	22.8	22.2	21.6	21.1	20.6
74	27.4	26.6	25.9	25.2	24.5	23.8	23.1	22.5	21.9	21.3	20.8	20.2
75	27.2	26.5	25.7	25.0	24.3	23.6	22.9	22.3	21.6	21.0	20.5	19.9
76	27.1	26.3	25.6	24.8	24.1	23.4	22.7	22.0	21.4	20.8	20.2	19.6
77	27.0	26.2	25.4	24.7	23.9	23.2	22.5	21.8	21.2	20.6	19.9	19.4
78	26.9	26.1	25.3	24.6	23.8	23.1	22.4	21.7	21.0	20.3	19.7	19.1
79	26.8	26.0	25.2	24.4	23.7	22.9	22.2	21.5	20.8	20.1	19.5	18.9
80	26.7	25.9	25.1	24.3	23.6	22.8	22.1	21.3	20.6	20.0	19.3	18.7
81	26.6	25.8	25.0	24.2	23.4	22.7	21.9	21.2	20.5	19.8	19.1	18.5
82	26.6	25.8	24.9	24.1	23.4	22.6	21.8	21.1	20.4	19.7	19.0	18.3
83	26.5	25.7	24.9	24.1	23.3	22.5	21.7	21.0	20.2	19.5	18.8	18.2
84	26.5	25.6	24.8	24.0	23.2	22.4	21.6	20.9	20.1	19.4	18.7	18.0
85	26.4	25.6	24.8	23.9	23.1	22.3	21.6	20.8	20.1	19.3	18.6	17.9
86	26.4	25.5	24.7	23.9	23.1	22.3	21.5	20.7	20.0	19.2	18.5	17.8
87	26.4	25.5	24.7	23.8	23.0	22.2	21.4	20.7	19.9	19.2	18.4	17.7
88	26.3	25.5	24.6	23.8	23.0	22.2	21.4	20.6	19.8	19.1	18.3	17.6
89	26.3	25.4	24.6	23.8	22.9	22.1	21.3	20.5	19.8	19.0	18.3	17.6
90	26.3	25.4	24.6	23.7	22.9	22.1	21.3	20.5	19.7	19.0	18.2	17.5

RMD Joint and Last Survivor Table - Life Expectancy											
Ages	71	72	73	74	75	76	77	78	79	80	81	82
71	20.9	20.5	20.1	19.7	19.4	19.1	18.8	18.5	18.3	18.1	17.9	17.7
72	20.5	20.0	19.6	19.3	18.9	18.6	18.3	18.0	17.7	17.5	17.3	17.1
73	20.1	19.6	19.2	18.8	18.4	18.1	17.8	17.5	17.2	16.9	16.7	16.5
74	19.7	19.3	18.8	18.4	18.0	17.6	17.3	17.0	16.7	16.4	16.2	15.9
75	19.4	18.9	18.4	18.0	17.6	17.2	16.8	16.5	16.2	15.9	15.6	15.4
76	19.1	18.6	18.1	17.6	17.2	16.8	16.4	16.0	15.7	15.4	15.1	14.9
77	18.8	18.3	17.8	17.3	16.8	16.4	16.0	15.6	15.3	15.0	14.7	14.4
78	18.5	18.0	17.5	17.0	16.5	16.0	15.6	15.2	14.9	14.5	14.2	13.9
79	18.3	17.7	17.2	16.7	16.2	15.7	15.3	14.9	14.5	14.1	13.8	13.5
80	18.1	17.5	16.9	16.4	15.9	15.4	15.0	14.5	14.1	13.8	13.4	13.1
81	17.9	17.3	16.7	16.2	15.6	15.1	14.7	14.2	13.8	13.4	13.1	12.7
82	17.7	17.1	16.5	15.9	15.4	14.9	14.4	13.9	13.5	13.1	12.7	12.4
83	17.5	16.9	16.3	15.7	15.2	14.7	14.2	13.7	13.2	12.8	12.4	12.1
84	17.4	16.7	16.1	15.5	15.0	14.4	13.9	13.4	13.0	12.6	12.2	11.8
85	17.3	16.6	16.0	15.4	14.8	14.3	13.7	13.2	12.8	12.3	11.9	11.5

RMD Joint and Last Survivor Table - Life Expectancy											
Ages	71	72	73	74	75	76	77	78	79	80	81	82
86	17.1	16.5	15.8	15.2	14.6	14.1	13.5	13.0	12.5	12.1	11.7	11.3
87	17.0	16.4	15.7	15.1	14.5	13.9	13.4	12.9	12.4	11.9	11.4	11.0
88	16.9	16.3	15.6	15.0	14.4	13.8	13.2	12.7	12.2	11.7	11.3	10.8
89	16.9	16.2	15.5	14.9	14.3	13.7	13.1	12.6	12.0	11.5	11.1	10.6
90	16.8	16.1	15.4	14.8	14.2	13.6	13.0	12.4	11.9	11.4	10.9	10.5

RMD Joint and Last Survivor Table - Life Expectancy							
Ages	83	84	85	86	87	88	89	90
83	11.7	11.4	11.1	10.9	10.6	10.4	10.2	10.1
84	11.4	11.1	10.8	10.5	10.3	10.1	9.9	9.7
85	11.1	10.8	10.5	10.2	9.9	9.7	9.5	9.3
86	10.9	10.5	10.2	9.9	9.6	9.4	9.2	9.0
87	10.6	10.3	9.9	9.6	9.4	9.1	8.9	8.6
88	10.4	10.1	9.7	9.4	9.1	8.8	8.6	8.3
89	10.2	9.9	9.5	9.2	8.9	8.6	8.3	8.1
90	10.1	9.7	9.3	9.0	8.6	8.3	8.1	7.8

Treas. Reg. Sec. 1.401(a)(9)-9

RMD MDIB Joint and Survivor Annuity Table (maximum percentage for survivor)					
Excess of Participant's Age over Beneficiary's Age	Applicable Percentage	Excess of Participant's Age over Beneficiary's Age	Applicable Percentage	Excess of Participant's Age over Beneficiary's Age	Applicable Percentage
10 or less	100	22	70	34	57
11	96	23	68	35	56
12	93	24	67	36	56
13	90	25	66	37	55
14	87	26	64	38	55
15	84	27	63	39	54
16	82	28	62	40	54
17	79	29	61	41	53
18	77	30	60	42	53
19	75	31	59	43	53
20	73	32	59	44 and greater	52
21	72	33	58		

Treas. Reg. Sec. 1.401(a)(9)-9

ONE YEAR TERM RATES

The following rates are used in computing the "cost" of pure life insurance protection that is taxable to the employee under: qualified pension and profit sharing plans split-dollar plans; and tax-sheltered annuities.[1]

For these purposes, the rate at insured's attained age is generally applied to the excess of the amount payable at death over the cash value of the policy at the end of the year.

Table 2001 can generally be used starting in 2001. P.S. 58 rates and other rates derived from Table 38 could generally be used in years prior to 2002. However, split dollar arrangements entered into before January 28, 2002, in which the contractual arrangement between the employer and the employee provides that P.S. 58 rates will be used may continue to use P.S. 58 rates. In 2001, either Table 2001 or the P.S. 58/Table 38 derived rates could generally be used.

---

1. Notice 2002-8, 2002-4 IRB 398; Rev. Rul. 66-110, 1966-1 CB 12.

Table 2001

One Year Term Premiums for $1,000 of Life Insurance Protection – One Life

Age		Premium	Age		Premium	Age		Premium
0	....	$0.70	34	....	$0.98	67	....	$15.20
1	....	0.41	35	....	0.99	68	....	16.92
2	....	0.27	36	....	1.01	69	....	18.70
3	....	0.19	37	....	1.04	70	....	20.62
4	....	0.13	38	....	1.06	71	....	22.72
5	....	0.13	39	....	1.07	72	....	25.07
6	....	0.14	40	....	1.10	73	....	27.57
7	....	0.15	41	....	1.13	74	....	30.18
8	....	0.16	42	....	1.20	75	....	33.05
9	....	0.16	43	....	1.29	76	....	36.33
10	....	0.16	44	....	1.40	77	....	40.17
11	....	0.19	45	....	1.53	78	....	44.33
12	....	0.24	46	....	1.67	79	....	49.23
13	....	0.28	47	....	1.83	80	....	54.56
14	....	0.33	48	....	1.98	81	....	60.51
15	....	0.38	49	....	2.13	82	....	66.74
16	....	0.52	50	....	2.30	83	....	73.07
17	....	0.57	51	....	2.52	84	....	80.35
18	....	0.59	52	....	2.81	85	....	88.76
19	....	0.61	53	....	3.20	86	....	99.16
20	....	0.62	54	....	3.65	87	....	110.40
21	....	0.62	55	....	4.15	88	....	121.85
22	....	0.64	56	....	4.68	89	....	133.40
23	....	0.66	57	....	5.20	90	....	144.30
24	....	0.68	58	....	5.66	91	....	155.80
25	....	0.71	59	....	6.06	92	....	168.75
26	....	0.73	60	....	6.51	93	....	186.44
27	....	0.76	61	....	7.11	94	....	206.70
28	....	0.80	62	....	7.96	95	....	228.35
29	....	0.83	63	....	9.08	96	....	250.01
30	....	0.87	64	....	10.41	97	....	265.09
31	....	0.90	65	....	11.90	98	....	270.11
32	....	0.93	66	....	13.51	99	....	281.05
33	....	0.96						

"P.S. No. 58" Rates

One Year Term Premiums for $1,000 of Life Insurance Protection – One Life

Age		Premium		Age		Premium	Age		Premium	
0	....	$42.10	*	35	....	$ 3.21	70	....	$ 48.06	
1	....	4.49	*	36	....	3.41	71	....	52.29	
2	....	2.37	*	37	....	3.63	72	....	56.89	
3	....	1.72	*	38	....	3.87	73	....	61.89	
4	....	1.38	*	39	....	4.14	74	....	67.33	
5	....	1.21	*	40	....	4.42	75	....	73.23	
6	....	1.07	*	41	....	4.73	76	....	79.63	
7	....	.98	*	42	....	5.07	77	....	86.57	
8	....	.90	*	43	....	5.44	78	....	94.09	
9	....	.85	*	44	....	5.85	79	....	102.23	
10	....	.83	*	45	....	6.30	80	....	111.04	
11	....	.91	*	46	....	6.78	81	....	120.57	
12	....	1.00	*	47	....	7.32	82	....	130.86	*
13	....	1.08	*	48	....	7.89	83	....	141.95	*
14	....	1.17	*	49	....	8.53	84	....	153.91	*
15	....	1.27		50	....	9.22	85	....	166.77	*
16	....	1.38		51	....	9.97	86	....	180.60	*
17	....	1.48		52	....	10.79	87	....	195.43	*
18	....	1.52		53	....	11.69	88	....	211.33	*
19	....	1.56		54	....	12.67	89	....	228.31	*
20	....	1.61		55	....	13.74	90	....	246.45	*
21	....	1.67		56	....	14.91	91	....	265.75	*
22	....	1.73		57	....	16.18	92	....	286.25	*
23	....	1.79		58	....	17.56	93	....	307.98	*
24	....	1.86		59	....	19.08	94	....	330.94	*
25	....	1.93		60	....	20.73	95	....	355.11	*
26	....	2.02		61	....	22.53	96	....	380.50	*
27	....	2.11		62	....	24.50	97	....	407.03	*
28	....	2.20		63	....	26.63	98	....	434.68	*
29	....	2.31		64	....	28.98	99	....	463.35	*
30	....	2.43		65	....	31.51	100	....	492.93	*
31	....	2.57		66	....	34.28	101	....	523.30	*
32	....	2.70		67	....	37.31	102	....	554.30	*
33	....	2.86		68	....	40.59	103	....	585.75	*
34	....	3.02		69	....	44.17	104	....	617.42	*

* Rates are derived by the editor from U.S. Life Table 38, and are based on the underlying actuarial assumptions of the P.S. 58 rates (see following pages).

P.S. 58 RATES CALCULATIONS

(Net annual premium per $1,000 – 1 year term)

For various tax purposes, P.S. 58 rates can be used for the net annual premium per $1,000 of one year term life insurance where there is only one insured. P.S. 58 equivalent rates (e.g., joint and joint and survivor rates) can also be determined where there is more than one insured (sometimes referred to as Table 38 rates). The derivation of such rates is described below for one and two insureds.

In each instance, the present value of $1,000 is discounted one year at 2.5% to $975.60. $975.60 is then multiplied by the probability of death of the insured(s) during the year. In each of the formulas below, substitute the appropriate q_x from Table 38 for each insured (where two insureds are involved, the second insured is referred to as y rather than x).

required interest rate = i = 2.5%
$1 \div (1 + i) = 1 \div 1.025 = .97560$
$\$1,000 \times .97560 = \$975.60$

q_x – probability of dying in each year of age (from Table 38)
  (e.g., q_x for person age 25 is .00198)

Where two lives are involved q_x and q_y are used
  q_x is probability at first person's age
  q_y is probability at second person's age
  (e.g., q_x for first person, age 35, is .00329 and q_y for second person, age 45, is .00646)

ONE LIFE
P.S. 58 rate = $\$975.60 \times q_x$
  (e.g., rate for person age 50
  = $\$975.60 \times .00945 = \$9.22$)

TWO LIFE (Joint and Survivor, Second to Die)
P.S. 58 equivalent rate = $\$975.60 \times q_x \times q_y$
  (e.g., rate for persons age 60 and 70 = $\$975.60 \times .02125 \times .04926 = \$1.02$)
  after first death use one life rate

TWO LIFE (Joint, First to Die)
P.S. 58 equivalent rate = $\$975.60 \times [(q_x + q_y) - (q_x \times q_y)]$
  (e.g., rate for persons age 60 and 70
  = $\$975.60 \times [(.02125 + .04926) - (.02125 \times .04926)]$
  = $\$67.77$)

Table 38					
Age x	q(x)	Age x	q(x)	Age x	q(x)
0	.04315	35	.00329	70	.04926
1	.00460	36	.00350	71	.05360
2	.00243	37	.00372	72	.05831
3	.00176	38	.00397	73	.06344
4	.00141	39	.00424	74	.06901
5	.00124	40	.00453	75	.07506
6	.00110	41	.00485	76	.08162
7	.00100	42	.00520	77	.08873
8	.00092	43	.00558	78	.09644
9	.00087	44	.00600	79	.10479
10	.00085	45	.00646	80	.11382
11	.00093	46	.00695	81	.12358
12	.00102	47	.00750	82	.13413
13	.00111	48	.00809	83	.14550
14	.00120	49	.00874	84	.15776
15	.00130	50	.00945	85	.17094
16	.00141	51	.01022	86	.18511
17	.00152	52	.01106	87	.20032
18	.00156	53	.01198	88	.21661
19	.00160	54	.01299	89	.23402
20	.00165	55	.01408	90	.25261
21	.00171	56	.01528	91	.27239
22	.00177	57	.01658	92	.29341
23	.00183	58	.01800	93	.31568
24	.00191	59	.01956	94	.33921
25	.00198	60	.02125	95	.36399
26	.00207	61	.02309	96	.39001
27	.00216	62	.02511	97	.41721
28	.00226	63	.02730	98	.44555
29	.00237	64	.02970	99	.47493
30	.00249	65	.03230	100	.50525
31	.00263	66	.03514	101	.53638
32	.00277	67	.03824	102	.56816
33	.00293	68	.04160	103	.60039
34	.00310	69	.04527	104	.63286
				105	1.00000

					One Year Term Premiums for $1,000 of Joint and Survivor Life Insurance Protection* (Second-to-Die)					
AGE	5	10	15	20	25	30	35	40	45	50
5	.00	.00	.00	.00	.00	.00	.00	.01	.01	.01
10	.00	.00	.00	.00	.00	.00	.00	.00	.01	.01
15	.00	.00	.00	.00	.00	.00	.00	.01	.01	.01
20	.00	.00	.00	.00	.00	.00	.01	.01	.01	.02
25	.00	.00	.00	.00	.00	.00	.01	.01	.01	.02
30	.00	.00	.00	.00	.00	.01	.01	.01	.02	.02
35	.00	.00	.00	.01	.01	.01	.01	.01	.02	.03
40	.01	.00	.01	.01	.01	.01	.01	.02	.03	.04
45	.01	.01	.01	.01	.01	.02	.02	.03	.04	.06
50	.01	.01	.01	.02	.02	.02	.03	.04	.06	.09
55	.02	.01	.02	.02	.03	.03	.05	.06	.09	.13
60	.03	.02	.03	.03	.04	.05	.07	.09	.13	.20
65	.04	.03	.04	.05	.06	.08	.10	.14	.20	.30
70	.06	.04	.06	.08	.10	.12	.16	.22	.31	.45
75	.09	.06	.10	.12	.14	.18	.24	.33	.47	.69
80	.14	.09	.14	.18	.22	.28	.37	.50	.72	1.05
85	.21	.14	.22	.28	.33	.42	.55	.76	1.08	1.58
90	.31	.21	.32	.41	.49	.61	.81	1.12	1.59	2.33
95	.44	.30	.46	.59	.70	.88	1.17	1.61	2.29	3.36
100	.61	.42	.64	.81	.98	1.23	1.62	2.23	3.18	4.66

AGE	55	60	65	70	75	80	85	90	95	100
5	.02	.03	.04	.06	.09	.14	.21	.31	.44	.61
10	.01	.02	.03	.04	.06	.09	.14	.21	.30	.42
15	.02	.03	.04	.06	.10	.14	.22	.32	.46	.64
20	.02	.03	.05	.08	.12	.18	.28	.41	.59	.81
25	.03	.04	.06	.10	.14	.22	.33	.49	.70	.98
30	.03	.05	.08	.12	.18	.28	.42	.61	.88	1.23
35	.05	.07	.10	.16	.24	.37	.55	.81	1.17	1.62
40	.06	.09	.14	.22	.33	.50	.76	1.12	1.61	2.23
45	.09	.13	.20	.31	.47	.72	1.08	1.59	2.29	3.18
50	.13	.20	.30	.45	.69	1.05	1.58	2.33	3.36	4.66
55	.19	.29	.44	.68	1.03	1.56	2.35	3.47	5.00	6.94
60	.29	.44	.67	1.02	1.56	2.36	3.54	5.24	7.55	10.47
65	.44	.67	1.02	1.55	2.37	3.59	5.39	7.96	11.47	15.92
70	.68	1.02	1.55	2.37	3.61	5.47	8.22	12.14	17.49	24.28
75	1.03	1.56	2.37	3.61	5.50	8.33	12.52	18.50	26.65	37.00
80	1.56	2.36	3.59	5.47	8.33	12.64	18.98	28.05	40.42	56.10
85	2.35	3.54	5.39	8.22	12.52	18.98	28.51	42.13	60.70	84.26
90	3.47	5.24	7.96	12.14	18.50	28.05	42.13	62.26	89.70	124.52
95	5.00	7.55	11.47	17.49	26.65	40.42	60.70	89.70	129.26	179.42
100	6.94	10.47	15.92	24.28	37.00	56.10	84.26	124.52	179.42	249.05

* Rates are derived from U.S. Life Table 38. They are based on the underlying actuarial assumptions of the P.S. 58 rates. The method for deriving the rates is also based upon an unofficial informational letter of Norman Greenberg, Chief, Actuarial Branch, Department of the Treasury. The letter indicates that after the first death, the single life regular P.S. 58 rates are to be used. Due to space limitations, the table is presented in 5-year age increments. For planning purposes, it is suggested that each actual age be rounded to the nearest corresponding age in the table, or do the calculation described earlier in this appendix.

INDEX

S

U

V

W